Dictionary

Norwegian – English
English – Norwegian

Ordbok

Norsk – Engelsk
Engelsk – Norsk

Berlitz Publishing / APA Publications GmbH & Co.
Verlag KG, Singapore Branch, Singapore

Contacting the Editors
Every effort has been made to provide accurate information in this publication, but changes are inevitable. The publisher cannot be responsible for any resulting loss, inconvenience or injury. We would appreciate it if readers would call our attention to any errors or outdated information by contacting Berlitz Publishing, 95 Progress Street, Union, NJ 07083, USA. Fax: 1-908-206-1103, e-mail: comments@berlitzbooks.com

Cover photo: ©ID Image Direkt CD-ROM GmbH, Germany

Contents

Innhold

Preface

In selecting the vocabulary and phrases for this dictionary, the editors have had the traveller's needs foremost in mind. This book will prove a useful companion to casual tourists and business travellers alike who appreciate the reassurance a small and practical dictionary can provide. It offers them—as well as beginners and students—all the basic vocabulary they will to encounter and have to use, giving the key words and expressions to allow them to cope in everyday situations.

Like our successful phrase books and travel guides, these dictionaries—created with the help of a computer data bank—are designed to slip into pocket or purse, and thus have a role as handy companions at all times.

Besides just about everything you normally find in dictionaries, there are these Berlitz bonuses:

- imitated pronunciation after each foreign-word entry, making it easy to read and enunciate words whose spelling may look forbidding

- a unique, practical glossary to simplify reading a foreign restaurant menu and to take the mystery out of complicated dishes and indecipherable names on bills of fare

- useful information on how to tell the time and how to count, on conjugating irregular verbs, commonly seen abbreviations and converting to the metric system, in addition to basic phrases.

While no dictionary of this size can pretend to completeness, we, we are confident this dictionary will help you get most out of your trip abroad.

Berlitz Publishing

Forord

I valget av ordforråd og uttrykk til denne ordboken har vi først og fremst tatt sikte på å dekke den reisendes behov. Denne boken vil derfor være en god følgesvenn for både turister og forretningsreisende som setter pris på den tryggheten en hendig ordbok gir. Også de som vil lære språket, nybegynnere såvel som viderekomne, finner her det grunnleggende ordforråd de vil komme i berøring med, dertil nøkkelord og -uttrykk som gjør det mulig å klare seg i dagligdagse situasjoner.

Ordboken er – i likhet med våre parlører og reiseguider – utarbeidet ved hjelp av en databank, og er laget for å kunne tas med i en veske eller lomme. Vi håper at den ved sitt praktiske format vil tiltale mange og være til god hjelp i alle situasjoner.

Foruten alt det en ordbok vanligvis inneholder, finner du følgende Berlitz-bonustillegg:

* imitasjon av uttalen etter hver oppføring på fremmedspråket, noe som gjør det enkelt å lese ordet og å bruke ord med en komplisert stavemåte

* en spesiell praktisk ordliste som gjør det lettere å forstå hva som skjuler seg bak et utenlandsk spisekart; slik blir kompliserte retter og uforklarlige gastronomiske begreper enkle å tyde

* en rekke praktiske opplysninger som tallord, vanlige forkortelser, hvordan man angir klokkeslett, bøyning av uregelmessige verb, samt et avsnitt med nyttige uttrykk.

Det sier seg selv at en ordbok av dette format ikke kan gjøre krav på å være fullstendig. Allikevel er vi overbevist om at denne ordboken vil være til uvurderlig hjelp når det gjelder å få det beste ut av utenlandsreisen din.

Berlitz Publishing

Norwegian-English

Norsk-Engelsk

Introduction

This dictionary has been designed to take account of your practical needs. Unnecessary linguistic information has been avoided. The entries are listed in alphabetical order, regardless of whether the entry is printed in a single word or in two or more separate words. As the only exception to this rule, a few idiomatic expressions are listed alphabetically as main entries by the most significant word of the expression. When an entry is followed by sub-entries, such as expressions and locutions, these are also listed in alphabetical order[1].

Each main-entry word is followed by a phonetic transcription (see guide to pronunciation). Following the transcription, the part of speech of the entry word is indicated, whenever applicable. If an entry word is used as more than one part of speech, the translations are grouped together after the respective part of speech.

In the regular indefinite plural, both common, masculine and neuter nouns take an -(e)r ending. Exceptions: masculine nouns ending in -er take ~e (e.g.: arbeider, pl arbeidere), and monosyllabic neuter nouns remain unchanged (e.g.: barn, pl barn).

All irregular plural forms of nouns not conforming to these rules are given in brackets after the part of speech.

Whenever an entry word is repeated in irregular forms or sub-entries, a tilde (~) is used to represent the full word. In plurals of long words, only the part that changes is written out fully, whereas the unchanged part is represented by a hyphen (-).

Entry word:	mus c (pl ~)	Plural:	mus
	vidunder nt (pl ~, ~e)		vidunder, vidundere
	antibiotikum nt (pl -ka)		antibiotika

An asterisk (*) in front of a verb indicates that it is irregular. For more detail, refer to the list of irregular verbs.

---

[1] Note that the Norwegian alphabet comprises 29 letters; æ, ø and å are considered independent characters and come after z, in that order.

Abbreviations

adj	adjective	*p*	past tense
adv	adverb	*pl*	plural
Am	American	*plAm*	plural (American)
art	article	*pp*	past participle
c	common gender	*pr*	present tense
conj	conjunction	*pref*	prefix
m	masculine	*prep*	preposition
n	noun	*pron*	pronoun
nAm	noun (American)	*suf*	suffix
nt	neuter	*v*	verb
num	numeral	*vAm*	verb (American)

Guide to Pronunciation

Each main entry in this part of the dictionary is followed by a phonetic transcription which shows you how to pronounce the words. This transcription should be read as if it were English. It is based on Standard British pronunciation, though we have tried to take account of General American pronunciation also. Below, only those letters and symbols are explained which we consider likely to be ambiguous or not immediately understood.

The syllables are separated by hyphens, and stressed syllables are printed in *italics*.

Of course, the sounds of any two languages are never exactly the same, but if you follow carefully our indications, you should be able to pronounce the foreign words in such a way that you'll be understood. To make your task easier, our transcriptions occasionally simplify slightly the sound system of the language while still reflecting the essential sound differences.

Consonants

g	always hard, as in go
kh	quite like h in huge, but with the tongue raised a little higher
r	rolled in the front of the mouth, except in south-western Norway, where it's pronounced in the back of the mouth
s	always hard, as in so

The consonants **d, l, n, s, t,** if preceded by **r,** are generally pronounced with the tip of the tongue turned up well behind the upper front teeth. The **r** then ceases to be pronounced.

Vowels and Diphthongs

aa	long **a**, as in c**a**r, without any **r**-sound
ah	a short version of **aa**; between **a** in c**a**t and **u** in c**u**t
aw	as in r**aw** (British pronunciation)
æ	like **a** in c**a**t
ææ	a long **æ**-sound
eh	like **e** in g**e**t
er	as in oth**er**, without any **r**-sound
ew	a "rounded **ee**-sound". Say the vowel sound **ee** (as in s**ee**), and while saying it, round your lips as for **oo** (as in s**oo**n), without moving your tongue; when your lips are in the **oo** position, but your tongue in the **ee** position, you should be pronouncing the correct sound
igh	as in s**igh**
o	always as in h**o**t (British pronunciation)
ou	as in l**ou**d
ur	as in f**ur**, but with rounded lips and no **r**-sound

1) A bar over a vowel symbol (e.g. $\overline{\text{ew}}$) shows that this sound is long.
2) Raised letters (e.g. ^{y}**aa**, **ew**^{ee}) should be pronounced only fleetingly.

Tones

In Norwegian there are two "tones": one is rising, the other consists of a falling pitch followed by a rise. As these tones are complex and very hard to copy, we do not indicate them, but mark their position as stressed.

A

-a (*aa*) *art* the

abbedi (ah-ber-*dee*) *nt* abbey

abonnement (ah-boo-ner-*mahngng*) *nt* subscription

abonnent (ah-boo-*nehnt*) *m* subscriber

abort (ah-*bott*) *m* abortion; miscarriage

absolutt (ahp-soo-*lewtt*) *adj* very, sheer; *adv* absolutely

abstrakt (ahp-*strahkt*) *adj* abstract

absurd (ahp-*sewrd*) *adj* absurd

adapter (ah-*dap*-terr) *m* adaptor

addisjon (ah-di-*shōōn*) *m* addition

adekvat (ah-deh-*kvaat*) *adj* adequate

adel (*aa*-derl) *m* nobility

adelig (aa-der-li) *adj* belonging to nobility

adgang (*aad*-gahng) *m* admission, entrance, admittance, entry; ~ **forbudt** no entry, no admittance

adjektiv (ahd-*ᵞ*ehk-tiv) *nt* adjective

adkomst (*aad*-komst) *m* access

*adlyde (*aad-lēw*-der) *v* obey

administrasjon (ahd-mi-ni-strah-*shōōn*) *m* administration

administrerende (ahd-mi-ni-*strāy*-rer-ner) *adj* administrative; executive

adoptere (ah-doop-*tāy*-rer) *v* adopt

adressat (ahd-reh-*saat*) *m* addressee

adresse (ah-*drehss*-ser) *c* address

adressere (ahd-reh-*sāy*-rer) *v* address

advare (*aad*-vaa-rer) *v* caution, warn

advarsel (*aad*-vah-sherl) *m* (pl -sler) warning

adverb (ahd-*værb*) *nt* adverb

advokat (ahd-voo-*kaat*) *m* lawyer, barrister; solicitor, attorney

affektert (ah-fehk-*tāyt*) *adj* affected

affære (ah-*fææ*-rer) *m* affair

Afrika (*aaf*-ri-kah) Africa

afrikaner (ahf-ri-*kaa*-nerr) *m* African

afrikansk (ahf-ri-*kaansk*) *adj* African

aftensmat (*ahf*-terns-maat) *m* supper

agent (ah-*gehnt*) *m* agent

agentur (ah-gehn-*tēwr*) *nt* agency

aggressiv (*ah*-greh-seev) *adj* aggressive

agn (ahngn) *nt* bait

agurk (ah-*gewrk*) *m* cucumber

AIDS (ayds) AIDS

airbag (*ehr*-bæg) *m* airbag

akademi (ah-kah-day-*mee*) *nt* academy

akkompagnere (ah-koom-pahn-*ᵞay*-rer) *v* accompany

akkreditiv (ah-kreh-di-*teev*) *nt* letter of credit

akkurat (ah-kew-*raat*) *adj* just; exact; *adv* exactly

aksel (*ahk*-serl) *m* (pl aksler) axle

akselerere (*ahk*-ser-ler-*rāy*-rer) *v* accelerate

aksent (ahk-*sahngng*) *m* accent

akseptere (ahk-sehp-*tāy*-rer) *v* accept

aksje (*ahk*-sher) *m* share, stock

aksjon (ahk-*shōōn*) *m* action

akt (ahkt) *m* act; nude

akte (*ahk*-ter) *v* esteem

aktelse (*ahk*-terl-ser) *m* respect; esteem

akterspeil (*ahk*-ter-shpayl) *nt* (pl ~) stern, rear

aktiv (*ahk*-tiv) *adj* active

aktivitet (ahk-ti-vi-*tāyt*) *m* activity

aktuell (ahk-tew-*ehll*) *adj* topical; current

akutt (ah-*kewtt*) *adj* acute

akvarell (ahk-vah-*rehll*) *m* watercolo(u)r

alarm (ah-*lahrm*) *m* alarm

alarmere (ah-lahr-*māy*-rer) *v* alarm

albue (*ahl*-bēw-er) *m* elbow

album (*ahl*-bewm) *nt* album

alder (*ahl*-derr) *m* (pl ~e, aldrer) age

alderdom (*ahl*-der-dom) *m* old age, age

aldri (*ahl*-dri) *adv* never

alene (ah-*lay*-ner) *adv* alone; only

ale opp (*aa*-ler) **breed, raise

alfabet (ahl-fah-*bayt*) *nt* alphabet

algebra (*ahl*-geh-brah) *m* algebra

Algerie (ahl-sheh-*ree*) Algeria

algerier (ahl-*shay*-ri-err) *m* Algerian

algerisk (ahl-*shay*-risk) *adj* Algerian

alkohol (ahl-koo-*hool*) *m* alcohol, *colloquial* booze

alkoholholdig (ahl-koo-*hool*-hol-di) *adj* alcoholic; **alkoholholdige drikker** spirits

all (ahll) *adj* all

allé (ah-*lay*) *m* avenue

allerede (ah-ler-*ray*-der) *adv* already

allergi (ahl-ær-*gee*) *m* allergy

allianse (ah-li-*ahng*-ser) *m* alliance

allierte (ah-li-*ay*-ter) *pl* Allies *pl*

allikevel (ah-*lee*-ker-vehl) *conj* yet

allmektig (*ahl*-mehk-ti) *adj* omnipotent

allmenn (*ahl*-*mayn*) *adj* public; general

allsidig (*ahl*-see-di) *adj* all-round

alltid (*ahl*-ti) *adv* always; ever; **for ~** forever, for ever

allting (*ahl*-ting) *pron* everything

alm (ahlm) *m* elm

almanakk (ahl-mah-*nahkk*) *m* diary

alminnelig (ahl-*min*-ner-li) *adj* plain, customary, common

alpelue (*ahl*-per-*lew*-er) *c* beret

alt (ahlt) *pron* everything; *adj* all; *m* alto

alter (*ahl*-terr) *nt* (pl altre) altar

alternativ (ahl-*tæ*-nah-teev) *nt* alternative

altfor (ahlt-for) *adv* too

altså (*ahlt*-so) *adv* consequently

alv (ahlv) *m* elf

alvor (*ahl*-vor) *nt* seriousness, gravity

alvorlig (ahl-*vaw*-li) *adj* serious, bad, grave

ambassade (ahm-bah-*saa*-der) *m* embassy

ambassadør (ahm-bah-sah-*dūrr*) *m* ambassador

ambisiøs (ahm-bi-si-*ūrss*) *adj* ambitious

ambulanse (ahm-bew-*lahng*-ser) *m* ambulance

Amerika (ah-*may*-ri-kah) America

amerikaner (ah-meh-ri-*kaa*-nerr) *m* American

amerikansk (ah-meh-ri-*kaansk*) *adj* American

ametyst (ah-mer-*tewst*) *m* amethyst

amme (*ahm*-mer) *v* nurse

amnesti (ahm-ner-*stee*) *nt* amnesty

amulett (ah-mew-*lehtt*) *nt* lucky charm, charm

analfabet (ahn-nahl-fah-*bayt*) *m* illiterate

analyse (ahn-ah-*lew*-ser) *m* analysis

analysere (ahn-ah-lew-*say*-rer) *v* analyse

analytiker (ahn-ah-*lewt*-ti-kerr) *m* analyst

ananas (*ahn*-nah-nahss) *m* pineapple

anarki (ahn-ahr-*kee*) *nt* anarchy

anatomi (ahn-ah-too-*mee*) *m* anatomy

anbefale (*ahn*-beh-faa-ler) *v* recommend

anbefaling (*ahn*-beh-faa-ling) *c* recommendation

and (ahnn) *c* (pl ender) duck

ane (*aa*-ner) *v* suspect, guess

anelse (*aa*-nerl-ser) *m* notion; suspicion

anemi (ahn-eh-*mee*) *m* anaemia

anerkjenne (*ahn*-nær-kheh-ner) *v* recognize, acknowledge

anerkjennelse (*ahn*-nær-kheh-nerl-ser) *m* recognition

anfall (*ahn*-fahl) *nt* (pl ∼) fit

anfører (*ahn*-fūr-rerr) *m* leader

anførselstegn (*ahn*-fur-sherls-tayn) *pl* quotation marks

anger (*ahng*-ngerr) *m* repentance

*****angi** (*ahn*-ᵞee) *v* indicate

angre (*ahng*-rer) *v* regret, repent

angrep (*ahn*-grāyp) *nt* (pl ∼) attack; raid

*****angripe** (*ahn*-gree-per) *v* attack, assault

angst (ahngst) *m* fright

*****angå** (*ahn*-gaw) *v* concern

angående (*ahn*-gaw-erner) *prep* regarding, about, as regards, concerning

ankel (*ahng*-kerl) *m* (pl ankler) ankle

anker (*ahng*-kerr) *nt* (pl ankre) anchor

anklage¹ (*ahn*-klaa-ger) *v* accuse, charge

anklage² (*ahn*-klaa-ger) *m* charge

anklagede (*ahn*-klaa-ger-der) accused

*****ankomme** (*ahn*-ko-mer) *v* arrive

ankomst (*ahn*-komst) *m* arrival

ankomsttid (*ahn*-komst-teed) *c* time of arrival

anledning (ahn-*lāyd*-ning) *m* chance, opportunity; *****ha ∼ til** afford

anlegg (*ahn*-lehg) *nt* (pl ∼) aptitude; construction

anliggende (*ahn*-li-ger-ner) *nt* affair, concern

anmassende (*ahn*-mah-ser-ner) *adj* presumptuous

anmelde (*ahn*-meh-ler) *v* report; review

anmeldelse (*ahn*-meh-lerl-ser) *m* review

anmode (*ahn*-mōō-der) *v* request

anmodning (*ahn*-mōōd-ning) *m* request

anneks (ah-*nehks*) *nt* annex

annektere (ah-nehk-*tāy*-rer) *v* annex

annen (*aa*-ern) *num* second; *pron* other

annerledes (*ahn*-ner-lāy-derss) *adv* otherwise; *adj* different

annetsteds (*aa*-ern-stehss) *adv* elsewhere

annonse (ah-*nong*-ser) *m* advertisement

annullere (ah-new-*lāy*-rer) *v* cancel; recall

anonym (ah-noo-*nēwm*) *adj* anonymous

ansatt (*ahn*-saht) *m* (pl ∼e) employee

*****anse** (*ahn*-sāy) *v* consider, regard

anseelse (*ahn*-sāy-erl-ser) *m* reputation

anselig (ahn-*sāy*-li) *adj* considerable, substantial

*****ansette** (*ahn*-seh-ter) *v* engage

ansikt (*ahn*-sikt) *nt* face

ansiktskrem (*ahn*-sikts-krāym) *m* face cream

ansiktstrekk (*ahn*-sikts-trehk) *nt* feature

ansjos (ahn-*shōōss*) *m* anchovy

anskaffe (*ahn*-skah-fer) *v* *****buy, *****get

anskaffelse (*ahn*-skah-ferl-ser) *m* purchase

anspennelse (*ahn*-speh-nerl-ser) *m* strain

anspent (*ahn*-spehnt) *adj* tense

anspore (*ahn*-spōō-rer) *v* incite

anstendig (ahn-*stehn*-di) *adj* decent

anstendighet (ahn-*stehn*-di-hāyt) *c* decency

anstrengelse (*ahn*-strayng-erl-ser) *m* effort, strain

anstrenge seg (*ahn*-streh-nger) labo(u)r; try

anstøt (*ahn*-stūrt) *nt* (pl ∼) offense *Am*, offence

anstøtelig (*ahn*-stūrt-eli) *adj* offensive

ansvar (*ahn*-svahr) *nt* liability, responsibility

ansvarlig (ahn-*svaa*-li) *adj* liable, responsible; ~ **for** in charge of

***anta** (*ahn*-taa) *v* assume, suppose; guess

antakelig (ahn-*taa*-ker-li) *adj* presumable

antall (*ahn*-tahl) *nt* (pl ~) number; quantity

antenne (ahn-*tehn*-ner) *c* aerial

antibiotikum (ahn-ti-bi-$\overline{oo}$-ti-kewm) *nt* (pl -ka) antibiotic

antikk (ahn-*tikk*) *adj* antique

antikvitet (ahn-ti-kvi-*t$\overline{ay}$t*) *m* antique

antikvitetshandler (ahn-ti-kvi-*t$\overline{ay}$ts*-hahnd-lerr) *m* antique dealer

antipati (ahn-ti-pah-*tee*) *m* dislike

antyde (*ahn*-t$\overline{ew}$-der) *v* indicate; imply; hint

antydning (*ahn*-t$\overline{ew}$-dning) *m* hint

anvende (*ahn*-veh-ner) *v* employ, apply; utilize

anvendelig (ahn-*vehn*-ner-li) *adj* usable

anvendelse (*ahn*-veh-nerl-ser) *m* application

anvise (*ahn*-vee-ser) *v* indicate

ape (*aa*-per) *c* monkey

aperitiff (ah-peh-ri-*tiff*) *m* aperitif

apotek (ah-poo-*t$\overline{ay}$k*) *nt* pharmacy, chemist's; drugstore *nAm*

apoteker (ah-poo-*t$\overline{ay}$*-kerr) *m* chemist

apparat (ah-pah-*raat*) *nt* apparatus; machine; appliance; gadget

appell (ah-*pehll*) *m* appeal

appelsin (ah-perl-*seen*) *m* orange

appetitt (ah-per-*titt*) *m* appetite

appetittlig (ah-per-*tit*-li) *adj* appetizing

appetittvekker (ah-per-*tit*-veh-kerr) *m* appetizer

applaudere (ahp-lou-*d$\overline{ay}$*-rer) *v* clap, applaud

applaus (ah-*plouss*) *m* applause

aprikos (ahp-ri-*k$\overline{oo}$ss*) *m* apricot

april (ah-*preel*) April

araber (ah-*raa*-berr) *m* Arab

arabisk (ah-*raa*-bisk) *adj* Arab

arbeid (*ahr*-bay) *nt* labo(u)r, work; employment

arbeide (ahr-*bay*-der) *v* work

arbeider (ahr-*bay*-derr) *m* labo(u)rer, worker, workman

arbeidsbesparende (*ahr*-bayss-beh-spaa-rer-ner) *adj* labo(u)r-saving

arbeidsdag (*ahr*-bayss-daag) *m* working day

arbeidsformidling (*ahr*-bayss-for-mid-ling) *c* employment exchange

arbeidsgiver (*ahr*-bayss-^{y}ee-verr) *m* employer

arbeidsledig (*ahr*-bayss-*l$\overline{ay}$*-di) *adj* unemployed, jobless

arbeidsledighet (*ahr*-bayss-*l$\overline{ay}$*-di-h$\overline{ay}$t) *c* unemployment

arbeidsløs (*ahr*-bayss-l$\overline{ur}$ss) *adj* unemployed, jobless

arbeidsløshet (*ahr*-bayss-l$\overline{ur}$ss-h$\overline{ay}$t) *c* unemployment

arbeidstillatelse (*ahr*-bayss-ti-laa-terl-ser) *m* work permit; labor permit *Am*

areal (ah-reh-*aal*) *nt* area

Argentina (ahr-gern-*tee*-nah) Argentina

argentiner (ahr-gern-*tee*-nerr) *m* Argentinian

argentinsk (ahr-gern-*teensk*) *adj* Argentinian

argument (ahr-gew-*mehnt*) *nt* argument

argumentere (ahr-gew-mehn-*t$\overline{ay}$*-rer) *v* argue

ark (ahrk) *nt* sheet

arkade (ahr-*kaa*-der) *m* arcade

arkeolog (ahr-keh-oo-*lawg*) *m* archaeologist

arkeologi (ahr-keh-oo-loo-*gee*) *m* archaeology

arkitekt (ahr-ki-*tehkt*) *m* architect

arkitektur (ahr-ki-tehk-*tewr*) *m* architecture

arkiv (ahr-*keev*) *nt* archives *pl*

arm (ahrm) *m* arm; **arm i arm** arm-in-arm

armbånd (*ahrm*-bon) *nt* (pl ~) bangle, bracelet

armbåndsur (*ahrm*-bons-ēwr) *nt* (pl ~) wrist-watch

armé (ahr-*māy*) *m* army

aroma (ah-*rōō*-mah) *m* aroma

arr (ahrr) *nt* scar

arrangere (ah-rahng-*shāy*-rer) *v* arrange

arrestasjon (ah-reh-stah-*shōōn*) *m* arrest, capture

arrestere (ah-reh-*stāy*-rer) *v* arrest

art (ahtt) *m* species

artikkel (ah-*tik*-kerl) *m* (pl artikler) article

artisjokk (ah-ti-*shokk*) *m* artichoke

artistisk (ah-*tiss*-tisk) *adj* artistic

arv (ahrv) *m* inheritance

arve (*ahr*-ver) *v* inherit

arvelig (*ahr*-ver-li) *adj* hereditary

arving (*ahrv*-ing) *m* heir; heiress

asbest (ahss-*behst*) *m* asbestos

asfalt (*ahss*-fahlt) *m* asphalt

Asia (*aa*-si-ah) Asia

asiat (ah-si-*aat*) *m* Asian

asiatisk (ah-si-*aa*-tisk) *adj* Asian

aske (*ahss*-ker) *c* ash

askebeger (*ahss*-ker-bāy-gerr) *nt* (pl -gre) ashtray

asparges (ah-*spahr*-gerss) *m* (pl ~) asparagus

aspekt (ah-*spehkt*) *nt* aspect

aspirin (ahss-pi-*reen*) *m* aspirin

assistanse (ah-si-*stahng*-ser) *m* assistance

assistent (ah-si-*stehnt*) *m* assistant

astma (*ahst*-mah) *m* asthma

astronomi (ah-stroo-noo-*mee*) *m* astronomy

asyl (ah-*sēwl*) *nt* asylum

at (ahtt) *conj* that

ateist (ah-teh-*ist*) *m* atheist

Atlanterhavet (aht-*lahn*-terr-haa-ver) Atlantic

atlet (aht-*lāyt*) *m* athlete

atmosfære (aht-mooss-*fææ*-rer) *m* atmosphere

atom (ah-*tōōm*) *nt* atom; **atom-** atomic

atskillelse (*aat*-shi-lerl-ser) *m* separation

atskillige (aht-*shil*-li-er) *adj* several

atskilt (*aat*-shilt) *adj* separate; *adv* apart

atspredelse (*aat*-sprāy-derl-ser) *m* amusement, diversion; recreation

atten (*aht*-tern) *num* eighteen

attende (*aht*-terner) *num* eighteenth

atter (*aht*-terr) *adv* again

attest (ah-*tehst*) *m* certificate

attestere (ah-*tehs*-tāy-rer) *v* attest

attraksjon (ah-trahk-*shōōn*) *m* attraction

attråverdig (*aht*-raw-vær-di) *adj* desirable

aubergine (o-behr-*sheen*) *m* eggplant

auditorium (ou-di-*tōō*-ri-ewm) *nt* (pl -ier) auditorium

august (ou-*gewst*) August

auksjon (ouk-*shōōn*) *m* auction

Australia (ou-*straa*-li-ah) Australia

australier (ou-*straa*-li-err) *m* Australian

australsk (ou-*straalsk*) *adj* Australian

autentisk (ou-*tehn*-tisk) *adj* authentic

automat (ou-too-*maat*) *m* slot machine; vending machine

automatisering (ou-too-mah-ti-*sāy*-ring) *c* automation

automatisk (ou-too-*maa*-tisk) *adj*

automatic
automobilklubb (ou-too-moo-*beel*-klewb) *m* automobile club
autorisasjon (ou-too-ri-sah-*shoon*) *m* authorization
autoritet (ou-too-ri-*tayt*) *m* authority
autoritær (ou-too-ri-*tæær*) *adj* authoritarian
av (aav) *prep* by, of, for, with, from; *adv* off, ~ **og til** sometimes, occasionally
avansert (ah-vahng-*sayt*) *adj* advanced
avbestille (*aav*-beh-sti-ler) *v* cancel
avbestilling (*aav*-beh-sti-ling) *c* cancellation
avbetale (*aav*-beh-tah-ler) *v* *pay on account; *pay instalments on
avbetalingskjøp (*aav*-beh-tah-lings-*khūrp*) *nt* (pl ~) hire purchase, *Am* instalment plan
***avbryte** (*aav*-*brēw*-ter) *v* interrupt
avbrytelse (*aav*-*brēwt*-erl-ser) *m* interruption
avdekke (*aav*-deh-ker) *v* uncover
avdeling (ahv-*dāy*-ling) *c* department; division, section
avdrag (*aav*-draag) *nt* (pl ~) instalment
aveny (ah-ver-*nēw*) *m* avenue
avfall (*aav*-fahl) *nt* rubbish, refuse, garbage, litter
avfatte (*aav*-fah-ter) *v* *draw up; compose
avføringsmiddel (*aav*-*fūr*-rings-mi-derl) *nt* (pl -midler) laxative
avgang (*aav*-gahng) *m* departure
avgangstid (*aav*-gahngs-teed) *c* time of departure
avgifter (*aav*-*ᵞif*-terr) *pl* dues *pl*
***avgjøre** (*aav*-*ᵞūr*-rer) *v* decide
avgjørelse (*aav*-*ᵞūr*-rerl-ser) *m* decision
avgrunn (*aav*-grewn) *m* abyss

avgud (*aav*-gēwd) *m* idol
avhandling (*aav*-hahnd-ling) *c* essay, treatise
avhengig (*aav*-heh-ngi) *adj* dependant
avhente (*aav*-hehn-ter) *v* collect, fetch
***avholde seg fra** (*aav*-ho-ler) abstain from
avholdsmann (*aav*-hols-mahn) *m* (pl -menn) teetotaller
avis (ah-*veess*) *c* newspaper
aviskiosk (ah-*veess*-khosk) *m* newsstand
avlang (*aav*-lahng) *adj* oblong
avleiring (*aav*-lay-ring) *c* deposit
avlevere (*aav*-leh-*vāy*-rer) *v* deliver
avling (*ahv*-ling) *c* harvest, crop
avløp (*aav*-lūrp) *nt* (pl ~) drain
avløse (*aav*-lūr-ser) *v* relieve
avreise (*aav*-ray-ser) *c* departure
avrundet (*aav*-rew-nert) *adj* rounded
avsende (*aav*-seh-ner) *v* dispatch, dispatch
avsender (*aav*-seh-nerr) *m* sender
avsides (*aav*-see-derss) *adj* out of the way, remote
avskaffe (*aav*-skah-fer) *v* abolish
avskjed (*aav*-*shāyd*) *m* parting; resignation
avskjedige (*aav*-*shāy*-di-er) *v* dismiss, fire
avskjedssøknad (*aav*-*shāyds*-*sūrk*-nah) *m* resignation
avskrekke (*aav*-skrehk-ker) *v* discourage
avsky¹ (*aav*-*shēw*) *v* hate, dislike, detest
avsky² (*aav*-*shēw*) *m* dislike, disgust
avskyelig (ahv-*shēw*-er-li) *adj* hideous, horrible, disgusting
avslag (*aav*-shlaag) *nt* (pl ~) refusal; discount, reduction
avslapning (*aav*-shlahp-ning) *m*

relaxation
avslappet (*aav*-shlah-pert) *adj* easy-going; relaxed
avslutning (*aav*-shlewt-ning) *m* ending
avslutte (*aav*-shlew-ter) *v* stop, finish; settle
avsløre (*aav*-shlūr-rer) *v* reveal; expose
avsløring (*aav*-shlūr-ring) *c* revelation
*****avslå** (*aav*-shlaw) *v* refuse
avsnitt (*aav*-snit) *nt* (pl ~) paragraph; passage
avspark (*aav*-spahrk) *nt* kick-off
avstamning (*aav*-stahm-ning) *m* origin
avstand (*aav*-stahn) *m* distance; space; way
avstandsmåler (*aav*-stahns-maw-lerr) *m* range finder
avstemning (*aav*-stehm-ning) *m* vote
*****avta** (*aav*-taa) *v* decrease
avtale (*aav*-taa-ler) *m* agreement, engagement; date, appointment
avtrekker (*aav*-treh-kerr) *m* trigger
avtrykk (*aav*-trewk) *nt* (pl ~) print
avveksling (*aav*-vehks-ling) *c* variation
avvente (*aa*-vehn-ter) *v* await
avverge (*aa*-vær-ger) *v* prevent
*****avvike** (*aa*-vee-ker) *v* deviate
avvise (*aa*-vee-ser) *v* reject

B

babord (*baa*-boor) port
baby (*bay*-bi) *m* baby
babybag (*bay*-bi-bæg) *m* carry-cot
bacon (*bay*-kern) *nt* bacon
bad (baad) *nt* bath, bathroom
bade (*baa*-der) *v* bathe; swim
badebukse (*baa*-der-book-ser) *c* swimming-trunks *pl*, bathing suit
badedrakt (*baa*-der-drahkt) *c* swimsuit, swimming suit *Am*, bathing suit
badehette (*baa*-der-heh-ter) *c* bathing cap
badehåndkle (*baa*-der-hong-kler) *nt* (pl -lær) bath towel
badekåpe (*baa*-der-kaw-per) *c* bathrobe
badested (*baa*-der-stāy) *nt* seaside resort
badevakt (*baa*-der-vakt) *c* pool attendant
badeværelse (*baa*-der-væl-ser) *nt* bathroom
badstue (*bahss*-tēwer) *c* sauna
bagasje (bah-*gaa*-sher) *m* luggage, baggage
bagasjehylle (bah-*gaa*-sher-hew-ler) *c* luggage rack
bagasjeoppbevaring (bah-*gaa*-sher-oop-ber-*vaa*-ring) *c* left luggage office; *Am* baggage deposit office
bagasjerom (bah-*gaa*-sher-room) *nt* (pl ~) boot; *nAm* trunk
bagasjevogn (bah-*gah*-sher-vongn) *c* luggage van
bak (baak) *prep* behind; *adv* behind; *m* bottom
bake (*baa*-ker) *v* bake
baker (*baa*-kerr) *m* baker
bakeri (bah-ker-*ree*) *nt* bakery
bakgrunn (*baak*-grewn) *m* background
bakhold (*baak*-hol) *nt* (pl ~) ambush
bakke (*bahk*-ker) *m* hill; earth

bakketopp (*bahk*-ker-top) *m* hilltop

baklengs (*baak*-lehngs) *adv*
backwards

baklykt (*baak*-lewkt) *c* rear light

baklys (*baak*-le̅wss) *nt* (pl ~) tail-light

bakside (*baak*-see-der) *c* rear; reverse

bakterie (bahk-*ta̅y*-ri-er) *m* bacterium

bakvaskelse (*baak*-vahss-kerl-ser) *m*
slander

bakverk (*baak*-værk) *nt* bakegoods;
finere ~ pastry

balanse (bah-*lahng*-ser) *m* balance

balkong (bahl-*kongng*) *m* balcony;
dress circle

ball (bahll) *m* ball; *nt* ball

ballett (bah-*lehtt*) *m* ballet

ballong (bah-*longng*) *m* balloon

bambus (*bahm*-bewss) *m* bamboo

banan (bah-*naan*) *m* banana

bandasje (bahn-*daa*-sher) *m* bandage

bande (*bahn*-der) *m* gang

banditt (bahn-*ditt*) *m* bandit

bane (*baa*-ner) *m* track

bank (bahngk) *m* bank; *m/nt* tap;
*sette i banken deposit

banke (*bahng*-ker) *v* knock, tap

bankett (bahng-*kehtt*) *m* banquet

bankhvelv (*bahngk*-vehlv) *nt* (pl ~)
vault

bankkonto (*bahng*-kon-too) *m* (pl
~er, -ti) bank account

banne (*bahn*-ner) *v* curse, *swear

banner (*bahn*-nerr) *nt* (pl ~, ~e)
banner

banning (*bahn*-ning) *c* curse

bar (baar) *adj* bare, naked; neat; *m*
bar, saloon

barberblad (bahr-*ba̅yr*-blaa) *nt* (pl ~)
razor blade

barbere seg (bahr-*ba̅y*-rer) shave

barberhøvel (bahr-*bair-hur*-verl) *m*
(pl -vler) safety razor, razor

barberkost (bahr-*ba̅yr*-koost) *m*
shaving brush

barbermaskin (bahr-*ba̅yr*-mah-
sheen) *m* electric razor, shaver

barberskum (bahr-*ba̅yr*-skoomm) *nt*
shaving foam

bare (*baarer*) *adv* only, merely

bark (bahrk) *m* bark

barm (bahrm) *m* bosom

barmhjertig (bahrm-ᵞæ-ti) *adj*
merciful

barmhjertighet (bahrm-ᵞæ-ti-ha̅yt) *c*
mercy

barn (baan) *nt* child; kid; **foreldreløst
~** orphan

barnebarn (baa-ner-baan) *nt*
grandchild

barnehage (*baa*-ner-haa-ger) *m*
kindergarten

barnepike (*baa*-ner-pee-ker) *m* nurse

barnevakt (*baa*-ner-vahkt) *c*
babysitter

barnevogn (*baa*-ner-voangn) *c* pram;
baby carriage *Am*

barneværelse (*baa*-ner-væ-rerl-ser)
nt nursery

barokk (bah-*rokk*) *adj* baroque

barometer (bah-roo-*ma̅y*-terr) *nt* (pl
-tre) barometer

barriere (bah-ri-*ææ*-rer) *m* barrier;
crash barrier

barsk (bahshk) *adj* bleak; tough

bart (bahtt) *m* moustache

bartender (*baa*-tehn-derr) *m*
bartender, barman

baryton (*bahr*-ri-ton) *m* baritone

basar (bah-*saar*) *m* fair

base (*baa*-ser) *m* base

basere (bah-*sa̅y*-rer) *v* base

basilika (bah-*see*-li-kah) *m* basilica

basill (bah-*sill*) *m* germ

basis (*baa*-siss) *m* basis, base

bass (bahss) *m* bass

bastard (bah-*stahrd*) *m* bastard

batteri (bah-ter-*ree*) *nt* battery

*be (ba̅y) *v* ask; beg; pray

bebo (beh-*boo*) v inhabit

beboelig (beh-*boo*-er-li) adj habitable, inhabitable

beboer (beh-*boo*-err) m occupant, inhabitant

bebreide (beh-*bray*-der) v blame, reproach

bebreidelse (beh-*bray*-derl-ser) m blame, reproach

bedervelig (beh-*dær*-ver-li) adj perishable

***bedra** (beh-*draa*) v deceive

bedrag (beh-*draag*) nt (pl ~) deceit

bedrageri (beh-drah-ger-*ree*) nt fraud

bedre (*bayd*-rer) adj better; superior

bedrift (beh-*drift*) m concern; feat

bedring (*bayd*-ring) c recovery

bedrøvelig (beh-*drūr*-ver-li) adj sad, dreary

bedrøvet (beh-*drūr*-vert) adj sad

bedyre (beh-*dew*-rer) v affirm

bedømme (beh-*durm*-mer) v judge

bedøvelse (beh-*dūr*-verl-ser) m anaesthesia

bedøvelsesmiddel (beh-*dūr*-verl-serss-mi-derl) nt (pl -midler) anaesthetic

bedårende (beh-*daw*-rer-ner) adj enchanting

befale (beh-*faa*-ler) v command

befaling (beh-*faa*-ling) c order, command

befalshavende (beh-*faals*-haa-ver-ner) m commander

befolkning (beh-*folk*-ning) m population

befrielse (beh-*free*-erl-ser) m liberation

befruktning (beh-*frewkt*-ning) m conception; fertilization

begavelse (beh-*gaa*-verl-ser) m talent, faculty

begavet (beh-*gaa*-vert) adj gifted, talented; clever, brilliant

begeistret (beh-*gayss*-trert) adj keen, enthusiastic

beger (*bay*-gerr) nt (pl ~, begre) tumbler

begge (behg-ger) pron both; either

begivenhet (beh-*ʲee*-vern-hāyt) c event, happening

begjær (beh-*ʲæær*) nt desire; lust

begjære (beh-*ʲææ*-rer) v desire

begrave (beh-*graa*-ver) v bury

begravelse (beh-*graa*-verl-ser) m funeral; burial

begrense (beh-*grehn*-ser) v limit

begrenset (beh-*grehn*-sert) adj limited

begrep (beh-*grāyp*) nt notion, idea

***begripe** (beh-*gree*-per) v *see, *understand

begunstige (beh-*gewns*-ti-er) v favo(u)r

begynne (beh-*ʲewn*-ner) v start, commence, *begin; ~ **igjen** recommence

begynnelse (beh-*ʲewn*-nerl-ser) m beginning; **i begynnelsen** at first; originally

***begå** (beh-*gaw*) v commit

behagelig (beh-*haa*-ger-li) adj agreeable, pleasing, enjoyable

behandle (beh-*hahnd*-ler) v handle, treat

behandling (beh-*hahnd*-ling) c treatment

***beholde** (beh-*hol*-ler) v *keep

beholder (beh-*hol*-lerr) m container

behov (beh-*hoov*) nt (pl ~) need; want

behøve (beh-*hūr*-ver) v need; demand

behå (beh-ho) m bra

beige (*baysh*) adj beige

bein (bayn) nt (pl ~) leg; bone

beinskinne (*bāyn*-shi-ner) c splint

beite (*bay*-ter) nt pasture; v graze

bekjempe (beh-*khehm*-per) v combat

bekjenne (beh-*kheh*-ner) v confess

bekjent (beh-*khehnt*) *m* acquaintance

***bekjentgjøre** (beh-*khehnt*-ᵞ*ūr*-rer) *v* announce

bekjentgjørelse (beh-*khehnt*-ᵞ*ūr*-rerl-ser) *m* announcement; bulletin

bekk (behkk) *m* stream, brook

bekken (*behk*-kern) *nt* pelvis

beklage (beh-*klaager*) *v* regret

beklagelse (beh-*klaa*-gerl-ser) *m* regret

beklager! (beh-*klaa*-gerr) sorry!

bekrefte (beh-*krehf*-ter) *v* confirm; acknowledge; affirm

bekreftelse (beh-*krehf*-terl-ser) *m* confirmation

bekreftende (beh-*krayf*-ter-ner) *adj* affirmative

bekvem (beh-*kvehmm*) *adj* comfortable; easy, convenient

bekvemmelighet (beh-*kvehm*-mer-li-hāyt) *c* comfort

bekymre seg (beh-*khewm*-rer) worry; **bekymre seg om** care about

bekymret (beh-*khewm*-rert) *adj* concerned, worried

bekymring (beh-*khewm*-ring) *c* anxiety, worry; concern, care

belastning (beh-*lahst*-ning) *m* load, strain

beleilig (beh-*lay*-li) *adj* convenient

beleiring (beh-*lay*-ring) *c* siege

Belgia (*behl*-gi-ah) Belgium

belgier (*behl*-gi-err) *m* Belgian

belgisk (*behl*-gisk) *adj* Belgian

beliggende (beh-*lig*-ger-ner) *adj* situated

beliggenhet (beh-*lig*-gern-hāyt) *c* location, site

belte (*behl*-ter) *nt* belt

belyse (beh-*lēw*-ser) *v* illuminate

belysning (beh-*lēwss*-ning) *m* lighting, illumination

belønne (beh-*lurn*-ner) *v* reward

belønning (beh-*lurn*-ning) *c* reward; prize

beløp (beh-*lūrp*) *nt* (pl ~) amount

***beløpe seg til** (beh-*lūr*-per) amount to

bemerke (beh-*mær*-ker) *v* note, notice; remark

bemerkelsesverdig (beh-*mær*-kerl-serss-vær-di) *adj* noticeable, remarkable

bemerkning (beh-*mærk*-ning) *m* remark

benekte (beh-*nehk*-ter) *v* deny

benektende (beh-*nehk*-ter-ner) *adj* negative

benevnelse (beh-*nehv*-nerl-ser) *m* name, designation, denomination

benk (behngk) *m* bench

bensin (behn-*seen*) *m* fuel, petrol; gas *nAm*, gasoline *nAm*; **blyfri ~** unleaded petrol

bensinpumpe (behn-*seen*-poom-per) *c* petrol pump; fuel pump *Am*

bensinstasjon (behn-*seen*-stah-shōōn) *m* service station, petrol station, filling station; gas station *Am*

bensintank (behn-*seen*-tahngk) *m* petrol tank, gas tank *Am*

benytte (beh-*newt*-ter) *v* use, make use of

benådning (beh-*nawd*-ning) *m* pardon

beordre (beh-*or*-drer) *v* order

beredt (beh-*reht*) *adj* prepared

beregne (beh-*ray*-ner) *v* calculate

berettiget (beh-*reht*-ti-ert) *adj* justified

berg (bærg) *nt* mountain

berglendt (*bærg*-lehnt) *adj* mountainous

berolige (beh-*rōō*-li-er) *v* reassure, calm down

beroligende (beh-*rōō*-li-er-ner) *adj* restful; **~ middel** sedative, tranquillizer

bero på (beh-*roo*) depend on
beruset (beh-*rew*-sert) *adj*
intoxicated, drunk
beryktet (beh-*rewk*-tert) *adj*
notorious
berømmelse (beh-*rurm*-merl-ser) *m*
fame, glory, celebrity
berømt (beh-*rurmt*) *adj* famous
berøre (beh-*rūr*-rer) *v* touch
berøring (beh-*rūr*-ring) *c* touch
besatt (beh-*sahtt*) *adj* possessed
beseire (beh-*say*-rer) *v* conquer
*besette (beh-*seht*-ter) *v* occupy·
besettelse (beh-*seht*-terl-ser) *m*
obsession
besittelse (beh-*sit*-terl-ser) *m*
possession
beskatning (beh-*skaht*-ning) *m*
taxation
beskjed (beh-*shēr*) *m* message
beskjeden (beh-*shāy*-dern) *adj*
modest
beskjedenhet (beh-*shāy*-dern-hāyt) *c*
modesty
beskjeftige (beh-*shehf*-ti-er) *v*
employ, occupy
beskjeftigelse (beh-*shehf*-ti-erl-ser)
m employment, occupation
*beskrive (beh-*skree*-ver) *v* describe
beskrivelse (beh-*skree*-verl-ser) *m*
description
beskylde (beh-*shewl*-ler) *v* accuse
beskytte (beh-*shewt*-ter) *v* protect
beskyttelse (beh-*shewt*-terl-ser) *m*
protection
*beslaglegge (beh-*shlaag*-leh-ger) *v*
confiscate
beslektet (beh-*shlehk*-tert) *adj*
related
beslutning (beh-*shlewt*-ning) *m*
decision
besluttsom (beh-*shlewt*-som) *adj*
resolute
best (behst) *adj* best

bestanddel (beh-*stahn*-dāyl) *m*
element, ingredient
bestefar (*behss*-ter-faar) *m* (pl -fedre)
grandfather, granddad
besteforeldre (*behss*-ter-fo-rehl-drer)
pl grandparents *pl*
bestemme (beh-*stehm*-mer) *v* define,
determine; designate, destine
bestemmelse (beh-*stehm*-merl-ser)
m regulation
bestemmelsessted (beh-*stehm*-merl-
serss-stāy) *nt* destination
bestemor (*behss*-ter-mōōr) *m* (pl
-mødre) grandmother
bestemt (beh-*stehmt*) *adj* definite;
resolute
*bestige (beh-*stee*-ger) *v* ascend;
mount
bestikk (beh-*stikk*) *nt* cutlery;
silverware *nAm*
*bestikke (beh-*stik*-ker) *v* corrupt,
bribe
bestikkelse (beh-*stik*-kerl-ser) *m*
corruption, bribery; bribe
bestille (beh-*stil*-ler) *v* order; book,
engage, reserve
bestilling (beh-*stil*-ling) *c* order;
booking; **laget på ~** made to order
bestrebelse (beh-*strāy*-berl-ser) *m*
effort
*bestride (beh-*stree*-der) *v* dispute
bestyre (beh-*stēw*-rer) *v* manage
bestyrer (beh-stew-rer) *m* manager
*bestå (beh-*staw*) *v* exist; pass a test; **~
av** consist of
besvare (beh-*svaa*-rer) *v* answer
besvime (beh-*svee*-mer) *v* faint
besvær (beh-*svæær*) *nt* trouble,
inconvenience
besværlig (beh-*svææ*-li) *adj*
inconvenient
besøk (beh-*sūrk*) *nt* (pl ~) call, visit
besøke (beh-*sūr*-ker) *v* call on, visit
besøkende (beh-*sūr*-ker-ner) *m*

visitor
besøkstid (beh-_sūrks_-teed) _c_ visiting hours
betagende (beh-_taa_-ger-ner) _adj_ moving; beautiful
betalbar (beh-_taal_-bahr) _adj_ due; payable
betale (beh-_taa_-ler) _v_ *pay
betaling (beh-_taa_-ling) _c_ payment
betegnende (beh-_tay_-ner-ner) _adj_ characteristic
betenkt (beh-_tehngkt_) _adj_ uneasy
betennelse (beh-_tehn_-nerl-ser) _m_ inflammation; *gå ~ i *become septic
betingelse (beh-_ting_-ngerl-ser) _m_ term; stipulation
betingelsesløs (beh-_ting_-ngerl-serss-lūrss) _adj_ unconditional
betinget (beh-_ting_-ngert) _adj_ conditional
betjene (beh-_t'ay_-ner) _v_ attend on; serve
betjening (beh-_t'ay_-ning) _c_ service
betong (beh-_tongng_) _m_ concrete
betoning (beh-_tōō_-ning) _c_ accent
betrakte (beh-_trahk_-ter) _v_ consider, regard; view, watch; **i betraktning av** considering
betraktelig (beh-_trahk_-ter-li) _adj_ considerable
betro (beh-_trōō_) _v_ confide in
betvile (beh-_tvee_-ler) _v_ query, doubt
bety (beh-_tēw_) _v_ *mean
betydelig (beh-_tēw_-der-li) _adj_ considerable
betydning (beh-_tēwd_-ning) _m_ sense; importance; *være av ~ matter
betydningsfull (beh-_tēwd_-nings-fewl) _adj_ important; significant
beundre (beh-_ewn_-drer) _v_ admire
beundrer (beh-_ewn_-drerr) _m_ fan
beundring (beh-_ewn_-dring) _c_ admiration
bevare (beh-_vaa_-rer) _v_ *keep;

*uphold
bevege (beh-_vāy_-ger) _v_ move
bevegelig (beh-_vāy_-ger-li) _adj_ mobile
bevegelse (beh-_vāy_-gerl-ser) _m_ motion, movement
bever (_bay_-verr) _m_ beaver
beverte (beh-_væ_-ter) _v_ entertain, treat
bevilge (beh-_veel_-ger) _v_ extend, grant; allow
bevis (beh-_veess_) _nt_ proof, evidence; token
bevise (beh-_vee_-ser) _v_ prove; demonstrate, *show
bevisst (beh-_vist_) _adj_ conscious
bevissthet (beh-_vist_-hāyt) _c_ consciousness
bevisstløs (beh-_vist_-lūrss) _adj_ unconscious
bevitne (beh-_vit_-ne) _v_ attest
bevokte (beh-_vok_-ter) _v_ watch, guard
bevæpne (beh-_vāyp_-ner) _v_ arm
bevæpnet (beh-_vayp_-nert) _adj_ armed
bibel (_bee_-berl) _m_ (pl bibler) bible
bibliotek (bi-bli-oo-_tāyk_) _nt_ library
bidrag (_bee_-draag) _nt_ (pl ~) contribution; allowance
bie (_bee_-er) _c_ bee
bielv (_bee_-ehlv) _c_ tributary
bifalle (_bee_-fah-ler) _v_ consent; applaud
biff (biff) _m_ steak
bikube (_bee_-kew-ber) _c_ beehive
bil (beel) _m_ automobile, car
bilde (_bil_-der) _nt_ picture, image
bile (_bee_-ler) _v_ motor
bilhorn (_beel_-hōōn) _nt_ (pl ~) hooter
bilisme (bi-_liss_-mer) _m_ motoring
bilist (bi-_list_) _m_ motorist
biljard (bil-_y_aad) _m_ billiards _pl_
bille (_bil_-ler) _m_ beetle; bug
billedhogger (_bil_-lerd-ho-gerr) _m_ sculptor
billett (bi-_lehtt_) _m_ ticket
billettautomat (bi-_lehtt_-ou-too-maat)

m ticket machine

billettkontor (bi-*leht*-koon-tóor) *nt* box office

billettluke (bi-*leht*-lew-ker) *c* box office window

billettpris (bi-*leht*-preess) *m* fare; admission fee

billig (*bil*-li) *adj* cheap, inexpensive

billigbok (*bil*-li-bóok) *c* paperback

bilpanser (*beel*-pahn-serr) *nt* bonnet; hood *nAm*

bilutleie (*beel*-oot-lay-er) *c* car hire; car rental *Am*

bind (binn) *nt* volume; sanitary napkin *Am*, sanitary towel

*binde (*bin*-ner) *v* *bind; tie; ~ **sammen** bundle

bindestrek (*bin*-ner-stráyk) *m* hyphen

biologi (bi-oo-loo-*gee*) *m* biology

biskop (*biss*-kop) *m* bishop

*bistå (*bee*-staw) *v* assist, aid

bit (beet) *m* bit, piece; scrap, morsel; bite

*bite (*bee*-ter) *v* *bite

bitter (*bit*-terr) *adj* bitter

bjelke (*b*ᵞ*ehl*-ker) *m* beam

bjelle (*b*ᵞ*ehl*-ler) *c* small bell

bjørk (b*ᵞ*urrk) *c* birch

bjørn (b*ᵞ*ūrn) *m* bear

bjørnebær (b*ᵞ*ū̄r-ner-bæær) *nt* (pl ~) blackberry

blad (blaa) *nt* leaf; blade

bladgull (*blaa*-gewl) *nt* gold leaf

bladsalat (*blaa*-sah-laht) *m* lettuce

blakk (blahkk) *adj* broke

blande (*blahn*-ner) *v* mix; ~ **seg inn i** interfere with

blandet (*blahn*-nert) *adj* mixed

blanding (*blahn*-ning) *c* mixture

blank (blahngk) *adj* glossy; blank

blankett (blahng-*kehtt*) *m* form

blant (blahnt) *prep* amid; among; ~ **annet** among other things

bleie (*blay*-er) *c* nappy; diaper *nAm*

blek (bl*ā̄y*k) *adj* pale

bleke (*bl*ā̄y-ker) *v* bleach

blekk (blehkk) *nt* ink

blekksprut (*blehk*-sprēwt) *m* octopus

blekne (*bl*ā̄yk-ner) *v* fade; *grow pale

blemme (*blehm*-mer) *c* blister

blende (*blehn*-ner) *v* blind

blendende (*blehn*-ner-ner) *adj* glaring

*bli (blee) *v* *become, *be, *get, *grow; stay; ~ **igjen** remain

blikk (blikk) *nt* glance, look; **kaste et ~** glance

blind (blinn) *adj* blind

blindgate (*blin*-gaa-ter) *c* cul-de-sac

blindtarm (*blin*-tahrm) *m* appendix

blindtarmbetennelse (*blin*-tahrm-beh-teh-nerl-ser) *m* appendicitis

blinklys (*blingk*-lēwss) *nt* (pl ~) trafficator; blinker *nAm*

blitzlampe (*blits*-lahm-per) *c* flash bulb

blod (bl*ōō*) *nt* blood

blodforgiftning (*bl*ōō-for-ᵞift-ning) *m* blood poisoning

blodkar (*bl*ōō-kaar) *nt* (pl ~) blood vessel

blodomløp (*bl*ōō-oom-lūrp) *nt* (pl ~) circulation

blodtrykk (*bl*ōō-trewk) *nt* (pl ~) blood pressure

blokk (blokk) *c* block

blokkere (blo-*k*ā̄y-rer) *v* block

blomkål (*blom*-kawl) *m* cauliflower

blomst (blomst) *m* flower, blossom

blomsterbed (*blom*-sterr-behd) *nt* (pl ~) flowerbed

blomsterforretning (*blom*-sterr-for-reht-ning) *c* flower shop

blomsterhandler (*blom*-sterr-hahnd-lerr) *m* florist

blomsterløk (*blom*-sterr-lūrk) *m* bulb

blomstre (blom-strer) *v* flower, blossom

blond (blonn) *adj* fair, blond
blondine (blon-*dee*-ner) *c* blonde
***blottlegge** (*blott*-leh-ger) *v* expose
bluse (*blew*-ser) *c* blouse
bly (blew) *nt* lead
blyant (*blew*-ahnt) *m* pencil
blyantspisser (*blew*-ahnt-spi-serr) *m* pencil sharpener
blyg (blewg) *adj* timid
blære (*blææ*-rer) *c* bladder
blærekatarr (*blææ*-rer-kah-tahr) *m* cystitis
blø (blur) *v* *bleed
blødning (*blurd*-ning) *m* h(a)emorrhage
bløt (blurt) *adj* mellow
bløte (*blur*-ter) *v* soak
***bløtgjøre** (*blurt*-ʸur-rer) *v* soften
blå (blaw) *adj* blue; **blått merke** bruise
blåse (*blaw*-ser) *v* *blow; **~ opp** inflate
blåsende (*blaw*-ser-ner) *adj* gusty
blåskjell (*blo*-shehl) *nt* (pl ~) mussel
bo (boo) *v* live, reside
bobil (*boo*-beel) *m* camper, caravan
boble (*bob*-ler) *c* bubble
bok (book) *c* (pl bøker) book
bokbind (*book*-bin) *nt* (pl ~) binding
bokføre (*book*-fur-rer) *v* enter, book
bokhandel (*book*-hahn-derl) *m* (pl -dler) bookstore
bokhandler (*book*-hahnd-lerr) *m* bookseller
boks (boks) *m* can, tin
bokse (*bok*-ser) *v* box
boksekamp (*bok*-ser-kahmp) *m* boxing match
bokstav (book-*staav*) *m* letter; **stor ~** capital letter
boksåpner (*boks*-awp-nerr) *m* can opener
bolig (*boo*-li) *m* house, residence
Bolivia (boo-*lee*-vi-ah) Bolivia
bolivianer (boo-li-vi-*aa*-nerr) *m* Bolivian
boliviansk (boo-li-vi-*aansk*) *adj* Bolivian
bolle (*bol*-ler) *m* bowl; basin; bun
bolt (bolt) *m* bolt
bom (boomm) *m* barrier; miss
bombardere (boom-bah-*day*-rer) *v* bomb
bombe (*boom*-ber) *c* bomb
bomme (*boom*-mer) *v* miss
bompenger (boomm-peh-ngerr) *pl* toll
bomull (*boom*-mewl) *m* cotton; **bomulls-** cotton
bomullsfløyel (*boom*-mewls-flurᵉʷ-erl) *m* velveteen
bomvei (*boom*-vay) *m* turnpike *nAm*
bonde (*boon*-ner) *m* (pl bønder) peasant, farmer
bondegård (*boon*-ner-gawr) *m* farm
bondekone (*boon*-ner-koo-ner) *c* farmer's wife
bong (bong) *m* voucher
bopel (*boo*-payl) *m* domicile
bor (borr) *nt* drill
bord (boor) *nt* table
bordell (boo-*dehll*) *m/nt* brothel
bordtennis (*boo*-teh-niss) *m* ping-pong, table tennis
bore (*boo*-rer) *v* bore, drill; **~plattform** drilling platform
borg (borg) *c* castle
borger (*bor*-gerr) *m* citizen; **borger-** civic
borgerlig (*bor*-ger-li) *adj* middle-class
borgermester (*bor*-ger-mehss-terr) *m* (pl -tre) mayor
bort (boott) *adv* away; ***gå ~** *leave, *go away
borte (*boot*-ter) *adv* gone; off
bortenfor (*boot*-tern-for) *adv* beyond; *prep* off; beyond
bortsett fra (*boot*-seht) apart from
bosatt (*boo*-saht) *adj* resident

boss (boss) *m* boss

bot (bōōt) *c* (pl bøter) fine

botanikk (boo-tah-*nikk*) *m* botany

botemiddel (*bōō*-ter-mi-derl) *nt* (pl -midler) remedy

bowlingbane (*bov*-ling-baa-ner) *m* bowling alley

bra (braa) *adj* good; *colloquial* super; **bra!** all right!

brann (brahnn) *m* fire

brannalarm (*brahn*-nah-lahrm) *m* fire alarm

brannmann (*brahn*-mahn) *m* firefighter

brannmannskap (*brahn*-mahn-skaap) *nt* firefighter

brannsikker (*brahn*-si-kerr) *adj* fireproof

brannslokker (*brahn*-shloo-kerr) *m* fire extinguisher

brannsår (*brahn*-sawr) *nt* (pl ~) burn

branntrapp (*brahn*-trahp) *c* fire escape

brannvesen (*brahn*-vāy-sern) *nt* fire brigade

Brasil (brah-*seel*) Brazil

brasilianer (brah-si-li-*aa*-nerr) *m* Brazilian

brasiliansk (brah-si-li-*aansk*) *adj* Brazilian

bratt (brahtt) *adj* steep

bred (brāy) *adj* wide, broad

bredd (brehdd) *m* shore, bank; embankment

bredde (*brehd*-der) *m* width, breadth

breddegrad (*brehd*-der-graad) *m* latitude

*brekke (brehk-ker) *v* fracture; **~ seg** vomit

brekkjern (*brehk*-ᵞæn) *nt* crowbar

bremse (*brehm*-ser) *c* brake; *v* slow down

bremselys (*brehm*-ser-lēwss) *pl* brake lights

bremsetrommel (*brehm*-ser-troo-merl) *m* (pl -tromler) brake drum

*brenne (*brehn*-ner) *v* *burn

brennemerke (*brehn*-ner-mær-ker) *nt* brand; stigma

brennpunkt (*brehn*-poongkt) *nt* focus

brensel (*brehn*-sherl) *nt* fuel

brenselolje (*brehn*-sherl-ol-ᵞer) *c* fuel oil

brett (brehtt) *nt* tray

brette (*breht*-ter) *v* fold; **~ ut** unfold

brev (brāyv) *nt* letter; **rekommandert ~** registered letter

brevpapir (*brāyv*-pah-peer) *nt* notepaper

brevveksle (*brāyvehk*-shler) *v* correspond

brevveksling (*brāyvehk*-shling) *c* correspondence

brikke (*brik*-ker) *c* chip; piece

briller (*bril*-lerr) *pl* spectacles, glasses

*bringe (*bring*-nger) *v* *bring; **~ tilbake** *bring back

bringebær (*bring*-nger-bæær) *nt* (pl ~) raspberry

bris (breess) *m* breeze

*briste (*briss*-ter) *v* *burst

brite (*brit*-ter) *m* Briton

britisk (*brit*-tisk) *adj* British

bro (brōō) *c* bridge

brodere (broo-*dāy*-rer) *v* embroider

broderi (broo-der-*ree*) *nt* embroidery

brokk (brokk) *m/nt* hernia

*brolegge (*brōō*-leh-ger) *v* pave

bronkitt (broong-*kitt*) *m* bronchitis

bronse (*brong*-sher) *m* bronze; **bronse-** bronze

bror (brōōr) *m* (pl brødre) brother

brorskap (*brōōsh*-kaap) *m/nt* fraternity, brotherhood

brosje (*brosh*-sher) *c* brooch

brosjyre (bro-*shēw*-rer) *m* brochure

brud (brēwd) *c* bride

brudd (brewdd) *nt* fracture, break

bruddstykke (*brewd*-stew-ker) *nt* fragment

brudgom (*brewd*-gom) *m* (pl ~mer) groom, bridegroom

bruk (brewk) *m* use

brukbar (*brewk*-baar) *adj* useful

bruke (*brew*-ker) *v* apply, use; *spend; ~ **opp** use up

bruker (*brew*-kerr) *m* user

bruksanvisning (*brewks*-ahn-viss-ning) *m* directions for use

brukt (brewkt) *adj* second-hand

brumme (*broom*-mer) *v* growl

brun (brewn) *adj* brown; tanned

brunette (brew-*neht*-ter) *m* brunette

brunfarge (*brewn-fahr*-ger) *m* suntan

brus (brewss) *m* fizz; *m* lemonade; soft drink *Am*

bruse (*brew*-ser) *v* roar

brusk (brewsk) *m* cartilage

brutal (brew-*taal*) *adj* brutal

brutto (*brewt*-too) *adj* gross

bry (brew) *v* trouble; *nt* bother; ~ **seg** bother; ~ **seg om** mind; care for

brydd (brewdd) *adj* embarrassed; ***gjøre** ~ embarrass

brygge (*brewg*-ger) *v* brew

bryggeri (brew-ger-*ree*) *nt* brewery

bryllup (*brewl*-lewp) *nt* wedding

bryllupsdag (*brewl*-lewps-daag) *m* anniversary

bryllupsreise (*brewl*-lewps-ray-ser) *c* honeymoon

brysom (*brew*-som) *adj*

bryst (brewst) *nt* chest, breast; bosom

brystholder (*brewst*-ho-lerr) *m* bra

brystkasse (*brewst*-kah-ser) *c* chest

brystsvømming (*brewst*-svur-ming) *c* breaststroke

***bryte** (*brew*-ter) *v* *break; ~ **sammen** collapse

bryter (*brew*-terr) *m* switch

brød (brur) *nt* bread; loaf; **ristet** ~ toast

brøkdel (*brurk*-dayl) *m* fraction

brøl (brurl) *nt* roar

brøle (*brur*-ler) *v* roar

brønn (brurnn) *m* well

bråk (brawk) *nt* din; fuss

bu (bew) *c* booth

bud (bewd) *nt* messenger; bid; **sende** ~ **etter** *send for

budsjett (bewd-*shehtt*) *nt* budget

bue (*bew*-er) *m* bow; arch

bueformet (*bew*-er-for-mert) *adj* arched

buegang (*bew*-er-gahng) *m* arcade

buet (*bew*-ert) *adj* curved

bukett (bew-*kehtt*) *m* bouquet, bunch

bukk (bookk) *m* buck

bukke (*book*-ker) *v* bow; ~ **under** succumb

bukse (*book*-ser) *c* trousers *pl*; pants *plAm*

buksedrakt (*book*-ser-drahkt) *c* pant suit

buksedress (*book*-ser-drehss) *m* pant suit

bukseseler (*book*-ser-*say*-lerr) *pl* braces *pl*; suspenders *plAm*

buksesmekk (*book*-ser-smehk) *m* fly

bukt (bookt) *c* bay

buktet (*book*-tert) *adj* winding

bulder (*bewl*-derr) *nt* noise

bulgarer (bewl-*gaa*-rerr) *m* Bulgarian

Bulgaria (bewl-*gaa*-ri-ah) Bulgaria

bulgarsk (bewl-*gaashk*) *adj* Bulgarian

bulk (bewlk) *m* dent

bunad (*boo*-nahd) *m* (Norwegian) national costume, national dress

bunke (*boong*-ker) *m* batch

bunn (bewnn) *m* bottom

bunnfall (*bewn*-fahl) *nt* (pl ~) deposit; sediment

bunt (bewnt) *m* bundle

bunte (*bewn*-ter) *v* bundle

buntmaker (*bewnt*-maa-kerr) *m* furrier

bur (bewr) *nt* cage
*burde (*bew*-der) *v* *ought to
busk (bewsk) *m* bush; shrub
buss (bewss) *m* bus; coach
butikk (bew-*tikk*) *m* shop; boutique
butikkeier (bew-*tikk*-ay-err) *m*
  tradeswoman, tradesman
butikkselger (bew-*tikk*-sehl-gerr) *m*
  shop assistant
butt (bewtt) *adj* blunt
by (bew) *m* town, city; **by-** urban
*by (bew) *v* bid
byfolk (*bew*-folk) *pl* townspeople *pl*
bygd (bewgd) *c* village
bygg (bewgg) *nt* barley; building
bygge (*bewg*-ger) *v* construct, *build
byggekunst (*bewg*-ger-kewnst) *m*
  architecture
bygning (*bewg*-ning) *m* construction,
  building
byll (bewll) *m* abscess, boil
byrde (*bewr*-der) *m* burden; charge
byrå (bew-*raw*) *nt* agency
byråkrati (bew-ro-krah-*tee*) *nt*
  bureaucracy
byste (*bewss*-ter) *c* bust
bytte (*bewt*-ter) *v* exchange, swap; *nt*
  exchange
bær (bæær) *nt* berry
*bære (*bææ*-rer) *v* carry, *bear;

support
bærer (*bæ*æ-rerr) *m* porter
bøddel (*burd*-derl) *m* (pl bødler)
  executioner
bøk (bürk) *m* beech
bølge (*burl*-ger) *c* wave
bølgelengde (*burl*-ger-lehng-der) *c*
  wave-length
bølget (*burl*-gert) *adj* wavy
bølle (*burl*-ler) *m* brute
bøllete (*burl*-ler-ter) *adj* rowdy
bønn (burnn) *m* prayer
bønne (*burn*-ner) *c* bean
*bønnfalle (*burn*-fah-ler) *v* beg
bør (bürr) *c* load
børs (bursh) *m* stock exchange
børste (*bursh*-ter) *v* brush; *m* brush
bøyd (bur^{ew}d) *adj* bent
bøye (*bur^{ew}*-er) *v* *bend; *m* buoy; ~
  seg *bend down
bøyelig (*bur^{ew}*-er-li) *adj* flexible,
  supple
bøyning (*bur^{ew}*-ning) *m* bend
både ... og (*baw*-der aw) both ... and
bål (bawl) *nt* bonfire
bånd (bonn) *nt* band; ribbon; tape;
  leash
bås (bawss) *m* booth
båt (bawt) *m* boat

C

campinggjest (*kæm*-ping-^{y}ehst) *m*
  camper
campingplass (*kæm*-ping-plahss) *m*
  camping site
campingvogn (*kæm*-ping-vongn) *c*
  caravan; trailer *nAm*
Canada (*kahn*-nah-dah) Canada
CD (*seh*-deh) *m* CD; **CD-spiller** *m* CD

player
CD-ROM (*seh*-deh-romm) *m* CD-
  ROM
celle (*sehl*-ler) *c* cell
cello (*chel*-lo, *sel*-lo) *m* cello
celsius (*sehl*-si-ewss) centigrade
cembalo (*shehm*-bah-loo) *m*
  harpsichord

centimeter (*sehn*-ti-may-terr) *m* (pl ~) centimeter *Am*, centimetre

champagne (shahm-*pahn*-ʸer) *m* champagne

charterflygning (*chaa*-terr-flewg-ning) *m* charter flight

Chile (*chee*-ler) Chile

chilener (chi-*lay*-nerr) *m* Chilean

chilensk (chi-*laynsk*) *adj* Chilean

cirka (*seer*-kah) *adv* approximately

clutch (klurch) *m* clutch

cocktail (*kok*-tayl) *m* cocktail

Colombia (koo-*loom*-bi-ah) Colombia

colombianer (koo-loom-bi-*aa*-nerr) *m* Colombian

colombiansk (koo-loom-bi-*aansk*) *adj* Colombian

container (koon-*tay*-nerr) *m* container

cricket (*kri*-kertt) *m* cricket

cruise (krewss) *nt* (pl ~) cruise

Cuba (*kew*-bah) Cuba

D

da (daa) *conj* when; *adv* then

daddel (*dahd*-derl) *m* (pl dadler) date

dag (daag) *m* day; **i ~** today; **om dagen** by day; **per ~** per day

dagbok (*daag*-book) *c* (pl -bøker) diary

daggry (*daa*-grew) *nt* daybreak, dawn

daglig (*daag*-li) *adj* everyday, daily

dagligdags (*daag*-li-dahks) *adj* ordinary

dagligstue (*daag*-li-stew-er) *c* living room

dagsavis (*dahks*-ahveess) *c* daily newspaper

dagslys (*dahks*-lewss) *nt* daylight

dagsorden (*dahk*-so-dern) *m* agenda

dagstur (*dahks*-tewr) *m* day trip

dal (daal) *m* valley

dam (dahmm) *m* (pl ~mer) pond; pool

dame (*daa*-mer) *c* lady

dameundertøy (*daa*-mer-ew-ner-tur^(ew)) *nt* lingerie

damp (dahmp) *m* steam, vapo(u)r

dampskip (*dahmp*-sheep) *nt* (pl ~) steamer

damspill (*dahm*-spil) *nt* (pl ~) draughts; checkers *plAm*

Danmark (*dahn*-mahrk) Denmark

dans (dahns) *m* dance

danse (*dahn*-ser) *v* dance

dansk (dahnsk) *adj* Danish

danske (*dahn*-sker) *m* Dane

dask (dahsk) *m* smack

datamaskin (*daa*-tah-mah-*sheen*) *m* computer

dato (*daa*-too) *m* date

datter (*daht*-terr) *c* (pl døtre) daughter

de (dee) *pron pl* (c den, nt det) those, they

debatt (deh-*baht*) *m* debate, discussion

debattere (deh-bah-*tay*-rer) *v* argue, discuss

debet (*day*-bert) *m* debit

defekt (deh-*fehkt*) *m* fault; *adj* faulty

definere (deh-fi-*nay*-rer) *v* define

definisjon (deh-fi-ni-*shoon*) *m* definition

deg (day) *pron* yourself; you

deig (day) *m* batter, dough

deilig (*day*-li) *adj* enjoyable, delicious; pleasant

dekk (dehkk) *nt* tire, tyre; deck;
øverste ~ main deck
dekke (*dehk*-ker) *v* cover
deklarasjon (dehk-lah-rah-*shoon*) *m*
declaration
deklarere (dehk-lah-*rāy*-rer) *v* declare
dekorasjon (dehk-koo-rah-*shoon*) *m*
decoration
del (dāyl) *m* part; share
dele (*dāy*-ler) *v* divide; share; **~ seg**
fork; **~ ut** *deal
delegasjon (deh-leh-gah-*shoon*) *m*
delegation
delikat (deh-li-*kaat*) *adj* delicate
delikatesse (deh-li-kah-*tehss*-ser) *m*
delicatessen
deling (*dāy*-ling) *c* division
***delta** (*dāyl*-taa) *v* participate
deltakelse (*dāyl*-taa-kerl-ser) *m*
participation
deltakende (*dāyl*-taa-ker-ner) *adj*
sympathetic
deltaker (*dāyl*-taa-kerr) *m* participant
delvis (*dāyl*-veess) *adv* partly; *adj*
partial
dem (dehmm) *pron* them
demning (*dehm*-ning) *m* dam; dike
demokrati (deh-moo-krah-*tee*) *nt*
democracy
demokratisk (deh-moo-*kraa*-tisk) *adj*
democratic
demonstrasjon (deh-moon-strah-
shoon) *m* demonstration
demonstrere (deh-moon-*strāy*-rer) *v*
demonstrate
den (dehnn) *pron* (nt det, pl de) it; that
denne (*dehn*-ner) *pron* (nt dette) this;
adj this
dens (dehnns) *pron* its
deodorant (deh-oo-doo-*rahnt*) *m*
deodorant
departement (deh-pah-ter-*mahngng*)
nt department; ministry
deponere (deh-poo-*nāy*-rer) *v*
deposit

depositum (deh-*poo*-si-tewm) *nt* (pl
-ta) deposit
depresjon (deh-preh-*shoon*) *m*
depression
deprimere (deh-pri-*māy*-rer) *v*
depress
deprimerende (deh-pri-*māy*-rer-ner)
adj depressing
deprimert (deh-pri-*māyt*) *adj*
depressed
der (dæær) *adv* there; **~ borte** over
there
dere (*dāy*-rer) *pron* you, yourselves
deres (*dāy*-rerss) *pron* your, yours;
their, theirs
derfor (*dær*-for) *adv* therefore
dersom (*dæ*-shom) *conj* if, in case
desember (deh-*sehm*-berr)
December
desertere (deh-sæ-*tāy*-rer) *v* desert
desimalsystem (deh-si-*maal*-sewss-
tāym) *nt* decimal system
desinfisere (dehss-sin-fi-*sāy*-rer) *v*
disinfect; **desinfiserende middel**
disinfectant
dessert (deh-*sæær*) *m* dessert; sweet
dessuten (deh-*sēw*-tern) *adv*
moreover, also, furthermore, besides
dessverre (dehss-*vær*-rer) *adv*
unfortunately
det (dāy) *pron* (c den, pl de) it; that
detalj (deh-*tahlʸ*) *m* detail
detaljert (deh-tahl-ʸ*āyt*) *adj* detailed
detaljhandel (deh-*tahlʸ*-hahn-derl) *m*
(pl -dler) retail trade
detektiv (*deht*-tehk-teev) *m* detective
dets (dehtts) *pron* its
devaluere (deh-vah-lew-*āy*-rer) *v*
devalue
devaluering (deh-vah-lew-*āy*-ring) *c*
devaluation
diabetes (di-ah-*bāy*-terss) *m* diabetes

diabetiker (di-ah-*bay*-ti-kerr) *m* diabetic

diagnose (di-ahg-*nōō*-ser) *m* diagnosis; **stille en ~** diagnose

diagonal (di-ah-goo-*naal*) *m* diagonal; *adj* diagonal

diagram (di-ah-*grahm*) *nt* (pl ~mer) chart, graph, diagram

dialekt (di-ah-*lehkt*) *m* dialect

diamant (di-ah-*mahnt*) *m* diamond

diaré (di-ah-*ray*) *m* diarrh(o)ea

diesel (*dee*-serl) *m* diesel

diett (di-*eht*) *m* diet

difteri (dif-ter-*ree*) *m* diphtheria

digital (dig-i-*taal*) *adj* digital

dikt (dikt) *nt* poem

diktat (dik-*taat*) *m* dictation

diktator (dik-*taa*-toor) *m* dictator

dikter (*dik*-terr) *m* poet

diktere (dik-*tay*-rer) *v* dictate

dimensjon (di-mehn-*shōōn*) *m* size; dimension

din (deen) *pron* your, yours

dine (*dee*-ner) *pron* your, yours

diplom (di-*plōōm*) *nt* certificate, diploma

diplomat (dip-loo-*maat*) *m* diplomat

direksjon (deer-ehk-*shōōn*) *m* board of directors

direkte (di-*rehk*-ter) *adj* direct

direktiv (di-rehk-*teev*) *nt* directive; direction

direktør (di-rehk-*turr*) *m* executive, manager, director

dirigent (di-ri-*gehnt*) *m* conductor

dirigere (di-ri-*gay*-rer) *v* conduct

dirre (*deer*-rer) *v* tremble

dis (deess) *m* mist, haze

disig (*dee*-si) *adj* hazy; misty

disiplin (di-si-*pleen*) *m* discipline

disk (disk) *m* counter

diskonto (diss-*kon*-too) *m* bank rate

diskusjon (diss-kew-*shōōn*) *m* discussion; argument

diskutere (diss-kew-*tay*-rer) *v* discuss; argue

disponibel (diss-poo-*nee*-berl) *adj* available

disposisjon (diss-poo-si-*shōōn*) *m* disposal

disse (*diss*-ser) *pron* these

distrikt (diss-*trikt*) *nt* district

dit (deet) *adv* there

diverse (di-*væsh*-sher) *adj* miscellaneous, various

djerv (d^yærv) *adj* fearless, bold

djevel (d^y*ay*-verl) *m* (pl -vler) devil

do (doo) *m*/*nt colloquial* toilet

dobbel (*dob*-berl) *adj* double

dobbeltseng (*dob*-berlt-sehng) *c* double bed

dokk (dokk) *m* dock

***dokksette** (*dok*-seh-ter) *v* dock

doktor (*dok*-toor) *m* doctor

dokument (doo-kew-*mehnt*) *nt* certificate, document

dokumentmappe (doo-kew-*mehnt*-mah-per) *c* attaché case, briefcase

dollar (dol-lar) *m* dollar, *colloquial* buck

dom (domm) *m* (pl ~mer) judgment; verdict, sentence

domfellelse (*dom*-feh-lerl-ser) *m* conviction

domfelt (*dom*-fehltt) *m* (pl ~e) convict

dominere (doo-mi-*nay*-rer) *v* dominate

domkirke (*dom*-kheer-ker) *c* cathedral

dommer (*dom*-merr) *m* judge; magistrate; umpire

domstol (*dom*-stōōl) *m* court, law court

donasjon (doo-nah-*shōōn*) *m* donation

dongeribukse (*dongh*-ri-book-se) *c* jeans

dose (*dōō*-ser) *m* dose

dott (dott) *m* wisp; tuft; wad

doven (*daw*-vern) *adj* lazy

*dra (draa) *v* pull; travel, *go; ~ **av sted** *set out

drake (*draa*-ker) *m* kite; dragon

drakt (drahkt) *c* costume

dram (drahmm) *m* drink of liquor

drama (*draa*-mah) *nt* drama

dramatiker (drah-*maa*-ti-kerr) *m* dramatist

dramatisk (drah-*maa*-tisk) *adj* dramatic

drap (draap) *nt* manslaughter, homicide

dreie (*dray*-er) *v* turn, resolve

dreining (*dray*-ning) *m* turn

drenere (dreh-*nāy*-rer) *v* drain

drepe (*drāy*-per) *v* kill

dress (drehss) *m* suit

dressere (dreh-*sāy*-rer) *v* train

dressjakke (*drehss*-ʸahk-ker) *c* jacket

dreven (*drāy*-vern) *adj* skilled, clever

drikk (drikk) *m* drink; beverage; **alkoholfri** ~ soft drink

*drikke (*drik*-ker) *v* *drink

drikkelig (*drik*-ker-li) *adj* drinkable

drikkepenger (*drik*-ker-peh-ngerr) *pl* tip, gratuity

drikkevann (*drik*-ker-vahn) *nt* drinking water

drink (dringk) *m* drink

dristig (*driss*-ti) *adj* bold, daring; risky

dristighet (*driss*-ti-hāyt) *c* daring

dritt (dritt) *m* *vulgar* crap

*drive frem (*dree*-ver) *propel

drivhus (*dreev*-hewss) *nt* (pl ~) greenhouse

drivkraft (*dreev*-krahft) *c* driving force

dronning (*droan*-ning) *c* queen

drosje (*drosh*-sher) *c* cab, taxi

drosjeholdeplass (*drosh*-sher-ho-ler-plahss) *m* taxi rank; taxi stand *Am*

drosjesjåfør (*drosh*-sher-sho-fūrr) *m* cab driver, taxi driver

druer (*drew*-err) *pl* grapes *pl*

drukne (*drook*-ner) *v* *be drowned; drown

dryppe (*drewp*-per) *v* drip

drøm (drurmm) *m* (pl ~mer) dream

drømme (*drurm*-mer) *v* *dream

dråpe (*draw*-per) *m* drop

du (dēw) *pron* you

due (*dēw*-er) *c* pigeon

duft (dewft) *m* scent

dugg (dewgg) *m* dew

duk (dēwk) *m* table-cloth

dukke (*dewk*-ker) *v* dive; *c* doll

dukketeater (*dewk*-ker-teh-*aa*-terr) *nt* (pl ~, -tre) puppet-show

dum (doomm) *adj* stupid, dumb; foolish, silly

dun (dēwn) *nt* down

dunke (*doong*-ker) *v* thump, bump

dunkel (*doong*-kerl) *adj* dim

dur (dēwr) *m* roar; major

dusin (dew-*seen*) *nt* (pl ~) dozen

dusj (dewshsh) *m* shower

duskregn (*dewsk*-rehngn) *nt* drizzle

DVD (dewe-dehr) *m* DVD

dverg (dværg) *m* dwarf

dybde (*dewb*-der) *m* depth

dyd (dēwd) *m* virtue

dykke (*dewk*-ker) *v* dive

dykkermaske (*dew*-ker-*mahss*-ker) *c* goggles *pl*

dyktig (*dewk*-ti) *adj* able, capable, skil(l)ful

dyktighet (*dewk*-ti-hāyt) *c* ability, skill

dynamo (dew-*naa*-moo) *m* dynamo

dyne (*dēw*-ner) *c* eiderdown

dyp (dēwp) *adj* deep; low

dypfryser (*dēwp*-frēw-serr) *m* deep-freeze

dypfryst mat (*dēwp*-frewst maat) frozen food

dypsindig (*dēwp*-sin-di) *adj* profound

dyr (dēwr) *nt* beast, animal; *adj* expensive

dyrebar (*dēw*-rer-baar) *adj* precious; dear

dyrekretsen (*dēw*-rer-kreht-sern) zodiac

dyrke (*dewr*-ker) *v* raise, cultivate, *grow

dyrlege (*dēwr*-lāy-ger) *m* veterinary surgeon

dyster (*dewss*-terr) *adj* gloomy, somber *Am*, sombre

dytt (*dewtt*) *m* push

dø (*dūr*) *v* die

død (*dūr*) *adj* dead; *m* death

dødelig (*dūr*-der-li) *adj* mortal, fatal

dødsfall (*durts*-fahl) *nt* (pl ~) death

dødsstraff (*durt*-strahf) *m* death penalty

døgn (durngn) *nt* twenty-four hours

dømme (*durm*-mer) *v* sentence; judge

døpe (*dūr*-per) *v* baptize, christen

dør (dūrr) *c* door

dørslag (*dūr*-shlaag) *nt* (pl ~) strainer

dørvokter (dūrr-vok-terr) *m* door-keeper

døv (dūrv) *adj* deaf

dåd (dawd) *m* exploit, achievement

dåkalv (*daw*-kahlv) *m* fawn

dåp (dawp) *m* christening, baptism

dårlig (*daw*-li) *adj* ill, bad; poor; ~ **luft** stale air

E

ebbe (*ehb*-ber) *m* ebb

Ecuador (ehk-vah-*dawr*) Ecuador

ecuadorianer (ehk-vah-do-ri-*aa*-nerr) *m* Ecuadorian

ed (āyd) *m* oath, vow

edderkopp (*ehd*-derr-kop) *m* spider

eddik (*ehd*-dik) *m* vinegar

edel (*āy*-derl) *adj* noble

edelstein (*āy*-derl-stāyn) *m* gem, precious stone

edru (*āyd*-rēw) *adj* sober

effekt (eh-*fehkt*) *m* effect

effektiv (*ehf*-fehk-tiv) *adj* effective; efficient

eføy (*āy*-fur^(ew)) *m* ivy

egen (*āy*-gern) *adj* own; peculiar, odd

egenskap (*āy*-gern-skaap) *m* quality, characteristic

egentlig (*āy*-gernt-li) *adv* really

egg (ehgg) *nt* egg

eggeglass (*ehg*-ger-glahss) *nt* (pl ~) egg-cup

eggeplomme (*ehg*-ger-plo-mer) *c* yolk, egg yolk

egn (ayn) *m* region

egnet (*ay*-nert) *adj* convenient, suitable, fit

egoisme (eh-goo-*iss*-mer) *m* selfishness

egoistisk (eh-goo-*iss*-tisk) *adj* egoistic

Egypt (eh-*gewpt*) Egypt

egypter (eh-*gewp*-terr) *m* Egyptian

egyptisk (eh-*gewp*-tisk) *adj* Egyptian

ei (āy) *art* a; *num* one

eie (*ay*-er) *v* own; possess, *nt* possession; **eiendeler** belongings *pl*

eiendom (*ay*-ern-dom) *m* (pl ~mer) property; estate; premises *pl*

eiendommelig (ay-ern-*dom*-li) *adj* peculiar; quaint

eiendommelighet (ay-ern-*dom*-li-hāyt) *c* peculiarity

eiendomsmegler (ay-ern-doms-mehg-lerr) *m* house-agent; realtor *nAm*

eier (*ay*-err) *m* owner, proprietor

eik (ayk) *c* oak

eike (*ay*-ker) *m* spoke

eikenøtt (*ay*-ker-nurt) *c* acorn

ekkel (*ehk*-kerl) *adj* nasty

ekko (*ehk*-koo) *nt* echo

ekorn (*ehk*-koon) *nt* squirrel

eksakt (ehk-*sahkt*) *adj* exact

eksamen (ehk-*saa*-mern) *m* exam *colloquial*, examination; ***ta ~** graduate

eksem (ehk-*saym*) *m*/*nt* eczema

eksempel (ehk-*sehm*-perl) *nt* (pl -pler) example, instance; **for ~** for instance, for example

eksemplar (ehk-sehm-*plaar*) *nt* specimen; copy

eksentrisk (ehk-*sehn*-trisk) *adj* eccentric

eksil (ehk-*seel*) *nt* exile

eksistens (ehk-si-*stehns*) *m* existence

eksistere (ehk-si-*stay*-rer) *v* exist

eksklusiv (*ehks*-klew-seev) *adj* exclusive

eksos (ehk-*sōōss*) *m* exhaust gases

eksospotte (ehk-*sōōss*-po-ter) *c* silencer; muffler *nAm*

eksosrør (ehk-*sōōss*-rūrr) *nt* (pl ~) exhaust pipe

eksotisk (ehk-*soo*-tisk) *adj* exotic

ekspedisjon (ehk-sper-di-*shōōn*) *m* expedition

ekspansjon (ehk-spang-*shōōn*) *m* expansion

ekspeditør (ehk-sper-di-*tūrr*) *m* shop assistant, salesman

eksperiment (ehk-speh-ri-*mehnt*) *nt* experiment

eksperimentere (ehk-speh-ri-mehn-*tay*-rer) *v* experiment

ekspert (ehk-*spæt*) *m* expert

eksplodere (ehk-sploo-*day*-rer) *v* explode, blow up

eksplosiv (ehk-sploo-*seev*) *adj* explosive

eksplosjon (ehk-sploo-*shōōn*) *m* blast, explosion

eksponere (ehk-spoo-*nay*-rer) *v* expose

eksponering (ehk-spoo-*nay*-ring) *c* exposure

eksport (ehk-*spot*) *m* exports *pl*

eksportere (ehk-spo-*tay*-rer) *v* export

ekspress- (ehk-*sprehss*) express

ekstase (ehk-*staa*-ser) *m* ecstasy

ekstra (*ehk*-strah) *adj* additional, extra; spare

ekstravagant (ehk-strah-vah-*gahnt*) *adj* extravagant

ekstrem (ehk-*straym*) *adj* extreme

ekte (*ehk*-ter) *adj* genuine, authentic, true; *v* marry

ektemann (*ehk*-ter-mahn) *m* (pl -menn) husband

ektepar (*ehk*-ter-paar) *nt* married couple

ekteskap (*ehk*-teh-skaap) *nt* matrimony, marriage

ekvator (ehk-*vaa*-toor) *m* equator

elastisk (eh-*lahss*-tisk) *adj* elastic

eldre (*ehl*-drer) *adj* older; elderly; **eldst** eldest

elefant (eh-ler-*fahnt*) *m* elephant

eleganse (eh-ler-*gahng*-ser) *m* elegance

elegant (eh-ler-*gahnt*) *adj* elegant

elektriker (eh-*lehk*-tri-kerr) *m* electrician

elektrisitet (eh-lehk-tri-si-*tayt*) *m* electricity

elektrisk (eh-*lehk*-trisk) *adj* electric

elektronisk (eh-lehk-*trōō*-nisk) *adj* electronic

element (eh-ler-*mehnt*) *nt* element

elementær (eh-ler-mehn-*tæær*) *adj* primary

elendig (eh-*lehn*-di) *adj* miserable

elendighet (eh-*lehn*-di-hayt) *c* misery

elev (eh-*layv*) *m* pupil

elfenbein (*ehl*-fern-bayn) *nt* ivory
elg (ehlg) *m* moose, elk
eliminere (eh-li-mi-*nay*-rer) *v* eliminate
eller (*ehl*-lerr) *conj* or; **enten ... eller** either ... or; **om ... eller** whether ... or
ellers (*ehl*-lersh) *adv* otherwise; else
elleve (*ehl*-ver) *num* eleven
ellevte (*ehl*-lerf-ter) *num* eleventh
elske (*ehl*-sker) *v* love
elsker (*ehl*-skerr) *m* lover
elskerinne (ehl-sker-*rin*-ner) *c* mistress
elsket (*ehl*-skert) *adj* beloved
elskling (*ehlsk*-ling) *m* sweetheart
elv (elv) *c* river
elvebredd (*el*-ver-brehd) *m* river bank, riverside
elvemunning (*el*-ver-mew-ning) *m* estuary
emalje (eh-*mahl*-Yer) *m* enamel
emaljert (eh-mahl-Y*ayt*) *adj* enamelled
embete (*ehm*-ber-ter) *nt* civil service office
embetsmann (*ehm*-berts-mahnn) *m* (pl -menn) civil servant
emblem (ehm-*blaym*) *nt* emblem
emigrant (eh-mi-*grahnt*) *m* emigrant
emigrasjon (eh-mi-grah-*shoon*) *m* emigration
emne (*ehm*-ner) *nt* topic, theme
en (*ayn*) *art* a; *num* one; **-en** the *art*
enakter (*ayn*-ahk-terr) *m* one-act play
ende (*ehn*-ner) *m* end
endelig (*ehn*-der-li) *adv* finally; eventually
endestasjon (*ehn*-ner-stah-*shoon*) *m* terminal
endetarm (*ehn*-ner-tahrm) *m* rectum
endossere (ahng-do-*say*-rer) *v* endorse
endre (*ehn*-drer) *v* alter; modify

endring (*ehn*-dring) *c* alteration; change
eneforhandler (*ay*-ner-for-hahnd-lerr) *m* sole distributor
energi (eh-nær-*gee*) *m* power, energy
energisk (eh-*nær*-gisk) *adj* energetic
eneste (*ay*-nerss-ter) *adj* sole, only
enestående (*ay*-ner-sto-er-ner) *adj* exceptional, unique; singular
eng (ehngng) *c* meadow
engangs- (*ayn*-gahngs) disposable
engel (*ehng*-ngerl) *m* (pl engler) angel
engelsk (eh-ngerlsk) *adj* English
engelskmann (eh-ngerlsk-mahn) *m* (pl -menn) Englishman; Briton
England (*ehng*-lahn) England
engroshandel (ahng-*graw*-hahn-derl) *m* (pl -dler) wholesale-trade
engstelig (*ehng*-ster-li) *adj* anxious; afraid
engstelse (*ehng*-sterl-ser) *m* fear
enhet (*ayn*-hayt) *m* unity; unit
enhver (ehn-*vær*) *pron* anyone; everybody, everyone
enig (*ay*-ni) *adj* unanimous, agreed; ***være ~** agree
enke (*ehng*-ker) *c* widow
enkel (*ehng*-kerl) *adj* simple; plain; single
enkelt (*ehng*-kerlt) *adj* individual
enkelte (*ehng*-kerl-ter) *pron* some
enkeltperson (*ehng*-kerlt-pæ-*shoon*) *m* individual
enkeltrom (*ehng*-kerlt-room) *nt* (pl ~) single room
enkemann (*ayng*-ker-mahn) *m* (pl -menn) widower
enn (ehnn) *conj* than
ennå (*ehn*-naw) *adv* yet
enorm (eh-*norm*) *adj* enormous; huge, immense, gigantic
ensartet (*ayn*-saa-tert) *adj* uniform
ensidig (*ayn*-see-di) *adj* one-sided
ensom (*ayn*-som) *adj* lonely

enstemmig (*ayn*-steh-mi) *adj* unanimous

entall (*ayn*-tahl) *nt* singular

entrénøkkel (ahng-*tray*-nur-kerl) *m* (pl -nøkler) latchkey

entreprenør (ahng-trer-preh-*nurr*) *m* contractor

entusiasme (ehn-tew-si-*ahss*-mer) *m* enthusiasm

entusiastisk (ehn-tew-si-*ahss*-tisk) *adj* enthusiastic

enveiskjøring (*ayn*-vayss-khur-ring) *c* one-way traffic

epidemi (eh-pi-der-*mee*) *m* epidemic

epilepsi (eh-pi-lehp-*see*) *m* epilepsy

epilog (eh-pi-*lawg*) *m* epilogue

episk (*ay*-pisk) *adj* epic

episode (eh-pi-*soo*-der) *m* episode

eple (*ehp*-ler) *nt* apple

epos (*ay*-pooss) *nt* epic

e-post (*ay*-poost) *m* e-mail

erfare (ær-*faa*-rer) *v* experience

erfaren (ær-*faa*-rern) *adj* experienced

erfaring (ær-*faa*-ring) *c* experience

ergerlig (*ær*-ger-li) *adj* annoying

ergre (*ær*-grer) *v* annoy; irritate

ergrelse (*ær*-grerl-ser) *m* annoyance

erindre (eh-*rin*-drer) *v* recall

erindring (eh-*rin*-dring) *c* remembrance

erkebiskop (*ær*-ker-biss-kop) *m* archbishop

erkjenne (ær-*khehn*-ner) *v* acknowledge; confess, admit

erklære (ær-*klææ*-rer) *v* declare; state

erklæring (ær-*klææ*-ring) *c* declaration, statement

erme (*ær*-mer) *nt* sleeve

erobre (e-*roob*-rer) *v* conquer; capture

erobrer (e-*roob*-rerr) *m* conqueror

erobring (æ-*roob*-ring) *c* conquest; capture

erstatning (æ-*shtaht*-ning) *m* indemnity; substitute

erstatte (æ-*shtaht*-ter) *v* replace, substitute

ert (ætt) *c* pea

erte (*æ*-ter) *v* tease

erverve (ær-*vær*-ver) *v* acquire; obtain

ervervelse (ær-*vær*-verl-ser) *m* acquisition

esel (*ay*-serl) *nt* (pl esler) donkey

eske (*ehss*-ker) *c* box

eskorte (ehss-*kot*-ter) *m* escort

eskortere (ehss-ko-*tay*-rer) *v* escort

essay (*ehss*-say) *nt* (pl ~, ~s) essay

essens (eh-*sehns*) *m* essence

et (*ayt*) *art* a; *num* one; **-et** the *art*

etablere (eh-tah-*blay*-rer) *v* establish

etappe (eh-*tahp*-per) *m* stage, leg

etasje (eh-*taa*-sher) *m* stor(e)y, floor; **første ~** ground floor

eter (*ay*-terr) *m* ether

etikett (eh-ti-*kehtt*) *m* label

Etiopia (eh-ti-*oo*-pi-ah) Ethiopia

etiopier (eh-ti-*oo*-pi-err) *m* Ethiopian

etiopisk (eh-ti-*oo*-pisk) *adj* Ethiopian

etsteds (eht-*stehss*) *adv* somewhere

etter (*eht*-terr) *prep* after; **~ at** after

etterforske (*eht*-terr-fosh-ker) *v* investigate

etterforskning (*eht*-terr-foshk-ning) *m* inquiry, investigation

*etterfølge (*eht*-terr-fur-ler) *v* succeed

etterkommer (*eht*-terr-ko-merr) *m* descendant

*etterlate (*eht*-ter-laa-ter) *v* *leave behind; *leave

etterligne (*eht*-ter-ling-ner) *v* copy, imitate

etterligning (*eht*-ter-ling-ning) *c* imitation

ettermiddag (*eht*-terr-mi-dah) *m* afternoon; **i ~** this afternoon

etternavn (*eht*-ter-nahvn) *nt* (pl ~) family name, surname

etterpå (*eht*-terr-paw) *adv* afterwards

ettersende (*eht*-ter-sheh-ner) *v*
forward

ettersom (*eht*-ter-shom) *conj* as,
because

etterspore (*eht*-ter-shpoo-rer) *v* trace

etterspørsel (*eht*-ter-shpur-sherl) *m*
demand

etui (eh-tew-*ee*) *nt* case

EU (eh-ew) EU

euro (ou-*roo*) *m* Euro

Europa (ou-*roo*-pah) Europe

europeer (ou-roo-*pay*-err) *m*
European

europeisk (ou-roo-*pay*-isk) *adj*
European

evakuere (eh-vah-kew-*ay*-rer) *v*
evacuate

evangelium (eh-vahng-*gay*-li-ewm) *nt*
(pl -ier) gospel

eventuell (eh-vehn-tew-*ehll*) *adj*
possible

eventyr (*ay*-vern-tewr) *nt* (pl ∼)
fairytale; tale; adventure

evig (*ay*-vi) *adj* eternal

evighet (*ay*-vi-hayt) *c* eternity

evne (*ehv*-ner) *c* faculty, gift; ability,
capacity

evolusjon (eh-voo-lew-*shoon*) *m*
evolution

F

fabel (*faa*-berl) *m* (pl fabler) fable

fabrikant (fahb-ri-*kahnt*) *m*
manufacturer

fabrikk (fahb-*rikk*) *m* works *pl*, mill,
plant, factory

fabrikkere (fahb-ri-*kay*-rer) *v*
manufacture

faen (fah-ahrn) *colloquial* damn!

fag (faag) *nt* profession

fagforening (*faag*-fo-reh-ning) *c* trade
union; union

fagmann (*faag*-mahnn) *m* (pl -menn)
expert

fakkel (*fahk*-kerl) *m* (pl fakler) torch

faks (fahks) *m* fax; **sende en ∼** send a
fax

faktisk (*fahk*-tisk) *adv* as a matter of
fact, really, actually, in effect, in fact;
adj actual, factual

faktor (*fahk*-toor) *m* factor

faktum (*fahk*-tewm) *nt* (pl -ta) fact

faktura (fahk-*tew*-rah) *m* invoice

fakturere (fahk-tew-*ray*-rer) *v* bill

fakultet (fah-kewl-*tayt*) *nt* faculty

fald (fahll) *m* hem

falk (fahlk) *m* hawk

fall (fahll) *nt* fall; **i alle ∼** at any rate; **i
hvert ∼** anyway, at any rate

*falle (*fahl*-ler) *v* *fall; **∼ sammen
med** coincide; ***la ∼** drop

falleferdig (*fahl*-ler-fæ-di) *adj*
ramshackle

fallitt (fah-*litt*) *adj* bankrupt

falme (*fahl*-mer) *v* fade

falsk (fahlsk) *adj* false

familie (fah-*mee*-li-er) *m* family

familiær (fah-mi-li-*æær*) *adj* familiar

fanatisk (fah-*naa*-tisk) *adj* fanatical

fang (fahng) *nt* lap

fange (*fahng*-nger) *v* capture; *catch;
m prisoner; ***ta til ∼** capture

fangenskap (*fahng*-ngern-skaap) *nt*
imprisonment

fangst (fahngst) *m* catch

fantasi (fahn-tah-*see*) *m* fantasy,
imagination, fancy

fantasifoster (fahn-tah-*seefooss*-terr) *nt* illusion

fantastisk (fahn-*tahss*-tisk) *adj* fantastic

fantom (fahn-*tōōm*) *nt* phantom

far (faar) *m* (pl fedre) father; dad

fare (*faa*-rer) *m* peril, danger; risk

farfar (*fahr*-faar) *m* (pl -fedre) grandfather

farge (*fahr*-ger) *m* colo(u)r; dye; *v* dye; ~ **av** discolo(u)r

fargeblind (*fahr*-ger-blin) *adj* colo(u)r-blind

fargerik (*fahr*-ger-reek) *adj* colo(u)rful; gay

farget (*fahr*-gert) *adj* colo(u)red

farlig (*faa*-li) *adj* dangerous

farmakologi (fahr-mah-koo-loo-*gee*) *m* pharmacology

farmor (*fahr*-mōōr) *c* (pl -mødre) grandmother

fart (fahtt) *m* rate, speed; **i full ~** in a hurry; **saktne farten** slow down; **øke farten** accelerate

fartsgrense (*fahts*-grehn-ser) *c* speed limit

fartsmåler (*fahts*-maw-lerr) *m* speedometer

fartøy (*faa*-tur^(ew)) *nt* vessel

fasade (fah-*saa*-der) *m* façade

fasan (fah-*saan*) *m* pheasant

fascisme (fah-*shiss*-mer) *m* fascism

fascist (fah-*shist*) *m* fascist

fascistisk (fah-*shiss*-tisk) *adj* fascist

fase (*faa*-ser) *m* stage, phase

fast (fahst) *adj* firm; fixed; permanent; *adv* tight

fastboende (*fahst*-bōō-er-ner) *m* (pl ~) resident

***fastholde** (*fahst*-ho-ler) *v* insist

fastland (*fahst*-lahn) *nt* mainland

***fastsette** (*fahst*-seh-ter) *v* determine; stipulate

***fastslå** (*fahst*-shlo) *v* establish; ascertain

fat (faat) *nt* dish; cask, barrel

fatal (fah-*taal*) *adj* fatal

fatning (*faht*-ning) *m* composure

fatøl *nt* draught beer

fatte (*faht*-ter) *v* *understand, grasp

fattig (*faht*-ti) *adj* poor

fattigdom (*faht*-ti-dom) *m* poverty

fattigslig (*faht*-tik-sli) *adj* poor

favoritt (fah-voo-*ritt*) *m* favo(u)rite

fe (fāy) *m* fairy

feber (*fāy*-berr) *m* fever

feberaktig (*fāy*-berr-ahk-ti) *adj* feverish

februar (feh-brew-*aar*) February

fedme (*fehd*-mer) *m* fatness, obesity

fedreland (*fāy*-drer-lahn) *nt* native country

feie (*fay*-er) *v* *sweep

feig (fayg) *adj* cowardly

feiging (*fay*-ging) *m* coward

feil (fayl) *m* (pl ~) fault, error, mistake; *adj* incorrect; ***ta ~** *be mistaken

feilaktig (fayl-*ahk*-ti) *adj* mistaken

feile (*fay*-ler) *v* err

feilfri (*fayl*-free) *adj* faultless

feiltakelse (*fayl*-taa-kerl-ser) *m* mistake, error

feiltrinn (*fayl*-trin) *nt* slip

feire (*fay*-rer) *v* celebrate

feiring (*fay*-ring) *c* celebration

fekte (*fehk*-ter) *v* fence

fele (*fai*-ler) *c* fiddle

felg (fehlg) *m* rim

felle (*fehl*-ler) *c* trap

felles (*fehl*-lerss) *adj* common; joint; **i fellesskap** jointly

fellesprosjekt *nt* joint venture

felt (fehlt) *nt* field

feltkikkert (*fehlt*-khi-kert) *m* field glasses

feltseng (*fehlt*-sehng) *c* camp bed; cot *nAm*

fem (fehmm) *num* five

feminin (feh-mi-*neen*) *adj* feminine

femte (*fehm*-ter) *num* fifth

femten (*fehm*-tern) *num* fifteen

femtende (*fehm*-ter-ner) *num* fifteenth

femti (*fehm*-ti) *num* fifty

fengsel (*fehng*-sherl) *nt* (pl -sler) jail, prison

fengsle (*fehng*-shler) *v* imprison; fascinate

ferdig (*fææ*-di) *adj* finished

ferdselsåre (*færd*-serls-*aw*-rer) *c* thoroughfare

ferge (*fær*-ger) *c* ferry-boat

ferie (*fay*-ri-er) *m* vacation, holiday; **på ~** on holiday

ferieleir (*fay*-ri-er-layr) *m* holiday camp

feriested (*fay*-ri-er-stay) *nt* holiday resort

ferje (*fær*-ʸer) *c* ferry-boat

fersk (fæshk) *adj* fresh

fersken (*fæsh*-kern) *m* peach

ferskvann (*fæshk*-vahn) *nt* fresh water

fest (fehst) *m* feast, party

feste (*fehss*-ter) *v* attach, fasten; **~ med nål** pin

festeinnretning (*fehss*-ter-in-reht-ning) *m* fastener

festival (fehss-ti-*vaal*) *m* festival

festlig (*fehst*-li) *adj* festive

festning (*fehst*-ning) *m* fortress; stronghold

fet (fayt) *adj* fat, obese

fett (fehtt) *nt* grease, fat

fetter (*feht*-terr) *m* cousin

fettet (*feht*-tert) *adj* greasy

fettholdig (*feht*-hol-di) *adj* fatty

fiasko (fi-*ahss*-koo) *m* failure

fiber (*fee*-berr) *m* (pl fibrer) fibre

fiende (*fee*-ern-der) *m* enemy

fiendtlig (*fee*-ern-tli) *adj* hostile

figur (fi-*gewr*) *m* figure

fik (feek) *m* slap, blow

fike (*fee*-ker) *v* slap

fiken (*fee*-kern) *m* fig

fiks (fiks) *adj* smart

fil (feel) *m* file; lane

filial (fi-li-*aal*) *m* branch

filipens (fi-li-*pehns*) *m* acne

Filippinene (fi-li-*pee*-ner-ner) Philippines *pl*

filippinsk (fi-li-*peensk*) *adj* Philippine

fille (*fil*-ler) *c* rag

film (film) *m* movie, film

filme (*fil*-mer) *v* film

filmkamera (*film*-kaa-mer-rah) *nt* camera

filmlerret (*film*-lær-rert) *nt* screen

filosof (fi-loo-*soof*) *m* philosopher

filosofi (fi-loo-soo-*fee*) *m* philosophy

filt (filt) *m* felt

filter (*fil*-terr) *nt* (pl -tre) filter

fin (feen) *adj* fine

finanser (fi-*nahng*-serr) *pl* finances *pl*

finansiell (fi-nahng-si-*ehll*) *adj* financial

finansiere (fi-nahng-si-*ay*-rer) *v* finance

finger (*fing*-ngerr) *m* (pl -gre) finger

fingeravtrykk (*fing*-ngerr-ahv-trewk) *nt* (pl ~) fingerprint

fingerbøl (*fing*-ngerr-burl) *nt* (pl ~) thimble

finhakke (*feen*-hah-ker) *v* mince

finke (*fing*-ker) *m* finch

Finland (*fin*-lahn) Finland

finmale (*feen*-maa-ler) *v* *grind

finne¹ (*fin*-ner) *m* Finn

*finne² (*fin*-ner) *v* *find; **~ igjen** recover; **~ skyldig** convict; **~ sted** *take place

finsk (finsk) *adj* Finnish

fint! (feent) all right!, okay!

fiol (fi-*ool*) *m* violet

fiolett (fi-oo-*lehtt*) *adj* violet

fiolin (fi-oo-*leen*) *m* violin

fire (*fee*-rer) *num* four

firfisle (*feer*-fis-ler) *c* lizard

firma (*feer*-mah) *nt* firm, company

fisk (fisk) *m* fish

fiske (*fiss*-ker) *v* fish; angle

fiskebein (*fiss*-ker-bayn) *nt* bone, fishbone

fiskeforretning (*fiss*-ker-fo-reht-ning) *c* fish shop

fiskegarn (*fiss*-ker-gaan) *nt* (pl ~) fishing net

fiskekort (*fiss*-ker-kot) *nt* (pl ~) fishing license *Am*, fishing licence

fiskekrok (*fiss*-ker-krook) *m* fishing hook

fisker (*fiss*-kerr) *m* fisherman

fiskeredskap (*fiss*-ker-rehss-kaap) *nt* fishing tackle

fiskeri (fiss-ker-*ree*) *nt* fishing industry

fiskesnøre (*fiss*-ker-snūr-rer) *nt* fishing line

fiskestang (*fiss*-ker-stahng) *c* (pl -stenger) fishing rod

fiskeutstyr (*fiss*-ker-ewt-stewr) *nt* fishing gear

fjell (f'ehll) *nt* mountain

fjellendt (f'ehl-lent) *adj* mountainous

fjellkjede (f'ehl-khāy-der) *m* mountain range

fjellklatring (f'ehl-klaht-ring) *c* mountaineering

fjerde (f'ææ-rer) *num* fourth

fjern (f'ææn) *adj* far-away, far, distant, remote, far-off

fjerne (f'ææ-ner) *v* *take away, remove

fjerning (f'ææ-ning) *c* removal

fjernsyn (f'ææn-sewn) *nt* television, *colloquial* telly

fjernsynsapparat (f'ææn-sewn-sah-pah-raat) *nt* television set

fjollet (f'ol-lert) *adj* foolish

i fjor (ee f'oor) last year

fjord (f'oor) *m* fjord

fjorten (f'oot-tern) *num* fourteen; ~

dager fortnight

fjortende (f'oot-ter-ner) *num* fourteenth

fjær (f'æær) *c* (pl ~) feather; spring

fjære (f'ææ-rer) *c* low tide

fjæring (f'ææ-ring) *c* suspension

fjærkre (f'æær-krāy) *nt* (pl ~) fowl, poultry

flagg (flahgg) *nt* flag

flakke (*flahk*-ker) *v* wander

flamingo (flah-*ming*-goo) *m* flamingo

flamme (*flahm*-mer) *m* flame

flanell (flah-*nehll*) *m* flannel

flaske (*flahss*-ker) *c* bottle; flask

flaskehals (*flahss*-ker-hahls) *m* bottleneck

flaskeåpner (*flahss*-ker-awp-nerr) *m* bottle opener

flass (flahss) *nt* dandruff

flat (flaat) *adj* flat; plane

flekk (flehkk) *m* spot, stain; speck, blot

flekke (*flehk*-ker) *v* stain

flekket (*flehk*-kert) *adj* spotted

flekkfjerner (flehk-f'æ-nerr) *m* stain remover

flere (*flāy*-rer) *adj* several; **flest** most

flertall (*flāy*-tahl) *nt* majority; plural

flid (fleed) *m* diligence

flink (flingk) *adj* clever, skil(l)ful, smart

flintstein (*flint*-stayn) *m* flint

flis (fleess) *c* chip; tile

flittig (*fli*-ti) *adj* diligent; industrious

flo (floo) *m* flood

flokk (flokk) *m* herd, flock; bunch

flott (flott) *adj* swell; *colloquial* super

flottør (flo-*tūrr*) *m* float

flue (*flēw*-er) *c* fly

flukt (flewkt) *c* escape

fluktstol (*flewkt*-stool) *m* deck chair

fly (flēw) *nt* aircraft, aeroplane, plane; airplane *nAm*

***fly** (flēw) *v* *fly

flybensin (flēw-behn-*seen*) *m*

kerosene

flygel (*flew*-gerl) *nt* (pl -gler) grand piano

flykaptein (*flew*-kahp-tayn) *m* captain

flykte (*flewk*-ter) *v* escape, flee

flyktig (*flewk*-ti) *adj* casual

flyktning (*flewkt*-ning) *m* refugee

flyndre (*flewnd*-rer) *c* sole

flyplass (*flew*-plahss) *m* airport, airfield

flyselskap (*flew*-sehl-skaap) *nt* airline

*flyte (*flew*-ter) *v* flow; float

flytende (*flew*-ter-ner) *adj* fluent; fluid, liquid

flyttbar (*flewt*-baar) *adj* movable

flytte (*flewt*-ter) *v* move

flytur (*flew*-tewr) *m* flight

flyulykke (*flew*-ew-lew-ker) *c* plane crash

flyvert (*flew*-væt) *m* steward

flyvertinne (*flew*-væ-ti-ner) *c* stewardess

fløte (*flur*-ter) *m* cream

fløteaktig (*flur*-ter-ahk-ti) *adj* creamy

fløyel (*flur*ᵉʷ-erl) *m* velvet

fløyte (*flur*ᵉʷ-ter) *c* flute; whistle

flå (flaw) *v* fleece

flåte (*flaw*-ter) *m* raft; fleet; navy

fnise (*fnee*-ser) *v* giggle

foajé (foo-ah-ʸaȳ) *m* foyer, lobby

fold (foll) *m* crease, fold

folde (*fol*-ler) *v* fold; ~ **sammen** fold; ~ **ut** *v* unfold

foldekniv (*fol*-ler-kneev) *m* clasp-knife

folk (folk) *nt* people, nation; *pl* people; **folke-** popular; national

folkedans (*fol*-ker-dahns) *m* folk dance

folkemengde (*fol*-ker-mehng-der) *m* crowd

folkerik (*fol*-ker-reek) *adj* populous

folkeslag (fol-ker-*shlaag*) *nt* (pl ~) people

folkevise (*fol*-ker-vee-ser) *c* folk song

folklore (folk-*law*-rer) *m* folklore

fond (fonn) *nt* fund

fondsbørs (*fons*-būrsh) *m* stock exchange

fondsmarked (*fons*-mahr-kerd) *nt* stock market

fonetisk (foo-*naȳ*-tisk) *adj* phonetic

for¹ (forr) *conj* for; *prep* for; ~ **hånden** available; ~ **å** in order to, to

fôr² (tōōr) *nt* lining; fodder

forakt (for-*ahkt*) *m* scorn, contempt

forakte (for-*ahk*-ter) *v* despise, scorn

foran (*for*-rahn) *prep* before, ahead of, in front of

forandre (for-*ahn*-drer) *v* change; vary, alter

forandring (for-*ahn*-dring) *c* variation, change; alteration

foranledning (*for*-rahn-*laȳd*-ning) *m* occasion

foranstaltning (*for*-rahn-stahlt-ning) *m* measure

forargelse (for-*ahr*-gerl-ser) *m* indignation

forbanne (for-*bahn*-ner) *v* curse

forbause (for-*bou*-ser) *v* astonish; amaze, surprise

forbauselse (for-*bou*-serl-ser) *m* astonishment; amazement

forbausende (for-*bou*-ser-ner) *adj* astonishing; amazing

forbedre (for-*bāȳd*-rer) *v* improve

forbedring (for-*bāȳd*-ring) *c* improvement

forbehold (*for*-ber-hol) *nt* qualification; reservation

forberede (for-ber-*rāȳ*-der) *v* prepare

forberedelse (for-ber-*rāȳ*-derl-ser) *m* preparation

forberedende (for-ber-*rāȳ*-der-ner) *adj* preliminary

forbi (for-*bee*) *prep* past, beyond, past; ***gå ~** pass by

*forbinde (for-*bin*-ner) v connect, link, join; dress; associate

forbindelse (for-*bin*-nerl-ser) m connection; relation, reference

forbipasserende (for-*bee*-pah-sāy-rer-ner) m (pl ∼) passer-by

*forbli (for-*blee*) v remain

forbløffe (for-blurf-fer) v astonish

forbokstav (*for*-book-staav) m initial

forbruk (*for*-brēwk) nt expenditure; consumption

forbruke (*for*-brēw-ker) v consume

forbruker (*for*-brēw-kerr) m consumer

forbrytelse (for-*brēw*-terl-ser) m crime

forbryter (for-*brēw*-terr) m criminal

forbrytersk (for-*brēw*-tershk) adj criminal

forbud (*for*-bēwd) nt (pl ∼) prohibition

forbudt (for-*bewtt*) adj prohibited; **forbikjøring forbudt** no passing Am

forbund (*for*-bewn) nt (pl ∼) league, union; **forbunds-** federal

forbundsfelle (*for*-bewns-feh-ler) m associate

forbundsstat (*for*-bewn-staat) m federation

*forby (for-*bēw*) v *forbid, prohibit

fordampe (fo-*dahm*-per) v evaporate

fordel (*for*-dāyl) m benefit, advantage, profit; ***ha ∼ av** benefit; **til ∼ for** for the benefit of

fordelaktig (fo-*dāyl*-ahk-ti) adj advantageous

fordele (fo-*dāy*-ler) v divide

fordi (fo-*dee*) conj as, because; since

fordom (*fo*-dom) m (pl ∼mer) prejudice

fordreid (fo-*drayd*) adj crooked, twisted

fordring (*fod*-ring) c claim

*fordrive (fo-*dree*-ver) v expel; chase

fordum (*fo*-dewm) adv formerly

fordømt (*fo*-dømt) adv damned; *colloquial* bloody

fordøye (fo-*dur*ᵉʷ-er) v digest

fordøyelig (fo-*dur*ᵉʷ-er-li) adj digestible

fordøyelse (fo-*dur*ᵉʷ-erl-ser) m digestion; **dårlig ∼** indigestion

forebygge (*faw*-rer-bew-ger) v prevent

forebyggende (*faw*-rer-bew-ger-ner) adj preventive

foredrag (*faw*-rer-draag) nt (pl ∼) lecture

*foregi (*faw*-rer-ʸee) v pretend

*foregripe (*faw*-rer-gree-per) v anticipate

foregående (*faw*-rer-gaw-er-ner) adj preceding, previous

*forekomme (*faw*-rer-ko-mer) v occur

forelder (for-*ehl*-derr) m parent

foreldet (for-*ehl*-dert) adj out of date

foreldre (for-*ehl*-drer) pl parents pl

*forelegge (*faw*-rer-leh-ger) v present

forelesning (*faw*-rer-lāyss-ning) m lecture

forelsket (for-*ehl*-skert) adj in love

foreløpig (*faw*-rer-lūr-pi) adj provisional, temporary

forene (fo-*rāy*-ner) v join, unite

forening (for-*āy*-ning) c association; club, society

forent (for-*āynt*) adj joint; **De forente stater** (di for-*āyn*-ter *staa*-terr) the States, United States

*foreskrive (*faw*-rer-skree-ver) v prescribe

*foreslå (*faw*-rer-shlaw) v propose, suggest

*forespørre (*faw*-rer-spur-rer) v inquire, query, enquire

forespørsel (*faw*-rer-spur-sherl) m (pl -sler) inquiry, query, enquiry

forestille (*faw*-rer-sti-ler) v represent; **∼ seg** conceive; imagine, fancy

forestilling (*faw*-rer-sti-ling) *c* show, performance; idea, conception

foretak (*faw*-rer-taak) *nt* undertaking; concern

*foretrekke (*faw*-rer-treh-ker) *v* prefer; **å ~** preferable

forfader (*for*-faa-derr) *m* (pl -fedre) ancestor

forfallen (for-*fahl*-lern) *adj* dilapidated

forfalske (for-*fahl*-sker) *v* counterfeit, forge

forfalskning (for-*fahlsk*-ning) *m* fake

forfalt (for-*fahlt*) *adj* overdue

forfatter (for-*faht*-terr) *m* author, writer

forfengelig (for-*fehng*-nger-li) *adj* vain

forferdelig (for-*fæ*-der-li) *adj* awful, dreadful, frightful, terrible

forfremme (for-*frehm*-mer) *v* promote

forfremmelse (for-*frehm*-merl-ser) *m* promotion

forfriske (for-*friss*-ker) *v* refresh

forfriskende (for-*friss*-ker-ner) *adj* refreshing

forfriskning (for-*frisk*-ning) *m* refreshment

*forfølge (for-*furl*-ler) *v* pursue, chase

forføre (for-*fūr*-rer) *v* seduce

forgasser (for-*gahss*-serr) *m* carburettor

forgifte (for-ʸ*if*-ter) *v* poison

forgjenger (for-ʸeh-ngerr) *m* predecessor

forgjeves (for-ʸ*āy*-verss) *adv* in vain; *adj* vain

forglemmelse (for-*glehm*-merl-ser) *m* oversight

forgrunn (*for*-grewn) *m* foreground

forgylt (for-ʸ*ewlt*) *adj* gilt

i forgårs (ee *for*-gosh) the day before yesterday

*forgå seg (for-*gaw*) offend

forhandle (for-*hahnd*-ler) *v* negotiate

forhandler (for-*hahnd*-lerr) *m* dealer

forhandling (for-*hahnd*-ling) *c* negotiation

forhastet (for-*hahss*-tert) *adj* rash; premature

forhekse (for-*hehk*-ser) *v* bewitch

forhenværende (*for*-hehn-væ-rer-ner) *adj* former

forhindre (for-*hin*-drer) *v* prevent; inhibit

forhold (*for*-hol) *nt* (pl ~) relation; affair

forholdsmessig (*for*-hols-meh-si) *adj* proportional

forhør (*for*-hūr) *nt* (pl ~) interrogation, examination

forhøre (for-*hūr*-rer) *v* interrogate; **~ seg** inquire

på forhånd (po *for*-hon) in advance

forhåndsbetalt (*for*-hons-beh-tahlt) *adj* prepaid

forhåndsvisning (*for*-hons-visning) *m* preview

forkaste (for-*kahss*-ter) *v* reject, turn down

forkjemper (*for*-khehm-perr) *m* champion

forkjærlighet (*for*-khææ-li-hāyt) *c* preference

forkjølelse (for-*khūr*-lerl-ser) *m* cold; ***bli forkjølet** *catch a cold

forkjørsrett (*for*-khūrsh-reht) *m* right of way

forklare (for-*klaa*-rer) *v* explain

forklaring (for-*klaa*-ring) *c* explanation

forklarlig (for-*klaa*-li) *adj* accountable

forkle (*for*-kler) *nt* (pl -lær) apron

forkledning (for-*klāyd*-ning) *m* disguise

forkle seg (for-*klāy*) disguise

forkorte (for-*kot*-ter) *v* shorten

forkortelse (for-_ko_-terl-ser) _m_
abbreviation

forlange (fo-_lahng_-nger) _v_ demand

*forlate (fo-_laa_-ter) _v_ check out,
*leave; desert

forleden (fo-_la͞y_-dern) _adv_ recently

forlegen (fo-_la͞y_-gern) _adj_
embarrassed; ***gjøre ~** embarrass

forlegenhet (fo-_la͞y_-gern-ha͞yt) _c_
embarrassment

*forlegge (fo-_leh_-ger) _v_ *mislay

forlegger (_fo_-leh-gerr) _m_ publisher

forlenge (fo-_lehng_-nger) _v_ lengthen;
extend

forlengelse (fo-_lehng_-ngerl-ser) _m_
extension

forlovede (fo-_law_-ver-der) _m_ fiancé;
fiancée

forlovelse (fo-_law_-verl-ser) _m_
engagement

forlovelsesring (fo-_law_-verl-serss-
ring) _m_ engagement ring

forlovet (fo-_law_-vert) _adj_ engaged

forlystelse (fo-_lewss_-terl-ser) _m_
entertainment, amusement

*forløpe (fo-_lu͞r_-per) _v_ pass

form (form) _c_ form, shape

formalitet (for-mah-li-_ta͞yt_) _m_
formality

formane (for-_maa_-ner) _v_ urge

formann (_for_-mahn) _m_ (pl -menn)
president, chairman, chairwoman;
foreman

format (for-_maat_) _nt_ size

forme (_for_-mer) _v_ shape, model, form

formel (_for_-merl) _m_ (pl -mler) formula

formell (for-_mehll_) _adj_ formal

formiddag (_for_-mi-dah) _m_ morning

formiddagsmat (_for_-mi-dahks-maat)
_m_ lunch

forminske (for-_min_-sker) _v_ lessen

formodning (for-_mo͞od_-ning) _m_ guess

formue (_for_-moo-er) _m_ fortune

formynder (for-_mewn_-derr) _m_
guardian

formynderskap (for-_mewn_-der-
shkaap) _nt_ custody

formørkelse (for-_murr_-kerl-ser) _m_
eclipse

formål (_for_-mawl) _nt_ (pl ~) purpose,
objective, object

formålstjenlig (_for_-mawls-t^y_a͞yn_-li)
adj appropriate

fornavn (_fo_-nahvn) _nt_ (pl ~) first
name, Christian name

fornemme (fo-_nehm_-mer) _v_ perceive

fornemmelse (fo-_nehm_-merl-ser) _m_
perception; sensation

fornuft (fo-_newft_) _m_ reason, sense

fornuftig (fo-_newf_-ti) _adj_ reasonable,
sensible

fornye (fo-_ne͞w_-er) _v_ renew

fornærme (fo-_nær_-mer) _v_ offend;
insult

fornærmelse (fo-_nær_-merl-ser) _m_
offense _Am_, offence; insult

fornøyd (for-_nur^ew_d) _adj_ pleased; glad

fornøyelse (fo-_nur^ew_-erl-ser) _m_
pleasure

forpakte bort (for-_pahk_-ter bot) lease

forpaktning (for-_pahkt_-ning) _m_ lease

forplikte (for-_plik_-ter) _v_ oblige; **~ seg**
engage; ***være forpliktet til** *be
obliged to

forpliktelse (for-_plik_-terl-ser) _m_
engagement

forresten (fo-_rehss_-tern) _adv_ besides;
by the way

forretning (fo-_reht_-ning) _c_ store, shop;
business

forretninger (fo-_reht_-ni-ngerr) _pl_
business; **i ~** on business

forretningskvinne (fo-_reht_-nings-
kvin-ner) _c_ businesswoman

forretningsmann (fo-_reht_-nings-
mahn) _m_ (pl -menn) businessman

forretningsmessig (fo-_reht_-nings-
meh-si) _adj_ business-like

forretningsreise (fo-*reht*-nings-ray-ser) *c* business trip

forretningssenter (fo-*reht*-ning-sehn-terr) *nt* (pl -trer) shopping centre, mall *nAm*

forrett (*for*-reht) hors d'œuvre

forrige (*for*-^yer) *adj* previous, last, past

forræder (fo-*ray*-derr) *m* traitor

forræderi (fo-reh-der-*ree*) *nt* treason

forråd (*foar*-rawd) *nt* (pl ~) supply

forråde (fo-*raw*-der) *v* betray

forsamling (fo-*shahm*-ling) *c* assembly, rally

forseelse (fo-*shay*-erl-ser) *m* offense *Am*, offence, misdemeanour

forsere (fo-*shay*-rer) *v* force

forside (*fo*-shee-der) *c* front

forsikre (fo-*shik*-rer) *v* assure; insure

forsikring (fo-*shik*-ring) *c* insurance

forsikringspolise (fo-*shik*-rings-poo-lee-ser) *m* insurance policy

forsikringspremie (fo-*shik*-rings-*pray*-mi-er) *m* premium

forsiktig (fo-*shik*-ti) *adj* careful, cautious; gentle; wary; ***være ~** watch out

forsiktighet (fo-*shik*-ti-hayt) *c* caution, precaution

forsinke (fo-*shing*-ker) *v* delay

forsinkelse (fo-*shing*-kerl-ser) *m* delay

forsinket (fo-*shing*-kert) *adj* overdue

forskjell (*fo*-shehl) *m* distinction, difference; ***gjøre ~** distinguish

forskjellig (fo-*shehl*-li) *adj* different, unlike, distinct; ***være ~** vary, differ

forskning (*foshk*-ning) *m* research

forskole (*fo*-shkoo-ler) *m* kindergarten

forskrekke (fo-*shkrehk*-ker) *v* frighten; ***bli forskrekket** **be frightened

forskrekkelig (fo-*shkrehk*-ker-li) *adj* frightful

forskudd (fo-*shkewd*) *nt* (pl ~) advance; **betale på ~** advance; **på ~** in advance

forslag (fo-*shlaag*) *nt* (pl ~) proposal, suggestion, proposition; motion

forsoning (fo-*shoo*-ning) *c* reconciliation

*forsove seg (fo-*shaw*-ver) *oversleep

forsprang (fo-*shprahng*) *nt* (pl ~) lead

forstad (fo-*shtaad*) *m* (pl -steder) suburb; **forstads-** suburban

forstand (fo-*shtahnn*) *m* reason; brain, wits *pl*, intellect

forstavelse (fo-*shtaa*-verl-ser) *m* prefix

forstmann (*fosht*-mahn) *m* (pl -menn) forester

forstoppelse (fo-*shtop*-perl-ser) *m* constipation

forstue (fo-*shtew*-er) *v* sprain

forstuing (fo-*shtew*-ing) *c* sprain

forstyrre (fo-*shtewr*-rer) *v* disturb; *upset

forstyrrelse (fo-*shtewr*-rerl-ser) *m* disturbance

forstørre (fo-*shturr*-rer) *v* enlarge; magnify

forstørrelse (fo-*shturr*-rerl-ser) *m* enlargement

forstørrelsesglass (fo-*shturr*-rerl-serss-glahss) *nt* (pl ~) magnifying glass

*forstå (fo-*shtaw*) *v* *understand; *see

forståelse (fo-*shtaw*-erl-ser) *m* understanding

forsvar (fo-*shvaar*) *nt* defense *Am*, defence

forsvare (fo-*shvaa*-rer) *v* defend

forsvarstale (*fo*-shvaa-sh-taa-ler) *m* plea

*forsvinne (fo-*shvin*-ner) *v* disappear, vanish

forsvunnet (fo-*shvewn*-nert) *adj* lost

forsyne (fo-shēw-ner) v provide, furnish, supply; ~ **med** furnish with

forsyning (fo-shēw-ning) c stock

forsøk (fo-shūrk) nt (pl ~) try, attempt; trial; experiment

forsøke (fo-shūr-ker) v try, attempt

forsømme (fo-shurm-mer) v neglect; fail

forsømmelse (fo-shurm-merl-ser) m neglect

fort (foott) adv quickly

*****forta seg** (fo-taa) *wear away

fortau (fo-tou) nt (pl ~) pavement; sidewalk nAm

fortauskant (fo-touss-kahnt) m curb

*****fortelle** (fo-tehl-ler) v *tell; relate

fortelling (fo-tehl-ling) c story, tale

forte seg (foot-ter) hurry

fortid (fo-teed) c past

fortjene (fo-tʸāy-ner) v deserve, merit

fortjeneste (fo-tʸāy-nerss-ter) m profit, gain; merit

fortred (fo-trāyd) m harm, mischief

fortrinnsrett (fo-trins-reht) m priority

fortryllelse (fo-trewl-lerl-ser) m spell

fortryllende (fo-trewl-ler-ner) adj charming

*****fortsette** (fot-seh-ter) v continue; *keep on, carry on, *go on, proceed, *go ahead

fortsettelse (fot-seh-terl-ser) m sequel

fortvile (fo-tvee-ler) v despair

fortvilet (fo-tvee-lt) adj desperate

fortynne (fo-tewn-ner) v dilute

forundre (for-ewn-drer) v amaze

forundring (for-ewn-dring) c wonder

forurense (for-rew-rehn-ser) v pollute

forurensning (for-rew-rehns-ning) m pollution

forurolige (for-rew-rōō-li-er) v alarm

foruroligende (for-rew-rōō-li-er-ner) adj scary

foruten (for-ēw-tern) prep besides

forutgående (for-rewt-gaw-er-ner) adj prior

forutsatt at (for-ēwt-sahtt ahtt) provided that, supposing that

*****forutse** (for-rēwt-sāy) v anticipate

*****forutsi** (for-rewt-see) v predict, forecast

forutsigelse (for-rewt-see-erl-ser) m prediction

forvaltende (for-vahl-ter-ner) adj administrative

forvaltningsrett (for-vahlt-nings-reht) m administrative law

forvandle (for-vahnd-ler) v transform; **forvandles til** turn into

forvaring (for-vaa-ring) c custody

forveksle (for-vehk-shler) v *mistake, confuse

forventning (for-vehnt-ning) m expectation

forvirre (for-veer-rer) v confuse

forvirret (for-veer-rert) adj confused

forvirring (for-veer-ring) c confusion; disturbance; muddle

forårsake (for-ro-shaa-ker) v cause

foss (foss) m waterfall

fossestryk (foss-ser-strēwk) nt (pl ~) rapids pl

fot (fōot) m (pl føtter) foot; **til fots** on foot, walking

fotball (foot-bahl) m soccer; football

fotballkamp (foot-bahl-kahmp) m football match

fotbrems (fōot-brehms) m foot brake

fotgjenger (fōot-ʸehng-err) m pedestrian

fotgjengerovergang (fōot-ʸayng-err-aw-verr-gahng) m crossing, pedestrian crossing; crosswalk nAm

fotoforretning (fōo-too-fo-reht-ning) c camera shop

fotograf (foo-too-graaf) m photographer

fotografere (foo-too-grah-fāy-rer) v

photograph
fotografering (foo-too-grah-*fāy*-ring)
c photography
fotografi (foo-too-grah-*fee*) nt
photograph, photo
fotografiapparat (foo-too-grah-*fee*-
ah-pah-raat) nt camera
fotokopi (*foot*-too-koo-pee) m
photocopy
fotokopiere (*fōō*-too-koo-pee-*āy*-rer)
v photocopy
fottur (*foot*-tewr) m hike
fra (fraa) prep from; out of; as from; ~
og med from, as from
fradrag (*fraa*-draag) nt (pl ~)
deduction; rebate
fraflytte (*fraa*-flew-ter) v vacate
frakk (frahkk) m coat, overcoat
frakt (frahkt) c cargo, freight
frankere (frahng-*kāy*-rer) v stamp
franko (*frahng*-koo) adv post-paid
Frankrike (*frahngk*-ree-ker) France
fransk (frahnsk) adj French
franskmann (*frahnsk*-mahn) m (pl
-menn) Frenchman
fraråde (fraa-*raw*-der) v dissuade
from
frastøtende (fraa-*stūr*-ter-ner) adj
revolting, repellent, repulsive
***frata** (fraa-taa) v deprive of
***fratre** (fraa-*trāy*) v resign
fravær (fraa-*væær*) nt (pl ~) absence
fraværende (fraa-*vææ*-rer-ner) adj
absent
fred (frāyd) m peace
fredag (*frāy*-dah) m Friday
fredelig (*frāy*-der-li) adj peaceful
frekk (frehkk) adj insolent, bold,
colloquial cheeky
frekkhet (*frehk*-hāyt) c impertinence
frekvens (freh-*kvehns*) m frequency
frelse (*frehl*-ser) v redeem, save; m
salvation
frem (frehmm) adv forward

fremad (*frehm*-maad) adv forward
fremadstrebende (*frehm*-maad-strāy-
ber-ner) adj go-ahead
***frembringe** (*frehm*-bri-nger) v effect
fremdeles (frehm-*dāy*-lerss) adv still
fremgang (*frehm*-gahng) m prosperity
fremgangsmåte (*frehm*-gahngs-maw-
ter) m approach; method, process,
procedure
***fremgå** (*frehm*-gaw) v appear
fremkalle (*frehm*-kah-ler) v develop
fremme (*frehm*-mer) v promote
fremmed (*frehm*-merd) adj strange;
foreign; m stranger
fremover (*frehm*-maw-verr) adv
onwards, ahead
fremragende (*frehm*-raa-ger-ner) adj
outstanding, excellent
fremskritt (*frehm*-skrit) nt (pl ~)
progress; advance; ***gjøre** ~ *get on,
advance
fremstille (*frehm*-sti-ler) v produce
fremstående (*frehm*-staw-er-ner) adj
distinguished
fremtid (*frehm*-tee) c future
fremtidig (*frehm*-tee-di) adj future
fremtoning (*frehm*-tōō-ning) m
appearance
***fremtre** (*frehm*-trāy) v appear
fremtredende (*frehm*-trāy-der-ner)
adj outstanding, distinguished
fremvise (*frehm*-vee-ser) v exhibit
fri (free) adj free
fribillett (*free*-bi-leht) m free ticket
frifinnelse (*free*-fi-nerl-ser) m
acquittal
frigjørelse (*free*-ʸūr-rerl-ser) m
emancipation
frihet (*free*-hāyt) c freedom, liberty
friidrett (*free*-id-reht) m athletics pl
friksjon (frik-*shōōn*) m friction
frikvarter (*free*-kvah-tāyr) nt break;
recess nAm
frimerke (*free*-mær-ker) nt postage

stamp, stamp
frimerkeautomat (*free*-mær-ker-ou-too-maat) *m* stamp machine
frisk (frisk) *adj* well; **bli ~** recover
frist (frist) *m* term
friste (*friss*-ter) *v* tempt
fristelse (*friss*-terl-ser) *m* temptation
frisyre (fri-*sew*-rer) *m* hair-do
frisør (fri-*surr*) *m* hairdresser
*frita (*free*-taa) *v* exempt; **~ for** discharge of
fritak (*free*-taak) *nt* exemption
fritatt (*free*-taht) *adj* exempt
fritid (*free*-teed) *c* spare time; leisure
frivillig[1] (*free*-vi-li) *adj* voluntary
frivillig[2] (*free*-vi-li) *m* (pl ~e) volunteer
frokost (*froo*-kost) *m* breakfast
from (fromm) *adj* pious
frontlys (front-*lewss*) *nt* (pl ~) headlamp, headlight
frontrute (front-*rew*-ter) *c* windscreen; windshield *nAm*
frosk (frosk) *m* frog
frossen (*fross*-sern) *adj* frozen
frost (frost) *m* frost
frotté (fro-*tay*) *m* towel(l)ing, terry(cloth)
frue (*frew*-er) *c* madam; mistress
frukt (frewkt) *m* fruit
fruktbar (*frewkt*-baar) *adj* fertile
frukthage (*frewkt*-haa-ger) *m* orchard
fruktsaft (*frewkt*-sahft) *m* squash
fryd (frewd) *m* delight, joy
frykt (frewkt) *m* fear, dread
frykte (*frewk*-ter) *v* fear, dread
fryktelig (*frewk*-ter-li) *adj* terrible, dreadful
frynse (*frewn*-ser) *c* fringe
fryse (*frew*-ser) *v* *freeze
*fryse (*frew*-ser) *v* *freeze
fryseboks (*frew*-ser-boks) *m* freezer
frysepunkt (*frew*-ser-pewngt) *nt* freezing point
fryser (*frew*-serr) *m* freezer

frysevæske (*frew*-ser-vehss-ker) *c* antifreeze
frø (frur) *nt* seed
fugl (fewl) *m* bird
fukte (*fook*-ter) *v* moisten, damp
fuktig (*fook*-ti) *adj* wet, damp, humid, moist
fuktighet (*fook*-ti-hayt) *c* damp, humidity, moisture
fuktighetskrem (*fook*-ti-hayts-kraym) *m* moisturizing cream
full (fewll) *adj* full; drunk
fullende (*fewl*-leh-ner) *v* accomplish, complete, finish
fullføre (*fewl*-*fur*-rer) *v* complete
fullkommen (*fewl*-ko-mern) *adj* perfect
fullkommenhet (*fewl*-ko-mern-hayt) *c* perfection
fullsatt (*fewl*-saht) *adj* full up
fullstappet (*fewl*-stah-pert) *adj* chockfull
fullstendig (fewl-*stehn*-di) *adv* altogether, *adj* total; utter, whole, complete
fundament (fewn-dah-*mehnt*) *nt* base
fundamental (fewn-dah-mehn-*taal*) *adj* fundamental
fungere (fewng-*gay*-rer) *v* work
funklende (*foongk*-ler-ner) *adj* sparkling
funksjon (fewngk-*shoon*) *m* function; operation
funksjonshemmet (fewngk-*shoons-hemmert*) *m* disabled
fure (*few*-rer) *m* groove
furu (*few*-rew) *c* pine
fusjon (few-*shoon*) *m* fusion; merger
fusjonere (few-shoon-*ay*-rer) *v* fusion; merge
fy! (few) shame!
fyldig (*fewl*-di) *adj* bulky; plump
fylke (*fewl*-ker) *nt* province
fyll (fewll) *nt* filling

fylle (*fewl*-ler) *v* fill; ~ **opp** fill up; ~ **ut** fill in; fill out *Am*

fyllepenn (*fewl*-ler-pehn) *m* fountainpen

fylt (fewlt) *adj* stuffed

fyr (fewr) *m* chap, fellow

fyring (*few*-ring) *c* heating

fyrstikk (*fewsh*-tik) *m* match

fyrstikkeske (*fewsh*-ti-kehss-ker) *c* match-box

fyrtårn (*few*-tawn) *nt* (pl ~) lighthouse

fysiker (*few*-si-kerr) *m* physicist

fysikk (few-*sikk*) *m* physics

fysiologi (few-si-oo-loo-*gee*) *m* physiology

fysisk (*few*-sisk) *adj* physical

føde (*fūr*-der) *c* nourishment

fødested (*fūr*-der-stāyd) *nt* place of birth

fødsel (*furt*-serl) *m* (pl -sler) birth; childbirth

fødselsdag (*furt*-serls-daag) *m* birthday

fødselsveer (*furt*-serls-vāy-err) *pl* labo(u)r pains

født (furtt) *adj* born

følbar (*fūrl*-baar) *adj* tangible

føle (*fūr*-ler) *v* *feel

følelig (*fūr*-ler-li) *adj* perceptible

følelse (*fūr*-lerl-ser) *m* sensation, feeling; emotion

følelsesløs (*fūr*-lerl-serss-lūrss) *adj* numb

følesans (*fūr*-ler-sahns) *m* touch

følge (*furl*-ler) *m* consequence; result;

v følge *holde ~ med* *keep up with

følge (*furl*-ler) *v* follow, accompany

følgende (*furl*-ger-ner) *adj* subsequent, following

følsom (*fūrl*-som) *adj* sensitive

før (fūrr) *conj* before; *prep* before

føre (*fūr*-rer) *v* *lead, conduct

fører (*fūr*-rerr) *m* leader; driver, conductor

førerhund (*fūr*-rerr-hewn) *m* guide dog

førerkort (*fūr*-rerr-kot) *nt* (pl ~) driving licence, driver's license *Am*

førerskap (*fūr*-rer-shkaap) *nt* leadership

førkrigs- (*fūrr*-kriks) pre-war

først (fursht) *adv* at first; ~ **og fremst** especially, essentially

første (*fursh*-ter) *num* first; *adj* foremost, primary

førstehjelp (*fursh*-ter-ʸehlp) *c* first aid

førstehjelpsskrin (*fursh*-ter-ʸehlp-skreen) *nt* first aid kit

førstehjelpsstasjon (*fursh*-ter-ʸehlp-stah-shōon) *m* first aid post

førsteklasses (*fursh*-ter-klah-serss) *adj* first-class, first-rate

førsterangs (*fursh*-ter-rahngs) *adj* first-rate

førti (*furt*-ti) *num* forty

føydal (fur^ew-daal) *adj* feudal

få (faw) *adj* few

*få (faw) *v* *get; obtain, receive; *have; ~ **til å** cause to

fårekjøtt (*faw*-rer-khurtt) *nt* mutton

G

*gi (ʸee) *v* *give; ~ **etter** indulge, *give in; ~ **opp** *v* *give up; ~ **seg** *give in

gift (ʸift) *c* poison

gifte seg (ʸif-ter) marry

giftig (ʸif-ti) *adj* toxic, poisonous

gikt (ʸikt) *c* gout

gips (ʸips) *m* plaster

gir (geer) *nt* gear; **skifte ~** change gear

girkasse (*geer*-kah-ser) *c* gear-box

girstang (*gee*-shtahng) *c* (pl -stenger) gear lever

gissel (*giss*-serl) *nt* (pl gisler) hostage

gitar (gi-*taar*) *m* guitar

gjedde (ʸ*ayd*-der) *c* pike

gjeld (ʸehll) *c* debt

***gjelde** (ʸ*ehl*-ler) *v* concern, apply

gjelle (ʸ*ehl*-ler) *c* gill

gjemme (ʸ*ehm*-mer) *v* *hide

gjenforene (ʸ*ehn*-fo-ra̅y̅-ner) *v* reunite

gjeng (ʸehngng) *m* gang

gjenlyd (ʸ*ehn*-le̅w̅d) *m* echo

gjennom (ʸ*ehn*-noom) *prep* through; ***gå ~** pass through

gjennombløte (ʸ*ehn*-noom-blu̅r̅-ter) *v* soak

gjennombore (ʸ*ehn*-noom-bo̅o̅-rer) *v* pierce

***gjennomgå** (ʸ*ehn*-noom-gaw) *v* *go through, suffer

gjennomreise (ʸ*ehn*-noom-ray-ser) *c* passage

gjennomsiktig (ʸ*ehn*-noom-sik-ti) *adj* sheer, transparent

gjennomsnitt (ʸ*ehn*-noom-snit) *nt* (pl ~) average, mean; **i ~** on the average

gjennomsnittlig (ʸ*ehn*-noom-snit-li) *adj* average, medium

gjennomtrenge (ʸ*ehn*-noom-treh-nger) *v* penetrate

gjenopplivelse (ʸ*ehn*-noop-lee-verl-ser) *m* revival

***gjenoppta** (ʸ*ehn*-nop-taa) *v* resume

gjensidig (ʸ*ehn*-see-di) *adj* mutual

gjenstand (ʸ*ehn*-stahn) *m* object; article

***gjenta** (ʸ*ehn*-taa) *v* repeat

gjentakelse (ʸ*ehn*-taa-kerl-ser) *m* repetition

gjerde (ʸ*ææ*-der) *nt* fence

gjerne (ʸ*ææ*-ner) *adv* willingly, gladly

gjerning (ʸ*ææ*-ning) *c* deed

gjerrig (ʸ*ær*-ri) *adj* stingy

gjespe (ʸ*ehss*-per) *v* yawn

gjest (ʸehst) *m* guest

gjesteværelse (ʸ*ehss*-ter-vææ-rerl-ser) *nt* guest room

gjestfri (ʸ*ehst*-free) *adj* hospitable

gjestfrihet (ʸ*ehst*-fri-ha̅y̅t) *c* hospitality

gjeter (ʸ*ay*-terr) *m* shepherd

gjette (ʸ*eht*-ter) *v* guess

gjær (ʸær) *m* yeast

gjære (ʸ*ææ*-rer) *v* ferment

gjø (ʸu̅r̅) *v* bark, bay

gjødsel (ʸ*urt*-serl) *c* manure, dung

gjødseldynge (ʸ*urt*-serl-dew-nger) *c* dunghill

gjøk (ʸu̅r̅k) *m* cuckoo

***gjøre** (ʸ*u̅r̅*-rer) *v* *do

glad (glaa) *adj* cheerful, glad, joyful, happy; ***være ~ i** love

glans (glahns) *m* gloss

glansløs (glahns-*lu̅r̅ss*) *adj* mat

glass (glahss) *nt* glass; **glass-** glass

glassmaleri (*glahss*-maa-ler-ree) *nt* stained glass window

glasur (glah-*se̅w̅r*) *m* icing, frosting

glatt (glahtt) *adj* slippery; smooth

glede (*gla̅y̅*-der) *c* gladness, joy, delight; *v* please, delight; ***ha ~ av** enjoy; **med ~** gladly

glemme (*glehm*-mer) *v* *forget

glemsom (*glehm*-som) *adj* forgetful

***gli** (glee) *v* *slide, glide; skid, slip

glidefly (*glee*-der-fle̅w̅) *nt* (pl ~) glider

glidelås (*glee*-der-lawss) *m* zip, zipper

glimrende (*glim*-rer-ner) *adj* splendid

glimt (glimt) *nt* flash; glimpse

glinse (*glin*-ser) *v* *shine

glis (gleess) *nt* grin

glise (glee-ser) *v* grin

globalisering (*glo̅o̅*-bah-li-sering) *c* globalization

globus (*glōō*-bewss) *m* globe

glød (glūrd) *m* glow

gløde (*glūr*-der) *v* glow

*gni (gnee) *v* rub

gnist (gnist) *m* spark

gobelin (goo-beh-*lehngng*) *nt* tapestry

god (gōō) *adj* good; kind

godkjenne (*gōō*-kheh-ner) *v* approve of, approve

godkjennelse (*gōō*-kheh-nerl-ser) *m* approval

godlynt (*gōō*-lewnt) *adj* good-humo(u)red

godmodig (gōō-*mōō*-di) *adj* good-tempered, good-natured

*godskrive (*gōō*-skree-ver) *v* credit

godstog (*goots*-tawg) *nt* (pl ∼) goods train; freight train *Am*

godsvogn (*goots*-vongn) wag(g)on*m* (goods)wagon; freight car *Am*

godt (gott) *adv* well

godter (*got*-terr) *pl* candy *nAm*, sweets

*godtgjøre (*got*-ᵞūr-rer) *v* *make good

godtgjørelse (*got*-ᵞūr-rerl-ser) *m* remuneration

godtroende (*gōō*-trōō-er-ner) *adj* credulous

godvilje (*gōō*-vil-ᵞer) *m* goodwill

golf (golf) *m* golf; gulf

golfbane (*golf*-baa-ner) *m* golf links, golf course

gondol (gon-*dōōl*) *m* gondola

grad (graad) *m* degree; grade; **i den ∼ so**

gradvis (*graad*-veess) *adv* gradually; *adj* gradual

grafisk (*graa*-fisk) *adj* graphic; ∼ **fremstilling** diagram

gram (grahmm) *nt* gram

grammatikk (grah-mah-*tikk*) *m* grammar

grammatisk (grah-*maa*-tisk) *adj*

grammatical

gran (graan) *c* fir tree

granitt (grah-*nitt*) *m* granite

granne (*grahn*-ner) *m* neighbo(u)r

grapefrukt (*grayp*-frewkt) *c* grapefruit

grasiøs (grah-si-*ūrss*) *adj* graceful

gratis (*graa*-tiss) *adj* free, gratis; free of charge

gratulasjon (grah-tew-lah-*shōōn*) *m* congratulation

gratulere (grah-too-*lay*-rer) *v* congratulate

grav (graav) *c* tomb, grave

grave (*graa*-ver) *v* *dig; ∼ **ned** bury

gravere (grah-*vay*-rer) *v* engrave

gravid (grah-*veed*) *adj* pregnant

gravlund (*graav*-lewn) *m* cemetery

gravstein (*graav*-stayn) *m* tombstone, gravestone

gravør (grah-*vūr*) *m* engraver

gre (greh) *v* comb

grei (gray) *adj* nice; **det er greit** that's fine; OK

greie (gray-er) *v* cope

greker (*gray*-kerr) *m* Greek

gren (grāyn) *c* branch

grense (*grehn*-ser) *c* limit, bound, boundary; frontier, border

grenseløs (*grehn*-ser-lūrss) *adj* unlimited

grep (grāyp) *nt* grasp; clutch, grip

gresk (grāysk) *adj* Greek

gress (grehss) *nt* grass

gresshoppe (*grehss*-ho-per) *c* grasshopper

gressløk (*grehss*-lūrk) *m* chives *pl*

gressplen (*grehss*-plāyn) *m* lawn

gresstrå (*greh*-straw) *nt* (pl ∼) blade of grass

greve (*grāy*-ver) *m* earl, count

grevinne (greh-*vin*-ner) *c* countess

grevskap (*grāyv*-skaap) *nt* county

gribb (gribb) *m* vulture

grille (*gril*-ler) v grill; barbecue

grind (grinn) c gate

*gripe (*gree*-per) v *take, *catch, grasp, seize, grip; ~ **inn** intervene, interfere

gris (greess) m pig

grisk (grisk) adj greedy

griskhet (*grisk*-hāyt) c greed

grop (grōōp) c pit

grossist (groos-*sist*) m wholesale dealer

grotte (*grot*-ter) c cave, grotto

grov (grawv) adj coarse, gross

grovsmed (*grawv*-smāy) m blacksmith

gru (grēw) m horror

grundig (*grewn*-di) adj thorough

grunn[1] (grewnn) m ground; reason; cause; **på ~ av** owing to, because of, for, on account of

grunn[2] (grewnn) adj shallow

grunnlag (*grewn*-laag) nt (pl ~) basis; basics

*grunnlegge (*grewn*-leh-ger) v found

grunnleggende (*grewn*-leh-ger-ner) adj basic

grunnlov (*grewn*-lawv) m constitution

grunnsetning (*grewn*-seht-ning) m principle

grunntall (*grewn*-tahll) nt cardinal number

gruppe (*grewp*-per) c group; party

gruppere (grew-*pāy*-rer) v classify

grus (grēwss) m gravel, grit

grusom (*grēw*-som) adj cruel, harsh; terrible, horrible, grim

gruve (*grēw*-ver) c pit, mine

gruvearbeider (*grēw*-ver-ahr-bay-derr) m miner

gruvedrift (*grēw*-ver-drift) c mining

gryte (*grēw*-ter) c pot

grøft (grurft) c ditch

grønn (grurnn) adj green; **grønt kort** green card

grønnsak (*grurn*-saak) c vegetable

grønnsakhandler (*grurn*-saak-hahnd-lerr) m greengrocer; vegetable man

grøt (grūrt) m porridge

grå (graw) adj grey

grådig (*graw*-di) adj greedy

*gråte (*graw*-ter) v *weep, cry

gud (gēwd) m god

guddommelig (gew-*dom*-mer-li) adj divine

gudfar (*gēw*-faar) m (pl -fedre) godfather

gudinne (gew-*din*-ner) c goddess

gudstjeneste (gewts-tʸāy-nerss-ter) m worship, service

guide (gighd) m guide

gul (gēwl) adj yellow

gull (gewll) nt gold

gullgruve (gewll-*grēw*-ver) c goldmine

gullsmed (*gewll*-smāy) m jeweller, goldsmith

gulrot (*gēwl*-rōōt) c (pl -røtter) carrot

gulsott (*gēwl*-sot) m jaundice

gulv (gewlv) nt floor

gulvteppe (*gewlv*-teh-per) nt carpet

gummi (*gewm*-mi) m rubber, gum

gunstig (*gewn*-sti) adj favo(u)rable; cheap

gurgle (*gewr*-gler) v gargle

gutt (gewtt) m boy; lad

guvernør (gew-veh-*nūrr*) m governor

gyldig (ʸewl-di) adj valid

gyllen (ʸewl-lern) adj golden

gymnastikk (gewm-nah-*stikk*) m physical education, PE; gymnastics pl

gymnastikksal (gewm-nah-*stik*-saal) m gymnasium

gynekolog (gew-ner-koo-*lawg*) m gynaecologist

gynge (ʸewng-nger) v rock

gys (ʸēwss) nt shudder

gøy (gurᵉʷ) m/nt fun

gøyal (gurᵉʷ-ahl) adj amusing

*gå (gaw) v *go, walk; pull out; ~ **bort**
*leave, *go away; pass away; ~ **forbi**
pass by; ~ **forut for** precede; ~ **fottur**
hike; ~ **fra borde** disembark; ~
gjennom pass through; ~ **hjem** *go
home; ~ **igjennom** *go through; ~ **i**
land land; ~ **inn** enter, *go in; ~ **med**
på agree; ~ **ned** descend; ~ **om bord**
embark; ~ **over** cross; ~ **sin vei**
depart; ~ **tilbake** *get back; ~ **til**
verks proceed; ~ **ut** *go out; ~ **videre**

*go ahead, *go on
i går (i-*gawr*) yesterday
gårdsplass (*gawsh*-plahss) m
backyard, courtyard
gås (gawss) c (pl gjess) goose
gåsehud (*gaw*-ser-hēwd) c goose
flesh
gåte (*gaw*-ter) c puzzle, enigma,
riddle
gåtefull (*gaw*-ter-fewl) adj mysterious

H

*ha (haa) v *have; ~ **noe imot** mind; ~
på seg *wear; ~ **det!** bye-bye
hage (*haa*-ger) m garden
hagl (hahgl) nt hail; buckshot
hai (high) m shark
haike (*high*-ker) v hitchhike
haiker (*high*-kerr) m hitchhiker
hake (*haa*-ker) c chin
hakke (*hahk*-ker) v chop
hale (*haa*-ler) m tail
hallo! (hah-*lōō*) hello!
halm (hahlm) m straw
halmtak (*hahlm*-taak) nt (pl ~)
thatched roof
hals (hahls) m throat, neck
halsbrann (*hahls*-brahn) m heartburn
halsbånd (*hahls*-bon) nt (pl ~) collar
halsesyke (*hahl*-ser-sēw-ker) m sore
throat
halskjede (*hahls*-khāy-der) nt
necklace
halt (hahlt) adj lame
halte (*hahl*-ter) v limp
halv (hahll) adj half; **halv-** semi-
halvdel (*hahl*-dāyl) m half
halvere (hahl-*vāy*-rer) v halve
halvsirkel (*hahl*-seer-kerl) m (pl

-kler) semicircle
halvt (hahlt) adv half
halvtid (*hahl*-teed) c half time
halvveis (*hahl*-vayss) adv halfway
halvøy (*hahl*-lur^(ew)) c peninsula
ham (hahmm) pron him
hamburger (hahmm-bur-gerr) m
hamburger, beefburger, burger
hammer (*hahm*-merr) m hammer
hamp (hahmp) m hemp
han (hahnn) pron he, him; **hann-** male
handel (*hahn*-derl) m (pl -dler)
commerce, business, trade; deal;
*drive ~ trade; **handels-** commercial
handelsmann (*hahn*-derls-mahn) m
(pl -menn) tradesman
handelsrett (*hahn*-derls-reht) m
commercial law
handelsvare (*hahn*-derls-vaa-rer) m
merchandise
handikap (*hahn*-di-kapp) nt handicap
handle (*hahnd*-ler) v shop; act; ~ **med**
*deal with
handlebag (*hahnd*-ler-bæg) m
shopping bag
handlende (*hahnd*-ler-ner) m (pl ~)
dealer

handling (*hahnd*-ling) *c* action, act, deed; plot

hane (*haa*-ner) *m* cock

hans (hahns) *pron* his

hanske (*hahn*-sker) *m* glove

hard (haar) *adj* hard

harddisk (haar-disk) *m* hard disk

hardnakket (*haanah*-kert) *adj* obstinate

hare (*haa*-rer) *m* hare

harmoni (hahr-moo-*nee*) *m* harmony

harpe (*hahr*-per) *c* harp

harpiks (*hahr*-piks) *m* resin

harsk (hahshk) *adj* rancid

hasselnøtt (*hahss*-serl-nurt) *c* hazelnut

hast (hahst) *m* haste

hastig (*hahss*-ti) *adj* hasty

hastighet (*hahss*-ti-hāyt) *c* speed

hastverk (*hahst*-værk) *nt* hurry

hat (haat) *nt* hatred, hate

hate (*haa*-ter) *v* hate, detest

hatt (hahtt) *m* hat

haug (hou) *m* pile, heap; mound

hauk (houk) *m* hawk

hav (haav) *nt* ocean

havmåke (*haav*-maw-ker) *c* seagull

havn (hahvn) *c* port, harbour

havnearbeider (*hahv*-ner-ahr-bay-derr) *m* docker

havneby (*hahv*-ner-bēw) *m* seaport

havre (*hahv*-rer) *m* oats *pl*

hebraisk (heh-*braa*-isk) *nt* Hebrew

hedensk (*hāy*-dernsk) *adj* pagan, heathen

heder (*hāy*-derr) *m* glory

hederlig (*hāy*-der-li) *adj* honourable

hedning (*hāyd*-ning) *m* pagan, heathen

hedre (*hāy*-drer) *v* honour

heftig (*hehf*-ti) *adj* severe, violent, fierce

hegre (*hāy*-grer) *m* heron

hei (hay) *c* heath, moor

heis (hayss) *m* lift; elevator *nAm*

heise (*hay*-ser) *v* hoist

heisekran (*hay*-ser-kraan) *m* crane

hekk (hehkk) *m* hedge

hekle (*hehk*-ler) *v* crochet

heks (hehks) *c* witch

hel (hāyl) *adj* entire, whole

helbrede (*hehl*-brāy-der) *v* cure, heal

helbredelse (*hehl*-brāy-derl-ser) *m* recovery, cure

heldig (*hehl*-di) *adj* lucky, fortunate

heldigvis (*hehl*-di-vis) *adv* luckily, fortunately

hele (*hāy*-ler) *nt* whole; **i det ~** altogether

helg (hehlg) *c* weekend

helgen (*hehl*-gern) *m* saint

helgenskrin (*hehl*-gern-skreen) *nt* (pl ~) reliquary

helikopter (*hehll*-ee-kopp-terr) *nt* helicopter

helkornbrød (*hāyl*-kōon-brūr) *nt* (pl ~) wholemeal bread

hell (hehll) *nt* luck

Hellas (*hehl*-lahss) Greece

helle (*hehl*-ler) *v* pour; slope

heller (*hehl*-lerr) *adv* sooner, rather

hellig (*hehl*-li) *adj* holy, sacred

helligbrøde (*hehl*-li-brūr-der) *m* sacrilege

helligdag (*hehl*-li-daag) *m* holiday, Sunday

helligdom (*hehl*-li-dom) *m* (pl ~mer) shrine

helling (*hehl*-ling) *c* gradient

helse (*hehl*-ser) *c* health

helseattest (*hehl*-ser-ah-tehst) *m* health certificate

helt[1] (hehlt) *m* hero

helt[2] (hāylt) *adv* wholly, entirely, quite, completely

heltinne (hehlt-*inn*-ner) *c* heroine

helvete (*hehl*-ver-ter) *nt* hell

hemme (*hehm*-mer) *v* inhibit

hemmelig (*hehm*-li) *adj* secret

hemmelighet (*hehm*-li-hayt) *c* secret

hemorroider (heh-moo-*ree*-derr) *pl* piles *pl*, haemorrhoids *pl*

hende (*hehn*-ner) *v* happen, occur

hendelse (*hehn*-nerl-ser) *m* incident, happening, occurrence

hendig (*hehn*-di) *adj* handy

***henge** (*hehng*-nger) *v* *hang

hengebro (*hehng*-nger-broo) *c* suspension bridge

hengekøye (*hehng*-nger-kur^(ew)-er) *c* hammock

hengelås (heh-nger-lawss) *m* padlock

henger (*hehng*-ngerr) *m* hanger

hengiven (*hehn*-^(y)ee-vern) *adj* affectionate

hengivenhet (*hehn*-^(y)ee-vern-hayt) *c* affection

hengsel (*hehng*-sherl) *nt* (pl -sler) hinge

henne (*hehn*-ner) *pron* her

hennes (*hehn*-nerss) *pron* her, hers

henrettelse (*hehn*-reh-terl-ser) *m* execution

henrivende (*hehn*-ree-ver-ner) *adj* adorable, delightful, enchanting

henrykt (*hehn*-rewkt) *adj* delighted

hensikt (*hehn*-sikt) *m* intention, purpose, design; ***ha til ~** intend

henstand (*hehn*-stahn) *m* respite

hensyn (*hehn*-sewn) *nt* regard; **med ~ til** as regards, regarding

hensynsfull (*hehn*-sewns-fewl) *adj* considerate

hensynsfullhet (*hehn*-sewns-fewl-hayt) *c* consideration

hente (*hehn*-ter) *v* fetch; *get, pick up, collect

henvende seg til (*hehn*-veh-ner) address

henvise til (*hehn*-vee-ser) refer to

henvisning (*hehn*-veess-ning) *m* reference

her (hæær) *adv* here

heretter (*hææ*-reh-terr) *adv* from now on

herkomst (*hæær*-komst) *m* origin

herlig (*hææ*-li) *adj* wonderful, lovely, delightful

hermetikk (hær-mer-*tikk*) *m* tinned food

hermetikkboks (hær-mer-*tik*-boks) *m* tin; can *nAm*

hermetikkåpner (hær-mer-*tik*-awp-nerr) *m* tin opener

hermetisere (hær-mah-ti-*say*-rer) *v* preserve

herre (*hær*-rer) *m* gentleman

herredømme (*hær*-rer-dur-mer) *nt* dominion

herregård (*hær*-rer-gawr) *m* mansion, manor house

herretoalett (*hær*-rer-too-ah-leht) *nt* men's room

herske (*hæsh*-ker) *v* reign, rule

hersker (*hæsh*-kerr) *m* sovereign

hertug (*hæt*-tewg) *m* duke

hertuginne (hæ-tew-*gin*-ner) *c* duchess

hes (hayss) *adj* hoarse

hest (hehst) *m* horse

hestekraft (*hehss*-ter-krahft) *c* (pl -krefter) horsepower

hestesko (*hehss*-ter-skoo) *m* (pl ~) horseshoe

hesteveddeløp (*hehss*-ter-veh-der-lurp) *nt* (pl ~) horserace

het (hayt) *adj* hot

hete (*hay*-ter) *m* heat

***hete** (*hay*-ter) *v* *be called

heteroseksuell (*hay*-ter-roo-sehk-sew-ehl) *adj* heterosexual

hette (*heht*-ter) *c* hood

heve (*hay*-ver) *v* raise; *draw, cash

hevelse (*hay*-verl-ser) *m* swelling

hevn (hehvn) *m* revenge

hi (hee) *nt* den

hierarki (hi-eh-rahr-*kee*) *nt* hierarchy

hikke (*hik*-ker) *m* hiccup

hilse (*hil*-ser) *v* greet; salute; ~ **på** say hello to

hilsen (*hil*-sern) *m* greeting

himmel (*him*-merl) *m* (pl himler) sky; heaven

hindre (*hin*-drer) *v* hinder, impede

hindring (*hin*-dring) *c* obstacle, impediment

hinsides (*heen*-see-derss) *prep* beyond

hint (hinnt) *nt* hint; *v* ~**e** hint

hissig (*hiss*-si) *adj* hot-tempered, quick-tempered

historie (hiss-*tōō*-ri-er) *c* history

historiker (hiss-*tōō*-ri-kerr) *m* historian

historisk (hiss-*tōō*-risk) *adj* historic, historical

hittegods (*hit*-ter-goots) *nt* lost and found

hittegodskontor (*hit*-ter-goots-koon-*tōōr*) *nt* lost property office

hittil (*heet*-til) *adv* so far

hjelm (*y*ehlm) *m* helmet

hjelp (*y*ehlp) *c* aid, assistance, help; relief

***hjelpe** (*y*ehl-per) *v* help, aid; support, assist

hjelper (*y*ehl-perr) *m* helper

hjelpsom (*y*ehlp-som) *adj* helpful

hjem (*y*ehmm) *nt* home

hjemlengsel (*y*ehm-lehng-serl) *m* homesickness

hjemme (*y*ehm-mer) *adv* at home

hjemmelaget (*y*ehm-mer-laa-gert) *adj* home-made

hjemover (*y*ehm-maw-verr) *adv* homeward

hjemreise (*y*ehm-ray-ser) *c* return journey

hjerne (*y*ææ-ner) *m* brain

hjernerystelse (*y*ææ-ner-rewss-terl-ser) *m* concussion

hjerte (*y*æt-ter) *nt* heart

hjerteanfall (*y*æt-ter-ahn-fahl) *nt* (pl ~) heart attack

hjerteklapp (*y*æt-ter-klahp) *m* palpitation

hjertelig (*y*æt-li) *adj* cordial, hearty

hjerteløs (*y*æt-ter-lūrss) *adj* heartless

hjort (*y*ott) *m* deer

hjul (*y*ēwl) *nt* wheel

hjørne (*y*ūr-ner) *nt* corner

hode (*hōō*-der) *nt* head; **på hodet** upside down

hodepine (*hōō*-der-pee-ner) *c* headache

hodepute (*hōō*-der-pēw-ter) *c* pillow

hoff (hoff) *nt* court

hofte (*hof*-ter) *c* hip

hold (holl) *nt* stitch

***holde** (*hol*-ler) *v* *hold; *keep; ~ **oppe** *hold up; ~ **opp med** stop; ~ **på** *hold; ~ **på med** *keep at; ~ **seg borte fra** *keep away from; ~ **seg fast** *hold on; ~ **tilbake** keep back, *withhold ~ **ut** *keep up; *bear, endure; ~ **utkikk etter** watch for

holdeplass (*hol*-ler-plahss) *m* stop

holdning (*hold*-ning) *m* position, attitude

Holland (*hol*-lahn) Holland

hollandsk (*hol*-lahnsk) *adj* Dutch

hollender (*hol*-lehn-derr) *m* Dutchman

homofil (*hōō*-moo-feel) *adj* homosexual, gay *colloquial*; lesbian

honning (*hon*-ning) *m* honey

honorar (hoo-noo-*raar*) *nt* fee

hop (hōōp) *m* lot; heap

hopp (hopp) *nt* jump, leap, hop

hoppe[1] (*hop*-per) *v* jump; skip; hop; *leap; ~ **over** skip

hoppe[2] (*hop*-per) *c* mare

hore (*hōō*-rer) *c* whore

horisont (hoo-ri-*sont*) *m* horizon

horisontal (hoo-ri-son-*taal*) *adj*
horizontal

horn (hoon) *nt* horn

hornorkester (hoo-nor-kehss-terr) *nt*
(pl -tre) brass band

hos (hooss) *prep* with; at

hospital (hooss-pi-*taal*) *nt* hospital

hoste (hooss-ter) *v* cough; *m* cough

hotell (hoo-*tehll*) *nt* hotel

hov (hoov) *m* hoof

hoved- (hoo-verd) capital, cardinal,
chief, main, primary, principal

hovedgate (hoo-verd-gaa-ter) *c* main
street

hovedkvarter (hoo-verd-kvah-*tayr*)
nt headquarters *pl*

hovedledning (hoo-verd-*layd*-ning)
m mains *pl*

hovedsakelig (hoo-verd-saa-ker-li)
adv mainly

hovedstad (hoo-verd-staad) *m* (pl
-steder) capital

hovedvei (hoo-verd-vay) *m*
thoroughfare, main road

hoven (haw-vern) *adj* snooty

hovmester (hawv-mehss-terr) *m* (pl
-tre) head waiter

hovmodig (hov-*moo*-di) *adj* haughty;
proud

hud (hewd) *c* skin

hudfarge (hewd-fahr-ger) *m*
complexion

hukommelse (hew-*kom*-merl-ser) *m*
memory

hul (hewl) *adj* hollow

hule (hew-ler) *c* cave, cavern

hull (hewll) *nt* hole

hulrom (hewl-room) *nt* (pl ~) cavity

humle (hoom-ler) *c* bumblebee; *m*
hops

hummer (hoom-merr) *m* lobster

humor (hew-moor) *m* humo(u)r

humoristisk (hew-moo-*riss*-tisk) *adj*
humorous

humpet (hoom-pert) *adj* bumpy

humør (hew-*mürr*) *nt* mood; spirits

hun (hewnn) *pron* she; **hunn-** female

hund (hewnn) *m* dog

hundehus (hewn-ner-hewss) *nt* (pl ~)
kennel

hunderem (hewn-ner-rehmm) *c* (pl
~mer) lead

hundre (hewn-drer) *num* hundred

hurtig (hewt-ti) *adj* fast, quick, rapid

hurtigtog (hewt-ti-tawg) *nt* (pl ~)
through train, express train

hus (hewss) *nt* house; **hus-** domestic

husarbeid (hewss-ahr-bayd) *nt*
housework

husbåt (hewss-bawt) *m* houseboat

husdyr (hewss-dewr) *nt* (pl ~)
domestic animal

huse (hew-ser) *v* lodge

huseier (hewss-ay-err) *m* landlord

hushjelp (hewss-*y*erlp) *c* maid,
housemaid

husholderske (hewss-ho-lersh-ker)
m housekeeper

husholdning (hewss-hol-ning) *m*
housekeeping

huske (hewss-ker) *v* remember;
recollect; *swing; *m* swing

huslærer (hewss-lææ-rerr) *m* tutor

husmor (hewss-moor) *c* (pl -mødre)
housewife

husrom (hewss-room) *nt*
accommodation; **skaffe ~**
accommodate

husstand (hew-stahn) *m* household

husvert (hewss-væt) *m* landlord,
landlady

hutre (hewt-rer) *v* shiver

hva (vaa) *pron* what; **~ enn** whatever;
~ som helst anything

hval (vaal) *m* whale

hvelv (vehlv) *nt* arch

hvelving (vehl-ving) *m* vault

hvem (vehmm) *pron* who; **~ som enn**

whoever; **~ som helst** anybody; **til ~** whom

hver (væær) *adj* every, each

hverandre (væ-*rahn*-drer) *pron* each other

hverdag (*væ*æ-daag) *m* weekday

hvete (*vay*-ter) *m* wheat

hvetebolle (*vay*-ter-bo-ler) *m* bun

hvetebrødsdager (*vay*-ter-brūrss-daa-gerr) *pl* honeymoon

hvile (*vee*-ler) *v#* rest; *m* rest

hvilehjem (*vee*-ler-ᵞehm) *nt* (pl ~) rest home

hvilken (*vil*-kern) *pron* which; **~ som helst** whichever; **hvilke som helst** any

hvin (veen) *nt* shriek

hvis (viss) *conj* if; in case

hviske (*viss*-ker) *v* whisper

hvisking (*viss*-king) *c* whisper

hvit (veet) *adj* white

hvitløk (*veet*-lūrk) *m* garlic

hvitting (*vit*-ting) *m* whiting

hvor (vōor) *adv* where; how; **~ enn** wherever; **~ mange** how many; **~ mye** how much; **~ som helst** anywhere

hvordan (*voo*-dahn) *adv* how

hvorfor (*voor*-for) *adv* why; what for

hyggelig (*hewg*-ger-li) *adj* pleasant, enjoyable

hygiene (hew-gi-*ay*-ner) *m* hygiene

hygienisk (hew-gi-*ay*-nisk) *adj* hygienic

hykler (*hewk*-lerr) *m* hypocrite

hykleri (hewk-ler-*ree*) *nt* hypocrisy

hyklersk (*hewk*-lehshk) *adj* hypocritical

hyl (hēwl) *nt* scream, yell

hyle (*hēw*-ler) *v* scream, yell

hylle (*hewl*-ler) *c* shelf; *v* *pay tribute to

hyllest (*hewl*-lerst) *m* homage, tribute

hymne (*hewm*-ner) *m* hymn

hypotek (hew-poo-*tāyk*) *nt* mortgage

hyppig (*hewp*-pi) *adj* frequent

hyppighet (*hewp*-pi-hāyt) *c* frequency

hyssing (*hewss*-sing) *m* twine

hysterisk (hewss-*tāy*-risk) *adj* hysterical

hytte (*hewt*-ter) *c* cabin, hut; chalet, lodge; cottage

hæl (hæl) *m* heel

høflig (*hurf*-li) *adj* polite, civil

høne (*hūr*-ner) *c* hen

hørbar (*hūr*-baar) *adj* audible

høre (*hūr*-rer) *v* *hear

hørsel (*hursh*-sherl) *m* hearing

høst (hurst) *m* autumn; fall *nAm*

høste (*hurss*-ter) *v* gather

høvding (*hurv*-ding) *m* chieftain

høvisk (*hūr*-visk) *adj* courteous

høy¹ (hur^(ew)) *adj* tall, high; loud

høy² (hur^(ew)) *nt* hay

høyde (*hur^(ew)*-der) *m* height; altitude, rise

høydepunkt (*hur^(ew)*-der-poongt) *nt* zenith, height

høyderygg (*hur^(ew)*-der-rewgg) *m* ridge

høyere (*hur^(ew)*-er-rer) *adj* superior, higher

høyland (*hur^(ew)*-lahn) *nt* (pl ~) uplands *pl*

høylydt (*hur^(ew)*-lewt) *adj* loud

høyre (*hur^(ew)*-rer) *adj* right; right-hand; **på ~ side** right-hand

høyrød (*hur^(ew)*-rūr) *adj* crimson

høysesong (*hur^(ew)*-seh-song) *m* peak season, high season

høyslette (*hur^(ew)*-shleh-ter) *c* plateau

høysnue (*hur^(ew)*-snew-er) *m* hay fever

høyst (hur^(ew)st) *adv* at most

høyt (hur^(ew)t) *adv* aloud

høytidelig (hur^(ew)-*tee*-der-li) *adj* solemn

høyttaler (*hur^(ew)*-taa-lerr) *m* loud-speaker

høyvann (*hur^(ew)*-vahn) *nt* high tide

hån (hawn) *m* mockery, scorn

hånd (honn) *c* (pl hender) hand; ***ta ~ om** attend to

håndarbeid (*hon*-nahr-bayd) *nt* needlework; handwork

håndbagasje (*hon*-bah-gaa-sher) *m* hand luggage; hand baggage *Am*

håndbok (*hon*-book) *c* (pl -bøker) handbook, manual

håndbrems (*hon*-brehms) *m* handbrake

håndflate (*hon*-flaa-ter) *c* palm

håndfull (*hon*-fewl) *m* handful

håndjern (*hon*-ʸæn) *pl* handcuffs *pl*

håndkle (*hong*-kler) *nt* (pl -lær) towel

håndkrem (*hon*-krāym) *m* hand cream

håndlaget (*hon*-laa-gert) *adj* handmade

håndledd (*hon*-lehd) *nt* (pl ~) wrist

håndskrift (*hon*-skrift) *c* handwriting

håndtak (*hon*-taak) *nt* (pl ~) handle

håndtere (hon-*tāy*-rer) *v* handle

håndterlig (hon-*tāy*-li) *adj* manageable

håndtrykk (*hon*-trewk) *nt* (pl ~) handshake

håndvask (*hon*-vahsk) *m* wash-basin; hand wash

håndverk (*hon*-værk) *nt* (pl ~) handicraft

håndveske (*hon*-vehss-ker) *c* bag, handbag

håne (*haw*-ner) *v* mock

håp (hawp) *nt* hope

håpe (*haw*-per) *v* hope

håpefull (*haw*-per-fewl) *adj* hopeful

håpløs (*hawp*-lūrss) *adj* hopeless

håpløshet (*hawp*-lūrss-hāyt) *c* despair

hår (hawr) *nt* hair

hårbalsam (*hawr*-bahl-sahm) *m* conditioner

hårbørste (*hawr*-bursh-ter) *m* hairbrush

håret (*haw*-rert) *adj* hairy

hårfrisyre (*hawr*-fri-sēw-rer) *m* hairdo

hårgelé (*hawr*-sheh-*lay*) *m* hair gel

hårklipp (*hawr*-klip) *m* haircut

hårlakk (*haw*-lahk) *m* hair spray

hårskill (*haw*-shil) *m* parting

hårspenne (*haw*-shpeh-ner) *c* hairpin; bobby pin *Am*

hårtørrer (*haw*-turr-rerr) *m* hairdrier, hairdryer

I

i (ee) *prep* in; for, at

*iaktta (i-*ahk*-tah) *v* observe, watch

iakttakelse (i-*ahk*-taa-kerl-ser) *m* observation

ibenholt (*ee*-bern-holt) *m/nt* ebony

idé (i-*dāy*) *m* idea

ideal (i-deh-*aal*) *nt* ideal

ideell (i-deh-*ehll*) *adj* ideal

identifisere (i-dehn-ti-fi-*sāy*-rer) *v* identify

identifisering (i-dehn-ti-fi-*sāy*-ring) *c* identification

identisk (i-*dehn*-tisk) *adj* identical

identitet (i-dehn-ti-*tāyt*) *m* identity

identitetskort (i-dehn-ti-*tāyts*-kot) *nt* (pl ~) identity card, ID

idiom (i-di-*ōōm*) *nt* idiom

idiomatisk (i-di-oo-*maa*-tisk) *adj* idiomatic

idiot (i-di-*ōōt*) *m* idiot

idiotisk (i-di-*oo*-tisk) *adj* idiotic

idol (i-*dool*) *nt* idol

idrettsmann (*eed*-rehts-mahn) *m* (pl -menn) sportsman

idrettskvinne (*eed*-rehts-*kvin*-ner) *c* sportswoman

ifølge (i-*furl*-ger) *prep* according to

igjen (i-*ʸehnn*) *adv* again

ignorere (ig-noo-*rāy*-rer) *v* ignore

ikke (*ik*-ker) *adv* not

ikke-røyker (*ik*-ker-*rurᵉʷ*-kerr) *m* non-smoker

ikon (i-*koon*) *m*/*nt* icon

ild (ill) *m* fire

ildfast (*il*-fahst) *adj* fireproof, ovenproof

ildsfarlig (*ils*-faa-li) *adj* inflammable

ildsted (*il*-*stāyd*) *nt* hearth

illegal (*il*-leh-gaal) *adj* illegal

illeluktende (*il*-ler-look-ter-ner) *adj* smelly

illevarslende (*il*-ler-vahsh-ler-ner) *adj* sinister, ominous

illusjon (i-lew-*shoon*) *m* illusion

illustrasjon (i-lew-strah-*shoon*) *m* illustration; picture

illustrere (i-lew-*strāy*-rer) *v* illustrate

imens (i-*mehns*) *adv* meanwhile, in the meantime

imidlertid (i-*mid*-ler-ti) *adv* though; in the meantime

imitasjon (i-mi-tah-*shoon*) *m* imitation

imitere (i-mi-*tāy*-rer) *v* imitate

immigrant (i-mi-*grahnt*) *m* immigrant

immigrasjon (i-mi-grah-*shoon*) *m* immigration

immigrere (i-mi-*grāy*-rer) *v* immigrate

immun: *gjøre ~ (ʾ*ūr*-rer i-*mēwn*) immunize

immunitet (i-mew-ni-*tāyt*) *m* immunity

imperium (im-*pāy*-ri-ewm) *nt* (pl -ier) empire

imponere (im-poo-*nāy*-rer) *v* impress

imponerende (im-poo-*nāy*-rer-ner) *adj* impressive, imposing

import (im-*pott*) *m* import

importavgift (im-*pot*-taav-ʸift) *c* import duty

importere (im-po-*tāy*-rer) *v* import

importvarer (im-*pot*-vaa-rerr) *pl* imported goods

importør (im-po-*tūrr*) *m* importer

impotens (im-poo-*tehns*) *m* impotence

impotent (im-poo-*tehnt*) *adj* impotent

improvisere (im-proo-vi-*sāy*-rer) *v* improvise

impuls (im-*pewls*) *m* impulse

impulsiv (*im*-pewl-seev) *adj* impulsive

imøtekommende (i-*mūr*-ter-ko-mer-ner) *adj* obliging

indeks (*in*-dehks) *m* index

inder (*in*-derr) *m* Indian

India (*in*-di-ah) India

indianer (in-di-*aa*-nerr) *m* Indian

indiansk (in-di-*aansk*) *adj* Indian

indirekte (*in*-di-rehk-ter) *adj* indirect

indisk (*in*-disk) *adj* Indian

individ (in-di-*veed*) *nt* individual

individuell (in-di-vi-dew-*ehll*) *adj* individual

Indonesia (in-doo-*nāy*-si-ah) Indonesia

indonesier (in-doo-*nāy*-si-err) *m* Indonesian

indonesisk (in-doo-*nāy*-sisk) *adj* Indonesian

indre (*in*-drer) *adj* internal; inside, inner

industri (in-dew-*stree*) *m* industry

industriell (in-dew-stri-*ehll*) *adj* industrial

industriområde (in-dew-*stree*-om-raw-der) *nt* industrial area

infanteri (in-fahn-ter-*ree*) *nt* infantry

infeksjon (in-fehk-*shōōn*) *m* infection

infinitiv (in-*fīn*-ni-teev) *m* infinitive

infisere (in-fi-*sāy*-rer) *v* infect

inflasjon (in-flah-*shōōn*) *m* inflation

influensa (in-flew-*ehn*-sah) *m* flu, influenza

informasjon (in-for-mah-*shōōn*) *m* information

informasjonskontor (in-for-mah-*shōōns*-koon-tōōr) *nt* inquiry office, information bureau

informere (in-for-*māy*-rer) *v* inform

infrarød (in-frah-rūr) *adj* infra-red

ingefær (*ing*-nger-fæær) *m* ginger

ingen (*ing*-ngern) *pron* nobody, no one; none; *adj* no; ~ **av dem** neither

ingeniør (in-shern-*yūr*) *m* engineer

ingensteds (*ing*-ngern-stehss) *adv* nowhere

ingenting (*ing*-ngern-ting) *pron* nil, nothing

ingrediens (ing-greh-di-*ehns*) *m* ingredient

initiativ (i-nit-si-ah-*teev*) *nt* initiative

injeksjon (in-*y*ehk-*shōōn*) *m* injection

inkludert (in-klew-*dāyt*) *adj* included; **alt** ~ all included

inklusive (*in*-klew-seever) *adv* inclusive

inkompetent (*in*-kom-per-tehnt) *adj* incompetent

inn (inn) *adv* in; ~ **i** into

innbefatte (*in*-beh-fah-ter) *v* comprise, include

innbille seg (*in*-bi-ler) imagine

innbilsk (*in*-bilsk) *adj* conceited

innbilt (*in*-bilt) *adj* imaginary

innblande (*in*-blah-ner) *v* involve

innblandet (*in*-blah-nert) *adj* concerned, involved

innblanding (*in*-blah-ning) *c* interference

innbringende (*in*-bri-nger-ner) *adj* profitable

innbrudd (*in*-brewd) *nt* burglary

innbruddstyv (*in*-brewds-tēwv) *m* burglar

*innby (in-bēw) *v* ask; invite

innbydelse (in-*bēw*-derl-ser) *m* invitation

innbygger (*in*-bew-gerr) *m* inhabitant

inndele (*in*-dāy-ler) *v* *break down, divide into

inne (*in*-ner) *adv* indoors; inside

*innebære (*in*-ner-bææ-rer) *v* imply

innehaver (*in*-ner-haa-verr) *m* owner, bearer

*inneholde (*in*-ner-ho-ler) *v* contain

innen (*in*-nern) *prep* inside; within

innendørs (*in*-nern-dūrsh) *adj* indoor

innenfor (*in*-nern-for) *prep* inside; within

innenlands (*in*-nern-lahns) *adj* domestic

innfall (*in*-fahl) *nt* (pl ~) idea; whim; brain wave

innfatning (*in*-faht-ning) *m* frame

innflytelse (*in*-flēw-terl-ser) *m* influence

innflytelsesrik (*in*-flēw-terl-serss-reek) *adj* influential

innfødt (*in*-furt) *m* (pl ~e) native

innføre (*in*-fūr-rer) *v* import; introduce; initiate

innførsel (*in*-fur-sherl) *m* import

innførselstoll (*in*-fur-sherls-tol) *m* duty

inngang (*in*-gahng) *m* entrance, entry; way in

inngangspenger (*in*-gahngs-peh-ngerr) *pl* entrance fee

innhold (*in*-hol) *nt* contents *pl*

innholdsfortegnelse (*in*-hols-fo-tay-nerl-ser) *m* table of contents

inni (*in*-ni) *adv prep* within; inside

innkassere (*in*-kah-sāy-rer) *v* collect

innledende (*in*-lāy-der-ner) *adj* preliminary

innledning (*in*-lāyd-ning) *m*
introduction

innlemme (*in*- lāym -mer) *v* integrate

innlysende (*in*-lēw-ser-ner) *adj*
obvious

innover (*in*-naw-verr) *adv* inwards

innpakning (*in*-pahk-ning) *m*
packing, wrapping

innpakningspapir (*in*-pahk-nings-
pah-peer) *nt* wrapping paper

innrede (*in*-reh-der) *v* furnish;
decorate

innredning (*in*-reh-dning) *m*
furnishing, decoration

innrette (*in*-reht-ter) *v* arrange

innretning (*in*-reht-tning) *m* facilities;
gadget

innrømme (*in*-rur-mer) *v*
acknowledge, admit

innsamler (*in*-sahm-lerr) *m* collector

innsats (*in*-sahts) *m* achievement;
contribution; stake

innsatt (*in*-saht) *m* (pl ~e) prisoner

***innse** (*in*-sāy) *v* realize, *see

innside (*in*-see-der) *c* inside; interior

innsikt (*in*-sikt) *m* insight

innsirkle (*in*-seer-kler) *v* encircle

innsjø (*in*-shūr) *m* lake

innskipning (*in*-ship-ning) *m*
embarkation

innskrenkning (*in*-skrehngk-ning) *m*
reduction, restriction

***innskrive** (*in*-skree-ver) *v* list, enter,
register; ~ seg register

***innskyte** (*in*-shēw-ter) *v* insert

innskytelse (*in*-shēw-terl-ser) *m*
impulse

innsprøyte (*in*-sprur^ew^-ter) *v* inject

innstendig (*in*-stehn-di) *adj* urgent

inntekt (*in*-tehkt) *c* income, earnings

inntektsskatt (*in*-tehkt-skaht) *m*
income tax

inntil (*in*-til) *conj* until, till; *prep* till

inntreden (*in*-trāy-dern) *m* entrance

inntrengende (*in*-treh-nger-ner) *adj*
pressing

inntrykk (*in*-trewk) *nt* impression;
*gjøre ~ på impress

innvende (*in*-veh-ner) *v* object; ~ mot
object to

innvendig (*in*-vehn-di) *adv* within

innvending (*in*-vehn-ning) *c* objection

innviklet (*in*-vik-lert) *adj* complex,
complicated

innvilge (*in*-vil-ger) *v* grant

innvoller (*in*-vo-lerr) *pl* insides,
entrails

innånde (*in*-no-ner) *v* inhale

insekt (*in*-sehkt) *nt* insect; bug *nAm*

insektmiddel (*in*-sehkt-mi-derl) *nt* (pl
-midler) insecticide, insect repellent

insinuere (*in*-si-new-āy-rer) *v* hint,
insinuate

insistere (in-si-stāy-rer) *v* insist

inskripsjon (in-skrip-shōōn) *m*
inscription

inspeksjon (*in*-spehk-shōōn) *m*
inspection

inspektør (in-spayk-tūrr) *m* inspector

inspirere (in-spi-rāy-rer) *v* inspire

inspisere (in-spi-sāy-rer) *v* inspect

installasjon (in-stah-lah-shōōn) *m*
installation

installere (in-stah-lāy-rer) *v* install

instinkt (in-stingt) *nt* instinct

institusjon (in-sti-tew-shōōn) *m*
institution

institutt (in-sti-*tewtt*) *nt* institution,
institute

instruktør (in-strewk-*tūrr*) *m*
instructor

instrument (in-strew-*mehnt*) *nt*
instrument

instrumentbord (in-strew-*mehnt*-
bōōr) *nt* (pl ~) dashboard

intakt (in-*tahkt*) *adj* intact; unbroken

integrere (in-teh-grāy-rer) *v* integrate

intellekt (in-teh-*lehkt*) *nt* intellect

intellektuell (in-teh-lehk-tew-*ehll*) *adj*
intellectual

intelligens (in-teh-li-*gehns*) *m*
intelligence

intelligent (in-teh-li-*gehnt*) *adj*
intelligent; clever

intens (in-*tehns*) *adj* intense

interessant (in-ter-reh-*sahngng*) *adj*
interesting

interesse (in-ter-*rehss*-ser) *m* interest

interessere (in-ter-reh-*sāy*-rer) *v*
interest

interessert (in-ter-reh-*sāyt*) *adj*
interested

internasjonal (*in*-ter-nah-shoo-naal)
adj international

Internett (in-terr-*nettl*) Internet

intervall (in-terr-*vahl*) *nt* interval

intervju (in-terr-*vᵛew*) *nt* interview

intet (*in*-tert) *nt* nothing

intetkjønn (*in*-tert-khurn) neuter

intetsigende (*in*-tert-see-er-ner) *adj*
insignificant, petty

intim (in-*teem*) *adj* intimate

intrige (in-*tree*-ger) *m* intrigue

introduksjonsskriv (in-troo-dewk-
shōōn-skreev) *nt* (pl ∼) letter of
recommendation

introdusere (in-troo-dew-*sāy*-rer) *v*
introduce

invadere (in-vah-*dāy*-rer) *v* invade

invasjon (in-vah-*shōōn*) *m* invasion

investere (in-vehss-*tāy*-rer) *v* invest

investering (in-vehss-*tāy*-ring) *c*
investment

invitere (in-vi-*tāy*-rer) *v* invite

Irak (i-*raak*) Iraq

iraker (i-*raa*-kerr) *m* Iraqi

irakisk (i-*raa*-kisk) *adj* Iraqi

Iran (i-*raan*) Iran

iraner (i-*raa*-nerr) *m* Iranian

iransk (i-*rahnsk*) *adj* Iranian

Irland (*eer*-lahn) Ireland

irlending (*eer*-leh-ning) *m* Irishman

ironi (i-roo-*nee*) *m* irony

ironisk (i-*rōō*-nisk) *adj* ironical

irritabel (i-ri-*taa*-berl) *adj* irritable

irritere (i-ri-*tāy*-rer) *v* irritate; annoy

irriterende (i-ri-*tāy*-rer-ner) *adj*
annoying

irsk (eeshk) *adj* Irish

is (eess) *m* ice

isbre (*eess*-brāy) *m* glacier

iskald (*eess*-kahl) *adj* freezing

iskrem (*eess*-krāym) *m* ice cream

Island (*eess*-lahn) Iceland

islandsk (*eess*-lahnsk) *adj* Icelandic

islending (*eess*-leh-ning) *m* Icelander

isolasjon (i-soo-lah-*shōōn*) *m*
isolation; insulation

isolator (i-soo-*laa*-toor) *m* insulator

isolere (i-soo-*lāy*-rer) *v* insulate;
isolate

isolert (i-soo-*lāyt*) *adj* isolated

Israel (*eess*-rah-ehl) Israel

israeler (iss-rah-*āy*-lerr) *m* Israeli

israelsk (iss-rah-*āy*lsk) *adj* Israeli

istedenfor (i-*stāy*-dern-for) *prep*
instead of

isvann (*eess*-vahn) *nt* iced water

især (i-*sæær*) *adv* especially

Italia (i-*taa*-li-ah) Italy

italiener (i-tah-li-*āy*-nerr) *m* Italian

italiensk (i-tah-li-*āy*nsk) *adj* Italian

iver (*ee*-verr) *m* zeal

ivrig (*eev*-ri) *adj* zealous; anxious,
eager

J

ja (ˈaa) yes; ~ **vel!** well!; OK!

jade (ˈaa-der) *m* jade

jage (ˈaa-ger) *v* hunt, chase; ~ **bort** chase

jakke (ˈahk-ker) *c* jacket

jakt (ˈahkt) *c* hunt; chase

jakte (ˈahk-ter) *v* hunt

jamre (ˈahm-rer) *v* moan

januar (ˈah-new-aar) January

Japan (ˈaa-pahn) Japan

japaner (ˈah-paa-nerr) *m* Japanese

japansk (ˈaa-pahnsk) *adj* Japanese

jeg (ˈay) *pron* I

jekk (ˈehkk) *m* jack

jeksel (ˈehk-serl) *m* (pl -sler) molar

jente (ˈehn-ter) *c* girl

jern (ˈææn) *nt* iron

jernbane (ˈææn-baa-ner) *m* railway; railroad *nAm*

jernbaneferje (ˈææn-baa-ner-fær-ˈer) *c* train ferry

jernbaneovergang (ˈææn-baa-ner-aw-verr-gahng) *m* crossing

jernbanevogn (ˈææn-baa-ner-vongn) *c* coach

jernvarehandel (ˈææn-vaa-rer-hahn-derl) *m* (pl -dler) hardware store

jernvarer (ˈææn-vaa-rerr) *pl* hardware

jersey (ˈæsh-shi) *m* jersey

jetfly (ˈeht-flew) *nt* (pl ~) jet

jevn (ˈehvn) *adj* level; smooth, even

jo (ˈoo) *adv* yes; certainly; **jo … jo** … the

jobb (ˈobb) *m* job

jockey (ˈok-ki) *m* jockey

jod (ˈodd) *m* iodine

jogge (ˈogg-er) *v* go jogging, go running

joggesko (ˈogg-er-skoo) *pl* running shoes; sneakers; tennis shoes

jolle (ˈol-ler) *c* dinghy

jomfru (ˈom-frew) *c* virgin; **gammel ~** spinster

jonglere (ˈon-gler-rer) *v* juggle

jonglør (ˈon-glūr) *m* juggler

jord (ˈoor) *c* earth; ground, soil

Jordan (ˈoo-dahn) Jordan

jordaner (ˈoo-daa-nerr) *m* Jordanian

jordansk (ˈoo-daansk) *adj* Jordanian

jordbruk (ˈoor-brewk) *nt* agriculture

jordbunn (ˈoor-bewn) *m* soil

jordbær (ˈoor-bæær) *nt* (pl ~) strawberry

jordklode (ˈoor-kloo-der) *m* globe

jordmor (ˈoor-moor) *c* (pl -mødre) midwife

jordskjelv (ˈoor-shehlv) *m*/*nt* (pl ~) earthquake

jordsmonn (ˈoosh-mon) *nt* soil

journalist (shoo-nah-*list*) *m* journalist

journalistikk (shoor-nah-li-*stikk*) *m* journalism

jubileum (ˈew-bi-*lay*-ewm) *nt* (pl -eer) jubilee; anniversary

jukse (ˈook-ser) *v* cheat

jul (ˈewl) *c* Christmas, Xmas; **gledelig ~!** Merry Christmas!

juli (ˈew-li) July

juling (ˈew-ling) *c* spanking

jungel (ˈoong-ngerl) *m* jungle

juni (ˈew-ni) June

junior (ˈew-ni-oor) *adj* junior

juridisk (ˈew-ree-disk) *adj* legal

jurisdiksjon (ˈew-ris-dik-*shoon*) *m* jurisdiction

jurist (ˈew-*rist*) *m* lawyer

jury (ˈew-ri) *m* jury

justere (ˈewss-*tay*-rer) *v* adjust

juvel (ˈew-vayl) *m* gem

jøde (ˈūr-der) *m* Jew

jødisk (ˈūr-disk) *adj* Jewish

K

kabaret (kah-bah-*ray*) *m* cabaret

kabel (*kaa*-berl) *m* (pl kabler) cable;
~**-TV** cable tv

kabelfjernsyn (*kaa*-berl-f*^y*ææn-*sewn*)
nt cable television

kabin (kah-*been*) *m* cabin

kabinett (kah-bi-*nehtt*) *nt* cabinet

kafé (kah-*fay*) *m* café

kafeteria (kah-feh-*tay*-ri-ah) *m*
cafeteria; self-service restaurant

kaffe (*kahf*-fer) *m* coffee

kaffein (kah-feh-*een*) *m* caffeine

kaffeinfri (kah-feh-*een*-free) *adj*
decaffeinated

kaffetrakter (*kahf*-fer-trahk-terr) *m*
percolator

kai (kigh) *c* dock, quay

kajakk (kah-*^yahkk*) *m* kayak

kake (*kaa*-ker) *c* cake

kaki (*kaa*-ki) *m* khaki

kald (kahll) *adj* cold

kalender (kah-*lehn*-derr) *m* (pl -drer)
calendar

kalk (kahlk) *m* lime

kalkulator (*kahl*-koo-lah-toor) *m*
calculator

kalkun (kahl-*kewn*) *m* turkey

kalle (*kahl*-ler) *v* call, name

kalori (kah-loo-*ree*) *m* calorie

kalsium (*kahl*-si-ewm) *nt* calcium

kalv (kahlv) *m* calf

kalvekjøtt (*kahl*-ver-khurt) *nt* veal

kalveskinn (*kahl*-ver-shin) *nt* (pl ~)
calf skin

kam (kahmm) *m* (pl ~mer) comb

kamerat (kah-mer-*raat*) *m* friend,
comrade, buddy

kamp (kahmp) *m* fight, battle,
combat; struggle; match

kampanje (kahm-*pahn*-*^y*er) *m*
campaign

kanadier (kah-*naa*-di-err) *m*
Canadian

kanadisk (kah-*naa*-disk) *adj*
Canadian

kanal (kah-*naal*) *m* channel, canal;
Den engelske ~ English Channel

kanarifugl (kah-*naa*-ri-*fewl*) *m* canary

kandidat (kahn-di-*daat*) *m* candidate

kanel (kah-*nayl*) *m* cinnamon

kanin (kah-*neen*) *m* rabbit

kano (*kaa*-noo) *m* canoe

kanon (kah-*noon*) *m* gun

kanskje (*kahn*-sher) *adv* perhaps,
maybe

kant (kahnt) *m* edge, verge, rim,
border

kantine (kahn-*tee*-ner) *c* canteen

kaos (*kaa*-oss) *nt* chaos

kaotisk (kah-*oo*-tisk) *adj* chaotic

kapasitet (kah-pah-si-*tayt*) *m* capacity

kapell (kah-*pehll*) *nt* chapel

kapellan (kah-peh-*laan*) *m* chaplain

kapital (kah-pi-*taal*) *m* capital

kapitalanbringelse (kah-pi-*taal*-ahn-
bri-ngerl-ser) *m* investment

kapitalisme (kah-pi-tah-*liss*-mer) *m*
capitalism

kapitulasjon (kah-pi-tew-lah-*shoon*)
m capitulation

kapp (kahpp) *nt* cape

kappe (*kahp*-per) *c* coat, cloak

kappløp (*kahp*-*lurp*) *nt* race

kapre (*kaap*-rer) *v* hijack

kaprer (*kaap*-rerr) *m* hijacker

kapsel (*kahp*-serl) *m* (pl -sler) capsule

kaptein (kahp-*tayn*) *m* captain

kar (kaar) *nt* vessel; *m* guy

karakter (kah-rahk-*tayr*) *m* character;
mark

karakterisere (kah-rahk-teh-ri-*say*-
rer) *v* characterize

karakteristisk (kah-rahk-teh-*riss*-tisk)
adj characteristic

karaktertrekk (kah-rahk-*tay*-trehk) *nt* (pl ~) characteristic

karamell (kah-rah-*mehll*) *m* caramel

karantene (kah-rahn-*tay*-ner) *m* quarantine

karat (kah-*raat*) *m* carat

kardinal (kahr-di-*naal*) *m* cardinal

karneval (*kaa*-ner-vahl) *nt* carnival

karosseri (kah-ro-ser-*ree*) *nt* bodywork; body *nAm*

karpe (*kahr*-per) *m* carp

karri (*kahr*-ri) *m* curry

karriere (kah-ri-*ææ*-rer) *m* career

kart (kahtt) *nt* map

kartong (kah-*tongng*) *m* carton; **kartong-** cardboard

karusell (kah-rew-*sehll*) *m* merry-go-round

kaserne (kah-*sææ*-ner) *m* barracks *pl*

kasino (kah-*see*-noo) *nt* casino

kasjmir (kahsh-*meer*) *m* cashmere

kasse (*kahss*-ser) *c* pay desk; crate

kassere (kah-*say*-rer) *v* discard

kasserer (kah-*say*-rerr) *m* cashier; treasurer; teller *nAm*

kasserolle (kah-ser-*rol*-ler) *m* saucepan

kassett (kah-sett) *m* cassette

kassettspiller (kah-sett-spi-lerr) *m* recorder

kast (kahst) *nt* throw, cast

kastanje (kah-*stahn-*yer) *m* chestnut

kaste (*kahss*-ter) *v* *cast, *throw; toss; ~ **opp** vomit

katakombe (kah-tah-*koom*-ber) *m* catacomb

katalog (kah-tah-*lawg*) *m* catalogue

katarr (kah-*tahrr*) *m* catarrh

katastrofal (kah-tah-stroo-*faal*) *adj* disastrous

katastrofe (kah-tah-*stroo*-fer) *m* catastrophe, calamity; disaster

katedral (kah-ter-*draal*) *m* cathedral

kategori (kah-ter-goo-*ree*) *m* category

kateter (kah-*tay*-terr) *nt* (pl -tre) desk; catheter

katolsk (kah-*toolsk*) *adj* catholic

katt (kahtt) *m* cat

kausjon (kou-*shoon*) *m* bail, security; guarantee

kaviar (kah-vi-*aar*) *m* caviar

keiser (*kay*-serr) *m* emperor

keiserdømme (*kay*-ser-dur-mer) *nt* empire

keiserinne (kay-ser-*rin*-ner) *c* empress

keiserlig (*kay*-ser-li) *adj* imperial

keivhendt (*khayv*-hehnt) *adj* left-handed

kelner (*kehl*-nerr) *m* waiter, waitress

kenguru (*kehng*-gew-rew) *m* kangaroo

kennel (*kehn*-nerl) *m* kennel

Kenya (*kehn-*yah) Kenya

keramikk (kheh-rah-*mikk*) *m* ceramics *pl*; pottery

kikke (*khik*-ker) *v* peep

kikkert (*khik*-kert) *m* binoculars *pl*

kilde (*khil*-der) *m* fountain, source, well, spring; **kildesortering** *c* waste separation

kile (*khee*-ler) *v* tickle; *m* wedge

kilo (*khee*-loo) *m/nt* kilogram

kilometer (*khil*-loo-*may*-terr) *m* (pl ~) kilometer *Am*, kilometre

kilometertall (*khil*-loo-*may*-ter-tahl) *nt* (pl ~) distance in kilometres (*Am* kilometers)

kim (kheem) *m* germ

Kina (*khee*-nah) China

kineser (khi-*nay*-serr) *m* Chinese

kinesisk (khi-*nay*-sisk) *adj* Chinese

kinn (khinn) *nt* cheek

kinnbein (*khin*-bayn) *nt* (pl ~) cheek-bone

kinnskjegg (*khin*-shehg) *nt* sideburns *pl*, whiskers *pl*

kino (*khee*-noo) *m* cinema, pictures;

movies *plAm*, movie theater *Am*

kiosk (khosk) *m* kiosk

kirke (*kheer*-ker) *c* church; chapel

kirkegård (*kheer*-ker-gawr) *m* graveyard, churchyard

kirketårn (*kheer*-ker-tawn) *nt* (pl ~) steeple

kirsebær (*khish*-sher-bæær) *nt* (pl ~) cherry

kirurg (khi-*rewrg*) *m* surgeon

kiste (*khiss*-ter) *c* chest; coffin

kjede (*khāy*-deh) *v* bore

kjedelig (*khāy*-der-li) *adj* dull, boring

kjeft (khehft) *m* mouth

kjeks (khehks) *m* (pl ~) cookie; biscuit

kjele (*khāy*-ler) *m* kettle

kjelke (*khæl*-ker) *m* sledge, sleigh

kjeller (*khehl*-lerr) *m* cellar

kjelleretasje (*khehl*-lerr-eh-taa-sher) *m* basement

kjemi (kheh-*mee*) *m* chemistry

kjemisk (*khāy*-misk) *adj* chemical

kjempe (*khehm*-per) *v* combat, *fight, struggle, battle; *m* giant

kjenne (*khehn*-ner) *v* *know; ~ igjen recognize

kjennelse (*khehn*-nerl-ser) *m* verdict

kjennemerke (*khehn*-ner-mær-ker) *nt* feature

kjenner (*khehn*-nerr) *m* connoisseur

kjennetegn (*khehn*-ner-tayn) *nt* (pl ~) characteristic

kjennetegne (*khehn*-ner-tay-ner) *v* mark, characterize

kjennskap (*khehn*-skaap) *nt* knowledge

kjent (khehnt) *adj* noted

kjepphest (*khehp*-hehst) *m* hobby-horse

kjerne (*khææ*-ner) *m* pip; heart, essence, core, nucleus; **kjerne-** nuclear

kjernehus (*khææ*-ner-hēwss) *nt* (pl ~) fruit core

kjernekraft (*khææ*-ner-krahft) *c* nuclear energy

kjerre (*khær*-rer) *c* cart

kjertel (*khæt*-terl) *m* (pl -tler) gland

kjetting (*kheht*-ting) *m* chain

kjeve (*khāy*-ver) *m* jaw

kjole (*khōō*-ler) *m* gown, dress; frock; **lang ~** robe

kjæledyr (*khāy*-ler-dēwr) *nt* (pl ~) pet

kjælenavn (*khāy*-ler-nahvn) *nt* (pl ~) nickname

kjær (khæær) *adj* dear

kjæreste (*khææ*-rerss-ter) *m* darling, girlfriend, boyfriend

kjærlig (*khææ*-li) *adj* affectionate

kjærlighet (*khææ*-li-hāyt) *c* love

kjærlighetshistorie (*khææ*-li-hāyts-hiss-tōō-ri-er) *c* love story

kjøkken (*khurk*-kern) *nt* kitchen

kjøkkenhage (*khurk*-kern-haager) *m* kitchen garden

kjøkkenhåndkle (*khurk*-kern-hong-kler) *nt* (pl -lær) kitchen towel

kjøkkenredskap (*t'urk*-kehn-reh-skaap) *nt* utensil

kjøkkensjef (*khurk*-kern-shāyf) *m* chef

kjøl (khūrl) *m* keel

kjøleskap (*khūr*-ler-skaap) *nt* (pl ~) refrigerator, fridge

kjølig (*khūr*-li) *adj* chilly, cool

kjønn (khurnn) *nt* sex; gender; **kjønns-** genital

kjønnssykdom (*khurn*-sēwk-dom) *m* venereal disease

kjøp (khūrp) *nt* purchase; **godt ~** bargain

kjøpe (*khūr*-per) *v* purchase, *buy

kjøper (*khūr*-perr) *m* purchaser, buyer

kjøpesenter (*khūr*-per-senterr) *nt* shopping centre, mall *nAm*

kjøpesum (*khūr*-per-sewm) *m* (pl ~mer) purchase price

kjøpmann (*khūrp*-mahn) *m* (pl

-menn) shopkeeper; trader, merchant

*kjøpslå (*khūrp*-shlo) *v* bargain

kjøre (*khūr*-rer) *v* *drive; *ride; ~ **forbi** *overtake; pass *vAm*; ~ **for fort** *speed

kjørebane (*khūr*-rer-baa-ner) *m* carriageway; roadway *nAm*

kjøretur (*khūr*-rer-tewr) *c* drive

kjøretøy (*khūr*-rer-tur^(ew)) *nt* vehicle

kjøtt (khurtt) *nt* meat; flesh

klage (*klaa*-ger) *v* complain; *m* complaint

klagebok (*klaa*-ger-book) *c* (pl -bøker) complaints book

klamre (*klahm*-rer) *v*: ~ **seg til** cling to

klandre (*klahn*-drer) *v* blame

klang (klahngng) *m* tone; sound

klappe (*klahp*-per) *v* clap, applaud

klar (klaar) *adj* clear; serene; ready; ***ha klart for seg** realize; ~ **over** aware

*klargjøre (*klaar*-^(y)ūr-rer) *v* elucidate, clarify

*klarlegge (*klaar*-leh-ger) *v* clarify

klart (klaart) *adv* certainly

klasse (*klahss*-ser) *c* class; form

klassekamerat (*klahss*-ser-kah-mer-raat) *m* class-mate

klasseværelse (*klahss*-ser-væ-rerl-ser) *nt* classroom

klassifisere (klah-si-fi-*sāy*-rer) *v* classify, class

klassisk (*klahss*-sisk) *adj* classical

klatre (*klaht*-rer) *v* climb

klatring (*klaht*-ring) *c* climb

klausul (*klou*-sewl) *m* clause

kle (klāy) *v* *become; suit; ~ **av seg** undress; ~ **på seg** dress; ~ **seg** dress; ~ **seg om** change

klebe (*klāy*-beh) *v* *stick

klebrig (*klāyb*-ri) *adj* sticky

klem (klehm) *m* (pl ~mer) hug

klemme (*klehm*-mer) *v* squeeze; cuddle, hug

klenge (*klehng*-er) *v* cling

klenodie (kleh-*noo*-di-er) *nt* gem

kleshenger (*klāyss*-heh-ngerr) *m* coat hanger

klesskap (*klāy*-skaap) *nt* (pl ~) wardrobe, closet *nAm*

klient (kli-*ehnt*) *m* client

klikk (klik) *m* set, clique; *nt* click

klikke (klik-ker) *v* click; ~ **på plass** click into place

klima (*klee*-mah) *nt* climate

klinikk (kli-*nikk*) *m* clinic

klinkekule (*kling*-ker-koo-ler) *c* marble

klippe (*klip*-per) *v* *cut; *m* cliff, rock; ~ **av** *cut off

klistre (*kliss*-trer) *v* paste; cling; ~**merke** *nt* sticker

klo (kloo) *c* (pl klør) claw

kloakk (kloo-*ahkk*) *m* sewer

klok (klook) *adj* clever; wise

klokke (*klok*-ker) *c* clock; bell; **klokken ...** at ... o'clock

klokkerem (*klok*-ker-rehm) *c* (pl ~mer) watch-strap

klokkespill (*klok*-ker-spil) *nt* chimes *pl*

klor (kloor) *m* chlorine

kloss (kloss) *m* block

klosset (*kloss*-sert) *adj* awkward, clumsy

kloster (*kloss*-terr) *nt* (pl -tre) convent, monastery, cloister

klovn (klovn) *m* clown

klubb (klewbb) *m* club

klubbe (*klewb*-ber) *c* club

klukke (*klook*-ker) *v* chuckle

klump (kloomp) *m* lump

klumpet (*kloom*-pert) *adj* lumpy

klut (klewt) *m* cloth

*klype (*klēw*-per) *v* pinch

klær (klæær) *pl* clothes *pl*

klø (klūr) *v* itch

kløe (*klūr*-er) *m* itch

kløft (klurft) *c* chasm, cleft

kløver (*klurv*-verr) *m* clover

kløyve (*klurᵉʷ*-ver) *v* *split

knagg (knahgg) *m* peg

knapp (knahpp) *m* button; *adj* scarce

knappe (*knahp*-per) *v* button; **~ opp** unbutton

knappenål (*knahp*-per-nawl) *c* pin

knapphet (*knahp*-hāyt) *c* scarcity, shortage

knapphull (*knahp*-hewl) *nt* buttonhole

knapt (knahpt) *adv* scarcely

kne (knāȳ) *nt* (pl knær) knee

kneipe (*knay*-per) *c* pub

*knekke (*knehk*-ker) *v* crack; break

knekt (knehkt) *m* knave

knele (*knāȳ*-ler) *v* *kneel

knep (knāȳp) *nt* trick

kneskål (*knāȳ*-skawl) *c* kneecap

knipetang (*knee*-per-tahng) *c* (pl -tenger) pincers *pl*

knipling (*knip*-ling) *m* lace

knirke (*kneer*-ker) *v* creak

kniv (kneev) *m* knife

knoke (*knōō*-ker) *m* knuckle

knopp (knopp) *m* bud

knott (knott) *m* knob

knulle (*knewl*-ler) *v* vulgar fuck

knurre (*knewr*-rer) *v* grumble

knuse (*knēw̄ser*) *v* *break; smash

knust (knēw̄st) *adj* broken

knute (*knēw̄*-ter) *m* knot

knutepunkt (*knēw̄*-ter-poongt) *nt* junction

knytte (*knēw̄*-ter) *v* tie, knot; **~ til** attach to; **~ opp** untie

knyttneve (*knewt*-nāȳ-ver) *m* fist

knyttneveslag (*knewt*-nāȳ-ver-shlaag) *nt* (pl ~) punch

koagulere (koo-ah-gew-*lāȳ*-rer) *v* coagulate

kobbe (*kob*-ber) *m* seal

kode (*kōō*-der) *m* code

koffert (*koof*-fert) *m* case, suitcase; trunk

kokain (koo-kah-*een*) *m/nt* cocaine

koke (*kōō*-ker) *v* boil

kokebok (*kōō*-ker-bōōk) *c* (pl -bøker) cookery book; cookbook *nAm*

kokk (kokk) *m* cook

kokosnøtt (*kook*-kooss-nurt) *c* coconut

koldtbord (kolt-bōōr) *nt* (pl ~) buffet

kolje (*kol*-ʸer) *c* haddock

kolle (*kol*-ler) *m* hill, peak

kollega (koo-*lāȳ*-gah) *m* colleague

kolleksjon (*kol*-lerk-*shōōn*) *n* collection *m*

kollektiv (*kol*-lerk-teev) *adj* collective

kollidere (koo-li-*dāȳ*-rer) *v* collide, crash

kollisjon (koo-li-*shōōn*) *m* crash, collision

koloni (koo-loo-*nee*) *m* colony

kolonne (koo-*lon*-ner) *m* column

kolossal (koo-loo-*saal*) *adj* enormous, tremendous

koma (*kōō*-mah) *m* coma

kombinasjon (koom-bi-nah-*shōōn*) *m* combination

kombinere (koom-bi-*nāȳ*-rer) *v* combine

komedie (koo-*māȳ*-di-er) *m* comedy

komfort (koom-*fawr*) *m* comfort

komfortabel (koom-fo-*taa*-berl) *adj* comfortable

komfyr (koom-*fēw̄r*) *m* cooker; stove

komiker (*kōō*-mi-kerr) *m* comedian

komisk (*kōō*-misk) *adj* funny, comic

komité (koo-mi-*tāȳ*) *m* committee

komma (*kom*-mah) *nt* comma

komme (*kom*-mer) *nt* coming

*komme (*kom*-mer) *v* *come; **~ an på** depend; **~ over** *come across; **~ på** *think of; **~ seg** recover; **~ tilbake** return

kommende (*kom*-mer-ner) *adj*

oncoming

kommentar (koo-mehn-*taar*) m
comment

kommentere (koo-mehn-*tāy*-rer) v
comment

kommersiell (koo-mæ-shi-*ehll*) adj
commercial

kommisjon (koo-mi-*shōōn*) m
commission

kommode (koo-*mōō*-der) m chest of
drawers; bureau nAm

kommunal (koo-mew-*naal*) adj
municipal

kommune (koo-*mēw*-ner) m local
authority, municipality

kommunestyre (koo-*mēw*-ner-stēw-
rer) nt local council

kommunikasjon (koo-mew-ni-kah-
shōōn) m communication

kommuniké (koo-mew-ni-*kāy*) nt
communiqué

kommunisme (koo-mew-*niss*-mer) m
communism

kommunist (koo-mew-*nist*) m
communist

kompakt (koom-*pahkt*) adj compact

kompani (koom-pah-*nee*) nt company

kompanjong (koom-pahn-*ᶦongng*) m
partner, associate

kompass (koom-*pahss*) m/nt compass

kompensasjon (koom-pehn-sah-
shōōn) m compensation

kompensere (koom-pehn-*sāy*-rer) v
compensate

kompetent (koom-per-*tehnt*) adj
qualified; capable

kompleks (koom-*plehks*) nt complex

komplett (koom-*plehtt*) adj complete

kompliment (koom-pli-*mahngng*) m
compliment

komplimentere (koom-pli-mehn-*tāy*-
rer) v compliment

komplisert (koom-pli-*sāyt*) adj
complicated

komplott (koom-*plott*) nt plot

komponist (koom-poo-*nist*) m
composer

komposisjon (koom-poo-si-*shōōn*) m
composition

kompromiss (koom-proo-*miss*) nt
compromise

kondisjon (koon-di-*shōōn*) m
physical fitness

konditori (koon-di-too-*ree*) nt pastry
shop

kondom (koon-*dom*) nt condom

kone (*kōō*-ner) c wife

konfekt (koon-*fehkt*) m chocolate

konferanse (koon-fer-*rahng*-ser) m
conference

konfidensiell (koon-fi-dehn-si-*ehll*)
adj confidential

konfiskere (koon-fiss-*kāy*-rer) v
confiscate

konflikt (koon-*flikt*) m conflict

konfrontere (kon-fron-*tāy*-rer) v face,
confront

konge (*kong*-nger) m king

kongelig (*kong*-nger-li) adj royal

kongerike (*kong*-nger-ree-ker) nt
kingdom

kongress (kong-*grehss*) m congress

konjakk (kon-ᶦ*ahkk*) m cognac

konklusjon (koong-klew-*shōōn*) m
conclusion

konkret (koong-*krāyt*) adj concrete

konkurranse (koong-kew-*rahng*-ser)
m contest, competition; rivalry

konkurrent (koong-kew-*rehnt*) m
rival, competitor

konkurrere (koong-kew-*rāy*-rer) v
compete

konkurs (koong-*kēwsh*) adj bankrupt

konsekvens (kon-ser-*kvehns*) m
consequence

konsentrasjon (koon-sehn-trah-
shōōn) m concentration

konsentrere (koon-sehn-*trāy*-rer) v

concentrate

konsert (koon-*sætt*) *m* concert

konsertsal (koon-*sæt*-saal) *m* concert hall

konservativ (koon-*sær*-vah-teev) *adj* conservative

konservatorium (koon-sær-vah-*tōō*-ri-ewm) *nt* (pl -ier) music academy

konservere (kon-sær-*vāy*-rer) *v* preserve

konservering (kon-sær-*vāy*-ring) *c* preservation

konsesjon (koon-seh-*shōōn*) *m* license *Am*, licence; concession

konsis (koon-*seess*) *adj* concise

konstant (koon-*stahnt*) *adj* constant; even

konstatere (koon-stah-*tāy*-rer) *v* note; diagnose, ascertain

konstruere (koon-strew-*āy*-rer) *v* construct

konstruksjon (koon-strewk-*shōōn*) *m* construction

konsul (*kon*-sewl) *m* consul

konsulat (koon-sew-*laat*) *nt* consulate

konsultasjon (kon-sewl-tah-*shōōn*) *m* consultation

konsum (koon-sewm) *nt* consumption

konsument (koon-sew-*mehnt*) *m* consumer

konsumere (koon-sew-*meh-rer*) *v* consume

kontakt (koon-*tahkt*) *m* touch, contact

kontakte (koon-*tahk*-ter) *v* contact

kontaktlinser (koon-*tahkt*-lin-serr) *pl* contact lenses

kontanter (koon-*tahn*-terr) *pl* cash

kontinent (koon-ti-*nehnt*) *nt* continent

kontinental (koon-ti-nehn-*taal*) *adj* continental

kontinuerlig (koon-ti-new-*āy*-li) *adj* continuous

konto (*kon*-too) *m* (pl ∼er, -ti) account

kontor (koon-*tōōr*) *nt* office

kontortid (koon-*tōō*-teed) *c* office hours, business hours

kontra (*kon*-trah) *prep* versus

kontrakt (koon-*trahkt*) *m* contract; agreement; pact

kontrast (koon-*trahst*) *m* contrast

kontroll (koon-*troll*) *m* control; inspection

kontrollere (koon-troo-*lāy*-rer) *v* verify, check, control

kontrollør (koon-troo-*lūrr*) *m* supervisor

kontroversiell (kon-troo-væ-shi-*ehll*) *adj* controversial

kontur (kon-*tōōr*) *m* outline

konversasjon (koon-væ-shah-*shōōn*) *m* conversation

konvolutt (koon-voo-*lewtt*) *m* envelope

kooperativ (koo-*op*-rah-teev) *adj* co-operative

koordinasjon (koo-o-di-nah-*shōōn*) *m* co-ordination

kopi (koo-*pee*) *m* copy

kopiere (koo-pi-*āy*-rer) *v* copy

kople (*kop*-ler) *v* connect; ∼ **til** connect

kopp (kopp) *m* cup

kopper (*kop*-perr) *pl* smallpox; *nt* copper

kor (*kōōr*) *nt* choir

korall (koo-*rahll*) *m* coral

kordfløyel (*kawd*-flur^(ew)-erl) *m* corduroy

kork (kork) *m* cork; stopper

korketrekker (*kor*-ker-treh-kerr) *m* corkscrew

korn (*kōōn*) *nt* grain, corn

kornåker (*kōō*-naw-kerr) *m* (pl -krer) cornfield

korpulent (kor-pew-*lehnt*) *adj* stout, corpulent

korrekt (koo-*rehkt*) *adj* correct

korrespondanse (koo-rer-spoon-*dahng*-ser) m correspondence

korrespondent (koo-rer-spoon-*dehnt*) m correspondent

korridor (koo-ri-*doōr*) m corridor

korrigere (koo-ri-*gāy*-rer) v correct

korrupt (koo-*rewpt*) adj corrupt

kors (koshsh) nt cross

korsett (ko-*shehtt*) nt corset

korsfeste (kosh-*fehss*-ter) v crucify

korsfestelse (kosh-*fehss*-terl-ser) m crucifixion

korstog (*kosh*-tawg) nt (pl ~) crusade

korsvei (*kosh*-vay) m road fork

kort (kott) adj short; brief; nt card

kortfattet (*kot*-fah-tert) adj brief

kortslutning (*kot*-slewt-ning) m short circuit

kortstokk m pack

kortvarig (*kot*-vaa-ri) adj momentary

koselig (*kōō*-ser-li) adj cosy; nice

kosmetika (koss-meh-*tikk*) pl cosmetics pl

kost[1] (kost) m fare; ~ **og losji** room and board, bed and board, board and lodging

kost[2] (koost) m broom

kostbar (*kost*-baar) adj expensive; precious

koste (*koss*-ter) v *cost

kostfri (*kost*-free) adj free of charge

kostnad (*kost*-nah) m cost

kotelett (ko-ter-*lehtt*) m chop

krabbe (*krahb*-ber) v crawl; c crab

kraft (krahft) c (pl krefter) force; energy, power

kraftig (*krahf*-ti) adj strong

kraftverk (*krahft*-værk) nt power station

krage (*kraa*-ger) m collar

kragebein (*kraa*-ger-bayn) nt (pl ~) collarbone

krampe (*krahm*-per) m cramp; clamp

krampetrekning (*krahm*-per-trehk-ning) m convulsion

kran (kraan) c crane; tap

krangel (*krahng*-ngerl) m/nt (pl -gler) dispute, row, quarrel

krangle (*krahng*-ler) v quarrel

krater (*kraa*-terr) nt crater

kratt (krahtt) nt scrub

krav (kraav) nt demand, claim; requirement

kreativ (kreh-*atieev*) adj creative

kreditor (*krāy*-di-toor) m creditor

kreditt (kreh-*ditt*) m credit

kredittkort (kreh-*dit*-kot) nt (pl ~) credit card

kreere (kreh-*āy*-rer) v create

kreft (krehft) m cancer

krem (krāym) m cream

kremasjon (kreh-*māy*-ring) m cremation

kremere (kreh-*māy*-rer) v cremate

kremgul (*krāy*-m-gēwl) adj cream

krenke (*krehng*-ker) v offend, injure; trespass

krenkelse (*krehng*-kerl-ser) m violation

krenkende (*krehng*-ker-ner) adj offensive

kresen (*krāy*-sern) adj particular

krets (krehts) m ring, circle

kretsløp (*krehts*-lūrp) nt (pl ~) cycle

kreve (*krāy*-ver) v require, claim; charge

krig (kreeg) m war

krigsfange (*kriks*-fah-nger) m prisoner of war

krigsmakt (*kriks*-mahkt) c armed forces

krigsskip (*krik*-sheep) nt warship

krim (kri-m) m detective story

kriminalitet (kri-mi-nah-li-*tāyt*) m criminality

kriminell (kri-mi-*nehll*) adj criminal

kringkaste (*kring*-kahss-ter) v *broadcast

kringkasting (*kring*-kahss-ting) *c*
  broadcast
krise (*kree*-ser) *c* crisis
kristen[1] (*kriss*-tern) *m* (pl -tne)
  Christian
kristen[2] (*kriss*-tern) *adj* Christian
Kristus (*kriss*-tewss) Christ
kritiker (*kree*-ti-kerr) *m* critic
kritikk (kri-*tikk*) *m* criticism
kritisere (kri-ti-*sāy*-rer) *v* criticize
kritisk (*kree*-tisk) *adj* critical
kritt (kritt) *nt* chalk
kro (krōō) *c* pub, tavern
krok (krōōk) *m* hook
kroket (*krōō*-kert) *adj* crooked
krokodille (kroo-koo-*dil*-ler) *c*
  crocodile
krom (kroomm) *m* chromium
kronblad (*krōōn*-blaa) *nt* (pl ∼) petal
krone (*krōō*-ner) *c* crown; *v* crown
kronisk (*krōō*-nisk) *adj* chronic
kronologisk (kroo-noo-*law*-gisk) *adj*
  chronological
kropp (kropp) *m* body
krukke (*krook*-ker) *c* jar; pitcher
krum (kroomm) *adj* curved
krumning (*kroom*-ning) *m* bend;
  curve
krus (krēwss) *nt* mug
krusifiks (krew-si-*fiks*) *nt* crucifix
krutt (krewtt) *nt* gunpowder
krybbe (*krewb*-ber) *c* manger
krydder (*krewd*-derr) *nt* (pl ∼) spice
krydderier (krew-der-*ree*-err) *pl*
  spices
krydret (*krewd*-rert) *adj* spiced, spicy
krykke (*krewk*-ker) *c* crutch
krympe (*krewm*-per) *v* *shrink
krympefri (*krewm*-per-free) *adj*
  shrinkproof
krypdyr (*krēwp*-dēwr) *nt* (pl ∼) reptile
*krype (*krēw*-per) *v* *creep
kryss (krewss) *nt* cross
krysse (*krewss*-ser) *v* cross

krysse av (*krewss*-ser) tick off
krystall (krew-*stahll*) *m*/*nt* crystal;
krystall- *adj* crystal
kroll (krurll) *m* curl
krolle (*krurl*-ler) *v* curl; crease
krollet (*krurl*-lert) *adj* curly
kråke (*kraw*-ker) *c* crow
ku (kēw) *c* (pl ∼er, kyr) cow
kubaner (kew-*baa*-nerr) *m* Cuban
kubansk (kew-*baansk*) *adj* Cuban
kubbe (*kewb*-ber) *m* log
kube (*kēw*-ber) *m* cube
kul[1] (kēwl) *m* lump
kul[2] (kēwl) *adj* colloquial super, cool
kulde (*kewl*-ler) *c* cold
kuldegysning (kewl-ler-*gēwss*-ning)
  m chill
kule (*kēw*-ler) *c* bullet; sphere
kulepenn (*kēw*-ler-pehn) *m* ballpoint
  pen, Biro
kull (kewll) *nt* coal; litter
kult (kēwlt) *adj* colloquial super, cool
kultivert (kewl-ti-*vāyt*) *adj* cultured
kultur (kewl-*tēwr*) *m* culture
kun (kewnn) *adv* only
kunde (*kewn*-der) *m* client, customer
*kunne (*kewn*-ner) *v* *can, *be able
  to; *may, *might
*kunngjøre (*kewn*-ʸūr-rer) *v*
  announce; proclaim
kunngjøring (*kewn*-ʸūr-ring) *c*
  announcement; notice
kunst (kewnst) *m* art; ∼ og håndverk
  arts and crafts; **skjønne kunster** fine
  arts
kunstakademi (*kewnst*-ah-kah-deh-
  mee) *nt* art school
kunstferdig (*kewnst*-fææ-di) *adj*
  elaborate
kunstgalleri (*kewnst*-gah-ler-ree) *nt*
  gallery, art gallery
kunsthistorie (*kewnst*-hiss-tōō-ri-er)
  c art history
kunsthåndverk (*kewnst*-hon-værk) *nt*

(pl ~) handicraft

kunstig (*kewn*-sti) *adj* artificial

kunstner (*kewnst*-nerr) *m* artist

kunstnerisk (*kewnst*-ner-risk) *adj* artistic

kunstsamling (*kewnst*-sahm-ling) *c* art collection

kunstutstilling (*kewnst*-ewt-sti-ling) *c* art exhibition

kunstverk (*kewnst*-værk) *nt* work of art

kupé (kew-*pay*) *m* compartment

kupert (kew-*payt*) *adj* hilly

kupong (kew-pongng) *m* coupon

kuppel (*kewp*-perl) *m* (pl kupler) dome

kur (kēwr) *m* cure

kurs (kēwsh) *nt* course; *m* course

kursted (*kēw*-shtāy) *nt* spa

kurv (kewrv) *m* basket; hamper

kurve (*kewr*-ver) *m* curve

kusine (kew-*see*-ner) *c* cousin

kusma (*kewss*-mah) *m* mumps

kutt (kewtt) *nt* cut

kuvertavgift (kew-*vææ*-raav-ⁱift) *c* cover charge

kuøye (*kēw*-ur^(ew)-er) *nt* porthole

kvadrat (kvah-*draat*) *nt* square

kvadratisk (kvah-*draa*-tisk) *adj* square

kvaksalver (*kvahk*-sahl-verr) *m* quack

kvalifikasjon (kvah-li-fi-kah-*shoon*) *m* qualification

kvalifisere seg (kvah-li-fi-*say*-rer) qualify

kvalifisert (kvah-li-fi-*sayt*) *adj* qualified

kvalitet (kvah-li-*tayt*) *m* quality

kvalm (kvahlm) *adj* sick

kvalme (*kvahl*-mer) *m* nausea; sickness

kvantitet (kvahn-ti-*tayt*) *m* quantity

kvart (kvahtt) *quarter*

kvartal (kvah-*taal*) *nt* quarter; house block *Am*; **kvartals-** quarterly

kvarter (kvah-*tāyr*) *nt* quarter of an hour; district; quarter

kveg (kvāyg) *nt* cattle *pl*

kveite (*kvay*-ter) *c* halibut

kveld (kvehll) *m* evening

kvele (*kvāy*-ler) *v* choke; strangle

kveles (*kvāy*-lerss) *v* choke

kveste (*kvehss*-ter) *v* injure

kvestelse (*kvehss*-terl-ser) *m* injury

kvikksølv (*kvik*-surl) *nt* mercury

kvinne (*kvin*-ner) *c* woman

kvinnelege (*kvin*-ner-lāy-ger) *m* gynaecologist

kvise (*kvee*-ser) *c* pimple

kvist (kvist) *m* twig

kvitt (kvit) *adj*: **bli ~** get rid of

kvittering (kvi-*tāy*-ring) *c* receipt

kvote (*kvoo*-ter) *m* quota

kylling (*khewl*-ling) *m* chicken

kyndig (*khewn*-di) *adj* skilled, skil(l)ful

kysk (khewsk) *adj* chaste

kyss (khewss) *nt* kiss

kysse (*khewss*-ser) *v* kiss

kyst (khewst) *m* coast; seashore, shore, seaside

kø (kūr) *m* line; queue; ***stå i ~** queue; stand in line *Am*

kølle (*kurl*-ler) *c* club; mallet

køye (*kur*^(ew)-er) *c* bunk

kål (kawl) *m* cabbage

kåpe (*kaw*-per) *c* coat

L

*la (laa) v *let; allow to; ~ **være** *keep off

laboratorium (lah-boo-rah-$\overline{too}$-ri-ewm) nt (pl -ier) laboratory

labyrint (lah-bew-*rint*) m labyrinth; maze

ladning (*lahd*-ning) m charge

lag (laag) nt layer; team

lage (*laa*-ger) v *make

lager (*laa*-gerr) nt (pl lagre) depository

lagerbeholdning (*laa*-gerr-beh-hold-ning) m stock

lagerbygning (*laagerr*-bewg-ning) m store house, warehouse

lagerplass (*laa*-gerr-plahss) m depot

lagre (*laag*-rer) v store; stock

lagring (*laag*-ring) c storage

lagune (lah-*gew*-ner) m lagoon

laken (*laa*-kern) nt sheet

lakk (lahkk) m varnish, lacquer

lakkere (lah-*kay*-rer) v varnish

lakris (*lahk*-riss) m liquorice

laks (lahks) m salmon

lam (lahmm) nt lamb; adj lame

lamme (*lahm*-mer) v paralyse

lammekjøtt (*lahm*-mer-khurt) nt lamb

lampe (*lahm*-per) c lamp

lampeskjerm (*lahm*-per-shærm) m lampshade

land (lahnn) nt country, land; ***gå i ~** disembark, land; **i ~** ashore; **på landet** in the country

landbruk (*lahn*-brewk) nt agriculture

lande (*lahn*-ner) v land

landemerke (*lahn*-ner-mær-ker) nt landmark

landflyktig m (pl ~e) exile

landgang (*lahn*-gahng) m gangway

landlig (*lahn*-li) adj rural

landområde (lahnn-om-*raw*-der) nt

landsby (*lahns*-bew) m village

landsens (*lahn*-serns) adj rustic

landskap (*lahn*-skaap) nt scenery, landscape

landsmann (*lahns*-mahn) m (pl -menn) countryman

landsted (*lahn*-st$\overline{ay}$) nt country house

landstryker (*lahn*-str$\overline{ew}$-kerr) m tramp

lang (lahngng) adj long; tall

langs (lahngs) prep past, along; **på ~** lengthways

langsom (*lahng*-som) adj slow

langvarig (*lahng*-vaa-ri) adj longlasting

lapp (lahp) m patch, scrap, note

larm (lahrm) m noise

last (lahst) c freight, cargo, load; bulk

laste (*lahss*-ter) v charge, load

lastebil (*lahss*-ter-beel) m lorry; truck nAm

lasterom (*lahss*-ter-room) nt (pl ~) hold

lat (laat) adj idle; lazy

*late som (*laa*-ter somm) pretend

*late til (*laa*-ter till) seem

Latin-Amerika (lah-*teen*-ah-m$\overline{ay}$-ri-kah) Latin America

latinamerikansk (lah-*tee*-nah-m$\overline{ay}$-ri-kaansk) adj Latin-American

latter (*laht*-terr) m laughter, laugh

latterlig (*laht*-ter-li) adj ridiculous; ludicrous

*latterliggjøre (*laht*-ter-li-$^y\overline{ur}$-rer) v ridicule

lav (laav) adj low

lavland (*laav*-lahn) nt (pl ~) lowlands pl

lavsesong (*laav*-seh-song) m low season

lavtrykk (*laav*-trewk) nt (pl ~) low

pressure; depression
lavvann (*laa*-vahn) *nt* low tide
*le (lay) *v* laugh
ledd[1] (lehdd) *nt* joint; **gått av ~** dislocated
ledd[2] (lehdd) *nt* link
lede (*lay*-der) *v* *lead, head
ledelse (*lay*-derl-ser) *m* management, administration; lead
ledende (*lay*-der-ner) *adj* leading
ledig (*lay*-di) *adj* vacant, unoccupied
ledning (*layd*-ning) *m* flex; electric cord
ledsager (*layd*-saa-gerr) *m* companion
legal (leh-*gaal*) *adj* legal
legalisering (leh-gah-li-*say*-ring) *c* legalization
legasjon (leh-gah-*shoon*) *m* legation
legat (leh-*gaat*) *nt* legacy
lege (*lay*-ger) *m* physician, doctor; *v* cure, heal; **allmennpraktiserende ~** general practitioner
legekontor (*lay*-ger-koon-*toor*) *nt* surgery
legeme (*lay*-ger-mer) *nt* body
legemiddel (*lay*-ger-mi-derl) *nt* (pl -midler) remedy, medicine
legevitenskap (*lay*-ger-vee-tern-skaap) *m* medical science
legg (lehgg) *m* calf
*legge (*lehg*-ger) *v* *put, *lay; pave; **~ igjen** *leave; **~ sammen** add; **~ seg** *go to bed; **~ seg ned** *lie down
lei av (lay) fed up with, tired of
leie (*lay*-er) *v* hire, rent, lease; *m* rent; **~ ut** *let; lease; **til ~** for hire
leieboer (*lay*-er-*boo*-err) *m* lodger, tenant
leiegård (*lay*-er-gawr) *m* block of flats; apartment house *Am*
leiekontrakt (*lay*-er-koon-trahkt) *m* tenancy agreement
lei for (lay) sorry

leilighet (*lay*-li-*hayt*) *c* flat, apartment *nAm*; occasion, opportunity
leir (layr) *m* camp
leire (*lay*-rer) *c* clay
lek (layk) *m* play
leke (*lay*-ker) *v* play
lekeplass (*lay*-ker-plahss) *m* recreation ground, playground
leketøy (*lay*-ker-tur*ew*) *nt* toy
leketøysforretning (*lay*-ker-tur*ew*ss-fo-reht-ning) *c* toyshop
lekk (lehkk) *adj* leaky
lekkasje (leh-*kaa*-sher) *m* leak
lekke (*lehk*-ker) *v* leak
lekker (*lehk*-kerr) *adj* delicious, nice
lekkerbisken (*lehk*-kerr-biss-kern) *m* delicacy
lekmann (*layk*-mahn) *m* (pl -menn) layman
leksikon (*lehk*-si-kon) *nt* (pl ~, ~er, -ka) encyclop(a)edia
leksjon (lehk-*shoon*) *m* lesson
lektor (*lehk*-toor) *m* master, teacher
lem (lehmm) *nt* (pl ~mer) limb
lene seg (*lay*-ner) *v* *lean
lenestol (*lay*-ner-*stool*) *m* armchair; easy chair
lengde (*lehng*-der) *c* length
lengdegrad (*lehng*-der-graad) *m* longitude
lenge (*lehng*-er) *adv* long
lengsel (*lehng*-serl) *m* (pl -sler) longing; wish
lengte etter (*lehng*-ter) long for
lenke (*lehng*-ker) *c* chain; link
leppe (*lehp*-per) *c* lip
leppepomade (*lehp*-per-poo-maa-der) *m* lip balm
leppestift (*lehp*-per-stift) *m* lipstick
lerke (*lær*-ker) *c* lark
lerret (*lær*-rert) *nt* canvas; screen
lesbisk (*les*-bisk) *adj* lesbian
lese (*lay*-ser) *v* *read
leselampe (*lay*-ser-lahm-per) *c*

reading lamp

leselig (*lāy*-ser-li) *adj* legible

lesesal (*lāy*-ser-saal) *m* reading room

lesning (*lāyss*-ning) *m* reading

lesse av (*lehss*-ser) discharge, unload

lete etter (*lāy*-ter) *v* look for, search; hunt for

leting (*lāy*-ting) *c* search

lett (lehtt) *adj* light; easy; gentle

lette (*leht*-ter) *v* *take off

lettelse (*leht*-terl-ser) *m* relief

letthet (*leht*-hāyt) *c* ease

leve (*lāy*-ver) *v* live

levebrød (*lāy*-ver-brūr) *nt* livelihood, living

levende (*lay*-ver-ner) *adj* alive, live

lever (*lehv*-verr) *c* liver

leveranse (leh-ver-*rahng*-ser) *m* delivery

levere (leh-*vāy*-rer) *v* deliver

levering (leh-*vāy*-ring) *c* delivery; supply

levestandard (*lāy*-ver-stahn-dahr) *m* standard of living

levetid (*lāy*-ver-teed) *c* lifetime

levning (*lehv*-ning) *m* remnant

li (lee) *c* hillside

libaneser (li-bah-*nāy*-serr) *m* Lebanese

libanesisk (li-bah-*nāy*-sisk) *adj* Lebanese

Libanon (*lee*-bah-non) Lebanon

liberal (li-beh-*raal*) *adj* liberal

Liberia (li-*bāy*-ri-ah) Liberia

liberier (li-*bāy*-ri-err) *m* Liberian

liberisk (li-*bāy*-risk) *adj* Liberian

***lide** (*lee*-der) *v* suffer

lidelse (*lee*-derl-ser) *m* suffering

lidenskap (*lee*-dern-skaap) *m* passion

lidenskapelig (lee-dern-*skaa*-per-li) *adj* passionate

liga (*lee*-gah) *m* league

***ligge** (*lig*-ger) *v* *lie

lighter (*ligh*-terr) *m* lighter

lik[1] (leek) *adj* alike, like; equal; ***være** ~ equal

lik[2] (leek) *nt* corpse

like (*lee*-ker) *v* *be fond of, fancy; like; *adv* equally, as; *adj* even

likedan (*lee*-ker-dahn) *adv* alike; *adj* alike

likefrem (*lee*-ker-frehm) *adj* direct; simple

likegyldig (*lee*-ker-*y*ewl-di) *adj* indifferent; careless

likeledes (*lee*-ker-*lāy*-derss) *adv* likewise; also

likesinnet (*lee*-ker-si-nert) *adj* like-minded

likestrøm (*lee*-ker-strurm) *m* direct current

likeså (*lee*-ker-so) *adv* likewise

likevekt (*lee*-ker-vehkt) *m* balance

likevel (*lee*-ker-vehl) *adv* yet, however; still

likhet (*leek*-hāyt) *c* equality; resemblance, similarity

likne (*lik*-ner) *v* resemble

liknende (*lik*-ner-ner) *adj* similar

liksom (*lik*-som) *conj* like, as

liktorn (*leek*-tōōn) *m* corn

likør (li-*kūr*) *m* liqueur

lilje (*lil*-*y*er) *c* lily

lilla (*lil*-lah) *adj* purple, mauve, violet

lillefinger (*lil*-ler-fi-ngerr) *m* (pl -gre) little finger

lim (leem) *nt* gum, glue

limbånd (*leem*-bon) *nt* (pl ~) adhesive tape

limett (li-*mehtt*) *m* lime

limonade (li-moo-*naa*-der) *m* lemonade

lind (linn) *m* lime

lindetre (*lin*-der-trāy) *nt* (pl -rær) limetree

lindre (*lin*-drer) *v* relieve

lindring (*lin*-dring) *c* relief

line (*lee*-ner) *c* line

linjal (lin-ʸaal) m ruler

linje (lin-ʸer) c line; extension

linse (lin-ser) c lens

lintøy (leen-turᵉʷ) nt linen

lisens (li-sehns) m license Am, licence

lisse (liss-ser) c lace

list (list) c cunning, ruse

liste (liss-ter) c list

lite (lee-ter) adj little

liten (lee-tern) adj (pl små) small, little; short; petty, minor; **bitte ~** tiny, minute

liter (lee-terr) m (pl ~) liter Am, litre

litt (litt) pron some

litteratur (li-ter-rah-tewr) m literature

litterær (li-ter-ræær) adj literary

liv (leev) nt life

livbelte (leev-behl-ter) nt lifebelt

livfull (leev-fewl) adj vivid

livlig (liv-li) adj lively, brisk

livmor (leev-moor) c womb

livsfarlig (lishs-faa-li) adj perilous

livsforsikring (lifs-fo-shik-ring) c life insurance

livvakt (lee-vahkt) m bodyguard

lodd (lodd) m destiny, lot

loddrett (lod-reht) adj perpendicular

loft (loft) nt attic

logikk (loo-gikk) m logic

logisk (loo-gisk) adj logical

lojal (loo-ʸaal) adj loyal

lokal (loo-kaal) adj local

lokalisere (loo-kah-li-saʸ-rer) v locate

lokaltog (loo-kaal-tawg) nt (pl ~) local train

lokk (lokk) nt cover, lid, top

lokomotiv (loo-koo-moo-teev) nt engine, locomotive

lomme (loom-mer) c pocket

lommebok (loom-mer-book) c (pl -bøker) wallet, pocketbook

lommekalkulator (loom-mer-kahl-koo-lah-too) m (pocket) calculator

lommekniv (loom-mer-kneev) m penknife, pocket-knife

lommelykt (loom-mer-lewkt) c torch, flash-light

lommeregner (loom-mer-ray-nerr) m (pocket) calculator

lommetørkle (loom-mer-turr-kler) nt (pl -lær) handkerchief

lord (lord) m lord

los (looss) m pilot

losji (loo-shee) nt accommodation, lodgings pl

loslitt (loo-shlit) adj threadbare

losse (loss-ser) v discharge

lotteri (lo-ter-ree) nt lottery

lov (lawv) m law; permission; ***ha ~ til** *be allowed to

love (law-ver) v promise

lovlig (lawv-li) adj lawful, legitimate

lubben (lewb-bern) adj plump

lue (lewer) c cap

luft (lewft) c air; sky; **luft-** pneumatic

lufte (lewf-ter) v air; ventilate; **~ ut** ventilate

lufthavn (lewft- hahvn) c airport

luftig (lewf-ti) adj airy

luftkondisjonering (lewft-koon-di-shoo-naʸ-ring) c air conditioning

luft-kondisjonert (lewft-koon-di-shoo-naʸt) adj air-conditioned

luftpost (lewft-post) m airmail

luftsyke (lewft-sēw-ker) m air-sickness

lufttett (lewf-teht) adj airtight

lufttrykk (lewft-trewkk) nt (pl ~) atmospheric pressure

lugar (lew-gaar) m cabin

luke (lēw-ker) c hatch

lukke (look-ker) v close, *shut; **~ opp** unlock

lukket (look-kert) adj closed, shut

luksuriøs (lewk-sew-ri-ūrss) adj luxurious

luksus (lewk-sewss) m luxury

lukt (lookt) *c* odo(u)r, smell
lukte (*look*-ter) *v* *smell
lumbago (loom-*baa*-goo) *m* lumbago
lund (lewnn) *m* grove
lune (l$\overline{ew}$-ner) *nt* mood, humo(u)r
lunge (*loong*-nger) *c* lung
lungebetennelse (*loong*-nger-beh-teh-nerl-ser) *m* pneumonia
lunken (*loong*-kern) *adj* lukewarm, tepid
lunsj (lurnsh) *m* luncheon, dinner, lunch
lunte (*lewn*-ter) *c* fuse
lur (l$\overline{ew}$r) *m* nap; *adj* smart, cunning
lus (l$\overline{ew}$ss) *c* (pl ~) louse
ly (l$\overline{ew}$) *nt* shelter, cover; ***gi ~** shelter
lyd (l$\overline{ew}$d) *m* sound; noise
lydbånd (*l$\overline{ew}$d*-bonn) *nt* (pl ~) tape
*lyde (*l$\overline{ew}$*-der) *v* sound
lydig (*l$\overline{ew}$*-di) *adj* obedient
lydighet (*l$\overline{ew}$*-di-h$\overline{ay}$t) *c* obedience
lydpotte (*l$\overline{ew}$d*-po-ter) *c* silencer; muffler *nAm*
lydtett (*l$\overline{ew}$*-d-teht) *adj* soundproof
lykke (*lewk*-ker) *c* happiness, fortune; **~ til!** good luck!
lykkelig (*lewk*-li) *adj* happy
lykkes (*lewk*-kerss) *v* manage, succeed
lykkønskning (*lewk*-kurnsk-ning) *m* congratulation
lykt (lewkt) *c* lantern
lyktestolpe (*lewk*-ter-stol-per) *m* lamp-post
lyn (l$\overline{ew}$n) *nt* lightning
lyng (lewngng) *m* heather
lys (l$\overline{ew}$ss) *nt* light; *adj* light; pale; **skarpt ~** glare
lysbilde (*l$\overline{ew}$ss*-bil-der) *nt* slide
lysende (*l$\overline{ew}$*-ser-ner) *adj* luminous
lyserød (*l$\overline{ew}$*-ser-r$\overline{ur}$) *adj* pink
lyshåret (*l$\overline{ew}$ss*-haw-rert) *adj* fair
lyskaster (*lewss*-kahss-terr) *m* searchlight
lyske (*lewss*-ker) *m* groin

lysmåler (*l$\overline{ew}$ss*-maw-lerr) *m* exposure meter
lysning (*l$\overline{ew}$ss*-ning) *m* clearing
lyspære (*l$\overline{ew}$ss*-pææ-rer) *c* light bulb
lyst (lewst) *c* desire; zest; ***ha ~ til** *feel like, fancy
lystbåt (*lewst*-bawt) *m* yacht
lystig (*lewss*-ti) *adj* cheerful, jolly
lystspill (*lewst*-spil) *nt* (pl ~) comedy
lytt (lewtt) *adj* noisy
lytte (*lewt*-ter) *v* listen; eavesdrop
lytter (*lewt*-terr) *m* listener
*lyve (*l$\overline{ew}$*-wer) *v* lie, *tell a lie
lær (læær) *nt* leather; **lær-** leather
lærd (læærd) *adj* scholarly
lære (*læ ǣ*-rer) *v* *learn; *teach; *c* teachings *pl*; **~ utenat** memorize
lærebok (*læ ǣ*-rer-b$\overline{oo}$k) *c* (pl -bøker) textbook
lærer (*læ ǣ*-rerr) *m* master, teacher, schoolmaster, schoolteacher
lærerik (*læ ǣ*-rer-reek) *adj* instructive
lærling (*læ ǣr*-ling) *m* apprentice, trainee
løfte (*lurf*-ter) *v* lift; *nt* vow; promise
løgn (lur^{ew}n) *c* lie
løk (lurk) *m* onion
løkke (*lurk*-ker) *c* loop
lønn (lurnn) *m* salary, pay, wages *pl*; maple
lønne (*lurn*-ner) *v* *pay; **~ seg** *be worthwhile
lønnsom (*lurn*-som) *adj* profitable
lønnstaker (*lurns*-taa-kerr) *m* employee
lønnstillegg (*lurns*-ti-lehg) *nt* (pl ~) *pay rise; raise *nAm*
løp (l$\overline{ur}$p) *nt* course
*løpe (*l$\overline{ur}$*-per) *v* *run
løper (*l$\overline{ur}$*-perr) *m* runner
lørdag (*l$\overline{ur}$*-dah) *m* Saturday
løs (l$\overline{ur}$ss) *adj* loose
løse (*l$\overline{ur}$*-ser) *v* solve; unfasten; **~ opp** *undo

løsepenger (*lūr*-ser-peh-ngerr) *pl* ransom

løsne (lurss-ner) *v* unfasten, detach; loosen

løsning (*lūrss*-ning) *m* solution

løve (*lūr*-ver) *m* lion

løvetann (*lūr*-ver-tahn) *c* dandelion

lån (lawn) *nt* loan

låne (*law*-ner) *v* borrow; ~ **bort** *lend

lår (lawr) *nt* thigh

lås (lawss) *m* lock

låse (*law*-ser) *v* lock; ~ **inne** lock up; ~ **opp** unlock

låve (*law*-ver) *m* barn

M

madrass (mahd-*rahss*) *m* mattress

mage (*maa*-ger) *m* stomach; belly; **mage-** gastric

mager (*maa*-gerr) *adj* lean, thin

magesår (*maa*-ger-sawr) *nt* (pl ~) gastric ulcer

magi (mah-*gee*) *m* magic

magisk (*maa*-gisk) *adj* magic

magnetisk (mahng-*nāy*-tisk) *adj* magnetic

mai (migh) May

mais (mighss) *m* maize; corn *nAm*

maiskolbe (*mighss*-kol-ber) *m* corn on the cob

major (mah-*ᵞōōr*) *m* major

makrell (mah-*krehll*) *m* mackerel

makt (mahkt) *c* might, power; rule

maktesløs (*mahk*-terss-*lūrss*) *adj* powerless

malaria (mah-*laa*-ri-ah) *m* malaria

Malaysia (mah-*ligh*-si-ah) Malaysia

malaysier (mah-*ligh*-sᵞerr) *m* Malay

malaysisk (mah-*ligh*-sisk) *adj* Malaysian

male (*maa*-ler) *v* paint; *grind

maler (*maa*-lerr) *m* painter

maleri (mah-ler-*ree*) *nt* picture, painting

malerisk (*maa*-ler-risk) *adj* picturesque

malerskrin (*maa*-ler-shkreen) *nt* (pl ~) paint-box

maling (*maa*-ling) *c* paint

malm (mahlm) *m* ore

malplassert (*maal*-plah-*sāyt*) *adj* misplaced

mamma (*mahm*-mah) *m* mom, mommy

mammut (*mahm*-mewt) *m* mammoth

man (mahnn) *pron* one

mandag (*mahn*-dah) *m* Monday

mandarin (mahn-dah-*reen*) *m* tangerine, mandarin

mandat (mahn-*daat*) *nt* mandate

mandel (*mahn*-derl) *m* (pl -dler) almond

mandler (*mahn*-dlerr) *pl* tonsils *pl*; **betente** ~ tonsilitis

manerer (mah-*nāy*-rerr) *pl* manners *pl*

manesje (mah-*nāy*-sher) *m* ring

manet (mah-*nāyt*) *m* jelly-fish

mange (*mahng*-nger) *pron* many; much

mangel (*mahng*-ngerl) *m* (pl -gler), want, lack, deficiency; shortage

mangelfull (*mahng*-ngerl-fewl) *adj* faulty, defective

mangle (*mahng*-ler) *v* fail, lack

manglende (*mahng*-ler-ner) *adj* missing, lacking

mani (mah-*nee*) *m* craze

manikyr (mah-ni-*kewr*) *m* manicure

manikyrere (mah-ni-kew-*ray*-rer) *v* manicure

mann (mahnn) *m* (pl menn) man; husband

mannekeng (mah-ner-*kehngng*) *m* model

mannskap (*mahn*-skaap) *nt* crew

mansjett (mahn-*shehtt*) *m* cuff

mansjettknapper (mahn-*sheht*-knahperr) *pl* cuff links *pl*

manuskript (mah-noo-*skript*) *nt* manuscript

marg (mahrg) *m* margin; marrow

margarin (mahr-gah-*reen*) *m* margarine

marine- (mah-*ree*-ner) naval

maritim (mah-ri-*teem*) *adj* maritime

mark (mahrk) *m* worm; *c* field

marked (*mahr*-kerd) *nt* market

markere (mahr-*kay*-rer) *v* mark; score

marmelade (mahr-mer-*laa*-der) *m* marmalade

marmor (*mahr*-moor) *m* marble

marokkaner (mah-ro-*kaa*-nerr) *m* Moroccan

marokkansk (mah-ro-*kaansk*) *adj* Moroccan

Marokko (mah-*rok*-koo) Morocco

mars (mahshsh) March

marsj (mahshsh) *m* march

marsjere (mah-*shay*-rer) *v* march

marsjfart (*mahsh*-faht) *c* cruising speed

marsvin (*maa*-shveen) *nt* (pl ~) guinea pig

martyr (*maa*-tewr) *m* martyr

mas (maass) *nt* fuss

maske (*mahss*-ker) *c* mask; mesh

maskin (mah-*sheen*) *m* machine, engine

maskineri (mah-shi-ner-ree) *nt* machinery

maskinskade (mah-*sheen*-skaa-der) *m* breakdown

maskulin (*mahss*-kew-leen) *adj* masculine

massasje (mah-*saa*-sher) *m* massage

masse (*mahss*-ser) *m* bulk

masseproduksjon (*mahss*-ser-proodewk-*shoon*) *m* mass production

massere (mah-*say*-rer) *v* massage

massiv (mah-*seev*) *adj* massive; solid

massør (mah-*surr*) *m* masseur

mast (mahst) *c* mast

mat (maat) *m* food; **lage ~** cook

mate (*maa*-ter) *v* *feed

matematikk (mah-ter-mah-*tikk*) *m* mathematics

matematisk (mah-ter-*maa*-tisk) *adj* mathematical

materiale (mah-ter-ri-*aa*-ler) *nt* material

materiell (mah-ter-ri-*ehll*) *adj* material

matforgiftning (maat-for-ˀift-ning) *m* food poisoning

matlyst (*maat*-lewst) *c* appetite

matolje (maat-ol-ˀer) *c* salad-oil

matt (mahtt) *adj* mat, dull, dim

matte (*maht*-ter) *c* mat

matvareforretning (*maat*-vaa-rer-foreht-ning) *c* grocer's

matvarehandler (maat-vaa-rerhahnd-lerr) *m* grocer

matvarer (*maat*-vaa-rerr) *pl* foodstuffs *pl*, groceries *pl*

maur (mour) *m* ant

mausoleum (mou-soo-*lay*-ewm) *nt* (pl -eer) mausoleum

med (*may*) *prep* with; by; **~ mindre** unless

medalje (meh-*dahl*-ˀer) *m* medal

***medbringe** (*may*-bri-nger) *v* *bring

meddele (*may*-day-ler) *v* communicate, inform; notify

meddelelse (*may*-day-lerl-ser) *m* information, communication

medfødt (*māy*-furt) *adj* inborn

medfølelse (*māyd*-fūr-lerl-ser) *m* sympathy

medfølende (*māyd*-fūr-leh-ner) *adj* sympathetic

medisin (meh-di-*seen*) *m* medicine; drug

medisinsk (meh-di-*seensk*) *adj* medical

meditere (meh-di-*tāy*-rer) *v* meditate

medlem (*māyd*-lehm) *nt* (pl ˷mer) member, associate

medlemskap (*māyd*-lehm-skaap) *nt* membership

medlidenhet (mehd-*lee*-dern-hāyt) *c* pity; **˷ha ˷ med** pity

medregne (*māyd*-ray-ner) *v* include, count in

medvirkning (*māyd*-veerk-ning) *m* co-operation

meg (may) *pron* me, myself

meget (*māy*-gert) *adv* very; far

megle (*mehg*-ler) *v* mediate

megler (*mehg*-lerr) *m* mediator; broker

meieri (may-er-*ree*) *nt* dairy

meisel (*may*-serl) *m* (pl -sler) chisel

mekaniker (meh-*kaa*-ni-kerr) *m* mechanic

mekanisk (meh-*kaa*-nisk) *adj* mechanical

mekanisme (meh-kah-*niss*-mer) *m* mechanism

meksikaner (mehks-i-*kaa*-nerr) *m* Mexican

meksikansk (mehks-i-*kaansk*) *adj* Mexican

mektig (*mehk*-ti) *adj* powerful, mighty

mel (māyl) *nt* flour

melankoli (meh-lahng-koo-*lee*) *m* melancholy

melde (*mehl*-ler) *v* report; bid; **˷ seg** report

melding (*mehl*-ling) *c* report

melk (mehlk) *c* milk

melkaktig (*mehl*-kahk-ti) *adj* milky

mellom (*mehl*-lom) *prep* between; among

mellommann (*mehl*-loo-mahn) *m* (pl -menn) intermediary

mellomrom (*mehl*-loom-room) *nt* (pl ˷) space

mellomspill (*mehl*-loom-spil) *nt* (pl ˷) interlude

mellomste (*mehl*-loom-ster) *adj* middle

mellomtid (*mehl*-loom-teed) *c* interim; **i mellomtiden** meanwhile

melodi (meh-loo-*dee*) *m* tune; melody

melodisk (meh-*lōō*-disk) *adj* tuneful

melodrama (meh-loo-*draa*-mah) *nt* melodrama

melon (meh-*lōōn*) *m* melon

membran (mehm-*braan*) *m* diaphragm

memorandum (meh-moo-*rahn*-dewm) *nt* (pl -da) memo

men (mehnn) *conj* but; only

mene (*māy*-ner) *v* *mean; consider

mened (*māyn*-āyd) *m* perjury

mengde (*mehng*-der) *m* lot, amount, mass; crowd

menighet (*māy*-ni-hāyt) *c* congregation

mening (*māy*-ning) *m* opinion; meaning, sense

meningsløs (*māy*-nings-lūrss) *adj* meaningless, senseless

meningsmåling (*māy*-nings-*maw*-ling) *c* poll

menneske (*mehn*-sker) *nt* human being, man

menneskehet (*mehn*-sker-hāyt) *c* humanity, mankind

menneskelig (*mehn*-sker-li) *adj* human

mens (mehns) *conj* while

menstruasjon (mehn-strew-ah-

shōōn) *m* menstruation

mental (mehn-*taal*) *adj* mental

meny (meh-*new*) *m* menu

mer (māyr) *adj* more; **litt ~** some more

merkbar (*mærk*-baar) *adj* perceptible, noticeable

merke[1] (*mær*-ker) *v* mark; *nt* tick, mark; brand

merke[2] (*mær*-ker) *v* sense; notice; ***legge ~ til** notice

merkelapp (*mær*-ker-lahp) *m* tag; ***sette ~ på** label

merkelig (*mær*-ker-li) *adj* funny, queer

merknad (*mærk*-nah) *m* note

merkverdig (mærk-*vær*-di) *adj* curious, strange

meslinger (*mehsh*-li-ngerr) *pl* measles

messe (*mehss*-ser) *m* Mass

messing (*mehss*-sing) *m* brass

mester (*mehss*-terr) *m* (pl ~e, -trer) master; champion

mesterverk (*mehss*-terr-vayrk) *nt* masterpiece

mestre (*mehss*-trer) *v* cope

metall (meh-*tahll*) *nt* metal; **metall-** metal

metalltråd (meh-*tahl*-traw) *m* wire

meter (māy-terr) *m* (pl ~) metre

metode (meh-*tōō*-der) *m* method

metodisk (meh-*tōō*-disk) *adj* methodical

metrisk (māyt-risk) *adj* metric

Mexico (*mehk*-si-koo) Mexico

middag (*mid*-dah) *m* dinner; midday; **spise ~** dine

middel (*mid*-derl) *nt* (pl midler) means

middelalderen (*mid*-derl-ahld-rern) Middle Ages

middelaldersk (*mid*-derl-ahl-dershk) *adj* mediaeval

Middelhavet (*mid*-derl-haa-vert) Mediterranean

middelklasse (*mid*-derl-klah-ser) *c* middle class

middelmådig (*mid*-derl-maw-di) *adj* average, commonplace

middels (*mid*-derls) *adj* medium

midje (*mid*-ʸer) *c* waist

midlertidig (*mid*-ler-tee-di) *adj* temporary

midnatt (*mid*-nahtt) *c* midnight

midte (*mit*-ter) *m* midst, middle

midtpunkt (*mit*-poongt) *nt* center *Am*, centre

midtsommer (*mit*-so-merr) *m* midsummer

migrene (mig-*rāy*-ner) *m* migraine

mikrobølgeovn (*mik*-roo-burl-ge-ovnn) *m* microwave oven

mikrofon (mik-roo-*fōōn*) *m* microphone

mikser (*mik*-serr) *m* mixer

mild (mill) *adj* mild; gentle

milestein (*mee*-ler-stayn) *m* milestone

militær- (mi-li-*tæær*) military

miljø (mil-ʸ*ur*) *nt* milieu; environment

miljøvern (mil-ʸ*ur*-vææn) *nt* environmental protection

milliard (mil-ʸ*ard*) *m* billion

million (mil-ʸ*ōōn*) *m* million

millionær (mil-ʸoo-*næær*) *m* millionaire

min (meen) *pron* my

mindre (*min*-drer) *adv* less; *adj* minor; **ikke desto ~** nevertheless

mindretall (*min*-drer-tahll) *nt* (pl ~) minority

mindreverdig (*min*-drer-vær-di) *adj* inferior

mindreårig (*min*-drer-aw-ri) *m* (pl ~e) minor

mineral (mi-ner-*raal*) *nt* mineral

mineralvann (mi-ner-*raal*-vahn) *nt* mineral water; soda (pop); lemonade

miniatyr (mi-ni-ah-*tewr*) *m* miniature

minibank (*mee*-ni-bahngk) *m* cash

dispenser, automatic teller (ATM)

minimum (*mee*-ni-moom) *nt* (pl -ima) minimum

mink (mingk) *m* mink

minke (*ming*-ker) *v* decrease

minne (*min*-ner) *nt* remembrance, memory; ~ **på** remind

minnes (*min*-nerss) *v* recall

minnesmerke (*min*-nerss-mær-ker) *nt* monument

minnestein (*min*-nerstayn) *m* memorial

minneverdig (*min*-ner-vær-di) *adj* memorable

minoritet (mi-noo-ri-*tayt*) *m* minority

minske (*min*-sker) *v* lessen, reduce, decrease

minst (minst) *adj* least; *adv* at least; **i det minste** at least

minus (*mee*-newss) *adv* minus

minutt (mi-*newtt*) *nt* minute

mirakel (mi-*raa*-kerl) *nt* (pl -kler) miracle

mirakuløs (mi-rah-kew-*lūrss*) *adj* miraculous

misbillige (*miss*-bi-li-er) *v* disapprove

misbruk (*miss*-brewk) *nt* abuse, misuse

misdannet (*miss*-dahn-nert) *adj* deformed

misfornøyd (*miss*-fo-nur^ew d) *adj* discontented

***misforstå** (*miss*-fo-shtaw) *v* *misunderstand

misforståelse (*miss*-fo-*shtaw*-erl-ser) *m* misunderstanding

mislike (*miss*-lee-ker) *v* dislike

mislykkes (*miss*-lew-kerss) *v* fail

mislykket (*miss*-lew-kert) *adj* unsuccessful

mistanke (*miss*-tahng-ker) *m* suspicion

miste (*miss*-ter) *v* miss; *lose

mistenke (*miss*-tehng-ker) *v* suspect

mistenkelig (miss-*tehng*-ker-li) *adj* suspicious

mistenksom (miss-*tehngk*-som) *adj* suspicious

mistenksomhet (*miss-tehngk*-som-hayt) *c* suspicion

mistenkt (*miss*-tehngt) *m* suspect

mistro (*miss*-trōō) *v* mistrust

mistroisk (*miss*-trōō-isk) *adj* distrustful

misunne (mi-*sewn*-ner) *v* envy; grudge

misunnelig (mi-*sewn*-li) *adj* envious

misunnelse (mi-*sewn*-nerl-ser) *m* envy

mobil (moo-*beel*) *adj* mobile

mobil(-telefon) (moo-*beel*-(teh-ler-fōōn)) *m* cellphone, mobile (phone)

modell (moo-*dehll*) *m* model

modellere (moo-der-*lay*-rer) *v* model

modem (*mōō*-dem) *nt* modem

moden (*mōō*-dern) *adj* ripe, mature

modenhet (*mōō*-dern-hayt) *c* maturity

moderat (moo-der-*raat*) *adj* moderate

moderne (moo-*dææ*-ner) *adj* modern; fashionable; trendy

modifisere (moo-di-fi-*say*-rer) *v* modify

modig (*mōō*-di) *adj* courageous, brave, plucky

moll (*moll*) *m* minor

molo (*mōō*-loo) *m* jetty

molte (*mol*-ter) *c* cloudberry

moms (merverdiomsetningsavgift) (*mooms*) *m* purchase tax, turnover tax, sales tax

monark (moo-*nahrk*) *m* monarch, ruler

monarki (moo-nahr-*kee*) *nt* monarchy

monolog (moo-noo-*lawg*) *m* monologue

monopol (moo-noo-*pōōl*) *nt* monopoly

monoton (moo-noo-*tōōn*) *adj* monotonous

monter (*moon*-terr) *m* (pl -trer) showcase

monument (moo-new-*mehnt*) *nt* monument

moped (moo-*pāyd*) *m* moped; motorbike *nAm*

mor (*mōōr*) *c* (pl mødre) mother

moral (moo-*raal*) *m* morality; moral

moralsk (moo-*raalsk*) *adj* moral

mord (moord) *nt* assassination, murder

morder (*moor*-derr) *m* murderer

more (*mōō*-rer) *v* amuse; entertain

morfar (*moor*-faar) *m* (pl -fedre) grandfather

morfin (moor-*feen*) *m* morphia, morphine

morgen (*maw*-ern) *m* morning; **i ~** tomorrow; **i morges** this morning

morgenavis (*maw*-ern-ah-veess) *c* morning paper

morgenkåpe (*maw*-ern-kaw-per) *c* dressing gown

morgenutgave (*maw*-ern-ēwt-gaa-ver) *c* morning edition

mormor (*moor*-mōōr) *c* (pl -mødre) grandmother

moro (*moor*-roo) *c* fun

morsmål (*mōōsh*-mawl) *nt* mother tongue, native language

morsom (*moosh*-shom) *adj* enjoyable, entertaining; humorous

mort (moot) *m* roach

mosaikk (moo-sah-*ikk*) *m* mosaic

mose (*mōō*-ser) *m* moss; *v* mash

moské (mooss-*kāy*) *m* mosque

moskito (mooss-*kee*-too) *m* mosquito

mot[1] (*mōōt*) *prep* against; towards

mot[2] (*mōōt*) *nt* courage; **ta motet fra** *v* discourage

motbydelig (moot-*bēw*-der-li) *adj* disgusting, revolting

mote (*mōō*-ter) *m* fashion

motell (moo-*tehll*) *nt* motel

motgang (*mōōt*-gahng) *m* adversity, hardship

motiv (moo-*teev*) *nt* motive; pattern

motivere (moo-tee-*vāy*-rer)) *v* motivate

motor (*mōō*-toor) *m* motor, engine

motorbåt (*mōō*-toor-bawt) *m* motorboat

motorstopp (*mōō*-toor-stop) *m/nt* (pl ~) breakdown

motorsykkel (*mōō*-toor-sew-kerl) *m* (pl -sykler) motor-cycle

motorvei (*mōō*-toor-vay) *m* motorway; highway *nAm*

motsatt (*mōōt*-saht) *adj* opposite, contrary; reverse; **det motsatte** the contrary

motsetning (*mōōt*-seht-ning) *m* contrast; reverse

*motsette seg** (*mōōt*-seh-ter) oppose

*motsi** (*mōōt*-see) *v* contradict

motstand (*mōōt*-stahn) *m* resistance

motstander (*mōōt*-stahn-derr) *m* opponent

motstridende (*mōōt*-stree-der-ner) *adj* contradictory

motsvarende (*mōōt*-svaa-rer-ner) *adj* equivalent

*motta** (*mōō*-taa) *v* receive; accept

mottakelse (*mōō*-taa-kerl-ser) *m* reception, receipt

motto (*moot*-too) *nt* motto

motvilje (*mōōt*-vil-ᵞer) *m* aversion, dislike, antipathy

mugg (mewgg) *m* mildew

mugge (*mewg*-ger) *c* jug

muggen (*mewg*-gern) *adj* mouldy

muldyr (*mewl*-dēwr) *nt* (pl ~) mule

mulesel (*mewl*-āy-serl) *nt* (pl -sler) mule

mulig (*mēw*-li) *adj* possible; eventual; realizable

muligens (*mew*-li-erns) *adv* perhaps

mulighet (*mew*-li-hāyt) *c* possibility

mulkt (mewlkt) *c* fine

multe (*mool*-ter) *c* cloudberry

multiplikasjon (mool-ti-pli-kah-*shōōn*) *m* multiplication

multiplisere (mool-ti-pli-*say*-rer) *v* multiply

munk (moongk) *m* monk

munkeorden (*moong*-ker-*or*-dern) *m* monastic order

munn (mewnn) *m* mouth

munning (*mewn*-ning) *m* outlet; estuary; muzzle

munnvann (*mewn*-vahn) *nt* mouthwash

munter (*mewn*-terr) *adj* merry, gay

muntlig (*mewnt*-li) *adj* oral, verbal

mur (*mēwr*) *m* brick wall

mure (*mēw*-rer) *v* *lay bricks

murer (*mēw*-rerr) *m* bricklayer

murpuss (*mēwr*-pewss) *m* plaster

murstein (*mēw*-shtayn) *m* brick

mus (*mēwss*) *c* (pl ~) mouse; **~matte** *c* mouse pad

museum (mew-*say*-ewm) *nt* (pl -eer) museum

musikal (*mēw*-si-kaarl) *m* musical

musikalsk (mew-si-*kaalsk*) *adj* musical

musiker (*mēw*-si-kerr) *m* musician

musikk (mew-*sikk*) *m* music

musikkinstrument (mew-*sikk*-in-strew-mehnt) *nt* musical instrument

musikkspill (mew-*sikk*-spil) *nt* (pl ~) musical comedy

muskatnøtt (mewss-*kaat*-nurt) *c* nutmeg

muskel (*mewss*-kerl) *m* (pl -kler) muscle

muskuløs (mewss-kew-*lūrss*) *adj* muscular

muslim (*mewss*-lim) *m* Muslim

musserende (mew-*say*-rer-ner) *adj* sparkling

mutter (*mewt*-terr) *m* (pl ~e, mutrer) nut

mye (*mēw*-er) *adj* much; *adv* much; **like ~** as much

mygg (mewgg) *m* (pl ~) mosquito

myggnett (*mewg*-neht) *nt* (pl ~) mosquito net

myk (*mēwk*) *adj* supple, smooth, soft; tender

mynde (*mewn*-der) *m* greyhound

myndig (*mewn*-di) *adj* of age

myndighet (*mewn*-di-hāyt) *c* authority; **utøvende ~** executive; **myndigheter** authorities *pl*

mynt (mewnt) *m* coin

mynte (*mewn*-ter) *c* mint

myntenhet (*mewnt*-āyn-hāyt) *m* monetary unit

myr (*mēwr*) *c* swamp, bog

myrde (*mēwr*-der) *v* murder

mysterium (mewss-*tay*-ri-ewm) *nt* (pl -ier) mystery

mystisk (*mewss*-tisk) *adj* mysterious

myte (*mēw*-ter) *m* myth

mytteri (mew-ter-*ree*) *nt* mutiny

møbler (*mūrb*-lerr) *pl* furniture

møblere (murb-*lay*-rer) *v* furnish

møkk (murkk) *c* muck

møll (murll) *m* (pl ~) moth

mølle (*murl*-ler) *c* mill

mønster (*murn*-sterr) *nt* (pl -tre) pattern

mør (*mūr*) *adj* tender

mørk (murrk) *adj* obscure, dark

mørke (*murr*-ker) *nt* dark; gloom

møte (*mūr*-ter) *v* encounter, *meet; *nt* encounter, meeting; appointment

møtende (*mūr*-ter-ner) *adj* oncoming

møtested (*mūr*-ter-stāy) *nt* meeting place

måke (*maw*-ker) *c* gull

mål (mawl) *nt* measure; goal; target; tongue, language

målbevisst (*mawl*-beh-vist) *adj* determined

måle (*maw*-ler) *v* measure

målebånd (*maw*-ler-bon) *nt* (pl ~) tape measure

måleinstrument (*maw*-ler-in-strew-mehnt) *nt* gauge

måler (*maw*-lerr) *m* meter

målestokk (*maw*-ler-stok) *m* scale

mållinje (*mawl*-lin-ᵞer) *c* finish

målløs (*mawl*-lūrss) *adj* speechless

målmann (*mawl*-mahn) *m* (pl -menn) goalkeeper

måltid (*mawl*-teed) *nt* meal

måne (*maw*-ner) *m* moon

måned (*maw*-nerd) *m* month

månedlig (*maw*-nerd-li) *adj* monthly

måneskinn (*maw*-ner-shin) *nt* moonlight

måte (*maw*-ter) *m* fashion, way, manner; **på hvilken som helst ~** any way; **på ingen ~** by no means

*måtte (*mot*-ter) *v* *must, *have to; *be bound to; need, need to

N

nabo (*naa*-boo) *m* neighbo(u)r

nabolag (*naa*-boo-laag) *nt* (pl ~) vicinity, neighbo(u)rhood

naiv (nah-*eev*) *adj* naïve

naken (*naa*-kern) *adj* nude, bare, naked

nakke (*nahk*-ker) *m* nape of the neck

narkoman (nahr-*koo*-mahn) *m* drug addict

narkose (nahr-*kōō*-ser) *m* narcosis

narkotika (nahr-*kōō*-ti-kah) *m* (pl ~) drug; **narkotisk middel** narcotic

narre (*nahr*-rer) *v* fool

nasjon (nah-*shōōn*) *m* nation

nasjonal (nah-shoo-*naal*) *adj* national

nasjonaldrakt (nah-shoo-*naal*-drahkt) *c* national dress

nasjonalisere (nah-shoo-nah-li-*sāy*-rer) *v* nationalize

nasjonalitet (nah-shoo-nah-li-*tāyt*) *m* nationality

nasjonalpark (nah-shoo-*naal*-pahrk) *m* national park

nasjonalsang (nah-shoo-*naal*-sahng) *m* national anthem

natt (nahtt) *c* (pl netter) night; **i ~** tonight; **om natten** by night

nattergal (*naht*-terr-gaal) *m* nightingale

nattkjole (*naht*-khōō-ler) *m* nightdress

nattklubb (*naht*-klewb) *m* cabaret, nightclub

nattkrem (*naht*-krāym) *m* night cream

nattlig (*naht*-li) *adj* nightly

natt-takst (*naht*-tahkst) *m* night rate

natt-tog (*naht*-tawg) *nt* (pl ~) night train

natur (nah-*tewr*) *m* nature

naturlig (nah-*tēw*-li) *adj* natural

naturligvis (nah-*tēw*-li-veess) *adv* of course, naturally

naturskjønn (nah-*tēw*-shurn) *adj* scenic

naturvitenskap (nah-*tewr*-vee-tern-skaap) *m* natural science

navigasjon (nah-vi-gah-*shōōn*) *m* navigation

navigere (nah-vi-*gāy*-rer) *v* navigate

navle (*nahv*-ler) *m* navel

navn (nahvn) *nt* name; **i ...s ~** on behalf of, in the name of

nebb (nehbb) *nt* beak

ned (nāyd) *adv* down; downstairs

nedbetale (nāyd-beh-taa-ler) *v* *pay off

nedbetaling (nāyd-beh-taa-ling) *c* down payment

nedbør (nāyd-būr) *m* precipitation

nede (nāy-der) *adv* below, downstairs

nedenfor (nāy-dern-for) *prep* under, below

nedenunder (nāy-dern-ew-nerr) *adv* underneath

nederlag (nāy-der-laag) *nt* (pl ~) defeat

Nederland (nāy-der-lahn) the Netherlands

nederlandsk (nāy-der-lahnsk) *adj* Dutch

nederlender (nāy-der-leh-nerr) *m* Dutchman

nedgang (nāyd-gahng) *m* decrease; depression

nedkomst (nāyd-komst) *m* delivery

nedover (nāy-do-verr) *adv* down, downwards

nedre (nāyd-rer) *adj* inferior, lower

nedrivning (nāyd-reev-ning) *m* demolition

nedslått (nāyd-shlot) *adj* down

nedstemt (nāyd-stehmt) *adj* depressed

nedstigning (nāyd-steeg-ning) *m* descent

nedtrykt (nāyd-trewkt) *adj* depressed

negativ (nāy-gah-teev) *adj* negative; *nt* negative

negl (nayl) *m* nail

neglebørste (nay-ler-bursh-ter) *m* nailbrush

neglefil (nay-ler-feel) *c* nail file

neglelakk (nay-ler-lahk) *m* nail polish

neglesaks (nay-ler-sahks) *c* nail scissors *pl*

nei (nay) no

nekte (nehk-ter) *v* deny

nemlig (nehm-li) *adv* namely

neon (nāy-oon) *m* neon

neppe (nehp-per) *adv* hardly

nerve (nær-ver) *m* nerve

nervøs (nær-vūrss) *adj* nervous

nese (nāy-ser) *c* nose

neseblod (nāy-ser-blōō) *nt* nosebleed

nesebor (nāy-ser-bōōr) *nt* (pl ~) nostril

nesevis (nāy-ser-veess) *adj* impertinent

neshorn (nāyss-hōōn) *nt* (pl ~) rhinoceros

neste (nehss-ter) *adj* next; following

nesten (nehss-tern) *adv* nearly, almost

nett (nehtt) *nt* net; Internet; *adj* neat

netthinne (neht-hi-ner) *c* retina

netto (neht-too) *adv* net

nettopp (neht-top) *adv* just

nettverk (neht-værk) *nt* network

nevne (nehv-ner) *v* mention

nevralgi (nehv-rahl-gee) *m* neuralgia

nevrose (nehv-rōō-ser) *m* neurosis

nevø (neh-vūr) *m* nephew

ni (nee) *num* nine

niende (nee-er-ner) *num* ninth

niese (ni-āy-ser) *c* niece

nifs (nifs) *adj* creepy

Nigeria (ni-gāy-ri-ah) Nigeria

nigerianer (ni-geh-ri-aa-nerr) *m* Nigerian

nigeriansk (ni-geh-ri-aansk) *adj* Nigerian

nikk (nikk) *nt* nod

nikke (nik-ker) *v* nod

nikkel (nik-kerl) *m* nickel

nikotin (ni-koo-teen) *m* nicotine

nitten (nit-tern) *num* nineteen

nittende (nit-ter-ner) *num* nineteenth

nitti (nit-ti) *num* ninety

nivellere (ni-ver-lāy-rer) *v* level

nivå (ni-vaw) *nt* level

noe (nōō-er) *pron* something

noen (nōō-ern) *pron* somebody, someone; some; ~ **gang** ever

nok (nokk) *adv* enough

nokså (nok-so) *adv* fairly, somewhat

nominasjon (noo-mi-nah-*shōōn*) *m* nomination

nominell (noo-mi-*nehll*) *adj* nominal

nominere (noo-mi-*nāy*-rer) *v* nominate

nonne (*non*-ner) *c* nun

nonnekloster (*non*-ner-kloss-terr) *nt* (pl -tre) nunnery

nonsens (*non*-serns) *nt* nonsense

nord (nōōr) *m* north

nordlig (nōō-li) *adj* north, northern; northerly

nordmann (*noor*-mahn) *m* (pl -menn) Norwegian

Nordpolen (nōōr-pōō-lern) North Pole

nordvest (noor-*vehst*) *m* north-west

nordøst (noor-*urst*) *m* north-east

Norge (*nor*-ger) Norway

norm (norm) *m* standard

normal (noor-maal) *adj* normal; regular

norsk (noshk) *adj* Norwegian

nota (nōō-tah) *m* bill

notar (noo-*taar*) *m* notary

notat (noo-*taat*) *nt* note

notere (noo-*tāy*-rer) *v* note

notis (noo-*teess*) *m* note

notisblokk (noo-*teess*-blok) *c* note pad

notisbok (noo-*teess*-bōōk) *c* (pl -bøker) notebook

nougat (noogaa) *m* nougat

november (noo-*vehm*-berr) November

null (newll) *nt* zero, nought

nummer (*noom*-merr) *nt* (pl numre) number; act

nummerskilt (*noom*-mer-shilt) *nt* registration plate; licence plate *Am*

ny (nēw) *adj* new; recent

nyanse (new-*ahng*-ser) *m* nuance; shade

nybegynner (nēw-beh-ʸew-nerr) *m* beginner; learner

nybygger (nēw-bew-gerr) *m* pioneer

nyhet (nēw-hāyt) *c* news; **nyheter** *pl* news

nykke (newk-ker) *nt* whim

nylig (nēw-li) *adv* recently, lately

nynne (newn-ner) *v* hum

nyre (nēw-rer) *c* kidney

*nyse (nēw-ser) *v* sneeze

nysgjerrig (new-*shær*-ri) *adj* curious; inquisitive; nosy *colloquial*

nysgjerrighet (new-*shær*-ri-hāyt) *c* curiosity

*nyte (nēw-ter) *v* enjoy

nytelse (nēw-terl-ser) *m* enjoyment

nytte (newt-ter) *c* utility, use; *v* *be of use

nytteløs (newt-ter-lūrss) *adj* idle

nyttig (newt-ti) *adj* useful

nyttår (newt-tawr) *nt* New Year

Ny-Zealand (nēw-*sāy*-lahn) New Zealand

nær (næær) *adv* near; *adj* close, near

nærende (næææ-rer-ner) *adj* nourishing, nutritious

nærhet (næær-hāyt) *c* vicinity

næring (nææær-ing) *c* nourishment; industry; economy; **næringsliv** economy

nærliggende (næææ-li-ger-ner) *adj* neighbo(u)ring, nearby

nærme seg (nær-mer) approach

nærsynt (næææ-shewnt) *adj* short-sighted

nærvær (næær-væær) *nt* presence

nød (nūrd) *c* misery, distress

nøde (nū-der) *v* compel; ***være nødt til** *be obliged to

nødsignal (nūrd-sing-naal) *nt* distress signal

nødssituasjon ($n\overline{u}$rd-si-tew-ah-$sh\overline{oo}n$) *m* emergency

nødstilfelle ($n\overline{u}$rds-til-feh-ler) *nt* emergency

nødtvunget ($n\overline{u}$rd-tvoo-ngert) *adv* by force

nødutgang ($n\overline{u}$rd-$\overline{ew}$t-gahng) *m* emergency exit

nødvendig (nurd-*vehn*-di) *adj* necessary

nødvendighet (nurd-*vehn*-di-h$\overline{ay}$t) *c* necessity, need

nøkkel (*nurk*-kerl) *m* (pl nøkler) key

nøkkelhull (*nurk*-kerl-hewl) *nt* keyhole

nøktern (*nurk*-tern) *adj* down-to-earth, sober

nøle ($n\overline{u}r$-ler) *v* hesitate

nøtt (nurtt) *c* nut

nøtteknekker (*nurt*-ter-kneh-kerr) *m* nutcrackers *pl*

nøtteskall (*nurt*-ter-skahl) *nt* (pl ∼) nutshell

nøyaktig (nur^{ew}-*ahk*-ti) *adj* accurate, precise, exact; careful

nøyaktighet (nur^{ew}-*ahk*-ti-h$\overline{ay}$t) *c* correctness

nøye seg med (nur^{ew}-er) *make do with

nøytral (nur^{ew}-*traal*) *adj* neutral

nå[1] (naw) *v* reach; *catch; *make

nå[2] (naw) *adv* now; ∼ og da occasionally, now and then

nåde (*naw*-der) *m* mercy, grace

nål (nawl) *c* needle

nåletre (*naw*-ler-tr$\overline{ay}$) *nt* (pl -rær) firtree

når (norr) *adv* when; *conj* when; ∼ enn whenever

nåtid (*naw*-teed) *c* present

nåtildags (*naw*-til-dahks) *adv* nowadays

nåværende (*naw*-væææ-er-ner) *adj* current, present

O

oase (oo-*aa*-ser) *m* oasis

obduksjon (ob-dewk-$sh\overline{oo}n$) *m* autopsy

oberst ($\overline{oo}$-bersht) *m* colonel

objekt (oob-^{y}*ehkt*) *nt* object

objektiv (ob-^{y}ehk-*teev*) *adj* objective

obligasjon (ob-li-gah-$sh\overline{oo}n$) *m* bond

obligatorisk (oob-li-gah-$\overline{oo}$-risk) *adj* obligatory, compulsory

observasjon (op-sehr-vah-$sh\overline{oo}n$) *m* observation

observatorium (op-sehr-vah-$\overline{oo}$-ri-ewm) *nt* (pl -ier) observatory

observere (op-sehr-*v$\overline{ay}$*-rer) *v* observe

odde (*od*-der) *m* headland

offensiv (*of*-fahng-seev) *adj* offensive; *m* offensive

offentlig (*of*-fernt-li) *adj* public

***offentliggjøre** (o-fernt-li-^{y}$\overline{ur}$-rer) *v* publish

offentliggjørelse (*of*-fernt-li-^{y}$\overline{ur}$-rerl-ser) *m* publication

offer (*of*-ferr) *nt* (pl ofre) victim; casualty; sacrifice

offiser (o-fi-*s$\overline{ay}$r*) *m* (pl ∼er) officer

offisiell (o-fi-si-*ehll*) *adj* official

ofre (*of*-rer) *v* sacrifice

ofte (*of*-ter) *adv* frequently, often

og (o) *conj* and

også (*oss*-so) *adv* also; as well, too

okkupasjon (o-kew-pah-$sh\overline{oo}n$) *m* occupation

okse (*ook*-ser) *m* ox

oksekjøtt (*ook*-ser-khurt) *nt* beef

oksygen (ok-sew-*gayn*) *nt* oxygen

oktober (ok-*too*-berr) October

olabukse (oo-*lah*-book-se) *c* jeans

oldtid (*ol*-teed) *c* antiquity

oliven (oo-*lee*-vern) *m* (pl ~, ~er) olive

olivenolje (oo-*lee*-vern-ol-*y*er) *c* olive oil

olje (*ol*-*y*er) *c* oil

oljebrønn (*ol*-*y*er-brurn) *m* oil well

oljefilter (*ol*-*y*er-fil-terr) *nt* (pl -tre) oil filter

oljemaleri (*ol*-*y*er-maa-ler-ree) *nt* oil painting

oljeraffineri (*ol*-*y*er-rah-fi-ner-ree) *nt* oil refinery

oljet (*ol*-*y*ert) *adj* oily

oljetrykk (*ol*-*y*er-trewk) *nt* (pl ~) oil pressure

om (oomm) *prep* round; about; in; *conj* whether, if

om bord (om boor) aboard

omdanne (*oom*-dah-ner) *v* transform

omdreining (*om*-dray-ning) *m* revolution

omegn (*oom*-mayn) *m* ~ surroundings *pl*

omelett (oo-mer-*lehtt*) *m* omelette

omfang (*oom*-fahng) *nt* extent

omfangsrik (*oom*-fahngs-reek) *adj* big, bulky, extensive

omfatte (*oom*-fah-ter) *v* comprise, include

omfattende (*oom*-fah-ter-ner) *adj* comprehensive, extensive

omfavne (*oom*-fahv-ner) *v* embrace, hug

omfavnelse (*oom*-fahv-nerl-ser) *m* embrace

omgang (*oom*-gahng) *m* round; half time

***omgi** (*oom*-*y*ee) *v* encircle, circle, surround

omgivelser (*oom*-*y*ee-verl-serr) *pl* environment; setting

***omgå** (*oom*-gaw) *v* by-pass

omgående (*oom*-gaw-er-ner) *adj* prompt

***omgås** (*oom*-gawss) *v* associate with; *~ med mix with

omhyggelig (oom-*hew*-ger-li) *adj* careful, thorough

omkjøring (oom-khur-ring) *c* detour, diversion

***omkomme** (*oom*-ko-mer) *v* perish

omkostninger (*oom*-kost-ni-ngerr) *pl* expenses *pl*

omkring (oom-*kringng*) *prep* round, around; *adv* about

omkringliggende (om-*kring*-li-ger-ner) *adj* surrounding

omløp (*oom*-lurp) *nt* circulation; orbit

omregne (*oom*-ray-ner) *v* convert

omregningstabell (*oom*-ray-nings-tah-behll) *m* conversion chart

omringe (*oom*-ri-nger) *v* encircle, circle, surround

omriss (*oom*-riss) *nt* (pl ~) contour, outline; **gi et ~ av** outline

område (*oom*-raw-der) *nt* zone, area, territory, region; sphere

omsetning (*oom*-seht-ning) *m* turnover

omslag (*oom*-shlaag) *nt* reverse; sleeve, jacket

omslutte (*oom*-shlewt-ter) *v* envelop

omsorg (*oom*-sorg) *c* care

omstendighet (oom-*stehn*-di-hayt) *c* condition, circumstance

omstridt (*oom*-strit) *adj* controversial

omtale (*oom*-taa-ler) *m* mention

omtanke (*oom*-tahng-ker) *m* consideration

omtenksom (oom-*tehngk*-som) *adj* thoughtful

omtrent (oom-*trehnt*) *adv* approximately; about

omtrentlig (oom-*trehnt*-li) *adj*
approximate

omvei (*oom*-vay) *m* detour

omvende (*oom*-veh-ner) *v* convert

ond (oonn) *adj* wicked, ill, evil

ondartet (*oon*-naa-tert) *adj* malignant

onde (*oon*-der) *nt* evil

ondsinnet (*oon*-si-nert) *adj* evil

ondskapsfull (*oon*-skaaps-fewl) *adj*
vicious, spiteful, malicious

onkel (*oong*-kerl) *m* (pl onkler) uncle

onsdag (*oons*-dah) *m* Wednesday

onyks ($\overline{oo}$-newks) *m* onyx

opal (oo-*paal*) *m* opal

opera (*oo*-per-rah) *m* opera; opera
house

operasjon (oo-per-rah-*shoon*) *m*
surgery, operation

operatør (oo-per-rah-*turr*) *m* operator

operere (oo-per-*ray*-rer) *v* operate

operette (oo-per-*reht*-ter) *m* operetta

opp (oopp) *adv* up

oppblåsbar (*oop*-blawss-baar) *adj*
inflatable

oppdage (*oop*-daa-ger) *v* discover,
detect; notice

oppdagelse (*oop*-daa-gerl-ser) *m*
discovery

oppdikte (*oop*-dik-ter) *v* invent

*oppdra (*oop*-draa) *v* educate; *bring
up; raise; rear

oppdrag (*oop*-draag) *nt* (pl ~)
assignment

oppdragelse (*oop*-draa-gerl-ser) *m*
up-bringing

oppdrette (*oop*-dreh-ter) *v* *breed

oppfatning (*oop*-faht-ning) *m*
opinion, view

oppfatte (*oop*-fah-ter) *v* conceive

*oppfinne (*oop*-fi-ner) *v* invent

oppfinnelse (*oop*-fi-nerl-ser) *m*
invention

oppfinner (*oop*-fi-nerr) *m* inventor

oppfinnsom (oop-*fin*-som) *adj*
inventive

oppfostre (*oop*-foost-rer) *v* educate;
*bring up; raise; rear

oppføre (*oop*-fur-rer) *v* construct; ~
seg act, behave

oppførelse (*oop*-fur-rerl-ser) *m* show;
construction

oppførsel (*oop*-fur-sherl) *m* conduct,
behavio(u)r

oppgave (*oop*-gaa-ver) *c* duty; task;
exercise

*oppgi (*oop*-^{y}ee) *v* declare; *give up

opphav (*oop*-haav) *nt* origin

opphisse (*oop*-hi-ser) *v* excite

opphisselse (*oop*-hi-serl-ser) *m*
excitement

opphisset (*oop*-hi-sert) *adj* excited

opphold (*oop*-hol) *nt* (pl ~) stay

*oppholde seg (*oop*-ho-ler) stay

oppholdstillatelse (*oop*-hols-ti-laa-
terl-ser) *m* residence permit

opphøre (*oop*-hur-rer) *v* finish, cease,
discontinue, expire, end

oppkalle (*oop*-kahl-ler) *v* name after

opplag (*oop*-laag) *nt* (pl ~) edition

opplagt (*oop*-lahkt) *adj* fit; self-
evident

oppleve (*oop*-*lay*-ver) *v* experience

opplyse (*oop*-*lew*-ser) *v* inform;
illuminate

opplysning (*oop*-*lewss*-ning) *m*
information

oppløp (*oop*-*lurp*) *nt* (pl ~) riot

oppløse (*oop*-*lur*-ser) *v* dissolve

oppløselig (oop-*lur*-ser-li) *adj* soluble

oppløsning (*oop*-*lurss*-ning) *m*
solution

oppmerksom (oop-*mærk*-som) *adj*
attentive; *være ~ *pay attention;
*være ~ **på** attend to, *pay attention
to

oppmerksomhet (oop-*mærk*-som-
hayt) *c* notice, attention

oppmuntre (*oop*-mewn-trer) *v*

encourage; cheer up

oppnå (*oop*-naw) *v* achieve, attain

oppnåelig (oop-*naw*-er-li) *adj* attainable; obtainable

opponere (oo-poo-*nay*-rer) *v* oppose

opposisjon (oo-poo-si-*shoon*) *m* opposition

oppover (*oop*-paw-verr) *adv* up, upwards

oppreist (*oop*-rayst) *adj* erect

opprette (*oop*-reh-ter) *v* found; institute

***opprettholde** (*oop*-reht-ho-ler) *v* maintain

oppriktig (oop-*rik*-ti) *adj* sincere, honest

oppringning (*oop*-ring-ning) *m* call

opprinnelig (oop-*rin*-ner-li) *adj* original, initial

opprinnelse (oop-*rin*-nerl-ser) *m* origin, source

opprør (*oop*-rūrr) *nt* (pl ~) revolt, rebellion; ***gjøre** ~ revolt

opprørende (*oop*-rūr-rer-ner) *adj* revolting

opprørt (*oop*-rūrt) *adj* *upset

oppsiktsvekkende (*oop*-sikts-veh-ker-ner) *adj* sensational, striking

oppskrift (*oop*-skrift) *c* recipe

oppslag (*oop*-slag) *nt* bulletin

oppslagstavle (*oop*-slags-tavle) *c*

oppspore (*oop*-spoo-rer) *v* trace

oppstand (*oop*-stahn) *m* rising, rebellion, revolt

oppstigning (*oop*-steeg-ning) *m* ascent; rise

oppstyr (*oop*-stēwr) *nt* fuss

***oppstå** (*oop*-staw) *v* *arise

oppsyn (*oop*-sēwn) *nt* (pl ~) supervision

oppsynsmann (*oop*-sēwns-mahn) *m* (pl -menn) warden

***oppta** (*oop*-taa) *v* *take up; occupy

opptak¹ (*oop*-taak) *nt* (pl ~) recording

opptak² (*oop*-taak) *nt* admission

opptatt (*oop*-taht) *adj* busy, engaged; occupied

opptog (*oop*-tawg) *nt* (pl ~) procession

opptre (*oop*-trāy) *v* perform

opptreden (*oop*-trāy-dern) *m* appearance

oppvakt (*oop*-vahkt) *adj* bright

oppvarte (*oop*-vah-ter) *v* wait on

oppvask (*oop*-vahsk) *m* washing-up; dirty dishes

oppvaskmaskin (*oop*-vahsk-mah-sheen) *m* dishwasher

oppvise (*oop*-vee-ser) *v* exhibit, show

oppå (*oop*-po) *prep* on top of

optiker (*oop*-ti-kerr) *m* optician

optimisme (oop-ti-*miss*-mer) *m* optimism

optimist (oop-t-*mist*) *m* optimist

optimistisk (oop-ti-*miss*-tisk) *adj* optimistic

oransje (oo-*rahng*-sher) *adj* orange

ord (ōōr) *nt* word

ordbok (ōōr-bōōk) *c* (pl -bøker) dictionary

orden (*o*-dern) *m* order; **i** ~ in order

ordentlig (*o*-dernt-li) *adj* tidy; neat

ordforråd (ōōr-fo-rawd) *nt* vocabulary

ordinær (o-di-*næær*) *adj* vulgar

ordliste (ōōr-liss-ter) *c* word list

ordne (*oord*-ner) *v* arrange, settle; sort; fix

ordning (*oord*-ning) *c* arrangement, method; settlement

ordre (*oord*-rer) *m* order

ordspill (ōōr-spil) *nt* (pl ~) pun

ordspråk (ōōr-sprawk) *nt* (pl ~) proverb

ordstrid (ōōr-streed) *m* dispute

ordveksling (ōōr-vehk-shling) *c* argument

organ (or-*gaan*) *nt* organ

organisasjon (or-gah-ni-sah-*shoon*)

m organization

organisere (or-gah-ni-*say*-rer) *v* organize

organisk (or-*gaa*-nisk) *adj* organic

orgel (*or*-gerl) *nt* (pl orgler) organ

orientalsk (o-ri-ehn-*taalsk*) *adj* oriental

Orienten (o-ri-ehn-tern) Orient

orientere seg (o-ri-ehn-*tay*-rer) orientate

original (o-ri-gi-*naal*) *adj* original

orkan (or-*kaan*) *m* hurricane

orke (*or*-ker) *v* sustain

orkester (or-*kehss*-terr) *nt* (pl -tre) orchestra; band

orkesterplass (or-*kehss*-terr-plahss) *m* stall; orchestra seat *Am*

ornament (o-nah-*mehnt*) *nt* ornament

ornamental (o-nah-mehn-*taal*) *adj* ornamental

ortodoks (o-too-*doks*) *adj* orthodox

oss (oss) *pron* us, ourselves

ost (oost) *m* cheese

ouverture (oo-ver-*tew*-rer) *m* overture

oval (oo-*vaal*) *adj* oval

ovenfor (*aw*-vern-for) *prep* above, over; *adv* above, overhead

ovenpå (*aw*-vern-paw) *adv* upstairs

over (*aw*-verr) *prep* across, over; *adv* over; **over-** upper; **~ ende** down, over

overall (*aw*-ver-rol) *m* overalls *pl*

overalt (o-ver-*rahlt*) *adv* everywhere, throughout

overanstrenge (*aw*-ver-rahn-streh-nger) *v* strain; **~ seg** overwork

overbevise (*aw*-verr-beh-vee-ser) *v* convince, persuade

overbevisning (*aw*-verr-beh-veess-ning) *m* conviction, persuasion

overdreven (*aw*-dray-vern) *adj* extravagant, excessive

***overdrive** (*aw*-ver-dree-ver) *v* exaggerate; magnify; overdo

overdrivelse (*aw*-verr-driv-erl-ser) *m* exaggeration

overenskomst (*aw*-ver-rehns-komst) *m* settlement, agreement

overensstemmelse (*aw*-ver-rehns-steh-merl-ser) *m* agreement; **i ~ med** in accordance with, according to

overfall (*aw*-verr-fahl) *nt* (pl ~) attack; robbery; hold-up

overfart (*aw*-verr-faht) *m* crossing, passage

overfladisk (*aw*-verr-flaa-disk) *adj* superficial

overflate (*aw*-verr-flaa-ter) *c* surface

overflod (*aw*-verr-flood) *m* abundance; plenty

overflødig (*aw*-verr-flur-di) *adj* superfluous; redundant

overfor (*aw*-verr-for) *prep* opposite, facing; towards

overfylt (*aw*-verr-fewlt) *adj* crowded

overføre (*aw*-verr-fur-rer) *v* transfer; remit

overgang (*aw*-verr-gahng) *m* transition

***overgi seg** (*aw*-verr-ʸee) surrender

overgivelse (*aw*-verr-ʸee-verl-ser) *m* surrender

overgrodd (*aw*-verr-grood) *adj* overgrown

***overgå** (*aw*-verr-gaw) *v* exceed, *outdo

overhale (*aw*-verr-haa-ler) *v* overhaul

overhodet (o-verr-*hoo*-der) *adv* at all

overlagt (*aw*-ver-lahkt) *adj* deliberate

***overlate** (*aw*-ver-laa-ter) *v* *leave to; entrust

overlegen (*aw*-ver-*lay*-gern) *adj* superior, haughty

overleve (*aw*-verr-*lay*-ver) *v* survive

overlærer (*aw*-ver-læ-rerr) *m* headmaster, head teacher

overmodig (*aw*-verr-*moo*-di) *adj* presumptuous

overoppsyn (*awv*-err-op-*sewn*) *nt*

supervision

overraske (*aw*-ver-rahss-ker) *v* surprise

overraskelse (*aw*-ver-rahss-kerl-ser) *m* surprise

*****overrekke** (*aw*-ver-reh-ker) *v* hand, *give

overrumple (*aw*-ver-roomp-ler) *v* *catch

*****overse** (*aw*-ver-sh$\overline{ay}$) *v* overlook

*****oversette** (*aw*-ver-sheh-ter) *v* translate

oversettelse (*aw*-ver-sheh-terl-ser) *m* translation; version

oversetter (*aw*-ver-sheh-terr) *m* translator

overside (*aw*-ver-shee-der) *c* top side, top

oversikt (*aw*-ver-shikt) *m* survey

oversjøisk (*aw*-ver-sh$\overline{u}$r-isk) *adj* overseas

*****overskride** (*aw*-ver-shkree-der) *v* exceed

overskrift (*aw*-ver-shkrift) *c* heading; headline

overskudd (*aw*-ver-shkewd) *nt* (pl ~) surplus

overskyet (*aw*-ver-sh$\overline{ew}$-ert) *adj* overcast, cloudy

overspent (*aw*-ver-shpehnt) *adj*

overstrung

overstrømmende (*aw*-ver-shtrur-mer-ner) *adj* exuberant

oversvømmelse (*aw*-ver-shvur-merl-ser) *m* flood

*****overta** (*aw*-ver-taa) *v* *take over

overtale (*aw*-ver-taa-ler) *v* persuade

overtrekk (*aw*-ver-trehkk) *nt* overdraft

overtrett (*aw*-ver-trehtt) *adj* overtired

overtro (*aw*-ver-tr$\overline{oo}$) *c* superstition

overveie (*aw*-verr-vay-er) *v* consider; deliberate

overveielse (*aw*-verr-vay-erl-ser) *m* consideration; deliberation

overvekt (*aw*-verr-vehkt) *c* overweight; predominance

overvelde (*aw*-verr-veh-ler) *v* overwhelm

*****overvinne** (*aw*-verr-vi-ner) *v* *overcome; defeat

*****overvære** (*aw*-verr-væ$\overline{æ}$-rer) *v* attend

overvåke (*awv*-err-vaw-ker) *v* supervise; patrol

overvåking (*awv*-err-vaw-king) *c* surveillance

ovn (ovnn) *m* stove, furnace

ozon (oo-s$\overline{oo}$n) *nt* ozone

P

padde (*pahd*-der) *c* toad

padleåre (*pahd*-ler-aw-rer) *c* paddle

Pakistan (pah-ki-*staan*) Pakistan

pakistaner (pah-ki-*staa*-nerr) *m* Pakistani

pakistansk (pah-ki-*staansk*) *adj* Pakistani

pakke[1] (*pahk*-ker) *c* package, parcel

pakke[2] (*pahk*-ker) *v* pack; ~ **inn** wrap; envelop ~ **ned** pack up; ~ **opp** unpack, unwrap

pakkhus (*pahk*-h$\overline{ew}$ss) *nt* (pl ~) warehouse

pakt (pahkt) *c* pact

palass (pah-*lahss*) *nt* palace

palme (*pahl*-mer) *m* palm

panel (pah-*nāyl*) *nt* panel

panelverk (pah-*nāyl*-værk) *nt* panelling

panikk (pah-*nikk*) *m* scare, panic

panne (*pahn*-ner) *c* forehead; pan

panser (*pahn*-serr) *nt* bonnet; hood *nAm*

pant (pahnt) *m* deposit

pantelån (*pahn*-ter-lawn) *nt* mortgage

pantelåner (*pahn*-ter-lawnerr) *m* pawnbroker

***pantsette** (*pahnt*-seh-ter) *v* pawn

papegøye (pah-per-*gur*ᵉʷ-er) *m* parrot; parakeet

papir (pah-*peer*) *nt* paper; **papir-**paper

papirhandel (pah-*peer*-hahn-derl) *m* (pl -dler) stationer's

papirkniv (pah-*peer*-kneev) *m* paper knife

papirkurv (pah-*peer*-kewrv) *m* wastepaper basket

papirlommetørkle (pah-*peer*-loo-mer-turr-kler) *nt* (pl -lær) tissue

papirpose (pah-*peer*-pōō-ser) *m* paper bag

papirserviett (pah-*peer*-sær-vi-eht) *m* paper napkin

papirvarer (pah-*peer*-vaa-rerr) *pl* stationery

papp (pahpp) *m* cardboard

pappa (*pahp*-pah) *m* dad, daddy

par (paar) *nt* pair; couple

parade (pah-*raa*-der) *m* parade

parabolantenne (pah-*raa*-bōōl-ahn-tehn-ner) *c* satellite dish

paradis (pah-*raa*-dis) *nt* paradise

parafin (pah-rah-*feen*) *m* paraffin

parallell (pah-rah-*lehll*) *m* parallel; *adj* parallel

paraply (pah-rah-*plēw*) *m* umbrella

parasoll (pah-rah-*soll*) *m* sunshade

parat (pah-*raat*) *adj* ready

parfyme (pahr-*fēw*-mer) *m* perfume

park (pahrk) *m* park; **offentlig parkanlegg** public garden

parkere (pahr-*kāy*-rer) *v* park

parkering (pahr-*kāy*-ring) *c* parking; **~ forbudt** no parking

parkeringsavgift (pahr-*kāy*-rings-aav-ʸift) *c* parking fee

parkeringslys (pahr-*kāy*-rings-lēwss) *nt* (pl ~) parking light

parkeringsplass (pahr-*kāy*-rings-plahss) *m* car park; parking lot *Am*

parkeringssone (pahr-*kāy*-ring-sōō-ner) *c* parking zone

parkometer (pahr-koo-*māy*-terr) *nt* (pl ~, -tre) parking meter

parlament (pahr-lah-*mehnt*) *nt* parliament; **parlamentarisk** *adj* parliamentary

parlør (pah-*lūr*) *m* phrase book

parti (pah-*tee*) *nt* party; side

partisk (*paa*-tisk) *adj* partial

partner (*paat*-nerr) *m* partner; associate

parykk (pah-*rewkk*) *m* wig

pasient (pah-si-*ehnt*) *m* patient

pasifisme (pah-si-*fiss*-mer) *m* pacifism

pasifist (pah-si-*fist*) *m* pacifist

pasifistisk (pah-si-*fiss*-tisk) *adj* pacifist

pass (pahss) *nt* passport; mountain pass

passasje (pah-*saa*-sher) *m* passage

passasjer (pah-sah-*shāyr*) *m* passenger

passasjerbåt (pah-sah-*shāyr*-bawt) *m* liner

passe (*pahss*-ser) *v* fit, suit; tend; look after; **~ på** mind, *take care of; **~ seg for** mind, look out; **~ til** match

passende (*pahss*-ser-ner) *adj* appropriate, convenient, adequate; proper, just

passere (pah-*sāy*-rer) *v* pass

passfoto (*pahss*-foo-too) *nt* (pl ~)
passport photograph

passiv (*pahss*-seev) *adj* passive

passkontroll (*pahss*-koon-trol) *m*
passport control

passord (*pahss*- oor) *m* password

pasta (*pahss*-tah) *m* paste; noodles

patent (pah-*tehnt*) *nt* patent

pater (*paa*-terr) *m* Father

patriot (paht-ri-oot) *m* patriot

patron (paht-roon) *m* cartridge

patrulje (paht-*rewl*-ʸer) *m* patrol

patruljere (pah-trewl-ʸay-rer) *v* patrol

pattedyr (*paht*-ter-dewr) *nt* (pl ~)
mammal

pause (*pou*-ser) *m* pause;
intermission, interval

pave (*paa*-ver) *m* pope

paviljong (pah-vil-ʸoangng) *m*
pavilion

peanøtt (*pee*-ah-nurt) *c* peanut

pedal (peh-*daal*) *m* pedal

peis (payss) *m* fireplace

peke (*pay*-ker) *v* point

pekefinger (*pay*-ker-fi-ngerr) *m* (pl
-grer) index finger

pelikan (peh-li-*kaan*) *m* pelican

pels (pehls) *m* fur

pelskåpe (pehls-kaw-per) *c* fur coat

pen (payn) *adj* good-looking,
handsome, pretty; fine, nice

pendler (*pehnd*-lerr) *m* commuter

pengeanbringelse (*pehng*-nger-ahn-
bri-ngerl-ser) *m* investment

pengepung (*pehng*-nger-poong) *m*
purse

penger (*pehng*-ngerr) *pl* money

pengeseddel (*pehng*-nger-seh-derl)
m (pl -sedler) banknote

pengeskap (*pehng*-nger-skaap) *nt* (pl
~) safe

pengeutpresning (*pehng*-nger-ewt-
prehss-ning) *m* blackmail; **presse
penger av** blackmail

penicillin (peh-ni-si-*leen*) *nt* penicillin

penn (pehnn) *m* pen

pensel (*pehn*-serl) *m* (pl -sler) paintbrush, brush

pensjon (pahng-*shoon*) *m* pension;
board; retirement; **full ~** full board,
board and lodging, bed and board; **gå
av med ~** retire

pensjonat (pahng-shoo-*naat*) *nt*
boarding-house, guest-house,
pension

pensjonatskole (pahng-shoo-*naat*-
skoo-ler) *m* boarding school

pensjonert (pahng-shoo-*nayt*) *adj*
retired

pepper (*pehp*-perr) *m* pepper

peppermynte (peh-perr-*mewn*-ter) *c*
peppermint

pepperrot (*pehp*-per-root) *c*
horseradish

per, pr. (pær) *prep* per

perfeksjon (pær-fehk-*shoon*) *m*
perfection

perfekt (pær-*fehkt*) *adj* perfect;
faultless

periode (peh-ri-oo-der) *m* period

periodevis (peh-ri-oo-der-veess) *adj*
periodical

perle (*pææ*-ler) *c* pearl, bead

perlekjede (*pææ*-ler-khay-der) *nt*
beads *pl*

perlemor (*pææ*-ler-moor) *nt* mother
of pearl

perm (pærm) *m* cover

permisjon (pær-mi-*shoon*) *m* leave;
permit

perrong (peh-*rongng*) *m* platform

perser (*pæsh*-sherr) *m* Persian

Persia (*pæsh*-shi-ah) Persia

persienne (pæ-shi-*ehn*-ner) *m* blind,
shutter

persille (pæ-*shil*-ler) *c* parsley

persisk (*pæsh*-shisk) *adj* Persian

person (pæ-*shoon*) *m* person; **per ~**

per person

personale (pæ-shoo-*naa*-ler) *nt* personnel, staff

personlig (pæ-*shoon*-li) *adj* personal; private

personlighet (pæ-*shoon*-li-hayt) *c* personality

persontog (pæ-*shoon*-tawg) *nt* (pl ~) passenger train

perspektiv (pæsh-pehk-*teev*) *nt* perspective

pertentlig (pæ-*tehnt*-li) *adj* precise

pese (*pay*-ser) *v* pant

pessimisme (peh-si-*miss*-mer) *m* pessimism

pessimist (peh-si-*mist*) *m* pessimist

pessimistisk (peh-si-*miss*-tisk) *adj* pessimistic

petisjon (peh-ti-*shoon*) *m* petition

petroleum (peht-*roo*-leh-ewm) *m* petroleum; kerosene

pianist (piah-*nist*) *m* pianist

piano (pi-*aa*-noo) *nt* piano

pigg (pigg) *m* spike; peak

pigge (*pigg*-ger) *v* spike; prod

piggtråd (*pigg*-traw) *m* barbed wire

pikant (pi-*kahnt*) *adj* savo(u)ry

pike (*pee*-ker) *m* girl

pikenavn (*pee*-ker-nahvn) *nt* (pl ~) maiden name

pikkolo (*pik*-koo-loo) *m* bellboy, page-boy

piknik (*pik*-nik) *m* picnic; ***dra på ~** picnic

pil (peel) *c* arrow; willow

pilegrim (*pil*-grim) *m* pilgrim

pilegrimsreise (*pil*-grims-ray-ser) *m* pilgrimage

pille (*pil*-ler) *c* pill

pilot (pi-*loot*) *m* pilot

pimpstein (*pimp*-stayn) *m* pumice stone

pine (*pee*-ner) *v* torment; *c* torment

pingvin (ping-*veen*) *m* penguin

pinlig (*peen*-li) *adj* embarrassing, awkward

pinnsvin (*pin*-sveen) *nt* (pl ~) hedgehog

pinse (*pin*-ser) *c* Whitsun, Pentecost

pinsett (pin-*sehtt*) *m* tweezers *pl*

pipe (*pee*-per) *c* pipe

pipetobakk (*pee*-per-too-bahk) *m* pipe tobacco

pisk (pisk) *m* whip

pistol (piss-*tool*) *m* pistol

pittoresk (pi-too-*rehsk*) *adj* picturesque

plage (*plaa*-ger) *v* bother; *m* nuisance

plagg (plahgg) *nt* garment

plakat (plah-*kaat*) *m* poster, placard

plan (plaan) *m* scheme, project, plan; map; *nt* level; *adj* even, flat, level

planet (plah-*nayt*) *m* planet

planetarium (plah-neh-*taa*-ri-ewm) *nt* (pl -ier) planetarium

planke (*plahng*-ker) *m* board, plank

*planlegge (*plaan*-leh-ger) *v* plan

planovergang (*plaa*-naw-verr-gahng) *m* level crossing

plantasje (plahn-*taa*-sher) *m* plantation

plante (*plahn*-ter) *m* plant; *v* plant

planteskole (*plahn*-ter-skooler) *m* nursery

plass (plahss) *m* square; room; seat

plassere (plah-*say*-rer) *v* *put, *lay

plaster (*plah*-sterr) *nt* (pl ~, -tre) plaster

plastikk (plahss-*tikk*) *m* plastic; **plastikk-** plastic

plate (*plaa*-ter) *c* plate; sheet; record

platespiller (*plaa*-ter-spi-lerr) *m* record player

platina (*plaa*-ti-nah) *m* platinum

pleie (*play*-er) *v* *be in the habit of; nurse

pleieforeldre (*play*-er-fo-rehl-drer) *pl* foster parents *pl*

pleiehjem (*play*-er-^yehm) *nt* (pl ~)
foster-home

plettfri (*pleht*-free) *adj* spotless,
stainless

plikt (plikt) *c* duty

plog (ploog) *m* plough

plombe (*ploom*-ber) *m* filling

plomme (*ploom*-mer) *c* plum

plugge inn (*plewg*-er-in) plug in

plukke (*plook*-ker) *v* pick

pluss (plewss) *adv* plus

plutselig (*plewt*-ser-li) *adj* suddenly;
sudden

plyndring (*plewn*-dring) *c* robbery

plystre (*plewss*-trer) *v* whistle

pløye (plur^{ew}-er) *v* plough

poengsum (po-*ehng*-sewm) *m* (pl
~mer) score

poesi (poo-eh-*see*) *m* poetry

pokal (poo-*kaal*) *m* cup

polakk (poo-*lahkk*) *m* Pole

Polen (*poo*-lern) Poland

polere (poo-*lay*-rer) *v* polish

polio (*poo*-li-oo) *m* polio

polise (poo-*lee*-ser) *m* policy

politi (poo-li-*tee*) *nt* police *pl*

politibetjent (poo-li-*tee*-beh-t^yehnt)
m policeman, policewoman

politiker (poo-*lee*-ti-kerr) *m* politician

politikk (poo-li-*tikk*) *m* politics; policy

politisk (poo-*lee*-tisk) *adj* political

politistasjon (poo-li-*tee*-stah-shoon)
m police station

polsk (poolsk) *adj* Polish

polstre (*pol*-strer) *v* upholster

pommes frites (pom fritt) chips;
French fries *Am*

ponni (*pon*-ni) *m* pony

popmusikk (*pop*-mew-sik) *m* pop
music

populær (poo-pew-*læær*) *adj* popular

porselen (poo-sher-*layn*) *nt* china,
porcelain

porsjon (poo-*shoon*) *m* portion;
helping

port (poott) *m* gate

portier (poo-ti-*æær*) *m* (pl ~er)
doorman

portner (*poot*-nerr) *m* porter

porto (*poot*-too) *m* postage

portrett (poot-*rehtt*) *nt* portrait

Portugal (*poo*-tew-gahl) Portugal

portugiser (poo-tew-*gee*-serr) *m*
Portuguese

portugisisk (poo-tew-*gee*-sisk) *adj*
Portuguese

pose (*poo*-ser) *m* bag

posisjon (poo-si-*shoon*) *m* position;
station

positiv (*poo*-si-teev) *adj* positive

post (post) *m* mail, post; item; **ledig ~**
vacancy; **poste restante** poste
restante

postbud (*post*-bewd) *nt* (pl ~)
postman

poste (*poss*-ter) *v* mail, post

postei (*poewss*-tei) *m* pasty

poster (*poewss*-terr) *m* poster

postkasse (*post*-kah-ser) *c* pillar-box,
letter-box; mailbox *nAm*

postkontor (*post*-koon-toor) *nt* post-
office

postkort (*post*-kot) *nt* (pl ~) postcard

postnummer (*post*-noo-merr) *nt* (pl
-numre) zip code *Am*

postvesen (*post*-vay-sern) *nt* postal
service

pote (*poo*-ter) *m* paw

potet (poo-*tayt*) *m* potato; **~stappe** *c*
mashed potatoes

praksis (*prahk*-siss) *m* practice

prakt (prahkt) *m* splendo(u)r

praktfull (*prahkt*-fewl) *adj*
magnificent, gorgeous, splendid

praktisere (prahk-ti-*say*-rer) *v*
practise

praktisk (*prahk*-tisk) *adj* practical; **~**
talt practically

prat (praat) *m/nt* chat

prate (*praa*-ter) *v* chat

preke (*prāy*-ker) *v* preach

preken (*prāy*-kern) *m* sermon

prekestol (*prāy*-ker-stool) *m* pulpit

premie (*prāy*-mi-er) *m* prize

preposisjon (preh-poo-si-*shoon*) *m* preposition

presang (preh-*sahngng*) *m* gift, present

presentasjon (preh-sahng-tah-*shoon*) *m* introduction, presentation

presentere (preh-sahng-*tāy*-rer) *v* present, introduce

president (preh-si-*dehnt*) *m* president

presis (preh-*seess*) *adj* punctual, precise

press (prehss) *nt* pressure

presse (*prehss*-ser) *v* press; squeeze; *c* press

pressekonferanse (*prehss*-ser-koon-feh-rahng-ser) *m* press conference

presserende (preh-*sāy*-rer-ner) *adj* urgent, pressing

prest (prehst) *m* clergyman, parson; rector, minister; **katolsk ~** priest

prestasjon (prehss-tah-*shoon*) *m* feat, achievement

prestegård (*prehss*-ter-gawr) *m* vicarage, parsonage

prestere (prehss-*tāy*-rer) *v* achieve

prestisje (prehss-*tee*-sher) *m* prestige

prevensjonsmiddel (preh-vahng-*shoons*-mi-derl) *nt* (pl -midler) contraceptive

prikk (*prik*) *m* dot

primær (pri-*mæær*) *adj* primary

prins (prins) *m* prince

prinsesse (prin-*sehss*-ser) *c* princess

prinsipp (prin-*sipp*) *nt* principle

prioritet (pri-oo-ri-*tāyt*) *m* priority

pris (preess) *m* cost, price; charge, rate; award

prisfall (*preess*-fahl) *nt* drop in price, slump

prisliste (*preess*-liss-ter) *c* price list

privat (pri-*vaat*) *adj* private

privatliv (pri-*vaat*-leev) *nt* privacy

privilegere (pri-vi-leh-*gāy*-rer) *v* favo(u)r

privilegium (pri-vi-*lāy*-gi-ewm) *nt* (pl -ier) privilege

problem (proo-*blāym*) *nt* problem; question

produksjon (proo-dook-*shoon*) *m* production; output

produkt (proo-*dewkt*) *nt* product; produce

produsent (proo-dew-*sehnt*) *m* producer

produsere (proo-dew-*sāy*-rer) *v* produce

profesjon (proo-feh-*shoon*) *m* profession

profesjonell (proo-feh-shoo-*nehll*) *adj* professional

professor (proo-*fehss*-soor) *m* professor

profet (proo-*fāyt*) *m* prophet

program (proo-*grahmm*) *nt* (pl ~mer) programme

programvare (proo-*grahmm-vaarer*) *m* software

progressiv (*proog*-reh-seev) *adj* progressive

promenade (proo-mer-*naa*-der) *m* promenade

pronomen (proo-*noo*-mern) *nt* pronoun

propaganda (proo-pah-*gahn*-dah) *m* propaganda

propell (proo-*pehll*) *m* propeller

proporsjon (proo-poo-*shoon*) *m* proportion

proppfull (*prop*-fewl) *adj* chock-full

prosent (proo-*sehnt*) *m* percent

prosentsats (proo-*sehnt*-sahts) *m* percentage

prosesjon (proo-seh-*shoon*) *m*
procession

prosess (proo-*sehss*) *m* process

prosjekt (proo-*shehkt*) *nt* project

prosjektør (proo-shehk-*turr*) *m*
spotlight

prospekt (proo-*spehkt*) *nt* prospectus

prospektkort (proo-*spehkt*-kot) *nt* (pl
~) picture postcard, postcard

prostituert (proo-sti-tew-*ayt*) *m*
prostitute

protein (proo-teh-*een*) *nt* protein

protest (proo-*tehst*) *m* protest

protestantisk (proo-ter-*stahn*-tisk)
adj Protestant

protestere (proo-ter-*stay*-rer) *v*
protest; object

protokoll (proo-too-*koll*) *m* record

proviant (proo-vi-*ahnt*) *m* provisions
pl

provins (proo-*vins*) *m* province

provinsiell (proo-vin-si-*ehll*) *adj*
provincial

prute (*prew*-ter) *v* bargain

prøve (*prur*-ver) *v* try, attempt; try on;
rehearse; *c* specimen; test; rehearsal;
på ~ on approval

prøverom (*prur*-ver-room) *nt* (pl ~)
fitting room

psykiater (sew-ki-*aa*-terr) *m*
psychiatrist

psykisk (*sew*-kisk) *adj* psychic

psykoanalytiker (sew-koo-ah-nah-
lewt-ti-kerr) *m* analyst,
psychoanalyst

psykolog (sew-koo-*lawg*) *m*
psychologist

psykologi (sew-koo-loo-*gee*) *m*
psychology

psykologisk (sew-koo-*law*-gisk) *adj*
psychological

publikum (*pewb*-li-kewm) *nt*
audience, public

publisitet (pewb-li-si-*tayt*) *m* publicity

pudder (*pewd*-derr) *nt* powder

puff (pewff) *nt* push

pule (*pew*-ler) *v vulgar* fuck

puls (pewls) *m* pulse

pulsåre (*pewls*-aw-rer) *c* artery

pult (pewlt) *m* desk

pumpe (*poom*-per) *v* pump; *c* pump

pund (pewnn) *nt* pound

pung (poongng) *m* purse; pouch

punkt (poongt) *nt* point; item

punktering (poong-*tay*-ring) *c*
puncture, blow-out; flat tyre

punktert (poong-*tayt*) *adj* punctured

punktlig (*poongt*-li) *adj* punctual

punktum (*pewng*-tewm) *nt* full stop,
period, dot

pur (pewr) *adj* sheer

purpurfarget (*pewr*-pewr-fahr-gert)
adj purple

pusekatt (*pew*-ser-kaht) *m* pussy-cat

pusle (*pewsh*-ler) *v* potter; busy
oneself

puslespill (*pewsh*-ler-spil) *nt* (pl ~)
jigsaw puzzle

pusse (*pewss*-ser) *v* polish

pussig (*pewss*-si) *adj* funny

pust (pewst) *m* breath

puste (*pewss*-ter) *v* breathe; **~ ut**
expire, exhale

pute (*pew*-ter) *c* cushion; pillow; pad

putevar (*pew*-ter-vaar) *nt* (pl ~)
pillow-case

putte (*pewt*-ter) *v* *put

pyjamas (pew-*shaa*-mahss) *m*
pyjamas *pl*

pynt (pewnt) *m* decoration

pynte (pewn-ter) *v* decorate

pytt (pewtt) *m* puddle

pære (*pææ*-rer) *c* pear

pæreholder (*pææ*-rer-hoa-lerr) *m*
socket

pølse (*purl*-ser) *c* sausage

på (paw) *prep* upon, on, at; to

***pådra seg** (*paw*-draa) contract

påfallende (*paw*-fah-ler-ner) *adj*
striking
påfugl (*paw*-fewl) *m* peacock
påkrevd (*paw*-krehvd) *adj* requisite
pålegg (*paw*-lehg) *nt* (pl ~) rise;
sandwich spread, cold cuts
***pålegge** (*paw*-lehg-er) *v* raise,
charge
pålitelig (po-*lee*-ter-li) *adj* sound,
reliable, trustworthy
påske (*pawss*-ker) *c* Easter

påskelilje (*pawss*-ker-lil-ʸer) *c*
daffodil
påskjønne (*paw*-shur-ner) *v*
appreciate
påskudd (*paw*-skewd) *nt* (pl ~)
pretext, pretence
***påstå** (*paw*-staw) *v* claim
***påta seg** (*paw*-taa) *take charge of
påvirke (*paw*-veer-ker) *v* affect,
influence

R

rabalder (rah-*bahl*-derr) *nt* racket
rabarbra (rah-*bahr*-brah) *m* rhubarb
rabatt (rah-*bahtt*) *m* discount, rebate
rabies (*raa*-bi-ehss) *m* rabies
racket (*rehk*-ket) *m* racket
rad (raad) *m* row
radering (rah-*dāy*-ring) *c* etching
radiator (rah-di-*aa*-toor) *m* radiator
radikal (rah-di-*kaal*) *adj* radical
radio (*raa*-di-oo) *m* radio
radius (*raa*-di-ewss) *m* (pl -ier) radius
raffineri (rah-fi-ner-*ree*) *nt* refinery
rak (raak) *adj* straight
rake (*raa*-ker) *c* rake
rakett (rah-*kehtt*) *m* rocket
ramme (*rahm*-mer) *c* frame; *v* *hit
rampe (*rahm*-per) *c* ramp
ran (raan) *nt* robbery
rand (rahnn) *m* (pl render) brim
rane (*raa*-ner) *v* rob
rang (rahngng) *m* rank
ransake (*rahn*-saa-ker) *v* search
ransel (*rahn*-serl) *m* (pl -sler) satchel
ransmann (*raans*-mahn) *m* (pl -menn)
robber
rapphøne (*rahp*-hūr-ner) *c* partridge
rapport (rah-*pott*) *m* report

rapportere (rah-po-*tāy*-rer) *v* report
rar (raar) *adj* odd
rase (*raa*-ser) *m* race; breed; *v* rage;
rase- racial
rasende (*raa*-ser-ner) *adj* mad,
furious
raseri (raa-ser-*ree*) *nt* rage, anger
rasjon (rah-*shōōn*) *m* ration
rask (rahsk) *adj* swift, fast; *nt* trash
raspe (*rahss*-per) *v* grate
rastløs (*rahst*-lūrss) *adj* restless
rastløshet (*rahst*-lūrss-hāyt) *c* unrest
ratt (rahtt) *nt* steering wheel
rattstamme (*raht*-stah-mer) *m*
steering column
rav (raav) *nt* amber
ravn (rahvn) *m* raven
reagere (reh-ah-ga*āy*-rer) *v* react
reaksjon (reh-ahk-*shōōn*) *m* reaction
realisere (reh-ah-li-*sāy*-rer) *v* realize
realistisk (reh-ah-*liss*-tisk) *adj* matter-
of-fact
redaktør (reh-dahk-*tūrr*) *m* editor
redd (rehdd) *adj* afraid; ***være ~** *be
afraid
redde (*rehd*-der) *v* rescue, save
reddik (*rehd*-dik) *m* radish

rede (*ray*-der) *nt* nest

redegjørelse (*ray*-der-*y*ur-rerl-ser) *m* account

redigere (reh-dig-ehrer) *v* edit

redning (*rehd*-ning) *m* rescue

redsel (*reht*-serl) *m* (pl -sler) terror, horror

redselsfull (*reht*-serls-fewl) *adj* awful, horrible

redskap (*rehss*-kaap) *nt* utensil, tool

reduksjon (reh-dewk-*shoon*) *m* reduction

redusere (reh-dew-*say*-rer) *v* reduce

referanse (reh-fer-*rahng*-ser) *m* reference

referat (reh-fer-raat) *nt* minutes

refill (ri-*fill*) *m* (pl ~) refill

refleks (reh-*flehks*) *m* reflection

reflektere (rehf-lehk-*tay*-rer) *v* reflect

reflektor (reh-*flehk*-toor) *m* reflector

Reformasjonen (reh-for-mah-*shoo*-nern) the Reformation

refundere (reh-fewn-*day*-rer) *v* refund

regatta (reh-*gaht*-tah) *m* regatta

regel (*ray*-gerl) *m* (pl regler) rule; regulation; **som ~** in general, as a rule

regelmessig (*ray*-gerl-meh-si) *adj* regular

regent (reh-*gehnt*) *m* ruler

regi (reh-*shee*) *m* direction, staging

regime (reh-*shee*-mer) *nt* régime

regional (reh-gi-oo-*naal*) *adj* regional

regissere (reh-shi-*sai*-rer) *v* direct

regissør (reh-shi-*surr*) *m* director

register (reh-*giss*-terr) *nt* (pl ~, -tre) index

registrere (reh-gi-*stray*-rer) *v* record

registrering (reh-gi-*stray*-ring) *c* registration

registreringsnummer (reh-gi-*stray*-rings-noo-merr) *nt* (pl -numre) registration number; licence number *Am*

regjere (reh-*y*a*y*-rer) *v* govern, rule

regjering (reh-*y*a*y*-ring) *c* government; rule

regjeringstid (reh-*y*a*y*rings-teed) *c* reign

regn (rayn) *nt* rain

regnbue (rayn-*bew*-er) *m* rainbow

regne[1] (*ray*-ner) *v* rain

regne[2] (*ray*-ner) *v* reckon; **~ ut** calculate

regnfrakk (rayn-frahk) *m* raincoat, mackintosh

regnfull (rayn-fewl) *adj* rainy

regning (*ray*-ning) *c* arithmetic; bill; check *nAm*

regnskur (rayn-skoor) *m* shower

regulere (reh-gew-*lay*-rer) *v* regulate

regulering (reh-gew-*lay*-ring) *c* regulation; brace

rehabilitering (reh-hah-bi-li-*tay*-ring) *c* rehabilitation

reinsdyr (rayns-*dewr*) *nt* (pl ~) reindeer

reise[1] (*ray*-ser) *v* travel; *c* voyage, journey, trip; **~ bort** depart

reise[2] (*ray*-ser) *v* erect; **~ seg** *rise

reisebyrå (*ray*-ser-bew-raw) *nt* travel agency, travel agent

reiseforsikring (*ray*-ser-fo-shik-ring) *c* travel insurance

reisehåndbok (*ray*-ser-hon-*book*) *c* (pl -bøker) travel guide

reisende (*ray*-ser-ner) *m* (pl ~) travel(l)er

reiseplan (*ray*-ser-plaan) *m* itinerary

reiserute (*ray*-ser-*rew*-ter) *c* itinerary

reisesjekk (*ray*-ser-shehk) *m* travel(l)er's cheque

reiseutgifter (*ray*-ser-*ewt*-*y*if-terr) *pl* travelling expenses

reke (*ray*-ker) *c* shrimp; prawn

rekke (*rehk*-ker) *c* rank, file; chain

***rekke** (*rehk*-ker) *v* pass, *catch

rekkefølge (*rehk*-ker-fur-ler) *m*

sequence, order

rekkevidde (*rehk*-ker-vi-der) *c* reach; range

rekkverk (*rehk*-værk) *nt* railing

reklame (reh-*klaa*-mer) *m* advertising; commercial

rekommandere (reh-koo-mahn-*dāy*-rer) *v* register

rekord (reh-koord) *m* record

rekreasjon (rehk-reh-ah-*shōōn*) *m* recreation

rekreasjonssenter (reh-kreh-ah-*shōōn*-sehn-terr) *nt* (pl -trer) recreation centre (*Am* center)

rekrutt (rehk-*rewtt*) *m* recruit

rektangel (rehk-*tahng*-ngerl) *nt* (pl -gler) oblong, rectangle

rektangulær (rehk-tahng-gew-*læær*) *adj* rectangular

rektor (*rehk*-toor) *m* headmaster, principal

relativ (*rehl*-lah-teev) *adj* comparative, relative

relieff (reh-li-*ehff*) *nt* relief

religion (reh-li-gi-*ōōn*) *m* religion

religiøs (reh-li-gi-*ūrss*) *adj* religious

relikvie (reh-*leek*-vi-er) *m* relic

rem (rehmm) *c* (pl ~mer) strap

remisse (reh-*miss*-ser) *m* remittance

ren (rāyn) *adj* clean; pure; **gjøre rent** clean

rengjøring (*rāyn*-ʸūr-ring) *c* cleaning

rengjøringsmiddel (*rāyn*-ʸūr-rings-mi-derl) *nt* (pl -midler) detergent

rennestein (*rehn*-ner-stayn) *m* gutter

rense (*rehn*-ser) *v* clean

rensemiddel (*rehn*-ser-mi-derl) *nt* (pl -midler) cleaning fluid

renseri (rehn-ser-*ree*) *nt* dry cleaner's

renslig (*rāyn*-shli) *adj* clean, cleanly

rente (*rehn*-ter) *c* interest

rep (rāyp) *nt* rope

reparasjon (reh-pah-rah-*shōōn*) *m* reparation, repair

reparere (reh-pah-*rāy*-rer) *v* repair; mend, fix

repertoar (reh-peh-too-*aar*) *nt* repertory

reporter (reh-*paw*-terr) *m* reporter

representant (reh-preh-sern-*tahnt*) *m* agent

representasjon (reh-preh-sern-tah-*shōōn*) *m* representation

representativ (reh-preh-*sehn*-tah-teev) *adj* representative

representere (reh-preh-sern-*tāy*-rer) *v* represent

reproduksjon (reh-proo-dewk-*shōōn*) *m* reproduction

reprodusere (reh-proo-dew-*sāy*-rer) *v* reproduce

republikansk (reh-pewb-li-*kaansk*) *adj* republican

republikk (reh-pew-*blikk*) *m* republic

resepsjon (reh-sehp-*shōōn*) *m* reception office

resepsjonist (reh-sehp-*shōōn*-ist) *m* receptionist

resept (reh-*sehpt*) *m* prescription

reservasjon (reh-sær-vah-*shōōn*) *m* reservation, booking

reserve (reh-*sær*-ver) *m* reserve; **reserve-** spare

reservedekk (reh-*sær*-ver-dehk) *nt* (pl ~) spare tyre

reservedel (reh-*sær*-ver-dāyl) *m* spare part

reservehjul (reh-*sær*-ver-ʸēwl) *nt* (pl ~) spare wheel

reservere (reh-sær-*vāy*-rer) *v* reserve; book

reservert (reh-sær-*vāyt*) *adj* reserved

reservoar (reh-sær-voo-*aar*) *nt* reservoir

resirkulerbar (*reh*-seer-kew-*lāyr*-bahr) *adj* recyclable

resirkulere (*reh*-seer-kew-*lāy*-rer) *v* recycle

resonnere (reh-soo-*nay*-rer) v reason

respekt (rehss-*pehkt*) m esteem, respect; regard

respektabel (rehss-pehk-*taa*-berl) adj respectable

respektere (rehss-pehk-*tay*-rer) v respect

respektiv (*rehss*-pehk-teev) adj respective

rest (rehst) m rest; remainder, remnant

restaurant (rehss-tew-*rahngng*) m restaurant

resterende (rehss-*tay*-rer-ner) adj remaining

resultat (reh-sewl-*taat*) nt result; outcome, issue

resultere (reh-sewl-*tay*-rer) v result

resymé (reh-sew-*may*) nt résumé

retning (*reht*-ning) m direction; way

retningslinje (*rehtt*-nings-lin-ʸer) c guideline

retningsnummer (*rehtt*-nings-*noom*-merr) nt area code

rett¹ (rehtt) m dish, course

rett² (rehtt) m law, justice; adj right; appropriate; adv straight; ***ha ~ *be** right; **~ frem** straight on, straight ahead

rette¹ (*reht*-ter) v correct; **med ~** rightly

rette² (*reht*-ter) v direct; **~ mot** aim at

rettelse (*reht*-terl-ser) m correction

rettergang (*reht*-terr-gahng) m trial

rettferdig (reht-*fær*-di) adj just, fair, right

rettferdiggjøre (reht-*fær*-di-ʸ*ūr*-rer) v justify

rettferdighet (reht-*fær*-di-hāyt) c justice

rettighet (*reht*-ti-hāyt) c right

rettslig (*reht*-shli) adj legal

rettssak (*reht*-saak) c lawsuit, trial

returnere (reh-tewr-*nay*-rer) v *send

back

reumatisme (rehv-mah-*tiss*-mer) rheumatism

rev (rāyv) m fox; nt reef

revers (reh-*væshss*) m reverse

revidere (reh-vi-*day*-rer) v revise

revisjon (reh-vi-*shōōn*) m revision

revolusjon (reh-voo-lew-*shōōn*) m revolution

revolusjonær (reh-voo-lew-shoo-*næær*) adj revolutionary

revolver (reh-*vol*-verr) m gun, revolver

revy (reh-*vēw*) m revue

revyteater (reh-*vēw*-teh-aa-terr) nt (pl ~, -tre) music hall

ribbein (*rib*-bayn) nt (pl ~) rib

ridder (*rid*-derr) m knight

*ride (*ree*-der) v *ride

rideskole (*ree*-der-skōō-ler) m riding school

ridning (*reed*-ning) m riding

rift (rift) c tear

rik (reek) adj wealthy, rich

rikdom (*reek*-dom) m (pl ~mer) wealth, riches pl

rike (*reeker*) nt kingdom

rikelig (*ree*-ker-li) adj plentiful; abundant

rikelighet (*reek*-li-hāyt) c plenty

riksvei (*riks*-vay) m highway

riktig (*rik*-ti) adj correct, just, right; proper; adv rather

rim (reem) nt rhyme

rimelig (*ree*-mer-li) adj reasonable

ring (ringng) m ring

ringe (*ring*-nger) v *ring; adj small; v call; ring up, phone; **call up** Am

ringeakt (*ring*-nger-ahkt) m contempt, disdain

ringeklokke (*ring*-nger-klo-ker) c doorbell, bell

ringvei (*ring*-vay) m by-pass

rips (rips) m (pl ~) (red)currant

ris (reess) *m* rice
risikabel (ri-si-*kaa*-berl) *adj* risky; precarious, critical
risikere (ri-si-*kay*-rer) *v* risk
risiko (*riss*-si-koo) *m* risk; hazard, chance
risp (risp) *nt* scratch
rispe (*riss*-per) *v* scratch
rist (rist) *c* grate
riste (*riss*-ter) *v* roast; *shake; toast
rival (ri-*vaal*) *m* rival
rivalisere (ri-vah-li-*say*-rer) *v* rival
rivalitet (ri-vah-li-*tayt*) *m* rivalry
*rive (*ree*-ver) *v* *tear; ~ **i stykker** rip; ~ **ned** demolish
rivjern (*reev*-^yæn) *nt* (pl ~) grater
ro¹ (r$\overline{oo}$) *m* quiet; **falle til** ~ calm down; **roe seg** calm down; ~ **og mak** leisure
ro² (r$\overline{oo}$) *v* row
robust (roo-*bewst*) *adj* robust
robåt (*r$\overline{oo}$*-bawt) *m* rowing boat
rogn (rongn) *c* roe
rolig (*r$\overline{oo}$*-li) *adj* quiet, calm, tranquil; serene
rom (roomm) *nt* room, chamber; space
roman (roo-*maan*) *m* novel
romanforfatter (roo-*maan*-for-faht-terr) *m* novelist
Romania (roo-*maa*-ni-ah) Rumania
romantisk (roo-*mahn*-tisk) *adj* romantic
romerbad (*r$\overline{oo}$*-merr-baad) *nt* (pl ~) Turkish bath
romersk-katolsk (*r$\overline{oo}$*-mersh-kah-t$\overline{oo}$lsk) *adj* Roman Catholic
romferge (*r$\overline{oo}$m*-fær-ger), **romferje** (*r$\overline{oo}$m*-fær-^yer) *c* space shuttle
romme (*room*-mer) *v* contain
rommelig (*room*-mer-li) *adj* spacious, roomy; large
rop (r$\overline{oo}$p) *nt* call, cry; shout
rope (*r$\overline{oo}$*-per) *v* cry, call; shout
ror (r$\overline{oo}$r) *nt* helm, rudder

rorgjenger (*r$\overline{oo}$r*-^yeh-ngerr) *m* helmsman
rormann (*r$\overline{oo}$r*-mahn) *m* (pl -menn) helmsman
ros (r$\overline{oo}$ss) *m* glory, praise
rosa (*r$\overline{oo}$*-sah) *adj* rose
rose (*r$\overline{oo}$*-ser) *c* rose; *v* praise
rosenkrans (*r$\overline{oo}$*-sern-krahns) *m* beads *pl*, rosary
rosenkål (*r$\overline{oo}$*-sern-kawl) *m* sprouts *pl*
rosin (roo-*seen*) *c* raisin
rot¹ (r$\overline{oo}$t) *c* (pl røtter) root
rot² (r$\overline{oo}$t) *nt* muddle, mess
rote (*r$\overline{oo}$*-ter) *v* muddle; ~ **til** mess up
rotte (*rot*-ter) *c* rat
rouge (r$\overline{oo}$sh) *m* rouge
rovdyr (*rawv*-dewr) *nt* (pl ~) beast of prey
ru (r$\overline{ew}$) *adj* rough; harsh
rubin (rew-*been*) *c* ruby
rubrikk (rew-*brikk*) *m* column
ruin (rew-*een*) *m* ruins
rulett (rew-*lehtt*) *m* roulette
rull (rewll) *m* roll
rulle (*rewl*-ler) *v* roll
rullegardin (*rewl*-ler-gah-deen) *m/nt* blind
rulleskøyteløping (rewl-ler-shur^{ew}-ter-l$\overline{oo}$p-ing) *c* roller-skating
rullestein (*rewl*-ler-stayn) *m* boulder
rullestol (*rewl*-ler-st$\overline{oo}$l) *m* wheelchair
rulletrapp (*rewl*-ler-trahp) *c* escalator
rumener (roo-*may*-nerr) *m* Rumanian
rumensk (roo-*maynsk*) *adj* Rumanian
rumpeballe (*room*-per-bah-ler) *m* buttock
rund (rewnn) *adj* round
runde (*rewn*-der) *m* round; lap
rundhåndet (*rewn*-ho-nert) *adj* generous
rundkjøring (*rewn*-kh$\overline{ew}$r-ring) *c* roundabout
rundreise (*rewn*-ray-ser) *c* tour

rundspørring (*rewn*-spur-ring) *c*
enquiry; poll

rundstykke (*rewn*-stew-ker) *nt* roll;
bun *nAm*

rundt (rewnt) *prep* about; *adv* around

rushtid (*rursh*-teed) *m* rush hour,
peak hour

russer (*rewss*-serr) *m* Russian

russisk (*rewss*-sisk) *adj* Russian

Russland (*rewss*-lahn) Russia

rust (rewst) *m* rust

rusten (*rewss*-tern) *adj* rusty

rustning (*rewst*-ning) *m* armour

rute (*rēw*-ter) *c* check; pane; route

ruteplan (*rēw*-ter-plaan) *m* schedule

rutet (*rēw*-tert) *adj* chequered

rutine (rew-*tee*-ner) *m* routine

rutsjebane (*rewt*-sher-baa-ner) *m*
slide

rydde opp (*rewd*-der) tidy up

rydde vekk (*rewd*-der vehkk) *put
away

rye (*rēw*-er) *c* rug

rygg (rewgg) *m* back

rygge (*rewg*-ger) *v* reverse

ryggrad (*rewg*-raad) *m* spine,
backbone

ryggsekk (*rewg*-sehk) *m* knapsack,
rucksack

ryggsmerter (*rewg*-smæ-terr) *pl*
backache

rykk (rewkk) *nt* wrench, tug

rykte (*rewk*-ter) *nt* rumour;
reputation, fame

rynke (*rewng*-ker) *c* wrinkle; crease

ryste (*rewss*-ter) *v* *shake

rytme (*rewt*-mer) *m* rhythm

rytter (*rewt*-terr) *m* horseman, rider

rød (*rūr*) *adj* red

rødbete (*rūr*-bāy-ter) *c* beetroot

rødme (*rurd*-mer) *v* blush

rødspette (*rūr*-speh-ter) *c* plaice

rødstrupe (*rūr*-strēw-per) *m* robin

røkelse (*rūr*-kerl-ser) *m* incense

rømling (*rurm*-ling) *m* runaway

rømme[1] (*rurm*-mer) *m* sour cream

rømme[2] (*rurm*-mer) *v* escape, flee

røntgenbilde (*rurnt*-kern-bil-der) *nt*
X-ray

røntgenfotografere (*rurnt*-kern-foo-
too-grah-fāy-rer) *v* X-ray

røpe (*rūr*-per) *v* *give away

rør (rūrr) *nt* tube, pipe; cane

røre (*rūr*-rer) *v* touch; stir; ~ seg move

rørende (*rūr*-rer-ner) *adj* touching

rørlegger (*rūr*-leh-gerr) *m* plumber

røyk (rur^(ew)k) *m* smoke

røyke (rur^(ew)-ker) *v* smoke; **røyking
forbudt** no smoking

røykekupé (rur^(ew)-ker-kew-pāy) *m*
smoking compartment, smoker

røyker (rur^(ew)-kerr) *m* smoker

rå (raw) *adj* raw

råd (rawd) *nt* advice; counsel, council;
*ha ~ til *can afford

råde (*raw*-der) *v* advise

rådgiver (*rawd*-^yee-verr) *m*
counsellor

rådhus (*rawd*-hēwss) *nt* (pl ~) town
hall

rådslagning (*rawd*-shlaag-ning) *m*
deliberation

***rådslå** (*rawd*-shlaw) *v* deliberate

rådsmedlem (*rawds*-māyd-lerm) *nt*
(pl ~mer) councillor

***rådspørre** (*rawd*-spur-rer) *v* consult

råmateriale (*raw*-mah-ter-ri-aa-ler) *nt*
raw material

råtten (*rot*-tern) *adj* rotten

S

safe (sayf) *m* safe

safir (sah-*feer*) *m* sapphire

saft (sahft) *c* juice

saftig (*sahf*-ti) *adj* juicy

sag (saag) *c* saw

sagbruk (*saag*-brōōk) *nt* (pl ~) sawmill

sagflis (*saag*-fleess) *c* sawdust

sak (saak) *c* matter, cause; case; issue

sakfører (*saak*-fūr-rerr) *m* solicitor

sakkyndig (*saak*-khewn-di) *adj* expert

saks (sahks) *c* scissors *pl*

sakte (*sahk*-ter) *adj* slow

sal (saal) *m* hall; saddle

salat (sah-*laat*) *m* salad, lettuce

saldo (*sahl*-doo) *m* balance

salg (sahlg) *nt* sale; **til salgs** for sale; **salgsfremmende tiltak** sales promotion

salgbar (*sahlg*-baar) *adj* saleable

salme (*sahl*-mer) *m* hymn

salmiakk (sahl-mi-*ahkk*) *m* ammonia

salong (sah-*longng*) *m* salon; lounge, drawing room

salt (sahlt) *nt* salt; *adj* salty

saltkar (*sahlt*-kaar) *nt* (pl ~) salt cellar, salt shaker Am

salve (*sahl*-ver) *c* ointment, salve

samarbeid (*sahm*-mahr-bayd) *nt* co-operation

samarbeide (*sahm*-mahr-bay-der) *v* collaborate

samarbeidsvillig (*sahm*-mahr-bayds-vi-li) *adj* co-operative

same (*saa*-mer) *m* Saami (aborigines of Northern Scandinavia)

samfunn (*sahm*-fewn) *nt* (pl ~) society; community; **samfunns-** social

samle (*sahm*-ler) *v* collect, gather; assemble; compile; ~ **inn** collect

samler (*sahm*-lerr) *m* collector

samles (*sahm*-lerss) *v* gather

samling (*sahm*-ling) *c* collection

samme (*sahm*-mer) *adj* same

sammen (*sahm*-mern) *adv* together

sammendrag (*sahm*-mern-draag) *nt* (pl ~) summary

sammenføye (*sahm*-mern-fur^(ew)-er) *v* join

sammenheng (*sahm*-mern-hehng) *m* connection; coherence

sammenkomst (*sahm*-mern-komst) *m* meeting, assembly

sammenligne (*sahm*-mern-ling-ner) *v* compare

sammenligning (*sahm*-mern-ling-ning) *m* comparison; **uten ~** by far

sammensetning (*sahm*-mern-seht-ning) *m* composition

sammensmeltning (*sahm*-mern-smehlt-ning) *m* merger

sammenstille (*sahm*-mern-sti-ler) *v* combine

sammenstøt (sahm-mern-st*ūr*t) *nt* (pl ~) collision

sammenvergelse (*sahm*-mern-svær-gerl-ser) *m* plot

sammensverge seg (*sahm*-mern-svær-ger) conspire

sammentreff (sahm-mern-trehf) *nt* (pl ~) coincidence

samordne (*sahm*-mor-dner) *v* co-ordinate

samtale (*sahm*-taa-ler) *m* talk, conversation; discussion

samtidig[1] (*sahm*-tee-di) *adj* simultaneous; contemporary; *adv* simultaneously

samtidig[2] (*sahm*-tee-di) *m* (pl ~e) contemporary

samtykke (*sahm*-tew-ker) *v* consent; *nt* consent

samvittighet (sahm-*vit*-ti-hāyt) *c*

conscience

sanatorium (sah-nah-*tōō*-ri-ewm) *nt* (pl -ier) sanatorium

sand (sahnn) *m* sand

sandal (sahn-*daal*) *m* sandal

sanddyne (*sahn*-dēw-ner) *c* dune

sandet (*sahn*-nert) *adj* sandy

sandpapir (*sahn*-pah-peer) *nt* sandpaper

sang (sahngng) *m* song

sanger (*sahng*-ngerr) *m* vocalist, singer

sanitetsbind (sah-ni-*tāyts*-bin) *nt* (pl ~) sanitary towel

sanitær (sah-ni-*tæær*) *adj* sanitary

sann (sahnn) *adj* true

sannferdig (sahn-*fær*-di) *adj* truthful

sannhet (*sahn*-hāyt) *c* truth

sannsynlig (sahn-*sēwn*-li) *adj* probable, likely

sannsynligvis (sahn-*sēwn*-li-veess) *adv* probably

sans (sahns) *m* sense

sardin (sah-*deen*) *m* sardine

satellitt (sah-ter-*litt*) *m* satellite; **~-TV** satellite tv

satellittoverføring (sah-ter-*litt*-aw-verr-*fūr*-ing) *c* satellite television

sateng (sah-*tehngng*) *m* satin

sau (sou) *m* sheep

Saudi-Arabia (*sou*-di-ah-rah-bi-ah) Saudi Arabia

saudiarabisk (*sou*-di-ah-raa-bisk) *adj* Saudi Arabian

saus (souss) *m* sauce

savn (sahvn) *nt* lack

savne (*sahv*-ner) *v* miss; lack; **savnet person** missing person

scene (*sāy*-ner) *m* stage; scene; shot

*se (sāy) *v* *see; look; notice; **~ opp** look out; **~ på** look at; **~ ut** look

sebra (*sāyb*-rah) *m* zebra

seder (*sāy*-derr) *pl* customs; morals

sedvane (*sāyd*-vaa-ner) *m* usage

sedvanlig (sehd-*vaan*-li) *adj* customary

seer (*sāy*-err) *m* spectator

seg (say) *pron* himself, herself, itself, oneself; themselves

segl (sayl) *nt* seal

seier (*say*-err) *m* victory

seig (say) *adj* tough

seil (sayl) *nt* sail

seilbar (*sayl*-baar) *adj* navigable

seilbåt (*sayl*-bawt) *m* sailing boat

seilduk (*sayl*-dēwk) *m* canvas

seile (*say*-ler) *v* sail

seilforening (*sayl*-fo-rāy-ning) *c* yacht club

seilsport (*sayl*-spot) *m* yachting

sekk (sehkk) *m* sack

sekretær (sehk-rer-*tæær*) *m* secretary; clerk

seks (sehks) *num* six

seksjon (sehk-*shōōn*) *m* section

seksten (*sayss*-tern) *num* sixteen

sekstende (*sayss*-ter-ner) *num* sixteenth

seksti (*sehks*-ti) *num* sixty

seksualitet (sehk-sew-ah-li-*tāyt*) *m* sexuality

seksuell (sehk-sew-*ehll*) *adj* sexual

sekund (seh-*kewnn*) *nt* second

sekundær (seh-kewn-*dæær*) *adj* secondary; subordinate

sel (sāyl) *m* seal

*selge (*sehl*-ler) *v* *sell

selleri (seh-ler-*ree*) *m* celery

selskap (*sehl*-skaap) *nt* party, company; society

selskapsantrekk (*sehl*-skaap-sahn-trehk) *nt* (pl ~) evening dress

selters (*sehl*-tersh) *m* soda water

selv (sehll) *pron* myself, yourself, herself, himself, itself, oneself, ourselves, yourselves, themselves; self, selves; **~ om** though, although

selvbetjening (*sehl*-beh-t^yāy-ning) *c*

self-service

selvbetjeningsvaskeri (*sehl*-beht^yay-nings-vahss-ker-ree) *nt*
launderette

selvfølgelig (sehl-*furl*-ger-li) *adv*
naturally, of course

selvgod (*sehl*-goo) *adj* conceited

selvisk (*sehl*-visk) *adj* selfish

selvmord (*sehl*-moord) *nt* (pl ~)
suicide

selvopptatt (*sehl*-lop-taht) *adj* self-centered *Am*, self-centred

selvstendig (sehl-*stehn*-di) *adj*
independent; self-employed

selvstyre (*sayl*-stew-rer) *nt* self-government

selvstyrt (*sehl*-stewt) *adj* autonomous

sement (seh-*mehnt*) *m* cement

semikolon (seh-mi-*koo*-lon) *nt* semicolon

sen (sayn) *adj* late; **for sent** too late;
senere afterwards

senat (seh-*naat*) *nt* senate

senator (seh-*naa*-toor) *m* senator

sende (*sehn*-ner) *v* *send; transmit; ~
av sted** dispatch, *send off; ~ bort**
dismiss; **~ tilbake** *send back

sendemann (*sehn*-ner-mahn) *m* (pl
-menn) envoy

sender (*sehn*-nerr) *m* transmitter

sending (*sehn*-ning) *c* consignment;
transmission

sene (*say*-ner) *c* sinew, tendon

seng (sehngng) *c* bed

sengeteppe (*sehng*-nger-teh-per) *nt*
bedspread

sengetøy (*sehng*-nger-tur^{ew}) *nt*
bedding

senil (seh-*neel*) *adj* senile

senit (*say*-nit) *nt* zenith

senke (*sehng*-ker) *v* lower

sennep (*sehn*-nerp) *m* mustard

sensasjon (sehn-sah-*shoon*) *m*
sensation

sensasjonell (sehn-sah-shoo-*nehll*)
adj sensational

sensur (sehn-*sewr*) *m* censorship

sentimental (sehn-ti-mehn-*taal*) *adj*
sentimental

sentral (sehn-*traal*) *adj* central

sentralbord (sehn-*traal*-boor) *nt* (pl
~) switchboard

sentralfyring (sehn-*traal*-few-ring) *c*
central heating

sentralisere (sehn-trah-li-*say*-rer) *v*
centralize

sentralstasjon (sehn-*traal*-stah-shoon) *m* central station

sentrum (*sehn*-trewm) *nt* (pl -ra) town
center *Am*, town centre, center *Am*,
centre

separat (seh-pah-*raat*) *adv* apart,
separately

separere (seh-pah-*ray*-rer) *v* separate

september (sehp-*tehm*-berr)
September

septisk (*sehp*-tisk) *adj* septic

seremoni (seh-reh-moo-*nee*) *m*
ceremony

serie (*say*-ri-er) *m* series, sequence

seriøs (seh-ri-*urss*) *adj* serious

serum (*say*-rewm) *nt* (pl sera) serum

servere (sær-*vay*-rer) *v* serve

serveringsavgift (sær-*vay*-ring-saav-^yift) *c* service charge

serviett (sær-vi-*ehtt*) *m* napkin,
serviette

servise (sær-*vee*-ser) *nt* dinner service

servitør (sær-vi-*thur*) *m* waiter,
waitress

sesjon (seh-*shoon*) *m* session

sesong (seh-*songng*) *m* season;
utenfor sesongen off season

sesongkort (seh-*song*-kot) *nt* (pl ~)
season ticket

sete (*say*-ter) *nt* seat; chair

setning (*seht*-ning) *m* sentence

sett (sehtt) *nt* set

*sette (*seht*-ter) *v* *lay, place, *set; **~ i gang** launch; **~ inn** insert; **~ i stand** enable; **~ opp** *make up; *draw up; **~ på** turn on; **~ sammen** compose, assemble; **~ seg** *sit down

severdighet (*sāy-vær*-di-hāyt) *c* sight; scenic place

sex (sehks) *m* sex

shorts (shawts) *m* (pl ~) shorts *pl*

*si (see) *v* *say, *tell

siamesisk (si-ah-*māy*-sisk) *adj* Siamese

side (*see*-der) *c* page; side; **på den andre siden** across; **på den andre siden av** across, beyond; **til ~** aside; **til siden** sideways; aside; **ved siden av** next to, beside

sidegate (*see*-der-gaa-ter) *c* sidestreet

siden (*see*-dern) *adv* since; *prep* since; *conj* since; **for ... siden** ago

siffer (*sif*-ferr) *nt* (pl ~, sifre) digit

sigar (si-*gaar*) *m* cigar

sigarett (si-gah-*rehtt*) *m* cigarette

sigarettetui (si-gah-*reht*-teh-tew-ee) *nt* cigarette case

sigarettobakk (si-gah-*reht*-too-bahk) *m* cigarette tobacco

signal (sing-naal) *nt* signal

signalement (sing-nah-ler-*mahngng*) *nt* description

signalere (sing-nah-*lāy*-rer) *v* signal

signatur (sing-nah-*tewr*) *m* signature

sikker (*sik*-kerr) *adj* secure, safe; certain, sure

sikkert (*sik*-kerrt) *adv* certainly

sikkerhet (*sik*-kerr-hāyt) *c* security, safety

sikkerhetsbelte (*sik*-kerr-hāyts-behl-ter) *nt* seat belt, safety belt

sikkerhetsforanstaltning (*sik*-kerr-hāyts-fo-rahn-stahlt-ning) *m* precaution

sikkerhetsnål (*sik*-kerr-hāyts-nawl) *c* safety pin

sikkert (*sik*-kert) *adv* surely; **helt ~** without fail

sikre seg (*sik*-rer) secure

sikring (*sik*-ring) *c* fuse

sikt (sikt) *m* visibility

sikte[1] (*sik*-ter) *nt* aim; ***ta ~ på** aim at

sikte[2] (*sik*-ter) *v* aim; **~ på** aim at

sil (seel) *m* sieve, strainer

sild (sill) *c* (pl ~) herring

sile (*see*-ler) *v* strain

silke (*sil*-ker) *m* silk

simpel (*sim*-perl) *adj* common; vulgar

simpelthen (*sim*-pehlt-hehn) *adv* simply

simulere (si-mew-*lāy*-rer) *v* simulate

sindig (*sin*-di) *adj* sedate, soberminded

sink (singk) *m* zinc

sinke (*sing*-ker) *v* impede

sinn (sinn) *nt* mind

sinne (*sin*-ner) *nt* anger, temper

sinnsbevegelse (*sins*-beh-vāy-gerl-ser) *m* emotion

sinnsforvirring (*sins*-for-vi-ring) *c* insanity

sinnssyk (*sin*-sēwk) *adj* insane, mad, crazy

sint (sint) *adj* cross, angry

sirene (si-*rāy*-ner) *c* siren

siriss (si-*riss*) *m* cricket

sirkel (*seer*-kerl) *m* (pl -kler) circle

sirkulasjon (seer-kew-lah-*shōōn*) *m* circulation

sirkus (*seer*-kewss) *nt* circus

sirup (*seer*-rewp) *m* syrup

sist (sist) *adj* last

siste (*siss*-ter) *adj* ultimate; **i det ~** lately

sitat (si-*taat*) *nt* quotation

sitere (si-*tāy*-rer) *v* quote

sitron (si-*trōōn*) *m* lemon

*sitte (*sit*-ter) *v* *sit

sitteplass (*sit*-ter-plahss) *m* seat

situasjon (si-tew-ah-*shōōn*) *m*

position, situation
siv (seev) *nt* rush, reed
sivil (si-*veel*) *adj* civil; civilian
sivilisasjon (si-vi-li-sah-*shōōn*) *m* civilization
sivilisert (si-vi-li-*sāyt*) *adj* civilized
sivilperson (si-*veel*-pæ-shōōn) *m* civilian
sivilrett (si-*veel*-reht) *m* civil law
sjakk (shahkk) *m* chess; **sjakk!** check!
sjakkbonde (*shahk*-boo-ner) *m* (pl -bønder) pawn
sjakkbrett (*shahk*-breht) *nt* (pl ~) chessboard; checkerboard *nAm*
sjal (shaal) *nt* shawl
sjalu (shah-*lēw*) *adj* jealous; envious
sjalusi (shah-lew-*see*) *m* jealousy
sjampinjong (shahm-pin-*ʸongng*) *m* mushroom
sjampo (*shahm*-poo) *m* shampoo
sjanse (*shahng*-ser) *m* chance
sjargong (*shaa*-gongng) *m* slang; jargon
sjarlatan (*shaa*-lah-tahn) *m* quack
sjarm (shahrm) *m* charm; glamour, attraction
sjarmerende (shahr-*māy*-rer-ner) *adj* charming
sjef (shāyf) *m* manager, boss, chief
sjekk (shehkk) *m* cheque; check *nAm*
sjekke (*shehk*-ker) *v* check
sjel (shāyl) *c* soul
sjelden (*shehl*-dern) *adv* rarely, seldom; *adj* rare, uncommon, infrequent
sjenere (sheh-*nāy*-rer) *v* embarrass
sjenert (sheh-*nāyt*) *adj* shy
sjenerthet (sheh-*nāyt*-hāyt) *c* timidity
sjetong (sheh-*tong*) *m* token
sjette (*sheht*-ter) *num* sixth
sjofel (*shōōf*-erl) *adj* mean
sjokk (shokk) *nt* shock
sjokkere (sho-*kāy*-rer) *v* shock
sjokkerende (sho-*kāy*-rer-ner) *adj* shocking

sjokolade (shoo-koo-*laa*-der) *m* chocolate
sju (shēw) *num* seven
sjuende (*shēw*-er-ner) *num* seventh
sjusket (*shewss*-kert) *adj* slovenly
sjø (shūr) *m* sea
sjøfugl (*shūr*-fēwl) *m* sea-bird
sjøkart (*shūr*kahrt) *nt* chart
sjømann (*shūr*-mahn) *m* (pl -menn) sailor, seaman
sjøpinnsvin (*shūr*-pin-sveen) *nt* (pl ~) sea urchin
sjøreise (*shūr*-ray-ser) *c* cruise
sjørøver (*shūr*-rūr-verr) *m* pirate
sjøsetning (*shūr*-seht-ning) *m* launching
sjøsyk (*shūr*-sēwk) *adj* seasick
sjøsyke (*shūr*-sēw-ker) *m* seasickness
sjøvann (*shūr*-vahn) *nt* sea water
sjåfør (sho-*fūrr*) *m* chauffeur
skade (*skaa*-der) *m* injury, damage; harm, mischief; *v* *hurt, harm, injure; damage
skadelig (*skaa*-der-li) *adj* harmful, hurtful
skadeserstatning (*skaa*-der-sææsh-taht-ning) *m* compensation, indemnity
skadet (*skaa*-dert) *adj* injured
skaffe (*skahf*-fer) *v* provide, furnish
skaft (skahft) *nt* handle
skala (*skaa*-lah) *m* scale
skall (skahll) *nt* shell; skin
skalldyr (*skahl*-dēwr) *nt* (pl ~) shellfish
skalle (*skahl*-ler) *m* skull
skallet (*skahl*-lert) *adj* bald
skam (skahmm) *c* shame, disgrace
skamfull (*skahm*-fewl) *adj* ashamed
skamme seg (*skahm*-mer) *be ashamed
skandale (skahn-*daa*-ler) *m* scandal
skandinav (skahn-di-*naav*) *m*

Scandinavian

Skandinavia (skahn-di-*naa*-vi-ah)
Scandinavia

skandinavisk (skahn-di-*naa*-visk) *adj*
Scandinavian

skap (skaap) *nt* cupboard; closet;
locker

skape (*skaaper*) *v* create

skapende (*skaa*-pene) *adj* creative

skapning (*skaap*-ning) *m* creature

skarlagenrød (skah-*laa*-gern-rur) *adj*
scarlet

skarp (skahrp) *adj* sharp; keen; bright

skatt (skahtt) *m* treasure; tax; darling

skattefri (*skaht*-ter-free) *adj* tax-free

***skattlegge** (*skaht*-leh-ger) *v* tax

ski (shee) *c* (pl ~) ski; ***gå på ~** ski

skibukse (*shee*-book-ser) *c* ski pants

skifer (*shee*-ferr) *m* slate

skift (shift) *nt* shift

skifte (*shif*-ter) *v* switch; change

skiftenøkkel (*shif*-ter-nur-kerl) *m* (pl
-nøkler) spanner; monkey wrench *Am*

skiheis (*shee*-hayss) *m* ski lift

skihopp (*shee*-hop) *nt* (pl ~) ski jump

skikk (shikk) *m* custom

skikkelse (*shi*-kerl-ser) *m* figure

skille (*shil*-ler) *v* separate, part; divide

skilles (*shil*-lerss) *v* divorce

skillevegg (*shil*-ler-vehg) *m* partition

skillevei (*shil*-ler-vay) *m* road fork

skilpadde (*shil*-pah-der) *c* turtle

skilsmisse (*shils*-mi-ser) *m* divorce

skiløper (*shee*-lūr-perr) *m* skier

skiløping (*shee*-lūr-ping) *c* skiing

skimte (*shim*-ter) *v* glimpse

skinke (*shing*-ker) *c* ham

skinn (shinn) *nt* skin; hide; glare;
semsket ~ suede; **skinn-** leather

skinne[1] (*shin*-ner) *v* *shine

skinne[2] (*shin*-ner) *c* rail; track

skinnende (*shin*-ner-ner) *adj* bright

skinnhellig (*shin*-heh-li) *adj*
hypocritical

skip (sheep) *nt* boat, ship

skipe (*shee*-per) *v* ship

skipsfart (*ships*-faht) *m* navigation,
navigation; shipping

skipsreder (*ships*-rāy-derr) *m*
shipowner

skipsverft (*ships*-værft) *nt* shipyard

skisse (*shiss*-ser) *c* sketch

skissere (shi-*sāy*-rer) *v* sketch

skistaver (*shee*-staa-verr) *pl* ski sticks;
ski poles *Am*

skistøvler (*shee*-sturv-lerr) *pl* ski
boots

skitt (shitt) *m* dirt

skitten (*shit*-tern) *adj* filthy, dirty, foul;
soiled

skive (*shee*-ver) *c* disc; slice

skiveprolaps (*shee*-ver-pro-lahps) *m*
slipped disc

skje[1] (shāy) *v* occur, happen

skje[2] (shāy) *c* spoon

skjebne (*shāyb*-ner) *m* destiny, fate;
fortune, luck

skjebnesvanger (*shāyb*-ner-svah-
ngerr) *adj* fatal

skjefull (*shāy*-fewl) *m* spoonful

skjegg (shehgg) *nt* beard

skjelett (sheh-*lehtt*) *nt* skeleton

skjell (shehll) *nt* shell, sea-shell; scale

skjelle (*shehl*-ler) *v* scold; **~ ut** call
names

skjelne (*shehl*-ner) *v* distinguish

***skjelve** (*shehl*-ver) *v* tremble, shiver

skjeløyd (*shāyl*-ur^(ew)d) *adj* cross-eyed

skjema (*shāy*-mah) *nt* scheme; form

skjemme bort (*shehm*-mer boot)
*spoil

skjenke (*shehng*-ker) *v* pour; donate

skjenne på (*shehn*-ner) *v* scold

skjerf (shærf) *nt* scarf

skjerm (shærm) *m* screen

skjermbrett (*shærm*-breht) *nt* folding
screen

skjev (shāyv) *adj* slanting

skjorte (*shoot*-ter) *c* shirt
skjul (*shewl*) *nt* cover
skjule (*shew*-ler) *v* *hide, conceal
skjær (*shæær*) *adj* sheer; *nt* rock
skjære (*shææ*-rer) *c* magpie
*skjære (*shææ*-rer) *v* *cut; carve; ~ av
*cut off; ~ i carve; ~ ned *cut; ~ ut
carve
skjødesløs (*shūr*-derss-lūrss) *adj*
careless
skjønn (shurnn) *adj* wonderful, lovely
skjønne (*shurn*-ner) *v* *understand,
*see
skjønnhet (*shurn*-hāyt) *c* beauty
skjønnhetspleie (*shurn*-hāyts-play-
er) *m* beauty treatment
skjønnhetssalong (*shurn*-hāyt-sah-
long) *m* beauty parlo(u)r, beauty
salon
skjønt (shurnt) *conj* though, although
skjør (shūrr) *adj* fragile
skjørt (shurtt) *nt* skirt
skjøteledning (*shūr*-ter-lāyd-ning) *m*
extension cord
skli (sklee) *v* slip
sko (skoo) *m* (pl ~) shoe
skog (skoog) *m* wood, forest
skogkledd (*skoog*-klehd) *adj* wooded
skogsområde (*skoogs*-oom-raw-der)
nt woodland
skokrem (*skoo*-krāym) *m* shoe polish
skole (*skoo*-ler) *m* school;
videregående ~ secondary school
skolebestyrer (*skoo*-ler-beh-stēw-
rerr) *m* principal
skolegutt (*skoo*-ler-gewt) *m*
schoolboy
skolepike (*skoo*-ler-pee-ker) *m*
schoolgirl
skolisse (*skoo*-li-ser) *c* shoe-lace
skomaker (*skoo*-maa-kerr) *m*
shoemaker
skorpe (*skor*-per) *c* crust
skorstein (*skosh*-tayn) *m* chimney

skotsk (skotsk) *adj* Scottish, Scotch
skotte (*skot*-ter) *m* Scot
Skottland (*skot*-lahn) Scotland
skotøy (*skoo*-tur^(ew)) *nt* footwear
skotøyforretning (*skoo*-tur^(ew)-fo-reht-
ning) *c* shoe shop
skramme (*skrahm*-mer) *c* scratch
skrap (skraap) *nt* junk
skrape (*skraa*-per) *v* scrape, scratch
skravle (*skrahv*-ler) *v* chat
skravlebøtte (*skrahv*-ler-bur-ter) *c*
chatterbox
skredder (*skrehd*-derr) *m* tailor
skreddersydd (*skrehd*-der-shewd)
adj tailor-made
skrekk (skrehkk) *m* fright
skrekkelig (*skreh*-ker-li) *adj* horrible,
grim
skrell (skrehll) *nt* peel
skrelle (*skrehl*-ler) *v* peel
skremme (*skrehm*-mer) *v* scare,
terrify
skremmende (*skrehm*-mer-ner) *adj*
terrifying
skremt (skrehmt) *adj* frightened
skrifte (*skrif*-ter) *v* confess
skriftemål (*skrif*-ter-mawl) *nt* (pl ~)
confession
skriftlig (*skrift*-li) *adj* in writing;
written
skrik (skreek) *nt* scream, cry
*skrike (*skree*-ker) *v* shout, scream,
cry; shriek
skritt (skritt) *nt* step, pace, move
*skrive (*skree*-ver) *v* *write; ~ inn
book; ~ ned *write down; ~ på data
type; ~ seg inn check in; ~ ut print
out
skriveblokk (*skree*-ver-blok) *c*;
writing pad
skrivebord (*skree*-ver-boor) *nt* desk,
bureau
skrivemaskin (*skree*-ver-mah-sheen)
m typewriter

skrivemaskinpapir (*skree*-ver-mah-sheen-pah-peer) *nt* typing paper

skrivepapir (*skree*-ver-pah-peer) *nt* writing paper

skriver (*skree*-verr) *m* printer

skru (skr$\overline{ew}$) *v* screw; ~ **av** turn off; ~ **på** turn on

skrubbe (*skrewb*-ber) *v* scrub

skrubbsår (*skrewb*-sawr) *nt* (pl ~) graze

skrue (*skr$\overline{ew}$*-er) *m* screw

skruestikke (*skr$\overline{ew}$*-er-sti-ker) *m* clamp

skrujern (*skr$\overline{ew}$*-ʸææn) *nt* (pl ~) screwdriver

skrukke (*skrook*-ker) *v* crease

skrunøkkel (*skr$\overline{ew}$*-nur-kerl) *m* (pl -nøkler) wrench

*skryte (*skr$\overline{ew}$*-ter) *v* boast

skrøne (*skr$\overline{ur}$*-ner) *v* *tell tall tales

skrøpelig (*skr$\overline{ur}$*-per-li) *adj* fragile

skrå (skraw) *adj* slanting

skråne (*skraw*-ner) *v* slant

skrånende (*skraw*-ner-ner) *adj* sloping, slanting

skråning (*skraw*-ning) *m* incline, slope

skudd (skewdd) *nt* shot

skuddår (*skewd*-dawr) *nt* (pl ~) leap year

skue (*sk$\overline{oo}$*-er) *nt* sight

skuespill (*sk$\overline{ew}$*-er-spil) *nt* (pl ~) drama

skuespiller (*sk$\overline{ew}$*-er-spi-lerr) *m* actor, actress *m*; comedian

skuespillforfatter (*sk$\overline{ew}$*-er-spil-for-fah-terr) *m* playwright

skuff (skooff) *m* drawer

skuffe (*skewf*-fer) *v* disappoint; ***være skuffet** *be disappointed

skuffelse (*skewf*-ferl-ser) *m* disappointment

skulder (*skewl*-derr) *c* (pl -drer) shoulder

skulke (*skewl*-ker) *v* play truant

*skulle (*skewl*-ler) *v* *shall; *should

skulptur (skewlp-*t$\overline{ew}$r*) *m* sculpture

skum (skoomm) *nt* froth, foam, lather

skumgummi (*skoom*-gew-mi) *m* foam rubber

skumme (*skoom*-mer) *v* foam

skumring (*skoom*-ring) *c* twilight

skur (sk$\overline{ew}$r) *nt* shed; *m* shower

skurd (skewrd) *m* carving

skurk (skewrk) *m* bastard, villain, rascal

skvette (*skveht*-ter) *v* splash

sky (sh$\overline{ew}$) *c* cloud; *adj* shy

skyet (*sh$\overline{ew}$*-ert) *adj* cloudy

skyffel (*shewf*-ferl) *m* (pl skyfler) shovel

skygge (*shewg*-ger) *m* shadow, shade

skyggefull (*shewg*-ger-fewl) *adj* shady

skyggelue (*shewg*-er-lew-er) *c* cap

skyhet (*sh$\overline{ew}$*-hāyt) *c* shyness

skyld (shewll) *c* blame, guilt

skylde (*shewl*-ler) *v* owe

skyldig (*shewl*-di) *adj* guilty; due; ***være ~** owe

skylle (*shewl*-ler) rinse

skylling (*shewl*-ling) *c* rinse

skynde seg (*shewn*-ner) hurry, hasten

skyskraper (*sh$\overline{ew}$*-skraa-perr) *m* skyscraper

*skyte (*sh$\overline{ew}$*-ter) *v* fire, *shoot

skyteskive (*sh$\overline{ew}$*-ter-shee-ver) *c* mark, target

*skyve (*sh$\overline{ew}$*-ver) *v* push

skyvedør (*sh$\overline{ew}$*-ver-d$\overline{ew}$r) *c* sliding door

skøyeraktig (*skur^{ew}*-er-rahk-ti) *adj* mischievous

skøyte (*shur^{ew}*-ter) *c* skate; ***gå på skøyter** skate

skøytebane (*shur^{ew}*-ter-baa-ner) *m* skating rink

skøyteløping (*shur^{ew}*-ter-l$\overline{ew}$r-ping) *c* skating

skål (skawl) *c* saucer; *m* toast

sladder (*shlahd*-derr) *m* gossip

sladre (*shlahd*-rer) *v* gossip

slag (shlaag) *nt* blow; smash; breed; battle; lapel

slaganfall (*shlaagahn*-fahl) *nt* (pl ~) stroke

slagord (shlaa-gōōr) *nt* (pl ~) slogan

slags (shlahks) *m/nt* sort; **alle ~** all sorts of

slakter (*shlahk*-terr) *m* butcher

slange (*shlahng*-nger) *m* snake

slang (shlahng) *m* slang

slank (shlahngk) *adj* slender, slim

slanke seg (shlahng-ker) slim

slapp (shlahpp) *adj* limp

slappe av (*shlahp*-per) relax

slave (*shlaa*-ver) *m* slave

slede (*shlay*-er) *m* sleigh, sledge

sleip (shlayp) *adj* slippery

slekt (shlehkt) *m* family; relatives

slektning (*shlehkt*-ning) *m* relation, relative

slem (shlehmm) *adj* naughty, bad

slenge (*shlehng*-nger) *v* *throw

slentre (*shlehn*-trer) *v* stroll

slepe (*shlay*-per) *v* haul, drag

slepebåt (*shlay*-per-bawt) *m* tug

slette (*shleht*-ter) *c* plain

slettvar (*shleht*-vaar) *m* brill

slik (shleek) *pron* such; *adv* thus, so, such; **~ at** so that; **~ som** such as

slikke (*shlik*-ker) *v* lick, lap

slips (shlips) *nt* tie, necktie

***slite** (*shlee*-ter) *v* labo(u)r; **~ ut** wear out

sliten (*shlee*-tern) *adj* weary, worn out

slitt (shlitt) *adj* worn

slokke (*shlook*-ker) *v* *put out, extinguish

slott (shlott) *nt* castle

slu (shlew) *adj* sly, cunning

sludder (*shlewd*-derr) *nt* rubbish

sluke (*shlew*-ker) *v* swallow

slukt (shlewkt) *m* gorge

slum (shlewmm) *m* slum

slump (shloomp) *m* chance; **på ~** by chance

slurk (shlewrk) *m* sip

slurvet (*shlewr*-vert) *adj* sloppy

sluse (*shlew*-ser) *m* lock, sluice

slutning (*shlewt*-ning) *m* conclusion; end

slutt (shlewtt) *m* finish, end; **til ~** at last; eventually

slutte (*shlewt*-ter) *v* finish, end; quit; **~ seg til** join

sluttresultat (*shlewt*-reh-sewl-taat) *nt* final result

slyngel (*shlewng*-ngerl) *m* (pl -gler) rascal

slør (shlürr) *nt* veil

sløse bort (*shlür*-ser boot) waste

sløseri (shlür-ser-*ree*) *nt* waste

sløv (shlürv) *adj* dull, blunt

sløyfe (*shlur*ew-fer) *c* bow; bow tie

slå (shlaw) *m* bolt

***slå** (shlaw) *v* *strike, *beat, *hit; punch; bruise; dial; **~ av** switch off; **hakk i** chip; **~ igjen** slam; **~ i hjel** kill; **~ i stykker** crack; **~ ned** knock down; **~ opp** look up; **~ på** switch on; **~ seg ned** settle down; **~ til** *strike

slående (*shlaw*-er-ner) *adj* striking

***slåss** (shloss) *v* *fight; struggle

smak (smaak) *m* taste; flavo(u)r; ***sette ~ på** flavo(u)r

smake (*smaa*-ker) *v* taste; **~ på** taste

smakløs (smaak-*lürss*) *adj* tasteless

smal (smaal) *adj* narrow

smaragd (smah-*rahgd*) *m* emerald

smart (smaat) *adj* smart, lur

smed (smay) *m* smith

smekke (*smehk*-ker) *v* smack

smell (smehll) *nt* crack

***smelle** (*smehl*-ler) *v* crack

smelte (*smehl*-ter) *v* melt, thaw

smerte (*smæt*-ter) *m* pain; grief,

sorrow

smertefri (*smæt*-ter-free) *adj* painless

smertefull (*smæ*-ter-fool) *adj* painful

smertestillende middel (*smæ*-ter-stil-lene mid-del) *nt* painkiller

*__smette__ (*smeht*-ter) *v* slip

smidig (*smee*-di) *adj* supple

smil (smeel) *nt* smile

smile (*smee*-ler) *v* smile

sminke (*sming*-ker) *c* make-up

smitte (*smit*-ter) *v* infect

smittende (*smi*-ter-ner) *adj* contagious

smittsom (*smit*-som) *adj* infectious, contagious

smoking (*smaw*-king) *m* dinner jacket; tuxedo *nAm*

smug (smewg) *nt* alley, lane

smugle (*smewg*-ler) *v* smuggle

smul (smewl) *adj* smooth

smule (*smew*-ler) *c* crumb; bit

smykke (*smewk*-ker) *nt* piece of jewellery (*Am* jewelry)

smør (smurr) *nt* butter

smørbrød (*smurr*-brur) *nt* (pl ~) open sandwich

*__smøre__ (*smur*-rer) *v* grease; lubricate

smøreolje (*smur*-rer-ol-yer) *c* lubrication oil

smøring (*smur*-ring) *c* lubrication

små (smaw) (pl liten) *adj* small

småbarn (*smaw*-baan) *nt* toddler

smågris (*smaw*-greess) *m* piglet

småkake (*smaw*-kaa-ker) *c* biscuit; cookie *nAm*

smålig (*smaw*-li) *adj* stingy

småpenger (*smaw*-peh-ngerr) *pl* petty cash, change

småstein (*smaw*-stayn) *m* pebble

snakke (*snahk*-ker) *v* *speak, talk

snakkesalig (*snahk*-ker-saa-li) *adj* talkative

snart (snaat) *adv* presently, soon, shortly; **så ~ som** as soon as

snegl (snayl) *m* snail

snekker (*snehk*-kerr) *m* carpenter

snever (*snay*-verr) *adj* narrow, restricted

sneversynt (*snay*-ver-shewnt) *adj* narrow-minded

snikskytter (*sneek*-shew-terr) *m* sniper

snill (snill) *adj* good, nice, kind

snitte (*snit*-ter) *v* *cut, slice

snitsel (*snit*-tsel) *m* cutlet

sno (snoo) *v* twist; **~ seg** *wind

snor (snoor) *c* string; cord

snorke (*snor*-ker) *v* snore

snorkel (*snor*-kerl) *m* (pl -kler) snorkel

snu (snew) *v* turn round; **~ om** invert; **~ seg** turn round

snuble (*snewb*-ler) *v* stumble

snurre (*snewr*-rer) *v* *spin

snute (*snew*-ter) *c* snout

*__snyte__ (*snew*-ter) *v* cheat

snø (snur) *v* snow; *m* snow

snøskred (*snur*-skrayd) *nt* (pl ~) avalanche

snøslaps (*snur*-shlahps) *nt* slush

snøstorm (*snur*-storm) *m* blizzard, snowstorm

sodavann (*soo*-dah-vahn) *nt* soda water

sofa (*soof*-fah) *m* sofa

software (*sooft*-vehr) *m* software

sogn (songn) *nt* parish

sogneprest (*song*-ner-prehst) *m* rector, vicar

sokk (sokk) *m* sock

sol (sool) *c* sun

solbrent (*sool*-brehnt) *adj* sunburned

solbriller (*sool*-bri-lerr) *pl* sun-glasses *pl*

solbær (*sool*-bæær) *nt* (pl ~) black-currant

soldat (sool-*daat*) *m* soldier

sole seg (*soo*-ler) sunbathe

solid (soo-*leed*) *adj* solid, firm

solistkonsert (soo-*list*-koon-sæt) *m* recital

sollys (*sool*-lewss) *nt* sunlight

solnedgang (*sool*-nay-gahng) *m* sunset

sololje (*soo*-lol-Yer) *c* suntan oil

soloppgang (*soo*-lop-gahng) *m* sunrise

solrik (*sool*-reek) *adj* sunny

solseil (*sool*-sayl) *nt* (pl ~) awning

solskinn (*sool*-shin) *nt* sunshine

solstikk (*sool*-stik) *nt* (pl ~) sunstroke

solsystem (*sool*-sewss-*taym*) *nt* solar system

som (somm) *pron* who, that, which; *conj* as; ~ **om** as if

somletog (*soom*-ler-tawg) *nt* (pl ~) slow train; milk train *Am*

sommer (*som*-merr) *m* (pl sommer) summer

sommerfugl (*som*-merr-*fewl*) *m* butterfly

sommertid (*som*-mer-teed) *c* summer time

sone (*soo*-ner) *c* zone

sopp (sopp) *m* mushroom; toadstool

sorg (sorg) *c* sorrow, grief; mourning

sort (sott) *m* kind, sort

sortere (so-*tay*-rer) *v* sort, assort

sortiment (so-ti-*mahngng*) *nt* assortment

sosial (soo-si-*aal*) *adj* social

sosialisme (soo-si-ah-*liss*-mer) *m* socialism

sosialist (soo-si-ah-*list*) *m* socialist

sosialistisk (soo-si-ah-*liss*-tisk) *adj* socialist

sosiologi (soo-si-oo-loo-*gee*) *m* sociology

*sove (*saw*-ver) *v* *sleep

sovende (*saw*-ver-ner) *adj* asleep

sovepille (*saw*-ver-pi-ler) *c* sleeping pill

sovepose (*saw*-ver-*poo*-ser) *m* sleeping bag

sovesal (*saw*-ver-saal) *m* dormitory

sovevogn (*saw*-ver-vongn) *c* sleeping car; Pullman

soveværelse (*saw*-ver-væææ-rerl-ser) *nt* bedroom

sovne (*sov*-ner) *v* *fall asleep

spade (*spaa*-er) *m* spade

spalte (*spahl*-ter) *c* column

spandere (spahn-*day*-rer) *v* *spend

Spania (*spaa*-ni-ah) Spain

spanier (*spaa*-ni-err) *m* Spaniard

spanjol (spahn-Yool) *m* Spaniard

spann (spahnn) *nt* pail, bucket

spansk (spahnsk) *adj* Spanish

spare (*spaa*-rer) *v* save; economize

sparebank (*spaa*-rer-bahngk) *m* savings bank

sparegris (*spaa*-rer-gris) *m* piggy bank

sparepenger (*spaa*-rer-peh-ngerr) *pl* savings *pl*

spark (spahrk) *nt* kick

sparke (*spahr*-ker) *v* kick; ***gi sparken** dismiss

sparsommelig (spaa-*shom*-mer-li) *adj* thrifty, economical

spasere (spah-*say*-rer) *v* walk

spaserstokk (spah-*say*-shtok) *m* walking stick

spasertur (spah-*say*-tewr) *m* stroll, walk

spedalskhet (speh-*daalsk*-hayt) *c* leprosy

spedbarn (*spay*-baan) *nt* (pl ~) infant

speider (*spay*-derr) *m* girl scout; boy scout

speil (spayl) *nt* looking-glass, mirror

speilbilde (*spayl*-bil-der) *nt* reflection

spekulere (speh-kew-*lay*-rer) *v* speculate

spenne (*spayn*-ner) *c* buckle

spennende (*spehn*-ner-ner) *adj*

exciting

spenning (*spehn*-ning) *m* tension; voltage

sperre (*spehr*-rer) *v* block; ~ **inne** lock up

spesialisere seg (speh-si-ah-li-*say*-rer) specialize

spesialist (speh-si-ah-*list*) *m* specialist

spesialitet (speh-si-ah-li-*tayt*) *m* speciality

spesiell (speh-si-*ehll*) *adj* particular, special

spesifikk (speh-si-*fikk*) *adj* specific

spidd (spidd) *nt* spit

spiker (*spee*-kerr) *m* (pl ~, -krer) nail

spill (spill) *nt* game

spille (*spil*-ler) *v* play; act

spillemerke (*spil*-ler-mær-ker) *nt* chip

spiller (*spil*-lerr) *m* player

spillkort (*spil*-kot) *nt* (pl ~) playing card

spillopper (spi-*lop*-perr) *pl* mischief

spinat (spi-*naat*) *m* spinach

spindelvev (*spin*-derl-vayv) *m* (pl ~) spider's web

*spinne (*spin*-ner) *v* *spin

spion (spi-*oon*) *m* spy

spir (speer) *nt* spire

spirituosa (spi-ri-tew-*oo*-sah) *pl* spirits

spise (*spee*-ser) *v* *eat

spisekart (*spee*-ser-kaht) *nt* menu

spiselig (*spee*-ser-li) *adj* edible

spisesal (*spee*-ser-saal) *m* dining room

spiseskje (*spee*-ser-shay) *c* tablespoon

spisestue (*spee*-ser-stew-er) *c* dining room

spisevogn (*spee*-ser-vongn) *c* dining car

spiskammer (*spiss*-kah-merr) *nt* (pl ~, -kamre) larder

spiss (spiss) *adj* pointed, sharp; *m* tip, point

spissborgerlig (*spiss*-bor-ger-li) *adj* bourgeois

spisse (*spiss*-ser) *v* sharpen

splint (splint) *m* splinter

splinter ny (*splin*-terr new) brand-new

spole (*spoo*-ler) *m* spool

spor (spoor) *nt* trace; trail, track

sport (spott) *m* sport

sportsbil (spotsh-beel) *m* sports car

sportsklær (*spotsh*-klær) *pl* sportswear

sprang (sprahng) *nt* jump

spray (spray) *m* atomizer; spray

sprayflaske (*spray*-flahss-ker) *c* atomizer

spre (spray) *v* *spread; scatter; *shed

sprekk (sprehkk) *m* crack

*sprekke (*sprehk*-ker) *v* *burst; crack

sprenge (*sprehng*-er) *v* blow up

sprengstoff (*sprehng*-stof) *nt* explosive

springvann (*spring*-vahn) *nt* (pl ~) fountain

sprit (spreet) *m* liquor

spritapparat (*spree*-tah-pah-raat) *nt* spirit stove

sprut (sprewt) *m* squirt

sprute (*sprewt*-er) *v* squirt; spray

sprø (sprür) *adj* crisp

sprøyte (*sprur*ᵉʷ-ter) *c* syringe; shot

språk (sprawk) *nt* language

spurv (spewrv) *m* sparrow

spyd (spewd) *nt* spear

spytt (spewtt) *nt* spit

spytte (*spewt*-ter) *v* *spit

spøk (spürk) *m* joke

spøkelse (*spür*-kerl-ser) *nt* ghost; spirit, spook

*spørre (*spurr*-rer) *v* ask

spørrelek (*spurr*-rer-layk) *m* quiz

spørsmål (*spursh*-mawl) *nt* (pl ~)

question; matter, issue

spørsmålstegn (*spursh*-mawls-tayn) *nt* (pl ~) question mark

spå (spaw) *v* predict, tell fortunes

sta (staa) *adj* dogged, head-strong, stubborn, pig-headed, obstinate

stabel (staa-berl) *m* (pl -bler) stack

stabil (stah-*beel*) *adj* stable

stable (*stahb*-ler) *v* pile

stadig (staa-di) *adj* continual, frequent

stadion (staa-di-oon) *nt* stadium

stadium (staa-di-ewm) *nt* (pl -ier) stage, phase

stakitt (stah-*kitt*) *nt* picket fence

stall (stahll) *m* stable

stallkar (stahll-kahrr) *m* groom

stamme (*stahm*-mer) *m* trunk; tribe; *v* stammer

stampe (*stahm*-per) *v* stamp

stand[1] (stahnn) *m* (pl stender) state; *gjøre i ~ mend; i ~ til able

stand[2] (stahnn) *m* stand

standard- (*stahn*-dahr) standard

standhaftig (stahn-*hahf*-ti) *adj* steadfast

stang (stahngng) *c* (pl stenger) bar, pole; rod

stanse (*stahn*-ser) *v* stop, halt, pull up

start (staat) *m* take-off; beginning, start

startbane (*staat*-baa-ner) *m* runway

starte (*staht*-ter) *v* start, *begin

stasjon (stah-*shōōn*) *m* station; depot *nAm*

stat (staat) *m* state; **stats-** national

statistikk (stah-ti-*stikk*) *m* statistics *pl*

statsborgerskap (staats-bor-ger-shkaap) *nt* citizenship

statskasse (staats-kahs-ser) *c* treasury

statsminister (staats-mi-niss-terr) *m* (pl ~e, -trer) premier, Prime Minister

statsoverhode (staat-saw-verr-hōō-der) *nt* head of state

statsråd (staats-rawd) *m* minister

statstjenestemann (staats-t³āy-ner-ster-mahn) *m* (pl -menn) civil servant

statue (staa-tew-er) *m* statue

stave (staa-ver) *v* *spell

stavelse (staa-verl-ser) *m* syllable

stavemåte (staa-ver-maw-ter) *m* spelling

stearinlys (steh-ah-*reen*-lēwss) *nt* (pl ~) candle

stebarn (*stāy*-baan) *nt* (pl ~) stepchild

sted (stāy) *nt* spot, site, place; locality

stedfortreder (*stāy*-fo-trāy-derr) *m* substitute; deputy

stedlig (*stāyd*-li) *adj* local; resident

stefar (*stāy*-faar) *m* (pl -fedre) stepfather

steg (stāyg) *nt* step

steil (stayl) *adj* steep

stein (stayn) *m* stone; **stein-** stone

steinbrudd (*stayn*-brewd) *nt* (pl ~) quarry

steinet (stay-nert) *adj* rocky

steintøy (*stayn*-tur³ᵂ) *nt* stoneware, crockery

steke (*stāy*-ker) *v* fry; roast

stekeovn (*stāy*-ker-ovn) *m* oven

stekepanne (*stāy*-ker-pah-ner) *c* frying pan

stemme (*stehm*-mer) *m* voice; vote; *v* vote; ~ **overens** agree

stemmerett (*stehm*-mer-reht) *m* franchise; suffrage

stemning (*stehm*-ning) *m* atmosphere; mood

stemor (*stāy*-mōōr) *c* (pl -mødre) stepmother

stempel (*stehm*-perl) *nt* (pl ~, -pler) stamp; piston

stenge (*stehng*-nger) *v* close; ~ **av** turn off; *cut off; ~ **inne** *shut in

stengt (stehngt) *adj* closed, shut

stereo (*stāyh*-rāyoo) *m* stereo

stereoanlegg (*stayh*-rayoo-ahn-lehg)
  nt stereo (unit)
steril (steh-*reel*) *adj* sterile
sterilisere (steh-ri-li-*say*-rer) *v*
  sterilize
sterk (stærk) *adj* strong; powerful
sti (stee) *m* trail, path
stift (stift) *m* staple
stifte (*stif*-ter) *v* found, institute
stiftelse (*stif*-terl-ser) *m* foundation
stige (*stee*-ger) *m* ladder
***stige** (*stee*-ger) *v* ascend, *rise; ~ av
  *get off; ~ opp ascend; ~ på *get on
stigning (*steeg*-ning) *m* increase;
  ascent
stikk (stikk) *nt* bite, sting; picture,
  engraving
***stikke** (*stik*-ker) *v* *sting
stikkelsbær (*stik*-kerls-bæær) *nt* (pl ~)
  gooseberry
stikkontakt (*stik*-koon-tahkt) *m* plug
stikkord (stikk-*oor*) *nt* catchword
stikkpille (*stik*-pi-ler) *c* suppository
stil (steel) *m* style; essay
stilk (stilk) *m* stem
stillas (sti-*laass*) *nt* scaffolding
stille (*stil*-ler) *adj* calm, quiet, still;
  silent; *v* place, *put; ~ inn tune in
Stillehavet (*stil*-ler-haa-ver) Pacific
  Ocean
stillestående (*stil*-ler-staw-er-ner) *adj*
  stationary
stillferdig (stil-*fæædi*) *adj* quiet
stillhet (*stil*-hayt) *c* silence, quiet
stilling (*stil*-ling) *c* position; job
stimulans (sti-mew-*lahngs*) *m*
  stimulant
stimulere (sti-mew-*lay*-rer) *v*
  stimulate
sting (stingng) *nt* stitch
***stinke** (*sting*-ker) *v* *smell, *stink
stipend (sti-*pehnd*) *nt* grant,
  scholarship
stirre (*steer*-rer) *v* stare, gaze

stiv (steev) *adj* stiff
***stjele** (*st*^y*ay*-ler) *v* *steal
stjerne (*st*^y*ææ*-ner) *c* star
stoff (stoff) *nt* cloth, material, fabric;
  matter
stokk (stokk) *m* cane, stick
stokke (*stok*-ker) *v* shuffle
stol (stool) *m* chair
stola (*stoo*-lah) *m* stole
stole på (*stoo*-ler) trust; rely on
stolpe (*stol*-per) *m* post; pillar
stolt (stolt) *adj* proud
stolthet (*stolt*-hayt) *c* pride
stopp! (stopp) stop!
stoppe (*stop*-per) *v* stop; quit; darn
stor (stoor) *adj* great, major, big; large
storartet (*stoo*-raa-tert) *adj* superb,
  grand, terrific
Storbritannia (*stoor*-bri-tah-ni-ah)
  Great Britain
stork (stork) *m* stork
storm (storm) *m* gale; storm
stormagasin (*stoor*-mah-gah-seen) *nt*
  department store
stormfull (*storm*-fewl) *adj* stormy
stormlykt (*storm*-lewkt) *c* hurricane
  lamp
storslått (*stoo*-shlot) *adj* magnificent
Stortinget (*stoor*-ti-nger) Norwegian
  Parliament
stortingsrepresentant (*stoo*-tings-)
  reh-preh-sern-*tahnt*) *m* Member of
  (the Norwegian) Parliament
straff (strahff) *m* punishment; penalty
straffe (*strahf*-fer) *v* punish
strafferett (*strahf*-fer-reht) *m* criminal
  law
straffespark (*strahf*-fer-spahrk) *nt* (pl
  ~) penalty kick
straks (strahks) *adv* instantly, at once,
  immediately
stram (strahmm) *adj* tight
stramme (*strahm*-mer) *v* tighten;
  strammes to be tightened

strand (strahnn) *c* (pl strender) beach

strebe (*strāy*-ber) *v* aspire; **~ etter** pursue, aim at

streife omkring (stray-fer) roam

streik (strayk) *m* strike

streike (stray-ker) *v* *strike

strek (strāyk) *m* line

strekning (strehk-ning) *m* stretch; distance

streng (strehngng) *adj* strict, severe, harsh; *m* string

stress (strehss) *nt* stress

strid (streed) *m* contest; fight, battle, struggle

*strides (stree-derss) *v* dispute

strikk (strikk) *m* rubber band

strikke (strik-ker) *v* *knit

strimmel (strim-merl) *m* (pl strimler) strip

stripe (stree-per) *c* stripe

stripet (stree-pert) *adj* striped

strofe (strōō-fer) *m* stanza

struktur (strewk-*tewr*) *m* structure; texture, fabric

strupekatarr (*strēw*per-kah-tahr) *m* laryngitis

struts (strewts) *m* ostrich

*stryke (*strēw*-ker) *v* iron; *strike; fail an exam

strykefri (*strēw*-ker-free) *adj* drip-dry, wash and wear

strykejern (*strēw*-ker-ᵞææn) *nt* (pl ~) iron

strøm (strurmm) *m* (pl ~mer) electricity; current, stream; **med strømmen** downstream; **mot strømmen** upstream

strømfordeler (*strurm*-fo-dāy-lerr) *m* distributor

strømme (*strurm*-mer) *v* flow, stream

strømpe (*strurm*-per) *c* stocking

strømpebukse (*strurm*-per-book-ser) *c* tights *pl*, panty hose

stråle (*straw*-ler) *m* beam, ray; spout, jet; *v* *shine

strålende (*straw*-ler-ner) *adj* brilliant; glorious

student (stew-*dehnt*) *m* student

studere (stew-*dāy*-rer) *v* study

studium (*stēw*-di-oom) *nt* (pl -ier) study; studies

stue (*stēw*-er) *c* sitting room

stuert (*stōō*-ert) *m* steward

stum (stewmm) *adj* mute, dumb

stund (stewnn) *c* while

stup (stēwp) *nt* precipice

stupe (*stēw*-per) *v* dive

stusse (stewss-ser) *v* trim

stygg (stewgg) *adj* ugly

stykke (stewk-ker) *nt* piece, fragment, lump, part; ***gå i stykker** *break down; **i stykker** broken; **stort ~** chunk

styrbord (stewr-bōōr) *nt* starboard

styre (*stēw*-rer) *v* direct; steer; *nt* board, direction; government; rule

styrke (stewr-ker) *m* power, strength; force; **væpnede styrker** armed forces

styrte (stewt-ter) *v* crash; rush, dash

stær (stæær) *m* starling

stø (stūr) *adj* steady

stønne (sturn-ner) *v* groan

støpejern (*stūr*-per-ᵞææn) *nt* (pl ~) cast iron

størkne (sturr-kner) *v* harden

størrelse (sturr-rerl-ser) *m* size; **stor ~** outsize

størsteparten (stursh-ter-pah-tern) *m* bulk, the greater part of

støt (stūrt) *nt* bump

støtdemper (*stūrt*-dehm-perr) *m* shock absorber

støte (*stūr*-ter) *v* bump; **~ på** run into, *come across; knock against; **~ sammen** bump

støtfanger (*stūrt*-fah-ngerr) *m* bumper

støtte (*sturt*-ter) *v* *hold up; *m* support

støv (stūrv) *nt* dust

støvel (*sturv*-verl) *m* (pl -vler) boot

støvet (*stūr*-vert) *adj* dusty

støvsuge (*stūrv*-sēw-ger) *v* hoover; vacuum *vAm*

støvsuger (*stūrv*-sēw-gerr) *m* vacuum cleaner

støy (stur^{ew}) *m* noise

støyende (*stur^{ew}*-er-ner) *adj* noisy

*stå (staw) *v* *stand; **~ opp** *get up; *rise

stående (*staw*-er-ner) *adj* erect

stål (stawl) *nt* steel; **rustfritt ~** stainless steel

ståltråd (*stawl*-traw) *m* wire

subjekt (sewb-^y*ehkt*) *nt* subject

substans (sewb-*stahns*) *m* substance

substansiell (sewb-stahn-si-*ehl*) *adj* substantial

substantiv (*sewp*-stahn-teev) *nt* noun

subtil (sewb-*teel*) *adj* subtle

suge (*sēw*-ger) *v* suck

suite (*svit*-ter) *m* suite

sukke (*sewk*-ker) *v* sigh

sukker (*sook*-kerr) *nt* sugar

sukkerbit (*sook*-kerr-beet) *m* lump of sugar

sukkersyke (*sook*-ker-shēw-ker) *m* diabetes

sukkersykepasient (*sook*-ker-shēw-ker-pah-si-ehnt) *m* diabetic

sukkertøy (*sook*-ker-tur^{ew}) *nt* sweet; candy *nAm*

sukre (*sook*-rer) *v* sweeten

suksess (sewk-*sehss*) *m* success; hit

sult (sewlt) *m* hunger

sulten (*sewl*-tern) *adj* hungry

sum (sewmm) *m* (pl ~mer) sum; amount

summing (sewm-ming) *c* buzz

sump (soomp) *m* marsh

sunn (sewnn) *adj* healthy; wholesome

superlativ (sew-*pæl*-lah-teev) *m* superlative

supermarked (*sēw*-perr-mahr-kerd) *nt* supermarket

suppe (*sewp*-per) *c* soup

suppeskje (*sewp*-per-shāy) *c* soup spoon

suppetallerken (*sewp*-per-tah-lær-kern) *m* soup plate

sur (sēwr) *adj* sour

surfingbrett (*surr*-fing-breht) *nt* surf-board

surstoff (*sēw*-shtof) *nt* oxygen

suspendere (sewss-pahng-*dāy*-rer) *v* suspend

suvenir (sew-ver-*neer*) *m* souvenir

svak (svaak) *adj* weak, feeble; faint; slight

svakhet (*svaak*-hāyt) *c* weakness

svale (*svaa*-ler) *c* swallow

svamp (svahmp) *m* sponge

svane (*svaa*-ner) *c* swan

svangerskap (*svahng*-ngerr-skaap) *nt* pregnancy

svar (svaar) *nt* answer, reply; **som ~** in reply

svare (*svaa*-rer) *v* answer, reply; **~ til** correspond

svart (svahtt) *adj* dirty; black

svartebørs (*svaht*-ter-būrsh) *m* black market

svarttrost (*svaht*-rost) *m* blackbird

sveise (*svay*-ser) *v* weld

Sveits (svayts) Switzerland

sveitser (*svayt*-serr) *m* Swiss

sveitsisk (*svayt*-sisk) *adj* Swiss

svelge (*svehl*-ger) *v* swallow

svelle (*svehl*-ler) *v* *swell

svensk (svehnsk) *adj* Swedish

svenske (*svehn*-sker) *m* Swede

sverd (sværd) *nt* sword

*sverge (*svær*-ger) *v* vow, *swear

Sverige (*svær*-^yer) Sweden

svette (*sveht*-ter) *v* perspire, sweat; *m*

perspiration, sweat

*svi (svee) v *burn

svigerdatter (svee-gerr-dah-terr) c daughter-in-law

svigerfar (svee-gerr-faar) m (pl -fedre) father-in-law

svigerforeldre (svee-gerr-fo-rehl-drer) pl parents-in-law pl

svigerinne (svee-ger-rin-ner) c sister-in-law

svigermor (svee-gerr-mōōr) c (pl -mødre) mother-in-law

svigersønn (svee-ger-shurn) m son-in-law

svikte (svik-ter) v *let down

svimmel (svim-merl) adj dizzy, giddy

svimmelhet (svim-merl-hāyt) c dizziness, giddiness

svindel (svin-derl) m swindle

svindle (svin-dler) v swindle

svindler (svin-dlerr) m swindler

svinekjøtt (svee-ner-khurt) nt pork

svinelær (svee-ner-læær) nt pigskin

sving (svingng) m turning, bend, turn

svingdør (sving-dūrr) c revolving door

svinge (sving-nger) v turn; *swing

sviske (sviss-ker) c prune

svoger (svaw-gerr) m (pl ~e, -grer) brother-in-law

svulst (svewlst) m tumo(u)r, growth

svær (svæær) adj huge

svært (svææt) adv very

svømme (svurm-mer) v *swim

svømmebasseng (svurm-mer-bah-sehng) nt swimming pool

svømmer (svurm-merr) m swimmer

svømmevest (svurm-me-vest) m life jacket

svømming (svurm-ming) c swimming

swahili (svah-hee-li) m Swahili

sy (sēw) v *sew; ~ sammen *sew up

syd (sēwd) m south

sydlig (sēwd-li) adj southerly

Sydpolen (sēwd-pōō-lern) South Pole

syk (sēwk) adj sick, ill

sykdom (sēwk-dom) m (pl ~mer) sickness, illness; disease

sykebil (sēw-ker-beel) m ambulance

sykehus (sēw-ker-hēwss) nt (pl ~) hospital

sykepleier (sēw-ker-play-er) m nurse

sykkel (sewk-kerl) m (pl sykler) bicycle, cycle, bike

sykle (sewk-kler) v bicycle, cycle, bike

syklist (sewk-list) m cyclist

syklus (sēwk-lewss) m cycle

sylinder (sew-lin-derr) m (pl ~e, -drer) cylinder

syltetøy (sewl-ter-tur^(ew)) nt jam

symaskin (sēw-mah-sheen) m sewing machine

symbol (sewm-bōōl) nt symbol

symfoni (sewm-foo-nee) m symphony

sympati (sewm-pah-tee) m sympathy

sympatisk (sewm-paa-tisk) adj nice

symptom (sewm-tōōm) nt symptom

syn (sēwn) vision; outlook, view; sight, spectacle

synagoge (sew-nah-gōō-ger) m synagogue

synd (sewnn) m sin; **så synd!** what a pity!; **synes ~ på** pity

synde (sewnn-der) v sin

syndebukk (sewn-der-book) m scapegoat

synder (sewnn-derr) m sinner

synes (sēw-nerss) v appear, look, seem; **jeg ~ I** think; I find

*synge (sewng-nger) v *sing

*synke (sewng-ker) v *sink

synlig (sēwn-li) adj visible

synonym (sew-noo-nēwm) nt synonym

synspunkt (sēwns-poongt) nt point of view

syntetisk (sewn-tāy-tisk) adj synthetic

syre (sēw-rer) c acid

syrer (*sēw*-rerr) *m* Syrian
Syria (*sēw*-ri-ah) Syria
syrisk (*sēw*-risk) *adj* Syrian
system (sewss-*tāym*) *nt* system
systematisk (sewss-teh-*maa*-tisk) *adj* systematic
sytten (*surt*-tern) *num* seventeen
syttende (*surt*-ter-ner) *num* seventeenth
sytti (*surt*-ti) *num* seventy
syv (*sēwv*) *num* seven
syvende (*sēw*-ver-ner) *num* seventh
sær (sæær) *adj* queer
særdeles (sæ-*dāy*-lerss) *adv* quite
særdeleshet: i ~ (ee sæ-***āy*-lerss-hāyt) in particular
særegen (*sææ*-reh-gern) *adj* particular
særlig (*sæær*-li) *adv* especially
særskilt (*sææ*-shilt) *adj* separate
søke (*sūr*-ker) *v* *seek, apply
søker (*sūr*-kerr) *m* view-finder
søknad (*sūrk*-nah) *m* application
søle (*sūr*-ler) *v* *spill; *m* mud
sølet (*sūr*-lert) *adj* muddy
sølv (surll) *nt* silver; **sølv-** silver
sølvsmed (*surl*-smāy) *m* silversmith
sølvtøy (*surl*-tur^ew) *nt* silverware
søm (surmm) *m* (pl ~mer) seam
sømmelig (*surm*-mer-li) *adj* proper
søndag (*surn*-daa) *m* Sunday
sønn (surnn) *m* son
søppel (*surp*-perl) *nt* garbage, litter

søppelbøtte (*surp*-perl-bur-ter) *c* rubbish bin; waste basket *Am*
søppelkasse (*surp*-perl-kah-ser) *c* dustbin; trash can *Am*
sør (sūrr) *m* south
Sør-Afrika (*sūr*-rahf-ri-kah) South Africa
sørge (*surr*-ger) *v* grieve; mourn; **~ for** see to, look after
sørlig (*sūr*-li) *adj* southern
sørvest (surr-*vehst*) *m* south-west
sørøst (surr-*urst*) *m* south-east
søster (surss-terr) *c* (pl -tre) sister
søt (sūrt) *adj* sweet
søtsaker (*sūrt*-saa-kerr) *pl* candy *nAm*
søvn (survn) *m* sleep
søvnig (*surv*-ni) *adj* sleepy
søvnløs (survn-*lūrss*) *adj* sleepless
søvnløshet (survn-*lūrss*-hāyt) *c* insomnia
søyle (sur^ew-ler) *c* column
så (saw) *adv* so; then; *conj* so, so that; *v* *sow; **~ vel som** as well as; **~ vidt** barely; as much
såkalt (*saw*-kahlt) *adj* so-called
såle (*saw*-ler) *m* sole
sånn (sonn) *adj* such
såpe (*saw*-per) *c* soap
sår (sawr) *nt* wound; ulcer, sore; *adj* sore
sårbar (*sawr*-baar) *adj* vulnerable
såre (*saw*-rer) *v* wound; *hurt

T

***ta** (taa) *v* *take; **~ bort** *take out; **~ ille opp** resent; *** ~ imot** accept; **~ inn** stay; **~ med** *bring; **~ med seg** *take away; **~ opp** pick up; *bring up; **~ på** *put on; **~ seg av** attend to, *deal with; **~ vare på** *take care of; **~ vekk** *take away
tabell (tah-*behll*) *m* chart, table
tablett (tahb-*lehtt*) *m* tablet
tabu (*taa*-bew) *nt* taboo

tak (taak) *nt* roof; ceiling; grip
takk (tahkk) thank you
takke (*tahk*-ker) *v* thank; ***ha å ~ for** owe
takknemlig (tahk-*nehm*-li) *adj* grateful, thankful
takknemlighet (tahk-*nehm*-li-hāyt) *c* gratitude
taksameter (tahk-sah-*māy*-terr) *nt* (pl ~, -tre) taxi-meter
taksere (tahk-*sāy*-rer) *v* value, estimate
takstein (*taak*-stayn) *m* tile
taktikk (tahk-*tikk*) *m* tactics *pl*
tale (*taa*-ler) *m* speech
talent (tah-*lehnt*) *nt* talent
talerstol (*taa*-ler-shtool) *m* pulpit
talkum (*tahl*-kewm) *m* talc powder
tall (tahll) *nt* figure, number
tallerken (tah-*lær*-kern) *m* plate, dish
tallord (*tahl*-loor) *nt* (pl ~) numeral
tallrik (*tahl*-reek) *adj* numerous
tam (tahmm) *adj* tame
tampong (tahm-*pongng*) *m* tampon
tang (tahngng) *c* (pl tenger) tongs *pl*, pliers *pl*
tank (tahngk) *m* tank
tankbåt (*tahngk*-bawt) *m* tanker
tanke (*tahng*-ker) *m* thought, idea
tankefull (*tahng*-ker-fewl) *adj* thoughtful
tankestrek (*tahng*-ker-strāyk) *m* dash
tann (tahnn) *c* (pl tenner) tooth
tannbørste (*tahn*-bursh-ter) *m* toothbrush
tannkjøtt (*tahn*-khurt) *nt* gum
tannkrem (*tahnn*-krāym) *m* toothpaste
tannlege (*tahn*-lāy-ger) *m* dentist
tannpasta (*tahn*-pahss-tah) *m* toothpaste
tannpine (*tahn*-pee-ner) *c* toothache
tannpirker (*tahn*-peer-kerr) *m* toothpick

tannregulering (*tahn*-reh-gew-*lāy*-ring) *c* brace
tannverk (*tahn*-værk) *m* toothache
tante (*tahn*-ter) *c* aunt
tap (taap) *nt* loss
tape (*taa*-per) *v* *lose
taper (*taa*-perr) *m* loser
tapet (tah-*pāyt*) *nt* wallpaper
tapper (*tahp*-perr) *adj* brave, courageous
tapperhet (*tahp*-perr-hāyt) *c* courage
tariff (tah-*riff*) *m* rate, tariff
tarm (tahrm) *m* intestine, gut; **tarmer** bowels *pl*, intestines
tast (tahst) *m* key
tastatur (tahsta-*tewr*) *nt* keyboard
taste (tahs-ter) *v* dial, type
tau (tou) *nt* cord
taue (*tou*-er) *v* tow, tug
taus (touss) *adj* silent
tavle (*tahv*-ler) *c* blackboard; board
taxi (*tahk*-si) *m* taxi
te (tāy) *m* tea
teater (teh-*aa*-terr) *nt* (pl ~, -tre) theater *Am*, theatre
teaterstykke (teh-*aa*-ter-shtew-ker) *nt* play
tegn (tayn) *nt* sign, token, signal; indication
tegne (*tay*-ner) *v* *draw; sketch; **~ opp** design
tegnefilm (*tay*-ner-film) *m* cartoon
tegnestift (*tay*-ner-stift) *m* drawing pin; thumbtack *nAm*
tegning (*tay*-ning) *c* sketch, drawing
tekanne (*tāy*-kah-ner) *c* teapot
tekniker (*tehk*-ni-kerr) *m* technician
teknikk (tehk-*nikk*) *m* technique
teknisk (*tehk*-nisk) *adj* technical
teknologi (tehk-noo-loo-*gee*) *m* technology
teknologisk (tehk-noo-loo-*gee*) *adj* technological
tekopp (*tāy*-kop) *m* teacup

tekst (tehkst) *m* text; subtitle

tekstil (tehk-*steel*) *m*/*nt* textile

telefaks (*teh*-ler-fahks) *m* fax; **sende en ~** send a fax

telefon (teh-ler-*foon*) *m* phone, telephone

telefonere (teh-ler-foo-*nay*-rer) *v* phone

telefonkatalog (teh-ler-*foon*-kah-tah-lawg) *m* telephone directory; telephone book *Am*

telefonkiosk (teh-ler-*foon*-khosk) *m* telephone booth

telefonkort (teh-ler-*foon*-kot) *nt* phone card

telefonrør (teh-ler-*foon*-rürr) *nt* (pl ~) receiver

telefonsamtale (teh-ler-*foon*-sahm-taa-ler) *m* telephone call

telefonsentral (teh-ler-*foon*-sehn-traal) *m* telephone exchange

telefonsvarer (teh-ler-*foon*-svaa-rerr) *m* answering machine

teleobjektiv (*tay*-ler-ob-ʸehk-teev) *nt* telephoto lens

telepati (teh-ler-pah-*tee*) *m* telepathy

***telle** (*tehl*-ler) *v* count; **~ opp** count

telt (tehlt) *nt* tent

tema (*tay*-mah) *nt* theme

temme (*tehm*-mer) *v* tame

temmelig (*tehm*-mer-li) *adv* rather, pretty, fairly, quite

tempel (*tehm*-perl) *nt* (pl ~, -pler) temple

temperatur (tehm-per-rah-*tewr*) *m* temperature

tempo (*tehm*-poo) *nt* pace

tendens (tehn-*dehns*) *m* tendency; ***ha ~ til** tend

tenke (*tehng*-ker) *v* *think; **~ over** *think over; **~ på** *think of; **~ seg** imagine, fancy; **~ ut** conceive

tenker (*tehng*-kerr) *m* thinker

tenne (*tehn*-ner) *v* *light

tenning (*tehn*-ning) *c* ignition

tennis (*tehn*-niss) *m* tennis

tennisbane (*tehn*-niss-baa-ner) *m* tennis court

tennissko (*tehn*-ni-skoo) *pl* tennis shoes

tennplugg (*tehn*-plewg) *m* sparking plug

tennspole (*tehn*-spoo-ler) *m* ignition coil

tenåring (*tay*-naw-ring) *m* teenager

teologi (teh-oo-loo-*gee*) *m* theology

teoretisk (teh-oo-*ray*-tisk) *adj* theoretical

teori (teh-oo-*ree*) *m* theory

teppe (*tehp*-per) *nt* blanket; carpet; curtain

terapi (teh-rah-*pee*) *m* therapy

termin (tær-*meen*) *m* term

termometer (tær-moo-*may*-terr) *nt* (pl ~, -tre) thermometer

termosflaske (*tær*-mooss-flahss-ker) *c* thermos flask

termostat (tær-moo-*staat*) *m* thermostat

terning (*tææ*-ning) *m* cube; dice *pl*

terpentin (tær-pehn-*teen*) *m* turpentine

terrasse (tæ-*rahss*-ser) *m* terrace

terreng (tæ-*rehngng*) *nt* terrain

terror (*tær*-roor) *m* terror

terrorisme (tæ-roo-*riss*-mer) *m* terrorism

terrorist (tæ-roo-*rist*) *m* terrorist

terskel (*tæsh*-kerl) *m* threshold

tesalong (*tay*-sah-long) *m* tea-shop

tese (*tay*-ser) *m* thesis

teservise (*tay*-sær-vee-ser) *nt* tea set

teskje (*tay*-shay) *c* teaspoon

test (tehst) *m* test

testamente (tehss-tah-*mehn*-ter) *nt* will

teste (*tehss*-ter) *v* test

tett (tehtt) *adj* dense, thick

tettpakket (*teht-pah-kert*) *adj*
crowded

Thailand (*tigh-lahn*) Thailand

thailandsk (*tigh-lahnsk*) *adj* Thai

thailender (*tigh-leh-nerr*) *m* Thai

ti (tee) *num* ten

tid (teed) *c* time; period; **hele tiden** all
the time; **i tide** in time

tidevann (*tee-der-vahn*) *nt* tide

tidlig (*tee-li*) *adj* early; **tidligere**
before, former, previous, formerly,
adv before; past

tidsbesparende (*tits-beh-spaa-rer-
ner*) *adj* time-saving

tidsfordriv (*tits-for-driv*) *nt* pastime

tidsskrift (*tit-skrift*) *nt* magazine,
periodical, review, journal

tie (*tee-er*) *v* *be silent, *keep quiet

tiende (*tee-er-ner*) *num* tenth

tiger (*tee-gerr*) *m* tiger

tigge (*tig-ger*) *v* beg

tigger (*tig-gerr*) *m* beggar

til (till) *prep* to; for; until, till; **en ~**
another; **~ og med** even

tilbake (til-*baa*-ker) *adv* back; ***gå ~**
*get back

tilbakebetale (til-*baa*-ker-beh-taa-
ler) *v* reimburse, *repay

tilbakebetaling (til-*baa*-ker-beh-taa-
ling) *c* repayment, refund

tilbakegang (til-*baa*-ker-gahng) *m*
recession

tilbakekalle (til-*baa*-ker-kah-ler) *v*
recall

tilbakekomst (til-*baa*-ker-komst) *m*
return

tilbakereise (til-*baa*-ker-ray-ser) *c*
return journey

tilbakevei (til-*baa*-ker-vay) *m* way
back

tilbakevise (til-*baa*-ker-vee-ser) *v*
reject

*tilbe (til-*bāy*) *v* worship

tilbehør (*til*-beh-hūrr) *nt* accessories
pl

tilberede (*til*-beh-rāy-der) *v* prepare;
cook

*tilbringe (*til*-bri-nger) *v* *spend

tilbud (*til*-bēwd) *nt* (pl ~) offer; supply;
bid

*tilby (*til*-bēw) *v* offer; *bid

tilbøyelig (til-*bur*ᵉʷ-er-li) *adj* inclined;
*være ~ til tend to

tilbøyelighet (til-*bur*ᵉʷ-er-li-hāyt) *c*
inclination, tendency

tildele (*til*-dāy-ler) *v* award; assign to;
administer

tilfeldig (*til*-fehl-di) *adj* incidental,
accidental, casual

tilfeldighet (til-*fehl*-di-hāyt) *c* chance,
coincidence

tilfeldigvis (til-*fehl*-di-veess) *adv* by
chance

tilfelle (*til*-feh-ler) *nt* case, instance;
chance; coincidence; **i ~ av** in case of

tilfluktssted (*til*-flewkt-steh) *nt*
shelter

tilfreds (til-*frehts*) *adj* content;
satisfied

tilfredshet (til-*frehts*-hāyt) *c*
contentment

tilfredsstille (*til*-freht-sti-ler) *v* satisfy

tilfredsstillelse (*til*-freht-sti-lerl-ser)
m satisfaction

tilfredsstillende (*til*-freht-sti-lerl-ner)
adj satisfactory

tilfredsstilt (*til*-freht-stilt) *adj* satisfied

tilførsel (*til*-fur-sherl) *m* (pl -sler)
supply

tilføye (*til*-furᵉʷ-er) *v* add; inflict

tilføyelse (*til*-furᵉʷ-erl-ser) *m* addition

tilgang (*til*-gahng) *m* access

*tilgi (*til*-ʸee) *v* *forgive

tilgivelse (*til*-ʸee-verl-ser) *m* pardon

tilgjengelig (til-ʸ*ehng*-nger-li) *adj*
available; accessible

tilhenger (*til*-heh-ngerr) *m* trailer;
supporter

tilhøre (*til*-hūr-rer) *v* belong, belong to

tilhører (*til*-hūr-rerr) *m* auditor

*tilintetgjøre (ti-*lin*-tert-ᵞ*ūr*-rer) *v* destroy; ruin

*tillate (*til*-laa-ter) *v* permit, allow; *være tillatt *be allowed

tillatelse (*til*-laa-terl-ser) *m* permission, authorization; permit; *gi ~ license

tillegg (*til*-lehg) *nt* (pl ~) supplement; surcharge; annex

tillit (*til*-leet) *m* faith, confidence, trust

tillitsfull (*til*-leets-fewl) *adj* confident

tilpasse (*til*-pah-ser) *v* adapt, suit; adjust; accommodate

tilrettevise (til-*reht*-ter-vee-ser) *v* reprimand

tilråde (*til*-raw-der) *v* recommend

tilsiktet (*til*-sik-tert) *adj* intentional

*tilskrive (*til*-skree-ver) *v* assign to

tilskudd (*til*-skewd) *nt* (pl ~) subsidy; grant

tilskuer (*til*-skēw-err) *m* spectator

tilsluttet (*til*-shlew-tert) *adj* affiliated

tilstand (*til*-stahn) *m* condition

tilstedeværelse (til-*stāy*-der-væærerl-ser) *m* presence

tilstedeværende (til-*stāy*-der-vææ-rer-ner) *adj* present

tilstrekkelig (til-*streh*-ker-li) *adj* enough, sufficient; adequate; *være ~ suffice; *do

tilstøtende (*til*-stūr-ter-ner) *adj* neighbo(u)ring, adjacent

*tilstå (*til*-staw) *v* confess, admit

tilståelse (*til*-staw-erl-ser) *m* confession

tilsvare (*til*-svaa-rer) *v* correspond

tilsvarende (*til*-svaa-rer-ner) *adj* equivalent

tilsynelatende (til-*sēw*-ner-laa-ter-ner) *adj* apparent

*tilta (*til*-taa) *v* increase

tiltakende (*til*-taa-ker-ner) *adj* progressive

*tiltrekke (*til*-treh-ker) *v* attract

tiltrekkende (*til*-treh-ker) *adj* attractive

tiltrekning (*til*-trehk-ning) *m* attraction

time (*tee*-mer) *m* hour; lesson; hver ~ hourly

timeplan (*ti*-mer-plaan) *m* schedule

timian (*tee*-mi-ahn) *m* thyme

tind (tinn) *m* peak

tine (*tee*-ner) *v* thaw

ting (tingng) *m* (pl ~) thing

tinn (tinn) *nt* pewter, tin

tinning (tin-ning) *m* temple

tirsdag (*teesh*-dah) *m* Tuesday

tispe (*tiss*-per) *c* bitch

tistel (*tiss*-terl) *m* (pl -tler) thistle

tittel (*tit*-terl) *m* (pl titler) title

tiur (tee-ēwr) *m* wood grouse

tjene (*tᵞāy*-ner) *v* earn; *make

tjener (*tᵞāy*-nerr) *m* boy, servant, domestic

tjeneste (*tᵞāy*-nerss-ter) *m* favo(u)r; service

tjue (*khēw*-er) *num* twenty

tjuende (*khēw*-er-ner) *num* twentieth

tjære (*khææ*-rer) *c* tar

to (tōō) *num* two

toalett (too-ah-*lehtt*) *nt* bathroom, lavatory, toilet; washroom, rest room *Am*

toalettpapir (too-ah-*leht*-pah-peer) *nt* toilet paper

toalettsaker (too-ah-*leht*-saa-kerr) *pl* toiletry

toalettveske (too-ah-*leht*-vehss-ker) *c* toilet case

tobakk (too-*bahkk*) *m* tobacco

tobakksforretning (too-*bahks*-fo-reht-ning) *c* tobacconist's

todelt (*tōō*-dehlt) *adj* two-piece

tog (tawg) *nt* train, parade

tolk (tolk) *m* interpreter

tolke (*tol*-ker) *v* interpret

toll (toll) *m* customs duty; customs *pl*

tollavgift (*tol*-laav-ᵞift) *c* customs duty

toller (*tol*-lerr) *m* customs officer

tollfri (*toll*-free) *adj* duty-free

tolv (toll) *num* twelve

tolvte (*tol*-ter) *num* twelfth

tom (tomm) *adj* empty

tomat (too-*maat*) *m* tomato

tomme (*tom*-me) *m* inch

tommelfinger (*tom*-merl-fi-ngerr) *m* (pl -gre) thumb

tomt (tomt) *c* grounds, plot

tone (*too*-ner) *m* note, tone

tonn (tonn) *nt* ton

topp (topp) *m* summit, top; peak

topplokk (*top*-lok) *nt* (pl ∿) cylinder head

torden (*too*-dern) *m* thunder

tordenvær (*too*-dern-væær) *nt* (pl ∿) thunderstorm

tordne (*tood*-ner) *v* thunder

***tore** (*too*-rer) *v* dare

torg (torg) *nt* market-place

torn (*toon*) *m* thorn

torsdag (*tawsh*-dah) *m* Thursday

torsk (toshk) *m* (pl ∿) cod

tortur (too-*tewr*) *m* torture

torturere (too-tew-*ray*-rer) *v* torture

tosk (tosk) *m* fool

tospråklig (*too*-sprawk-li) *adj* bilingual

total (too-*taal*) *adj* total; overall; utter

totalisator (too-tah-li-*saa*-toor) *m* bookmaker

totalitær (too-tah-li-*tæær*) *adj* totalitarian

totalsum (too-*taal*-sewm) *m* (pl ∿mer) total

totalt (too-*taalt*) *adv* completely

tradisjon (trah-di-*shoon*) *m* tradition

tradisjonell (trah-di-shoo-*nehll*) *adj* traditional

trafikk (trah-*fikk*) *m* traffic

trafikk-kork (trah-*fik*-kork) *m* jam, traffic jam

trafikklys (trah-*fik*-lewss) *nt* (pl ∿) traffic light

tragedie (trah-*gay*-di-er) *m* tragedy

tragisk (*traa*-gisk) *adj* tragic

trakt (trahkt) *c* region; funnel

traktat (trahk-*taat*) *m* treaty

traktor (*trahk*-toor) *m* tractor

trang (trahngng) *adj* tight, narrow; *m* urge

transaksjon (trahn-sahk-*shoon*) *m* deal, transaction

transatlantisk (*trahn*-saht-lahn-tisk) *adj* transatlantic

transformator (trahn-for-*maa*-toor) *m* transformer

transpirasjon (trahn-spi-rah-*shoon*) *m* perspiration

transpirere (trahn-spi-*ray*-rer) *v* perspire

transport (trahns-*pott*) *m* transport, transportation

transportabel (trahns-po-*taa*-berl) *adj* portable

transportere (trahns-po-*tay*-rer) *v* transport

trapp (trahpp) *c* stairs *pl*, staircase

travel (*traa*-verl) *adj* busy

travelhet (*traa*-verl-hayt) *c* bustle

***tre** (tray) *v* step; thread

tre[1] (tray) *num* three

tre[2] (tray) *nt* (pl trær) tree; wood; **tre-** wooden

tredje (*trayd*-ᵞer) *num* third

***treffe** (*trehf*-fer) *v* *hit; *meet

treg (trayg) *adj* slack

trekant (*tray*-kahnt) *m* triangle

trekantet (*tray*-kahn-tert) *adj* triangular

trekk (trehkk) *nt* move; trait; *m* draught

***trekke** (*trehk*-ker) *v* pull, *draw; upholster; ∿ **fra** deduct; subtract; ∿

opp *wind; uncork; ~ **tilbake**
  *withdraw; ~ **ut** extract
trekløver (*trāy*-klur-verr) *m* shamrock
trekning (*trehk*-ning) *m* draw
trekull (*trāy*-kewl) *nt* charcoal
trene (*trāy*-ner) *v* drill; train
trener (*trāy*-nerr) *m* coach; trainer
trenge (*trehng*-nger) *v* need; ~ **seg**
  frem push
trening (*trāy*-ning) *c* training
treskjærerarbeid (*trāy*-shææ-rerr-
  ahr-bayd) *nt* wood carving
tresko (*trāy*-skōō) *m* (pl ~) wooden
  shoe
trett (trehtt) *adj* tired, weary
trette (*treht*-ter) *v* argue, quarrel; tire;
  m quarrel
tretten (*treht*-tern) *num* thirteen
trettende (*treht*-ter-ner) *num*
  thirteenth; *adj* tiring
tretti (*treht*-ti) *num* thirty
trettiende (*treht*-ti-er-ner) *num*
  thirtieth
trevle opp (*trehv*-ler) fray
tribune (tri-*bew*-ner) *m* stand
trick (trikk) *nt* trick
trikk (trikk) *m* tram; streetcar *nAm*
trillebår (*tril*-ler-bawr) *c* wheelbarrow
trinn (trinn) *nt* step
trinse (*trin*-ser) *c* pulley
trist (trist) *adj* sad
triumf (tri-*ewmf*) *m* triumph
triumfere (tri-ewm-*fāy*-rer) *v* triumph
triumferende (tri-ewm-*fāy*-rer-ner)
  adj triumphant
tro (trōō) *v* believe; reckon; *c* belief,
  faith; *adj* faithful
trofast (*trōō*-fahst) *adj* faithful, true
trolig (*trōō*-li) *adj* credible
trolldom (*trol*-dom) *m* magic
tromme (*troom*-mer) *c* drum
trommehinne (*troom*-mer-hi-ner) *c*
  ear-drum
trompet (troom-*pāyt*) *m* trumpet

trone (*trōō*-ner) *c* throne
tropene (*trōō*-per-ner) *pl* tropics *pl*
tropisk (*trōō*-pisk) *adj* tropical
tropper (*trop*-perr) *pl* troops *pl*
tross (tross) *prep* in spite of, despite;
  til ~ for in spite of
trost (trost) *m* thrush
true (*trēw*-er) *v* threaten
truende (*trēw*-er-ner) *adj* threatening
trumf (trewmf) *m* trump, trump card
trupp (trewpp) *m* band; company
truse (*trēw*-ser) *c* briefs *pl*, panties *pl*;
  underpants *plAm*
trussel (*trewss*-serl) *m* (pl -sler) threat
trygle (*trēw*-ger-ler) *v* plead, beseech,
  beg
trykk[1] (trewkk) *nt* pressure
trykk[2] (trewkk) *nt* engraving, print
trykk[3] (trewkk) *nt* stress; *legge ~ på
  stress
trykke[1] (*trewk*-ker) *v* press; ~ **på** press
trykke[2] (*trewk*-ker) *v* print
trykkende (*trewk*-ker-ner) *adj* stuffy
trykknapp (*trewk*-knahp) *m* push
  button; press-stud
trykkoker (trewk-*kōō*-kerr) *m*
  pressure cooker
tryllekunstner (*trewl*-ler-kewnst-
  nerr) *m* magician
trøbbel (*trurb*-berl) *nt* trouble
trøffel (*trur*-ferl) *m* truffle
trøst (trurst) *c* comfort
trøste (*trurss*-ter) *v* comfort
trøstepremie (*trurss*-ter-prāy-mi-er)
  m consolation prize
trå (traw) *v* step
tråd (traw) *m* thread
tube (*tēw*-ber) *m* tube
tuberkulose (tew-bær-kew-*lōō*-ser) *m*
  tuberculosis
tulipan (tew-li-*paan*) *m* tulip; ~**løk**
  tulip bulb
tull (tewll) *nt* rubbish
tunfisk (*tēwn*-fisk) *m* tuna

tung (toongng) *adj* heavy

tunge (*toong*-nger) *c* tongue

tungnem (*toong*-nehm) *adj* slow

tunika (*tew*-ni-kah) *m* tunic

Tunisia (tew-*nee*-si-ah) Tunisia

tunisier (tew-*nee*-si-err) *m* Tunisian

tunisisk (tew-*nee*-sisk) *adj* Tunisian

tunnel (tew-*nehll*) *m* tunnel

tur (tewr) *m* ride, trip; turn

turbin (tewr-*been*) *m* turbine

turbojet (*tewr*-boo-^yeht) *m* turbojet

turgjenger (*tewr*-^yeh-ngerr) *m* walker

turist (tew-*rist*) *m* tourist

turistklasse (tew-*rist*-klah-ser) *c* tourist class

turistkontor (tew-*rist*-koon-tōōr) *nt* tourist office

turisttrafikk (tew-*riss*-trah-fik) *m* tourism

turner (*tew*-nerr) *m* gymnast

turnering (tew-*nāy*-ring) *c* tournament

turnsko (*tēwn*-skōō) *pl* gym shoes; sneakers *plAm*

tur-retur (*tēwr*-reh-tēwr) round trip

tusen (*tēw*-sern) *num* thousand

tusmørke (*tewss*-murr-ker) *nt* dusk

tut (tēwt) *m* nozzle

tute (*tēw*-ter) *v* hoot; honk *vAm*, toot *vAm*

TV (*tēwehr*) *m colloquial* TV

tvang (tvahng) *m* constraint; force

tverr (tværr) *adj* cross

tvert imot (tvæt i-*mōōt*) on the contrary

tvert om (tvæt om) the other way round

tvetydig (tvāy-tēw-di) *adj* ambiguous

tvil (tveel) *m* doubt; **uten ~** without doubt

tvile (*tvee*-ler) *v* doubt

tvillinger (*tvil*-li-ngerr) *pl* twins *pl*

tvilsom (*tveel*-som) *adj* doubtful

***tvinge** (*tving*-nger) *v* force

tvist (tvist) *m* dispute

tydelig (*tēw*-der-li) *adj* clear, distinct, plain; evident, apparent; explicit

tyfus (*tēw*-fewss) *m* typhoid

tygge (tewg-ger) *v* chew

tyggegummi (*tewg*-ger-gew-mi) *m* chewing gum

tykk (tewkk) *adj* thick; corpulent, big

tykkelse (*tewk*-kerl-ser) *m* thickness

tykkfallen (*tewk*-fah-lern) *adj* stout

tykne (*tewk*-ner) *v* thicken

tyngde (tewng-der) *m* weight

tyngdekraft (tewng-der-krahft) *c* gravity

tynge (tewng-nger) *v* oppress

tynn (tewnn) *adj* thin; sheer; weak

type (*tēw*-per) *m* type

typisk (*tēw*-pisk) *adj* typical

tyr (tēwr) *m* bull

tyrann (tew-*rahnn*) *m* tyrant

tyrefektning (*tēw*-rer-fehkt-ning) *m* bullfight

tyrker (*tewr*-kerr) *m* Turk

Tyrkia (*tewr*-ki-ah) Turkey

tyrkisk (*tewr*-kisk) *adj* Turkish

tysk (tewsk) *adj* German

tysker (*tewss*-kerr) *m* German

Tyskland (*tewsk*-lahn) Germany

tyv (tēwv) *m* thief

tyve (*tēw*-ver) *num* twenty

tyvende (*tēw*-ver-ner) *num* twentieth

tyveri (tēw-ver-*ree*) *nt* robbery, theft

tøffel (*turf*-ferl) *m* (pl tøfler) slipper

tømme (*turm*-mer) *v* empty

tømmer (*turm*-merr) *nt* timber

tømmermenn (*turm*-merr-mehn) *pl* hangover

tømming (*turm*-ming) *c* emptying

tønne (*turn*-ner) *c* cask, barrel

tørke (*turr*-ker) *c* drought; *v* wipe, dry; **~ av** wipe; **~ bort** wipe

tørkeapparat (*turr*-ker-ah-pah-raat) *nt* dryer

tørr (turrr) *adj* dry

tørst (tursht) *adj* thirsty; *m* thirst
tøvær (*tūr*-væær) *nt* thaw
tøye (*tur^ew*-er) *v* stretch
tøyelig (*tur^ew*-er-li) *adj* elastic
tøyelighet (*tur^ew*-er-li-hāyt) *c* elasticity
tøyle (*tur^ew*-ler) *v* curb; restrain
tå (taw) *c* (pl tær) toe
tåke (*taw*-ker) *c* mist, fog

tåkelykt (*taw*-ker-lewkt) *c* foglamp
tåket (*taw*-kert) *adj* foggy
tålmodig (tol-*mōō*-di) *adj* patient
tålmodighet (tol-*mōō*-di-hāyt) *c* patience
tåpelig (*taw*-per-li) *adj* silly, foolish; crazy
tåre (*taw*-rer) *c* tear
tårn (tawn) *nt* tower

U

uakseptabel (e**w-ahk-sep-ta*abel*) *adj* unacceptable
ualminnelig (ew-ahl-*mi*-ner-li) *adj* unusual
uanselig (ew-ahn-*sāy*-li) *adj* inconspicuous, insignificant
uanstendig (*ēw*-ahn-stehn-di) *adj* indecent; obscene
uavbrutt (*ēw*-ahv-brewt) *adj* continuous
uavhengig (*ēw*-ahv-heh-ngi) *adj* independent
uavhengighet (*ēwahv*-heh-ngi-hāyt) *c* independence
ubebodd (*ēw*-beh-bood) *adj* uninhabited
ubeboelig (*ēw*-beh-*bōō*-er-li) *adj* uninhabitable
ubegrenset (*ēw*-beh-grehn-sert) *adj* unlimited
ubehagelig (*ēw*-beh-haa-ger-li) *adj* disagreeable, unpleasant; nasty
ubekvem (*ēw*-beh-kvehm) *adj* uncomfortable
ubekymret (*ēw*-beh-khewm-rert) *adj* carefree
ubeleilig (*ēw*-beh-lay-li) *adj* inconvenient
ubeleilighet (*ēw*-beh-lay-li-hāyt) *c*

inconvenience
ubesindig (*ēw*-beh-sin-di) *adj* rash
ubeskjeden (*ēw*-beh-shāy-dern) *adj* immodest
ubeskyttet (*ēw*-beh-shew-tert) *adj* unprotected
ubestemt (*ēw*-beh-stehmt) *adj* indefinite
ubesvart (*ēw*-beh-svaat) *adj* unanswered
ubetydelig (*ēw*-beh-*tēw*-der-li) *adj* insignificant; slight, petty
ubevisst (ew-ber-vist) *adj* unconscious
ubotelig (ew-*bōō*-ter-li) *adj* irreparable
ubåt (ew-bawt) *m* submarine
udugelig (ew-*dēw*-ger-li) *adj* incapable
udyrket (ew-dewr-kert) *adj* uncultivated
uegnet (*ēw*-ay-nert) *adj* unsuitable, unfit
uekte (*ēw*-ehk-ter) *adj* false
uendelig (ew-*ehn*-ner-li) *adj* endless, infinite
uenig: **være ~* (*vææ*-rer ew-*āy*-ni) disagree
uerfaren (*ēw*-ær-faa-rern) *adj*

inexperienced

ufaglært ($\overline{ew}$-faag-lææt) *adj* unskilled

uflaks ($\overline{ew}$-flahks) *m* bad luck

uforklarlig ($\overline{ew}$-for-*klaa*-li) *adj* unaccountable

uformell ($\overline{ew}$-for-mehll) *adj* casual, informal

uforskammet ($\overline{ew}$-fo-shkah-mert) *adj* insolent, impertinent; impudent; rude, *colloquial* cheeky

uforskammethet ($\overline{ew}$-fo-shkah-mert-hāyt) *c* insolence

uforståelig ($\overline{ew}$-fo-shtaw-er-li) *adj* puzzling

ufortjent ($\overline{ew}$-fo-t'āynt) *adj* unearned

ufremkommelig ($\overline{ew}$-frehm-ko-mer-li) *adj* impassable

ufullkommen ($\overline{ew}$-fewl-ko-mern) *adj* imperfect

ufullstendig ($\overline{ew}$-fewl-stehn-di) *adj* incomplete

ufølsom ($\overline{ew}$-fur-l-som) *adj* insensitive

ufør ($\overline{ew}$-*fūr*) *adj* disabled

ugift ($\overline{ew}$-'ift) *adj* single

ugjenkallelig (ew-'ehn-*kahl*-ler-li) *adj* irrevocable

ugle (*ewg*-ler) *c* owl

ugress ($\overline{ew}$-grehss) *nt* weed

ugunstig ($\overline{ew}$-gewn-sti) *adj* unfavo(u)rable

ugyldig ($\overline{ew}$-'ewl-di) *adj* invalid, void

uhelbredelig ($\overline{ew}$-hehl-*brāy*-der-li) *adj* incurable

uheldig (ew-*hehl*-di) *adj* unfortunate, unlucky

uheldigvis (ew-*hehl*-di-veess) *adv* unfortunately

uhell ($\overline{ew}$-hehl) *nt* misfortune; accident; mishap

uhyggelig (ew-*hew*-ger-li) *adj* creepy; ominous

uhøflig (ew-*hurf*-li) *adj* impolite

ujevn ($\overline{ew}$-'ehvn) *adj* uneven

uke ($\overline{ew}$-ker) *c* week

ukentlig ($\overline{ew}$-kernt-li) *adj* weekly

ukjent ($\overline{ew}$-khehnt) *adj* unknown, unfamiliar

uklar ($\overline{ew}$-klaar) *adj* obscure, dim

uklok ($\overline{ew}$-kl$\overline{oo}$k) *adj* unwise

uknuselig (ew-*kn$\overline{ew}$*-ser-li) *adj* unbreakable

ukvalifisert ($\overline{ew}$-kvah-li-fi-sāyt) *adj* unqualified

uleilighet (ew-*lay*-li-hāyt) *c* trouble

ulempe ($\overline{ew}$-lehm-per) *m* disadvantage

uleselig (ew-*lāy*-ser-li) *adj* illegible

ulik ($\overline{ew}$-leek) *adj* unequal, uneven

ulike ($\overline{ew}$-lee-ker) *adj* odd

ull (ewll) *c* wool; **ull-** wool(l)en

ulljakke (*ewl-y*ah-ker) *c* sweater, cardigan

ulovlig ($\overline{ew}$-lawv-li) *adj* illegal, unlawful

ultrafiolett (*ewl*-trah-fi-oo-leht) *adj* ultraviolet

ulv (ewlv) *m* wolf

ulykke ($\overline{ew}$-lew-ker) *c* accident, misfortune; calamity, disaster; misery

ulykkelig (ew-*lewk*-ker-li) *adj* unhappy; miserable

ulærd ($\overline{ew}$-læærd) *adj* uneducated

umake ($\overline{ew}$-maa-ker) *m* pains; ***være umaken verd** *be worthwhile

umiddelbart ($\overline{ew}$-mi-derl-baat) *adv* immediately, instantly

umoderne ($\overline{ew}$-moo-dææ-ner) *adj* out of date; old-fashioned

umulig (ew-*mēw*-li) *adj* impossible

umyndig ($\overline{ew}$-mewn-di) *adj* under age

umåtelig (ew-*maw*-ter-li) *adj* vast, immense

under[1] (*ewn*-derr) *nt* wonder

under[2] (*ewn*-nerr) *prep* below, during, beneath, under; *adv* beneath

underbukse (*ewn*-nerr-book-ser) *c* panties *pl*, drawers, pants *pl*; shorts *plAm*

underdrive (*ewn*-nerr-driver) *v*
understate

underdrivelse (*ewn*-nerr-driv-erl-ser)
n understatement

underernæring (*ewn*-nerr-æ-næær-ring) *c* malnutrition

undergang (*ewn*-nerr-gahng) *m* ruin,
destruction

undergrunnsbane (*ewn*-nerr-grewns-baa-ner) *m* underground; subway
nAm

****underholde** (*ewn*-nerr-ho-ler) *v*
entertain, amuse

underholdende (*ewn*-nerr-ho-ler-ner) *adj* entertaining

underholdning (*ewn*-nerr-hol-ning)
m entertainment

underjordisk (*ewn*-nerr-ᵛoor-disk)
adj underground

underkaste seg (*ewn*-nerr-kahss-ter)
submit

underkue (*ewn*-nerr-kēw-er) *v*
subject

underlegen (*ewn*-ner-lāy-gern) *adj*
inferior

underlig (*ewn*-der-li) *adj* odd, strange,
queer; peculiar

underordnet (*ewn*-ner-oord-nert) *adj*
subordinate; minor, secondary;
additional

underretning (*ewn*-ner-reht-ning) *m*
notice

underrette (*ewn*-ner-reh-ter) *v*
inform; notify

underskrift (*ewn*-nerr-skrift) *c*
signature

underskudd (*ewn*-ner-shkewd) *nt* (pl
~) deficit

understreke (*ewn*-ner-shtrāy-ker) *v*
underline; emphasize

understrøm (*ewn*-ner-shtrurm) *m* (pl
~mer) undercurrent

undersøke (*ewn*-ner-shūr-ker) *v*

enquire; examine

undersøkelse (*ewn*-ner-shūr-kerl-ser) *m* investigation, enquiry; check-up, examination

undersått (*ewn*-ner-shot) *m* subject

undertegne (*ewn*-ner-tay-ner) *v* sign

undertrykke (*ewn*-ner-trew-ker) *v*
oppress, suppress

undertøy (*ewn*-ner-tur^(ew)) *pl*
underwear

undervanns- (*ewn*-nerr-vahns)
underwater

undervise (*ewn*-nerr-vee-ser) *v*
**teach; instruct

undervisning (*ewn*-nerr-veess-ning) *c*
tuition, instruction

undervurdere (*ewn*-nerr-vew-dāy-rer) *v* underestimate

undre seg (*ewn*-drer) wonder; marvel

ung (oongng) *adj* young

ungarer (oong-gaa-rerr) *m*
Hungarian

Ungarn (ewng-gaan) Hungary

ungarsk (ewng-gaashk) *adj*
Hungarian

ungdom (oong-dom) *m* (pl ~mer)
youth; **ungdoms-** juvenile

ungdomsherberge (oong-doms-hær-bær-ger) *nt* youth hostel

unge (oong-nger) *m* kid

ungkar (oong-kaar) *m* bachelor

uniform (ew-ni-*form*) *c* uniform

union (ew-ni-*ōon*) *m* union

univers (ew-ni-*væshsh*) *nt* universe

universell (ew-ni-væ-*shehll*) *adj*
universal

universitet (ew-ni-væ-shi-*tāyt*) *nt*
university

****unngå** (*ewn*-gaw) *v* avoid; escape

unnskyld! (*ewn*-shewl) sorry!

unnskylde (*ewn*-shew-ler) *v* excuse

unnskyldning (*ewn*-shewl-ning) *m*
apology, excuse; **be om ~* apologize

****unnslippe** (*ewn*-shli-per) *v* escape

unntak (*ewn*-taak) *nt* (pl ~) exception

unntaksvis (*ewn*-taaks-vis) *adv* for a change

unntatt (*ewn*-taht) *prep* except

***unnvike** (*ewn*-vee-ker) *v* avoid

***unnvære** (*ewn*-vææ-rer) *v* spare

unyttig (*ēw*-new-ti) *adj* useless

ûnødvendig (*ēw*-nurd-vern-di) *adj* unnecessary

unøyaktig (*ēw*-nur^ew-ahk-ti) *adj* inaccurate

uoffisiell (*ēw*-o-fi-si-erl) *adj* unofficial

uopphørlig (*ēw*-oop-hūr-li) *adv* continually

uorden (*ēw*-o-dern) *m* disorder; **i ~** out of order; broken

uordentlig (*ēw*-ont-li) *adj* untidy

uoverkommelig (*ēw*-o-verr-ko-mer-li) *adj* prohibitive, insurmountable

uovertruffen (*ēw*-o-ver-troo-fern) *adj* unsurpassed

upartisk (*ēw*-paa-tisk) *adj* impartial

upassende (*ēw*-pah-ser-ner) *adj* improper

upersonlig (*ēw*-pæ-shōōn-li) *adj* impersonal

upopulær (*ēw*-poo-pew-læær) *adj* unpopular

upålitelig (*ēw*-po-lee-ter-li) *adj* unreliable, untrustworthy

ur (*ēw*r) *nt* watch

uregelmessig (*ēw*-rāy-gerl-meh-si) *adj* irregular

urett (*ēw*-reht) *m* wrong, injustice; ***gjøre ~** wrong; ***ha ~** *be wrong

urettferdig (*ēw*-reht-fæ-di) *adj* unfair, unjust

uriktig (ew-*rik*-ti) *adj* incorrect, wrong

urimelig (ew-*ree*-mer-li) *adj* unreasonable; absurd

urin (ew-*reen*) *m* urine

urmaker (*ēw*r-maa-kerr) *m* watch-maker

uro (*ēw*-rōō) *m* unrest

urolig (ew-*rōō*-li) *adj* restless; uneasy

urskog (*ēw*-shkōōg) *m* jungle; primeval forest

urt (ewtt) *c* herb

urtids- (*ēw*-tits) ancient

Uruguay (ew-rew-gew-*igh*) Uruguay

uruguayaner (ew-rew-gew-igh-*aa*-nerr) *m* Uruguayan

uruguayansk (ew-rew-gew-igh-*aansk*) *adj* Uruguayan

usann (*ēw*-sahn) *adj* untrue

usannsynlig (*ēw*-sahn-*sēw*n-li) *adj* improbable, unlikely

usedvanlig (ew-sehd-*vaan*-li) *adj* uncommon, extraordinary, exceptional

uselvisk (*ēw*-sehl-visk) *adj* unselfish

usikker (*ēw*-si-kerr) *adj* uncertain; doubtful; unsafe

uskadd (*ēw*-skahd) *adj* unhurt; whole

uskadelig (ew-*skaa*-der-li) *adj* harmless

uskikkelig (ew-*shik*-ker-li) *adj* naughty

uskyld (*ēw*-shewl) *c* innocence

uskyldig (ew-*shewl*-di) *adj* innocent

uspiselig (ew-*spee*-ser-li) *adj* inedible

ustabil (*ēw*-stah-beel) *adj* unstable

ustadig (ew-*staa*-di) *adj* unsteady

ustø (*ēw*-stūr) *adj* unsteady

usunn (*ēw*-sewn) *adj* unhealthy, unsound

usympatisk (*ēw*-sewm-paa-tisk) *adj* unpleasant

usynlig (ew-*sēwn*-li) *adj* invisible

ut (*ēw*t) *adv* out; ***gå ~** *go out; **~ over** beyond

utad (*ēw*-taad) *adv* outwards

utakknemlig (*ēw*-tahk-nehm-li) *adj* ungrateful

utbre (*ēw*t-brāy) *v* expand

utbredelse (*ēw*t-bred-*ehl*-ser) *m* expansion

utbrudd (*ēw*t-brewd) *nt* (pl ~)

outbreak

*utbryte (ēwt-brēw-ter) v exclaim

utbytte (ēwt-bew-ter) nt benefit; profit; ***ha ~ av** profit

utdanne (ēwt-dah-ner) v educate

utdannelse (ēwt-dah-nerl-ser) m education; background

utdele (ēwt-dāy-ler) v distribute

utdrag (ēwt-draag) nt (pl ~) extract, excerpt

utdype (ēwt-dēw-per) v elaborate

ute (ēw-ter) adv out

*utelate (ēw-ter-laa-ter) v omit, *leave out

utelukke (ēw-ter-loo-ker) v exclude

utelukkende (ēw-ter-loo-ker-ner) adv solely, exclusively

uten (ēw-tern) prep without

utenat (ēw-ter-naht) adv by heart

utendørs (ēw-tern-dūrsh) adv outdoors

utenfor (ēw-tern-for) prep outside; adv outside

utenkelig (ew-tehng-ker-li) adj inconceivable

utenlands (ēw-tern-lahns) adv abroad

utenlandsk (ēw-tern-lahnsk) adj alien, foreign

utflukt (ēwt-flookt) c trip, excursion, outing

utfolde (ēwt-fo-ler) v unfold, display

utfordre (ēwt-foord-rer) v challenge; dare; **utfordrende** challenging, defiant

utforske (ēwt-fosh-ker) v explore

utføre (ēwt-fūr-rer) v execute, perform, implement, carry out; export

utførlig (ewt-fūr-li) adj detailed

utførsel (ēwt-fur-sherl) m (pl -sler) exportation, export

utgang (ēwt-gahng) m way out, exit; outcome

utgangspunkt (ēwt-gahngs-poongt)

nt starting point

utgave (ēwt-gaa-ver) c edition

*utgi (ēwt-ʸee) v publish; issue; edit

utgift (ēwt-ʸift) c expense; **utgifter** expenditure

utgravning (ēwt-graav-ning) m excavation

*utgyte (ēwt-ʸew-ter) v *shed

utholde (ēwt-ho-ler) v endure

utholdelig (ēwt-ho-ler-li) adj tolerable

utilfreds (ēw-til-frehts) adj dissatisfied

utilfredsstillende (ēw-til-freht-sti-ler-ner) adj unsatisfactory

utilgjengelig (ēw-til-ʸeh-nger-li) adj inaccessible

utilsiktet (ēw-til-sik-tert) adj unintentional

utilstrekkelig (ēw-til-streh-ker-li) adj insufficient; inadequate

utiltalende (ēw-til-taa-ler-ner) adj unpleasant

utjevne (ēwt-ʸehv-ner) v equalize

utkant (ēwt-kahnt) m outskirts pl

utkast (ēwt-kahst) nt draft

utkjørsel (ēwt-khur-sherl) m exit, driveway

utkople (ēwt-kop-ler) v disconnect

utlede (ēwt-lāy-der) v deduce, infer

utlending (ēwt-lehn-ing) m alien, foreigner

utligne (ēwt-ling-ner) v level

utluftning (ēwt-lewft-ning) m ventilation

utløp (ēwt-lūrp) nt (pl ~) expiry

*utløpe (ēwt-lūr-per) v expire

utløpt (ēwt-lurpt) adj expired

utmatte (ēwt-mah-ter) v exhaust

utmattet (ēwt-mah-tert) adj tired

utmerke seg (ēwt-mær-ker) excel

utmerket (ēwt-mær-kert) adj fine, excellent

utnevne (ēwt-nehv-ner) v appoint

utnevnelse (ēwt-nehv-nerl-ser) m

nomination, appointment

utnytte (*ewt*-new-ter) *v* exploit

utpresse (*ewt*-preh-ser) *v* extort

utpressing (*ewt*-preh-sing) *c* extortion

utregning (*ewt*-ray-ning) *c* calculation

utrivelig (ew-*tree*-ver-li) *adj* unpleasant

utro (*ew*-troo) *adj* unfaithful

utrolig (ew-*troo*-li) *adj* incredible; amazing

utrop (*ewt*-roop) *nt* (pl ~) exclamation

utruste (*ewt*-rewss-ter) *v* equip

utrustning (*ewt*-rewst-ning) *m* outfit

utsalg (*ewt*-sahlg) *nt* (pl ~) sales

utseende (*ewt*-say-er-ner) *nt* look, appearance; semblance

utsending (*ewt*-seh-ning) *m* delegate

***utsette** (*ewt*-seh-ter) *v* postpone, delay, *put off, adjourn; expose; **utsatt for** liable to; subject to

utsettelse (*ewt*-seh-terl-ser) *m* delay

utside (*ewt*-seeer) *c* outside; exterior

utsikt (*ewt*-sikt) *m* view; prospect, outlook

utskeielse (*ewt*-shay-erl-ser) *m* excess

utskrift (*ewt*-skrift) *c* printout

utslett (*ewt*-sleht) *nt* rash

utslitt (*ewt*-shlit) *adj* worn-out

utsolgt (*ewt*-solt) *adj* sold out

utstedelse (*ewt*-stay-derl-ser) *m* issue

utstikker (*ewt*-sti-kerr) *m* pier

utstille (*ewt*-sti-ler) *v* *show, exhibit; display

utstilling (*ewt*-sti-ling) *c* exposition, exhibition, show, display

utstillingsdukke (*ewt*-sti-lings-dew-ker) *c* mannequin

utstillingslokale (*ewt*-sti-lings-loo-kaa-ler) *nt* showroom

utstillingsvindu (*ewt*-sti-lings-vin-dew) *nt* shop-window

utstrakt (*ewt*-strahkt) *adj* extensive, broad

utstyr (*ewt*-stewr) *nt* equipment; kit, gear

utstyre (*ewt*-stew-rer) *v* equip

utsøkt (*ewt*-surkt) *adj* exquisite, select

uttale (*ew*-taa-ler) *m* pronunciation; *v* pronounce; ~ **galt** mispronounce

uttrykk (*ew*-trewk) *nt* (pl ~) expression; phrase; term; *gi ~ for express

uttrykke (*ew*-trew-ker) *v* express

uttrykkelig (ew-*trewk*-ker-li) *adj* explicit, express

utvalg (*ewt*-vahlg) *nt* (pl ~) choice, selection; variety, assortment; committee

utvalgt (*ewt*-vahlt) *adj* select

utvandre (*ewt*-vahn-drer) *v* emigrate

utvei (*ewt*-vay) *m* way out; course

utveksle (*ewt*-vehk-shler) *v* exchange

utveksling (*ewt*-vehk-shling) *c* exchange

***utvelge** (*ewt*-vehl-ger) *v* select

utvendig (*ewt*-vehn-di) *adj* external, outward

utvide (*ewt*-vee-der) *v* widen; extend, expand, enlarge

utvidelse (*ewt*-vee-derl-ser) *m* extension; expansion

utvikle (*ewt*-vik-ler) *v* develop

utvikling (*ewt*-vik-ling) *c* development

utvilsomt (ew-*tveel*-somt) *adv* undoubtedly

utvise (*ewt*-vee-ser) *v* expel

utvungenhet (*ew*-tvoo-ngern-hayt) *c* ease

utydelig (ew-*tew*-der-li) *adj* dim

utøve (*ew*-tūr-ver) *v* exercise

utålelig (ew-*taw*-ler-li) *adj* intolerable

utålmodig (*ew*-tol-moo-di) *adj* eager, impatient

uunngåelig (ew-ewng-*gaw*-er-li) *adj* unavoidable, inevitable

uunnværlig (ew-ewn-*vææ*-li) *adj* essential

uutholdelig (ew-ewt-*hol*-ler-li) *adj*
unbearable

uvanlig (ew-*vahn*-li) *adj* unusual

uvant ($\overline{ew}$-vahnt) *adj* unaccustomed

uvedkommende ($\overline{ew}$-vā̄yd-ko-mer-ner) *m* (pl ~) trespasser

uvel ($\overline{ew}$-vehl) *adj* unwell

uvennlig ($\overline{ew}$-vehn-li) *adj* unkind, unfriendly

uventet ($\overline{ew}$-vehn-tert) *adj* unexpected

uvesentlig (ew-*vā̄y*-sernt-li) *adj* insignificant

uviktig ($\overline{ew}$-vik-ti) *adj* unimportant

uvillig ($\overline{ew}$-vi-li) *adj* unwilling; averse

uvirkelig ($\overline{ew}$-veer-ker-li) *adj* unreal

uvirksom ($\overline{ew}$-veerk-som) *adj* idle

uviss (ew-viss) *adj* uncertain

uvitende ($\overline{ew}$-vi-ter-ner) *adj* ignorant

uvurderlig ($\overline{ew}$-vew-*dā̄y*-li) *adj* priceless

uvær (ew-væær) *nt* (pl ~) tempest

uærlig ($\overline{ew}$-ææ-li) *adj* dishonest; crooked

uønsket ($\overline{ew}$-urn-skert) *adj* undesirable

V

vaffel (*vahf*-ferl) *m* (pl vafler) waffle

vag (vaag) *adj* vague, faint

vakker (*vahk*-kerr) *adj* handsome, fair, beautiful

vakle (*vahk*-ler) *v* falter

vaklende (*vahk*-ler-ner) *adj* shaky

vaksinasjon (vahk-si-nah-*shōōn*) *m* inoculation

vaksinere (vahk-si-*nā̄y*-rer) *v* vaccinate, inoculate

vaksinering (vahk-si-*nā̄y*-ring) *c* vaccination

vakt (vahkt) *m* guard; attendant

vaktel (*vahk*-terl) *m* (pl -tler) quail

vaktmester (*vahkt*-mehss-terr) *m* (pl ~e, -trer) caretaker, janitor

vakuum (*vaa*-kewm) *nt* vacuum

valen (*vaa*-lern) *adj* numb

valg (vahlg) *nt* choice, pick; election

valgfri (*vahlg*-free) *adj* optional

valgkrets (*vahlg*-krehts) *m* constituency

valgspråk (*vahlg*-sprawk) *nt* (pl ~) slogan

valmue (*vahl*-mēwer) *m* poppy

valnøtt (*vaal*-nurt) *c* walnut

vals (vahls) *m* waltz

valuta (vah-*lewt*-tah) *m* currency

valutakurs (vah-*lewt*-tah-kēwsh) *m* rate of exchange, exchange rate

vandre (*vahn*-drer) *v* wander

vandrerhjem (*vahn*-drer-ʸehmm) *nt* youth hostel

vane (*vaa*-ner) *m* custom, habit

vanilje (vah-*nil*-ʸer) *m* vanilla

vanlig (*vaan*-li) *adj* common, usual, ordinary, habitual; customary, regular, simple

vanligvis (*vaan*-li-veess) *adv* as a rule, usually

vann (vahnn) *nt* water; **innlagt ~** running water

vannfarge (*vahn*-fahr-ger) *m* watercolo(u)r

vannkopper (*vahn*-ko-perr) *pl* chickenpox

vannkran (*vahn*-kraan) *c* faucet *nAm*

vannmelon (*vahn*-meh-*lōōn*) *m* watermelon

vannski (*vahn*-shee) *c* water ski

vannstoff (*vahn*-stof) *nt* hydrogen; ~ **hyperoksyd** peroxide

vanntett (*vahn*-teht) *adj* rainproof, waterproof

vanskapt (*vahn*-skahpt) *adj* deformed

vanskelig (*vahn*-sker-li) *adj* difficult; hard

vanskelighet (*vahn*-sker-li-hāyt) *c* difficulty

vant (vahnt) *adj* accustomed; ***være ~ til** *be used to

vanvidd (*vahn*-vid) *nt* lunacy

vanvittig (*vahn*-vi-ti) *adj* mad

vaporisator (vah-poo-ri-*saa*-toor) *m* atomizer

vare (*vaa*-rer) *v* last; *c* ware

varebil (*vaa*-rer-beel) *m* pick-up van, van, delivery van

varehus (*vaa*-rer-hēwss) *nt* (pl ~) department store

varemerke (*vaa*-rer-mær-ker) *nt* trademark

varemesse (*vaa*-rer-meh-ser) *c* fair

vareopptelling (*vaa*-rer-oop-teh-ling) *c* inventory

vareprøve (*vaarer*-prūr-ver) *c* sample

varer (*vaa*-rerr) *pl* merchandise, wares *pl*, goods *pl*

varetekt (*vaa*-rer-tehkt) *c* custody

variabel (vah-ri-*aa*-berl) *adj* variable

variere (vah-ri-*āy*-rer) *v* vary

variert (vah-ri-*āyt*) *adj* varied

varig (*vaa*-ri) *adj* lasting; permanent

varighet (*vaa*-ri-hāyt) *c* duration

varm (vahrm) *adj* hot, warm

varme (*vahr*-mer) *m* heat, warmth; *v* warm; ~ **opp** heat

varmeflaske (*vahr*-mer-flahss-ker) *c* hot-water bottle

varmeovn (*vahr*-mer-ovn) *m* heater

varmepute (*vahr*-mer-pēw-ter) *c* heating pad

varsle (*vahsh*-ler) *v* forecast; notify

vase (*vaa*-ser) *m* vase

vask (vahsk) *m* washing; laundry; sink

vaskbar (*vahsk*-baar) *adj* washable

vaske (*vahss*-ker) *v* wash; ~ **opp** wash up

vaskemaskin (*vahss*-ker-mah-sheen) *m* washing machine

vaskepulver (*vahss*-ker-pewl-verr) *nt* washing powder

vaskeri (vahss-ker-*ree*) *nt* laundry

vasse (*vahss*-ser) *v* wade

vatt (vahtt) *m* cotton wool

vatt-teppe *nt* quilt

ved (vāy) *m* firewood; *prep* by; on; ~ **siden av** beside, next to

vedde (*vehd*-der) *v* *bet

veddeløp (*vehd*-der-lūrp) *nt* race

veddeløpsbane (*vehd*-der-lūrps-baa-ner) *m* race-course; racetrack

veddeløpshest (*vehd*-der-lūrps-hehst) *m* race-horse

veddemål (*vehd*-der-mawl) *nt* (pl ~) bet

vedlegg (*vāy*-lehg) *nt* enclosure; attachment

*vedlegge (*vāy*-leh-ger) *v* attach, enclose

vedlikehold (veh-*lee*-ker-hol) *nt* maintenance, upkeep

vedrøre (*vāy*-rūr-rer) *v* affect

vedrørende (*vāy*-rūr-rer-ner) *prep* with reference to, concerning

*vedta (*vāy*-taa) *v* adopt, decide

vedvarende (*vāy*-vaa-rer-ner) *adj* permanent

veg (vay) *m* road; way

vegetarianer (veh-ger-tah-ri-*aa*-nerr) *m* vegetarian

vegg (vehgg) *m* wall

veggedyr (*vehg*-ger-dēwr) *nt* (pl ~) bug

vei (vay) *m* road; way; **på ~ til** bound for

veiarbeid (*vay*-ahr-bayd) *nt* road work

veidekke (*vay*-deh-ker) *nt* pavement

veie (*vay*-er) *v* weigh

veikant (*vay*-kahnt) *m* roadside, wayside

veikart (*vay*-kaht) *nt* road map

veikryss (*vay*-krewss) *nt* (pl ~) intersection, junction

veilede (*vay*-lāy-der) *v* direct

veinett (*vay*-neht) *nt* (pl ~) road system

veiskilt (*vay*-shilt) *nt* road sign

veiviser (*vay*-vee-serr) *m* signpost

vekk (vehkk) *adv* off; away

vekke (*vehk*-ker) *v* *wake, *awake

vekkeklokke (*vehk*-ke-klo-ker) *c* alarm-clock

vekselstrøm (*vehk*-serl-strurm) *m* alternating current

vekselvis (*vehk*-sherl-veess) *adv* alternate

veksle (*vehk*-shler) *v* change; exchange

vekslepenger (*vehk*-shler-peh-ngerr) *pl* change

vekslingskontor (*vehk*-shlings-koon-tōōr) *nt* money exchange, exchange office

vekst (vehkst) *m* growth

vekt (vehkt) *c* weight; scales *pl*; ***legge ~ på** stress

vektstang (*vehkt*-stahng) *c* (pl -tenger) lever

velbegrunnet (*vehl*-beh-grew-nert) *adj* well-founded

velbehag (*vehl*-beh-haag) *nt* pleasure

veldig (*vehl*-di) *adj* huge; immense

velferd (*vehl*-fæær) *m* welfare

***velge** (*vehl*-ger) *v* *choose; pick; elect; ~ **ut** select

velgjørenhet (*vehl*-ʸūr-rern-hāyt) *c* charity

velhavende (*vehl*-haa-ver-ner) *adj* well-to-do

velkjent (*vehl*-khehnt) *adj* familiar; well-known

velkommen (vehl-*kom*-mern) *adj* welcome; **hilse ~** welcome

velkomst (*vehl*-komst) *m* welcome

vellykket (*vehl*-lew-kert) *adj* successful

velsigne (vehl-*sing*-ner) *v* bless

velsignelse (vehl-*sing*-nerl-ser) *m* blessing

velsmakende (*vehl*-smaa-ker-ner) *adj* tasty, savo(u)ry

velstand (*vehl*-stahn) *m* prosperity

velstående (*vehl*-stawer-ner) *adj* prosperous

velvære (*vehl*-vææ-rer) *nt* comfort

vemmelig (*vehm*-mer-li) *adj* nasty

vemod (*vāy*-mōōd) *nt* sadness

vemodig (*vāy*-mōō-di) *adj* sad

vende (*vehn*-ner) *v* turn; ~ **bort** avert; ~ **om** turn over; ~ **tilbake** return; *go back, turn back

vendepunkt (*vehn*-ner-pewngt) *nt* turning point

vending (*vehn*-ning) *c* turn

Venezuela (veh-neh-sew-*āy*-lah) Venezuela

venezuelaner (veh-neh-sew-eh-*laa*-nerr) *m* Venezuelan

venezuelansk (veh-neh-sew-eh-*laansk*) *adj* Venezuelan

venn (vehnn) *m* (male, female) friend

venne (*vehn*-ner) *v* accustom

venninne (veh-*nin*-ner) *c* (female) friend

vennlig (*vehn*-li) *adj* kind, friendly; **med ~ hilsen, mvh** best regards; yours sincerely

vennligst (*vehn*-likst) please

vennskap (*vehn*-skaap) *nt* friendship

vennskapelig (vehn-*skaa*-per-li) *adj* friendly

venstre (*vehn*-strer) *adj* left; left-hand

vente (*vehn*-ter) *v* wait; expect; ~ **på** await

venteliste (*vehn*-ter-liss-ter) *c*

waitinglist

ventet (vehn-tert) adj due

venteværelse (vehn-ter-vææ-rerl-ser) nt waiting room

ventil (vehn-teel) m valve

ventilasjon (vehn-ti-lah-shoon) m ventilation

ventilator (vehn-ti-laa-toor) m ventilator

ventilere (vehn-ti-lay-rer) v ventilate

venting (vehn-ting) m waiting

veps (vehps) m wasp

veranda (væ-rahn-dah) m veranda

verb (værb) nt verb

verd (værd) nt worth; ***være ~** *be worth

verden (vær-dern) m world

verdensberømt (vær-derns-beh-rurmt) adj world-famous

verdensdel (vær-derns-dayl) m continent

verdenskrig (vær-derns-kreeg) m world war

verdensomfattende (vær-dern-soom-fah-ter-ner) adj global

verdensomspennende (vær-dern-soom-speh-ner-ner) adj world-wide

verdensrom (vær-derns-room) nt space

verdi (væædee) m value

verdifull (væ-dee-fewl) adj valuable

verdig (væ-di) adj dignified; worthy of

verdighet (væ-di-hayt) c dignity

verdiløs (væ-dee-lurss) adj worthless

verdipapirer (væ-dee-pah-pee-rerr) pl stocks and shares

verdisaker (væ-dee-saa-kerr) pl valuables pl

*verdsette (værd-seh-ter) v appreciate estimate

verdsettelse (værd-seh-terl-ser) m appreciation

verk (værk) m ache; pus

verke (vær-ker) v ache

verken ... eller (vær-kern ... ehl-err) neither ... nor

verksted (værk-stay) nt workshop

verktøy (værk-tur^ew) nt implement, tool

vern (væn) nt defense Am, defence

vernepliktig (væ-ner-plik-ti) m conscript

verre (vær-rer) adv worse; adj worse; **verst** worst

vers (væshss) nt verse

versjon (væ-shoon) m version

vert (vætt) m host; landlord

vertikal (væ-ti-kaal) adj vertical

vertinne (væ-tin-ner) c hostess; landlady

vertshus (væts-hewss) nt (pl ~) public house; inn; m roadside restaurant

vesen (vay-sern) nt being; essence

vesentlig (vay-sernt-li) adj essential; vital

veske (vehss-ker) c bag

vest (vehst) m west; waistcoat; vest nAm

vestlig (vehst-li) adj western, westerly

veterinær (veh-ter-ri-næær) m veterinary surgeon

vett (vehtt) nt brains, sense

vev (vayv) m loom; nt tissue

veve (vay-ver) v *weave

vi (vee) pron we

via (vee-ah) prep via

viadukt (vi-ah-dewkt) m viaduct

vibrasjon (vi-brah-shoon) m vibration

vibrere (vi-bray-rer) v vibrate

vid (vee) adj wide

vidd (vidd) nt wit

vidde (vee-er) c plateau

videokamera (vid-eoo-kah-meh-raa) nt video camera

videokassett (vid-eoo-kah-sehtt) m video cassette

videospiller (vid-eoo-spil-lerr) m video recorder

videre (*vee*-der-rer) *adj* further;
farther; **og så ~** and so on, etcetera
vidstrakt (*vee*-strahkt) *adj* vast, broad
vidunder (vi-*dewn*-derr) *nt* (pl ~, ~e)
marvel
vidunderlig (vi-*dewn*-der-li) *adj*
wonderful, marvel(l)ous
vie (*vee*-er) *v* marry; devote; dedicate
vielse (*vee*-erl-ser) *m* wedding
vielsesring (*vee*-erl-serss-ring) *m*
wedding ring
vifte (*vif*-ter) *c* fan
vifterem (*vif*-ter-rehm) *c* fan belt
vik (veek) *c* inlet, creek
vikle (*vik*-ler) *v* *wind
viktig (*vik*-ti) *adj* important; big,
capital
viktighet (*vik*-ti-hāyt) *c* importance
vilje (*vil*-ʸer) *m* will; **med ~** on purpose
viljestyrke (*vil*-ʸer-stewr-ker) *m* willpower
vilkår (*vil*-kawr) *nt* condition
vilkårlig (vil-*kaw*-li) *adj* arbitrary
vill (vill) *adj* savage, wild; fierce; **gått ~**
lost
villa (*vil*-lah) *m* villa
*ville (*vil*-ler) *v* *will, want
villig (*vil*-li) *adj* willing
vilt (vilt) *nt* game, quarry
vin (veen) *m* wine
vind (vinn) *m* wind
vindebro (*vin*-ner-brōō) *c* drawbridge
vindhard (*vin*-haar) *adj* windy
vindkast (*vin*-kahst) *nt* (pl ~) blow,
gust
vindmølle (*vin*-mur-ler) *c* windmill
vindu (*vin*-dew) *nt* window
vindusvisker (*vin*-dewss-viss-kerr) *m*
windscreen wiper; windshield wiper
Am
vinge (vingng-er) *m* wing
vink (vingk) *nt* sign
vinkart (*veen*-kaht) *nt* wine list
vinke (*ving*-ker) *v* wave

vinkel (*ving*-kerl) *m* (pl -kler) angle
vinkjeller (*veen*-kheh-lerr) *m* wine
cellar
vinmonopol (*veen*-moo-noo-pōōl) *nt*
off-licence, *Am* liquor store
*vinne (*vin*-ner) *v* gain, *win
vinnende (*vin*-ner-ner) *adj* winning
vinner (*vin*-nerr) *m* winner
vinranke (*veen*-rahng-ker) *m* vine
vinter (*vin*-terr) *m* (pl -trer) winter
vintersport (*vin*-ter-shpot) *m* winter
sports
vipe (*vee*-per) *c* pewit
vippe (*vip*-per) *c* seesaw
virke (*veer*-ker) *v* work; operate
virkelig (*veer*-ker-li) *adj* actual, real;
very, true; substantial; *adv* indeed,
really
virkelighet (*veer*-ker-li-hāyt) *c* reality;
i virkeligheten as a matter of fact
virkemåte (*veer*-ker-maw-ter) *m*
mode of operation
virkning (*veerk*-ning) *m* effect
virkningsfull (*veerk*-nings-fewl) *adj*
effective, efficient
virkningsløs (*veerk*-nings-lūrss) *adj*
inefficient, ineffective
virksom (*veerk*-som) *adj* active
virksomhet (*veerk*-som-hāyt) *c*
enterprise, business
virvar (*veer*-vahr) *nt* muddle
vis (veess) *adj* wise; *nt* way, manner
visdom (*veess*-dom) *m* wisdom
vise (*vee*-ser) *v* *show; point out;
display; **~ frem** *show; **~ seg** appear;
prove
visepresident (*vee*-ser-preh-si-dehnt)
m vice president
visitere (vi-si-*tāy*-rer) *v* search
visitt (vi-*sitt*) *m* call, visit
visittkort (vi-*sit*-kot) *nt* (pl ~) card,
business card
viskelær (*viss*-ker-læær) *nt* (pl ~)
rubber, eraser

vispe (*viss*-per) *v* whip

viss (viss) *adj* certain

visse (*viss*-ser) *pron* some

visum (*vee*-sewm) *nt* (pl visa) visa

vitamin (vi-tah-*meen*) *nt* vitamin

***vite** (*vee*-ter) *v* *know

vitebegjærlig (*vee*-ter-beh-ʸææ-li) *adj* curious

vitenskap (*vee*-tern-skaap) *m* science

vitenskapelig (*vee*-tern-skaaper-li) *adj* scientific

vitenskapskvinne (*vee*-tern-skaaps-kvin-ner) *c* (female) scientist

vitenskapsmann (*vee*-tern-skaaps-mahn) *m* (pl -menn) (male) scientist

vitne (*vit*-ner) *nt* witness; *v* testify

vitnesbyrd (*vit*-nerss-bewrd) *nt* certificate

vits (vits) *m* joke

vittig (*vit*-ti) *adj* humorous, witty

vogn (voangn) *c* carriage

vokal (voo-*kaal*) *m* vowel; *adj* vocal

voks (voks) *m* wax

vokse (*vok*-ser) *v* *grow

voksen[1] (*vok*-sern) *m* (pl -sne) adult, grown-up

voksen[2] (*vok*-sern) *adj* adult, grown-up

vokskabinett (*voks*-kah-bi-neht) *nt* waxworks *pl*

vokte seg (*vok*-ter) beware

vold (voll) *m* violence; force

volde (*vol*-ler) *v* cause

voldsom (*vol*-som) *adj* violent

***voldta** (*vol*-taa) *v* rape

voldtekt (*vol*-tekt) *c* rape

vollgrav (*vol*-graav) *c* moat

volt (volt) *m* volt

volum (voo-*lewm*) *nt* volume

vond (voonn) *adj* bad, painful; evil; ***gjøre vondt** *hurt; ***ha vondt** *have a pain

vorte (*vor*-ter) *c* wart

votter (*vot*-terr) *pl* mittens *pl*

vrak (vraak) *nt* wreck

vrengt (vrehngt) *adj* inside out

***vri** (vree) *v* twist, wrench; ~ **om** turn

vridning (*vreed*-ning) *m* twist

vrien (*vree*-ern) *adj* difficult

vrøvle (*vrurv*-ler) *v* talk rubbish

vugge (*vewg*-ger) *c* cradle

vulgær (vewl-*gæær*) *adj* vulgar

vulkan (vewl-*kaan*) *m* volcano

vurdere (vew-*dāy*-rer) *v* evaluate; value, estimate

vurdering (vew-*dāy*-ring) *c* estimate; appreciation

vær (væær) *nt* weather

***være** (*vææ*-rer) *v* *be; **vær så god** here you are

værelse (*vææ*-rerl-ser) *nt* room; ~ **med frokost** bed and breakfast

værelsesbetjening (*vææ*-rerl-serss-beh-tʸāy-ning) *c* room service

værelsestemperatur (*vææ*-rerl-serss-tehm-peh-rah-tewr) *m* room temperature

værmelding (*væær*-meh-ling) *c* weather forecast

væske (*vehss*-ker) *c* fluid

våge (*vaw*-ger) *v* dare; venture

vågemot (*vaw*-ger-mōōt) *nt* guts

våken (*vaw*-kern) *adj* awake

våkne (*vok*-ner) *v* wake up

våningshus (*vaw*-nings-hēwss) *nt* (pl ~) farmhouse

våpen (*vaw*-pern) *nt* (pl ~) arm, weapon

våpenstillstand (*vaw*-pern-still-stann) *m* ceasefire

vår[1] (vawr) *pron* our; ours

vår[2] (vawr) *m* spring; springtime

våt (vawt) *adj* wet; moist

W

watt (vahtt) *m* watt

Y

ydmyk (*ēwd*-mēwk) *adj* humble

ynde (*ewn*-der) *m* grace

yndig (*ewn*-di) *adj* lovely, graceful

yndling (*ewnd*-ling) *m* favo(u)rite;
 yndlings- pet, favo(u)rite

ynkelig (*ewng*-ker-li) *adj* lamentable

yrke (*ewr*-ker) *nt* trade; occupation

yte (*ēw*-ter) *v* yield, produce

ytre (*ewt*-rer) *v* utter; express; *adj*
 exterior

ytterlig (*ewt*-ter-li) *adj* extreme

ytterligere (*ewt*-ter-li-er-rer) *adj*
 additional, further

ytterlighet (*ewt*-ter-li-hāyt) *c* extreme

ytterside (*ewt*-ter-shee-der) *c* outside

ytterst (*ewt*-tersht) *adj* utmost,
 extreme

Z

zoo (sōō) *m* zoo; **zoologisk hage**
 zoological gardens

zoologi (soo-loo-*gi*) *m* zoology

zoomlinse (*sōōm*-lin-ser) *c* zoom lens

Æ

ærbødig (ær-*būr*-di) *adj* respectful

ærbødighet (ær-*būr*-di-hāyt) *c* respect

ære (*ææ*-rer) *c* honour; glory; *v*
 honour

ærefull (*ææ*-rer-fewl) *adj* honourable

ærend (*ææ*-rern) *nt* errand

æresfølelse (*ææ*-rerss-*fūr*-erl-ser) *m*
 sense of honour

ærgjerrig (ær-ʸær-ri) *adj* ambitious

ærgjerrighet (ær-ʸær-ri-hāyt) *c*
 ambition

ærlig (*ææ*-li) *adj* honest; straight

ærlighet (*ææ*-li-hāyt) *c* honesty

ærverdig (ær-*vær*-di) *adj* venerable

Ø

øde (*ūr*-der) *adj* desert; waste

*ødelegge (*ūr*-der-leh-ger) *v* wreck; smash; destroy; ruin; *spoil

ødeleggelse (*ūr*-der-leh-gerl-ser) *m* destruction

ødsel (*urt*-serl) *adj* wasteful; lavish

øke (*ūr*-ker) *v* increase; raise

økning (*ūrk*-ning) *m* increase

økologi (ur-koo-loo-*gee*) *m* ecology

økologisk (ur-koo-loo-*gisk*) *adj* ecologic; ecological

økonom (ur-koo-*nōōm*) *m* economist

økonomi (ur-koo-noo-*mee*) *m* economy

økonomisk (ur-koo-*nōō*-misk) *adj* economic; economical

øks (urks) *c* axe

øl (urll) *nt* beer; ale

øm (urmm) *adj* sore; gentle, tender

ønske (*urns*-ker) *v* wish, want, desire; *nt* wish, desire; ~ til lykke congratulate

ønskelig (*urns*-ker-li) *adj* desirable

øre (*ūr*-rer) *nt* ear

øredobb (*ūr*-rer-dob) *m* earring

øreverk (*ūr*-rer-værk) *m* earache

ørken (*urr*-kern) *m* desert

ørn (*ūrn*) *c* eagle

ørret (*urr*-rert) *m* trout

øsregn (*ūrss*-rayn) *nt* downpour

øst (urst) *m* east

Østerrike (*urss*-ter-ree-ker) Austria

østerriker (*urss*-ter-ree-kerr) *m* Austrian

østerriksk (*urss*-ter-reeksk) *adj* Austrian

østers (*urss*-tersh) *m* (pl ~) oyster

østlig (*urst*-li) *adj* eastern; easterly

østre (*urst*-rer) *adj* eastern

øve (*ūr*-ver) *v* exercise; ~ seg practise

øvelse (*ūrv*-erl-ser) *m* exercise

øverst (*ūr*-versht) *adj* top

øvre (*ūrv*-rer) *adj* upper

for øvrig (for *ūrv*-ri) moreover

øy (ur^(ew)) *c* island

øye (ur^(ew)-er) *nt* (pl øyne) eye

øyeblikk (ur^(ew)-er-blik) *nt* instant, second, moment

øyeblikkelig (ur^(ew)-er-*blik*-li) *adv* instantly, immediately; *adj* immediate

øyenbryn (ur^(ew)-ern-br^(ēwn)) *nt* (pl ~) eyebrow

øyenbrynsblyant (ur^(ew)-ern-br^(ēwns)-blew-ahnt) *m* eyebrow pencil

øyenlege (ur^(ew)-ern-*lāy*-ger) *m* oculist

øyenlokk (ur^(ew)-ern-lok) *nt* eyelid

øyenskygge (ur^(ew)-ern-shew-ger) *m* eye shadow

øyensverte (ur^(ew)-ern-svæ-ter) *c* mascara

øyensynlig (ur^(ew)-ern-*sēwn*-li) *adv* apparently

øyenvippe (ur^(ew)-ern-vi-per) *m* eyelash

øyenvitne (ur^(ew)-ern-vit-ner) *nt* eyewitness

Å

åbor (*ob*-boor) *m* bass, perch

åk (awk) *nt* yoke

åker (*aw*-kerr) *m* (pl åkrer) field

ål (awl) *m* eel

ånd (onn) *m* spirit; ghost

åndedrett (*on*-der-dreht) *nt* breathing, respiration

åndelig (*on*-der-li) *adj* spiritual

åpen (*aw*-pern) *adj* open

åpenbare (*aw*-pern-baa-rer) *v* reveal

åpenbart (*aw*-pern-baat) *adv* apparently

åpenhjertig (*aw*-pern-ᵞæ-ti) *adj* open

åpne (*awp*-ner) *v* open; *undo

åpning (*awp*-ning) *c* opening; breach, gap

åpningstid (*awp*-nings-teed) *c* business hours

år (awr) *nt* year; **per ~** per annum

årbok (*awr*-bōōk) *c* (pl -bøker) annual

åre (*aw*-rer) *m* oar; vein

åreknute (*aw*-rer-knēw-ter) *m* varicose vein

århundre (*awr*-hewn-drer) *nt* century

årlig (*aw*-li) *adj* yearly, annual

årsak (*aw*-shaak) *c* reason, cause

årsdag (*awsh*-daag) *m* anniversary

årstid (*awsh*-teed) *c* season

årvåken (*awr*-vaw-kern) *adj* vigilant

åtte (*ot*-ter) *num* eight

åttende (*ot*-ter-ner) *num* eighth

åtti (*ot*-ti) *num* eighty

Menu Reader
Food

agurk cucumber

ananas pineapple

and duck

ansjos anchovies

appelsin orange

aprikos apricot

arme riddere French toast; slices of
  bread dipped in batter and fried,
  served with jam

asparges asparagus
  ~ bønne French bean (US green
    bean)
  ~ topp asparagus tip

bakt baked

banan banana

bankebiff slices or chunks of beef
  simmered in gravy

bekkørret river trout

benløse fugler rolled slices of veal
  stuffed with minced meat

betasuppe thick soup of meat and
  vegetables

biff beefsteak
  ~ med løk with fried onions
  ~ tartar steak tartare, minced raw
    steak

bjørnebær blackberry

blandede grønnsaker mixed
  vegetables

blodpudding black pudding (US
  blood sausage)

blomkål cauliflower

bløtkake rich sponge layer cake

blåbær bilberry (US blueberry)

blåskjell mussel

brekkbønne French bean (US green
  bean)

bringebær raspberry

brisling sprat

broiler specially fed 2-months-old

chicken

brød bread

buljong broth, consommé

bønne bean

daddel (pl dadler) date

dagens meny day's menu

dagens rett day's special

drue grape

dyrestek roast venison

eddik vinegar

egg egg
  ~ og bacon bacon and eggs
  bløtkokt ~ soft-boiled
  forlorent ~ poached
  hardkokt ~ hard-boiled
  kokt ~ boiled
  speil~ fried (US sunny side up)

eggerøre scrambled eggs

elgstek roast elk (US moose)

eple apple
  ~ kake apple cake

ert pea

ertesuppe pea soup

estragon tarragon

fasan pheasant

fenalår cured leg of mutton

fersken peach

ferskt kjøtt og suppe meat-and-
  vegetable soup

fiken fig

fisk fish

fiskebolle fish ball

fiskegrateng fish casserole

fiskekabaret fish and shellfish in aspic

fiskekake fried fish ball

fiskepudding fish pudding

fiskesuppe fish soup

flatbrød thin wafer of rye and
  sometimes barley

fleskepannekake thick pancake with

bacon

fleskepølse pork sandwich spread

flyndrefilet fillet of flounder

fløte cream

~ **ost** cream cheese

~ **vaffel** cream-enriched waffle often served with jam

forrett first course, starter

frokost breakfast

fromasj mousse, blancmange

frukt fruit

~ **is** water-ice, sherbet

~ **salat** fruit salad

~ **terte** fruit tart

fugl fowl

fyll stuffing, forcemeat

fårefrikassé mutton or lamb fricassee

fårekjøtt mutton

fårestek leg of lamb

fårikål mutton or lamb in cabbage stew

gaffelbiter salt- and sugar-cured herring fillets

gammelost a semi-hard cheese with grainy texture and strong flavour

geitekilling kid

geitost a bitter-sweet brown cheese made from goat's milk

gjedde pike

grapefrukt grapefruit

gravet ørret salt-cured trout flavoured with dill

gravlaks salt- and sugar-cured salmon flavoured with dill, often served with creamy dill-and-mustard sauce

gressløk chive

griljert breaded

grillet grilled

grovbrød brown bread

grønnsak vegetable

grøt porridge, cereal

gudbrandsdalsost a slightly sweet brown cheese made from goat's and cow's milk

gulrot (pl **gulrøtter**) carrot

gås goose

gåselever(postei) goose liver (paste)

gåsestek roast goose

hasselnøtt hazelnut

havre oats

~ **grøt** oatmeal (porridge)

~ **kjeks** oatmeal biscuit (US oatmeal cookie)

helkornbrød wholemeal (US whole-wheat) bread

hellefisk halibut

helstekt roasted whole

hjemmelaget home-made

hoffdessert layers of meringue and whipped cream, topped with chocolate sauce and toasted almonds

honning honey

hummer lobster

hvalbiff steak of whale

hvetebolle sweet roll, bun

~ **med rosiner** with raisins

hvitløk garlic

hvitting whiting

hønsefrikassé chicken fricassée

is ice, water ice (US sherbet)

~ **krem** ice-cream

italiensk salat salad of diced cold meat or ham, apples, potatoes, gherkins and other vegetables in mayonnaise

jordbær strawberry

julekake rich fruit cake (Christmas speciality)

kake cake, tart

kalkun turkey

kalvekjøtt veal

kalvekotelett veal chop

kalvemedaljong a small round fillet of veal

kalvetunge calf's tongue

kanel cinnamon

karamellpudding caramel blancmange (US pudding)

karbonadekake hamburger steak
kardemomme cardamom
karri curry
karve caraway seed
kastanje chestnut
kirsebær cherry
kjeks biscuit (US cracker or cookie)
kjøtt meat
~ **bolle** meat ball
~ **deig** minced meat
~ **kake** small hamburger steak
~ **pudding** meat loaf
~ **suppe** broth with diced meat or sausage
klippfisk salted and dried cod
knekkebrød crisp bread (US hardtack)
kokosmakron coconut macaroon
kokosnøtt coconut
kokt cooked, boiled
koldtbord a buffet of cold dishes such as fish, meat, salad, cheese and dessert
kolje haddock
korint currant
kotelett chop, cutlet
krabbe crab
kransekake cone-shaped pile of almond-macaroon rings
krem whipped cream
kreps crayfish
kringle ring-twisted bread with raisins
kryddersild soused herring
kumle potato dumpling
kylling chicken
~ **bryst** breast
~ **lår** leg, thigh
~ **vinge** wing
kål cabbage
~ **ruletter** cabbage leaves stuffed with minced meat
laks salmon
lammebog shoulder of lamb
lammebryst brisket of lamb

lammekotelett lamb chop
lapskaus thick stew of diced or minced meat (generally beef, lamb or pork), potatoes, onions and other vegetables
lefse thin pancake (without eggs)
lettstekt sautéed
lever liver
~ **postei** liver paste
loff white bread
lompe kind of potato pancake
lungemos hash of pork lungs and onions
lutefisk boiled stockfish, served with white sauce or melted butter and potatoes
løk onion
makrell mackerel
mandel (pl **mandler**) almond
marengs meringue
marinert marinated
medisterkake hamburger steak made of pork
meny bill of fare, menu
middag dinner
molte Arctic cloudberry
morell morello cherry
morkel (pl **morkler**) morel mushroom
multe Arctic cloudberry
musling mussel
mysost a brown whey cheese similar to *gudbrandsdalsost*
mørbrad rumpsteak
napoleonskake custard slice (US napoleon)
normannaost blue cheese
nype rose hip
nyre kidney
nøtt nut
oksefilet fillet of beef
oksehalesuppe oxtail soup
oksekjøtt beef
okserull rolled stuffed beef, served cold

oksestek roast beef
omelett med sjampinjonger button mushroom omelet
ost cheese
pai pie
pale young coalfish
panert breaded
pannekake pancake
pepperkake ginger biscuit (US ginger snap)
pepperrot horse-radish
 ~ saus horse-radish sauce
persille parsley
pinnekjøtt salted and fried ribs of mutton roasted on twigs (Christmas speciality)
pir small mackerel
pisket krem whipped cream
plomme plum
 ~ grøt med fløtemelk stewed plums and cream
plukkfisk poached fish (usually dried cod or haddock) in white sauce
pommes frites potato chips (US French fries)
postei 1) vol-au-vent 2) meat or fish pie
potet potato
 ~ chips crisps (US chips)
 ~ gull crisps (US chips)
 ~ kake potato fritter
pultost a soft, sometimes fermented cheese, usually flavoured with caraway seeds
purre leek
pyttipanne diced meat and potatoes fried with onions, sometimes topped with a fried egg
pære pear
pølse sausage
rabarbra rhubarb
rakørret salt-cured trout
rapphøne partridge
reddik radish

regnbueørret rainbow trout
reinsdyrstek roast reindeer
reke shrimp
remuladesaus mayonnaise mixed with cream, chopped gherkins and parsley
rips redcurrant
ris rice
risengrynsgrøt rice pudding sprinkled with cinnamon and sugar, served warm
riskrem boiled rice mixed with whipped cream, served with raspberry or strawberry sauce
rislapp small sweet rice cake
ristet grilled, sautéed, toasted
rogn roe
rosenkål brussels sprout
rosin raisin
rundstykke roll
rype ptarmigan, snow grouse
rødbete beetroot
rødgrøt fruit pudding served with vanilla custard or cream
rødkål red cabbage
rødspette plaice
røkelaks smoked salmon
røkt smoked
rømme thick sour cream
 ~ grøt boiled and served with sugar
rørte tyttebær cranberry jam made without cooking
rå raw
 ~ stekt underdone
saus sauce
sei coalfish
selleri celery
sennep mustard
service inkludert service included
sild herring
sildekake herring patty
sildesalat salad of diced salt herring, cucumber, onions, vegetables, spices and mayonnaise

sirupssnipp ginger biscuit (US ginger snap)
sitron lemon
~ **fromasj** lemon blancmange (US lemon custard)
sjampinjong button mushroom, champignon
sjokolade chocolate
sjøtunge sole
sjøørret sea trout
skalldyr shellfish
skilpaddesuppe turtle soup
skinke ham
skive slice
slangeagurk cucumber
smør butter
~ **brød** open-faced sandwich
småkake biscuit (US cookie)
snittebønner sliced French beans
solbær blackcurrant
sopp mushroom
speilegg fried egg
spekemat cured meat (beef, mutton, pork, reindeer), often served with scrambled eggs and chives
spekepølse large air-dried sausage
spekesild salted herring, often served with cabbage, potatoes and pickled beetroot
spekeskinke cured ham
spinat spinach
stangselleri branch celery
stek roast
stekt fried, roasted
stikkelsbær gooseberry
stuet creamed
sukker sugar
~ **brød** sponge cake
~ **ert** sugar pea
suppe soup

surkål boiled cabbage flavoured with sugar, vinegar and caraway seeds
sursild soused herring
svinekjøtt pork
svinekotelett pork chop
svineribbe spare-rib
svinestek roast pork
sviske prune
~ **grøt** stewed prunes
sylte brawn (US head cheese)
~ **agurk** pickled gherkin (US pickle)
syltelabb boiled and salt-cured pig's trotter (US pig's foot)
syltetøy jam
terte tart, cake
tilslørte bondepiker dessert made from layers of apple sauce and bread-crumbs, topped with whipped cream
timian thyme
torsk cod
torskerogn cod roe
torsketunge cod tongue
trøffel (pl **trøfler**) truffle
tunfisk tunny (US tuna)
tunge tongue
tyttebær kind of cranberry
vaffel waffle
vaktel quail
valnøtt walnut
vannbakkels cream puff
vannis water-ice (US sherbet)
vilt game
voksbønne butter bean (US wax bean)
vørterkake spiced malt bread
wienerbrød Danish pastry
ørret (salmon) trout
østers oyster
ål eel
årfugl black grouse

Drinks

akevitt spirits distilled from potatoes or grain, often flavoured with aromatic seeds and spices
alkoholfri non-alcoholic
aperitiff aperitif
bar neat (US straight)
brennevin brandy, spirit
brus fizzy (US carbonated) fruit drink, soft drink
dobbel double
dram shot of spirit
eplemost applejuice
fløte cream
fruktsaft fruit juice
gløgg similar to mulled wine, with spirits and spices
is ice
  med ~ on the rocks
jus / juice orange juice
kaffe coffee
  ~ med fløte with cream
  ~ uten fløte black
  ~is~ iced
kakao cocoa
kefir kefir, fermented milk
konjakk cognac
likør liqueur

melk milk
  kald ~ cold
  varm ~ warm
mineralvann mineral water; soft drink
pils lager
pjolter long drink of whisky or brandy and soda water
portvin port (wine)
rom rum
rødvinstoddi mulled wine
saft squash (US fruit drink)
sjokolade chocolate drink
te tea
  ~ med sitron with lemon
vann water
vin wine
  hvit~ white
  musserende ~ sparkling
  rød~ red
  tørr ~ dry
øl beer
  bayer~ medium-strong, dark
  bokk~ bock
  export~ strong, light coloured
  lager~ light lager
  vørter~ non-alcoholic beer

Mini Norwegian Grammar

Articles

Norwegian nouns are either masculine, feminine, or neuter. The majority of feminine nouns also have a masculine form, so we have chosen to use the denotations *m* (masculine), *c* (common) and *nt* (neuter). In this way, you will have to learn only two sets of articles, as masculine and common words can have the same article:

1. Indefinite article (a/an)

masculine:	**en bil**	*a* car
common*:	**en dør**	*a* door
neuter:	**et eple**	*an* apple

2. Definite article (the)
Where we, in English, say "the house" Norwegians tag the definite article onto the end of the noun and say "house-the". In masculine and common nouns "the" is **-(e)n**, in neuter nouns **-(e)t**.

masculine:	**bilen**	*the* car
common*:	**døren**	*the* door
neuter:	**eplet**	*the* apple

Nouns

The plural of most nouns is formed by an **-(e)r** ending (indefinite plural) and an **-(e)ne** ending (definite plural).

masculine:	**biler**	cars	**bilene**	*the* cars
common*:	**dører**	doors	**dørene**	*the* doors
neuter:	**epler**	apples	**eplene**	*the* apples

Many monosyllabic nouns have irregular plurals.

| **en mann** | a man | **menn** | men | **mennene** | the men |
| **en sko** | a shoe | **sko** | shoes | **skoene** | the shoes |

Adjectives

1. Adjectives agree with the noun in gender and number. For the indefinite form, the neuter is generally formed by adding **-t**, the plural by adding **-e**.

| **(en) stor hund** | (a) big dog | **store hunder** | big dogs |
| **(et) stort hus** | (a) big house | **store hus** | big houses |

---

* In the feminine form "a door, the door" would be *ei* dør, *døra*; the common form is *en* dør, *døren*. In plural there is no difference.

2. The ending **-e** (masculine, common, neuter and plural) is used when the adjective is preceded by **den, det, de** (the definite article used with adjectives) or by a demonstrative or a possessive adjective.

den store hunden	the big dog	**det store huset**	the big house
de store hundene	the big dogs	**de store husene**	the big houses

3. Comparative and superlative

The comparative and superlative are normally formed either by adding the endings **-(e)re** and **-(e)st**, respectively, to the adjective or by putting **mer** (more) and **mest** (most) before the adjective.

stor/ større/ størst	big/bigger/biggest
lett/lettere/lettest	easy/easier/easiest
imponerende/mer impone-	impressive/more impressive/
rende/mest imponerende	the most impressive

4. Possessive adjectives agree in number and gender with the noun they modify, i.e. with the thing possessed and not the possessor.

	common	neuter	plural
my	**min**	**mitt**	**mine**
your	**din**	**ditt**	**dine**
his	**sin, hans**	**sitt, hans**	**sine, hans**
her	**sin, hennes**	**sitt, hennes**	**sine, hennes**
its	**sin, dens/dets***	**sitt, dens/dets**	**sine, dens/dets**
our	**vår**	**vårt**	**våre**
their	**sin, deres**	**sitt, deres**	**sine, deres**

Personal pronouns

	subject	object	genitive
I	**jeg**	**meg**	–
you	**du**	**deg**	–
he	**han**	**ham/han**	**hans**
she	**hun**	**henne**	**hennes**
it	**den/det**	**den/det**	**dens/dets**
we	**vi**	**oss**	–
you (plural)	**dere**	**dere**	–
they	**de**	**dem**	**deres**

---

* Use **dens** if "it" is of common gender and **dets** if "it" is neuter.

Verbs

The present tense is simple, because it has the same form for all persons.

	to ask	to buy	to go	to do
Infinitive	å spørre	å kjøpe	å gå	å gjøre
Present tense	spør	kjøper	går	gjør
Imperative	spør	kjøp	gå	gjør

There is no equivalent to the English present continuous tense. Thus:

Jeg reiser.   I travel/I am travelling.

Negation is expressed by using the adverb **ikke** (not). It is usually placed immediately after the verb in a main clause. In compound tenses, **ikke** appears between the auxiliary and the main verb.

Jeg snakker norsk.   I speak Norwegian.
Jeg snakker ikke norsk.   I do not speak Norwegian.

Irregular Verbs

There is a large number of prefixes in Norwegian, like *an-*, *av-*, *be-*, *etter-*, *for-*, *fra-*, *frem-*, *inn-*, *med-*, *ned-*, *om-*, *opp-*, *over-*, *på-*, *til-*, *under-*, *unn-*, *unna-*, *ut-*, *ved-*, etc. A prefixed verb is conjugated in the same way as the stem verb.

Infinitive	Preterite	Past participle	
be	ba	bedt	*ask, pray*
binde	bandt	bundet	*bind, tie*
bite	bet	bitt	*bite*
bli	ble	blitt	*become, remain*
brekke	brakk	brukket	*break*
brenne	brant/brente*	brent	*burn*
bringe	brakte	brakt	*bring*
briste	brast	bristet	*burst*
bryte	brøt	brutt	*break*
by	bydde/bød	budt	*offer; command*
bære	bar	båret	*bear*
dra	dro(g)	dradd/dratt	*pull; go, travel*
drikke	drakk	drukket	*drink*
drive	drev	drevet	*lead, manage; drift*
ete	åt	ett	*eat (animals)*
falle	falt	falt	*fall*
fare	fór	faret/fart	*go away, leave*
finne	fant	funnet	*find*
fly	fløy	fløyet	*fly*
flyte	fløt	flytt	*flow, float*
forstå	forsto(d)	forstått	*understand*
forsvinne	forsvant	forsvunnet	*disappear*
fortelle	fortalte	fortalt	*tell, relate*
fryse	frøs	frosset	*be cold, freeze*
følge	fulgte	fulgt	*follow*
få	fikk	fått	*get*
gi	ga(v)	gitt	*give*
gjelde	gjaldt	gjeldt	*concern; be valid*
gjøre	gjorde	gjort	*do, make*
gli	gled	glidd	*slide, glide*
gnage	gnagde/gnog	gnagd	*gnaw*
gni	gnidde/gned	gnidd	*rub*
grave	gravde/grov	gravd	*dig*
gripe	grep	grepet	*catch, seize*
gråte	gråt	grått	*weep, cry*

* These verbs are regular when used transitively, i.e. when they take an object.

gyte	gytte/gjøt	gytt	*spawn*
gå	gikk	gått	*walk, go*
ha	hadde	hatt	*have*
henge	hang/hengte*	hengt	*hang*
hete	het/hette	hett	*be called*
hive	hev	hevet	*throw*
hjelpe	hjalp	hjulpet	*help*
holde	holdt	holdt	*hold*
klinge	klang	kling(e)t	*ring*
klype	klypte/kløp	klypt/kløpet	*pinch*
klyve	kløv	kløvet	*climb*
knekke	knakk/knekte*	knekt/knekket	*crack, break*
knipe	knep	knepet	*pinch*
komme	kom	kommet	*come*
krype	krøp	krøpet	*creep, crawl*
kunne (kan)	kunne	kunnet	*can*
kveppe	kvapp	kveppet	*startle*
la(te)	lot	latt	*let*
le	lo	ledd	*laugh*
legge	la	lagt	*lay, put*
lide	led	lidd	*suffer*
ligge	lå	ligget	*lie*
lyde	lød	lydt	*sound*
lyge	løy	løyet	*tell a lie*
løpe	løp	løpt	*run*
måtte (må)	måtte	måttet	*must*
nyse	nyste/nøs	nyst	*sneeze*
nyte	nøt	nytt	*enjoy*
pipe	pep	pepet	*chirp*
rekke	rakte/rakk	rakt/rukket	*reach; hand*
renne	rant/rente*	rent	*run, flow*
ri(de)	red	ridd	*ride*
rive	rev	revet	*tear*
ryke	røk	røket	*smoke*
se	så	sett	*see*
selge	solgte	solgt	*sell*
sette	satte	satt	*set*
si	sa	sagt	*say*
sitte	satt	sittet	*sit*
skjelve	skalv	skjelvet	*tremble*
skjære	skar	skåret	*cut*
skri(de)	skred	skredet/skridd	*stride, stalk*

---

* These verbs are regular when used transitively, i.e. when they take an object.

skrike	skrek	skreket	*scream*
skrive	skrev	skrevet	*write*
skryte	skrøt	skrytt	*boast*
skulle (skal)	skulle	skullet	*shall*
skvette	skvatt/skvettet*	skvettet	*startle; splash*
skyte	skjøt	skutt	*shoot*
skyve	skjøv	skjøvet	*push, shove*
slenge	slang/slengte*	slengt	*throw, fling*
slippe	slapp	sluppet	*let go, drop*
slite	slet	slitt	*pull, tear*
slå	slo	slått	*strike, beat*
slåss	sloss	slåss	*fight*
smelle	smalt/smelte*	smelt	*smack, slam*
smette	smatt	smettet	*slip away*
smøre	smurte	smurt	*smear*
snike	snek	sneket	*sneak*
snyte (seg)	snøt	snytt	*blow one's nose; cheat*
sove	sov	sovet	*sleep*
spinne	spant	spunnet	*spin; purr*
sprekke	sprakk	sprukket	*burst*
sprette	spratt	sprettet	*bound*
springe	sprang	sprunget	*run; jump*
spørre	spurte	spurt	*ask*
stige	steg	steget	*rise, climb*
stikke	stakk	stukket	*sting*
stjele	stjal	stjålet	*steal*
strekke	strakk	strukket	*stretch*
stri(de)	stridde/stred	stridd	*quarrel*
stryke	strøk	strøket	*iron; cross out*
stå	sto	stått	*stand*
sverge	sverget/svor	sverget/svoret	*swear*
svi	sved/svidde*	svidd	*singe*
svike	svek	sveket	*betray, disappoint*
svinge	svang	sving(e)t/svunget	*swing*
synge	sang	sunget	*sing*
synke	sank	sunket	*sink*
ta	tok	tatt	*take*
telle	talte/telte	talt/telt	*count*
tie	tidde	tidd	*be/keep silent*
tigge	tigget/tagg	tigget/tigd	*beg*
tre	trådte	trådt	*tread, step*

---

* These verbs are regular when used transitively, i.e. when they take an object.

treffe	traff	truffet	*meet; hit*
trekke	trakk	trukket	*pull*
tvinge	tvang	tvunget	*force*
tygge	tygde	tygd	*chew*
vekke	vakte	vakt	*wake*
velge	valgte	valgt	*choose, elect*
vike	vek	veket	*yield*
ville (vil)	ville	villet	*will*
vinde	vandt	vundet	*wind*
vinne	vant	vunnet	*win*
vite	visste	visst	*know*
vri	vred	vridd	*wrench, twist*
være	var	vært	*be*

Norwegian Abbreviations

adm.dir.	*administrerende direktør*	managing director
alm.	*alminnelig(het)*	general(ly)
A/S	*aksjeselskap*	Ltd., Inc.
dvs.	*det vil si*	i.e.
e.Kr.	*etter Kristi fødsel*	A.D.
el.	*eller*	or
EU	*Den europeiske union*	European Union
f.eks.	*for eksempel*	e.g.
fj.	*fjord*	fjord
f.Kr.	*før Kristi fødsel*	B.C.
flt.	*flertall*	plural
FN	*De forente nasjoner*	UN, United Nations
gen.sekr.	*generalsekretær*	secretary general
...gt.	*gate*	street
iflg.	*ifølge*	according to
KFUK	*Kristelig Forening av Unge Kvinner*	YWCA, Young Women's Christian Association
KFUM	*Kristelig Forening av Unge Menn*	YMCA, Young Men's Christian Association
kl.	*klokken*	hour, o'clock
KNM	*Den Kongelige Norske Marine*	Royal Norwegian Navy
kr	*krone*	crown (currency)
LO	*Landsorganisasjonen i Norge*	Association of Norwegian Trade Unions
mht.	*med hensyn til*	concerning
moms	*meromsetningsskatt*	VAT, value added tax
mots.	*motsatt*	contrary
N	*Norge*	Norway
nr.	*nummer*	number
NRK	*Norsk Rikskringkasting*	Norwegian Broadcasting Service
NSB	*Norges Statsbaner*	Norwegian National Railways
NTB	*Norsk Telegrambyrå*	Norwegian News Agency
NUH	*Norske ungdomsherberger*	Norwegian Youth Hostels
o.a.	*og annet, og andre*	etc., and others
osv.	*og så videre*	etc., and so on
stk.	*stykke(r)*	piece(s)
tlf.	*telefon*	telephone
...vn.	*veien, vegen*	road
årh.	*århundre*	century

Numerals

Cardinal numbers

0	null
1	en
2	to
3	tre
4	fire
5	fem
6	seks
7	syv/sju
8	åtte
9	ni
10	ti
11	elleve
12	tolv
13	tretten
14	fjorten
15	femten
16	seksten
17	sytten
18	atten
19	nitten
20	tyve/tjue
21	enogtyve/tjueen
30	tredve/tretti
31	enogtredve/trettien
40	førti
41	enogførti/førtien
50	femti
51	enogfemti/femtien
60	seksti
61	enogseksti/sekstien
70	sytti
71	enogsytti/syttien
80	åtti
81	enogåtti/åttien
90	nitti
91	enognitti/nittien
100	hundre
101	hundre og en
1 000	tusen
1 000 000	en million

Ordinal numbers

1.	første
2.	annen
3.	tredje
4.	fjerde
5.	femte
6.	sjette
7.	syvende/sjuende
8.	åttende
9.	niende
10.	tiende
11.	ellevte
12.	tolvte
13.	trettende
14.	fjortende
15.	femtende
16.	sekstende
17.	syttende
18.	attende
19.	nittende
20.	tyvende/tjuende
21.	enogtyvende/tjueførste
22.	toogtyvende/tjueandre
23.	treogtyvende/tjuetredje
24.	firogtyvende/tjuefjerde
25.	femogtyvende/tjuefemte
26.	seksogtyvende/tjuesjette
27.	syvogtyvende/tjuesjuende
28.	åtteogtyvende/tjueåttende
29.	niogtyvende/tjueniende
30.	tredevte/trettiende
40.	førtiende
50.	femtiende
60.	sekstiende
70.	syttiende
80.	åttiende
90.	nittiende
100.	hundrede
1 000.	tusende

Time

Although official time in Norway is based on the 24-hour clock, the 12-hour system is used in conversation.

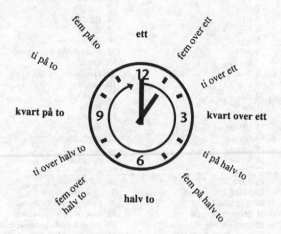

If you have to indicate that it is a.m. or p.m., add *om morgenen*, *om formiddagen*, *om ettermiddagen*, *om kvelden*, *om natten*.

Thus:

klokken syv om morgenen	7 a.m.
klokken elleve om formiddagen	11 a.m.
klokken to om ettermiddagen	2 p.m.
klokken åtte om kvelden	8 p.m.
klokken to om natten	2 a.m.

Days of the Week

søndag	Sunday	*torsdag*	Thursday
mandag	Monday	*fredag*	Friday
tirsdag	Tuesday	*lørdag*	Saturday
onsdag	Wednesday		

Some Basic Phrases

Noen vanlige uttrykk

Hello!	Hei!
Please.	Vær så snill.
Thank you very much.	Tusen takk.
Don't mention it.	Ingen årsak..
Good morning.	God morgen.
Good afternoon.	God dag.
Good evening.	God kveld.
Good night.	God natt.
Good-bye.	Ha det (bra)!
See you later.	Vi ses!
Where is/Where are...?	Hvor er...?
What do you call this?	Hva heter (kalles) dette?
What does that mean?	Hva betyr det?
Do you speak English?	Snakker du engelsk?
Do you speak German?	Snakker du tysk?
Do you speak French?	Snakker du fransk?
Do you speak Spanish?	Snakker du spansk?
Do you speak Italian?	Snakker du italiensk?
Could you speak more slowly, please?	Kunne du snakke litt langsommere?
I don't understand.	Jeg forstår ikke.
Can I have...?	Kan jeg få...?
Can you show me...?	Kan du vise meg...?
Can you tell me...?	Kan du si meg...?
Can you help me, please?	Kan du være så vennlig å hjelpe meg?
I'd like...	Jeg ville gjerne ha...
We'd like...	Væi ville gjerne ha...
Please give me...	Vær så snill å gi meg...
Please bring me...	Vær så snill å la meg få...
I'm hungry.	Jeg er sulten.
I'm thirsty.	Jeg er tørst.
I'm lost.	Jeg har gått meg vill.
Hurry up!	Skynd deg!
There is/There are...	Det finnes...
There isn't/There aren't...	Det finnes ikke...

Arrival

Ankomst

Your passport, please.	Passet, takk.
Have you anything to declare?	Har du noe å fortolle?
No, nothing at all.	Nei, ingenting.
Can you help me with my luggage, please?	Kan du hjelpe meg med bagasjen?

Where's the bus to the centre of town, please?	Hvor tar man bussen til sentrum?
This way, please.	Denne veien.
Where can I get a taxi?	Hvor kan jeg få tak i en drosje?
What's the fare to...?	Hva koster det til...?
Take me to this address, please.	Vær så snill å kjøre meg til denne adressen.
I'm in a hurry.	Jeg har det travelt.

Hotel / Hotell

My name is...	Mitt navn er...
Have you a reservation?	Har du bestilt?
I'd like a room with a bath.	Jeg vil gjerne ha et rom med bad.
What's the price per night?	Hva koster det for en natt?
May I see the room?	Kan jeg få se rommet?
What's my room number, please?	Hvilket værelsesnummer har jeg?
There's no hot water.	Det er ikke noe varmt vann.
May I see the manager, please?	Kan jeg få snakke med direktøren?
Did anyone telephone me?	Har det vært noen telefon til meg?
Is there any mail for me?	Er det noe post til meg?
May I have my bill (check), please?	Kan jeg få regningen, takk.

Eating out / Restaurant

Do you have a fixed-price menu?	Har dere en fast meny?
May I see the menu?	Kan jeg få se spisekartet?
May we have an ashtray, please?	Kan vi få et askebeger, takk?
Where's the toilet, please?	Hvor er toalettet?
I'd like an hors d'œuvre (starter).	Jeg vil gjerne ha en forrett.
Have you any soup?	Har dere suppe?
I'd like some fish.	Jeg vil gjerne ha fisk.
What kind of fish do you have?	Hva slags fisk har dere?
I'd like a steak.	Jeg vil gjerne ha en biff.
What vegetables have you got?	Hvilke grønnsaker har dere?
Nothing more, thanks.	Takk, jeg er forsynt.
What would you like to drink?	Hva vil du ha å drikke?
I'll have a beer, please.	Jeg vil gjerne ha en øl, takk.
I'd like a bottle of wine.	Jeg vil gjerne ha en flaske vin.
May I have the bill (check), please?	Regningen, takk!
Is service included?	Er service inkludert?
Thank you, that was a very good meal.	Takk. Det smakte utmerket.

Travelling / På reise

Where's the railway station, please?	Hvor er jernbanestasjonen?
Where's the ticket office, please?	Unnskyld, kan du si meg hvor billettluken er?

I'd like a ticket to...	Jeg vil gjerne ha en billett til...
First or second class?	Første eller annen klasse?
First class, please.	Første, takk.
Single or return (one way or roundtrip)?	Enkeltbillett eller tur-retur?
Do I have to change trains?	Må jeg bytte tog?
What platform does the train for... leave from?	Fra hvilken plattform går toget til...?
Where's the nearest underground (subway) station?	Hvor er nærmeste undergrunnsstasjon?
Where's the bus station, please?	Hvor er buss-stasjonen?
When's the first bus to...?	Når går den første bussen til...?
Please let me off at the next stop.	Kan du slippe meg av på neste holdeplass?

Relaxing / Fornøyelser

What's on at the cinema (movies)?	Hva går på kino?
What time does the film begin?	Når begynner filmen?
Are there any tickets for tonight?	Er det noen billetter igjen til i kveld?
Where can we go dancing?	Hvor kan vi gå for å danse?

Meeting people / Bekjentskap

How do you do.	God dag.
How are you?	Hvordan står det til?
Very well, thank you. And you?	Bare bra, takk. Og med deg?
May I introduce...?	Kan jeg få presentere...?
My name is...	Mitt navn er...
I'm very pleased to meet you.	Gleder meg (å treffe deg).
How long have you been here?	Hvor lenge har du vært her?
It was nice meeting you.	Det var hyggelig å treffe deg.
Do you mind if I smoke?	Har du noe imot at jeg røyker?
Do you have a light, please?	Unnskyld, kan du gi meg fyr?
May I get you a drink?	Kan jeg by deg på en drink?
May I invite you for dinner tonight?	Vil du spise middag med meg i kveld?
Where shall we meet?	Hvor skal vi møtes?

Shops, stores and services / Forretninger, varehus, etc.

Where's the nearest bank, please?	Unnskyld, hvor er nærmeste bank?
Where can I cash some travellers' cheques?	Hvor kan jeg løse inn reisesjekker?
Can you give me some small change, please?	Kan du gi meg litt vekslepenger?

Where's the nearest chemist's (pharmacy)?	Hvor er nærmeste apotek?
How do I get there?	Hvordan kommer jeg dit?
Is it within walking distance?	Er det langt å gå dit?
Can you help me, please?	Kan du være så snill å hjelpe meg?
How much is this? And that?	Hvor mye koster dette? Og det?
It's not quite what I want.	Det er ikke akkurat det jeg vil ha.
I like it.	Jeg liker det.
Can you recommend something for sunburn?	Kan du anbefale noe mot solbrenthet?
I'd like a haircut, please.	Jeg vil gjerne ha håret klippet.
I'd like a manicure, please.	Jeg vil gjerne ha en manikyr.

Street directions

Vi spør om veien

Can you show me on the map where I am?	Kan du vise meg på dette kartet hvor jeg er?
You are on the wrong road.	Du er på feil vei.
Go/Walk straight ahead.	Kjør/Gå rett frem.
It's on the left/on the right.	Det er på venstre/på høyre side.

Emergencies

Ulykker

Call a doctor quickly.	Tilkall en lege – fort.
Call an ambulance.	Ring etter en sykebil.
Please call the police.	Tilkall politiet.

Engelsk-Norsk

English-Norwegian

Veiledning

Ved utarbeidelsen av denne ordboken har vi først og fremst tatt sikte på å gjøre den så praktisk og anvendelig som mulig. Mindre viktige språklige opplysninger er utelatt. Oppslagsordene står i alfabetisk rekkefølge uansett om uttrykket skrives i ett ord, med bindestrek, eller i to eller flere ord. Det eneste unntaket fra denne regelen er noen få idiomatiske uttrykk, som du vil finne under det meningsbærende ordet. Når et oppslagsord følges av flere sammensetninger eller uttrykk, er også disse satt i alfabetisk rekkefølge.

Hvert hovedoppslagsord er fulgt av lydskrift (se Uttale), og vanligvis av ordklasse. I fall et oppslagsord tilhører flere ordklasser, er oversettelsene gruppert sammen etter de respektive ordklassene.

Dersom et substantiv har uregelmessig flertallsform, er denne angitt. I tilfeller der det kan oppstå tvil, har vi gitt eksempler på bruken.

Bølgestrek (~) er brukt som gjentagelsestegn for oppslagsordet når dette forekommer senere i artikkelen (f.eks. ved uregelmessig flertallsform, sammensatte ord, etc.).

Når det gjelder uregelmessig flertallsform av sammensatte ord, er bare den delen som forandres, skrevet helt ut; en kort strek (-) står for den uforandrede delen.

En stjerne (*) foran et verb betyr at verbet er uregelmessig. Bøyningsmønstret finner du i listen over uregelmessige verb.

I denne ordboken har vi anvendt vanlig engelsk stavemåte. Alle ord som må regnes som amerikanske, er merket *Am* (se listen over forkortelser).

Forkortelser

adj	adjektiv	*p*	imperfektum
adv	adverb	*pl*	flertall
Am	amerikansk	*plAm*	flertall (amerikansk)
art	artikkel	*pp*	perfektum partisipp
c	felleskjønn	*pr*	presens
conj	konjunksjon	*pref*	prefiks (forstavelse)
m	hankjønn	*prep*	preposisjon
n	substantiv	*pron*	pronomen
nAm	substantiv (amerikansk)	*suf*	suffiks (endelse)
nt	intetkjønn	*v*	verb
num	tallord	*vAm*	verb (amerikansk)

Uttale

I denne delen av ordboken er hvert stikkord fulgt av internasjonal lydskrift (IPA). Hvert enkelt tegn i denne fonetiske skriften står for en bestemt lyd. Tegn som her ikke er nærmere forklart, uttales omtrent som de tilsvarende norske bokstavene.

Konsonanter

ð	en slags lespende, stemt s-lyd; uttales med tungespissen løftet mot overtennene
g	alltid som i gå, aldri som i gi
k	alltid som i ku, aldri som i kinn
ŋ	som ng i lang
r	en stemt r-lyd som dannes ved at tungebladet heves mot den bakre del av gommene
ʃ	som sj i øst- og nordnorsk sjø
θ	en slags lespende, stemmeløs s-lyd
w	som o i ost, men meget svak
z	stemt s-lyd
ʒ	stemt sj-lyd

Merk: Transkripsjonen [sj] skal alltid uttales som en s fulgt av en j-lyd, ikke som i øst- og nordnorsk sjø.

Vokaler

ɑː	som a i far
æ	omtrent som æ i lærd
ʌ	omtrent som a i katt
e	som i telegram
ɛ	som e i penn
ə	som e i gate
ɔ	som o i tolv
u	som o i ost

1) Et kolon [ː] etter en vokal angir lang vokallyd.
2) Noen franske låneord har nasalert vokal (dvs. at ved uttalen går luften ut både gjennom munn og nese); dette er angitt med en tilde over vokalen (f. eks. = [ã]).

Diftonger

En diftong består av to vokaler hvorav den ene er sterk (betont) og den andre svak (ubetont), og uttales som en glidende lyd som bare utgjør én stavelse, som f. eks. **ei** i st**ei**n. I engelske diftonglyder er det alltid den andre vokalen som er svak. Dersom diftongen etterfølges av en [ə] medfører dette en ytterligere svekkelse av den andre vokalen.

Trykk

Tegnet ['] står foran den trykksterke stavelsen, [ˌ] foran stavelser med bitrykk.

Amerikansk uttale

Lydskriften her i boken følger britisk uttale. Selv om amerikansk uttale varierer sterkt fra den ene delen av USA til den annen, kan en sette opp visse regler for forskjellen mellom amerikansk og britisk uttale. Her er noen av dem:

1) I motsetning til på britisk engelsk uttales **r** både når den etterfølges av konsonant og på slutten av ord.
2) I mange ord (f. eks. *ask*, *castle*, *laugh*, osv.) blir [ɑː] til [æ].
3) Lyden [ɔ] uttaler amerikanerne som [ɑ] eller [ɔː].
4) I ord som *duty*, *tune*, *new*, osv. utelates ofte [j]-lyden som på britisk engelsk går forut for [uː].
5) Mange ord har trykkforskyvning i forhold til britisk uttale.

a [ei,ə] *art* (an) en; ei; et *art*

abbey ['æbi] *n* abbedi *nt*

abbreviation [ə,bri:vi'eiʃən] *n* forkortelse *m*

ability [ə'biləti] *n* dyktighet *c*; evne *c*

able ['eibəl] *adj* i stand til, dyktig; *be ~ to *være i stand til; *kunne

aboard [ə'bɔːd] *adv* om bord

abolish [ə'bɔliʃ] *v* avskaffe

abortion [ə'bɔːʃən] *n* abort *m*

about [ə'baut] *prep* om; angående; rundt; *adv* omtrent, omkring

above [ə'bʌv] *prep* over; ovenfor; *adv* over; ovenfor

abroad [ə'brɔːd] *adv* utenlands

abscess ['æbses] *n* byll *m*

absence ['æbsəns] *n* fravær *nt*

absent ['æbsənt] *adj* fraværende

absolutely ['æbsəluːtli] *adv* absolutt

abstain from [əb'stein] *avholde seg fra

abstract ['æbstrækt] *adj* abstrakt

absurd [əb'səːd] *adj* urimelig, absurd

abundance [ə'bʌndəns] *n* overflod *m*

abundant [ə'bʌndənt] *adj* rikelig

abuse [ə'bjuːs] *n* misbruk *nt*

abyss [ə'bis] *n* avgrunn *m*

academy [ə'kædəmi] *n* akademi *nt*

accelerate [ək'seləreit] *v* akselerere, øke farten

accelerator [ək'seləreitə] *n* gasspedal *m*

accent ['æksənt] *n* aksent *m*; betoning *c*

accept [ək'sept] *v* akseptere, *ta imot, *motta

access ['ækses] *n* tilgang *m*

accessible [ək'sesəbəl] *adj* tilgjengelig

accessories [ək'sesəriz] *pl* tilbehør *nt*

accident ['æksidənt] *n* ulykke *c*, uhell *nt*

accidental [,æksi'dentəl] *adj* tilfeldig

accommodate [ə'kɔmədeit] *v* tilpasse; skaffe husrom

accommodation [ə,kɔmə'deiʃən] *n* husrom *nt*, losji *nt*

accompany [ə'kʌmpəni] *v* følge; akkompagnere

accomplish [ə'kʌmpliʃ] *v* fullende; fullføre

accordance: in ~ with [in ə'kɔːdəns wið] i overensstemmelse med

according to [ə'kɔːdiŋ tuː] ifølge; i overensstemmelse med

account [ə'kaunt] *n* konto *m*; redegjørelse *m*; ~ for avlegge regnskap for; on ~ of på grunn av

accountable [ə'kauntəbəl] *adj* ansvarlig; forklarlig

accurate ['ækjurət] *adj* nøyaktig

accuse [ə'kjuːz] *v* beskylde; anklage

accused [ə'kjuːzd] *n* anklagede *m*

accustom [ə'kʌstəm] *v* venne; accustomed vant

ache [eik] *v* verke; *n* verk *m*

achieve [ə'tʃiːv] *v* oppnå; prestere

achievement [ə'tʃiːvmənt] *n* prestasjon *m*

acid ['æsid] *n* syre *c*

acknowledge [ək'nɔlidʒ] *v* erkjenne; innrømme; bekrefte

acne ['ækni] *n* filipens *m*

acorn ['eikɔːn] *n* eikenøtt *c*

acquaintance [ə'kweintəns] *n* bekjent *m*

acquire [ə'kwaiə] *v* erverve

acquisition [,ækwi'ziʃən] *n* ervervelse *m*

acquittal [ə'kwitəl] *n* frifinnelse *m*

across [ə'krɔs] *prep* over; på den andre siden av; *adv* på den andre siden

act [ækt] n handling c; akt m; nummer nt; v handle, oppføre seg; spille

action ['ækʃən] n handling c, aksjon m

active ['æktiv] adj aktiv; virksom

activity [æk'tivəti] n aktivitet m

actor ['æktə] n skuespiller m

actress ['æktris] n skuespiller m

actual ['æktʃuəl] adj faktisk, virkelig

actually ['æktʃuəli] adv faktisk

acute [ə'kju:t] adj akutt

adapt [ə'dæpt] v tilpasse

adaptor [ə'dæptə] n adapter m

add [æd] v *legge sammen; tilføye

addition [ə'diʃən] n addisjon m; tilføyelse m

additional [ə'diʃənəl] adj ekstra; ytterligere

address [ə'dres] n adresse c; v adressere; henvende seg til

addressee [,ædre'si:] n adressat m

adequate ['ædikwət] adj tilstrekkelig; passende, adekvat

adjective ['ædʒiktiv] n adjektiv nt

adjourn [ə'dʒə:n] v *utsette

adjust [ə'dʒʌst] v justere; tilpasse

administer [əd'ministə] v bestyre; tildele

administration [əd,mini'streiʃən] n administrasjon m; ledelse m

administrative [əd'ministrətiv] adj administrerende; forvaltende; ~ law forvaltningsrett m

admiration [,ædmə'reiʃən] n beundring c

admire [əd'maiə] v beundre

admission [əd'miʃən] n adgang m; opptak nt

admit [əd'mit] v *oppta; innrømme, erkjenne

admittance [əd'mitəns] n adgang m; **no ~** adgang forbudt

adopt [ə'dɔpt] v adoptere; *vedta

adorable [ə'dɔ:rəbəl] adj henrivende

adult ['ædʌlt] n voksen m; adj voksen

advance [əd'vɑ:ns] n fremskritt nt; forskudd nt; v *gjøre fremskritt; betale på forskudd; **in ~** på forhånd, på forskudd

advanced [əd'vɑ:nst] adj avansert

advantage [əd'vɑ:ntidʒ] n fordel m

advantageous [,ædvən'teidʒəs] adj fordelaktig

adventure [əd'ventʃə] n eventyr nt

adverb ['ædvə:b] n adverb nt

advertisement [əd'və:tismənt] n annonse m

advertising ['ædvətaiziŋ] n reklame m

advice [əd'vais] n råd nt

advise [əd'vaiz] v råde

advocate ['ædvəkət] n talsmann m

aerial ['ɛəriəl] n antenne c

aeroplane ['ɛərəplein] n fly nt

affair [ə'fɛə] n anliggende nt; affære m, forhold nt

affect [ə'fekt] v påvirke; vedrøre

affected [ə'fektid] adj affektert

affection [ə'fekʃən] n hengivenhet c

affectionate [ə'fekʃənit] adj hengiven, kjærlig

affiliated [ə'filieitid] adj tilsluttet

affirm [ə'fə:m] v bedyre; bekrefte

affirmative [ə'fə:mətiv] adj bekreftende

afford [ə'fɔ:d] v *ha råd til

afraid [ə'freid] adj redd, engstelig; *be ~ *være redd

Africa ['æfrikə] Afrika

African ['æfrikən] adj afrikansk; n afrikaner m

after ['ɑ:ftə] prep etter; conj etter at

afternoon [,ɑ:ftə'nu:n] n ettermiddag m; **this ~** i ettermiddag

afterwards ['ɑ:ftəwədz] adv senere; etterpå

again [ə'gen] adv igjen; ~ **and again** gang på gang

against [əˈgenst] *prep* mot

age [eidʒ] *n* alder *m*; alderdom *m*; **of ~** myndig; **under ~** umyndig

aged [ˈeidʒid] *adj* gammel

agency [ˈeidʒənsi] *n* agentur *nt*; byrå *nt*

agenda [əˈdʒendə] *n* dagsorden *m*

agent [ˈeidʒənt] *n* agent *m*, representant *m*

aggressive [əˈgresiv] *adj* aggressiv

ago [əˈgou] *adv* for … siden

agree [əˈgriː] *v* *være enig; *gå med på; stemme overens

agreeable [əˈgriːəbəl] *adj* behagelig

agreement [əˈgriːmənt] *n* kontrakt *m*; overenskomst *m*, avtale *m*; overensstemmelse *m*

agriculture [ˈægrikʌltʃə] *n* jordbruk *nt*

ahead [əˈhed] *adv* fremover; **~ of** foran; ***go ~** *gå videre; **straight ~** rett frem

aid [eid] *n* hjelp *c*; *v* *hjelpe, *bistå

AIDS [eidz] *n* AIDS

aim [eim] *n* sikte *nt*; **~ at** rette mot, sikte på; strebe etter, *ta sikte på

air [ɛə] *n* luft *c*; *v* lufte

airbag [ˈɛə bæg] *n* airbag *m*

air conditioning [ˈɛəkən,diʃəniŋ] *n* luftkondisjonering *c*; **air-conditioned** *adj* luftkondisjonert

aircraft [ˈɛəkrɑːft] *n* (pl ~) fly *nt*

airfield [ˈɛəfiːld] *n* flyplass *m*

airline [ˈɛəlain] *n* flyselskap *nt*

airmail [ˈɛəmeil] *n* luftpost *m*

airplane [ˈɛəplein] *nAm* fly *nt*

airport [ˈɛəpɔːt] *n* lufthavn *c*, flyplass *m*

airsickness [ˈɛə,siknəs] *n* luftsyke *m*

airtight [ˈɛətait] *adj* lufttett

airy [ˈɛəri] *adj* luftig

aisle [ail] *n* sideskip *nt*; midtgang *m*

alarm [əˈlɑːm] *n* alarm *m*; *v* alarmere, forurolige; **~clock** vekkeklokke *c*

album [ˈælbəm] *n* album *nt*

alcohol [ˈælkəhɔl] *n* alkohol *m*

alcoholic [,ælkəˈhɔlik] *adj* alkoholholdig

ale [eil] *n* øl *nt*

algebra [ˈældʒibrə] *n* algebra *m*

Algeria [ælˈdʒiəriə] Algerie

Algerian [ælˈdʒiəriən] *adj* algerisk; *n* algerier *m*

alien [ˈeiliən] *n* utlending *m*; *adj* utenlandsk

alike [əˈlaik] *adj* likedan, lik; *adv* likedan

alive [əˈlaiv] *adj* levende

all [ɔːl] *adj* all; **~ in** alt inkludert; **~ right!** fint!, ålreit; **at ~** overhodet

allergic [əˈlɔːdʒik] *adj* allergisk

allergy [ˈælədʒi] *n* allergi *m*

alley [ˈæli] *n* smug *nt*

alliance [əˈlaiəns] *n* allianse *m*

allow [əˈlau] *v* *tillate, bevilge; **~ to** *la; ***be allowed** *være tillatt; ***be allowed to** *ha lov til

allowance [əˈlauəns] *n* bidrag *nt*

all-round [,ɔːlˈraund] *adj* allsidig

almond [ˈɑːmənd] *n* mandel *m*

almost [ˈɔːlmoust] *adv* nesten

alone [əˈloun] *adv* alene

along [əˈlɔŋ] *prep* langs

aloud [əˈlaud] *adv* høyt

alphabet [ˈælfəbet] *n* alfabet *nt*

already [ɔːlˈredi] *adv* allerede

also [ˈɔːlsou] *adv* også; dessuten, likeledes

altar [ˈɔːltə] *n* alter *nt*

alter [ˈɔːltə] *v* forandre, endre

alteration [,ɔːltəˈreiʃən] *n* forandring *c*, endring *c*

alternate [ɔːlˈtəːnət] *adj* vekselvis

alternative [ɔːlˈtəːnətiv] *n* alternativ *nt*

although [ɔːlˈðou] *conj* skjønt

altitude [ˈæltitjuːd] *n* høyde *m*

alto [ˈæltou] *n* (pl ~s) alt *m*

altogether [ˌɔːltəˈgeðə] *adv* fullstendig; i det hele

always [ˈɔːlweiz] *adv* alltid

am [æm] *v* (pr be)

amaze [əˈmeiz] *v* forbause, forundre

amazement [əˈmeizmənt] *n* forbauselse *m*

amazing [əˈmeiziŋ] *adj* forbausende; utrolig

ambassador [æmˈbæsədə] *n* ambassadør *m*

amber [ˈæmbə] *n* rav *nt*

ambiguous [æmˈbigjuəs] *adj* tvetydig

ambition [æmˈbiʃən] *n* ærgjerrighet *c*

ambitious [æmˈbiʃəs] *adj* ærgjerrig

ambulance [ˈæmbjuləns] *n* ambulanse *m*, sykebil *m*

ambush [ˈæmbuʃ] *n* bakhold *nt*

America [əˈmerikə] Amerika

American [əˈmerikən] *adj* amerikansk; *n* amerikaner *m*

amethyst [ˈæmiθist] *n* ametyst *m*

amid [əˈmid] *prep* blant, midt i

ammonia [əˈmouniə] *n* salmiakk *m*

amnesty [ˈæmnisti] *n* amnesti *m*

among [əˈmʌŋ] *prep* blant, mellom; ~ **other things** blant annet

amount [əˈmaunt] *n* mengde *m*; beløp *nt*, sum *m*; ~ **to** *beløpe seg til

amuse [əˈmjuːz] *v* more, *underholde

amusement [əˈmjuːzmənt] *n* fornøyelse *m*, atspredelse *m*

amusing [əˈmjuːziŋ] *adj* morsom, gøyal

anaemia [əˈniːmiə] *n* anemi *m*

anaesthesia [ˌænisˈθiːziə] *n* bedøvelse *m*

anaesthetic [ˌænisˈθetik] *n* bedøvelsesmiddel *nt*

analyse [ˈænəlaiz] *v* analysere

analysis [əˈnæləsis] *n* (pl -ses) analyse *m*

analyst [ˈænəlist] *n* analytiker *m*; psykoanalytiker *m*

anarchy [ˈænəki] *n* anarki *m*

anatomy [əˈnætəmi] *n* anatomi *m*

ancestor [ˈænsestə] *n* forfader *m*

anchor [ˈæŋkə] *n* anker *nt*

anchovy [ˈæntʃəvi] *n* ansjos *m*

ancient [ˈeinʃənt] *adj* gammel; foreldet, gammeldags; urtids-

and [ænd, ənd] *conj* og

angel [ˈeindʒəl] *n* engel *m*

anger [ˈæŋgə] *n* sinne *nt*; raseri *nt*

angle [ˈæŋgəl] *v* fiske; *n* vinkel *m*

angry [ˈæŋgri] *adj* sint

animal [ˈæniməl] *n* dyr *nt*

ankle [ˈæŋkəl] *n* ankel *m*

annex¹ [ˈæneks] *n* anneks *nt*; tillegg *nt*

annex² [əˈneks] *v* annektere

anniversary [ˌæniˈvɔːsəri] *n* årsdag *m*, bryllupsdag *m*

announce [əˈnauns] *v* *kunngjøre, *bekjentgjøre

announcement [əˈnaunsmənt] *n* kunngjøring *c*, bekjentgjørelse *m*

annoy [əˈnɔi] *v* ergre, irritere

annoyance [əˈnɔiəns] *n* ergrelse *m*

annoying [əˈnɔiiŋ] *adj* ergerlig, irriterende

annual [ˈænjuəl] *adj* årlig; *n* årbok *c*

anonymous [əˈnɔniməs] *adj* anonym

another [əˈnʌðə] *adj* en til; en annen

answer [ˈɑːnsə] *v* svare; besvare; *n* svar *nt*

answering machine [ˈɑːnsəriŋ məˈʃiːn] *n* telefonsvarer *m*

ant [ænt] *n* maur *m*

antibiotic [ˌæntibaiˈɔtik] *n* antibiotikum *nt*

anticipate [ænˈtisipeit] *v* *forutse, *foregripe

antifreeze [ˈæntifriːz] *n* frysevæske *c*

antipathy [ænˈtipəθi] *n* motvilje *m*

antique [ænˈtiːk] *adj* antikk; *n* antikvitet *m*; ~ **dealer**

antikvitetshandler m

antiquity [æn'tikwəti] n oldtid c

anxiety [æŋ'zaiəti] n bekymring c

anxious ['æŋkʃəs] adj ivrig; engstelig

any ['eni] adj hvilke som helst

anybody ['enibɔdi] pron hvem som helst

anyhow ['enihau] adv på hvilken som helst måte

anyone ['eniwʌn] pron enhver

anything ['eniθiŋ] pron hva som helst

anyway ['eniwei] adv i hvert fall

anywhere ['eniweə] adv hvor som helst

apart [ə'pɑːt] adv atskilt, separat; ~ **from** bortsett fra

apartment [ə'pɑːtmənt] nAm leilighet c; ~ **house** Am leiegård m

aperitif [ə'perətiv] n aperitiff m

apologize [ə'pɔlədʒaiz] v *be om unnskyldning

apology [ə'pɔlədʒi] n unnskyldning m

apparatus [ˌæpə'reitəs] n apparat nt

apparent [ə'pærənt] adj tilsynelatende; tydelig

apparently [ə'pærəntli] adv åpenbart; øyensynlig

appeal [ə'piːl] n appell m

appear [ə'piə] v *se ut til, synes; *fremgå; vise seg; *fremtre

appearance [ə'piərəns] n fremtoning m; utseende nt; opptreden m

appendicitis [əˌpendi'saitis] n blindtarmbetennelse m

appendix [ə'pendiks] n (pl -dices, -dixes) blindtarm m

appetite ['æpətait] n matlyst c, appetitt m

appetizer ['æpətaizə] n appetittvekker m

appetizing ['æpətaiziŋ] adj appetittlig

applause [ə'plɔːz] n applaus m

applaud [ə'plɔːd] v applaudere

apple ['æpəl] n eple nt

appliance [ə'plaiəns] n apparat nt

application [ˌæpli'keiʃən] n anvendelse m; søknad m

apply [ə'plai] v anvende, bruke; søke; *gjelde

appoint [ə'pɔint] v utnevne

appointment [ə'pɔintmənt] n avtale m, møte nt; utnevnelse m

appreciate [ə'priːʃieit] v *verdsette; påskjønne

appreciation [əˌpriːʃi'eiʃən] n vurdering c; verdsettelse m

apprentice [ə'prentis] n lærling m

approach [ə'prəutʃ] v nærme seg; n fremgangsmåte m

appropriate [ə'prəupriət] adj formålstjenlig, passende, rett

approval [ə'pruːvəl] n godkjennelse m; billigelse m; **on** ~ på prøve

approve [ə'pruːv] v godkjenne

approximate [ə'prɔksimət] adj omtrentlig

approximately [ə'prɔksimətli] adv cirka, omtrent

apricot ['eiprikɔt] n aprikos m

April ['eiprəl] april

apron ['eiprən] n forkle nt

Arab ['ærəb] adj arabisk; n araber m

arbitrary ['ɑːbitrəri] adj vilkårlig

arcade [ɑː'keid] n buegang m, arkade m

arch [ɑːtʃ] n bue m; hvelv m

archaeologist [ˌɑːki'ɔlədʒist] n arkeolog m

archaeology [ˌɑːki'ɔlədʒi] n arkeologi m

archbishop [ˌɑːtʃ'biʃəp] n erkebiskop m

arched [ɑːtʃt] adj bueformet

architect ['ɑːkitekt] n arkitekt m

architecture ['ɑːkitektʃə] n byggekunst m, arkitektur m

archives ['ɑːkaivz] *pl* arkiv *nt*
are [ɑː] *v* (pr be)
area ['ɛəriə] *n* område *nt*; areal *nt*; ~ **code** retningsnummer *nt*
Argentina [,ɑːdʒən'tiːnə] Argentina
Argentinian [,ɑːdʒən'tiniən] *adj* argentinsk; *n* argentiner *m*
argue ['ɑːgjuː] *v* diskutere, debattere, argumentere; trette
argument ['ɑːgjumənt] *n* argument *nt*; diskusjon *m*
***arise** [ə'raiz] *v* *oppstå
arithmetic [ə'riθmətik] *n* regning *c*
arm [ɑːm] *n* arm *m*; våpen *nt*; *v* bevæpne
armchair ['ɑːmtʃɛə] *n* lenestol *m*
armed [ɑːmd] *adj* bevæpnet; ~ **forces** væpnede styrker
armour ['ɑːmə] *n* rustning *m*
army ['ɑːmi] *n* armé *m*
aroma [ə'roumə] *n* aroma *m*
around [ə'raund] *prep* omkring; *adv* rundt
arrange [ə'reindʒ] *v* ordne; arrangere
arrangement [ə'reindʒmənt] *n* ordning *c*
arrest [ə'rest] *v* arrestere; *n* arrestasjon *m*, pågripelse *m*
arrival [ə'raivəl] *n* ankomst *m*
arrive [ə'raiv] *v* *ankomme
arrow ['ærou] *n* pil *c*
art [ɑːt] *n* kunst *m*; kunstferdighet *m*; ~ **collection** kunstsamling *m*; ~ **exhibition** kunstutstilling *c*; ~ **gallery** kunstgalleri *nt*; ~ **history** kunsthistorie *c*; **arts and crafts** kunst og håndverk; ~ **school** kunstakademi *nt*
artery ['ɑːtəri] *n* pulsåre *c*
artichoke ['ɑːtitʃouk] *n* artisjokk *m*
article ['ɑːtikəl] *n* gjenstand *m*; artikkel *m*
artificial [,ɑːti'fiʃəl] *adj* kunstig
artist ['ɑːtist] *n* kunstner *m*

artistic [ɑː'tistik] *adj* kunstnerisk, artistisk
as [æz] *conj* liksom, som; like; fordi, ettersom; ~ **from** fra; fra og med; ~ **if** som om
asbestos [æz'bestɔs] *n* asbest *m*
ascend [ə'send] *v* *stige; *stige opp; *bestige
ascent [ə'sent] *n* stigning *m*; oppstigning *m*
ascertain [,æsə'tein] *v* konstatere; forvisse seg om, *fastslå
ash [æʃ] *n* aske *c*
ashamed [ə'ʃeimd] *adj* skamfull; *be ~ skamme seg
ashore [ə'ʃɔː] *adv* i land
ashtray ['æʃtrei] *n* askebeger *nt*
Asia ['eiʃə] Asia
Asian ['eiʃən] *adj* asiatisk; *n* asiat *m*
aside [ə'said] *adv* til siden, til side
ask [ɑːsk] *v* *spørre; *be; *innby
asleep [ə'sliːp] *adj* sovende
asparagus [ə'spærəgəs] *n* asparges *m*
aspect ['æspekt] *n* utseende *nt*; aspekt *nt*
asphalt ['æsfælt] *n* asfalt *m*
aspire [ə'spaiə] *v* strebe
aspirin ['æspərin] *n* aspirin *m*
assassination [ə,sæsi'neiʃən] *n* mord *nt*
assault [ə'sɔːlt] *v* *angripe; *overfalle
assemble [ə'sembəl] *v* samle, *sette sammen
assembly [ə'sembli] *n* forsamling *c*, sammenkomst *m*
assignment [ə'sainmənt] *n* oppdrag *nt*
assign to [ə'sain] *v* tildele; *tilskrive
assist [ə'sist] *v* *bistå, *hjelpe; ~ **at** *hjelpe til med
assistance [ə'sistəns] *n* hjelp *c*; assistanse *m*, understøttelse *m*
assistant [ə'sistənt] *n* assistent *m*
associate[1] [ə'souʃiət] *n* partner *m*,

kompanjong *m*; forbundsfelle *m*;
medlem *nt*
associate² [ə'souʃieit] *v* *forbinde; ~
with *omgås
association [ə,sousi'eiʃən] *n*
forening *c*
assort [ə'sɔːt] *v* sortere
assortment [ə'sɔːtmənt] *n* utvalg *nt*,
sortiment *nt*
assume [ə'sjuːm] *v* *anta, formode
assure [ə'ʃuə] *v* forsikre
asthma ['æsmə] *n* astma *m*
astonish [ə'stɔniʃ] *v* forbløffe,
forbause
astonishing [ə'stɔniʃiŋ] *adj*
forbausende
astonishment [ə'stɔniʃmənt] *n*
forbauselse *m*
astronaut ['æstrɔnɔːt] *n* astronaut *m*
astronomy [ə'strɔnəmi] *n* astronomi
m
asylum [ə'sailəm] *n* asyl *nt*
at [æt] *prep* på, hos, i
ate [et] *v* (p eat)
atheist ['eiθiist] *n* ateist *m*
athlete ['æθliːt] *n* idrettsutøver *m*
athletics [æθ'letiks] *pl* friidrett *m*
Atlantic [ət'læntik] Atlanterhavet
ATM [,eiti'em] *n* minibank *m*
atmosphere ['ætməsfiə] *n* atmosfære
m; stemning *m*
atom ['ætəm] *n* atom *nt*
atomic [ə'tɔmik] *adj* atom-
atomizer ['ætəmaizə] *n* sprayflaske *c*;
spray *m*, vaporisator *m*
attach [ə'tætʃ] *v* feste; *vedlegge;
attached to knyttet til
attachment [ə'tætʃmənt] *n* vedlegg *m*
attack [ə'tæk] *v* *angripe; *n* angrep *nt*
attain [ə'tein] *v* oppnå
attainable [ə'teinəbəl] *adj* oppnåelig
attempt [ə'tempt] *v* forsøke, prøve; *n*
forsøk *nt*
attend [ə'tend] *v* *overvære; ~ on

betjene; ~ to *ta hånd om, *ta seg av;
*være oppmerksom på
attendance [ə'tendəns] *n* deltakelse
m
attendant [ə'tendənt] *n* vakt *c*
attention [ə'tenʃən] *n*
oppmerksomhet *c*; *pay ~ *være
oppmerksom
attentive [ə'tentiv] *adj* oppmerksom
attest [ə'test] *v* attestere, bevitne
attic ['ætik] *n* loft *nt*
attitude ['ætitjuːd] *n* holdning *m*
attorney [ə'tɔːni] *n* advokat *m*
attract [ə'trækt] *v* *tiltrekke
attraction [ə'trækʃən] *n* attraksjon *m*;
tiltrekning *m*, sjarm *m*
attractive [ə'træktiv] *adj* tiltrekkende
auction ['ɔːkʃən] *n* auksjon *m*
audible ['ɔːdibəl] *adj* hørbar
audience ['ɔːdiəns] *n* publikum *nt*
auditor ['ɔːditə] *n* tilhører *m*
auditorium [,ɔːdi'tɔːriəm] *n*
auditorium *nt*
August ['ɔːgəst] august
aunt [ɑːnt] *n* tante *c*
Australia [ɔ'streiliə] Australia
Australian [ɔ'streiliən] *adj* australsk;
n australier *m*
Austria ['ɔstriə] Østerrike
Austrian ['ɔstriən] *adj* østerriksk; *n*
østerriker *m*
authentic [ɔː'θentik] *adj* autentisk;
ekte
author ['ɔːθə] *n* forfatter *m*
authoritarian [ɔː,θɔri'tɛəriən] *adj*
autoritær
authority [ɔː'θɔrəti] *n* autoritet *m*;
myndighet *c*
authorization [,ɔːθərai'zeiʃən] *n*
tillatelse *m*; autorisasjon *m*
automatic [,ɔːtə'mætik] *adj*
automatisk; ~ teller minibank *m*
automation [,ɔːtə'meiʃən] *n*
automatisering *c*

automobile [ˈɔːtəməbiːl] n bil m; ~
club automobilklubb m

autonomous [ɔːˈtɔnəməs] adj
selvstyrt

autopsy [ˈɔːtɔpsi] n obduksjon m

autumn [ˈɔːtəm] n høst m

available [əˈveiləbəl] adj tilgjengelig,
disponibel, for hånden

avalanche [ˈævəlɑːnʃ] n snøskred nt

avenue [ˈævənjuː] n aveny m; gate c

average [ˈævəridʒ] adj
gjennomsnittlig; n gjennomsnitt nt;
on the ~ i gjennomsnitt

averse [əˈvəːs] adj uvillig

aversion [əˈvəːʃən] n motvilje m

avert [əˈvəːt] v vende bort

avoid [əˈvɔid] v *unngå; *unnvike

await [əˈweit] v vente på, avvente

awake [əˈweik] adj våken

***awake** [əˈweik] v vekke

award [əˈwɔːd] n pris m; v tildele

aware [əˈwɛə] adj klar over

away [əˈwei] adv bort; ***go ~** reise bort

awful [ˈɔːfəl] adj forferdelig,
redselsfull

awkward [ˈɔːkwəd] adj pinlig; klosset

awning [ˈɔːniŋ] n markise m

axe [æks] n øks c

axle [ˈæksəl] n aksel m

B

baby [ˈbeibi] n baby m; ~ carriage Am
barnevogn c

babysitter [ˈbeibi,sitə] n barnevakt c

bachelor [ˈbætʃələ] n ungkar m

back [bæk] n rygg m; adv tilbake; ***go
~** vende tilbake

backache [ˈbækeik] n ryggsmerter pl

backbone [ˈbækboun] n ryggrad m

background [ˈbækgraund] n
bakgrunn m

backwards [ˈbækwədz] adv baklengs

bacon [ˈbeikən] n bacon nt

bacterium [bækˈtiːriəm] n (pl -ria)
bakterie m

bad [bæd] adj dårlig; alvorlig; slem

bag [bæg] n pose m; veske c,
håndveske c; reiseveske c

baggage [ˈbægidʒ] n bagasje m; ~
deposit office Am
bagasjeoppbevaring c; **hand ~**
håndbagasje m

bail [beil] n kausjon m

bait [beit] n agn nt

bake [beik] v bake

baker [ˈbeikə] n baker m

bakery [ˈbeikəri] n bakeri nt

balance [ˈbæləns] n likevekt c;
balanse m; saldo m

balcony [ˈbælkəni] n balkong m

bald [bɔːld] adj skallet

ball [bɔːl] n ball m; ball nt

ballet [ˈbælei] n ballett m

balloon [bəˈluːn] n ballong m

ballpoint pen [ˈbɔːlpɔintpen] n
kulepenn m

bamboo [bæmˈbuː] n (pl ~s) bambus
m

banana [bəˈnɑːnə] n banan m

band [bænd] n orkester nt; bånd nt

bandage [ˈbændidʒ] n bandasje m

bandit [ˈbændit] n banditt m

bangle [ˈbæŋgəl] n armbånd nt

bank [bæŋk] n bredd m; bank m; v
*sette i banken; ~ account
bankkonto m

banknote [ˈbæŋknout] n pengeseddel

m

bank rate ['bæŋkreit] *n* diskonto *m*

bankrupt ['bæŋkrʌpt] *adj* konkurs, fallitt

banner ['bænə] *n* banner *nt*

banquet ['bæŋkwit] *n* bankett *m*

baptism ['bæptizəm] *n* dåp *m*

baptize [bæp'taiz] *v* døpe

bar [baː] *n* bar *m*; stang *c*

barbecue ['baːbikjuː] *n* grillfest *m*, grilling *c*; *v* grille

barbed wire ['baːbd waiə] *n* piggtråd *m*

barber ['baːbə] *n* frisør *m*

bare [beə] *adj* naken, bar

barely ['beəli] *adv* så vidt

bargain ['baːgin] *n* godt kjøp; *v* *kjøpslå, prute

baritone ['bæritoun] *n* baryton *m*

bark [baːk] *n* bark *m*; *v* gjø

barley ['baːli] *n* bygg *m*

barman ['baːmən] *n* (pl -men) bartender *m*

barn [baːn] *n* låve *m*

barometer [bə'rɔmitə] *n* barometer *nt*

baroque [bə'rɔk] *adj* barokk

barracks ['bærəks] *pl* kaserne *m*

barrel ['bærəl] *n* fat *nt*, tønne *c*

barrier ['bæriə] *n* barriere *m*; bom *m*

barrister ['bæristə] *n* advokat *m*

bartender ['baː,tendə] *n* bartender *m*

base [beis] *n* base *m*, basis *m*; fundament *nt*; *v* basere

baseball ['beisbɔːl] *n* baseball *m*

basement ['beismənt] *n* kjelleretasje *m*

basic ['beisik] *adj* grunnleggende; **basics** *npl* grunnlag *nt/pl*

basilica [bə'zilikə] *n* basilika *m*

basin ['beisən] *n* bolle *m*

basis ['beisis] *n* (pl bases) basis *m*, grunnlag *nt*

basket ['baːskit] *n* kurv *m*

bass¹ [beis] *n* bass *m*

bass² [bæs] *n* (pl ~) åbor *m*

bastard ['baːstəd] *n* bastard *m*; skurk *m*

batch [bætʃ] *n* bunke *m*

bath [baːθ] *n* bad *nt*; ~ **towel** badehåndkle *nt*

bathe [beið] *v* bade

bathing cap ['beiðiŋkæp] *n* badehette *c*

bathing suit ['beiðiŋsuːt] *n* badedrakt *c*; badebukse *c*

bathrobe ['baːθroub] *n* badekåpe *c*

bathroom ['baːθruːm] *n* bad *nt*, badeværelse *nt*; toalett *nt*

batter ['bætə] *n* deig *m*

battery ['bætəri] *n* batteri *nt*

battle ['bætəl] *n* slag *nt*; kamp *m*, strid *m*; *v* kjempe

bay [bei] *n* bukt *c*; *v* gjø

***be** [biː] *v* *være

beach [biːtʃ] *n* strand *c*; **nudist** ~ nudistbadestrand *c*

bead [biːd] *n* perle *c*; **beads** *pl* perlekjede *nt*; rosenkrans *m*

beak [biːk] *n* nebb *nt*

beam [biːm] *n* stråle *m*; bjelke *m*

bean [biːn] *n* bønne *c*

bear [beə] *n* bjørn *m*

***bear** [beə] *v* *bære; tåle; *holde ut

beard [biəd] *n* skjegg *nt*

bearer ['beərə] *n* innehaver *m*

beast [biːst] *n* dyr *nt*; ~ **of prey** rovdyr *nt*

beat [biːt] *n* rytme *m*; slag *nt*

***beat** [biːt] *v* *slå

beautiful ['bjuːtifəl] *adj* vakker

beauty ['bjuːti] *n* skjønnhet *c*; ~ **parlo(u)r** skjønnhetssalong *m*; ~ **treatment** skjønnhetspleie *m*

beaver ['biːvə] *n* bever *m*

because [bi'kɔz] *conj* fordi; ettersom; ~ **of** på grunn av

***become** [bi'kʌm] *v* *bli; kle

bed [bed] *n* seng *c*; ~ **and board** kost

og losji, helpensjon *m*; **~ and breakfast** værelse med frokost

bedding ['bediŋ] *n* sengetøy *nt*

bedroom ['bedru:m] *n* soveværelse *nt*

bee [bi:] *n* bie *c*

beech [bi:tʃ] *n* bøk *m*

beef [bi:f] *n* oksekjøtt *nt*

beefburger [bi:fbə:gə] *n* hamburger *m*

beehive ['bi:haiv] *n* bikube *m*

been [bi:n] *v* (pp be)

beer [biə] *n* øl *nt*

beetle ['bi:təl] *n* bille *m*

beetroot ['bi:tru:t] *n* rødbete *c*

before [bi'fɔ:] *prep* før; foran; *conj* før; *adv* tidligere

beg [beg] *v* tigge; *bønnfalle; *be

beggar ['begə] *n* tigger *m*

***begin** [bi'gin] *v* begynne; starte

beginner [bi'ginə] *n* nybegynner *m*

beginning [bi'giniŋ] *n* begynnelse *m*; start *m*

behalf: on ~ of [ɔn bi'hɑ:f ɔv] på vegne av; til fordel for

behave [bi'heiv] *v* oppføre seg

behavio(u)r [bi'heivjə] *n* oppførsel *m*

behind [bi'haind] *prep* bak; *adv* bak

beige [beiʒ] *adj* beige

being ['bi:iŋ] *n* vesen *nt*

Belgian ['beldʒən] *adj* belgisk; *n* belgier *m*

Belgium ['beldʒəm] Belgia

belief [bi'li:f] *n* tro *c*

believe [bi'li:v] *v* tro

bell [bel] *n* klokke *c*; ringeklokke *c*

bellboy ['belbɔi] *n* pikkolo *m*

belly ['beli] *n* mage *m*

belong [bi'lɔŋ] *v* tilhøre

belongings [bi'lɔŋiŋz] *pl* eiendeler

beloved [bi'lʌvd] *adj* elsket

below [bi'lou] *prep* nedenfor; under; *adv* nede

belt [belt] *n* belte *nt*

bench [bentʃ] *n* benk *m*

bend [bend] *n* sving *m*, bøyning *m*; krumning *m*

***bend** [bend] *v* bøye; **~ down** bøye seg

beneath [bi'ni:θ] *prep* under; *adv* under

benefit ['benifit] *n* utbytte *nt*; fordel *m*; *v* *ha fordel av

bent [bent] *adj* (pp bend) bøyd

beret ['berei] *n* alpelue *c*

berry ['beri] *n* bær *nt*

beside [bi'said] *prep* ved siden av

besides [bi'saidz] *adv* dessuten; forresten; *prep* foruten

best [best] *adj* best

bet [bet] *n* veddemål *nt*; innsats *m*

***bet** [bet] *v* vedde

betray [bi'trei] *v* forråde

better ['betə] *adj* bedre

between [bi'twi:n] *prep* mellom

beverage ['bevəridʒ] *n* drikk *m*

beware [bi'wɛə] *v* vokte seg

bewitch [bi'witʃ] *v* forhekse

beyond [bi'jɔnd] *prep* hinsides; på den andre siden av; ut over; *adv* bortenfor

bible ['baibəl] *n* bibel *m*

bicycle ['baisikəl] *n* sykkel *m*

bid [bid] *n* bud *nt*; tilbud *nt*

***bid** [bid] *v* *tilby; *by

big [big] *adj* stor; omfangsrik; tykk; viktig

bike [baik] *n* *colloquial* sykkel *m*; *v* sykle

bile [bail] *n* galle *m*

bilingual [bai'liŋgwəl] *adj* tospråklig

bill [bil] *n* regning *c*, nota *m*; *v* fakturere

billiards ['biljədz] *pl* biljard *m*

billion ['biljən] *n* milliard *m*

***bind** [baind] *v* *binde

binding ['baindiŋ] *n* bokbind *nt*

binoculars [bi'nɔkjələz] *pl* kikkert *m*

biology [bai'ɔlədʒi] *n* biologi *m*

birch [bə:tʃ] *n* bjørk *c*

bird [bə:d] n fugl m

birth [bə:θ] n fødsel m

birthday ['bə:θdei] n fødselsdag m

biscuit ['biskit] n småkake c

bishop ['biʃəp] n biskop m

bit [bit] n bit m; smule m

bitch [bitʃ] n tispe c

bite [bait] n bit m; stikk nt

*bite [bait] v *bite

bitter ['bitə] adj bitter

black [blæk] adj svart; ~ market svartebørs m

blackberry ['blækbəri] n bjørnebær nt

blackbird ['blækbə:d] n svarttrost m

blackboard ['blækbɔ:d] n tavle c

blackcurrant [,blæk'kʌrənt] n solbær nt

blackmail ['blækmeil] n pengeutpresning m; v presse penger av

blacksmith ['blæksmiθ] n grovsmed m

bladder ['blædə] n blære c

blade [bleid] n blad nt; ~ of grass gresstrå nt

blame [bleim] n skyld c; bebreidelse m; v klandre, bebreide

blank [blæŋk] adj blank

blanket ['blæŋkit] n ullteppe nt; teppe nt

blast [blɑ:st] n eksplosjon m

bleach [bli:tʃ] v bleke

bleak [bli:k] adj ødslig, barsk

*bleed [bli:d] v blø; flå

bless [bles] v velsigne

blessing ['blesiŋ] n velsignelse m

blind [blaind] n persienne m, rullegardin c/nt; adj blind; v blende

blister ['blistə] n blemme c, gnagsår nt

blizzard ['blizəd] n snøstorm m

block [blɔk] v sperre, blokkere; n kloss m; kvartal nt; ~ of flats leiegård m

blond [blɔnd] adj blond

blonde [blɔnd] n blondine c, blond person m

blood [blʌd] n blod nt; ~ poisoning blodforgiftning m; ~ pressure blodtrykk nt; ~ vessel blodkar nt

bloody [blʌdi] adj blodig; colloquial fordømt

blossom ['blɔsəm] n blomst m; v blomstre

blot [blɔt] n flekk m

blouse [blauz] n bluse c

blow [blou] n fik m, slag nt; vindkast m

*blow [blou] v blåse; ~ up sprenge; eksplodere

blowout ['blouaut] n punktering c; utblåsning m

blue [blu:] adj blå; nedtrykt

blunt [blʌnt] adj sløv; butt

blush [blʌʃ] v rødme

board [bɔ:d] n planke m; tavle c; oppslagstavle c; pensjon m; styre nt; ~ and lodging kost og losji, helpensjon m

boardinghouse ['bɔ:diŋhaus] n pensjonat nt

boarding school ['bɔ:diŋsku:l] n pensjonatskole m

boast [boust] v *skryte

boat [bout] n båt m, skip nt

body ['bɔdi] n kropp m; legeme nt

bodyguard ['bɔdigɑ:d] n livvakt c

body-work ['bɔdiwə:k] n karosseri nt

bog [bɔg] n myr c

boil [bɔil] v koke; n byll m

bold [bould] adj dristig; frekk

Bolivia [bə'liviə] Bolivia

Bolivian [bə'liviən] adj boliviansk; n bolivianer m

bolt [boult] n slå c; bolt m

bomb [bɔm] n bombe c; v bombardere

bond [bɔnd] n obligasjon m

bone [boun] n bein nt; fiskebein nt; v skjære ut bein

bonnet ['bɔnit] n bilpanser nt

book [buk] n bok c; v reservere, bestille; bokføre

booking ['bukiŋ] n bestilling c, reservasjon m

bookmaker ['buk,meikə] n totalisator m

bookseller ['buk,selə] n bokhandler m

bookstand ['bukstænd] n bokstand m

bookstore ['bukstɔ:] n bokhandel m

boot [bu:t] n støvel m; bagasjerom nt

booth [bu:ð] n bu c; bås m

booze [bu:z] n colloquial alkohol m; v drikke alkohol

border ['bɔ:də] n grense c; kant m

bore¹ [bɔ:] v kjede; bore; n kjedelig person m

bore² [bɔ:] v (p bear)

boring ['bɔ:riŋ] adj kjedelig

born [bɔ:n] adj født

borrow ['bɔrou] v låne

bosom ['buzəm] n barm m; bryst nt

boss [bɔs] n boss m, sjef m

botany ['bɔtəni] n botanikk m

both [bouθ] adj begge; **both ... and** både ... og

bother ['bɔðə] v plage; bry seg; n bry nt

bottle ['bɔtəl] n flaske c; ~ **opener** flaskeåpner m; **hot-water ~** varmeflaske c

bottleneck ['bɔtəlnek] n flaskehals m

bottom ['bɔtəm] n bunn m; akterspeil nt, bak m; adj underste

bought [bɔ:t] v (p, pp buy)

boulder ['bouldə] n rullestein m

bound [baund] n grense c; *be ~ to **måtte; ~ for på vei til

boundary ['baundəri] n grense c

bouquet [bu'kei] n bukett m

bourgeois ['buəʒwɑ:] adj spissborgerlig

boutique [bu'ti:k] n butikk m

bow¹ [bau] v bukke

bow² [bou] n bue m; ~ **tie** sløyfe c

bowels [bauəlz] pl tarmer

bowl [boul] n bolle m

bowling ['bouliŋ] n bowling m; ~ **alley** bowlingbane m

box¹ [bɔks] v bokse; **boxing match** boksekamp m

box² [bɔks] n eske c

box office ['bɔks,ɔfis] n billettluke c, billettkontor nt

boy [bɔi] n gutt m; tjener m

boyfriend ['bɔifrend] n kjæreste m

bra [brɑ:] n brystholder m, behå m

brace ['breis] n (tann-)regulering c

bracelet ['breislit] n armbånd nt

braces ['breisiz] pl bukseseler pl;

brain [brein] n hjerne m; forstand m; ~ **wave** innfall nt

brake [breik] n brems m; ~ **drum** bremsetrommel m; ~ **lights** bremselys pl

branch [brɑ:ntʃ] n gren m; filial m

brand [brænd] n merke nt; brennemerke m

brand-new [,brænd'nju:] adj splinter ny

brass [brɑ:s] n messing m; ~ **band** hornorkester m

brave [breiv] adj modig, tapper

Brazil [brə'zil] Brasil

Brazilian [brə'ziljən] adj brasiliansk; n brasilianer m

breach [bri:tʃ] n åpning c

bread [bred] n brød nt; **wholemeal ~** helkornbrød nt

breadth [bredθ] n bredde m

break [breik] n brudd nt; m pause m; frikvarter nt

***break** [breik] v *bryte; ~ **down** *gå i stykker; inndele

breakdown ['breikdaun] n maskinskade m, motorstopp m/nt

breakfast ['brekfəst] n frokost m

breast [brest] n bryst nt

breaststroke ['breststrouk] n brystsvømming c

breath [breθ] n pust m

breathe [briːð] v puste

breathing ['briːðiŋ] n åndedrett nt

breed [briːd] n rase m; slag nt

*breed [briːd] v ale opp, oppdrette

breeze [briːz] n bris m

brew [bruː] v brygge

brewery ['bruːəri] n bryggeri nt

bribe [braib] v *bestikke

bribery ['braibəri] n bestikkelse m

brick [brik] n murstein m

bricklayer ['brikleiə] n murer m

bride [braid] n brud c

bridegroom ['braidgruːm] n brudgom m

bridge [bridʒ] n bro c; bridge m

brief [briːf] adj kort; kortfattet

briefcase ['briːfkeis] n dokumentmappe c

briefs [briːfs] pl truse c

bright [brait] adj skinnende; oppvakt

brighten ['braitən] v lyse opp

brill [bril] n slettvar m

brilliant ['briljənt] adj strålende; begavet

brim [brim] n rand m

*bring [briŋ] v *ta med, *bringe; *medbringe; ~ back *bringe tilbake; ~ up *oppdra; *ta opp

brisk [brisk] adj livlig

Britain ['britən] Britannia

British ['britiʃ] adj britisk

Briton ['britən] n brite m

broad [brɔːd] adj bred; utstrakt, vidstrakt; allmenn

broadcast ['brɔːdkɑːst] n sending c

*broadcast ['brɔːdkɑːst] v kringkaste

brochure ['brouʃuə] n brosjyre m

broke¹ [brouk] v (p break)

broke² [brouk] adj blakk

broken ['broukən] adj (pp break) knust, i stykker; i uorden

broker ['broukə] n megler m

bronchitis [brɔŋ'kaitis] n bronkitt m

bronze [brɔnz] n bronse m; adj bronse-

brooch [broutʃ] n brosje c

brook [bruk] n bekk m

broom [bruːm] n kost m

brothel ['brɔθəl] n bordell nt

brother ['brʌðə] n bror m

brother-in-law ['brʌðərinlɔː] n (pl brothers-) svoger m

brought [brɔːt] v (p, pp bring)

brown [braun] adj brun

bruise [bruːz] n blått merke; v *slå

brunette [bruː'net] n brunette m

brush [brʌʃ] n børste m; pensel m; v børste

brutal ['bruːtəl] adj brutal

bubble ['bʌbəl] n boble c

buck [bʌk] n bukk m; colloquial dollar m

bucket ['bʌkit] n spann nt

buckle ['bʌkəl] n spenne c

bud [bʌd] n knopp m

buddy ['bʌdi] n colloquial kamerat m

budget ['bʌdʒit] n budsjett nt

buffet ['bufei] n koldtbord nt

bug [bʌg] n veggedyr nt; bille m; insekt nt

*build [bild] v bygge

building ['bildiŋ] n bygning m

bulb [bʌlb] n blomsterløk m; light ~ lyspære c

Bulgaria [bʌl'gɛəriə] Bulgaria

Bulgarian [bʌl'gɛəriən] adj bulgarsk; n bulgarer m

bulk [bʌlk] n last c; masse m; størsteparten m

bulky ['bʌlki] adj fyldig, omfangsrik

bull [bul] n tyr m, okse m

bullet ['bulit] n kule c

bulletin ['bulitin] n bekjentgjørelse m, oppslag m

bullfight ['bulfait] n tyrefektning m

bump [bʌmp] v støte; støte sammen; dunke; n støt nt

bumper ['bʌmpə] n støtfanger m

bumpy ['bʌmpi] adj humpet

bun [bʌn] n hvetebolle m

bunch [bʌntʃ] n bukett m; flokk m

bundle ['bʌndəl] n bunt m; v bunte, *binde sammen

bunk [bʌŋk] n køye c

buoy [bɔi] n bøye m

burden ['bəːdən] n byrde m

bureau ['bjuərou] n (pl ~x, ~s) skrivebord nt; kommode m

bureaucracy [bjuə'rɔkrəsi] n byråkrati nt

burger [bəːgə] n hamburger

burglar ['bəːglə] n innbruddstyv m

burgle ['bəːgəl] v *begå innbrudd

burial ['beriəl] n begravelse m

burn [bəːn] n brannsår nt

burn [bəːn] v *brenne; *svi

burst [bəːst] v *sprekke; *briste

bury ['beri] v begrave; grave ned

bus [bʌs] n buss m

bush [buʃ] n busk m

business ['biznəs] n forretninger pl,

handel m; virksomhet c, forretning c; yrke nt; ~ **card** visittkort nt; ~ **hours** åpningstid c, kontortid c; ~ **trip** forretningsreise c; **on** ~ i forretninger

business-like ['biznislaik] adj forretningsmessig

businessman ['biznəsmən] n (pl -men) forretningsmann m

businesswoman ['biznəswumən] n (pl -women) forretningskvinne c

bust [bʌst] n byste c

bustle ['bʌsəl] n travelhet c

busy ['bizi] adj opptatt; travel

but [bʌt] conj men; dog; prep unntatt

butcher ['butʃə] n slakter m

butter ['bʌtə] n smør nt

butterfly ['bʌtəflai] n sommerfugl m; ~ **stroke** butterfly m

buttock ['bʌtək] n rumpeballe m

button ['bʌtən] n knapp m; v knappe

buy [bai] v kjøpe; anskaffe

buyer ['baiə] n kjøper m

buzz [bʌs] n summing c

by [bai] prep av; med; ved

bye-bye [bai'bai] colloquial ha det!

by-pass ['baipaːs] n ringvei m; bypass m; v *omgå

C

cab [kæb] n drosje c, taxi m

cabaret ['kæbərei] n kabaret m; nattklubb m

cabbage ['kæbidʒ] n kål m

cab driver ['kæb,draivə] n drosjesjåfør m, taxisjåfør m

cabin ['kæbin] n kabin m; hytte c; omkledningskabin m; lugar m

cable ['keibəl] n kabel m; ~ **tv** kabelfjernsyn, nt kabel-TV nt

café ['kæfei] n kafé m

cafeteria [,kæfə'tiəriə] n kafeteria m

caffeine ['kæfiːn] n kaffein m

cage [keidʒ] n bur nt

cake [keik] n kake c

calamity [kə'læməti] n ulykke c, katastrofe m

calcium ['kælsiəm] n kalsium nt

calculate ['kælkjuleit] v regne ut

calculation [,kælkju'leiʃən] n utregning c

calculator ['kælkjuleitə] n kalkulator

m, lommeregner *m*
calendar ['kæləndə] *n* kalender *m*
calf [kɑːf] *n* (pl calves) kalv *m*; legg *m*;
~ **skin** kalveskinn *nt*
call [kɔːl] *v* rope; kalle; ringe opp; *n*
rop *nt*; besøk *nt*, visitt *m*; oppringning
m; ***be called** *hete; ~ **names** skjelle
ut; ~ **on** besøke; ~ **up** *Am* ringe opp
calm [kɑːm] *adj* stille, rolig; ~ **down**
berolige; roe seg, falle til ro
calorie ['kæləri] *n* kalori *m*
came [keim] *v* (p come)
camel ['kæməl] *n* kamel *m*
cameo ['kæmiou] *n* (pl ~s) kamé *m*
camera ['kæmərə] *n* fotografiapparat
nt; filmkamera *nt*; ~ **shop**
fotoforretning *c*
camp [kæmp] *n* leir *m*; *v* campe; ~ **bed**
feltseng *c*
campaign [kæm'pein] *n* kampanje *m*
camper ['kæmpə] *n* campinggjest *m*;
bobil *m*
camping ['kæmpiŋ] *n* camping *m*; ~
site campingplass *m*
can [kæn] *n* boks *m*; ~ **opener**
boksåpner *m*
*can [kæn] *v* *kan
Canada ['kænədə] Canada
Canadian [kə'neidiən] *adj* kanadisk;
n kanadier *m*
canal [kə'næl] *n* kanal *m*
canary [kə'neəri] *n* kanarifugl *m*
cancel ['kænsəl] *v* annullere;
avbestille
cancellation [,kænsə'leiʃən] *n*
avbestilling *c*
cancer ['kænsə] *n* kreft *m*
candid ['kændid] *adj* åpen, oppriktig
candidate ['kændidət] *n* kandidat *m*
candle ['kændəl] *n* stearinlys *nt*
candy ['kændi] *nAm* sukkertøy *nt*;
godter *pl*, søtsaker *pl*
cane [kein] *n* rør *nt*; stokk *m*
canister ['kænistə] *n* boks *m*

canoe [kə'nuː] *n* kano *m*
canteen [kæn'tiːn] *n* kantine *c*
canvas ['kænvəs] *n* lerret *nt*, seilduk
m
cap [kæp] *n* lue *c*, skyggelue *c*
capable ['keipəbəl] *adj* dyktig,
kompetent
capacity [kə'pæsəti] *n* kapasitet *m*;
evne *c*
cape [keip] *n* cape *m*; kapp *nt*
capital ['kæpitəl] *n* hovedstad *m*;
kapital *m*; *adj* viktig, hoved-; ~ **letter**
stor bokstav
capitalism ['kæpitəlizəm] *n*
kapitalisme *m*
capitulation [kə,pitju'leiʃən] *n*
kapitulasjon *m*
capsule ['kæpsjuːl] *n* kapsel *m*
captain ['kæptin] *n* kaptein *m*;
flykaptein *m*
capture ['kæptʃə] *v* fange, *ta til
fange; erobre; *n* arrestasjon *m*;
erobring *c*
car [kɑː] *n* bil *m*; ~ **hire** bilutleie *m*; ~
park parkeringsplass *m*; ~ **rental** *Am*
bilutleie *c*
caramel ['kærəməl] *n* karamell *m*
carat ['kærət] *n* karat *m*
caravan ['kærəvæn] *n* bobil *m*
carburettor [,kɑːbju'retə] *n* forgasser
m
card [kɑːd] *n* kort *nt*; visittkort *nt*
cardboard ['kɑːdbɔːd] *n* papp *m*; *adj*
kartong-
cardigan ['kɑːdigən] *n* ulljakke *c*
cardinal ['kɑːdinəl] *n* kardinal *m*; *adj*
hoved-; ~ **number** grunntall *nt*
care [keə] *n* omsorg *c*; bekymring *c*; ~
about bekymre seg om; ~ **for** bry seg
om; ***take ~ of** passe på, *ta vare på
career [kə'riə] *n* karriere *m*
carefree ['keəfriː] *adj* ubekymret
careful ['keəfəl] *adj* forsiktig;
omhyggelig, nøyaktig

careless ['kɛələs] adj likegyldig, skjødesløs

caretaker ['kɛə,teikə] n vaktmester m

cargo ['kɑːgou] n (pl ~es) last c, frakt c

carnival ['kɑːnivəl] n karneval nt

carp [kɑːp] n (pl ~) karpe m

carpenter ['kɑːpintə] n snekker m

carpet ['kɑːpit] n gulvteppe nt, teppe nt

carriage ['kæridʒ] n hestevogn c, vogn c

carriageway ['kæridʒwei] n kjørebane m

carrot ['kærət] n gulrot c

carry ['kæri] v *bære; føre; ~ on *fortsette; ~ out utføre

carrycot ['kærikɔt] n babybag m

cart [kɑːt] n kjerre c

cartilage ['kɑːtilidʒ] n brusk m

carton ['kɑːtən] n kartong m

cartoon [kɑːˈtuːn] n tegnefilm m

cartridge ['kɑːtridʒ] n patron m

carve [kɑːv] v *skjære; *skjære i, *skjære ut

carving ['kɑːviŋ] n utskjæring c, skurd m

case [keis] n tilfelle nt; sak c; koffert m; etui nt; **attaché ~ dokumentmappe** c; **in ~** hvis

cash [kæʃ] n kontanter pl; v innkassere, heve; ~ **dispenser** minibank m

cashier [kæˈʃiə] n kasserer m

cashmere ['kæʃmiə] n kasjmir c

casino [kəˈsiːnou] n (pl ~s) kasino nt

cask [kɑːsk] n fat nt, tønne c

cassette [kəˈset] n kassett m

cast [kɑːst] n kast nt

***cast** [kɑːst] v kaste; **cast iron** støpejern nt

castle ['kɑːsəl] n slott nt, borg c

casual ['kæʒuəl] adj uformell; tilfeldig, flyktig

casualty ['kæʒuəlti] n ulykke c; offer nt

cat [kæt] n katt m

catacomb ['kætəkoum] n katakombe m

catalogue ['kætəlɔg] n katalog m

catarrh [kəˈtɑː] n katarr m

catastrophe [kəˈtæstrəfi] n katastrofe m

***catch** [kætʃ] v fange; *gripe; overrumple; nå, *rekke

catchword ['kætʃwəːd] n stikkord nt

category ['kætigəri] n kategori m

caterer [,keitərər] n catering m

cathedral [kəˈθiːdrəl] n katedral m, domkirke c

catheter [kəˈθiːdər] n kateter nt

catholic ['kæθəlik] adj katolsk

cattle ['kætəl] pl kveg nt

caught [kɔːt] v (p, pp catch)

cauliflower ['kɔliflauə] n blomkål m

cause [kɔːz] v forårsake; volde; n årsak c; grunn m; sak c; ~ **to** *få til å

caution ['kɔːʃən] n forsiktighet c; v advare

cautious ['kɔːʃəs] adj forsiktig

cave [keiv] n grotte c; hule c

cavern ['kævən] n hule c

caviar ['kævɑː] n kaviar m

cavity ['kævəti] n hulrom nt

CD [siːˈdiː] n CD m; ~ **player** CD-spiller

CD (-ROM) [siːˈdiː(rɔm)] n CD-ROM m

cease [siːs] v opphøre

ceasefire [siːsfaiə] n våpenstillstand m

ceiling ['siːliŋ] n tak nt

celebrate ['selibreit] v feire

celebration [,seliˈbreiʃən] n feiring c

celebrity [siˈlebrəti] n berømmelse m

celery ['seləri] n selleri m

cell [sel] n celle c

cellar ['selə] n kjeller m

cellphone ['selfoun] n mobil(-telefon) m

cement [si'ment] n sement m

cemetery ['semitri] n gravlund m

censorship ['sensəʃip] n sensur m

center ['sentə] nAm sentrum nt; midtpunkt nt

centigrade ['sentigreid] celsius

centimeter Am, centimetre ['sentimi:tə] n centimeter m

central ['sentrəl] adj sentral; ~ heating sentralfyring c; ~ station sentralstasjon m

centralize ['sentrəlaiz] v sentralisere

center Am, centre ['sentə] n sentrum nt; midtpunkt nt

century ['sentʃəri] n århundre nt

ceramics [si'ræmiks] pl keramikk m

ceremony ['serəməni] n seremoni m

certain ['sə:tən] adj sikker; viss

certainly ['sə:tənli] adv sikkert; klart

certificate [sə'tifikət] n attest m; vitnesbyrd nt, diplom nt, dokument nt

chain [tʃein] n kjede nt , kjetting m

chair [tʃɛə] n stol m; sete nt

chairman ['tʃɛəmən] n (pl -men) formann m, leder m

chairwoman ['tʃɛəwumən] n (pl -women) formann m, leder m

chalet ['ʃælei] n hytte c

chalk [tʃɔ:k] n kritt nt

challenge ['tʃæləndʒ] v utfordre; n utfordring c

chamber ['tʃeimbə] n rom nt

champagne [ʃæm'pein] n champagne m

champion ['tʃæmpjən] n mester m; forkjemper m

chance [tʃɑ:ns] n slump m; sjanse m, anledning m; risiko m; tilfelle nt; by ~ tilfeldigvis

change [tʃeindʒ] v forandre; veksle; kle seg om; skifte; n forandring c,

endring c; småpenger pl, vekslepenger pl; vekslepenger pl; for a ~ til avveksling; unntaksvis

channel ['tʃænəl] n kanal m; English Channel Den engelske kanal

chaos ['keiɔs] n kaos nt

chaotic [kei'ɔtik] adj kaotisk

chap [tʃæp] n fyr m

chapel ['tʃæpəl] n kapell nt, kirke c

chaplain ['tʃæplin] n kapellan m

character ['kærəktə] n karakter m

characteristic [,kærəktə'ristik] adj betegnende, karakteristisk; n kjennetegn nt; karaktertrekk nt

characterize ['kærəktəraiz] v karakterisere

charcoal ['tʃɑ:koul] n trekull nt

charge [tʃɑ:dʒ] v kreve; *pålegge; anklage; laste; n pris m; ladning m, byrde m, belastning m; anklage m; free of ~ kostfri; in ~ of ansvarlig for; *take ~ of *påta seg

charity ['tʃærəti] n velgjørenhet c

charm [tʃɑ:m] n sjarm m; amulett m

charming ['tʃɑ:miŋ] adj sjarmerende

chart [tʃɑ:t] n tabell m; diagram nt; sjøkart nt; conversion ~ omregningstabell m

chase [tʃeis] v *forfølge; jage bort, *fordrive; n jakt c

chasm ['kæzəm] n kløft c

chassis ['ʃæsi] n (pl ~) chassis nt

chaste [tʃeist] adj kysk

chat [tʃæt] v prate, skravle; n prat m/nt

chatterbox ['tʃætəbɔks] n skravlebøtte c

chauffeur ['ʃoufə] n sjåfør m

cheap [tʃi:p] adj billig; gunstig

cheat [tʃi:t] v jukse, *snyte

check [tʃek] v sjekke, kontrollere; n rute c; regning c; sjekk m; check! sjakk!; ~ in sjekke inn; ~ out sjekke ut

checkbook ['tʃekbuk] nAm

sjekkhefte nt

checkerboard ['tʃekəbɔːd] nAm
  sjakkbrett nt

checkers ['tʃekəz] plAm damspill nt

checkroom ['tʃekruːm] nAm
  garderobe m

checkup ['tʃekʌp] n undersøkelse m

cheek [tʃiːk] n kinn nt

cheekbone ['tʃiːkboun] n kinnbein nt

cheeky [tʃiːki] adj colloquial frekk,
  uforskammet

cheer [tʃiə] v hylle, juble; ~ up
  oppmuntre

cheerful ['tʃiəfəl] adj lystig, glad

cheese [tʃiːz] n ost m

chef [ʃef] n kjøkkensjef m

chemical ['kemikəl] adj kjemisk

chemist ['kemist] n apoteker m;
  chemist's apotek nt

chemistry ['kemistri] n kjemi m

cheque [tʃek] n sjekk m

chequered ['tʃekəd] adj rutet

cherry ['tʃeri] n kirsebær nt

chess [tʃes] n sjakk m

chest [tʃest] n bryst nt; brystkasse c;
  kiste c; ~ **of drawers** kommode m

chestnut ['tʃesnʌt] n kastanje m

chew [tʃuː] v tygge

chewing gum ['tʃuːiŋgʌm] n
  tyggegummi m

chicken ['tʃikin] n kylling m

chickenpox ['tʃikinpɔks] n
  vannkopper pl

chief [tʃiːf] n sjef m; adj hoved-, over-

chieftain ['tʃiːftən] n høvding m

child [tʃaild] n (pl children) barn nt

childbirth ['tʃaildbəːθ] n fødsel m

childhood ['tʃaildhud] n barndom m

Chile ['tʃili] Chile

Chilean ['tʃiliən] adj chilensk; n
  chilener m

chill [tʃil] n kuldegysning m

chilly ['tʃili] adj kjølig

chimes [tʃaimz] pl klokkespill nt

chimney ['tʃimni] n skorstein m

chin [tʃin] n hake c

China ['tʃainə] Kina

china ['tʃainə] n porselen nt

Chinese [tʃai'niːz] adj kinesisk; n
  kineser m

chip [tʃip] n flis c; chip m; brikke c; v
  *slå hakk i, snitte; **chips** pommes
  frites

chisel ['tʃizəl] n meisel m

chives [tʃaivz] pl gressløk m

chlorine ['klɔːriːn] n klor m

chock-full [tʃɔk'ful] adj proppfull,
  fullstappet

chocolate ['tʃɔklət] n sjokolade m;
  konfekt m

choice [tʃɔis] n valg nt; utvalg nt

choir [kwaiə] n kor nt

choke [tʃouk] v kveles; kvele; n choke
  m

***choose** [tʃuːz] v *velge

chop [tʃɔp] n kotelett m; v hakke

Christ [kraist] Kristus

christen ['krisən] v døpe

christening ['krisəniŋ] n dåp m

Christian ['kristʃən] adj kristen; ~
  name fornavn nt

Christmas ['krisməs] n jul c

chromium ['kroumiəm] n krom m

chronic ['krɔnik] adj kronisk

chronological [,krɔnə'lɔdʒikəl] adj
  kronologisk

chuckle ['tʃʌkəl] v klukke, *le

chunk [tʃʌŋk] n stort stykke

church [tʃəːtʃ] n kirke c

churchyard ['tʃəːtʃjaːd] n kirkegård
  m

cigar [si'gaː] n sigar m

cigarette [,sigə'ret] n sigarett m; ~
  case sigarettetui nt; ~ **lighter**
  [,sigə'ret,laitə] n lighter m

cinema ['sinəmə] n kino m

cinnamon ['sinəmən] n kanel m

circle ['səːkəl] n sirkel m; krets m;

balkong *m*; *v* *omgi, omringe

circulation [,səːkjuˈleiʃən] *n*
sirkulasjon *m*; blodomløp *nt*; omløp
nt

circumstance [ˈsəːkəmstæns] *n*
omstendighet *c*

circus [ˈsəːkəs] *n* sirkus *nt*

citizen [ˈsitizən] *n* borger *m*

citizenship [ˈsitizənʃip] *n*
statsborgerskap *nt*

city [ˈsiti] *n* by *m*

civic [ˈsivik] *adj* borger-

civil [ˈsivəl] *adj* sivil; høflig; ~ **law**
sivilrett *m*; ~ **servant**
statstjenestemann *m*

civilian [siˈviljən] *adj* sivil; *n*
sivilperson *m*

civilization [,sivəlaiˈzeiʃən] *n*
sivilisasjon *m*

civilized [ˈsivəlaizd] *adj* sivilisert

claim [kleim] *v* kreve; *påstå; *n* krav
nt, fordring *c*

clamp [klæmp] *n* krampe *m*;
skruestikke *c*

clap [klæp] *v* klappe, applaudere

clarify [ˈklærifai] *v* *klarlegge,
*klargjøre

class [klaːs] *n* klasse *c*

classical [ˈklæsikəl] *adj* klassisk

classify [ˈklæsifai] *v* gruppere

classmate [ˈklaːsmeit] *n*
klassekamerat *m*

classroom [ˈklaːsruːm] *n*
klasseværelse *nt*

clause [kloːz] *n* klausul *m*

claw [kloː] *n* klo *c*

clay [klei] *n* leire *c*

clean [kliːn] *adj* ren; *v* rense, gjøre
rent

cleaning [ˈkliːniŋ] *n* rengjøring *c*; ~
fluid vaskemiddel *nt*

clear [kliə] *adj* klar; tydelig; *v* rydde

clearing [ˈkliəriŋ] *n* lysning *m*

cleft [kleft] *n* kløft *c*

clergyman [ˈkləːdʒimən] *n* (pl -men)
prest *m*

clerk [klaːk] *n* sekretær *m*,
kontorpersonale *nt*

clever [ˈklevə] *adj* intelligent; flink,
begavet, klok

click [klik] *v* klikke; ~ **into place**
klikke på plass

client [ˈklaiənt] *n* kunde *m*; klient *m*

cliff [klif] *n* klippe *m*

climate [ˈklaimit] *n* klima *nt*

climb [klaim] *v* klatre; *n* klatring *c*

cling [kliŋ] *v* klistre, klenge; ~ **to**
klamre seg til

clinic [ˈklinik] *n* klinikk *m*

cloak [klouk] *n* kappe *c*

cloakroom [ˈkloukruːm] *n* garderobe
m

clock [klɔk] *n* klokke *c*; **at ... o'clock**
klokken / klokka ...

cloister [ˈkloistə] *n* kloster *nt*

close[1] [klouz] *v* lukke; **closed** *adj*
stengt, lukket

close[2] [klous] *adj* nær

closet [ˈklɔzit] *nAm* skap *nt*;
garderobeskap *nt*

close-up [ˈklousʌp] *n* nærbilde *nt*

cloth [klɔθ] *n* stoff *nt*; klut *m*

clothes [klouðz] *pl* klær *pl*

clothing [ˈklouðiŋ] *n* klær *pl*

cloud [klaud] *n* sky *c*

cloudberry [klaudbəri] *n* molte *c*,
multe *c*

cloudy [ˈklaudi] *adj* skyet, overskyet

clover [ˈklouvə] *n* kløver *m*

clown [klaun] *n* klovn *m*

club [klʌb] *n* klubb *m*, forening *c*;
kølle *c*, klubbe *c*

clumsy [ˈklʌmzi] *adj* klosset

clutch [klʌtʃ] *n* clutch *m*; grep *nt*

coach [koutʃ] *n* buss *m*; jernbanevogn
c; trener *m*

coal [koul] *n* kull *nt*

coarse [kɔːs] *adj* grov

coast [koust] *n* kyst *m*

coat [kout] *n* frakk *m*, kåpe *c*; kappe *c*; **~ hanger** kleshenger *m*

cocaine [kou'kein] *n* kokain *m/nt*

cock [kɔk] *n* hane *m*

cocktail ['kɔkteil] *n* cocktail *m*

coconut ['koukənʌt] *n* kokosnøtt *c*

cod [kɔd] *n* (pl ~) torsk *m*

code [koud] *n* kode *m*

coffee ['kɔfi] *n* kaffe *m*

cognac ['kɔnjæk] *n* konjakk *m*

coherence [kou'hiərəns] *n* sammenheng *m*

coin [kɔin] *n* mynt *m*

coincide [,kouin'said] *v* *falle sammen med

coincidence [,kouin'sidens] *m* tilfelle *nt*, tilfeldighet *c*

cold [kould] *adj* kald; *n* kulde *c*; forkjølelse *m*; *catch a ~ *bli forkjølet

collaborate [kə'læbərait] *v* samarbeide

collapse [kə'læps] *v* *bryte sammen

collar ['kɔlə] *n* halsbånd *nt*; krage *m*

collarbone ['kɔləboun] *n* kragebein *nt*

colleague ['kɔliːg] *n* kollega *m*

collect [kə'lekt] *v* samle; hente, avhente; samle inn

collection [kə'lekʃən] *n* samling *c*; kolleksjon *m*

collective [kə'lektiv] *adj* kollektiv

collector [kə'lektə] *n* samler *m*; innsamler *m*

college ['kɔlidʒ] *n* høyere læreinstitusjon; høyskole *m*

collide [kə'laid] *v* kollidere

collision [kə'liʒən] *n* sammenstøt *nt*, kollisjon *m*

Colombia [kə'lɔmbiə] Colombia

Colombian [kə'lɔmbiən] *adj* colombiansk; *n* colombianer *m*

colonel ['kəːnəl] *n* oberst *m*

colony ['kɔləni] *n* koloni *m*

colo(u)r ['kʌlə] *n* farge *m*; *v* farge

colo(u)rcolo(u)r-blind ['kʌləblaind] *adj* fargeblind

colo(u)red ['kʌləd] *adj* farget

colo(u)rful ['kʌləfəl] *adj* fargerik

column ['kɔləm] *n* søyle *c*, spalte *c*; kolonne *m*

coma ['koumə] *n* koma *m*

comb [koum] *v* gre; *n* kam *m*

combat ['kɔmbæt] *n* kamp *m*; *v* bekjempe, kjempe

combination [,kɔmbi'neiʃən] *n* kombinasjon *m*

combine [kəm'bain] *v* kombinere; sammenstille

***come** [kʌm] *v* *komme; **~ across** støte på; *komme over

comedian [kə'miːdiən] *n* skuespiller *m*; komiker *m*

comedy ['kɔmədi] *n* komedie *m*, lystspill *nt*

comfort ['kʌmfət] *n* komfort *m*, bekvemmelighet *c*, velvære *nt*; trøst *m*; *v* trøste

comfortable ['kʌmfətəbəl] *adj* bekvem, komfortabel

comic ['kɔmik] *adj* komisk

comics ['kɔmiks] *pl* tegneserie *m*

coming ['kʌmiŋ] *n* komme *nt*; *adj* kommende

comma ['kɔmə] *n* komma *nt*

command [kə'mɑːnd] *v* befale; *n* befaling *c*

commander [kə'mɑːndə] *n* befalshavende *m*

commemoration [kə,memə'reiʃən] *n* minnefest *m*; **in ~ of** til minne om

commence [kə'mens] *v* begynne

comment ['kɔment] *n* kommentar *m*; *v* kommentere

commerce ['kɔməːs] *n* handel *m*

commercial [kə'məːʃəl] *adj* handels-, kommersiell; *n* reklame *m*; **~ law**

handelsrett *m*

commission [kə'miʃən] *n* kommisjon *m*

commit [kə'mit] *v* *overlate, betro; *begå

committee [kə'miti] *n* komité *m*

common ['komən] *adj* felles; vanlig, alminnelig; simpel

commune ['komju:n] *n* kommune *m*

communicate [kə'mju:nikeit] *v* meddele

communication [kə,mju:ni'keiʃən] *n* kommunikasjon *m*; meddelelse *m*

communism ['komjunizəm] *n* kommunisme *m*

communist ['komjunist] *n* kommunist *m*

community [kə'mju:nəti] *n* samfunn *nt*

commuter [kə'mju:tə] *n* pendler *m*

compact ['kompækt] *adj* kompakt

companion [kəm'pænjən] *n* ledsager *m* ; guide *m*

company ['kʌmpəni] *n* selskap *nt*, firma *nt*

comparative [kəm'pærətiv] *adj* relativ

compare [kəm'pɛə] *v* sammenligne

comparison [kəm'pærisən] *n* sammenligning *c*

compartment [kəm'pɑ:tmənt] *n* kupé *m*

compass ['kʌmpəs] *n* kompass *m/nt*; passer *m*

compel [kəm'pel] *v* tvinge; nøde

compensate ['kompənseit] *v* kompensere, erstatte

compensation [,kompən'seiʃən] *n* kompensasjon *m*; skadeserstatning *m*

compete [kəm'pi:t] *v* konkurrere

competition [,kompə'tiʃən] *n* konkurranse *m*

competitor [kəm'petitər] *n* konkurrent *m*

compile [kəm'pail] *v* samle

complain [kəm'plein] *v* klage

complaint [kəm'pleint] *n* klage *c*

complete [kəm'pli:t] *adj* fullstendig, komplett; *v* fullende

completely [kəm'pli:tli] *adv* helt, totalt

complex ['kompleks] *n* kompleks *nt*; *adj* innviklet

complexion [kəm'plekʃən] *n* hudfarge *m*

complicated ['komplikeitid] *adj* komplisert, innviklet

compliment ['komplimənt] *n* kompliment *m*; *v* komplimentere

compose [kəm'pouz] *v* *sette sammen; komponere

composer [kəm'pouzə] *n* komponist *m*

composition [,kompə'ziʃən] *n* komposisjon *m*; sammensetning *m*

comprehensive [,kompri'hensiv] *adj* omfattende

comprise [kəm'praiz] *v* innbefatte, omfatte

compromise ['komprəmaiz] *n* kompromiss *nt*

compulsory [kəm'pʌlsəri] *adj* obligatorisk

computer [kom'pju:tə] *n* datamaskin *m*, PC *m*

comrade ['komreid] *n* kamerat *m*

conceal [kən'si:l] *v* skjule

conceited [kən'si:tid] *adj* selvgod; innbilsk *colloquial*

conceive [kən'si:v] *v* oppfatte, tenke ut; forestille seg

concentrate ['konsəntreit] *v* konsentrere

concentration [,konsən'treiʃən] *n* konsentrasjon *m*

conception [kən'sepʃən] *n* forestilling *c*; befruktning *m*

concern [kən'sə:n] *v* *gjelde, *angå; *n*

bekymring *c*; anliggende *nt*; bedrift *m*, foretak *nt*, konsern *nt*

concerned [kən'sə:nd] *adj* bekymret; innblandet

concerning [kən'sə:niŋ] *prep* angående, vedrørende

concert ['kɔnsət] *n* konsert *m*; ~ **hall** konsertsal *m*

concession [kən'seʃən] *n* konsesjon *m*

concierge [,kōsi'ɛɔʒ] *n* portner *m*

concise [kən'sais] *adj* konsis

conclusion [kən'klu:ʒən] *n* konklusjon *m*, slutning *m*

concrete ['kɔŋkri:t] *adj* konkret; *n* betong *m*

concurrence [kən'kʌrəns] *n* overensstemmelse *m*

concussion [kən'kʌʃən] *n* hjernerystelse *m*

condition [kən'diʃən] *n* vilkår *nt*; kondisjon *m*, tilstand *m*; omstendighet *c*

conditional [kən'diʃənəl] *adj* betinget

conditioner [kən'diʃənə] *n* hårbalsam *m*

condom ['kɔndəm] *n* kondom *nt*

conduct¹ ['kɔndʌkt] *n* oppførsel *m*

conduct² [kən'dʌkt] *v* ledsage; dirigere

conductor [kən'dʌktə] *n* leder *m*; dirigent *m*

conference ['kɔnfərəns] *n* konferanse *m*

confess [kən'fes] *v* *tilstå; skrifte; bekjenne

confession [kən'feʃən] *n* tilståelse *m*; skriftemål *nt*

confidence ['kɔnfidəns] *n* tillit *m*

confident ['kɔnfidənt] *adj* tillitsfull

confidential [,kɔnfi'denʃəl] *adj* konfidensiell

confirm [kən'fə:m] *v* bekrefte

confirmation [,kɔnfə'meiʃən] *n*

bekreftelse *m*

confiscate ['kɔnfiskeit] *v* *beslaglegge, konfiskere

conflict ['kɔnflikt] *n* konflikt *m*

confuse [kən'fju:z] *v* forvirre

confusion [kən'fju:ʒən] *n* forvirring *c*

congratulate [kəŋ'grætʃuleit] *v* gratulere

congratulation [kəŋ,grætʃu'leiʃən] *n* gratulasjon *m*, lykkønskning *m*

congregation [,kɔŋgri'geiʃən] *n* menighet *c*; forsamling *c*

congress ['kɔŋgres] *n* kongress *m*

connect [kə'nekt] *v* *forbinde; kople; kople til

connection [kə'nekʃən] *n* forbindelse *m*; sammenheng *m*

connoisseur [,kɔnə'sə:] *n* kjenner *m*

conquer ['kɔŋkə] *v* erobre; beseire

conqueror ['kɔŋkərə] *n* erobrer *m*

conquest ['kɔŋkwest] *n* erobring *c*

conscience ['kɔnʃəns] *n* samvittighet *c*

conscious ['kɔnʃəs] *adj* bevisst

consciousness ['kɔnʃəsnəs] *n* bevissthet *c*

conscript ['kɔnskript] *n* vernepliktig *m*

consent [kən'sent] *v* samtykke; bifalle; *n* samtykke *nt*

consequence ['kɔnsikwəns] *n* følge *m*, konsekvens *m*

consequently ['kɔnsikwəntli] *adv* altså

conservative [kən'sə:vətiv] *adj* konservativ

consider [kən'sidə] *v* betrakte; overveie; *anse, mene

considerable [kən'sidərəbəl] *adj* betraktelig; betydelig, anselig

considerate [kən'sidərət] *adj* hensynsfull

consideration [kən,sidə'reiʃən] *n*

overveielse *m*; omtanke *m*; hensyn *nt*

considering [kən'sidəriŋ] *prep* i betraktning av

consignment [kən'sainmənt] *n* sending *c*

consist of [kən'sist] *bestå av

conspire [kən'spaiə] *v* sammensverge seg

constant ['kɔnstənt] *adj* konstant

constipation [ˌkɔnsti'peiʃən] *n* forstoppelse *m*

constituency [kən'stitʃuənsi] *n* valgkrets *m*

constitution [ˌkɔnsti'tjuːʃən] *n* grunnlov *m*

construct [kən'strʌkt] *v* konstruere; bygge, oppføre

construction [kən'strʌkʃən] *n* konstruksjon *m*; oppførelse *m*, bygning *m*

consul ['kɔnsəl] *n* konsul *m*

consulate ['kɔnsjulət] *n* konsulat *nt*

consult [kən'sʌlt] *v* *rådspørre

consultation [ˌkɔnsəl'teiʃən] *n* konsultasjon *m*

consume [kən'sjuːm] *v* konsumere, forbruke; *ødelegge

consumer [kən'sjuːmə] *n* forbruker *m*

consumption [kən'sʌmpʃən] *n* forbruk *nt*, konsum *nt*

contact ['kɔntækt] *n* kontakt *m*; *v* kontakte; ~ **lenses** kontaktlinser *pl*

contagious [kən'teidʒəs] *adj* smittsom, smittende

contain [kən'tein] *v* *inneholde; romme

container [kən'teinə] *n* beholder *m*; container *m*

contemporary [kən'tempərəri] *adj* samtidig

contempt [kən'tempt] *n* ringeakt *m*, forakt *m*

content [kən'tent] *adj* tilfreds

contentment [kən'tentmənt] *n* tilfredshet *c*

contents ['kɔntents] *pl* innhold *nt*

contest ['kɔntest] *n* strid *m*; konkurranse *m*

continent ['kɔntinənt] *n* kontinent *nt*, verdensdel *m*

continental [ˌkɔnti'nentəl] *adj* kontinental

continual [kən'tinjuəl] *adj* stadig; **continually** *adv* uopphørlig

continue [kən'tinjuː] *v* *fortsette

continuous [kən'tinjuəs] *adj* uavbrutt, kontinuerlig

contour ['kɔntuə] *n* omriss *nt*

contraceptive [ˌkɔntrə'septiv] *n* prevensjonsmiddel *nt*

contract[1] ['kɔntrækt] *n* kontrakt *m*

contract[2] [kən'trækt] *v* *pådra seg

contractor [kən'træktə] *n* entreprenør *m*

contradict [ˌkɔntrə'dikt] *v* *motsi

contradictory [ˌkɔntrə'diktəri] *adj* motstridende

contrary ['kɔntrəri] *n* det motsatte; *adj* motsatt; **on the** ~ tvert imot

contrast ['kɔntrɑːst] *n* kontrast *m*, motsetning *m*

contribution [ˌkɔntri'bjuːʃən] *n* bidrag *nt*

control [kən'troul] *n* kontroll *m*; *v* kontrollere

controversial [ˌkɔntrə'vəːʃəl] *adj* kontroversiell, omstridt

convenience [kən'viːnjəns] *n* bekvemmelighet *c*

convenient [kən'viːnjənt] *adj* bekvem; passende, egnet, beleilig

convent ['kɔnvənt] *n* nonnekloster *nt*

conversation [ˌkɔnvə'seiʃən] *n* samtale *m*

convert [kən'vəːt] *v* omvende; omregne

convict[1] [kən'vikt] *v* *finne skyldig

convict² ['kɔnvikt] n domfelt m

conviction [kən'vikʃən] n
overbevisning m; domfellelse m

convince [kən'vins] v overbevise

convulsion [kən'vʌlʃən] n
krampetrekning m

cook [kuk] n kokk m; v lage mat,
tilberede

cookbook ['kukbuk] nAm kokebok c

cooker ['kukə] n komfyr m; gas ~
gasskomfyr m

cookery book ['kukəribuk] n
kokebok c

cookie ['kuki] nAm småkake c

cool [ku:l] adj kjølig

cooperation [kou,ɔpə'reiʃən] n
samarbeid nt; medvirkning m

co-operative [kou'ɔpərətiv] adj
kooperativ; samarbeidsvillig

coordinate [kou'ɔ:dineit] v samordne

coordination [kou,ɔ:di'neiʃən] n
koordinasjon m

cope [koup] v greie, mestre

copper ['kɔpə] n kopper nt

copy ['kɔpi] n kopi m; eksemplar nt; v
kopiere; etterligne

coral ['kɔrəl] n korall m

cord [kɔ:d] n tau nt; snor c

cordial ['kɔ:diəl] adj hjertelig

corduroy ['kɔ:dərɔi] n kordfløyel m

core [kɔ:] n kjerne m; kjernehus nt

cork [kɔ:k] n kork m

corkscrew ['kɔ:kskru:] n
korketrekker m

corn [kɔ:n] n korn nt; liktorn m; ~ on
the cob maiskolbe m

corner ['kɔ:nə] n hjørne nt

cornfield ['kɔ:nfi:ld] n kornåker m

corpse [kɔ:ps] n lik nt

corpulent ['kɔ:pjulənt] adj
korpulent; tykk, fyldig

correct [kə'rekt] adj korrekt, riktig; v
rette, korrigere

correction [kə'rekʃən] n rettelse m

correctness [kə'rektnəs] n
nøyaktighet c

correspond [,kɔri'spɔnd] v
brevveksle; svare til, tilsvare

correspondence [,kɔri'spɔndəns] n
korrespondanse m, brevveksling c

correspondent [,kɔri'spɔndənt] n
korrespondent m

corridor ['kɔridɔ:] n korridor m

corrupt [kə'rʌpt] adj korrupt; v
*bestikke

corruption [kə'rʌpʃən] n bestikkelse
m

corset ['kɔ:sit] n korsett nt

cosmetics [kɔz'metiks] pl kosmetika
pl

cost [kɔst] n kostnad m; pris m

*cost [kɔst] v koste

cosy ['kouzi] adj koselig

cot [kɔt] nAm feltseng c

cottage ['kɔtidʒ] n hytte c

cotton ['kɔtən] n bomull m; bomulls-;
~ wool ['kɔtənwul] n vatt m

couch [kautʃ] n sofa m

cough [kɔf] n hoste m; v hoste

could [kud] v (p can)

council ['kaunsəl] n råd nt;
rådsforsamling c

councillor ['kaunsələ] n rådsmedlem
nt

counsel ['kaunsəl] n råd nt

counsellor ['kaunsələ] n rådgiver m

count [kaunt] v *telle; *telle opp;
medregne; *anse; n greve m

counter ['kauntə] n disk m

counterfeit ['kauntəfi:t] v forfalske

countess ['kauntis] n grevinne c

country ['kʌntri] n land nt;
landområde nt; ~ house landsted nt

countryman ['kʌntrimən] n (pl -men)
landsmann m

county ['kaunti] n grevskap nt

couple ['kʌpəl] n par nt

coupon ['ku:pɔn] n kupong m

courage ['kʌridʒ] n tapperhet c, mot nt

courageous [kə'reidʒəs] adj tapper, modig

course [kɔ:s] n kurs m; rett m; løp nt; kurs nt; **intensive ~** intensivkurs nt; **of ~** naturligvis, selvfølgelig

court [kɔ:t] n domstol m; hoff nt; gårdsplass m

courteous ['kə:tiəs] adj høflig

cousin ['kʌzən] n kusine c, fetter m

cover ['kʌvə] v dekke; n ly nt, skjul nt; lokk nt; perm m; **~ charge** kuvertavgift c

cow [kau] n ku c

coward ['kauəd] n feiging m

cowardly ['kauədli] adj feig

crab [kræb] n krabbe c

crack [kræk] n smell nt; sprekk m; v *smelle; *slå i stykker, *knekke, *sprekke

cracker ['krækə] nAm kjeks m

cradle ['kreidəl] n vugge c

cramp [kræmp] n krampe m

crane [krein] n kran c

crap [kræp] n vulgar dritt m

crash [kræʃ] n kollisjon m; v kollidere; styrte; **~ barrier** barriere m

crate [kreit] n kasse c

crater ['kreitə] n krater nt

crawl [krɔ:l] v krabbe; n crawl m

craze [kreiz] n mani m

crazy ['kreizi] adj gal; sinnssyk

creak [kri:k] v knirke

cream [kri:m] n krem m; fløte m; adj kremgul

creamy ['kri:mi] adj fløteaktig

crease [kri:s] v skrukke, krølle; n fold m; rynke c; press m

create [kri'eit] v skape; kreere

creative [kri'eitiv] adj kreativ, skapende

creature ['kri:tʃə] n skapning m

credible ['kredibəl] adj troverdig

credit ['kredit] n kreditt m; v *godskrive; **~ card** kredittkort nt

creditor ['kreditə] n kreditor m

credulous ['kredjuləs] adj godtroende

creek [kri:k] n vik c

***creep** [kri:p] v *krype

creepy ['kri:pi] adj nifs, uhyggelig

cremate [kri'meit] v kremere

cremation [kri'meiʃən] n kremasjon m

crew [kru:] n mannskap nt

cricket ['krikit] n cricket m; siriss m

crime [kraim] n forbrytelse m

criminal ['kriminəl] n forbryter m; adj forbrytersk, kriminell; **~ law** strafferett m

criminality [,krimi'næləti] n kriminalitet m

crimson ['krimzən] adj høyrød

crisis ['kraisis] n (pl crises) krise c

crisp [krisp] adj sprø

critic ['kritik] n kritiker m

critical ['kritikəl] adj kritisk; risikabel

criticism ['kritisizəm] n kritikk m

criticize ['kritisaiz] v kritisere

crochet ['krouʃei] v hekle

crockery ['krɔkəri] n steintøy nt

crocodile ['krɔkədail] n krokodille c

crooked ['krukid] adj kroket, fordreid; uærlig

crop [krɔp] n avling c

cross [krɔs] v *gå over; adj tverr, sint; n kors nt

cross-eyed ['krɔsaid] adj skjeløyd

crossing ['krɔsiŋ] n overfart m; kryss nt; fotgjengerovergang m; jernbaneovergang m

crossroads ['krɔsroudz] n gatekryss nt

crosswalk ['krɔswɔ:k] nAm fotgjengerovergang m

crow [krou] n kråke c

crowbar ['kroubɑ:] n brekkjern nt

crowd [kraud] *n* mengde *m*, folkemengde *m*

crowded ['kraudid] *adj* overfylt; tettpakket

crown [kraun] *n* krone *c*; *v* krone

crucifix ['kru:sifiks] *n* krusifiks *nt*

crucifixion [ˌkru:si'fikʃən] *n* korsfestelse *m*

crucify ['kru:sifai] *v* korsfeste

cruel [kruəl] *adj* grusom

cruise [kru:z] *n* sjøreise *c*, cruise *nt*

crumb [krʌm] *n* smule *m*

crusade [kru:'seid] *n* korstog *nt*

crust [krʌst] *n* skorpe *c*

crutch [krʌtʃ] *n* krykke *c*

cry [krai] *v* *gråte; *skrike; rope; *n* skrik *nt*; rop *nt*

crystal ['kristəl] *n* krystall *m/nt*; *adj* krystall-

Cuba ['kju:bə] Cuba

Cuban ['kju:bən] *adj* kubansk; *n* kubaner *m*

cube [kju:b] *n* kube *m*; terning *m*

cuckoo ['kuku:] *n* gjøk *m*

cucumber ['kju:kəmbə] *n* agurk *m*

cuddle ['kʌdəl] *v* kjæle med; klemme

cuff [kʌf] *n* mansjett *m*; ~ **links** *pl* mansjettknapper *pl*

cul-de-sac ['kʌldəsæk] *n* blindgate *c*

cultivate ['kʌltiveit] *v* dyrke

culture ['kʌltʃə] *n* kultur *m*

cultured ['kʌltʃəd] *adj* kultivert

cunning ['kʌniŋ] *adj* slu

cup [kʌp] *n* kopp *m*; pokal *m*

cupboard ['kʌbəd] *n* skap *nt*

curb [kə:b] *n* fortauskant *m*; *v* tøyle

cure [kjuə] *v* helbrede, lege; *n* kur *m*; helbredelse *m*

curiosity [ˌkjuəri'ɔsəti] *n* nysgjerrighet *c*

curious ['kjuəriəs] *adj* vitebegjærlig, nysgjerrig; merkverdig

curl [kə:l] *v* krølle; *n* krøll *m*

curly ['kə:li] *adj* krøllet

currant ['kʌrənt] *n* rips *m*; solbær *nt*

currency ['kʌrənsi] *n* valuta *m*; **foreign** ~ utenlandsk valuta

current ['kʌrənt] *n* strøm *m*; *adj* nåværende, aktuell; **alternating** ~ vekselstrøm *m*; **direct** ~ likestrøm *m*

curry ['kʌri] *n* karri *m*

curse [kə:s] *v* banne; forbanne; *n* banning *c*; forbannelse *m*

curtain ['kə:tən] *n* gardin *m/nt*; teppe *nt*

curve [kə:v] *n* kurve *m*; krumning *m*

curved [kə:vd] *adj* krum, buet

cushion ['kuʃən] *n* pute *c*

custody ['kʌstədi] *n* varetekt *c*; forvaring *c*; formynderskap *nt*

custom ['kʌstəm] *n* vane *m*; skikk *m*

customary ['kʌstəməri] *adj* alminnelig, sedvanlig, vanlig

customer ['kʌstəmə] *n* kunde *m*

customs ['kʌstəmz] *pl* toll *m*; ~ **duty** tollavgift *c*; ~ **officer** toller *m*

cut [kʌt] *n* kutt *nt*

***cut** [kʌt] *v* *skjære; klippe; *skjære ned; ~ **off** *skjære av; klippe av; stenge av

cutlery ['kʌtləri] *n* bestikk *nt*

cutlet ['kʌtlət] *n* snitsel *m*

cycle ['saikəl] *n* sykkel *m*; kretsløp *nt*, syklus *m*

cycling ['saikliŋ] *n* sykling *c*

cyclist ['saiklist] *n* syklist *m*

cylinder ['silində] *n* sylinder *m*; ~ **head** topplokk *nt*

cystitis [si'staitis] *n* blærekatarr *m*

D

dad [dæd], **daddy** ['dædi] n pappa m

daffodil ['dæfədil] n påskelilje c

daily ['deili] adj daglig; n dagsavis c

dairy ['dɛəri] n meieri nt; melkebutikk m

dam [dæm] n demning c

damage ['dæmidʒ] n skade m; v skade

damn [dæm] v forbanne; ~! faen colloquial

damp [dæmp] adj fuktig; n fuktighet c; v fukte

dance [dɑːns] v danse; n dans m

dandelion ['dændilaiən] n løvetann c

dandruff ['dændrəf] n flass nt

Dane [dein] n danske m

danger ['deindʒə] n fare m

dangerous ['deindʒərəs] adj farlig

Danish ['deiniʃ] adj dansk; ~ **pastry** wienerbrød nt

dare [dɛə] v *tore, våge; utfordre

daring ['dɛəriŋ] adj dristig

dark [dɑːk] adj mørk; n mørke nt

darling ['dɑːliŋ] n kjæreste m, skatt m

darn [dɑːn] v stoppe

dash [dæʃ] v styrte; n tankestrek c

dashboard ['dæʃbɔːd] n instrumentbord nt

data ['deitə] pl data pl

date[1] [deit] n dato m; avtale m; stevnemøte nt; v datere; **out of ~** umoderne

date[2] [deit] n daddel m

daughter ['dɔːtə] n datter c

daughter-in-law ['dɔːtərinlɔ] n (pl daughters-) svigerdatter c

dawn [dɔːn] n daggry nt

day [dei] n dag m; **by ~** om dagen; ~ **trip** dagstur m; **per ~** per dag; **the ~ before yesterday** i forgårs

daybreak ['deibreik] n daggry nt

daylight ['deilait] n dagslys nt; ~ **saving time** sommertid c

dead [ded] adj død

deaf [def] adj døv

deal [diːl] n transaksjon m, handel c

***deal** [diːl] v dele ut; ~ **with** *ta seg av; handle med

dealer ['diːlə] n forhandler m; dealer m

dear [diə] adj kjær; dyr; dyrebar

death [deθ] n død m; ~ **penalty** dødsstraff c

debate [di'beit] n debatt m

debit ['debit] n debet m

debt [det] n gjeld c

decaffeinated [di'kæfineitid] adj kaffeinfri

deceit [di'siːt] n bedrag m

deceive [di'siːv] v *bedra

December [di'sembə] desember

decency ['diːsənsi] n anstendighet c

decent ['diːsənt] adj anstendig

decide [di'said] v *avgjøre

decision [di'siʒən] n beslutning m, avgjørelse m

deck [dek] n dekk nt; ~ **chair** fluktstol m

declaration [,deklə'reiʃən] n erklæring c; deklarasjon m

declare [di'klɛə] v erklære; *oppgi; deklarere

decorate [,dekə'reit] v pynte; innrede

decoration [,dekə'reiʃən] n dekorasjon m

decrease [diː'kriːs] v minke, minske; *avta; n nedgang m

dedicate ['dedikeit] v vie

deduce [di'djuːs] v utlede; avlede; konkludere

deduct [di'dʌkt] v *trekke fra

deed [diːd] n handling c, gjerning c

deep [diːp] adj dyp

deep-freeze [,diːp'friːz] n dypfryser m

deer [diə] n (pl ~) hjort m

defeat [di'fi:t] v *overvinne; n nederlag nt

defective [di'fektiv] adj mangelfull

defense, **defence** [di'fens] n forsvar nt; vern nt

defend [di'fend] v forsvare

deficiency [di'fiʃənsi] n mangel m

deficit ['defisit] n underskudd nt

define [di'fain] v bestemme, definere

definite ['definit] adj bestemt

definition [,defi'niʃən] n definisjon m

deformed [di'fɔ:md] adj misdannet, vanskapt

degree [di'gri:] n grad m

delay [di'lei] v forsinke; *utsette; n forsinkelse m; utsettelse m

delegate ['deligət] n utsending m

delegation [,deli'geiʃən] n delegasjon m

deliberate[1] [di'libəreit] v overveie, *rådslå

deliberate[2] [di'libərət] adj overlagt

deliberation [di,libə'reiʃən] n overveielse m, rådslagning m

delicacy ['delikəsi] n lekkerbisken m; finfølelse m

delicate ['delikət] adj delikat

delicatessen [,delikə'tesən] n delikatesse m; matvareforretning c

delicious [di'liʃəs] adj deilig, lekker

delight [di'lait] n glede c, fryd m; v glede; **I'm ~ed** gleder meg

delightful [di'laitfəl] adj henrivende, herlig

deliver [di'livə] v levere, avlevere

delivery [di'livəri] n levering c, leveranse m; nedkomst m; ~ **van** varebil m

demand [di'mɑ:nd] v behøve, forlange; n krav nt; etterspørsel m

democracy [di'mɔkrəsi] n demokrati nt

democratic [,demə'krætik] adj demokratisk

demolish [di'mɔliʃ] v *rive ned; *ødelegge

demolition [,demə'liʃən] n nedrivning m

demonstrate ['demənstreit] v bevise; demonstrere

demonstration [,demən'streiʃən] n demonstrasjon m

den [den] n hi nt; hule c

Denmark ['denmɑ:k] Danmark

denomination [di,nɔmi'neiʃən] n benevnelse m; trosretning m; verdienhet m

dense [dens] adj tett

dent [dent] n bulk m

dentist ['dentist] n tannlege m

denture ['dentʃə] n gebiss nt

deny [di'nai] v benekte; nekte

deodorant [di:'oudərənt] n deodorant m

depart [di'pɑ:t] v reise bort, *gå sin vei; *avgå ved døden

department [di'pɑ:tmənt] n avdeling c, departement nt; ~ **store** stormagasin nt, varehus nt

departure [di'pɑ:tʃə] n avreise c; avgang m

dependant [di'pendənt] adj avhengig

depend on [di'pend] bero på; **that depends** det kommer an på

deposit [di'pɔzit] n depositum nt; pant m; bunnfall nt, avleiring c; v deponere

depository [di'pɔzitəri] n lager nt

depot ['depou] n lagerplass m; stasjon m

depress [di'pres] v tynge ned

depressing [di'presiŋ] adj deprimerende

depression [di'preʃən] n depresjon m; lavtrykk nt; nedgang m

deprive of [di'praiv] *frata

depth [depθ] n dybde m

deputy ['depjuti] *n* deputert *m*; stedfortreder *m*

descend [di'send] *v* *gå ned

descendant [di'sendənt] *n* etterkommer *m*

descent [di'sent] *n* nedstigning *m*

describe [di'skraib] *v* *beskrive

description [di'skrip∫ən] *n* beskrivelse *m*; signalement *nt*

desert¹ ['dezət] *n* ørken *m*; *adj* øde

desert² [di'zə:t] *v* desertere; *forlate

deserve [di'zə:v] *v* fortjene

design [di'zain] *v* tegne opp; *n* design *m*; utkast *nt*; hensikt *m*

designate ['dezigneit] *v* peke ut

desirable [di'zaiərəbəl] *adj* attråverdig, ønskelig

desire [di'zaiə] *n* ønske *nt*; lyst *c*, begjær *nt*; *v* ønske, begjære

desk [desk] *n* skrivebord *nt*; kateter *nt*; pult *m*

despair [di'speə] *n* håpløshet *c*; *v* fortvile

despatch [di'spæt∫] *v* avsende

desperate ['despərət] *adj* fortvilet

despise [di'spaiz] *v* forakte

despite [di'spait] *prep* tross

dessert [di'zə:t] *n* dessert *m*

destination [,desti'nei∫ən] *n* bestemmelsessted *nt*

destine ['destin] *v* bestemme

destiny ['destini] *n* skjebne *m*, lodd *m*

destroy [di'strɔi] *v* *ødelegge, *tilintetgjøre

destruction [di'strʌk∫ən] *n* ødeleggelse *m*; undergang *m*

detach [di'tæt∫] *v* løsne

detail ['di:teil] *n* detalj *m*

detailed ['di:teild] *adj* detaljert, utførlig

detect [di'tekt] *v* oppdage

detective [di'tektiv] *n* detektiv *m*; ~ **story** krim *m*

detergent [di'tə:dʒənt] *n* vaskepulver *nt*

determine [di'tə:min] *v* *fastsette, bestemme

determined [di'tə:mind] *adj* bestemt

detest [di'test] *v* avsky, hate

detour ['di:tuə] *n* omvei *m*; omkjøring *c*

devaluation [,di:vælju'ei∫ən] *n* devaluering *c*

devalue [,di:'vælju:] *v* devaluere

develop [di'veləp] *v* utvikle; fremkalle

development [di'veləpmənt] *n* utvikling *c*

deviate ['di:vieit] *v* *avvike

devil ['devəl] *n* djevel *m*

devote [di'vout] *v* hengi

dew [dju:] *n* dugg *m*

diabetes [,daiə'bi:ti:z] *n* sukkersyke *m*, diabetes *m*

diabetic [,daiə'betik] *n* diabetiker *m*, sukkersykepasient *m*

diagnose [,daiəg'nouz] *v* stille en diagnose; konstatere

diagnosis [,daiəg'nousis] *n* (pl -ses) diagnose *m*

diagonal [dai'ægənəl] *n* diagonal *m*; *adj* diagonal

diagram ['daiəgræm] *n* diagram *nt*; grafisk fremstilling

dial ['daiəl] *n* urskive *c*; *v* slå, taste

dialect ['daiəlekt] *n* dialekt *m*

diamond ['daiəmənd] *n* diamant *m*

diaper ['daiəpə] *nAm* bleie *c*

diaphragm ['daiəfræm] *n* mellomgulv *nt*

diarrh(o)ea [daiə'riə] *n* diaré *m*

diary ['daiəri] *n* almanakk *m*; dagbok *c*

dictate [dik'teit] *v* diktere

dictation [dik'tei∫ən] *n* diktat *m*

dictator [dik'teitə] *n* diktator *m*

dictionary ['dik∫ənəri] *n* ordbok *c*

did [did] *v* (p do)

die [dai] *v* dø
diesel ['di:zəl] *n* diesel *m*
diet ['daiət] *n* diett *m*
differ ['difə] *v* *være forskjellig
difference ['difərəns] *n* forskjell *m*
different ['difərənt] *adj* forskjellig;
annerledes
difficult ['difikəlt] *adj* vanskelig; vrien
difficulty ['difikəlti] *n* vanskelighet *c*
*dig [dig] *v* grave
digest [di'dʒest] *v* fordøye
digestible [di'dʒestəbəl] *adj*
fordøyelig
digestion [di'dʒestʃən] *n* fordøyelse
m
digit ['didʒit] *n* siffer *nt*
digital ['didʒitəl] *adj* digital
dignified ['dignifaid] *adj* verdig
dignity ['digniti] *n* verdighet *c*
dilapidated [di'læpideitid] *adj*
forfallen
diligence ['dilidʒəns] *n* flid *m*
diligent ['dilidʒənt] *adj* flittig
dilute [dai'lju:t] *v* fortynne
dim [dim] *adj* dunkel, matt; uklar,
utydelig
din [din] *n* bråk *nt*
dine [dain] *v* spise middag
dinghy ['diŋgi] *n* jolle *c*
dining car ['dainiŋka:] *n* spisevogn *c*
dining room ['dainiŋru:m] *n*
spisestue *c*; spisesal *m*
dinner ['dinə] *n* middag *m*; lunsj *m*,
aftensmat *m*; **~ jacket** smoking *m*; **~
service** servise *nt*
diphtheria [dif'θiəriə] *n* difteri *m*
diploma [di'ploumə] *n* diplom *nt*
diplomat ['dipləmæt] *n* diplomat *m*
direct[1] ['direkt] *adj* direkte, likefrem
direct[2] [di'rekt] *v* rette; veilede; styre;
regissere
direction [di'rekʃən] *n* retning *m*;
direktiv *nt*; regi *m*; styre *nt*,
veiledning *m*; **directional signal** *Am*

retningsviser *m*; **directions for use**
bruksanvisning *m*
directive [di'rektiv] *n* direktiv *nt*
director [di'rektə] *n* direktør *m*;
regissør *m*
directory [di'rektəri] *n* adressebok *c*;
telefonkatalog *m*
dirt [də:t] *n* skitt *m*
dirty ['də:ti] *adj* skitten, svart
disabled [di'seibəld] *adj*
funksjonshemmet, ufør
disadvantage [,disəd'va:ntidʒ] *n*
ulempe *m*
disagree [,disə'gri:] *v* *være uenig
disagreeable [,disə'gri:əbəl] *adj*
ubehagelig
disappear [,disə'piə] *v* *forsvinne
disappoint [,disə'pɔint] *v* skuffe
disappointment [,disə'pɔintmənt] *n*
skuffelse *m*
disapprove [,disə'pru:v] *v* misbillige
disaster [di'za:stə] *n* katastrofe *m*;
ulykke *c*
disastrous [di'za:strəs] *adj*
katastrofal
disc [disk] *n* skive *c*; plate *c*; **slipped ~**
skiveprolaps *m*
discard [di'ska:d] *v* kassere
discharge [dis'tʃa:dʒ] *v* lesse av,
losse; **~ of** *frita for
discipline ['disiplin] *n* disiplin *m*
discolo(u)r [di'skʌlə] *v* farge av
disconnect [,diskə'nekt] *v* utkople;
*ta ut kontakten
discontented [,diskən'tentid] *adj*
misfornøyd
discontinue [,diskən'tinju:] *v* stanse,
opphøre
discount ['diskaunt] *n* rabatt *m*,
avslag *nt*
discourage ['diskʌrədʒ] *v* *ta motet
fra, avskrekke
discover [di'skʌvə] *v* oppdage
discovery [di'skʌvəri] *n* oppdagelse

m

discuss [di'skʌs] *v* diskutere; debattere

discussion [di'skʌʃən] *n* diskusjon *m*; samtale *m*, debatt *m*

disease [di'ziːz] *n* sykdom *m*

disembark [,disim'bɑːk] *v* *gå fra borde, *gå i land

disgrace [dis'greis] *n* skam *c*

disguise [dis'gaiz] *v* forkle seg; *n* forkledning *m*

disgust [dis'gʌst] *n* avsky *m*

disgusting [dis'gʌstiŋ] *adj* motbydelig, avskyelig

dish [diʃ] *n* tallerken *m*; fat *nt*; rett *m*; **dirty dishes** oppvask *m*

dishonest [di'sɔnist] *adj* uærlig

dishwasher [di'swɔʃə] *n* oppvaskmaskin *m*

disinfect [,disin'fekt] *v* desinfisere

disinfectant [,disin'fektənt] *n* desinfiserende middel

dislike [dis'laik] *v* mislike, avsky; *n* motvilje *m*, avsky *m*, antipati *m*

dislocated ['disləkeitid] *adj* gått av ledd

dismiss [dis'mis] *v* sende bort; *gi sparken, avskjedige

disorder [di'sɔːdə] *n* uorden *m*

dispatch [di'spætʃ] *v* avsende, sende av sted

display [di'splei] *v* utstille; vise; *n* utstilling *c*

disposable [di'spouzəbəl] *adj* engangs-

disposal [di'spouzəl] *n* disposisjon *m*

dispose of [di'spouz] kvitte seg med

dispute [di'spjuːt] *n* ordstrid *m*; krangel *m/nt*, tvist *m*; *v* *strides, *bestride

dissatisfied [di'sætisfaid] *adj* utilfreds

dissolve [di'zolv] *v* oppløse

dissuade from [di'sweid] fraråde

distance ['distəns] *n* avstand *m*; strekning *m*; ~ **in kilometres (kilometers** *Am)* kilometertall *nt*

distant ['distənt] *adj* fjern

distinct [di'stiŋkt] *adj* tydelig; forskjellig

distinction [di'stiŋkʃən] *n* forskjell *m*

distinguish [di'stiŋgwiʃ] *v* skjelne, *gjøre forskjell

distinguished [di'stiŋgwiʃt] *adj* fremstående

distress [di'stres] *n* nød *c*; bedrøvelse *m*; ~ **signal** nødsignal *nt*

distribute [di'stribjuːt] *v* utdele

distributor [di'stribjutə] *n* eneforhandler *m*; strømfordeler *m*

district ['distrikt] *n* distrikt *nt*; kvartal *nt*

disturb [di'stəːb] *v* forstyrre

disturbance [di'stəːbəns] *n* forstyrrelse *m*; forvirring *c*

ditch [ditʃ] *n* grøft *c*

dive [daiv] *v* dukke, stupe

diversion [dai'vəːʃən] *n* omkjøring *c*; atspredelse *m*

divide [di'vaid] *v* dele; fordele; skille

divine [di'vain] *adj* guddommelig

division [di'viʒən] *n* deling *c*; atskillelse *m*; avdeling *c*

divorce [di'vɔːs] *n* skilsmisse *m*; *v* skilles

dizziness ['dizinəs] *n* svimmelhet *c*

dizzy ['dizi] *adj* svimmel

***do** [duː] *v* *gjøre; *være tilstrekkelig

dock [dɔk] *n* dokk *m*; kai *c*; *v* *dokksette; *legge til kai

docker ['dɔkə] *n* havnearbeider *m*

doctor ['dɔktə] *n* lege *m*; doktor *m*

document ['dɔkjumənt] *n* dokument *nt*

dog [dɔg] *n* hund *m*

dogged ['dɔgid] *adj* sta

doll [dɔl] *n* dukke *c*

dollar [dɔl] *n* dollar *m*

dome [doum] n kuppel m
domestic [dəˈmestik] adj hus-; innenlands; ~ **animal** husdyr nt
domicile [ˈdɔmisail] n bopel m
dominate [ˌdɔmiˈneit] v dominere
dominion [dəˈminjən] n herredømme nt
donate [douˈneit] v skjenke
donation [douˈneiʃən] n donasjon m
done [dʌn] v (pp do)
donkey [ˈdɔŋki] n esel nt
donor [ˈdounə] n donator m; giver m
door [dɔː] n dør c; **revolving ~** svingdør c; **sliding ~** skyvedør c
doorbell [ˈdɔːbel] n ringeklokke c
doorkeeper [ˈdɔːˌkiːpə] n dørvokter m
doorman [ˈdɔːmən] n (pl -men) portier m
dormitory [ˈdɔːmitri] n sovesal m
dose [dous] n dose m
dot [dɔt] n punkt nt, punktum nt, prikk m
double [ˈdʌbəl] adj dobbel; ~ **bed** dobbeltseng c
doubt [daut] v tvile, betvile; n tvil m; **without ~** uten tvil
doubtful [ˈdautfəl] adj tvilsom; usikker
dough [dou] n deig m; colloquial penger pl
down[1] [daun] adv ned, nedover; over ende; adj nedslått; prep nedover, langs; ~ **payment** nedbetaling c
down[2] [daun] n dun nt
downpour [ˈdaunpɔː] n øsregn nt
downstairs [ˌdaunˈstɛəz] adv ned; nede
downstream [ˌdaunˈstriːm] adv med strømmen
down-to-earth [ˌdauntuˈəːθ] adj nøktern
downwards [ˈdaunwədz] adv nedover

dozen [ˈdʌzən] n (pl ~, ~s) dusin nt
draft [drɑːft] n utkast nt
drag [dræg] v slepe
dragon [ˈdrægən] n drake m
drain [drein] v drenere; n avløp nt
drama [ˈdrɑːmə] n drama nt; skuespill nt
dramatic [drəˈmætik] adj dramatisk
dramatist [ˈdræmətist] n dramatiker m
drank [dræŋk] v (p drink)
draught [drɑːft] n trekk m; ~ **beer** fatøl nt; **draughts** damspill nt
draw [drɔː] n trekning m
***draw** [drɔː] v tegne; *trekke; heve; ~ **up** avfatte, *sette opp
drawbridge [ˈdrɔːbridʒ] n vindebro c
drawer [ˈdrɔːə] n skuff m; **drawers** underbukse c
drawing [ˈdrɔːiŋ] n tegning c; ~ **pin** tegnestift m; ~ **room** salong m
dread [dred] v frykte; n frykt m
dreadful [ˈdredfəl] adj fryktelig, forferdelig
dream [driːm] n drøm m
***dream** [driːm] v drømme
dress [dres] v kle på; kle på seg, kle seg; *forbinde; n kjole m
dressing gown [ˈdresiŋgaun] n morgenkåpe c
dressmaker [ˈdresˌmeikə] n skredder m
drill [dril] v bore; trene; n bor nt; **drilling platform** boreplattform nt
drink [driŋk] n drink m; drikk m
***drink** [driŋk] v *drikke
drinking water [ˈdriŋkiŋˌwɔːtə] n drikkevann nt
drip-dry [ˌdripˈdrai] adj strykefri
drive [draiv] n vei m; kjøretur m
***drive** [draiv] v kjøre; føre
driver [ˈdraivə] n fører m; sjåfør m
driver's license nAm, **driving licence** n førerkort nt

drizzle ['drizəl] *n* duskregn *nt*

drop [drɔp] *v* *la falle; *n* dråpe *m*

drought [draut] *n* tørke *c*

drown [draun] *v* drukne; *be drowned* drukne

drug [drʌg] *n* narkotika *m*; medisin *m*; ~ **addict** narkoman *m*

drugstore ['drʌgstɔː] *nAm* apotek *nt*

drum [drʌm] *n* tromme *c*

drunk [drʌŋk] *adj* (pp drink) full, beruset

dry [drai] *adj* tørr; *v* tørke

dry-clean [ˌdrai'kliːn] *v* rense

dry cleaner's [ˌdrai'kliːnəz] *n* renseri *nt*

dryer ['draiə] *n* tørketrommel *m*, tørkeapparat *nt*

duchess [dʌtʃis] *n* hertuginne *c*

duck [dʌk] *n* and *c*

due [djuː] *adj* ventet; skyldig; forfalt til betaling

dues [djuːz] *pl* avgifter *pl*

dug [dʌg] *v* (p, pp dig)

duke [djuːk] *n* hertug *m*

dull [dʌl] *adj* kjedelig; matt; sløv

dumb [dʌm] *adj* stum; dum

dune [djuːn] *n* sanddyne *c*

dung [dʌŋ] *n* gjødsel *c*

dunghill ['dʌŋhil] *n* gjødseldynge *c*

duration [dju'reiʃən] *n* varighet *c*

during ['djuəriŋ] *prep* under, i løpet av

dusk [dʌsk] *n* tusmørke *nt*

dust [dʌst] *n* støv *nt*

dustbin ['dʌstbin] *n* søppelkasse *c*

dusty ['dʌsti] *adj* støvet

Dutch [dʌtʃ] *adj* hollandsk, nederlandsk

Dutchman ['dʌtʃmən] *n* (pl -men) nederlender *m*, hollender *m*

duty ['djuːti] *n* plikt *m*; oppgave *c*; innførselstoll *m*; **customs** ~ tollavgift *c*

duty-free [ˌdjuːti'friː] *adj* tollfri

DVD [diviː'diː] *n* DVD *m*

dwarf [dwɔːf] *n* dverg *m*

dye [dai] *v* farge; *n* farge *m*

dynamo ['dainəmou] *n* (pl ~s) dynamo *m*

E

each [iːtʃ] *adj* hver; ~ **other** hverandre

eager ['iːgə] *adj* ivrig, utålmodig

eagle ['iːgəl] *n* ørn *c*

ear [iə] *n* øre *nt*

earache ['iəreik] *n* øreverk *m*

eardrum ['iədrʌm] *n* trommehinne *c*

earl [əːl] *n* greve *m*

early ['əːli] *adj* tidlig

earn [əːn] *v* tjene; fortjene

earnest ['əːnist] *n* alvor *nt*

earnings ['əːniŋz] *pl* inntekt *c*

earring ['iəriŋ] *n* øredobb *m*

earth [əːθ] *n* jord *c*; bakke *m*

earthquake ['əːθkweik] *n* jordskjelv *m/nt*

ease [iːz] *n* letthet *c*, utvungenhet *c*

east [iːst] *n* øst *m*

Easter ['iːstə] *n* påske *c*

easterly ['iːstəli] *adj* østlig

eastern ['iːstən] *adj* østlig, østre

easy ['iːzi] *adj* lett; bekvem; ~ **chair** lenestol *m*

easy-going ['iːziˌgouiŋ] *adj* avslappet

*eat [iːt] *v* spise

eavesdrop ['iːvzdrɔp] *v* sniklytte

ebony ['ebəni] *n* ibenholt *m/nt*

eccentric [ik'sentrik] *adj* eksentrisk

echo ['ekou] *n* (pl ~es) gjenlyd *m*, ekko *nt*

eclipse [i'klips] *n* formørkelse *m*

economic [,i:kə'nɔmik] *adj* økonomisk

economical [,i:kə'nɔmikəl] *adj* økonomisk, sparsommelig

economist [i'kɔnəmist] *n* økonom *m*

economize [i'kɔnəmaiz] *v* spare

economy [i'kɔnəmi] *n* økonomi *m*; næring *c*, næringsliv *nt*

ecstasy ['ekstəzi] *n* ekstase *m*

Ecuador ['ekwədɔ:] Ecuador

Ecuadorian [,ekwə'dɔ:riən] *n* ecuadorianer *m*

eczema ['eksimə] *n* eksem *m/nt*

edge [edʒ] *n* kant *m*

edible ['edibəl] *adj* spiselig

edit ['edit] *v* utgi, redigere

edition [i'diʃən] *n* utgave *c*; opplag *nt*; **morning** ~ morgenutgave *c*

editor ['editə] *n* redaktør *m*

educate ['edʒukeit] *v* *oppdra, utdanne

education [,edʒu'keiʃən] *n* utdannelse *m*; oppdragelse *m*

eel [i:l] *n* ål *m*

effect [i'fekt] *n* effekt *m*, virkning *m*; *v* *frembringe; **in** ~ faktisk

effective [i'fektiv] *adj* effektiv, virkningsfull

efficient [i'fiʃənt] *adj* virkningsfull, effektiv

effort ['efət] *n* anstrengelse *m*; bestrebelse *m*; prestasjon *m*

egg [eg] *n* egg *nt*; ~ **yolk** eggeplomme *c*

eggcup ['egkʌp] *n* eggeglass *nt*

eggplant ['egplɑ:nt] *n* aubergine *c*

egoistic [,egou'istik] *adj* egoistisk

Egypt ['i:dʒipt] Egypt

Egyptian [i'dʒipʃən] *adj* egyptisk; *n* egypter *m*

eiderdown ['aidədaun] *n* ederdun *nt*; dyne *c*

eight [eit] *num* åtte

eighteen [,ei'ti:n] *num* atten

eighteenth [,ei'ti:nθ] *num* attende

eighth [eitθ] *num* åttende

eighty ['eiti] *num* åtti

either ['aiðə] *pron* den ene eller den andre; **either ... or** enten ... eller

elaborate [i'læbəreit] *v* utdype

elastic [i'læstik] *adj* elastisk; tøyelig; ~ **band** strikk *m*

elasticity [,elæ'stisəti] *n* tøyelighet *c*

elbow ['elbou] *n* albue *m*

elder ['eldə] *adj* eldre

elderly ['eldəli] *adj* eldre

elect [i'lekt] *v* *velge

election [i'lekʃən] *n* valg *nt*

electric [i'lektrik] *adj* elektrisk; ~ **cord** ledning *m*; ~ **razor** barbermaskin *m*

electrician [,ilek'triʃən] *n* elektriker *m*

electricity [,ilek'trisəti] *n* elektrisitet *m*

electronic [ilek'trɔnik] *adj* elektronisk

elegance ['eligəns] *n* eleganse *m*

elegant ['eligənt] *adj* elegant

element ['elimənt] *n* element *nt*, bestanddel *m*

elephant ['elifənt] *n* elefant *m*

elevator ['eliveitə] *nAm* heis *m*

eleven [i'levən] *num* elleve

eleventh [i'levənθ] *num* ellevte

elf [elf] *n* (pl elves) alv *m*

eliminate [i'limineit] *v* fjerne; avskaffe

elm [elm] *n* alm *m*

else [els] *adv* ellers

elsewhere [,el'sweə] *adv* annetsteds

elucidate [i'lu:sideit] *v* *klargjøre

e-mail ['i: meil] *n* e-post *m*; *v* sende (med) e-post

emancipation [i,mænsi'peiʃən] n
frigjøring c

embankment [im'bæŋkmənt] n
bredd m; demning m

embargo [em'ba:gou] n (pl ~es)
beslag nt; handelsforbud nt

embark [im'ba:k] v *gå om bord

embarkation [,emba:'keiʃən] n
innskipning c

embarrass [im'bærəs] v *gjøre brydd,
*gjøre forlegen; sjenere;
embarrassed brydd, flau, forlegen;
embarrassing pinlig;
embarrassment forlegenhet c

embassy ['embəsi] n ambassade m

emblem ['embləm] n emblem nt;
symbol nt

embrace [im'breis] v omfavne; n
omfavnelse m

embroider [im'brɔidə] v brodere

embroidery [im'brɔidəri] n broderi nt

emerald ['emərəld] n smaragd m

emergency [i'mə:dʒənsi] n
krisesituasjon m, nødstilfelle nt; ~
exit nødutgang m

emigrant ['emigrənt] n utvandrer m

emigrate ['emigreit] v utvandre

emigration [,emi'greiʃən] n
emigrasjon m

emotion [i'mouʃən] n sinnsbevegelse
m, følelse m

emperor ['empərə] n keiser m

emphasize ['emfəsaiz] v understreke

empire ['empaiə] n imperium nt,
keiserdømme nt

employ [im'plɔi] v *ansette; anvende

employee [,emplɔi'i:] n lønnstaker m,
ansatt m

employer [im'plɔiə] n arbeidsgiver m

employment [im'plɔimənt] n
beskjeftigelse m, arbeid nt; ~
exchange arbeidsformidling c

empress ['empris] n keiserinne c

empty ['empti] adj tom; v tømme

enable [i'neibəl] vm*sette i stand

enamel [i'næməl] n emalje m

enamelled [i'næməld] adj emaljert

enchanting [in'tʃa:ntiŋ] adj
bedårende, henrivende

encircle [in'sə:kəl] v omringe, *omgi;
innsirkle

enclose [iŋ'klouz] v *vedlegge

enclosure [iŋ'klouʒə] n vedlegg nt

encounter [iŋ'kauntə] v møte; n møte
nt

encourage [iŋ'kʌridʒ] v oppmuntre

encyclop(a)edia [en,saiklə'pi:diə] n
leksikon nt

end [end] n ende m, slutt m; v slutte;
opphøre

ending ['endiŋ] n avslutning c

endless ['endləs] adj uendelig

endorse [in'dɔ:s] v endossere

endure [in'djuə] v *utholde

enemy ['enəmi] n fiende m

energetic [,enə'dʒetik] adj energisk

energy ['enədʒi] n energi m; kraft c

engage [iŋ'geidʒ] v *ansette; bestille;
forplikte seg; engaged forlovet;
opptatt

engagement [iŋ'geidʒmənt] n
forlovelse m; forpliktelse m; avtale m;
~ ring forlovelsesring m

engine ['endʒin] n maskin m, motor
m; lokomotiv nt

engineer [,endʒi'niə] n ingeniør m

England ['iŋglənd] England

English ['iŋgliʃ] adj engelsk

Englishman ['iŋgliʃmən] n (pl -men)
engelskmann m

engrave [iŋ'greiv] v gravere

engraving [iŋ'greiviŋ] n trykk nt;
kopperstikk nt

enigma [i'nigmə] n gåte c

enjoy [in'dʒɔi] v *nyte, *ha glede av

enjoyable [in'dʒɔiəbəl] adj behagelig,
hyggelig, morsom; deilig

enjoyment [in'dʒɔimənt] n nytelse m

enlarge [in'lɑ:dʒ] v forstørre; utvide

enlargement [in'lɑ:dʒmənt] n forstørrelse m

enormous [i'nɔ:məs] adj enorm, kolossal

enough [i'nʌf] adv nok; adj tilstrekkelig

enquire [iŋ'kwaiə] v *forespørre; undersøke

enquiry [iŋ'kwaiəri] n forespørsel m; undersøkelse m; rundspørring c

enter ['entə] v *gå inn, *tre inn i; *innskrive

enterprise ['entəpraiz] n virksomhet c; driftighet c

entertain [,entə'tein] v *underholde, more; beverte

entertainer [,entə'teinə] n underholder m

entertaining [,entə'teiniŋ] adj morsom, underholdende

entertainment [,entə'teinmənt] n underholdning m, forlystelse m

enthusiasm [in'θju:ziæzəm] n entusiasme m

enthusiastic [in,θju:zi'æstik] adj entusiastisk

entire [in'taiə] adj hel

entirely [in'taiəli] adv helt

entrails ['entreilz] n innvoller

entrance ['entrəns] n inngang m; adgang m; inntreden m; ~ fee inngangspenger pl

entry ['entri] n inngang m, adgang m; oppføring c; no ~ adgang forbudt

envelop [in'veləp] v pakke inn, omslutte

envelope ['envəloup] n konvolutt m

envious ['enviəs] adj sjalu, misunnelig

environment [in'vaiərənmənt] n miljø nt; omgivelser pl; **environmental protection** miljøvern nt

envoy ['envɔi] n sendemann m

envy ['envi] n misunnelse m; v misunne

epic ['epik] n epos nt; adj episk

epidemic [,epi'demik] n epidemi m

epilepsy ['epilepsi] n epilepsi m

epilogue ['epilɔg] n epilog m

episode ['episoud] n episode m

equal ['i:kwəl] adj lik; n likemann m; v måle seg med

equality [i'kwɔləti] n likhet c

equalize ['i:kwəlaiz] v utjevne

equally ['i:kwəli] adv like

equator [i'kweitə] n ekvator m

equip [i'kwip] v utruste, utstyre

equipment [i'kwipmənt] n utstyr nt

equivalent [i'kwivələnt] adj motsvarende, tilsvarende

eraser [i'reizə] n viskelær nt

erect [i'rekt] v reise; adj oppreist, stående

err [ə:] v feile

errand ['erənd] n ærend nt

error ['erə] n feiltakelse m, feil m

escalator ['eskəleitə] n rulletrapp c

escape [i'skeip] v *unnslippe; *unngå, flykte; n flukt c

escort¹ ['eskɔ:t] n eskorte m

escort² [i'skɔ:t] v ledsage

especially [i'speʃəli] adv især, først og fremst, særlig

essay ['esei] n essay nt; stil m, avhandling c

essence ['esəns] n essens m; vesen nt, kjerne m

essential [i'senʃəl] adj uunnværlig; vesentlig

essentially [i'senʃəli] adv først og fremst

establish [i'stæbliʃ] v etablere; *fastslå

estate [i'steit] n eiendom m

esteem [i'sti:m] n aktelse m, respekt m; v akte

estimate¹ ['estimeit] v vurdere, taksere, *verdsette

estimate² ['estimət] n vurdering c

estuary ['estʃuəri] n elvemunning m

etcetera [et'setərə] og så videre

etching ['etʃiŋ] n radering c

eternal [i'tə:nəl] adj evig

eternity [i'tə:nəti] n evighet c

ether ['i:θə] n eter m

Ethiopia [iθi'oupiə] Etiopia

Ethiopian [iθi'oupiən] adj etiopisk; n etiopier m

EU ['i:'ju] EU, Den europeiske union m

Euro ['ju:rou] n euro m

Europe ['juərəp] Europa

European [,juərə'pi:ən] adj europeisk; n europeer m

evacuate [i'vækjueit] v evakuere

evaluate [i'væljueit] v vurdere

evaporate [i'væpəreit] v fordampe

even ['i:vən] adj jevn, like, plan; konstant; adv til og med

evening ['i:vniŋ] n kveld m; ~ dress selskapsantrekk m

event [i'vent] n begivenhet c

eventual [i'ventʃuəl] adj mulig; endelig

eventually [i'ventʃuəli] adv endelig; til slutt

ever ['evə] adv noen gang; alltid

every ['evri] adj hver

everybody ['evri,bɔdi] pron enhver

everyday ['evridei] adj daglig

everyone ['evriwʌn] pron enhver

everything ['evriθiŋ] pron alt

everywhere ['evriwɛə] adv overalt

evidence ['evidəns] n bevis nt

evident ['evidənt] adj tydelig

evil ['i:vəl] n onde nt; adj ondsinnet, ond

evolution [,i:və'lu:ʃən] n evolusjon m

exact [ig'zækt] adj nøyaktig

exactly [ig'zæktli] adv akkurat

exaggerate [ig'zædʒəreit] v *overdrive

exam [ig'zæm] colloquial, **examination** [ig,zæmi'neiʃən] n eksamen m; undersøkelse m; forhør nt

examine [ig'zæmin] v undersøke

example [ig'zɑ:mpəl] n eksempel nt; **for ~** for eksempel

excavation [,ekskə'veiʃən] n utgravning m

exceed [ik'si:d] v *overskride; *overgå

excel [ik'sel] v utmerke seg

excellent ['eksələnt] adj fremragende, utmerket

except [ik'sept] prep unntatt

exception [ik'sepʃən] n unntak nt

exceptional [ik'sepʃənəl] adj usedvanlig, enestående

excerpt ['eksə:pt] n utdrag nt

excess [ik'ses] n utskeielse m; overdrivelse m

excessive [ik'sesiv] adj overdreven

exchange [iks'tʃeindʒ] v bytte, veksle, utveksle; n bytte nt; børs m; ~ **office** vekslingskontor nt; ~ **rate** valutakurs m

excite [ik'sait] v opphisse

excited [ik'saitəd] adj opphisset

excitement [ik'saitmənt] n opphisselse m; spenning m

exciting [ik'saitiŋ] adj spennende

exclaim [ik'skleim] v *utbryte

exclamation [,eksklə'meiʃən] n utrop nt

exclude [ik'sklu:d] v utelukke

exclusive [ik'sklu:siv] adj eksklusiv

exclusively [ik'sklu:sivli] adv utelukkende

excursion [ik'skə:ʃən] n utflukt c

excuse¹ [ik'skju:s] n unnskyldning m

excuse² [ik'skju:z] v unnskylde

execute ['eksikju:t] v utføre

execution [,eksi'kju:ʃən] n
henrettelse m

executioner [,eksi'kju:ʃənə] n
bøddel m

executive [ig'zekjutiv] adj
administrerende; n utøvende makt;
direktør m

exempt [ig'zempt] v *frita; adj fritatt

exemption [ig'zempʃən] n fritak nt

exercise ['eksəsaiz] n øvelse m;
oppgave c; v øve; utøve

exhale [eks'heil] v puste ut

exhaust [ig'zɔːst] n eksosrør nt; v
utmatte; ~ gases eksos m

exhibit [ig'zibit] v utstille; fremvise,
oppvise

exhibition [,eksi'biʃən] n utstilling c

exile ['eksail] n eksil nt; landflyktig m

exist [ig'zist] v eksistere

existence [ig'zistəns] n eksistens m

exit ['eksit] n utgang m; utkjørsel m

exotic [ig'zɔtik] adj eksotisk

expand [ik'spænd] v utvide; utbre;
utfolde

expansion [ik'spænʃən] n utbredelse;
utvidelse, ekspansjon

expect [ik'spekt] v vente

expectation [,ekspek'teiʃən] n
forventning m

expedition [,ekspə'diʃən] n
ekspedisjon m

expel [ik'spel] v utvise

expenditure [ik'spendit ʃə] n forbruk
nt

expense [ik'spens] n utgift c;
expenses pl omkostninger pl,
kostnader pl

expensive [ik'spensiv] adj dyr;
kostbar

experience [ik'spiəriəns] n erfaring c;
v oppleve, erfare; experienced
erfaren

experiment [ik'sperimənt] n
eksperiment nt, forsøk nt; v
eksperimentere

expert ['ekspə:t] n fagmann m,
ekspert m; adj sakkyndig

expire [ik'spaiə] v *utløpe, opphøre;
utånde; expired utløpt

explain [ik'splein] v forklare

explanation [,eksplə'neiʃən] n
forklaring c

explicit [ik'splisit] adj tydelig,
uttrykkelig

explode [ik'sploud] v eksplodere

exploit [ik'splɔit] v utnytte

explore [ik'splɔ:] v utforske

explosion [ik'splouʒən] n eksplosjon
m

explosive [ik'splousiv] adj eksplosiv;
n sprengstoff nt

export¹ [ik'spɔ:t] v eksportere, utføre

export² ['ekspɔ:t] n eksport m,
utførsel m

exportation [,ekspɔ:'teiʃən] n
eksport m, utførsel m

exports ['ekspɔ:ts] pl eksport m

expose [ik'spous] v utsette; avsløre;
eksponere

exposition [,ekspə'ziʃən] n utstilling
c

exposure [ik'spouʒə] n utsatthet c;
eksponering c; ~ meter lysmåler m

express [ik'spres] v uttrykke; *gi
uttrykk for, ytre; adj ekspress-;
uttrykkelig; ~ train hurtigtog nt

expression [ik'spreʃən] n uttrykk nt

exquisite [ik'skwizit] adj utsøkt

extend [ik'stend] v forlenge; utvide;
bevilge

extension [ik'stenʃən] n forlengelse
m; utvidelse m; linje c; ~ cord
skjøteledning m

extensive [ik'stensiv] adj
omfangsrik; utstrakt, omfattende

extent [ik'stent] n omfang nt

exterior [ek'stiəriə] adj ytre; n utside c

external [ek'stə:nəl] adj utvendig

extinguish [ik'stiŋgwiʃ] v slokke

extort [ik'stɔːt] v utpresse

extortion [ik'stɔːʃən] n utpressing c

extra ['ekstrə] adj ekstra

extract[1] [ik'strækt] v *trekke ut

extract[2] ['ekstrækt] n utdrag nt

extradite ['ekstrədait] v utlevere en forbryter

extraordinary [ik'strɔːdənri] adj usedvanlig

extravagant [ik'strævəgənt] adj ekstravagant, overdreven

extreme [ik'striːm] adj ekstrem; ytterst, ytterlig; n ytterlighet c

exuberant [ig'zjuːbərənt] adj overstrømmende

eye [ai] n øye nt; ~ **shadow** øyenskygge m

eyebrow ['aibrau] n øyenbryn nt

eyelash ['ailæʃ] n øyenvippe m

eyelid ['ailid] n øyenlokk nt

eyewitness ['ai,witnəs] n øyenvitne nt

F

fable ['feibəl] n fabel m; sagn nt

fabric ['fæbrik] n stoff nt; struktur m

façade [fə'sɑːd] n fasade m

face [feis] n ansikt nt; v konfrontere; ~ **cream** ansiktskrem m

facilities [fə'silətis] pl innretning(er) pl; **cooking** ~ mulighet til å lage mat

facing overfor

fact [fækt] n kjensgjerning c, faktum nt; **in** ~ faktisk

factor ['fæktə] n faktor m

factory ['fæktəri] n fabrikk m

factual ['fæktʃuəl] adj faktisk

faculty ['fækəlti] n evne c; begavelse m, anlegg nt; fakultet nt

fade [feid] v blekne, falme

fail [feil] v mislykkes; mangle; forsømme; dumpe, *stryke; **without** ~ helt sikkert

failure ['feiljə] n fiasko m

faint [feint] v besvime; adj svak, vag

fair [fɛə] n basar m; varemesse c; adj rettferdig; lyshåret, blond; vakker

fairly ['fɛəli] adv nokså, temmelig, ganske

fairy ['fɛəri] n fe m

fairytale ['fɛəriteil] n eventyr nt

faith [feiθ] n tro c; tillit m

faithful ['feiðful] adj trofast

fake [feik] n forfalskning m

fall [fɔːl] n fall nt; høst m

*fall [fɔːl] v *falle

false [fɔːls] adj falsk; gal, uekte; ~ **teeth** gebiss nt

falter ['fɔːltə] v vakle; stamme

fame [feim] n berømmelse m; rykte nt

familiar [fə'miljə] adj velkjent; fortrolig

family ['fæməli] n familie m; slekt c; ~ **name** etternavn nt

famous ['feiməs] adj berømt

fan [fæn] n vifte c; beundrer m; ~ **belt** vifterem c

fanatical [fə'nætikəl] adj fanatisk

fancy ['fænsi] v *ha lyst til, like; tenke seg, forestille seg; n lune nt; fantasi m

fantastic [fæn'tæstik] adj fantastisk

fantasy ['fæntəzi] n fantasi m

far [fɑː] adj fjern; adv meget; **by** ~ uten sammenligning; **so** ~ hittil; ~ **away** langt borte

far-away ['fɑːrəwei] adj fjern

fare [feə] n billettpris m; kost m

farm [fɑːm] n bondegård m

farmer ['fɑːmə] n bonde m

farmhouse ['fɑːmhaus] n våningshus nt

far-off ['fɑːrɔf] adj fjern

farther ['fɑːðə] adj videre

fascinate ['fæsineit] v fengsle, fjetre

fascism ['fæʃizəm] n fascisme m

fascist ['fæʃist] adj fascistisk; n fascist m

fashion ['fæʃən] n mote m; måte m

fashionable ['fæʃənəbəl] adj moderne

fast [fɑːst] adj rask, hurtig; fast

fasten ['fɑːsən] v feste; stenge

fastener ['fɑːsənə] n festeinnretning m

fat [fæt] adj tykk, fet; n fett nt

fatal ['feitəl] adj dødelig, skjebnesvanger, fatal

fate [feit] n skjebne m

father ['fɑːðə] n far m; pater m

father-in-law ['fɑːðərinlɔː] n (pl fathers-) svigerfar m

fatigue [fəti:g] n utmattelse m, tretthet c

fatness ['fætnəs] n fedme m

fatty ['fæti] adj fettholdig

faucet ['fɔːsit] nAm vannkran c

fault [fɔːlt] n feil m, defekt m

faultless ['fɔːltləs] adj feilfri; perfekt

faulty ['fɔːlti] adj defekt, mangelfull

favo(u)r ['feivə] n tjeneste m; v privilegere, begunstige

favo(u)rable ['feivərəbəl] adj gunstig

favo(u)rite ['feivərit] n favoritt m, yndling m; adj yndlings-

fax [fæks] n telefaks m, faks m; send a ~ sende en faks

fear [fiə] n frykt m, engstelse m; v frykte

feasible ['fiːzəbəl] adj mulig, gjennomførbart

feast [fiːst] n fest m

feat [fiːt] n prestasjon m

feather ['feðə] n fjær c

feature ['fiːtʃə] n kjennemerke nt; ansiktstrekk nt

February ['februəri] februar

federal ['fedərəl] adj forbunds-

federation [,fedə'reiʃən] n forbundsstat m

fee [fiː] n honorar nt; gebyr nt

feeble ['fiːbəl] adj svak

*feed [fiːd] v mate; fed up with lei av

*feel [fiːl] v føle; ~ like *ha lyst til

feeling ['fiːliŋ] n følelse m

feet (pl foot)

fell [fel] v (p fall)

fellow ['felou] n fyr m

felt¹ [felt] n filt m

felt² [felt] v (p, pp feel)

female ['fiːmeil] adj hunn-

feminine ['feminin] adj feminin

fence [fens] n gjerde nt; stakitt nt; v fekte

ferment [fə'ment] v gjære

ferry-boat ['feribout] n ferge c; ferje c

fertile ['fəːtail] adj fruktbar

festival ['festivəl] n festival m

festive ['festiv] adj festlig

fetch [fetʃ] v hente *innbringe

feudal ['fjuːdəl] adj føydal

fever ['fiːvə] n feber m

feverish ['fiːvəriʃ] adj feberaktig

few [fjuː] adj få

fiancé [fi'ɑːsei] n forlovede m

fiancée [fi'ɑːsei] n forlovede m

fibre ['faibə] n fiber m

fiction ['fikʃən] n skjønnlitteratur m, oppdiktning m

field [fiːld] n mark c, åker m; felt nt; ~ glasses feltkikkert m

fierce [fiəs] adj vill; heftig

fifteen [,fif'tiːn] num femten

fifteenth [,fif'tiːnθ] num femtende

fifth [fifθ] num femte

fifty ['fifti] *num* femti

fig [fig] *n* fiken *m*

fight [fait] *n* strid *m*, kamp *m*

*fight [fait] *v* kjempe, *slåss

figure ['figə] *n* skikkelse *m*, figur *m*; tall *nt*

file [fail] *n* kartotek *nt*, fil *m*; dokumentsamling *c*; rekke *c*

fill [fil] *v* fylle; ~ in fylle ut; ~ out *Am* fylle ut; ~ up fylle opp; filling station bensinstasjon *m*

filling ['filiŋ] *n* plombe *m*; fyll *nt*

film [film] *n* film *m*; *v* filme

filter ['filtə] *n* filter *nt*

filthy ['filθi] *adj* skitten

final ['fainəl] *adj* endelig

finally ['fainəli] *adv* endelig, til slutt

finance [fai'næns] *v* finansiere

finances [fai'nænsiz] *pl* finanser *pl*

financial [fai'nænʃəl] *adj* finansiell

finch [fintʃ] *n* finke *m*

*find [faind] *v* *finne

fine [fain] *n* mulkt *c*; *adj* fin; pen; skjønn, utmerket; ~ arts skjønne kunster

finger ['fiŋgə] *n* finger *m*; little ~ lillefinger *m*

fingerprint ['fiŋgəprint] *n* fingeravtrykk *nt*

finish ['finiʃ] *v* fullende, avslutte, slutte; opphøre; *n* slutt *m*; mållinje *c*; finished ferdig

Finland ['finlənd] Finland

Finn [fin] *n* finne *m*

Finnish ['finiʃ] *adj* finsk

fire [faiə] *n* ild *m*; brann *m*; *v* *skyte; avskjedige; ~ alarm brannalarm *m*; ~ brigade brannvesen *nt*; ~ escape branntrapp *c*; ~ extinguisher brannslokker *m*

firefighter ['faiə,faitə] *n* brannmannskap *nt*

fireplace ['faiəpleis] *n* peis *m*

fireproof ['faiəpru:f] *adj* brannsikker;

ildfast

firm [fə:m] *adj* fast; solid; *n* firma *nt*

first [fə:st] *num* første; at ~ først; i begynnelsen; ~ name fornavn *nt*

first aid [,fə:st'eid] *n* førstehjelp *c*; ~ kit førstehjelpsutstyr *nt*; ~ post førstehjelpsstasjon *m*

first-class [,fə:st'kla:s] *adj* førsteklasses

first-rate [,fə:st'reit] *adj* førsteklasses, førsterangs

fir tree ['fə:tri:] *n* nåletre *nt*, gran *c*

fish¹ [fiʃ] *n* (pl ~, ~es) fisk *m*; ~ shop fiskeforretning *c*

fish² [fiʃ] *v* fiske; fishing gear fiskeutstyr *nt*; fishing hook fiskekrok *m*; fishing industry fiskeri *nt*; fishing license *Am*, fishing licence fiskekort *nt*; fishing line fiskesnøre *nt*; fishing net fiskegarn *nt*; fishing rod fiskestang *c*; fishing tackle fiskeredskap *c*

fishbone ['fiʃboun] *n* fiskebein *nt*

fisherman ['fiʃəmən] *n* (pl -men) fisker *m*

fist [fist] *n* knyttneve *m*

fit [fit] *adj* egnet; *n* anfall *nt*; *v* passe; fitting room prøverom *nt*

five [faiv] *num* fem

fix [fiks] *v* reparere, ordne

fixed [fikst] *adj* fast

fizz [fiz] *n* brusing *c*

fjord [fjɔ:d] *n* fjord *m*

flag [flæg] *n* flagg *nt*

flame [fleim] *n* flamme *m*

flamingo [flə'miŋgou] *n* (pl ~s, ~es) flamingo *m*

flannel ['flænəl] *n* flanell *m*

flash [flæʃ] *n* glimt *nt*; ~ bulb blitzlampe *c*

flashlight ['flæʃlait] *n* lommelykt *c*

flask [fla:sk] *n* flaske *c*; thermos ~ termosflaske *c*

flat [flæt] *adj* flat, plan; *n* leilighet *c*; ~

tyre punktering *c*

flavo(u)r ['fleivə] *n* smak *m*; *v* *sette smak på

flaw [flɔ:] *n* sprekk *m*; svakhet *c*

flee [fli:] *v* flykte, rømme

fleet [fli:t] *n* flåte *m*

flesh [fleʃ] *n* kjøtt *nt*

flew [flu:] *v* (p fly)

flex [fleks] *n* ledning *m*; *v* bøye

flexible ['fleksibəl] *adj* bøyelig

flight [flait] *n* flytur *m*; **charter ~** chartertur *m*

flint [flint] *n* flintstein *m*

float [flout] *v* *flyte; *n* flottør *m*

flock [flɔk] *n* flokk *m*

flood [flʌd] *n* oversvømmelse *m*; flo *m*

floor [flɔ:] *n* gulv *nt*; etasje *m*; **first ~** annen etasje; *Am* første etasje; **~ show** floor-show *nt*

florist ['flɔrist] *n* blomsterhandler *m*

flour [flauə] *n* mel *nt*

flow [flou] *v* strømme, *flyte

flower [flauə] *n* blomst *m*; **~ shop** blomsterforretning *c*

flowerbed ['flauəbed] *n* blomsterbed *nt*

flown [floun] *v* (pp fly)

flu [flu:] *n* influensa *m*

fluent ['flu:ənt] *adj* flytende

fluid ['flu:id] *adj* flytende; *n* væske *c*

flute [flu:t] *n* fløyte *c*

fly [flai] *n* flue *c*; buksesmekk *m*

*fly [flai] *v* *fly

foam [foum] *n* skum *nt*; *v* skumme; **~ rubber** skumgummi *m*

focus ['foukəs] *n* brennpunkt *nt*

fog [fɔg] *n* tåke *c*

foggy ['fɔgi] *adj* tåket

foglamp ['fɔglæmp] *n* tåkelykt *m*

fold [fould] *v* brette, folde; folde sammen; *n* fold *m*

folk [fouk] *n* folk *nt*; **~ dance** folkedans *m*; **~ song** folkevise *c*

folklore ['fouklɔ:] *n* folklore *m*

follow ['fɔlou] *v* *følge; **following** *adj* neste, følgende

fond: *be ~ of [bi: fɔnd ɔv] like

food [fu:d] *n* mat *m*; føde *c*; **~ poisoning** matforgiftning *m*

foodstuffs ['fu:dstʌfs] *pl* matvarer *pl*

fool [fu:l] *n* tosk *m*; *v* narre

foolish ['fu:liʃ] *adj* fjollet, tåpelig; dum

foot [fut] *n* (pl feet) fot *m*; **on ~** til fots

football ['futbɔ:l] *n* fotball *m*; **~ match** fotballkamp *m*

foot brake ['futbreik] *n* fotbrems *m*

footpath ['futpɑ:θ] *n* gangsti *m*

footwear ['futwɛə] *n* skotøy *nt*

for [fɔ:, fə] *prep* til; i; på grunn av, av, for; *conj* for

*forbid [fə'bid] *v* *forby

force [fɔ:s] *v* *tvinge; forsere; *n* kraft *c*, styrke *m*; vold *m*; **by ~** nødtvunget; **driving ~** drivkraft *c*

forecast ['fɔ:kɑ:st] *n* varsel *nt*; *v* *forutsi, varsle

foreground ['fɔ:graund] *n* forgrunn *m*

forehead ['fɔred] *n* panne *c*

foreign ['fɔrin] *adj* utenlandsk; fremmed

foreigner ['fɔrinə] *n* utlending *m*

foreman ['fɔ:mən] *n* (pl -men) formann *m*

foremost ['fɔ:moust] *adj* fremst, forrest

forest ['fɔrist] *n* skog *m*

forester ['fɔristə] *n* forstmann *m*

forever, for ever [fə'revə] *adv* for alltid; stadig

forge [fɔ:dʒ] *v* forfalske

*forget [fə'get] *v* glemme

forgetful [fə'getfəl] *adj* glemsom

*forgive [fə'giv] *v* *tilgi

fork [fɔ:k] *n* gaffel *m*; skillevei *m*; *v* dele seg

form [fɔ:m] *n* form *c*; blankett *m*;

skjema *nt*; klasse *c*; *v* forme

formal ['fɔːməl] *adj* formell

formality [fɔːˈmæləti] *n* formalitet *m*

former ['fɔːmə] *adj* forhenværende; tidligere; **formerly** før i tiden

formula ['fɔːmjulə] *n* (pl ~e, ~s) formel *m*

fortnight ['fɔːtnait] *n* fjorten dager

fortress ['fɔːtris] *n* festning *m*

fortunate ['fɔːtʃənət] *adj* heldig

fortunately ['fɔːtʃənətli] *adv* heldigvis

fortune ['fɔːtʃuːn] *n* formue *m*; skjebne *m*, lykke *c*

forty ['fɔːti] *num* førti

forward ['fɔːwəd] *adv* frem, fremad; *v* ettersende

foster parents ['fɔstə,pɛərənts] *pl* pleieforeldre *pl*

fought [fɔːt] *v* (p, pp fight)

foul [faul] *adj* skitten; gemen

found¹ [faund] *v* (p, pp find)

found² [faund] *v* *grunnlegge, opprette, stifte

foundation [faunˈdeiʃən] *n* grunnlag *nt*; stiftelse *m*

fountain ['fauntin] *n* springvann *nt*; kilde *m*

fountain pen ['fauntinpen] *n* fyllepenn *m*

four [fɔː] *num* fire

fourteen [,fɔːˈtiːn] *num* fjorten

fourteenth [,fɔːˈtiːnθ] *num* fjortende

fourth [fɔːθ] *num* fjerde

fowl [faul] *n* (pl ~s, ~) fjærkre *nt*

fox [fɔks] *n* rev *m*

foyer ['fɔiei] *n* foajé *m*

fraction ['frækʃən] *n* brøkdel *m*

fracture ['fræktʃə] *v* *brekke; *n* brudd *nt*

fragile ['frædʒail] *adj* skjør; skrøpelig

fragment ['frægmənt] *n* bruddstykke *nt*; stykke *nt*

frame [freim] *n* ramme *c*; innfatning

m

France [frɑːns] Frankrike

franchise ['fræntʃaiz] *n* stemmerett *m*

frank [fræŋk] *adj* oppriktig

fraternity [frəˈtɔːnəti] *n* brorskap *m*/*nt*

fraud [frɔːd] *n* bedrageri *nt*

fray [frei] *v* trevle opp

free [friː] *adj* fri; gratis; ~ **of charge** gratis; ~ **ticket** fribillett *m*

freedom ['friːdəm] *n* frihet *c*

***freeze** [friːz] *v* *fryse; fryse

freezer ['friːzə] *n* fryser *m*, fryseboks *m*

freezing ['friːziŋ] *adj* iskald

freezing point ['friːziŋpɔint] *n* frysepunkt *nt*

freight [freit] *n* last *c*, frakt *c*

freight train ['freittrein] *nAm* godstog *nt*

French [frentʃ] *adj* fransk; **the** ~ *pl* franskmennene; ~ **fries** *pl* pommes frites

Frenchman ['frentʃmən] *n* (pl -men) franskmann *m*

frequency ['friːkwənsi] *n* frekvens *m*; hyppighet *c*

frequent ['friːkwənt] *adj* stadig, hyppig; **frequently** ofte

fresh [freʃ] *adj* fersk; forfriskende; ~ **water** ferskvann *nt*

friction ['frikʃən] *n* friksjon *m*

Friday ['fraidi] fredag *m*

fridge [fridʒ] *n* kjøleskap *nt*

friend [frend] *n* venn *m*; venninne *c*

friendly ['frendli] *adj* vennlig; vennskapelig

friendship ['frendʃip] *n* vennskap *nt*

fright [frait] *n* skrekk *m*, angst *m*

frighten ['fraitən] *v* forskrekke

frightened ['fraitənd] *adj* skremt; ***be** ~ *bli forskrekket

frightful ['fraitfəl] *adj* forferdelig, forskrekkelig

fringe [frindʒ] *n* frynse *c*

frock [frɔk] *n* kjole *m*

frog [frɔg] *n* frosk *m*

from [frɔm] *prep* fra; av; fra og med

front [frʌnt] *n* forside *c*; **in ~ of** foran

frontier ['frʌntiə] *n* grense *c*

frost [frɔst] *n* frost *m*

froth [frɔθ] *n* skum *nt*

frozen ['frouzən] *adj* frossen; **~ food** dypfryst mat

fruit [fru:t] *n* frukt *c*

fry [frai] *v* steke

frying pan ['fraiiŋpæn] *n* stekepanne *c*

fuck [fʌk] *v vulgar* knulle, pule

fuel ['fju:əl] *n* brensel *nt*; bensin *m*; **~ pump** *Am* bensinpumpe *c*

full [ful] *adj* full; **~ board** helpensjon *m*; **~ stop** punktum *nt*; **~ up** fullsatt

fun [fʌn] *n* moro *c*, gøy *m/nt*

function ['fʌŋkʃən] *n* funksjon *m*

fund [fʌnd] *n* fond *nt*

fundamental [,fʌndə'mentəl] *adj* fundamental

funeral ['fju:nərəl] *n* begravelse *m*

funnel ['fʌnəl] *n* trakt *c*

funny ['fʌni] *adj* pussig, komisk; merkelig

fur [fə:] *n* pels *m*; **~ coat** pelskåpe *c*

furious ['fjuəriəs] *adj* rasende

furnace ['fə:nis] *n* ovn *m*

furnish ['fə:niʃ] *v* forsyne, skaffe; møblere, innrette; **~ with** forsyne med

furniture ['fə:nitʃə] *n* møbler *pl*

furrier ['fʌriə] *n* buntmaker *m*

further ['fə:ðə] *adj* videre; ytterligere

furthermore ['fə:ðəmɔ:] *adv* dessuten

furthest ['fə:ðist] *adj* fjernest; lengst

fuse [fju:z] *n* sikring *c*; lunte *c*

fuss [fʌs] *n* bråk *nt*; oppstyr *nt*, mas *nt*

future ['fju:tʃə] *n* fremtid *c*; *adj* fremtidig

G

gable ['geibəl] *n* gavl *m*

gadget ['gædʒit] *n* innretning *m*, apparat *nt*

gain [gein] *v* *vinne; *n* fortjeneste *m*

gale [geil] *n* storm *m*

gall [gɔ:l] *n* galle *m*; **~ bladder** galleblære *c*

gallery ['gæləri] *n* galleri *nt*; kunstgalleri *nt*

gallon ['gælən] *n* gallon *m* (Brit 4,55 l; Am 3,79 l)

gallop ['gæləp] *n* galopp *m*

gallows ['gælouz] *pl* galge *m*

gallstone ['gɔ:lstoun] *n* gallestein *m*

game [geim] *n* spill *nt*; vilt *nt*

gang [gæŋ] *n* bande *m*; gjeng *m*

gangway ['gæŋwei] *n* landgang *m*

gap [gæp] *n* åpning *c*

garage ['gærɑ:ʒ] *n* garasje *m*; *v* *sette i garasje

garbage ['gɑ:bidʒ] *n* avfall *nt*, søppel *nt*

garden ['gɑ:dən] *n* hage *m*; **public ~** offentlig parkanlegg; **zoological gardens** zoologisk hage

gardener ['gɑ:dənə] *n* gartner *m*

gargle ['gɑ:gəl] *v* gurgle

garlic ['gɑ:lik] *n* hvitløk *m*

garment [,gɑ:mənt] *n* klesplagg *nt*

gas [gæs] *n* gass *m*; bensin *m*; **~**

cooker gasskomfyr *m*; ~ **pump** *Am* bensinpumpe *c*; ~ **station** bensinstasjon *m*; ~ **stove** gasovn *m*

gasoline ['gæsəli:n] *nAm* bensin *m*

gastric ['gæstrik] *adj* mage-; ~ **ulcer** magesår *nt*

gasworks ['gæswə:ks] *n* gassverk *nt*

gate [geit] *n* port *m*; grind *c*

gather ['gæðə] *v* samle; samles; høste

gauge [geidʒ] *n* måleinstrument *nt*

gave [geiv] *v* (p give)

gay [gei] *adj* munter; fargerik; *colloquial* homofil

gaze [geiz] *v* stirre

gear [giə] *n* gir *nt*; utstyr *nt*; **change** ~ skifte gir; ~ **lever** girstang *c*

gearbox ['giəbɔks] *n* girkasse *c*

geese [dʒi:z] *n* (pl goose) gjess *pl*

gem [dʒem] *n* edelstein *m*, juvel *m*; klenodie *nt*

gender ['dʒendə] *n* kjønn *nt*

general ['dʒenərəl] *adj* generell; *n* general *m*; ~ **practitioner** allmennpraktiserende lege; **in** ~ som regel

generate ['dʒenəreit] *v* *frembringe

generation [,dʒenə'reiʃən] *n* generasjon *m*

generator ['dʒenəreitər] *n* generator *m*

generosity [,dʒenə'rɔsəti] *n* gavmildhet *c*

generous ['dʒenərəs] *adj* gavmild

genital ['dʒenitəl] *adj* kjønns-

genius ['dʒi:niəs] *n* geni *nt*

gentle ['dʒentəl] *adj* mild; lett; øm; forsiktig

gentleman ['dʒentəlmən] *n* (pl -men) herre *m*

genuine ['dʒenjuin] *adj* ekte

geography [dʒi'ɔgrəfi] *n* geografi *m*

geology [dʒi'ɔlədʒi] *n* geologi *m*

geometry [dʒi'ɔmətri] *n* geometri *m*

germ [dʒə:m] *n* basill *m*; kim *m*

German ['dʒə:mən] *adj* tysk; *n* tysker *m*

Germany ['dʒə:məni] Tyskland

gesticulate [dʒi'stikjuleit] *v* gestikulere

get-together sammenkomst *m*

***get** [get] *v* *få; hente; *bli; ~ **back** *gå tilbake; ~ **off** *stige av; ~ **on** *stige på; *gjøre fremskritt; ~ **up** *stå opp

ghost [goust] *n* spøkelse *nt*; ånd *m*

giant ['dʒaiənt] *n* kjempe *m*

giddiness ['gidinəs] *n* svimmelhet *c*

giddy ['gidi] *adj* svimmel

gift [gift] *n* presang *m*, gave *c*; evne *c*

gifted ['giftid] *adj* begavet

gigantic [dʒai'gæntik] *adj* enorm

giggle ['gigəl] *v* fnise

gill [gil] *n* gjelle *c*

gilt [gilt] *adj* forgylt

ginger ['dʒindʒə] *n* ingefær *m*

girl [gə:l] *n* pike *m*

girlfriend ['gə:lfrend] *n* kjæreste *m*

***give** [giv] *v* *gi; *overrekke; ~ **away** røpe; ~ **in** *gi seg, *gi etter; ~ **up** *oppgi, *gi opp

glacier ['glæsiə] *n* isbre *m*

glad [glæd] *adj* fornøyd, glad; **gladly** med glede, gjerne

gladness ['glædnəs] *n* glede *c*

glamorous ['glæmərəs] *adj* betagende, fortryllende

glamour ['glæmə] *n* sjarm *m*

glance [glɑ:ns] *n* blikk *nt*; *v* kaste et blikk

gland [glænd] *n* kjertel *m*

glare [gleə] *n* skarpt lys; skinn *nt*

glaring ['gleəriŋ] *adj* blendende

glass [glɑ:s] *n* glass *nt*; glass-; **glasses** briller *pl*; **magnifying** ~ forstørrelsesglass *nt*

glaze [gleiz] *v* glasere

glide [glaid] *v* *gli

glider ['glaidə] *n* glidefly *nt*

glimpse [glimps] *n* glimt *nt*; *v* skimte

global ['gloubəl] *adj* verdensomfattende

globalization [,gloubəli'zeiʃən] *n* globalisering *c*

globe [gloub] *n* globus *m*, jordklode *m*

gloom [glu:m] *n* mørke *nt*

gloomy ['glu:mi] *adj* dyster

glorious ['glɔ:riəs] *adj* strålende

glory ['glɔ:ri] *n* ære *c*, berømmelse *m*; ros *m*, heder *m*

gloss [glɔs] *n* glans *m*

glossy ['glɔsi] *adj* blank

glove [glʌv] *n* hanske *m*

glow [glou] *v* gløde; *n* glød *m*

glue [glu:] *n* lim *nt*

*****go** [gou] *v* *gå; reise; ~ **ahead** *fortsette; ~ **away** reise bort; ~ **back** vende tilbake; ~ **home** *gå hjem; ~ **in** *gå inn; ~ **on** *fortsette, *gå videre; ~ **out** *gå ut; ~ **through** *gjennomgå, *gå igjennom

goal [goul] *n* mål *nt*

goalkeeper ['goul,ki:pə] *n* målmann *m*

goat [gout] *n* geit *c*

god [gɔd] *n* gud *m*

goddess ['gɔdis] *n* gudinne *c*

godmother ['gɔd,mʌðə] *n* gudmor *c*; fadder *m*

godfather ['gɔd,fɑ:ðə] *n* gudfar *m*; fadder *m*

goggles ['gɔgəlz] *pl* dykkerbriller *pl*, snøbriller *pl*

gold [gould] *n* gull *nt*; ~ **leaf** bladgull *nt*

golden ['gouldən] *adj* gyllen

goldmine ['gouldmain] *n* gullgruve *c*

goldsmith ['gouldsmiθ] *n* gullsmed *m*

golf [gɔlf] *n* golf *m*; ~ **course** golfbane *m*; ~ **links** golfbane *m*

golfclub ['gɔlfklʌb] *n* golfkølle *c*; golfklubb *m*

gondola ['gɔndələ] *n* gondol *m*

gone [gɔn] *adv* (pp go) borte

good [gud] *adj* bra, god; snill

goodbye! [,gud'bai] adjø!

good-humo(u)red [,gud'hju:məd] *adj* godlynt

good-looking [,gud'lukiŋ] *adj* pen

good-natured [,gud'neitʃəd] *adj* godmodig

goods [gudz] *pl* varer *pl*; ~ **train** godstog *nt*

good-tempered [,gud'tempəd] *adj* godmodig

goodwill [,gud'wil] *n* godvilje *m*

goose [gu:s] *n* (pl geese) gås *c*; ~ **flesh** gåsehud *c*

gooseberry ['guzbəri] *n* stikkelsbær *nt*

gorge [gɔ:dʒ] *n* kløft *c*; *v* proppe seg

gorgeous ['gɔ:dʒəs] *adj* praktfull

gospel ['gɔspəl] *n* evangelium *nt*

gossip ['gɔsip] *n* sladder *m*; *v* sladre

got [gɔt] *v* (p, pp get)

gout [gaut] *n* gikt *c*

govern ['gʌvən] *v* regjere

government ['gʌvənmənt] *n* styre *nt*, regjering *c*

governor ['gʌvənə] *n* guvernør *m*

gown [gaun] *n* kjole *m*

grace [greis] *n* ynde *m*; nåde *m*

graceful ['greisfəl] *adj* yndig, grasiøs

grade [greid] *n* grad *m*; klasse *c*, *v* klassifisere; gradere

gradient ['greidiənt] *n* helling *c*

gradual ['grædʒuəl] *adj* gradvis

graduate ['grædʒueit] *v* *ta avsluttende eksamen

grain [grein] *n* korn *nt*

gram [græm] *n* gram *nt*

grammar ['græmə] *n* grammatikk *m*; ~ **book** grammatikk *m*

grammatical [grə'mætikəl] *adj* grammatisk

grand [grænd] *adj* storartet

grandchild ['græn,tʃaild] *n*

barnebarn *nt*

granddad ['grændæd], **grandfather** ['græn,fɑːðə] *n* farfar *m*; morfar *m*; bestefar *m*

grandma ['grænmɑ], **grandmother** ['græn,mʌðə] *n* farmor *c*; mormor *c*; bestemor *c*

grandparents ['græn,peərənts] *pl* besteforeldre *pl*

granite ['grænit] *n* granitt *m*

grant [grɑːnt] *v* bevilge; innvilge; *n* stipend *nt*, tilskudd *nt*

grapefruit ['greipfruːt] *n* grapefrukt *c*

grapes [greips] *pl* druer *pl*

graph [græf] *n* diagram *nt*

graphic ['græfik] *adj* grafisk

grasp [grɑːsp] *v* *gripe; *n* grep *nt*

grass [grɑːs] *n* gress *nt*

grasshopper ['grɑːs,hɔpə] *n* gresshoppe *c*

grate [greit] *n* rist *c*; *v* raspe

grateful ['greitfəl] *adj* takknemlig

grater ['greitə] *n* rivjern *nt*; rasp *c*

gratis ['grætis] *adj* gratis

gratitude ['grætitjuːd] *n* takknemlighet *c*

gratuity [grə'tjuːəti] *n* drikkepenger *pl*

grave [greiv] *n* grav *c*; *adj* alvorlig

gravel ['grævəl] *n* grus *m*

gravestone ['greivstoun] *n* gravstein *m*

graveyard ['greivjɑːd] *n* kirkegård *m*

gravity ['grævəti] *n* tyngdekraft *c*; alvor *nt*

gravy ['greivi] *n* saus *m*

graze [greiz] *v* beite; *n* skrubbsår *nt*

grease [griːs] *n* fett *nt*; *v* *smøre

greasy ['griːsi] *adj* fettet

great [greit] *adj* stor; **Great Britain** Storbritannia

Greece [griːs] Hellas

greed [griːd] *n* griskhet *c*

greedy ['griːdi] *adj* grisk; grådig

Greek [griːk] *adj* gresk; *n* greker *m*

green [griːn] *adj* grønn; **~ card** grønt kort

greengrocer ['griːn,grousə] *n* grønnsakhandler *m*

greenhouse ['griːnhaus] *n* drivhus *nt*

greens [griːnz] *pl* grønnsaker *pl*

greet [griːt] *v* hilse

greeting ['griːtiŋ] *n* hilsen *m*

grey [grei] *adj* grå

greyhound ['greihaund] *n* mynde *m*

grief [griːf] *n* sorg *c*; smerte *m*

grieve [griːv] *v* sørge

grill [gril] *n* grill *m*; *v* grille

grim [grim] *adj* grusom, skrekkelig

grin [grin] *v* glise, smile bredt; *n* glis *nt*

*grind [graind] *v* male; finmale

grip [grip] *v* *gripe; *n* grep *nt*, tak *nt*

grit [grit] *n* grus *m*; fasthet *c*

groan [groun] *v* stønne

grocer ['grousə] *n* matvarehandler *m*; **grocer's** matvareforretning *c*

groceries ['grousəriz] *pl* matvarer *pl*

groin [grɔin] *n* lyske *m*

groom [gruːm] *n* hestepleier *m*, stallkar *m*; brudgom *m*; *v* pleie

groove [gruːv] *n* fure *m*

gross [grous] *adj* grov; brutto

grotto ['grɔtou] *n* (pl ~es, ~s) grotte *c*

ground[1] [graund] *n* jord *c*, grunn *m*; **~ floor** første etasje; **grounds** tomt *m*

ground[2] [graund] *v* (p, pp grind)

group [gruːp] *n* gruppe *c*

grouse [graus] *n* (pl ~) rype *c*

grove [grouv] *n* lund *m*

*grow [grou] *v* vokse; dyrke; *bli

growl [graul] *v* brumme

grown-up ['grounʌp] *adj* voksen; *n* voksen *m*

growth [grouθ] *n* vekst *m*; svulst *m*

grudge [grʌdʒ] *v* misunne

grumble ['grʌmbəl] *v* knurre, klage

guarantee [,gærən'tiː] *n* garanti *m*; kausjon *m*; *v* garantere

guard [gɑːd] *n* vakt *c*; *v* bevokte

guardian ['gɑːdiən] *n* formynder *m*

guess [ges] *v* gjette; *anta; *n* formodning *m*

guest [gest] *n* gjest *m*; ~ **room** gjesteværelse *nt*

guesthouse ['gesthaus] *n* pensjonat *nt*

guide [gaid] *n* guide *m*; *v* vise vei

guidebook ['gaidbuk] *n* reisehåndbok *c*

guide dog ['gaiddɔg] *n* førerhund *m*

guideline ['gaidlain] *n* retningslinje *c*

guilt [gilt] *n* skyld *c*

guilty ['gilti] *adj* skyldig

guinea pig ['ginipig] *n* marsvin *nt*; forsøksdyr *nt*

guitar [gi'tɑː] *n* gitar *m*

gulf [gʌlf] *n* golf *m*; vik *c*

gull [gʌl] *n* måke *c*

gum [gʌm] *n* tannkjøtt *nt*; gummi *m*; lim *nt*

gun [gʌn] *n* revolver *m*, gevær *nt*; kanon *m*

gunpowder ['gʌn,paudə] *n* krutt *nt*

gust [gʌst] *n* vindkast *nt*

gusty ['gʌsti] *adj* blåsende

gut [gʌt] *n* tarm *m*; **guts** vågemot *nt*

gutter ['gʌtə] *n* rennestein *m*

guy [gai] *n* kar *m*

gymnasium [dʒim'neiziəm] *n* (pl ~s, -sia) gymnastikksal *m*

gymnast ['dʒimnæst] *n* turner *m*

gymnastics [dʒim'næstiks] *pl* gymnastikk *m*

gynaecologist [,gainə'kɔlədʒist] *n* kvinnelege *m*, gynekolog *m*

H

habit ['hæbit] *n* vane *m*

habitable ['hæbitəbəl] *adj* beboelig

habitual [hə'bitʃuəl] *adj* vanemessig

had [hæd] *v* (p, pp have)

haddock ['hædək] *n* (pl ~) kolje *c*

h(a)emorrhage ['heməridʒ] *n* blødning *m*

haemorrhoids ['hemərɔidz] *pl* hemorroider *pl*

hail [heil] *n* hagl *nt*

hair [hɛə] *n* hår *nt*; ~ **gel** hårgelé

hairbrush ['hɛəbrʌʃ] *n* hårbørste *m*

haircut ['hɛəkʌt] *n* hårklipp *m*

hairdo ['hɛəduː] *n* frisyre *m*

hairdresser ['hɛə,dresə] *n* frisør *m*

hairdrier, hairdryer ['hɛədraiə] *n* hårtørrer *m*

hairpin ['hɛəpin] *n* hårspenne *c*

hair spray ['hɛəsprei] *n* hårlakk *m*

hairy ['hɛəri] *adj* håret

half¹ [hɑːf] *adj* halv

half² [hɑːf] *n* (pl halves) halvdel *m*

half time [,hɑːf'taim] *n* halvtid *c*

halfway [,hɑːf'wei] *adv* halvveis

halibut ['hælibət] *n* (pl ~) kveite *c*

hall [hɔːl] *n* vestibyle *m*; sal *m*

halt [hɔːlt] *v* stanse

halve [hɑːv] *v* halvere

ham [hæm] *n* skinke *c*

hamlet ['hæmlət] *n* liten landsby

hammer ['hæmə] *n* hammer *m*

hammock ['hæmək] *n* hengekøye *c*

hamper ['hæmpə] *n* kurv *m*

hand [hænd] *n* hånd *c*; *v* *overrekke; ~ **cream** håndkrem *m*

handbag ['hændbæg] *n* håndveske *c*

handbook ['hændbuk] *n* håndbok *c*

handbrake ['hændbreik] *n*

håndbrems *m*

handcuffs ['hændkʌfs] *pl* håndjern *pl*

handful ['hændful] *n* håndfull *m*

handicraft ['hændikrɑːft] *n* håndverk *nt*; kunsthåndverk *nt*

handicap ['hændikæp] *n* handikap *nt*; funksjonshemming *c*

handkerchief ['hæŋkətʃif] *n* lommetørkle *nt*

handle ['hændəl] *n* skaft *nt*, håndtak *nt*; *v* håndtere; behandle

hand-made [,hænd'meid] *adj* håndlaget

handshake ['hændʃeik] *n* håndtrykk *nt*

handsome ['hænsəm] *adj* pen

handwork ['hændwɜːk] *n* håndarbeid *nt*

handwriting ['hænd,raitiŋ] *n* håndskrift *c*

handy ['hændi] *adj* hendig

*****hang** [hæŋ] *v* *henge

hanger ['hæŋə] *n* henger *m*

hangover ['hæŋ,ouvə] *n* bakrus *m*, tømmermenn *pl*

happen ['hæpən] *v* hende, skje

happening ['hæpəniŋ] *n* hendelse *m*, begivenhet *c*

happiness ['hæpinəs] *n* lykke *c*

happy ['hæpi] *adj* lykkelig, glad

harbour ['hɑːbə] *n* havn *c*

hard [hɑːd] *adj* hard; vanskelig; **~ disk** harddisk; **hardly** neppe

hardware ['hɑːdweə] *n* jernvarer *pl*; **~ store** jernvarehandel *m*

hare [hɛə] *n* hare *m*

harm [hɑːm] *n* skade *m*; fortred *m*; *v* skade

harmful ['hɑːmfəl] *adj* skadelig

harmless ['hɑːmləs] *adj* uskadelig; harmløs

harmony ['hɑːməni] *n* harmoni *m*

harp [hɑːp] *n* harpe *c*

harpsichord ['hɑːpsikɔːd] *n* cembalo

m

harsh [hɑːʃ] *adj* streng; grusom

harvest ['hɑːvist] *n* avling *c*

has [hæz] *v* (pr have)

haste [heist] *n* hast *m*

hasten ['heisən] *v* skynde seg

hasty ['heisti] *adj* hurtig; forhastet

hat [hæt] *n* hatt *m*

hatch [hætʃ] *n* luke *c*; *v* ruge ut

hate [heit] *v* avsky; hate; *n* hat *nt*

hatred ['heitrid] *n* hat *nt*

haughty ['hɔːti] *adj* hovmodig

haul [hɔːl] *v* slepe

*****have** [hæv] *v* *ha; *få; **~ to** *måtte

hawk [hɔːk] *n* hauk *m*; falk *m*

hay [hei] *n* høy *nt*; **~ fever** høysnue *m*

hazard ['hæzəd] *n* risiko *m*

haze [heiz] *n* dis *m*

hazelnut ['heizəlnʌt] *n* hasselnøtt *c*

hazy ['heizi] *adj* disig

he [hiː] *pron* han

head [hed] *n* hode *nt*; *v* lede; **~ of state** statsoverhode *nt*; **~ teacher** overlærer *m*; **~ waiter** hovmester *m*

headache ['hedeik] *n* hodepine *c*

heading ['hediŋ] *n* overskrift *c*

headlamp ['hedlæmp] *n* frontlys *nt*

headland ['hedlənd] *n* odde *m*

headlight ['hedlait] *n* frontlys *nt*

headline ['hedlain] *n* overskrift *c*

headmaster [,hed'mɑːstə] *n* overlærer *m*; rektor *m*

headquarters [,hed'kwɔːtəz] *pl* hovedkvarter *nt*

headrest ['hedrest] *n* nakkestøtte *c*

head-strong ['hedstrɔŋ] *adj* sta

heal [hiːl] *v* hele, lege

health [helθ] *n* helse *c*; **~ certificate** helseattest *m*

healthy ['helθi] *adj* sunn

heap [hiːp] *n* hop *m*, haug *m*

*****hear** [hiə] *v* høre

hearing ['hiəriŋ] *n* hørsel *m*

heart [hɑːt] *n* hjerte *nt*; kjerne *m*; **by ~**

utenat; ~ **attack** hjerteanfall nt

heartburn ['hɑːtbɜːn] n halsbrann m

hearth [hɑːθ] n ildsted nt

heartless ['hɑːtləs] adj hjerteløs

hearty ['hɑːti] adj hjertelig

heat [hiːt] n hete m, varme m; v varme opp; **heating pad** varmepute c

heater ['hiːtə] n varmeovn m

heath [hiːθ] n hei c

heathen ['hiːðən] n hedning m; adj hedensk

heather ['heðə] n lyng m

heating ['hiːtiŋ] n fyring c

heaven ['hevən] n himmel m

heavy ['hevi] adj tung

Hebrew ['hiːbruː] n hebraisk nt

hedge [hedʒ] n hekk m

hedgehog ['hedʒhɔg] n pinnsvin nt

heel [hiːl] n hæl m

height [hait] n høyde m; høydepunkt nt

heir [ɛə] n arving m

heiress [ɛərəs] n kvinnelig arving m

helicopter ['helikʌptə] n helikopter nt

hell [hel] n helvete nt

hello! [he'lou] hei!, hallo!; **say hello to** hilse på

helm [helm] n ror nt

helmet ['helmit] n hjelm m

helmsman ['helmzmən] n rormann m

help [help] v *hjelpe; n hjelp c

helper ['helpə] n hjelper m

helpful ['helpfəl] adj hjelpsom

helping ['helpiŋ] n porsjon m

hem [hem] n fald m; søm m

hemp [hemp] n hamp m

hen [hen] n høne c

her [hɜː] pron henne; hennes

herb [hɜːb] n urt c

herd [hɜːd] n flokk m; bøling m

here [hiə] adv her; ~ **you are!** vær så god!

hereditary [hi'reditəri] adj arvelig

hernia ['hɜːniə] n brokk m/nt

hero ['hiərou] n (pl ~es) helt m

heron ['herən] n hegre m

herring ['heriŋ] n (pl ~, ~s) sild c

herself [hɜː'self] pron seg; selv

hesitate ['heziteit] v nøle

heterosexual [,hetərə'sekʃuəl] adj heteroseksuell

hiccup ['hikʌp] n hikke c

hide [haid] n skinn nt

*hide** [haid] v gjemme; skjule

hideous ['hidiəs] adj avskyelig

hierarchy ['haiərɑːki] n hierarki nt

high [hai] adj høy

highway ['haiwei] n riksvei m; motorvei m

hijack ['haidʒæk] v kapre

hijacker ['haidʒækə] n kaprer m

hike [haik] v *gå fotturer

hill [hil] n bakke m

hillside ['hilsaid] n li c; bakke m

hilltop ['hiltɔp] n bakketopp m

hilly ['hili] adj kupert

him [him] pron han, ham

himself [him'self] pron seg; selv

hinder ['hində] v hindre

hinge [hindʒ] n hengsel nt

hint [hint] n hint; antydning

hip [hip] n hofte c

hire [haiə] v leie; **for ~** til leie

hire purchase [,haiə'pɜːtʃəs] n avbetalingskjøp nt

his [hiz] adj hans

historian [hi'stɔːriən] n historiker m

historic [hi'stɔrik] adj historisk

historical [hi'stɔrikəl] adj historisk

history ['histəri] n historie c

hit [hit] n suksess m; slag nt; treff nt

*hit** [hit] v *slå; ramme, *treffe

hitchhike ['hitʃhaik] v haike

hitchhiker ['hitʃ,haikə] n haiker m

hoarse [hɔːs] adj hes

hobby ['hɔbi] n hobby m

hobbyhorse ['hɔbihɔːs] n kjepphest

m

hockey ['hɔki] *n* hockey *m*

hoist [hɔist] *v* heise

hold [hould] *n* lasterom *nt*

*hold [hould] *v* *holde, *holde på; *beholde; ~ **on** *holde seg fast; ~ **up** *holde oppe, støtte

hold-up ['houldʌp] *n* overfall *nt*

hole [houl] *n* hull *nt*

holiday ['hɔlədi] *n* ferie *m*; helligdag *m*; ~ **camp** ferieleir *m*; ~ **resort** feriested *nt*; **on** ~ på ferie

Holland ['hɔlənd] Holland

hollow ['hɔlou] *adj* hul

holy ['houli] *adj* hellig

homage ['hɔmidʒ] *n* hyllest *m*

home [houm] *n* hjem *nt*; pleiehjem *nt*; *adv* hjemover, hjemme; **at** ~ hjemme

homework ['houmwəːk] *n* hjemmelekser *pl*, lekser *pl*

home-made [,houm'meid] *adj* hjemmelaget

homesickness ['houm,siknəs] *n* hjemlengsel *m*

homosexual [,houmə'sekʃuəl] *adj* homoseksuell; homofil

honest ['ɔnist] *adj* ærlig; oppriktig

honesty ['ɔnisti] *n* ærlighet *c*

honey ['hʌni] *n* honning *m*

honeymoon ['hʌnimuːn] *n* hvetebrødsdager *pl*, bryllupsreise *c*

honk [hʌŋk] *vAm* tute

honour ['ɔnə] *n* ære *c*; *v* hedre, ære

honourable ['ɔnərəbəl] *adj* ærefull, hederlig; rettskaffen

hood [hud] *n* hette *c*; motorpanser *nt*

hoof [huːf] *n* hov *m*

hook [huk] *n* krok *m*

hoot [huːt] *v* tute

hooter ['huːtə] *n* bilhorn *nt*

hop[1] [hɔp] *v* hoppe; *n* hopp *nt*

hop[2] [hɔp] *n* humle *c*

hope [houp] *n* håp *nt*; *v* håpe

hopeful ['houpfəl] *adj* håpefull

hopeless ['houpləs] *adj* håpløs

horizon [hə'raizən] *n* horisont *m*

horizontal [,hɔri'zɔntəl] *adj* horisontal

horn [hɔːn] *n* horn *nt*; signalhorn *nt*

horrible ['hɔribəl] *adj* redselsfull; grusom, avskyelig, skrekkelig

horror ['hɔrə] *n* gru *m*, redsel *m*

hors d'œuvre [ɔːˈdəːvr] *n* forrett *m*

horse [hɔːs] *n* hest *m*

horseman ['hɔːsmən] *n* (pl -men) rytter *m*

horsepower ['hɔːs,pauə] *n* hestekraft *c*

horserace ['hɔːsreis] *n* hesteveddeløp *m*

horseradish ['hɔːs,rædiʃ] *n* pepperrot *c*

horseshoe ['hɔːsʃuː] *n* hestesko *m*

hospitable ['hɔspitəbəl] *adj* gjestfri

hospital ['hɔspitəl] *n* sykehus *nt*, hospital *nt*

hospitality [,hɔspi'tæləti] *n* gjestfrihet *c*

host [houst] *n* vert *m*

hostage ['hɔstidʒ] *n* gissel *nt*

hostess ['houstis] *n* vertinne *c*

hostile ['hɔstail] *adj* fiendtlig

hot [hɔt] *adj* het, varm

hotel [hou'tel] *n* hotell *nt*

hot-tempered [,hɔt'tempəd] *adj* hissig

hour [auə] *n* time *m*

hourly ['auəli] *adj* hver time

house [haus] *n* hus *nt*; bolig *m*; ~ **agent** eiendomsmegler *m*; ~ **block** *Am* kvartal *nt*; **public** ~ vertshus *nt*

houseboat ['hausbout] *n* husbåt *m*

household ['haushould] *n* husstand *m*

housekeeper ['haus,kiːpə] *n* husholderske *c*

housekeeping ['haus,kiːpiŋ] *n* husholdning *m*

housemaid ['hausmeid] n hushjelp c
housewife ['hauswaif] n husmor c
housework ['hauswə:k] n husarbeid nt
how [hau] adv hvordan; hvor; ~ **many** hvor mange; ~ **much** hvor mye
however [hau'evə] conj likevel
hug [hʌg] v omfavne; klemme; n klem m
huge [hju:dʒ] adj svær, veldig, enorm
hum [hʌm] v nynne
human ['hju:mən] adj menneskelig; ~ **being** menneske nt
humanity [hju'mænəti] n menneskehet c
humble ['hʌmbəl] adj ydmyk
humid ['hju:mid] adj fuktig
humidity [hju'midəti] n fuktighet c
humorous ['hju:mərəs] adj vittig, morsom, humoristisk
humo(u)r ['hju:mə] n humor m
hundred ['hʌndrəd] n hundre
Hungarian [hʌŋ'gəəriən] adj ungarsk; n ungarer m
Hungary ['hʌŋgəri] Ungarn

hunger ['hʌŋgə] n sult m
hungry ['hʌŋgri] adj sulten
hunt [hʌnt] v jakte; n jakt c; ~ **for** lete etter
hunter ['hʌntə] n jeger m
hurricane ['hʌrikən] n orkan m; ~ **lamp** stormlykt c
hurry ['hʌri] v forte seg, skynde seg; n hastverk nt; **in a** ~ i full fart
*****hurt** [hə:t] v *gjøre vondt, skade; såre
hurtful ['hə:tfəl] adj skadelig
husband ['hʌzbənd] n ektemann m; mann m
hut [hʌt] n hytte c
hydrogen ['haidrədʒən] n vannstoff nt
hygiene ['haidʒi:n] n hygiene m
hygienic [hai'dʒi:nik] adj hygienisk
hymn [him] n hymne m, salme m
hyphen ['haifən] n bindestrek m
hypocrisy [hi'pɔkrəsi] n hykleri nt
hypocrite ['hipəkrit] n hykler m
hypocritical [,hipə'kritikəl] adj hyklersk, skinnhellig
hysterical [hi'sterikəl] adj hysterisk

I

I [ai] pron jeg
ice [ais] n is m; ~ **cream** iskrem m
Iceland ['aislənd] Island
Icelander ['aisləndə] n islending m
Icelandic [ais'lændik] adj islandsk
icon ['aikɔn] n ikon m/nt
ID [ai'di:] n identitetskort nt
idea [ai'diə] n idé m; tanke m, innfall nt; begrep nt, forestilling c
ideal [ai'diəl] adj ideell; n ideal nt
identical [ai'dentikəl] adj identisk
identification [ai,dentifi'keiʃən] n identifisering c

identify [ai'dentifai] v identifisere
identity [ai'dentəti] n identitet m; ~ **card** identitetskort nt
idiom ['idiəm] n idiom nt
idiomatic [,idiə'mætik] adj idiomatisk
idiot ['idiət] n idiot m
idiotic [,idi'ɔtik] adj idiotisk
idle ['aidəl] adj uvirksom; lat; nytteløs
idol ['aidəl] n avgud m; idol nt
if [if] conj hvis; om
ignition [ig'niʃən] n tenning c; ~ **coil** tennspole m

ignorant ['ignərənt] *adj* uvitende
ignore [ig'nɔ:] *v* ignorere
ill [il] *adj* syk; dårlig
illegal [i'li:gəl] *adj* illegal, ulovlig
illegible [i'ledʒəbəl] *adj* uleselig
illiterate [i'litərət] *n* analfabet *m*
illness ['ilnəs] *n* sykdom *m*
illuminate [i'lu:mineit] *v* opplyse, belyse
illumination [i,lu:mi'neiʃən] *n* belysning *m*
illusion [i'lu:ʒən] *n* illusjon *m*; fantasifoster *nt*
illustrate ['iləstreit] *v* illustrere
illustration [,ilə'streiʃən] *n* illustrasjon *m*
image ['imidʒ] *n* bilde *nt*
imaginary [i'mædʒinəri] *adj* innbilt
imagination [i,mædʒi'neiʃən] *n* fantasi *m*
imagine [i'mædʒin] *v* forestille seg; innbille seg; tenke seg
imitate ['imiteit] *v* imitere, etterligne
imitation [,imi'teiʃən] *n* imitasjon *m*, etterligning *c*
immediate [i'mi:djət] *adj* øyeblikkelig
immediately [i'mi:djətli] *adv* straks, øyeblikkelig, umiddelbart
immense [i'mens] *adj* enorm, veldig, umåtelig
immigrant ['imigrənt] *n* innvandrer *m*
immigrate ['imigreit] *v* immigrere
immigration [,imi'greiʃən] *n* immigrasjon *m*
immodest [i'mɔdist] *adj* ubeskjeden
immunity [i'mju:nəti] *n* immunitet *m*
immunize ['imjunaiz] *v* *gjøre immun
impartial [im'pɑ:ʃəl] *adj* upartisk
impassable [im'pɑ:səbəl] *adj* ufremkommelig
impatient [im'peiʃənt] *adj* utålmodig
impede [im'pi:d] *v* hindre, sinke

impediment [im'pedimənt] *n* hindring *c*
imperfect [im'pə:fikt] *adj* ufullkommen
imperial [im'piəriəl] *adj* keiserlig; riks-
impersonal [im'pə:sənəl] *adj* upersonlig
impertinence [im'pə:tinəns] *n* frekkhet *c*
impertinent [im'pə:tinənt] *adj* uforskammet, nesevis
implement¹ ['implimənt] *n* verktøy *nt*
implement² ['impliment] *v* iverksette, implementere
imply [im'plai] *v* antyde; *innebære
impolite [,impə'lait] *adj* uhøflig
import¹ [im'pɔ:t] *v* importere, innføre
import² ['impɔ:t] *n* innførsel *m*, importvarer *pl*, import *m*; ~ **duty** importavgift *c*
importance [im'pɔ:təns] *n* viktighet *c*, betydning *m*
important [im'pɔ:tənt] *adj* betydningsfull, viktig
importer [im'pɔ:tə] *n* importør *m*
imposing [im'pouziŋ] *adj* imponerende
impossible [im'pɔsəbəl] *adj* umulig
impotence ['impətəns] *n* impotens *m*
impotent ['impətənt] *adj* impotent; avmektig
impress [im'pres] *v* *gjøre inntrykk på, imponere
impression [im'preʃən] *n* inntrykk *nt*
impressive [im'presiv] *adj* imponerende
imprison [im'prizən] *v* fengsle
imprisonment [im'prizənmənt] *n* fangenskap *nt*
improbable [im'prɔbəbəl] *adj* usannsynlig
improper [im'prɔpə] *adj* upassende
improve [im'pru:v] *v* forbedre

improvement [im'pruːvmənt] *n*
forbedring *c*

improvise ['imprəvaiz] *v* improvisere

impudent ['impjudənt] *adj*
uforskammet

impulse ['impʌls] *n* impuls *m*;
innskytelse *m*

impulsive [im'pʌlsiv] *adj* impulsiv

in [in] *prep* i; om; *adv* inn

inaccessible [i‚næk'sesəbəl] *adj*
utilgjengelig

inaccurate [i'nækjurət] *adj*
unøyaktig

inadequate [i'nædikwət] *adj*
utilstrekkelig

incapable [iŋ'keipəbəl] *adj* udugelig

incense ['insens] *n* røkelse *m*

inch ['intʃ] *n* tomme *m* (2,54 cm)

incident ['insidənt] *n* hendelse *m*

incidental [‚insi'dentəl] *adj* tilfeldig

incite [in'sait] *v* anspore, egge

inclination [‚iŋkli'neiʃən] *n*
tilbøyelighet *c*

incline [iŋ'klain] *n* skråning *m*

inclined [iŋ'klaind] *adj* tilbøyelig

include [iŋ'kluːd] *v* innbefatte,
omfatte; **included** inkludert

inclusive [iŋ'kluːsiv] *adj* inklusive

income ['iŋkəm] *n* inntekt *c*; ~ **tax**
inntektsskatt *m*

incompetent [iŋ'kɔmpətənt] *adj*
inkompetent; udugelig

incomplete [‚inkəm'pliːt] *adj*
ufullstendig

inconceivable [‚iŋkən'siːvəbəl] *adj*
utenkelig

inconspicuous [‚iŋkən'spikjuəs] *adj*
uanselig

inconvenience [‚iŋkən'viːnjəns] *n*
ubeleilighet *c*, besvær *nt*

inconvenient [‚iŋkən'viːnjənt] *adj*
ubeleilig; besværlig

incorrect [‚iŋkə'rekt] *adj* uriktig, feil

increase[1] [iŋ'kriːs] *v* øke; forsterke,

*tilta

increase[2] ['iŋkriːs] *n* vekst *m*; stigning *m*

incredible [iŋ'kredəbəl] *adj* utrolig

incurable [iŋ'kjuərəbəl] *adj*
uhelbredelig

indecent [in'diːsənt] *adj* uanstendig

indeed [in'diːd] *adv* virkelig

indefinite [in'definit] *adj* ubestemt;
uklar

indemnity [in'demnəti] *n*
skadeserstatning *m*; erstatning *m*

independence [‚indi'pendəns] *n*
uavhengighet *c*

independent [‚indi'pendənt] *adj*
uavhengig; selvstendig

index ['indeks] *n* fortegnelse *m*,
register *nt*; ~ **finger** pekefinger *m*

India ['indiə] India

Indian ['indiən] *adj* indisk; indiansk; *n*
inder *m*; indianer *m*

indicate ['indikeit] *v* antyde, anvise,
*angi

indication [‚indi'keiʃən] *n* tegn *nt*

indicator ['indikeitə] *n* blinklys *nt*

indifferent [in'difərənt] *adj* likegyldig

indigestion [‚indi'dʒestʃən] *n* dårlig
fordøyelse

indignation [‚indig'neiʃən] *n*
forargelse *m*

indirect [‚indi'rekt] *adj* indirekte

individual [‚indi'vidʒuəl] *adj*
individuell, enkelt; *n* enkeltperson *m*,
individ *nt*

Indonesia [‚ində'niːziə] Indonesia

Indonesian [‚ində'niːziən] *adj*
indonesisk; *n* indonesier *m*

indoor ['indɔː] *adj* innendørs

indoors [‚in'dɔːz] *adv* inne

indulge [in'dʌldʒ] *v* *gi etter; *hengi
seg til

industrial [in'dʌstriəl] *adj* industriell;
~ **area** industriområde *nt*

industrious [in'dʌstriəs] *adj* flittig

industry ['indəstri] n industri m; næring c

inedible [i'nedibəl] adj uspiselig

inefficient [,ini'fiʃənt] adj udugelig; ineffektiv

inevitable [i'nevitəbəl] adj uunngåelig

inexpensive [,inik'spensiv] adj billig

inexperienced [,inik'spiəriənst] adj uerfaren

infant ['infənt] n spedbarn nt

infantry ['infəntri] n infanteri nt

infect [in'fekt] v infisere, smitte

infection [in'fekʃən] n smitte m

infectious [in'fekʃəs] adj smittsom

infer [in'fə:] v utlede

inferior [in'fiəriə] adj dårligere, underlegen; mindreverdig; nedre

infinite ['infinət] adj uendelig

infinitive [in'finitiv] n infinitiv m

inflammable [in'flæməbəl] adj ildsfarlig

inflammation [,inflə'meiʃən] n betennelse m

inflatable [in'fleitəbəl] adj oppblåsbar

inflate [in'fleit] v blåse opp

inflation [in'fleiʃən] n inflasjon m

inflict [in'flikt] v tilføye

influence ['influəns] n innflytelse m; v påvirke

influential [,influ'enʃəl] adj innflytelsesrik

influenza [,influ'enzə] n influensa m

inform [in'fɔ:m] v opplyse, informere; underrette, meddele

informal [in'fɔ:məl] adj uformell

information [,infə'meiʃən] n informasjon m; meddelelse m, opplysning m; ~ bureau informasjonskontor nt

infra-red [,infrə'red] adj infrarød

infrequent [in'fri:kwənt] adj sjelden

ingredient [iŋ'gri:diənt] n bestanddel

m, ingrediens m

inhabit [in'hæbit] v bebo

inhabitable [in'hæbitəbəl] adj beboelig

inhabitant [in'hæbitənt] n innbygger m; beboer m

inhale [in'heil] v innånde

inherit [in'herit] v arve

inheritance [in'heritəns] n arv m

inhibit [in'hibit] v hemme; forhindre

initial [i'niʃəl] adj opprinnelig, begynnelses-; n forbokstav m; v merke med initialer

initiate [i'niʃieit] v innføre; *ta initiativet til

initiative [i'niʃətiv] n initiativ nt

inject [in'dʒekt] v innsprøyte

injection [in'dʒekʃən] n injeksjon m

injure ['indʒə] v skade, kveste; krenke

injury ['indʒəri] n skade m; krenkelse m

injustice [in'dʒʌstis] n urett m

ink [iŋk] n blekk nt

inlet ['inlet] n vik c

inn [in] n vertshus nt

inner ['inə] adj indre

innkeeper ['in,ki:pə] n vertshusholder m

innocence ['inəsəns] n uskyld c

innocent ['inəsənt] adj uskyldig

inoculate [i'nɔkjuleit] v vaksinere

inoculation [i,nɔkju'leiʃən] n vaksinasjon m

inquire [iŋ'kwaiə] v *forespørre, forhøre seg

inquiry [iŋ'kwaiəri] n forespørsel m; etterforskning m; ~ office informasjonskontor m

inquisitive [iŋ'kwizətiv] adj nysgjerrig

insane [in'sein] adj sinnssyk

inscription [in'skripʃən] n inskripsjon m

insect ['insekt] n insekt nt; ~

repellent insektmiddel *nt*

insecticide [in'sektisaid] *n* insektmiddel *nt*

insensitive [in'sensətiv] *adj* ufølsom

insert [in'sə:t] *v* *sette inn, *innskyte

inside [,in'said] *n* innside *c*; *adj* indre; *adv* inne; inni; *prep* innen, innenfor; ~ **out** vrengt; **insides** innvoller *pl*

insight [in'sait] *n* innsikt *m*

insignificant [,insig'nifikənt] *adj* ubetydelig; intetsigende, uanselig; uvesentlig

insist [in'sist] *v* insistere; *fastholde

insolence ['insələns] *n* uforskammethet *c*

insolent ['insələnt] *adj* uforskammet, frekk

insomnia [in'somniə] *n* søvnløshet *c*

inspect [in'spekt] *v* inspisere

inspection [in'spekʃən] *n* inspeksjon *m*; kontroll *m*

inspector [in'spektə] *n* inspektør *m*

inspire [in'spaiə] *v* inspirere

install [in'stɔ:l] *v* installere

installation [,instə'leiʃən] *n* installasjon *m*

instal(l)ment [in'stɔ:lmənt] *n* avdrag *nt*; **installment plan** *Am* avbetalingskjøp *nt*

instance ['instəns] *n* eksempel *nt*; tilfelle *nt*; **for** ~ for eksempel

instant ['instənt] *n* øyeblikk *nt*

instantly ['instəntli] *adv* øyeblikkelig, straks, umiddelbart

instead of [in'sted ɔv] istedenfor

instinct ['instiŋkt] *n* instinkt *nt*

institute ['institju:t] *n* institutt *nt*; forordning *m*; *v* opprette, stifte

institution [,insti'tju:ʃən] *n* institusjon *m*, stiftelse *m*

instruct [in'strʌkt] *v* undervise

instruction [in'strʌkʃən] *n* undervisning *c*; veiledning *m*

instructive [in'strʌktiv] *adj* lærerik

instructor [in'strʌktə] *n* instruktør *m*

instrument ['instrumənt] *n* instrument *nt*; **musical** ~ musikkinstrument *nt*

insufficient [,insə'fiʃənt] *adj* utilstrekkelig

insulate ['insjuleit] *v* isolere

insulation [,insju'leiʃən] *n* isolasjon *m*

insulator ['insjuleitə] *n* isolator *m*

insult[1] [in'sʌlt] *v* fornærme

insult[2] ['insʌlt] *n* fornærmelse *m*

insurance [in'ʃuərəns] *n* forsikring *c*; ~ **policy** forsikringspolise *m*

insure [in'ʃuə] *v* forsikre

intact [in'tækt] *adj* intakt

integrate ['intəgreit] *integrere*; *innlemme*

intellect ['intəlekt] *n* intellekt *nt*, forstand *m*

intellectual [,intə'lektʃuəl] *adj* intellektuell

intelligence [in'telidʒəns] *n* intelligens *m*

intelligent [in'telidʒənt] *adj* intelligent

intend [in'tend] *v* *ha til hensikt

intense [in'tens] *adj* intens

intention [in'tenʃən] *n* hensikt *m*

intentional [in'tenʃənəl] *adj* tilsiktet

intercourse ['intəkɔ:s] *n* omgang *m*

interest ['intrəst] *n* interesse *m*; rente *c*; *v* interessere

interested ['intristid] *adj* interessert

interesting ['intrəstiŋ] *adj* interessant

interfere [,intə'fiə] *v* *gripe inn; ~ **with** blande seg inn i

interference [,intə'fiərəns] *n* innblanding *c*

interim ['intərim] *n* mellomtid *c*; *adj* foreløpig

interior [in'tiəriə] *n* innside *c*

interlude ['intəlu:d] *n* mellomspill *nt*

intermediary [,intə'mi:djəri] *n*

mellommann *m*

intermission [ˌintə'miʃən] *n* pause *m*

internal [in'tə:nəl] *adj* indre

international [ˌintə'næʃənəl] *adj* internasjonal

Internet [in'tənet] *n* Internett *nt*, nett *nt*

interpret [in'tə:prit] *v* tolke

interpreter [in'tə:pritə] *n* tolk *m*

interrogate [in'terəgeit] *v* forhøre

interrogation [inˌterə'geiʃən] *n* forhør *nt*

interrupt [ˌintə'rʌpt] *v* *avbryte

interruption [ˌintə'rʌpʃən] *n* avbrytelse *m*

intersection [ˌintə'sekʃən] *n* veikryss *nt*

interval ['intəvəl] *n* pause *m*; intervall *nt*

intervene [ˌintə'vi:n] *v* *gripe inn

interview ['intəvju:] *n* intervju *nt*

intestine [in'testin] *n* tarm *m*; **intestines** tarmer

intimate ['intimət] *adj* intim

into ['intu] *prep* inn i

intolerable [in'tɔlərəbəl] *adj* utålelig

intoxicated [in'tɔksikeitid] *adj* beruset

intrigue [in'tri:g] *n* intrige *m*

introduce [ˌintrə'dju:s] *v* introdusere, presentere, innføre

introduction [ˌintrə'dʌkʃən] *n* presentasjon *m*; innledning *m*

invade [in'veid] *v* trenge inn

invalid¹ ['invəli:d] *n* funksjonshemmet *m*, ufør *m*; *adj* funksjonshemmet, ufør

invalid² [in'vælid] *adj* ugyldig

invasion [in'veiʒən] *n* invasjon *m*

invent [in'vent] *v* *oppfinne; oppdikte

invention [in'venʃən] *n* oppfinnelse *m*

inventive [in'ventiv] *adj* oppfinnsom

inventor [in'ventə] *n* oppfinner *m*

inventory ['invəntri] *n* inventar *nt*; inventarliste *c*

invert [in'və:t] *v* snu om

invest [in'vest] *v* investere

investigate [in'vestigeit] *v* etterforske

investigation [inˌvesti'geiʃən] *n* undersøkelse *m*; etterforskning *m*

investment [in'vestmənt] *n* investering *c*; kapitalanbringelse *m*, pengeanbringelse *m*

invisible [in'vizəbəl] *adj* usynlig

invitation [ˌinvi'teiʃən] *n* innbydelse *m*

invite [in'vait] *v* *innby, invitere

invoice ['invɔis] *n* faktura *m*

involve [in'vɔlv] *v* innblande

inwards ['inwədz] *adv* innover

iodine ['aiədi:n] *n* jod *m*

Iran [i'ra:n] Iran

Iranian [i'reiniən] *adj* iransk; *n* iraner *m*

Iraq [i'ra:k] Irak

Iraqi [i'ra:ki] *adj* irakisk; *n* iraker *m*

Ireland ['aiələnd] Irland

Irish ['aiəriʃ] *adj* irsk

Irishman ['aiəriʃmən] *n* (pl -men) irlending *m*

iron ['aiən] *n* jern *nt*; strykejern *nt*; jern-; *v* *stryke

ironical [ai'rɔnikəl] *adj* ironisk

irony ['aiərəni] *n* ironi *m*

irregular [i'regjulə] *adj* uregelmessig

irreparable [i'repərəbəl] *adj* ubotelig

irrevocable [i'revəkəbəl] *adj* ugjenkallelig

irritable ['iritəbəl] *adj* irritabel

irritate ['iriteit] *v* irritere, ergre

is [iz] *v* (pr be)

island ['ailənd] *n* øy *c*

isolate ['aisəleit] *v* isolere

isolation [ˌaisə'leiʃən] *n* isolasjon *m*

Israel ['izreil] Israel

Israeli [iz'reili] *adj* israelsk; *n* israeler *m*

issue ['iʃu:] *v* utstede; *utgi; *n* utstedelse *m*; utgivelse *m*; spørsmål *nt*, sak *c*; utgang *m*, resultat *nt*, følge *m*, sluttresultat *nt*; utvei *m*

it [it] *pron* det

Italian [i'tæljən] *adj* italiensk; *n* italiener *m*

Italy ['itəli] Italia

itch [itʃ] *n* kløe *m*; *v* klø

item ['aitəm] *n* post *m*; punkt *nt*

itinerary [ai'tinərəri] *n* reiserute *c*, reiseplan *m*

its [its] *pron* dens, dets

itself [it'self] *pron* seg; seg selv; selv; **by ~** alene; av seg selv

ivory ['aivəri] *n* elfenbein *nt*

ivy ['aivi] *n* eføy *m*

J

jack [dʒæk] *n* jekk *m*

jacket ['dʒækit] *n* dressjakke *c*, jakke *c*; omslag *nt*

jade [dʒeid] *n* jade *m*

jail [dʒeil] *n* fengsel *m*

jam [dʒæm] *n* syltetøy *nt*; trafikkkork *m*

janitor ['dʒænitə] *n* vaktmester *m*

January ['dʒænjuəri] januar

Japan [dʒə'pæn] Japan

Japanese [,dʒæpə'ni:z] *adj* japansk; *n* japaner *m*

jar [dʒɑ:] *n* krukke *c*

jargon [dʒɑ:gən] *n* sjargong *m*

jaundice ['dʒɔ:ndis] *n* gulsott *m*

jaw [dʒɔ:] *n* kjeve *m*

jealous ['dʒeləs] *adj* sjalu

jealousy ['dʒeləsi] *n* sjalusi *m*

jeans [dʒi:nz] *pl* dongeribukse *c*, jeans *m*, olabukse *c*

jelly ['dʒeli] *n* gelé *m*

jellyfish ['dʒelifiʃ] *n* manet *m*

jersey ['dʒə:zi] *n* jersey *m*; genser *m*

jet [dʒet] *n* stråle *m*; jetfly *nt*

jetty ['dʒeti] *n* molo *m*

Jew [dʒu:] *n* jøde *m*

jewel ['dʒu:əl] *n* smykke *nt*

jewelry ['dʒu:əlri] *nAm* smykker *pl*

jeweller ['dʒu:ələ] *n* gullsmed *m*

jewellery ['dʒu:əlri] *n* smykker *pl*

Jewish ['dʒu:iʃ] *adj* jødisk

job [dʒɔb] *n* jobb *m*; stilling *c*

jobless ['dʒɔbles] *adj* arbeidsløs

jockey ['dʒɔki] *n* jockey *m*

join [dʒɔin] *v* *forbinde; slutte seg til; forene, sammenføye

joint [dʒɔint] *n* ledd *nt*; *adj* felles, forent; **~ venture** fellesprosjekt *nt*

jointly ['dʒɔintli] *adv* i fellesskap

joke [dʒouk] *n* vits *m*, spøk *m*

jolly ['dʒɔli] *adj* lystig

Jordan ['dʒɔ:dən] Jordan

Jordanian [dʒɔ:'deiniən] *adj* jordansk; *n* jordaner *m*

journal ['dʒə:nəl] *n* tidsskrift *nt*

journalism ['dʒə:nəlizəm] *n* journalistikk *m*

journalist ['dʒə:nəlist] *n* journalist *m*

journey ['dʒə:ni] *n* reise *c*

joy [dʒɔi] *n* glede *c*, fryd *m*

joyful ['dʒɔifəl] *adj* glad

jubilee ['dʒu:bili:] *n* jubileum *nt*

judge [dʒʌdʒ] *n* dommer *m*; *v* dømme; bedømme

judgment ['dʒʌdʒmənt] *n* dom *m*

jug [dʒʌg] *n* mugge *c*

juice [dʒuːs] n saft m
juicy ['dʒuːsi] adj saftig
July [dʒu'lai] juli
jump [dʒʌmp] v hoppe; n hopp nt, sprang nt
junction ['dʒʌŋkʃən] n veikryss nt; knutepunkt nt
June [dʒuːn] juni
jungle ['dʒʌŋgəl] n urskog m, jungel m
junior ['dʒuːnjə] adj junior

junk [dʒʌŋk] n skrap nt
jurisdiction [dʒuərisdikʃən] n jurisdiksjon m
jury ['dʒuəri] n jury m
just [dʒʌst] adj rettferdig, passende; riktig; adv nettopp; akkurat
justice ['dʒʌstis] n rett m; rettferdighet c
justify ['dʒʌstifai] v rettferdiggjøre
juvenile ['dʒuːvənail] adj ungdoms-

K

kangaroo [ˌkæŋgə'ruː] n kenguru m
kayak ['kaijæk] n kajakk m
keel [kiːl] n kjøl m
keen [kiːn] adj begeistret; skarp
*keep [kiːp] v *holde; bevare; *holde på med; ~ **away from** m*holde seg borte fra; ~ **off** *la være; ~ **on** *fortsette; ~ **quiet** tie; ~ **up** *holde ut; ~ **up with** *holde følge med
kennel ['kenəl] n hundehus nt; kennel m
Kenya ['kenjə] Kenya
kerosene ['kerəsiːn] n petroleum m; kerosin m, flybensin m
kettle ['ketəl] n kjele m
key [kiː] n nøkkel m
keyhole ['kiːhoul] n nøkkelhull nt
khaki ['kɑːki] n kaki m
kick [kik] v sparke; n spark nt
kickoff [ˌki'kɔf] n avspark nt
kid [kid] n barn nt, unge m; v skrøne
kidney ['kidni] n nyre c
kill [kil] v drepe, *slå i hjel
kilogram ['kiləgræm] n kilo m/nt
kilometer Am, **kilometre** ['kiləˌmiːtə] n kilometer m
kind [kaind] adj snill, vennlig; god; n

sort m
kindergarten ['kindəˌgɑːtən] n barnehage m, førskole m
king [kiŋ] n konge m
kingdom ['kiŋdəm] n kongerike nt; rike nt
kiosk ['kiːɔsk] n kiosk m
kiss [kis] n kyss nt; v kysse
kit [kit] n utstyr nt
kitchen ['kitʃin] n kjøkken nt; ~ **garden** kjøkkenhage m; ~ **towel** kjøkkenhåndkle nt
knapsack ['næpsæk] n ryggsekk m; ransel m
knave [neiv] n knekt m
knee [niː] n kne nt
kneecap ['niːkæp] n kneskål c
*kneel [niːl] v knele
knew [njuː] v (p know)
knife [naif] n (pl knives) kniv m
knight [nait] n ridder m
*knit [nit] v strikke; **knitting wool** garn nt
knob [nɔb] n knott m
knock [nɔk] v banke; n bank nt; ~ **against** støte på; ~ **down** *slå ned
knot [nɔt] n knute m; v knytte

*know [nou] v *vite; *kunne, kjenne
knowledge ['nɔlidʒ] n kjennskap nt;

kunnskap m
knuckle ['nʌkəl] n knoke m

L

label ['leibəl] n etikett m; v *sette
merkelapp på
laboratory [lə'bɔrətəri] n
laboratorium nt
labo(u)r ['leibə] n arbeid nt;
fødselsveer pl; v *slite, anstrenge seg;
labor permit Am arbeidstillatelse m
labo(u)rer ['leibərə] n arbeider m
labo(u)r-saving ['leibə,seiviŋ] adj
arbeidsbesparende
labyrinth ['læbərinθ] n labyrint m
lace [leis] n kniplinger pl; lisse c
lack [læk] n savn nt, mangel m; v
mangle
lacquer ['lækə] n lakk m
lad [læd] n gutt m
ladder ['lædə] n stige m
lady ['leidi] n dame c; **ladies' room**
dametoalett nt
lagoon [lə'gu:n] n lagune m
lake [leik] n innsjø m
lamb [læm] n lam nt; lammekjøtt nt
lame [leim] adj lam, halt
lamentable ['læməntəbəl] adj
beklagelig
lamp [læmp] n lampe c
lamppost ['læmppoust] n lyktestolpe
m
lampshade ['læmpʃeid] n
lampeskjerm m
land [lænd] n land nt; v lande; *gå i
land
landlady ['lænd,leidi] n vertinne c
landlord ['lændlɔ:d] n vert m, huseier
m; husvert m
landmark ['lændmɑ:k] n landemerke

nt
landscape ['lændskeip] n landskap nt
lane [lein] n smug nt, smal vei; fil m
language ['læŋgwidʒ] n språk nt
lantern ['læntən] n lykt c
lap [læp] n fang nt; runde m; v slikke
lapel [lə'pel] n jakkeslag nt
larder ['lɑ:də] n spiskammer nt
large [lɑ:dʒ] adj stor; rommelig
lark [lɑ:k] n lerke c
laryngitis [,lærin'dʒaitis] n
strupekatarr m
last [lɑ:st] adj sist; forrige; v vare; **at ~**
til slutt
lasting ['lɑ:stiŋ] adj varig
latchkey ['lætʃki:] n entrénøkkel m
late [leit] adj sen; for sent
lately ['leitli] adv i det siste, nylig
lather ['lɑ:ðə] n skum nt
Latin America ['lætin ə'merikə]
Latin-Amerika
Latin-American [,lætinə'merikən]
adj latinamerikansk
latitude ['lætitju:d] n breddegrad m
laugh [lɑ:f] v *le; n latter m
laughter ['lɑ:ftə] n latter m
launch [lɔ:ntʃ] v *sette i gang; *skyte
opp; n motorbåt m
launching ['lɔ:ntʃiŋ] n sjøsetning n
launderette [,lɔ:ndə'ret] n
selvbetjeningsvaskeri nt
laundry ['lɔ:ndri] n vaskeri nt; vask m
lavatory ['lævətəri] n toalett nt
lavish ['læviʃ] adj ødsel
law [lɔ:] n lov m; rett m; **~ court**
domstol m

lawful ['lɔ:fəl] *adj* lovlig
lawn [lɔ:n] *n* gressplen *m*
lawsuit ['lɔ:su:t] *n* rettssak *c*
lawyer ['lɔ:jə] *n* advokat *m*; jurist *m*
laxative ['læksətiv] *n* avføringsmiddel
nt
*****lay** [lei] *v* plassere, *legge, *sette; ~
bricks mure
layer [leiə] *n* lag *nt*
layman ['leimən] *n* lekmann *m*
lazy ['leizi] *adj* doven; lat
*****lead** [li:d] *v* lede
lead[1] [li:d] *n* forsprang *nt*; ledelse *m*;
hunderem *c*
lead[2] [led] *n* bly *nt*
leader ['li:də] *n* fører *m*, anfører *m*
leadership ['li:dəʃip] *n* ledelse *m*;
lederskap *nt*
leading ['li:diŋ] *adj* ledende
leaf [li:f] *n* (pl leaves) blad *nt*
league [li:g] *n* forbund *nt*; liga *m*
leak [li:k] *v* lekke; *n* lekkasje *m*
leaky ['li:ki] *adj* lekk
lean [li:n] *adj* mager
*****lean** [li:n] *v* lene seg
leap [li:p] *n* hopp *nt*
*****leap** [li:p] *v* hoppe
leap year ['li:pjiə] *n* skuddår *nt*
*****learn** [lə:n] *v* lære
learner ['lə:nə] *n* nybegynner *m*
lease [li:s] *n* leiekontrakt *m*;
forpaktning *m*; *v* forpakte bort, leie
ut; leie; lease
leash [li:ʃ] *n* koppel *nt*, bånd *nt*
least [li:st] *adj* minst; **at ~** i det minste;
minst
leather ['leðə] *n* lær *nt*; skinn-, lær-
leave [li:v] *n* permisjon *m*
*****leave** [li:v] *v* *forlate, *gå bort;
*legge igjen, *etterlate; ~ **behind**
*etterlate; ~ **out** *utelate
Lebanese [,lebə'ni:z] *adj* libanesisk;
n libaneser *m*
Lebanon ['lebənən] Libanon

lecture ['lektʃə] *n* foredrag *nt*,
forelesning *m*
left[1] [left] *adj* venstre
left[2] [left] *v* (p, pp leave)
left-hand ['lefthænd] *adj* venstre
left-handed [,left'hændid] *adj*
keivhendt
leg [leg] *n* bein *nt*
legacy ['legəsi] *n* legat *nt*
legal ['li:gəl] *adj* legal; rettslig;
juridisk
legalization [,li:gəlai'zeiʃən] *n*
legalisering *c*
legation [li'geiʃən] *n* legasjon *m*
legible ['ledʒibəl] *adj* leselig
legitimate [li'dʒitimət] *adj* lovlig
leisure ['leʒə] *n* fritid *c*; ro og mak
lemon ['lemən] *n* sitron *m*
lemonade [,lemə'neid] *n* limonade *m*;
brus *m*
*****lend** [lend] *v* låne bort
length [leŋθ] *n* lengde *c*
lengthen ['leŋθən] *v* forlenge
lengthways ['leŋθweiz] *adv* på langs
lens [lenz] *n* linse *c*; **telephoto ~**
teleobjektiv *nt*; **zoom ~** zoomlinse *c*
leprosy ['leprəsi] *n* spedalskhet *c*
lesbian ['lesbiən] *adj* lesbisk
less [les] *adv* mindre
lessen ['lesən] *v* minske, forminske
lesson ['lesən] *n* leksjon *m*, time *m*
*****let** [let] *v* *la; leie ut; ~ **down** svikte
lethal ['li:θəl] *adj* dødelig
letter ['letə] *n* brev *nt*; bokstav *m*; ~ **of**
credit akkreditiv *nt*; ~ **of**
recommendation anbefalingsbrev *nt*
letterbox ['letəbɔks] *n* postkasse *c*
lettuce ['letis] *n* bladsalat *m*
level ['levəl] *adj* jevn; plan; *n* plan *nt*,
nivå *nt*; *v* nivellere, utligne; ~
crossing planovergang *m*
lever ['li:və] *n* vektstang *c*
liability [,laiə'biləti] *n* ansvar *nt*;
forpliktelse *m*

liable ['laiəbəl] adj ansvarlig; ~ to utsatt for

liar ['laiə] n løgner m

liberal ['libərəl] adj liberal; rundhåndet, gavmild

liberation [,libə'reiʃən] n befrielse m

Liberia [lai'biəriə] Liberia

Liberian [lai'biəriən] adj liberisk; n liberier m

liberty ['libəti] n frihet c

library ['laibrəri] n bibliotek nt

licence ['laisəns] n, license nAm bevilling c; tillatelse m; driving ~, driver's ~ Am førerkort nt; ~ number Am registreringsnummer nt; ~ plate nummerskilt nt

license ['laisəns] v *gi tillatelse

lick [lik] v slikke

lid [lid] n lokk nt

lie [lai] v lyve; n løgn c

*lie [lai] v *ligge; ~ down *legge seg ned

life [laif] n (pl lives) liv nt; ~ insurance livsforsikring c; ~ jacket svømmevest m

lifebelt ['laifbelt] n livbelte nt

lifetime ['laiftaim] n levetid c

lift [lift] v løfte; n heis m

light [lait] n lys nt; adj lett; lys; ~ bulb lyspære c

*light [lait] v tenne

lighter ['laitə] n lighter m

lighthouse ['laithaus] n fyrtårn nt

lighting ['laitiŋ] n belysning m

lightning ['laitniŋ] n lyn nt

like [laik] v like; adj lik; conj liksom; prep liksom

likely ['laikli] adj sannsynlig

like-minded [,laik'maindid] adj likesinnet

likewise ['laikwaiz] adv likeså, likeledes

lily ['lili] n lilje c

limb [lim] n lem nt; gren c

lime [laim] n kalk m; lind m; limett m

limetree ['laimtri:] n lindetre nt

limit ['limit] n grense c; v begrense

limp [limp] v halte; adj slapp

line [lain] n linje c; strek m; line c; kø m; stand in ~ Am stå i kø

linen ['linin] n lin nt, lintøy nt

liner ['lainə] n passasjerbåt m

lingerie ['lõʒəri:] n dameundertøy nt

lining ['lainiŋ] n fôr nt

link [liŋk] v *forbinde; n lenke m; ledd nt; link m

lion ['laiən] n løve m

lip [lip] n leppe c; ~ balm leppepomade m

lipstick ['lipstik] n leppestift m

liqueur [li'kjuə] n likør m

liquid ['likwid] adj flytende; n væske c

liquor ['likə] n sprit m; brennevin nt; ~ store Am alkoholutsalg nt

liquorice ['likəris] n lakris m

list [list] n liste c; v *innskrive, regne opp

listen ['lisən] v lytte

listener ['lisnə] n lytter m

liter ['li:tə] nAm liter m

literary ['litrəri] adj litterær

literature ['litrətʃə] n litteratur m

litre ['li:tə] n liter m

litter ['litə] n avfall nt, søppel nt; kull nt

little ['litəl] adj liten; lite

live¹ [liv] v leve; bo

live² [laiv] adj levende; direkte

livelihood ['laivlihud] n levebrød c

lively ['laivli] adj livlig

liver ['livə] n lever c

living ['liviŋ] n liv nt; levebrød nt; adj levende; ~ room dagligstue c; stue c

lizard ['lizəd] n firfisle c

load [loud] n last c; bør c; v laste

loaf [louf] n (pl loaves) brød nt

loan [loun] n lån nt

lobby ['lɔbi] n vestibyle m; foajé m; lobby m

lobster ['lɔbstə] n hummer m

local ['loukəl] adj lokal, stedlig; ~ **call** lokalsamtale m; ~ **train** lokaltog nt

locality [lou'kæləti] n sted nt

locate [lou'keit] v lokalisere

location [lou'keiʃən] n beliggenhet c

lock [lɔk] v låse; n lås m; sluse c; ~ **up** låse opp, sperre inne

locker ['lɔkə] n skap nt

locomotive [,loukə'moutiv] n lokomotiv nt

lodge [lɔdʒ] v huse; n hytte c

lodger ['lɔdʒə] n leieboer m

lodgings ['lɔdʒiŋz] pl losji nt

log [lɔg] n kubbe m; ~ **in** v logge inn; ~ **off** v logge ut

logic ['lɔdʒik] n logikk m

logical ['lɔdʒikəl] adj logisk

lonely ['lounli] adj ensom

long [lɔŋ] adj lang; langvarig; ~ **for** lengte etter; **no longer** ikke lenger

longing ['lɔŋiŋ] n lengsel m

longitude ['lɔndʒitjuːd] n lengdegrad m

look [luk] v *se; synes, *se ut; n blikk nt; utseende nt; ~ **after** sørge for, passe; ~ **at** *se på; ~ **for** lete etter; ~ **out** *se opp, passe seg for; ~ **up** *slå opp

looking-glass ['lukiŋglɑːs] n speil nt

loop [luːp] n løkke c

loose [luːs] adj løs

loosen ['luːsən] v løsne

lord [lɔːd] n lord m; herre m

lorry ['lɔri] n lastebil m

***lose** [luːz] v tape, miste

loser ['luːz ə] n taper m

loss [lɔs] n tap nt

lost [lɔst] adj gått vill; forsvunnet; ~ **and found** hittegods nt; ~ **property office** hittegodskontor nt

lot [lɔt] n lodd m; mengde m, hop m

lotion ['louʃən] n hudkrem m; **aftershave** ~ barbervann nt

lottery ['lɔtəri] n lotteri nt

loud [laud] adj høylydt, høy

loudspeaker [,laud'spiːkə] n høyttaler m

lounge [laundʒ] n salong m; vestibyle m

louse [laus] n (pl lice) lus c

love [lʌv] v elske, *være glad i; n kjærlighet c; **in** ~ forelsket

lovely ['lʌvli] adj yndig, herlig, skjønn

lover ['lʌvə] n elsker m

love story ['lʌv,stɔːri] n kjærlighetshistorie c

low [lou] adj lav; dyp; nedstemt; ~ **tide** fjære c

lower ['louə] v senke; adj lavere

lowlands ['loulændz] pl lavland nt

loyal ['lɔiəl] adj lojal

lubricate ['luːbrikeit] v *smøre

lubrication [,luːbri'keiʃən] n smøring c; ~ **oil** smøreolje c

luck [lʌk] n hell nt; tilfeldighet c; **bad** ~ uflaks m; **good** ~ ! lykke til!

lucky ['lʌki] adj heldig; ~ **charm** amulett m

ludicrous ['luːdikrəs] adj latterlig

luggage ['lʌgidʒ] n bagasje m; **hand** ~ håndbagasje m; **left** ~ **office** bagasjeoppbevaring c; ~ **rack** bagasjehylle c; ~ **van** bagasjevogn c

lukewarm ['luːkwɔːm] adj lunken

lumbago [lʌm'beigou] n lumbago m

luminous ['luːminəs] adj lysende

lump [lʌmp] n klump m, stykke nt; kul m; ~ **of sugar** sukkerbit m; ~ **sum** rund sum

lumpy ['lʌmpi] adj klumpet

lunch [lʌntʃ] n formiddagsmat m, lunsj m

luncheon ['lʌntʃən] n lunsj m

lung [lʌŋ] n lunge c

lust [lʌst] n begjær nt

luxurious [lʌg'ʒuəriəs] adj luksuriøs

luxury ['lʌkʃəri] n luksus m

M

machine [mə'ʃiːn] n maskin m, apparat nt

machinery [mə'ʃiːnəri] n maskineri nt

mackerel ['mækrəl] n (pl ~) makrell m

mackintosh ['mækintɔʃ] n regnfrakk m

mad [mæd] adj gal, vanvittig, rasende

madam ['mædəm] n frue c

madness ['mædnəs] n galskap m

magazine [,mægə'ziːn] n tidsskrift nt

magic ['mædʒik] n magi m, trolldom m; adj magisk

magician [mə'dʒiʃən] n tryllekunstner m

magistrate ['mædʒistreit] n dommer m

magnetic [mæg'netik] adj magnetisk

magnificent [mæg'nifisənt] adj praktfull, storslått

magnify [mæg'nifai] v forstørre, overdrive

magpie ['mægpai] n skjære c

maid [meid] n hushjelp c

maiden name ['meidən neim] pikenavn nt

mail [meil] n post m; v poste; ~ order Am postanvisning m

mailbox ['meilbɔks] nAm postkasse c

main [mein] adj hoved-; størst; ~ deck øverste dekk nt; ~ road hovedvei m; ~ street hovedgate c

mainland ['meinlənd] n fastland nt

mainly ['meinli] adv hovedsakelig

mains [meinz] pl hovedledning m

maintain [mein'tein] v *opprettholde

maintenance ['meintənəns] n vedlikehold nt

maize [meiz] n mais m

major ['meidʒə] adj større; eldre; n major m; dur m

majority [mə'dʒɔrəti] n flertall nt

*make [meik] v lage; tjene; nå; ~ do with nøye seg med; ~ good *godtgjøre; ~ up *sette opp

make-up ['meikʌp] n sminke c

malaria [mə'lɛəriə] n malaria m

Malay [mə'lei] n malaysier m

Malaysia [mə'leiziə] Malaysia

Malaysian [mə'leiziən] adj malaysisk

male [meil] adj hann-

malicious [mə'liʃəs] adj ondskapsfull

malignant [mə'lignənt] adj ondartet

mall [mɔːl] nAm kjøpesenter nt

mallet ['mælit] n kølle c

malnutrition [,mælnju'triʃən] n underernæring c

mammal ['mæməl] n pattedyr nt

mammoth ['mæməθ] n mammut m

man [mæn] n (pl men) mann m; menneske nt; men's room herretoalett nt

manage ['mænidʒ] v bestyre; lykkes

manageable ['mænidʒəbəl] adj håndterlig

management ['mænidʒmənt] n ledelse m; administrasjon m

manager ['mænidʒə] n sjef m, direktør m

mandarin ['mændərin] n mandarin m

mandate ['mændeit] n mandat nt

manger ['meindʒə] n krybbe c

manicure ['mænikjuə] n manikyr m

mankind [mæn'kaind] n menneskehet c

mannequin ['mænəkin] n utstillingsdukke c

manner ['mænə] n måte m, vis nt; manners pl manerer pl

man-of-war [,mænəv'wɔː] n krigsskip nt

manor house ['mænəhaus] n herregård m

mansion ['mænʃən] n herregård m

manual ['mænjuəl] adj hånd-, manuell

manufacture [,mænju'fæktʃə] v fabrikkere

manufacturer [,mænju'fæktʃərə] n fabrikant m

manure [mə'njuə] n gjødsel c

manuscript ['mænjuskript] n manuskript nt

many ['meni] adj mange

map [mæp] n kart nt

maple ['meipəl] n lønn c

marble ['ma:bəl] n marmor m; klinkekule c

March [ma:tʃ] mars

march [ma:tʃ] v marsjere; n marsj m

mare [meə] n hoppe c

margarine [,ma:dʒə'ri:n] n margarin m

margin ['ma:dʒin] n marg m

maritime ['mæritaim] adj maritim

mark [ma:k] v markere; merke; kjennetegne; n merke nt; karakter m; skyteskive c

market ['ma:kit] n marked nt

marketplace ['ma:kitpleis] n torg nt

marmalade ['ma:məleid] n marmelade m

marriage ['mæridʒ] n ekteskap nt

marrow ['mærou] n marg m

marry ['mæri] v gifte seg; **married couple** ektepar nt

marsh [ma:ʃ] n sump m

martyr ['ma:tə] n martyr m

marvel ['ma:vəl] n vidunder nt; v undre seg

marvel(l)ous ['ma:vələs] adj vidunderlig

mascara [mæ'ska:rə] n øyensverte c

masculine ['mæskjulin] adj maskulin

mash [mæʃ] v mose; **mashed**

potatoes npl potetstappe c

mask [ma:sk] n maske c

Mass [mæs] n messe m

mass [mæs] n mengde m; ~ production masseproduksjon m

massage ['mæsa:ʒ] n massasje m; v massere

masseur [mæ'sə:] n massør m

massive ['mæsiv] adj massiv

mast [ma:st] n mast c

master ['ma:stə] n mester m; lektor m, lærer m; v mestre, beherske

masterpiece ['ma:stəpi:s] n mesterverk nt

mat [mæt] n matte c; adj glansløs, matt

match [mætʃ] n fyrstikk m; kamp m; v passe til

matchbox ['mætʃbɔks] n fyrstikkeske c

material [mə'tiəriəl] n materiale nt; stoff nt; adj materiell

mathematical [,mæθə'mætikəl] adj matematisk

mathematics [,mæθə'mætiks] n matematikk m

matrimony ['mætriməni] n ekteskap nt

matter ['mætə] n stoff nt; spørsmål nt, sak c; v *være av betydning; **as a ~ of fact** faktisk, i virkeligheten

matter-of-fact [,mætərəv'fækt] adj realistisk

mattress ['mætrəs] n madrass m

mature [mə'tjuə] adj moden

maturity [mə'tjuərəti] n modenhet c

mausoleum [,mɔ:sə'li:əm] n mausoleum nt

mauve [mouv] adj lilla

May [mei] mai

***may** [mei] v *kunne

maybe ['meibi:] adv kanskje

mayor [meə] n borgermester m

maze [meiz] n labyrint m

me [mi:] *pron* meg
meadow ['medou] *n* eng *c*
meal [mi:l] *n* måltid *nt*
mean [mi:n] *adj* sjofel; *n* gjennomsnitt *nt*
*mean [mi:n] *v* bety; mene
meaning ['mi:niŋ] *n* mening *m*
meaningless ['mi:niŋləs] *adj* meningsløs
means [mi:nz] *n* middel *nt*; **by no ~** på ingen måte
meantime: in the ~ [in ðə 'mi:ntaim] i mellomtiden, imens
meanwhile ['mi:nwail] *adv* i mellomtiden, imens
measles ['mi:zəlz] *n* meslinger *pl*
measure ['meʒə] *v* måle; *n* mål *nt*; foranstaltning *m*
meat [mi:t] *n* kjøtt *nt*
mechanic [mi'kænik] *n* mekaniker *m*
mechanical [mi'kænikəl] *adj* mekanisk
mechanism ['mekənizəm] *n* mekanisme *m*
medal ['medəl] *n* medalje *m*
media ['mi:diə] *pl* media *pl*
mediaeval [,medi'i:vəl] *adj* middelaldersk
mediate ['mi:dieit] *v* megle
mediator ['mi:dieitə] *n* megler *m*
medical ['medikəl] *adj* medisinsk
medicine ['medsin] *n* medisin *m*; legevitenskap *m*
meditate ['mediteit] *v* meditere
Mediterranean [,meditə'reiniən] Middelhavet
medium ['mi:diəm] *adj* gjennomsnittlig, middels
*meet [mi:t] *v* møte; *treffe
meeting ['mi:tiŋ] *n* møte *nt*, sammenkomst *m*
meeting place ['mi:tiŋpleis] *n* møtested *nt*

melancholy ['melənkəli] *n* melankoli *m*
mellow ['melou] *adj* bløt; moden
melodrama ['melə,drɑ:mə] *n* melodrama *nt*
melody ['melədi] *n* melodi *m*
melon ['melən] *n* melon *m*
melt [melt] *v* smelte
member ['membə] *n* medlem *nt*; **Member of Parliament** parlamentsrepresentant *m*
membership ['membəʃip] *n* medlemskap *nt*
memo ['memou] *n* (pl ~s) memorandum *nt*
memorable ['memərəbəl] *adj* minneverdig
memorial [mə'mɔ:riəl] *n* minnestein *m*
memorize ['meməraiz] *v* lære utenat
memory ['meməri] *n* hukommelse *m*; minne *nt*
mend [mend] *v* reparere, *gjøre i stand
menstruation [,menstru'eiʃən] *n* menstruasjon *m*
mental ['mentəl] *adj* mental
mention ['menʃən] *v* nevne; *n* omtale *m*
menu ['menju:] *n* spisekart *nt*, meny *m*
merchandise ['mə:tʃəndaiz] *n* varer *pl*, handelsvare *m*
merchant ['mə:tʃənt] *n* kjøpmann *m*
merciful ['mə:sifəl] *adj* barmhjertig
mercury ['mə:kjuri] *n* kvikksølv *nt*
mercy ['mə:si] *n* barmhjertighet *c*, nåde *m*
merely ['miəli] *adv* bare
merge [mə:dʒ] *v* sammensmelte; fusjonere
merger ['mə:dʒə] *n* sammensmeltning *m*; fusjon *m*

merit ['merit] v fortjene; n fortjeneste m

merry ['meri] adj munter

merry-go-round ['merigou,raund] n karusell m

mesh [meʃ] n nett nt, maske c

mess [mes] n rot nt; ~ **up** rote til

message ['mesidʒ] n beskjed m

messenger ['mesindʒə] n budbringer m

metal ['metəl] n metall nt; metall-

meter ['mi:tə] n måler m

method ['meθəd] n metode m, fremgangsmåte m; ordning c

methodical [mə'θɔdikəl] adj metodisk

metre ['mi:tə] n meter m

metric ['metrik] adj metrisk

Mexican ['meksikən] adj meksikansk; n meksikaner m

Mexico ['meksikou] Mexico

mice (pl mouse)

microphone ['maikrəfoun] n mikrofon m

microwave oven ['maikrəweiv 'ʌvən] n mikrobølgeovn m

midday ['middei] n middag m; midt på dagen

middle ['midəl] n midte m; adj mellomste; **Middle Ages** middelalderen; ~ **class** middelklasse c; **middle-class** adj borgerlig

midnight ['midnait] n midnatt c

midst [midst] n midte m

midsummer ['mid,sʌmə] n midtsommer m

midwife ['midwaif] n (pl -wives) jordmor c

might [mait] n makt c

***might** [mait] v *kunne

mighty ['maiti] adj mektig

migraine ['migrein] n migrene m

mild [maild] adj mild

mildew ['mildju] n mugg m

mile [mail] n engelsk mil

milage ['mailidʒ] n distanse m

milepost ['mailpoust] n veiskilt nt

milestone ['mailstoun] n milestein m

milieu ['mi:ljə:] n miljø nt

military ['militəri] adj militær-; ~ **force** krigsmakt c

milk [milk] n melk c

milkshake ['milkʃeik] n milkshake m

milky ['milki] adj melkaktig

mill [mil] n mølle c; fabrikk m

million ['miljən] n million m

millionaire [,miljə'nɛə] n millionær m

mince [mins] v finhakke

mind [maind] n sinn nt; v *ha noe imot; passe på, passe seg for, bry seg om

mine [main] n gruve c

miner ['mainə] n gruvearbeider m

mineral ['minərəl] n mineral nt; ~ **water** naturlig mineralvann nt

mingle ['miŋgl] v blande (seg) med; blande seg inn

miniature ['minjətʃə] n miniatyr m

minimum ['miniməm] n minimum nt

mining ['mainiŋ] n gruvedrift c

minister ['ministə] n statsråd m; prest m; **Prime Minister** statsminister m

ministry ['ministri] n departement nt; prestegjerning c

mink [miŋk] n mink m

minor ['mainə] adj mindre, liten; underordnet; n mindreårig m; moll c

minority [mai'nɔrəti] n mindretall nt

mint [mint] n mynte c

minus ['mainəs] prep minus

minute¹ ['minit] n minutt nt; **minutes** referat nt

minute² [mai'nju:t] adj bitte liten

miracle ['mirəkəl] n mirakel nt

miraculous [mi'rækjuləs] adj mirakuløs

mirror ['mirə] n speil nt

misbehave [,misbi'heiv] v oppføre

seg dårlig

miscarriage [mis'kæridʒ] *n* spontan abort *m*

miscellaneous [,misə'leiniəs] *adj* diverse

mischief ['mistʃif] *n* spillopper *pl*; ugagn *m*, skade *m*

mischievous ['mistʃivəs] *adj* skøyeraktig

miserable ['mizərəbəl] *adj* elendig, ulykkelig

misery ['mizəri] *n* elendighet *c*, ulykke *c*; nød *c*

misfortune [mis'fɔːtʃen] *n* ulykke *c*, uhell *nt*

mishap ['mishæp] *n* ulykke *c*, uhell *nt*

*****mislay** [mis'lei] *v* *forlegge

misplaced [mis'pleist] *adj* malplassert; mistet

mispronounce [,misprə'nauns] *v* uttale galt

miss¹ [mis] frøken *c* (*obsolete*)

miss² [mis] *v* miste

missing ['misiŋ] *adj* manglende; ~ **person** savnet person

mist [mist] *n* dis *m*, tåke *c*

mistake [mi'steik] *n* feiltakelse *m*, feil *m*

*****mistake** [mi'steik] *v* forveksle

mistaken [mi'steikən] *adj* feilaktig; *****be** ~ *ta feil

mister ['mistə] herr, herre *m* (*obsolete*)

mistress ['mistrəs] *n* frue *c*; bestyrer *m*; elskerinne *c*

mistrust [mis'trʌst] *v* mistro

misty ['misti] *adj* disig

*****misunderstand** [,misʌndə'stænd] *v* *misforstå

misunderstanding [,misʌndə'stændiŋ] *n* misforståelse *m*

misuse [mis'juːs] *n* misbruk *nt*

mitten ['mitən] *n* vott *m*

mix [miks] *v* blande; ~ **with** *omgås med

mixed [mikst] *adj* blandet

mixer ['miksə] *n* mikser *m*

mixture ['mikstʃə] *n* blanding *c*

moan [moun] *v* jamre

moat [mout] *n* vollgrav *c*

mobile ['moubail] *adj* bevegelig, mobil; ~ **(phone)** mobil(telefon) *m*

mock [mɔk] *v* håne

mockery ['mɔkəri] *n* hån *m*

model ['mɔdəl] *n* modell *m*; mannekeng *m*; *v* modellere, forme

modem ['moudem] *n* modem *nt*

moderate ['mɔdərət] *adj* moderat; middelmådig

modern ['mɔdən] *adj* moderne

modest ['mɔdist] *adj* beskjeden

modesty ['mɔdisti] *n* beskjedenhet *c*

modify ['mɔdifai] *v* modifisere, endre

moist [mɔist] *adj* fuktig, våt

moisten ['mɔisən] *v* fukte

moisture ['mɔistʃə] *n* fuktighet *c*; **moisturizing cream** fuktighetskrem *m*

molar ['moulə] *n* jeksel *m*

mom ['mɔm], **mommy** ['mɔmi] mamma *m*

moment ['moumənt] *n* øyeblikk *nt*

momentary ['mouməntəri] *adj* kortvarig

monarch ['mɔnək] *n* monark *m*

monarchy ['mɔnəki] *n* monarki *nt*

monastery ['mɔnəstri] *n* kloster *nt*

Monday ['mʌndi] mandag *m*

monetary ['mʌnitəri] *adj* penge-; ~ **unit** myntenhet *m*

money ['mʌni] *n* penger *pl*; ~ **exchange** vekslingskontor *nt*; ~ **order** postanvisning *m*

monk [mʌŋk] *n* munk *m*

monkey ['mʌŋki] *n* ape *c*

monologue ['mɔnɔlɔg] n monolog m

monopoly [mə'nɔpəli] n monopol nt

monotonous [mə'nɔtənəs] adj monoton

month [mʌnθ] n måned m

monthly ['mʌnθli] adj månedlig

monument ['mɔnjumənt] n monument nt, minnesmerke nt

mood [muːd] n humør m, stemning m

moon [muːn] n måne m

moonlight ['muːnlait] n måneskinn nt

moor [muə] n hei c, lyngmo m; myr c

moose [muːs] n (pl ~, ~s) elg m

moped ['mouped] n moped m

moral ['mɔrəl] n moral m; adj moralsk, sedelig

morality [mə'ræləti] n moral m

more [mɔː] adj mer; once ~ en gang til

moreover [mɔː'rouvə] adv dessuten, for øvrig

morning ['mɔːniŋ] n morgen m, formiddag m; ~ paper morgenavis c; this ~ i morges

Moroccan [mə'rɔkən] adj marokkansk; n marokkaner m

Morocco [mə'rɔkou] Marokko

morphia ['mɔːfiə] n morfin m

morphine ['mɔːfiːn] n morfin m

morsel ['mɔːsəl] n bit m

mortal ['mɔːtəl] adj dødelig

mortgage ['mɔːgidʒ] n pantelån nt

mosaic [mə'zeiik] n mosaikk m

mosque [mɔsk] n moské m

mosquito [mə'skiːtou] n (pl ~es) mygg m; moskito m; ~ net myggnett nt

moss [mɔs] n mose m

most [moust] adj flest; at ~ høyst; ~ of all mest

mostly ['moustli] adv for det meste

motel [mou'tel] n motell nt

moth [mɔθ] n møll m; nattsvermer m

mother ['mʌðə] n mor c; ~ of pearl perlemor m; ~ tongue morsmål m

mother-in-law ['mʌðərinlɔː] n (pl mothers-) svigermor c

motion ['mouʃən] n bevegelse m; forslag nt

motive ['moutiv] n motiv nt

motivate ['moutiveit] v motivere

motor ['moutə] n motor m; v bile; ~ body nAm karosseri nt; **starter** ~ starter m

motorbike ['moutəbaik] nAm moped m

motorboat ['moutəbout] n motorbåt m

motorcycle ['moutə,saikəl] n motorsykkel m

motoring ['moutəriŋ] n bilkjøring c

motorist ['moutərist] n bilist m

motorway ['moutəwei] n motorvei m

motto ['mɔtou] n (pl ~es, ~s) motto nt

mould [mould] n haug m

mount [maunt] v *bestige; n berg nt

mountain ['mauntin] n fjell nt; ~ pass pass nt; ~ range fjellkjede m

mountaineering [,maunti'niəriŋ] n fjellklatring c

mountainous ['mauntinəs] adj fjellendt

mourning ['mɔːniŋ] n sorg c

mouse [maus] n (pl mice) mus c; ~ pad musmatte c

moustache [mə'stɑːʃ] n bart m

mouth [mauθ] n munn m; kjeft m, gap nt; munning m

mouthwash ['mauθwɔʃ] n munnvann nt

movable ['muːvəbəl] adj flyttbar

move [muːv] v bevege; flytte; røre seg; n trekk nt, skritt nt; flytting c

movement ['muːvmənt] n bevegelse m; sats m

movie ['muːvi] n film m; **movies** plAm kino m; ~ theater kino m

much [mʌtʃ] *adj* mange, mye; *adv* mye; **as ~** like mye; så vidt

muck [mʌk] *n* møkk *c*

mud [mʌd] *n* søle *c*

muddle ['mʌdəl] *n* forvirring *c*, rot *nt*, virvar *nt*; *v* rote

muddy ['mʌdi] *adj* sølet

muffler ['mʌflə] *nAm* lydpotte *c*

mug [mʌg] *n* krus *nt*

mule [mjuːl] *n* mulesel *nt*, muldyr *nt*

multiplication [,mʌltipli'keiʃən] *n* multiplikasjon *m*

multiply ['mʌltiplai] *v* multiplisere

mumps [mʌmps] *n* kusma *m*

municipal [mjuː'nisipəl] *adj* kommunal, by-

municipality [mjuː,nisi'pæləti] *n* kommune *m*

murder ['məːdə] *n* mord *nt*; *v* myrde

murderer ['məːdərə] *n* morder *m*

muscle ['mʌsəl] *n* muskel *m*

muscular ['mʌskjulə] *adj* muskuløs

museum [mjuː'ziːəm] *n* museum *nt*

mushroom ['mʌʃruːm] *n* sjampinjong *m*; sopp *m*

music ['mjuːzik] *n* musikk *m*; **~ academy** konservatorium *nt*; **~ hall** revyteater *nt*

musical ['mjuːzikəl] *adj* musikalsk; *n* musikal *m*

musician [mjuː'ziʃən] *n* musiker *m*

mussel ['mʌsəl] *n* blåskjell *nt*

Muslim ['mʌslim] *n* muslim *m*

*must [mʌst] *v* *måtte

mustard ['mʌstəd] *n* sennep *m*

mute [mjuːt] *adj* stum

mutiny ['mjuːtini] *n* mytteri *nt*

mutton ['mʌtən] *n* fårekjøtt *nt*

mutual ['mjuːtʃuəl] *adj* gjensidig

my [mai] *adj* min

myself [mai'self] *pron* meg; selv

mysterious [mi'stiəriəs] *adj* gåtefull, mystisk

mystery ['mistəri] *n* mysterium *nt*

myth [miθ] *n* myte *m*

N

nail [neil] *n* negl *m*; spiker *m*; **~ file** neglefil *c*; **~ polish** neglelakk *m*; **~ scissors** *pl* neglesaks *c*

nailbrush ['neilbrʌʃ] *n* neglebørste *m*

naïve [naː'iːv] *adj* naiv

naked ['neikid] *adj* naken; bar

name [neim] *n* navn *nt*; *v* oppkalle, kalle; **in the ~ of** i ...s navn

namely ['neimli] *adv* nemlig

nap [næp] *n* lur *m*

napkin ['næpkin] *n* serviett *m*

nappy ['næpi] *n* bleie *c*

narcosis [naː'kousis] *n* (pl -ses) narkose *m*

narcotic [naː'kɔtik] *n* narkotisk middel

narrow ['nærou] *adj* trang, smal, snever

narrow-minded [,nærou'maindid] *adj* sneversynt

nasty ['naːsti] *adj* ubehagelig, vemmelig; ekkel

nation ['neiʃən] *n* nasjon *m*; folk *nt*

national ['næʃənəl] *adj* nasjonal; folke-; stats-; **~ anthem** nasjonalsang *m*; **~ dress** nasjonaldrakt *c*; bunad *m*; **~ park** nasjonalpark *m*

nationality [,næʃə'næləti] *n* nasjonalitet *m*

nationalize ['næʃənəlaiz] *v*

nasjonalisere

native ['neitiv] n innfødt m; adj født; ~ **country** fedreland nt; hjemland nt; ~ **language** morsmål nt

natural ['nætʃərəl] adj naturlig; medfødt

naturally ['nætʃərəli] adv selvfølgelig, naturligvis

nature ['neitʃə] n natur m

naughty ['nɔ:ti] adj uskikkelig, slem

nausea ['nɔ:siə] n kvalme m

naval ['neivəl] adj marine-

navel ['neivəl] n navle m

navigable ['nævigəbəl] adj seilbar

navigate ['nævigeit] v navigere

navigation [,nævi'geiʃən] n navigasjon m; seilas m

navy ['neivi] n flåte m

near [niə] prep nær; adj nær

nearby ['niəbai] adj nærliggende, tilstøtende

nearly ['niəli] adv nesten

neat [ni:t] adj nett, ordentlig

necessary ['nesəsəri] adj nødvendig

necessity [nə'sesəti] n nødvendighet c

neck [nek] n hals m; **nape of the ~** nakke m

necklace ['nekləs] n halskjede nt

necktie ['nektai] n slips nt

need [ni:d] v behøve, trenge; n behov nt; nødvendighet c; ~ **to** *måtte

needle ['ni:dəl] n nål c

needlework ['ni:dəlwə:k] n håndarbeid nt

negative ['negətiv] adj negativ, benektende; n negativ nt

neglect [ni'glekt] v forsømme; n forsømmelse m

negligee ['negliʒei] n neglisjé m/nt

negotiate [ni'gouʃieit] v forhandle

negotiation [ni,gouʃi'eiʃən] n forhandling c

neighbo(u)r ['neibə] n granne m,

nabo m

neighbo(u)rhood ['neibəhud] n nabolag m

neighbo(u)ring ['neibəriŋ] adj tilstøtende, nærliggende

neither ['naiðə] pron ingen av dem; **neither ... nor** verken ... eller

neon ['ni:ɔn] n neon m

nephew ['nefju:] n nevø m

nerve [nə:v] n nerve m; dristighet c

nervous ['nə:vəs] adj nervøs

nest [nest] n rede nt

net [net] n nett nt; adj netto

Netherlands: the ~ ['neðələndz] Nederland

network ['netwə:k] n nettverk c

neuralgia [njuə'rældʒə] n nevralgi m

neurosis [njuə'rousis] n nevrose m

neuter ['nju:tə] adj intetkjønns-

neutral ['nju:trəl] adj nøytral

never ['nevə] adv aldri

nevertheless [,nevəðə'les] adv ikke desto mindre

new [nju:] adj ny; **New Year** nyttår nt

news [nju:z] n nyheter pl, nyhet c

newspaper ['nju:z,peipə] n avis c

newsstand ['nju:zstænd] n aviskiosk m

New Zealand [nju: 'zi:lənd] Ny-Zealand

next [nekst] adj neste; ~ **to** ved siden av

next-door [,nekst'dɔ:] adv ved siden av, nabo-

nice [nais] adj koselig, snill, pen; lekker; sympatisk

nickel ['nikəl] n nikkel m; 5-cent-mynt

nickname ['nikneim] n kjælenavn nt

nicotine ['nikəti:n] n nikotin m

niece [ni:s] n niese c

Nigeria [nai'dʒiəriə] Nigeria

Nigerian [nai'dʒiəriən] adj nigeriansk; n nigerianer m

night [nait] n natt c; kveld m; **by ~** om

natten; ~ **rate** natt-takst *m*; ~ **train**
natt-tog *nt*
nightclub ['naitklʌb] *n* nattklubb *m*
night cream ['naitkri:m] *n* nattkrem
m
nightdress ['naitdres] *n* nattkjole *m*
nightingale ['naitiŋgeil] *n* nattergal
m
nightly ['naitli] *adj* nattlig
nil [nil] ingenting; null
nine [nain] *num* ni
nineteen [,nain'ti:n] *num* nitten
nineteenth [,nain'ti:nθ] *num* nittende
ninety ['nainti] *num* nitti
ninth [nainθ] *num* niende
nitrogen ['naitrədʒən] *n* kvelstoff *nt*
no [nou] nei; *adj* ingen; ~ **one** ingen
nobility [nou'biləti] *n* adel *m*
noble ['noubəl] *adj* adelig; edel
nobody ['noubɔdi] *pron* ingen
nod [nɔd] *n* nikk *nt*; *v* nikke
noise [nɔiz] *n* lyd *m*; bulder *nt*, larm
m, støy *m*
noisy ['nɔizi] *adj* støyende
nominal ['nɔminəl] *adj* nominell
nominate ['nɔmineit] *v* nominere
nomination [,nɔmi'neiʃən] *n*
nominasjon *m*; utnevnelse *m*
none [nʌn] *pron* ingen
nonsense ['nɔnsəns] *n* nonsens *nt*
non-smoker [,nɔn'smoukə] *n* ikke-
røyker *m*
noodles [nu:dəls] *pl*
nudler *pl*, pasta *m*
noon [nu:n] *n* klokken (klokka) tolv
normal ['nɔ:məl] *adj* normal
north [nɔ:θ] *n* nord *m*; *adj* nordlig;
North Pole Nordpolen
north-east [,nɔ:θ'i:st] *n* nordøst *m*
northerly ['nɔ:ðəli] *adj* nordlig
northern ['nɔ:ðən] *adj* nordlig
north-west [,nɔ:θ'west] *n* nordvest *m*
Norway ['nɔ:wei] Norge
Norwegian [nɔ:'wi:dʒən] *adj* norsk; *n*

nordmann (pl -menn) *m*
nose [nouz] *n* nese *c*
nosebleed ['nouzbli:d] *n* neseblod *nt*
nostril ['nɔstril] *n* nesebor *nt*
nosy ['nouzi] *adj colloquial* nysgjerrig
not [nɔt] *adv* ikke
notary ['noutəri] *n* notar *m*
notary public *Am* notarius publicus
note [nout] *n* merknad *m*, notis *m*;
notat *nt*; tone *m*; *v* notere; bemerke,
konstatere
notebook ['noutbuk] *n* notisbok *c*
noted ['noutid] *adj* kjent
notepaper ['nout,peipə] *n* brevpapir
nt
nothing ['nʌθiŋ] *n* ingenting, intet *nt*
notice ['noutis] *v* merke, bemerke,
*legge merke til, oppdage; *se; *n*
underretning *m*, kunngjøring *c*;
oppmerksomhet *c*
noticeable ['noutisəbəl] *adj* merkbar;
bemerkelsesverdig
notify ['noutifai] *v* meddele;
underrette; varsle
notion ['nouʃən] *n* anelse *m*, begrep
nt
notorious [nou'tɔ:riəs] *adj* beryktet
nougat ['nu:ga:] *n* nougat *m*
nought [nɔ:t] *n* null *m/nt*
noun [naun] *n* substantiv *nt*
nourishing ['nʌriʃiŋ] *adj* nærende
nourishment ['nʌriʃment] *n* næring *c*
novel ['nɔvəl] *n* roman *m*
novelist ['nɔvəlist] *n* romanforfatter
m
November [nou'vembə] november
now [nau] *adv* nå; ~ **and then** nå og
da; **from ~ on** heretter
nowadays ['nauədeiz] *adv* nåtildags
nowhere ['nouweə] *adv* ingensteds,
ingen steder
nozzle ['nɔzəl] *n* tut *m*
nuance [nju:'ā:s] *n* nyanse *m*
nuclear ['nju:kliə] *adj* kjerne-; ~

energy kjernekraft *c*
nucleus ['njuːkliəs] *n* kjerne *m*
nude [njuːd] *adj* naken; *n* akt *m*
nuisance ['njuːsəns] *n* plage *m*
numb [nʌm] *adj* følelsesløs; valen
number ['nʌmbə] *n* nummer *nt*; tall
nt, antall *nt*
numeral ['njuːmərəl] *n* tallord *nt*
numerous ['njuːmərəs] *adj* tallrik
nun [nʌn] *n* nonne *c*
nunnery ['nʌnəri] *n* nonnekloster *nt*

nurse [nəːs] *n* sykepleier *m*;
barnepike *m*; *v* pleie; amme
nursery ['nəːsəri] *n* barneværelse *nt*;
planteskole *m*
nut [nʌt] *n* nøtt *c*; mutter *m*
nutcrackers ['nʌt,krækəz] *pl*
nøtteknekker *m*
nutmeg ['nʌtmeg] *n* muskatnøtt *c*
nutritious [njuː'triʃəs] *adj* nærende
nutshell ['nʌtʃel] *n* nøtteskall *nt*

O

oak [ouk] *n* eik *c*
oar [ɔː] *n* åre *c*
oasis [ou'eisis] *n* (pl oases) oase *m*
oath [ouθ] *n* ed *m*
oats [outs] *pl* havre *m*
obedience [ə'biːdiəns] *n* lydighet *c*
obedient [ə'biːdiənt] *adj* lydig
obese [ou'biːs] *adj* fet
obesity [ou'biːsiti] *n* fedme *m*
obey [ə'bei] *v* *adlyde
object[1] ['ɔbdʒikt] *n* objekt *nt*;
gjenstand *m*; formål *nt*
object[2] [əb'dʒekt] *v* protestere,
innvende
objection [əb'dʒekʃən] *n* innvending
c
objective [əb'dʒektiv] *adj* objektiv; *n*
formål *nt*
obligatory [ə'bligətəri] *adj*
obligatorisk
oblige [ə'blaidʒ] *v* forplikte; *be
obliged to* *være forpliktet til; *være
nødt til
obliging [ə'blaidʒiŋ] *adj*
imøtekommende
oblong ['ɔblɔŋ] *adj* avlang; *n*
rektangel *nt*

obscene [əb'siːn] *adj* uanstendig;
obskøn
obscure [əb'skjuə] *adj* uklar, mørk
observation [,ɔbzə'veiʃən] *n*
iakttakelse *m*, observasjon *m*
observatory [əb'zɔːvətri] *n*
observatorium *nt*
observe [əb'zɔːv] *v* *iaktta, observere
obsession [əb'seʃən] *n* besettelse *m*
obstacle ['ɔbstəkəl] *n* hindring *c*
obstinate ['ɔbstinət] *adj* sta;
hardnakket
obtain [əb'tein] *v* erverve, *få
obtainable [əb'teinəbəl] *adj*
oppnåelig
obvious ['ɔbviəs] *adj* innlysende
occasion [ə'keiʒən] *n* tilfelle *nt*;
foranledning *m*
occasionally [ə'keiʒənəli] *adv* av og
til, nå og da
occupant ['ɔkjupənt] *n* beboer *m*
occupation [,ɔkju'peiʃən] *n*
beskjeftigelse *m*; okkupasjon *m*
occupy ['ɔkjupai] *v* *besette;
beskjeftige; **occupied** *adj* opptatt
occur [ə'kəː] *v* hende, *forekomme,
skje

occurrence [ə'kʌrəns] n hendelse m
ocean ['ouʃən] n hav nt
October [ɔk'toubə] oktober
octopus ['ɔktəpəs] n blekksprut m
oculist ['ɔkjulist] n øyenlege m
odd [ɔd] adj underlig, rar; ulike
odo(u)r ['oudə] n lukt c
of [ɔv, əv] prep av; fra; i
off [ɔf] adv av; vekk; prep av
offence [ə'fens] n forseelse m;
krenkelse m; anstøt nt, fornærmelse
m
offend [ə'fend] v krenke, fornærme;
*forgå seg
offense [ə'fens] nAm forseelse m;
krenkelse m; anstøt nt, fornærmelse
m
offensive [ə'fensiv] adj offensiv;
støtende, krenkende
offer ['ɔfə] v *tilby; yte; n tilbud nt
office ['ɔfis] n kontor nt; embete nt; ~
hours kontortid c
officer ['ɔfisə] n offiser m
official [ə'fiʃəl] adj offisiell
off-licence ['ɔf,laisəns] n
alkoholutsalg nt
often ['ɔfən] adv ofte
oil [ɔil] n olje c; fuel ~ brenselolje c; ~
filter oljefilter nt; ~ painting
oljemaleri nt; ~ pressure oljetrykk
nt; ~ refinery oljeraffineri nt; ~ well
oljebrønn m; ~ drilling platform
boreplattform nt
oily ['ɔili] adj oljet; glatt
ointment ['ɔintmənt] n salve c
okay!, OK! [,ou'kei] greit! ok!
old [ould] adj gammel; ~ age
alderdom m
old-fashioned [,ould'fæʃənd] adj
gammeldags
olive ['ɔliv] n oliven m; ~ oil olivenolje
c
omelette ['ɔmlət] n omelett m
ominous ['ɔminəs] adj illevarslende

omit [ə'mit] v *utelate
omnipotent [ɔm'nipətənt] adj
allmektig
on [ɔn] prep på; ved
once [wʌns] adv en gang; at ~ straks;
for ~ for en gangs skyld; ~ more en
gang til
oncoming ['ɔn,kʌmiŋ] adj
kommende; møtende
one [wʌn] num en; pron man
oneself [wʌn'self] pron selv
one-way ['wʌn-wei] adj enkel
only ['ounli] adj eneste; adv bare,
alene, kun; conj men
onwards ['ɔnwədz] adv fremover
onyx ['ɔniks] n onyks m
opal ['oupəl] n opal m
open ['oupən] v åpne; adj åpen;
åpenhjertig
opener ['oupənə]
n (flaske-)åpner m; åpningsnummer nt
opening ['oupəniŋ] n åpning c
opera ['ɔpərə] n opera m; ~ house
opera m
operate ['ɔpəreit] v virke, *drive;
operere
operation [,ɔpə'reiʃən] n virksomhet
c; operasjon m
operator ['ɔpəreitə] n operatør m
operetta [,ɔpə'retə] n operette m
opinion [ə'pinjən] n oppfatning m,
mening m
opponent [ə'pounənt] n motstander
m
opportunity [,ɔpə'tjuːnəti] n leilighet
c, anledning m
oppose [ə'pouz] v *motsette seg,
opponere
opposite ['ɔpəzit] prep overfor; adj
motsatt
opposition [,ɔpə'ziʃən] n opposisjon
m
oppress [ə'pres] v undertrykke,
knuge

optician [ɔp'tiʃən] n optiker m

optimism ['ɔptimizəm] n optimisme m

optimist ['ɔptimist] n optimist m

optimistic [,ɔpti'mistik] adj optimistisk

optional ['ɔpʃənəl] adj valgfri

or [ɔ:] conj eller

oral ['ɔ:rəl] adj muntlig

orange ['ɔrindʒ] n appelsin m; adj oransje

orbit ['ɔ:bit] n omløp nt

orchard ['ɔ:tʃəd] n frukthage m

orchestra ['ɔ:kistrə] n orkester nt; ~ seat Am orkesterplass m

order ['ɔ:də] v beordre; bestille; n rekkefølge m, orden m; ordre m, befaling c; bestilling c; in ~ i orden; in ~ to for å; made to ~ laget på bestilling; out of ~ i uorden

ordinary ['ɔ:dənri] adj vanlig, dagligdags

ore [ɔ:] n malm m

organ ['ɔ:gən] n organ nt; orgel nt

organic [ɔ:'gænik] adj organisk

organization [,ɔ:gənai'zeiʃən] n organisasjon m

organize ['ɔ:gənaiz] v organisere

Orient ['ɔ:riənt] n Orienten

oriental [,ɔ:ri'entəl] adj orientalsk

orientate ['ɔ:riənteit] v orientere seg

origin ['ɔridʒin] n avstamning m, opphav nt; herkomst m

original [ə'ridʒinəl] adj original, opprinnelig

originally [ə'ridʒinəli] adv i begynnelsen

ornament ['ɔ:nəmənt] n utsmykning m

ornamental [,ɔ:nə'mentəl] adj dekorativ

orphan ['ɔ:fən] n foreldreløst barn

orthodox ['ɔ:θədɔks] adj ortodoks

ostrich ['ɔstritʃ] n struts m

other ['ʌðə] adj annen

otherwise ['ʌðəwaiz] conj ellers; adv annerledes

*ought to [ɔ:t] *burde

ounce ['auns] n vektenhet, ca 30 g

our, ours [auə] adj vår

ourselves [auə'selvz] pron oss; selv

out [aut] adv ute, ut; ~ of sluppet opp for

outbreak ['autbreik] n utbrudd nt

outcome ['autkʌm] n resultat nt

*outdo [,aut'du:] v *overgå

outdoors [,aut'dɔ:z] adv utendørs

outer ['autə] adj ytre

outfit ['autfit] n utrustning m; klesdrakt m

outing ['autiŋ] n utflukt c

outline ['autlain] n kontur m, omriss nt; v gi et omriss av

outlook ['autluk] n utsikt m; syn nt

output ['autput] n produksjon m

outrage ['autreidʒ] n fornærmelse m; krenkelse m

outside [,aut'said] adv utenfor; prep utenfor; n utside c, ytterside c

outsize ['autsaiz] n stor størrelse

outskirts ['autskə:ts] pl utkant m

outstanding [,aut'stændiŋ] adj fremtredende, fremragende

outward ['autwəd] adj utvendig

outwards ['autwədz] adv utad

oval ['ouvəl] adj oval

oven ['ʌvən] n stekeovn m

over ['ouvə] prep over, ovenfor; adv over; over ende; ~ there der borte

overall ['ouvərɔ:l] adj total

overalls ['ouvərɔ:lz] pl overall m

overcast ['ouvəka:st] adj overskyet

overcoat ['ouvəkout] n frakk m

*overcome [,ouvə'kʌm] v *overvinne

overdo [,ouvə'du:] v overdrive

overdraft ['ouvədra:ft]

n overtrekk *nt*

overdue [,ouvə'djuː] *adj* forsinket; forfalt

overgrown [,ouvə'groun] *adj* overgrodd

overhaul [,ouvə'hɔːl] *v* overhale

overhead [,ouvə'hed] *adv* ovenfor

overlook [,ouvə'luk] *v* *overse

overnight [,ouvə'nait] *adv* natten over

overseas [,ouvə'siːz] *adj* oversjøisk

oversight ['ouvəsait] *n* forglemmelse *m*

*oversleep [,ouvə'sliːp] *v* *forsove seg

overstrung [,ouvə'strʌŋ] *adj* overspent

*overtake [,ouvə'teik] *v* kjøre forbi;

no overtaking forbikjøring forbudt

over-tired [,ouvə'taiəd] *adj* overtrett

overture ['ouvətʃə] *n* ouverture *m*

overweight ['ouvəweit] *n* overvekt *c*; *adj* overvektig

overwhelm [,ouvə'welm] *v* overvelde

overwork [,ouvə'wəːk] *v* overanstrenge seg

owe [ou] *v* *være skyldig, skylde; *ha å takke for; **owing to** på grunn av

owl [aul] *n* ugle *c*

own [oun] *v* eie; *adj* egen

owner ['ounə] *n* eier *m*, innehaver *m*

ox [ɔks] *n* (pl oxen) okse *m*

oxygen ['ɔksidʒən] *n* surstoff *nt*

oyster ['ɔistə] *n* østers *m*

ozone ['ouzoun] *n* ozon *nt*

P

pace [peis] *n* skritt *nt*; tempo *nt*

Pacific Ocean [pə'sifik 'ouʃən] Stillehavet

pacifism ['pæsifizəm] *n* pasifisme *m*

pacifist ['pæsifist] *n* pasifist *m*; pasifistisk

pack [pæk] *v* pakke; *nAm* kortstokk *m*; ~ **up** pakke ned

package ['pækidʒ] *n* pakke *c*

packet ['pækit] *n* liten pakke, småpakke *c*

packing ['pækiŋ] *n* innpakning *m*

pact [pækt] *n* pakt *c*; kontrakt *m*

pad [pæd] *n* pute *m*; notisblokk *c*

paddle ['pædəl] *n* padleåre *c*

padlock ['pædlɔk] *n* hengelås *m/nt*

pagan ['peigən] *adj* hedensk; *n* hedning *m*

page [peidʒ] *n* side *c*

pageboy ['peidʒbɔi] *n* pikkolo *m*

pail [peil] *n* spann *nt*

pain [pein] *n* smerte *m*; **pains** umake *m*

painful ['peinfəl] *adj* smertefull

painkiller ['peinkilə] *n* smertestillende middel *nt*

painless ['peinləs] *adj* smertefri

paint [peint] *n* maling *c*; *v* male

paintbox ['peintbɔks] *n* malerskrin *nt*

paintbrush ['peintbrʌʃ] *n* pensel *m*

painter ['peintə] *n* maler *m*

painting ['peintiŋ] *n* maleri *nt*

pair [pɛə] *n* par *nt*

Pakistan [,pɑːki'stɑːn] Pakistan

Pakistani [,pɑːki'stɑːni] *adj* pakistansk; *n* pakistaner *m*

palace ['pæləs] *n* palass *nt*

pale [peil] *adj* blek; lyse-

palm [pɑːm] *n* palme *m*; håndflate *c*

palpable ['pælpəbəl] *adj* følelig, merkbar

palpitation [,pælpi'teiʃən] *n* hjerteklapp *m*

pan [pæn] *n* panne *c*; kasserolle *m*

pane [pein] *n* vindusrute *c*

panel ['pænəl] *n* panel *nt*

panelling ['pænəliŋ] *n* panelverk *nt*

panic ['pænik] *n* panikk *m*

pant [pænt] *v* pese

panties ['pæntiz] *pl* underbukse *c*, truse *c*

pants [pænts] *pl* underbukse *c*; bukse *c*

pant suit ['pæntsu:t] *n* buksedrakt *c*, buksedress *m*

panty hose ['pæntihouz] *n* strømpebukse *c*

paper ['peipə] *n* papir *nt*; avis *c*; papir-; **~ bag** papirpose *m*; **~ napkin** papirserviett *m*; **~ knife** papirkniv *m*; **wrapping ~** innpakningspapir *nt*

paperback ['peipəbæk] *n* billigbok *c*

parade [pə'reid] *n* parade *m*; tog *nt*

paradise ['pærədais] *n* paradis *nt*

paraffin ['pærəfin] *n* parafin *m*

paragraph ['pærəgrɑ:f] *n* avsnitt *nt*; paragraf *m*

parakeet ['pærəki:t] *n* papegøye *m*

parallel ['pærəlel] *adj* parallell; *n* parallell *m*

paralyse ['pærəlaiz] *v* lamme

parcel ['pɑ:səl] *n* pakke *c*

pardon ['pɑ:dən] *n* tilgivelse *m*; benådning *m*

parent ['pɛərənt] *n* forelder *m*

parents ['pɛərənts] *pl* foreldre *pl*

parents-in-law ['pɛərəntsinlɔ:] *pl* svigerforeldre *pl*

parish ['pæriʃ] *n* sogn *nt*

park [pɑ:k] *n* park *m*; *v* parkere

parking ['pɑ:kiŋ] *n* parkering *c*; **no ~** parkering forbudt; **~ fee** parkeringsavgift *c*; **~ light**

parkeringslys *nt*; **~ lot** *Am*

parkeringsplass *m*; **~ meter** parkometer *nt*; **~ zone** parkeringssone *c*

parliament ['pɑ:ləmənt] *n* parlament *nt*

parliamentary [,pɑ:lə'mentəri] *adj* parlamentarisk

parrot ['pærət] *n* papegøye *m*

parsley ['pɑ:sli] *n* persille *c*

parson ['pɑ:sən] *n* prest *m*

parsonage ['pɑ:sənidʒ] *n* prestegård *m*

part [pɑ:t] *n* del *m*; stykke *nt*; *v* skille; **spare ~** reservedel *m*

partial ['pɑ:ʃəl] *adj* delvis; partisk

participant [pɑ:'tisipənt] *n* deltaker *m*

participate [pɑ:'tisipeit] *v* *delta

particular [pə'tikjulə] *adj* spesiell, særegen; kresen; **in ~** i særdeleshet

parting ['pɑ:tiŋ] *n* avskjed *m*; hårskill *m*

partition [pɑ:'tiʃən] *n* skillevegg *m*

partly ['pɑ:tli] *adv* delvis

partner ['pɑ:tnə] *n* partner *m*; kompanjong *m*

partridge ['pɑ:tridʒ] *n* rapphøne *c*

party ['pɑ:ti] *n* parti *nt*; selskap *nt*; gruppe *c*

pass [pɑ:s] *v* *forløpe, passere; *rekke; *bestå; **no passing** *Am* forbikjøring forbudt; **~ by** *gå forbi; **~ through** *gå gjennom

passage ['pæsidʒ] *n* passasje *m*; overfart *m*; avsnitt *nt*; gjennomreise *c*

passenger ['pæsəndʒə] *n* passasjer *m*; **~ train** persontog *nt*

passer-by [,pɑ:sə'bai] *n* forbipasserende *m*

passion ['pæʃən] *n* lidenskap *m*

passionate ['pæʃənət] *adj* lidenskapelig

passive ['pæsiv] *adj* passiv

passport ['pɑːspɔːt] n pass nt; ~
  control passkontroll m; ~
  photograph passfoto nt
password ['pɑːswəːd] n passord nt
past [pɑːst] n fortid c; adj forrige,
  tidligere; prep forbi, langs
paste [peist] n lim nt; v klistre
pastime ['pɑːstaim] n tidsfordriv nt
pastry ['peistri] n finere bakverk nt; ~
  shop konditori nt
pasture ['pɑːstʃə] n beite nt
pasty ['peisti] n postei m
patch [pætʃ] n lapp m
patent ['peitənt] n patent nt
path [pɑːθ] n sti m
patience ['peiʃəns] n tålmodighet c
patient ['peiʃənt] adj tålmodig; n
  pasient m
patriot ['peitriət] n patriot m
patrol [pə'troul] n patrulje m; v
  patruljere; overvåke
pattern ['pætən] n mønster nt, motiv
  nt
pause [pɔːz] n pause m; v *holde
  pause
pave [peiv] v *legge veidekke;
  *brolegge
pavement ['peivmənt] n fortau nt;
  veidekke m
pavilion [pə'viljən] n paviljong m
paw [pɔː] n pote m
pawn [pɔːn] v *pantsette; n
  sjakkbonde m
pawnbroker ['pɔːnˌboukə] n
  pantelåner m
pay [pei] n gasje m, lønn c
*pay [pei] v betale; lønne seg; ~
  attention to *være oppmerksom på;
  ~ **off** nedbetale; ~ **on account**
  avbetale; **paying** lønnsom
pay desk ['peidesk] n kasse c
payment ['peimənt] n betaling c
pea [piː] n ert c
peace [piːs] n fred m

peaceful ['piːsfəl] adj fredelig
peach [piːtʃ] n fersken m
peacock ['piːkɔk] n påfugl m
peak [piːk] n tind m; topp m; ~ **hour**
  rushtid c; ~ **season** høysesong m
peanut ['piːnʌt] n peanøtt m c
pear [pɛə] n pære c
pearl [pəːl] n perle c
peasant ['pezənt] n bonde m
pebble ['pebəl] n småstein m
peculiar [pi'kjuːljə] adj underlig;
  eiendommelig
peculiarity [piˌkjuːli'ærəti] n
  eiendommelighet c
pedal ['pedəl] n pedal m
pedestrian [pi'destriən] n fotgjenger
  m; ~ **crossing** fotgjengerovergang m;
  no pedestrians ikke for fotgjengere
peel [piːl] v skrelle; n skrell nt
peep [piːp] v kikke
peg [peg] n knagg m
pelican ['pelikən] n pelikan m
pelvis ['pelvis] n bekken nt
pen [pen] n penn m
penalty ['penəlti] n bot c; straff m; ~
  kick straffespark m
pencil ['pensəl] n blyant m; ~
  sharpener blyantspisser m
penetrate ['penitreit] v trenge
  gjennom
penguin ['peŋgwin] n pingvin m
penicillin [ˌpeni'silin] n penicillin nt
peninsula [pə'ninsjulə] n halvøy c
penknife ['pennaif] n (pl -knives)
  lommekniv m
penny ['peni]
  n (pl pennies, pence) penny m
pension[1] ['pãsiõ] n pensjonat nt
pension[2] ['penʃən] n pensjon m
Pentecost ['pentikəst] n pinse c
people ['piːpəl] pl folk pl; n folk nt,
  folkeslag nt
pepper ['pepə] n pepper m
peppermint ['pepəmint] n

peppermynte *c*

per [pə:] *prep* per, pr.; ~ **cent** prosent

perceive [pə'si:v] *v* fornemme

percent [pə'sent] *n* prosent *m*

percentage [pə'sentidʒ] *n* prosentsats *m*

perceptible [pə'septibəl] *adj* merkbar

perception [pə'sepʃən] *n* fornemmelse *m*

perch [pə:tʃ] (pl ~) åbor *m*

percolator ['pə:kəleitə] *n* kaffetrakter *m*

perfect ['pə:fikt] *adj* fullkommen, perfekt

perfection [pə'fekʃən] *n* perfeksjon *m*, fullkommenhet *c*

perform [pə'fɔ:m] *v* utføre; *opptre; utøve

performance [pə'fɔ:məns] *n* forestilling *c*

perfume ['pə:fju:m] *n* parfyme *m*

perhaps [pə'hæps] *adv* kanskje; muligens

peril ['peril] *n* fare *m*

perilous ['periləs] *adj* livsfarlig

period ['piəriəd] *n* periode *m*, tid *c*; punktum *nt*

periodical [,piəri'ɔdikəl] *n* tidsskrift *nt*; *adj* periodevis

perish ['periʃ] *v* *omkomme; *forgå

perishable ['periʃəbəl] *adj* bedervelig

perjury ['pə:dʒəri] *n* mened *m*

permanent ['pə:mənənt] *adj* varig, permanent, vedvarende, fast

permission [pə'miʃən] *n* tillatelse *m*; lov *m*

permit[1] [pə'mit] *v* *tillate

permit[2] ['pə:mit] *n* tillatelse *m*, permisjon *m*

peroxide [pə'rɔksaid] *n* vannstoff hyperoksyd

perpendicular [,pə:pən'dikjulə] *adj* loddrett

persecute ['pə:sikju:t] *v* *forfølge,

plage

Persia ['pə:ʃə] Persia

Persian ['pə:ʃən] *adj* persisk; *n* perser *m*

person ['pə:sən] *n* person *m*; **per ~** per person

personal ['pə:sənəl] *adj* personlig

personality [,pə:sə'næləti] *n* personlighet *c*

personnel [,pə:sə'nel] *n* personale *nt*

perspective [pə'spektiv] *n* perspektiv *nt*

perspiration [,pə:spə'reiʃən] *n* svette *m*

perspire [pə'spaiə] *v* transpirere, svette

persuade [pə'sweid] *v* overtale; overbevise

persuasion [pə'sweiʒən] *n* overbevisning *m*; overtaling *c*

pessimism ['pesimizəm] *n* pessimisme *m*

pessimist ['pesimist] *n* pessimist *m*

pessimistic [,pesi'mistik] *adj* pessimistisk

pet [pet] *n* kjæledyr *nt*; kjæledegge *m*; *adj* yndlings-

petal ['petəl] *n* kronblad *nt*

petition [pi'tiʃən] *n* bønn *m*; petisjon *m*

petrol ['petrəl] *n* bensin *m*; **unleaded ~** blyfri bensin; ~ **pump** bensinpumpe *c*; ~ **station** bensinstasjon *m*; ~ **tank** bensintank *m*

petroleum [pi'trouliəm] *n* petroleum *m*

petty ['peti] *adj* smålig, ubetydelig, liten; ~ **cash** småpenger *pl*

phantom ['fæntəm] *n* fantasibilde *nt*; gjenferd *nt*

pharmacology [,fɑ:mə'kɔlədʒi] *n* farmakologi *m*

pharmacy ['fɑ:məsi] *n* apotek *nt*

phase [feiz] n fase m

Philippine ['filipain] adj filippinsk

Philippines ['filipi:nz] pl Filippinene

philosopher [fi'lɔsəfə] n filosof m

philosophy [fi'lɔsəfi] n filosofi m

phone [foun] n telefon m; v
telefonere, ringe; ~ card telefonkort
nt

phonetic [fə'netik] adj fonetisk

phoney ['founi] adj falsk; n
bløffmaker m

photo ['foutou] n (pl ~s) fotografi nt

photocopy ['foutəkɔpi] n fotokopi m;
v (foto)kopiere

photograph ['foutəgrɑ:f] n fotografi
nt; v fotografere

photographer [fə'tɔgrəfə] n fotograf
m

photography [fə'tɔgrəfi] n
fotografering c

phrase [freiz] n uttrykk nt

phrase book ['freizbuk] n parlør m

physical ['fizikəl] adj fysisk

physician [fi'ziʃən] n lege m

physicist ['fizisist] n fysiker m

physics ['fiziks] n fysikk m

physiology [,fizi'ɔlədʒi] n fysiologi m

pianist ['pi:ənist] n pianist m

piano [pi'ænou] n piano nt; grand ~
flygel nt

pick [pik] v plukke; *velge; n valg nt; ~
up *ta opp; hente; pick-up van
varebil m

picnic ['piknik] n piknik m; v *dra på
piknik

picture ['piktʃə] n maleri nt;
illustrasjon m, stikk nt; bilde nt; ~
postcard prospektkort nt; pictures
kino m

picturesque [,piktʃə'resk] adj
pittoresk, malerisk

piece [pi:s] n stykke nt, bit m; brikke c

pier [piə] n utstikker m

pierce [piəs] v gjennombore

pig [pig] n gris m

pigeon ['pidʒən] n due c

piggy bank ['pigibæŋk]
n sparegris m

pig-headed [,pig'hedid] adj sta

piglet ['piglət] n smågris m

pigskin ['pigskin] n svinelær nt

pike [paik] n (pl ~) gjedde c

pile [pail] n haug m; v stable; piles pl
hemorroider pl

pilgrim ['pilgrim] n pilegrim m

pilgrimage ['pilgrimidʒ] n
pilegrimsreise c

pill [pil] n pille c

pillar ['pilə] n søyle c

pillarbox ['piləbɔks] n postkasse c

pillow ['pilou] n pute c, hodepute c

pillowcase ['piloukeis] n putevar nt

pilot ['pailət] n pilot m; los m

pimple ['pimpəl] n kvise c

pin [pin] n knappenål c; v feste med
nål; bobby ~ Am hårspenne c

pincers ['pinsəz] pl knipetang c

pinch [pintʃ] v *klype

pineapple ['pai,næpəl] n ananas m

ping-pong ['piŋpɔŋ] n bordtennis m

pink [piŋk] adj lyserød, rosa

pioneer [,paiə'niə] n nybygger m;
pioner m

pious ['paiəs] adj from

pip [pip] n kjerne m

pipe [paip] n pipe c; rør nt; ~ cleaner
piperenser m; ~ tobacco pipetobakk
m

pirate ['paiərət] n sjørøver m

pistol ['pistəl] n pistol m

piston ['pistən] n stempel nt

pit [pit] n grop c; gruve c

pitcher ['pitʃə] n krukke c

pity ['piti] n medlidenhet c; v synes
synd på, *ha medlidenhet med; what
a pity! så synd!

placard ['plækɑ:d] n plakat m

place [pleis] n sted nt; v *sette, stille; ~

of birth fødested *nt*; ***take ~** *finne sted

plague [pleig] *n* plage *c*; pest *m*

plaice [pleis] (pl ~) rødspette *c*

plain [plein] *adj* tydelig; alminnelig, enkel; *n* slette *c*

plan [plæn] *n* plan *m*; *v* *planlegge

plane [plein] *adj* flat; *n* fly *nt*; **~ crash** flyulykke *c*

planet ['plænit] *n* planet *m*

planetarium [,plæni'teəriəm] *n* planetarium *nt*

plank [plæŋk] *n* planke *m*

plant [plɑːnt] *n* plante *c*; fabrikk *m*; *v* plante

plantation [plæn'teiʃən] *n* plantasje *m*

plaster ['plɑːstə] *n* murpuss *m*, gips *m*; plaster *nt*

plastic ['plæstik] *adj* plastikk-; *n* plastikk *m*

plate [pleit] *n* tallerken *m*; plate *c*

plateau ['plætou] *n* (pl ~x, ~s) vidde *c*; høyslette *c*

platform ['plætfɔːm] *n* perrong *m*

platinum ['plætinəm] *n* platina *m*

play [plei] *n* lek *m*; teaterstykke *nt*; *v* leke; spille; **one-act ~** enakter *m*; **~ truant** skulke

player [pleiə] *n* spiller *m*

playground ['pleigraund] *n* lekeplass *m*

playing card ['pleiiŋkɑːd] *n* spillkort *nt*

playwright ['pleirait] *n* skuespillforfatter *m*

plea [pliː] *n* påstand *m*; bønn *m*

plead [pliːd] *v* føre en sak; trygle

pleasant ['plezənt] *adj* hyggelig, deilig

please [pliːz] vennligst; *v* glede; **pleased** fornøyd; **pleasing** behagelig

pleasure ['pleʒə] *n* behag *nt*,

fornøyelse *m*

plentiful ['plentifəl] *adj* rikelig

plenty ['plenti] *n* rikelighet *c*; overflod *m*

pliers [plaiəz] *pl* tang *c*

plot [plɔt] *n* komplott *nt*, sammensvergelse *m*; handling *c*; tomt *c*

plough [plau] *n* plog *m*; *v* pløye

plucky ['plʌki] *adj* modig

plug [plʌg] *n* stikkontakt *m*; **~ in** sette i kontakten, plugge inn

plum [plʌm] *n* plomme *c*

plumber ['plʌmə] *n* rørlegger *m*

plump [plʌmp] *adj* lubben

plural ['pluərəl] *n* flertall *m*

plus [plʌs] *prep* pluss

pneumatic [njuː'mætik] *adj* luft..., pneumatisk

pneumonia [njuː'mouniə] *n* lungebetennelse *m*

poach [poutʃ] *v* **~ed eggs** pocherte egg

pocket ['pɔkit] *n* lomme *c*

pocketbook ['pɔkitbuk] *nAm* lommebok *c*

pocketknife ['pɔkitnaif] *n* (pl -knives) lommekniv *m*

poem ['pouim] *n* dikt *nt*

poet ['pouit] *n* dikter *m*

poetry ['pouitri] *n* poesi *m*

point [pɔint] *n* punkt *nt*; spiss *m*; *v* peke; **~ of view** synspunkt *nt*; **~ out** vise

pointed ['pɔintid] *adj* spiss

poison ['pɔizən] *n* gift *c*; *v* forgifte

poisonous ['pɔizənəs] *adj* giftig

Poland ['poulənd] Polen

Pole [poul] *n* polakk *m*

pole [poul] *n* stang *c*

police [pə'liːs] *pl* politi *nt*; **~ station** politistasjon *m*

policeman [pə'liːsmən] *n* (pl -men) politibetjent *m*

policewoman [pə'liːswumən] *n* (pl -women) politibetjent *m*

policy ['pɔlisi] *n* politikk *m*; polise *m*

Polish ['pouliʃ] *adj* polsk

polish ['pɔliʃ] *v* pusse, polere

polite [pə'lait] *adj* høflig

political [pə'litikəl] *adj* politisk

politician [,pɔli'tiʃən] *n* politiker *m*

politics ['pɔlitiks] *n* politikk *m*

poll [poul] *n* meningsmåling *c*; valg; **go to the polls** velge

pollute [pə'luːt] *v* forurense

pollution [pə'luːʃən] *n* forurensning *m*

pond [pɔnd] *n* dam *m*

pony ['pouni] *n* ponni *m*

pool [puːl] *n* dam *m*; svømmebasseng *nt*; ~ **attendant** badevakt *c*

poor [puə] *adj* fattig; fattigslig; dårlig

pope [poup] *n* pave *m*

pop music [pɔp 'mjuːzik] popmusikk *m*

poppy ['pɔpi] *n* valmue *m*

popular ['pɔpjulə] *adj* populær; folke-

population [,pɔpju'leiʃən] *n* befolkning *m*

populous ['pɔpjuləs] *adj* folkerik

porcelain ['pɔːsəlin] *n* porselen *nt*

porcupine ['pɔːkjupain] *n* pinnsvin *nt*

pork [pɔːk] *n* svinekjøtt *nt*

port [pɔːt] *n* havn *c*; babord

portable ['pɔːtəbəl] *adj* transportabel

porter ['pɔːtə] *n* bærer *m*; portier *m*

porthole ['pɔːthoul] *n* kuøye *nt*

portion ['pɔːʃən] *n* porsjon *m*

portrait ['pɔːtrit] *n* portrett *nt*

Portugal ['pɔːtjugəl] Portugal

Portuguese [,pɔːtju'giːz] *adj* portugisisk; *n* portugiser *m*

position [pə'ziʃən] *n* posisjon *m*; situasjon *m*; holdning *m*; stilling *c*

positive ['pɔzətiv] *adj* positiv; *n* positivt bilde

possess [pə'zes] *v* eie; **possessed** *adj* besatt

possession [pə'zeʃən] *n* besittelse *m*; **possessions** eiendeler *pl*

possibility [,pɔsə'biləti] *n* mulighet *c*

possible ['pɔsəbəl] *adj* mulig; eventuell

post [poust] *n* stolpe *m*; post *m*; *v* poste; **post-office** postkontor *nt*

postage ['poustidʒ] *n* porto *m*; ~ **paid** portofri; ~ **stamp** frimerke *nt*

postcard ['poustkaːd] *n* postkort *nt*; prospektkort *nt*

poster ['poustə] *n* plakat *m*

poste restante [poust re'stɑːt] poste restante

postman ['poustmən] *n* (pl -men) postbud *nt*

post-paid [,poust'peid] *adj* frankert

postpone [pə'spoun] *v* *utsette

pot [pɔt] *n* gryte *c*

potato [pə'teitou] *n* (pl ~es) potet *m*

pottery ['pɔtəri] *n* keramikk *m*; steintøy *nt*

pouch [pautʃ] *n* pung *m*

poultry ['poultri] *n* fjærkre *nt*

pound [paund] *n* pund *nt*

pour [pɔː] *v* helle, skjenke

poverty ['pɔvəti] *n* fattigdom *m*

powder ['paudə] *n* pudder *nt*

power [pauə] *n* kraft *c*, styrke *m*; energi *m*; makt *c*; ~ **station** kraftverk *nt*

powerful ['pauəfəl] *adj* mektig; sterk

powerless ['pauələs] *adj* maktesløs

practical ['præktikəl] *adj* praktisk

practically ['præktikli] *adv* praktisk talt

practice ['præktis] *n* praksis *m*

practise ['præktis] *v* praktisere; øve seg

praise [preiz] *v* rose; *n* ros *m*

pram [præm] *n* barnevogn *c*

prawn [prɔːn] *n* reke *c*

pray [prei] v *be

prayer [preə] n bønn m

preach [priːtʃ] v preke

precarious [pri'kɛəriəs] adj risikabel; utrygg

precaution [pri'kɔːʃən] n forsiktighet c; sikkerhetstiltak nt

precede [pri'siːd] v *gå forut for

preceding [pri'siːdiŋ] adj foregående

precious ['preʃəs] adj kostbar; dyrebar; ~ **stone** edelstein m

precipice ['presipis] n stup nt

precipitation [pri,sipi'teiʃən] n nedbør m

precise [pri'sais] adj presis, nøyaktig; pertentlig

predecessor ['priːdisesə] n forgjenger m

predict [pri'dikt] v spå

prefer [pri'fəː] v *foretrekke

preferable ['prefərəbəl] adj til å foretrekke

preference ['prefərəns] n forkjærlighet c

prefix ['priːfiks] n forstavelse m

pregnant ['pregnənt] adj gravid

pregnancy ['pregnənsi] n svangerskap nt

prejudice ['predʒədis] n fordom m

preliminary [pri'liminəri] adj innledende; forberedende

premature ['premətʃuə] adj forhastet; for tidlig

premier ['premiə] n statsminister m

premises ['premisiz] pl eiendom m

premium ['priːmiəm] n forsikringspremie m

prepaid [,priː'peid] adj forhåndsbetalt

preparation [,prepə'reiʃən] n forberedelse m

prepare [pri'pɛə] v forberede; tilberede

prepared [pri'pɛəd] adj beredt

preposition [,prepə'ziʃən] n

preposisjon m

prescribe [pri'skraib] v *foreskrive

prescription [pri'skripʃən] n resept m

presence ['prezəns] n nærvær nt; tilstedeværelse m

present¹ ['prezənt] n presang m, gave c; nåtid c; adj nåværende; tilstedeværende

present² [pri'zent] v presentere; *forelegge

presentation [pri'zent'eiʃən] v presentasjon

presently ['prezəntli] adv snart

preservation [,prezə'veiʃən] n konservering c

preserve [pri'zəːv] v konservere; hermetisere

president ['prezidənt] n president m; formann m

press [pres] n presse m; v trykke på, trykke; presse; ~ **conference** pressekonferanse m

pressing ['presiŋ] adj presserende, inntrengende

pressure ['preʃə] n trykk nt; press nt; **atmospheric** ~ lufttrykk nt; ~ **cooker** trykkoker m

prestige [pre'stiːʒ] n prestisje m

presumable [pri'zjuːməbəl] adj antakelig

presumptuous [pri'zʌmpʃəs] adj overmodig; anmassende

pretence [pri'tens] n påskudd nt

pretend [pri'tend] v *foregi, *late som

pretext ['priːtekst] n påskudd nt

pretty ['priti] adj pen; adv ganske, temmelig

prevent [pri'vent] v avverge, forhindre; forebygge

preventive [pri'ventiv] adj forebyggende

preview ['priːvjuː] n forhåndsvisning m

previous ['priːviəs] adj foregående,

tidligere, forrige

pre-war [,pri:'wɔ:] adj førkrigs-

price [prais] n pris m; v prise

priceless ['praisləs] adj uvurderlig

price list ['prais,list] n prisliste c

pride [praid] n stolthet c

priest [pri:st] n katolsk prest

primary ['praiməri] adj primær; hoved-, første; elementær

primeval forest [praim'i:vəl 'fɔrist] n urskog m

prince [prins] n prins m

princess [prin'ses] n prinsesse c

principal ['prinsəpəl] adj hoved-; n rektor m, skolebestyrer m

principle ['prinsəpəl] n prinsipp nt, grunnsetning m

print [print] v trykke; n avtrykk nt; trykk nt

printer ['printə] n printer m, skriver m

printout ['printaut] n utskrift c

prior ['praiə] adj forutgående

priority [prai'ɔrəti] n fortrinnsrett m, prioritet m

prison ['prizən] n fengsel nt

prisoner ['prizənə] n fange m, innsatt m; ~ of war krigsfange m

privacy ['praivəsi] n privatliv nt

private ['praivit] adj privat; personlig

privilege ['priviliʤ] n privilegium nt

prize [praiz] n premie m; belønning c

probable ['prɔbəbəl] adj sannsynlig

probably ['prɔbəbli] adv sannsynligvis

problem ['prɔbləm] n problem nt; spørsmål nt

procedure [prə'si:dʒə] n fremgangsmåte m

proceed [prə'si:d] v *fortsette; *gå til verks

process ['prouses] n prosess m, fremgangsmåte m; rettergang m

procession [prə'seʃən] n opptog nt, prosesjon m

proclaim [prə'kleim] v *kunngjøre

produce¹ [prə'dju:s] v fremstille, produsere

produce² ['prɔdju:s] n landbruksprodukter pl; avling c

producer [prə'dju:sə] n produsent m

product ['prɔdʌkt] n produkt nt

production [prə'dʌkʃən] n produksjon m

profession [prə'feʃən] n yrke nt; fag nt

professional [prə'feʃənəl] adj profesjonell

professor [prə'fesə] n professor m

profit ['prɔfit] n fortjeneste c, fordel m; v *ha utbytte av

profitable ['prɔfitəbəl] adj innbringende

profound [prə'faund] adj dypsindig; grundig

programme ['prougræm] n program nt

progress¹ ['prougres] n fremskritt nt

progress² [prə'gres] v *gjøre fremskritt

progressive [prə'gresiv] adj progressiv, fremadstrebende; tiltagende

prohibit [prə'hibit] v *forby

prohibition [,proui'biʃən] n forbud nt

prohibitive [prə'hibitiv] adj uoverkommelig

project ['prɔʤekt] n plan m, prosjekt nt

promenade [,prɔmə'nɑ:d] n promenade m

promise ['prɔmis] n løfte nt; v love

promote [prə'mout] v forfremme, fremme

promotion [prə'mouʃən] n forfremmelse m; sales ~ salgsfremmende tiltak

prompt [prɔmpt] adj omgående, straks

pronoun ['prəunaun] *n* pronomen *nt*

pronounce [prə'nauns] *v* uttale

pronunciation [,prənʌnsi'eiʃən] *n* uttale *m*

proof [pru:f] *n* bevis *nt*

propaganda [,prɔpə'gændə] *n* propaganda *m*

propel [prə'pel] *v* *drive frem

propeller [prə'pelə] *n* propell *m*

proper ['prɔpə] *adj* passende; sømmelig, riktig

property ['prɔpəti] *n* eiendeler *pl*, eiendom *m*; egenskap *m*

prophet ['prɔfit] *n* profet *m*

proportion [prə'pɔ:ʃən] *n* proporsjon *m*

proportional [prə'pɔ:ʃənəl] *adj* forholdsmessig

proposal [prə'pouzəl] *n* forslag *nt*

propose [prə'pouz] *v* *foreslå

proposition [,prɔpə'ziʃən] *n* forslag *nt*

proprietor [prə'praiətə] *n* eier *m*

prosecute ['prɔsikju:t] *v* saksøke, anklage

prospect ['prɔspekt] *n* utsikt *m*

prosperity [prɔ'sperəti] *n* fremgang *m*, velstand *m*

prosperous ['prɔspərəs] *adj* velstående

prostitute ['prɔstitju:t] *n* prostituert *m*

protect [prə'tekt] *v* beskytte

protection [prə'tekʃən] *n* beskyttelse *m*

protein ['prouti:n] *n* protein *nt*

protest¹ ['proutest] *n* protest *m*

protest² [prə'test] *v* protestere

Protestant ['prɔtistənt] *adj* protestantisk

proud [praud] *adj* stolt; hovmodig

prove [pru:v] *v* bevise; vise seg

proverb ['prɔvə:b] *n* ordspråk *nt*

provide [prə'vaid] *v* forsyne, skaffe;

provided that forutsatt at

province ['prɔvins] *n* fylke *nt*; provins *m*

provincial [prə'vinʃəl] *adj* provinsiell

provisional [prə'viʒənəl] *adj* foreløpig

provisions [prə'viʒɔnz] *pl* proviant *m*

prudent ['pru:dənt] *adj* klok; varsom

prune [pru:n] *n* sviske *c*

psychiatrist [sai'kaiətrist] *n* psykiater *m*

psychic ['saikik] *adj* psykisk

psychoanalyst [,saikou'ænəlist] *n* psykoanalytiker *m*

psychological [,saikɔ'lɔdʒikəl] *adj* psykologisk

psychologist [sai'kɔlədʒist] *n* psykolog *m*

psychology [sai'kɔlədʒi] *n* psykologi *m*

pub [pʌb] *n* kro *c*, kneipe *c*, pub *m*

public ['pʌblik] *adj* offentlig; allmenn; *n* publikum *nt*; ~ **garden** offentlig parkanlegg; ~ **house** vertshus *nt*

publication [,pʌbli'keiʃən] *n* offentliggjørelse *m*

publicity [pʌ'blisəti] *n* publisitet *m*

publish ['pʌbliʃ] *v* *utgi, *offentliggjøre

publisher ['pʌbliʃə] *n* forlegger *m*

puddle ['pʌdəl] *n* pytt *m*

pull [pul] *v* *trekke; ~ **out** *trekke seg; *dra av sted; ~ **up** stanse

pulley ['puli] *n* (pl ~s) trinse *c*

Pullman ['pulmən] *n* sovevogn *c*

pullover ['pu,louvə] *n* genser *m*

pulpit ['pulpit] *n* prekestol *m*, talerstol *m*

pulse [pʌls] *n* puls *m*

pump [pʌmp] *n* pumpe *c*; *v* pumpe

pun [pʌn] *n* ordspill *nt*

punch [pʌntʃ] *v* *slå; *n* knyttneveslag *nt*; punsj *m*

punctual ['pʌŋktʃuəl] *adj* punktlig,

presis
puncture ['pʌŋktʃə] *n* punktering *c*
punctured ['pʌŋktʃəd] *adj* punktert
punish ['pʌniʃ] *v* straffe
punishment ['pʌniʃmənt] *n* straff *m*
pupil ['pjuːpəl] *n* elev *m*
puppet-show ['pʌpitʃou] *n* dukketeater *nt*
purchase ['pəːtʃəs] *v* kjøpe; *n* kjøp *nt*, anskaffelse *m*; ~ **price** kjøpesum *m*; ~ **tax** moms *m*
purchaser ['pəːtʃəsə] *n* kjøper *m*
pure [pjuə] *adj* ren
purple ['pəːpəl] *adj* purpurfarget, lilla
purpose ['pəːpəs] *n* hensikt *m*, formål *nt*; **on** ~ med vilje

purse [pəːs] *n* pengepung *m*, håndveske *c*
pursue [pə'sjuː] *v* *forfølge; strebe etter
pus [pʌs] *n* verk *m*; materie *m*
push [puʃ] *n* dytt *m*, støt *nt*; *v* *skyve; trenge seg frem
push button ['puʃ,bʌtən] *n* trykknapp *m*
***put** [put] *v* stille, *legge, plassere; putte; ~ **away** rydde vekk; ~ **off** *utsette; ~ **on** *ta på; ~ **out** slokke
puzzle ['pʌzəl] *n* puslespill *nt*; gåte *c*; *v* volde hodebry; **jigsaw** ~ puslespill *nt*
puzzling ['pʌzliŋ] *adj* uforståelig
pyjamas [pə'dʒɑːməz] *pl* pyjamas *m*

Q

quack [kwæk] *n* sjarlatan *m*, kvakksalver *m*
quail [kweil] *n* (pl ~, ~s) vaktel *m*
quaint [kweint] *adj* eiendommelig; gammeldags
qualification [,kwɔlifi'keiʃən] *n* kvalifikasjon *m*; forbehold *nt*, innskrenkning *m*
qualified ['kwɔlifaid] *adj* kvalifisert; kompetent
qualify ['kwɔlifai] *v* kvalifisere seg
quality ['kwɔləti] *n* kvalitet *m*; egenskap *m*
quantity ['kwɔntəti] *n* kvantitet *m*; antall *nt*
quarantine ['kwɔrəntiːn] *n* karantene *m*
quarrel ['kwɔrəl] *v* trette, krangle; *n* krangel *m*/*nt*, trette *c*
quarry ['kwɔri] *n* steinbrudd *nt*
quarter ['kwɔːtə] *n* kvart; kvartal *nt*; kvarter *nt*; *Am* 25-cent-mynt; ~ **of an**

hour kvarter *nt*
quarterly ['kwɔːtəli] *adj* kvartals-
quay [kiː] *n* kai *c*
queen [kwiːn] *n* dronning *c*
queer [kwiə] *adj* merkelig, underlig; sær
query ['kwiəri] *n* forespørsel *m*; *v* *forespørre; betvile
question ['kwestʃən] *n* spørsmål *nt*, problem *nt*; *v* *spørre ut; *dra i tvil; ~ **mark** spørsmålstegn *nt*
queue [kjuː] *n* kø *m*; *v* *stå i kø
quick [kwik] *adj* hurtig
quick-tempered [,kwik'tempəd] *adj* hissig
quiet ['kwaiət] *adj* stille, rolig, stillferdig; *n* stillhet *c*, ro *m*
quilt [kwilt] *n* vatt-teppe *nt*
quit [kwit] *v* slutte, stoppe
quite [kwait] *adv* helt; ganske, temmelig, særdeles
quiz [kwiz] *n* (pl ~zes) spørrelek *m*;

razor

prøve c
quota ['kwoutə] n kvote m
quotation [kwou'teiʃən] n sitat nt; ~

marks anførselstegn pl
quote [kwout] v sitere

R

rabbit ['ræbit] n kanin m
rabies ['reibiz] n hundegalskap m, rabies m
race [reis] n kappløp nt, veddeløp nt; rase m
racecourse ['reiskɔːs] n veddeløpsbane m
racehorse ['reishɔːs] n veddeløpshest m
racetrack ['reistræk] n veddeløpsbane m
racial ['reiʃəl] adj rase-
racket ['rækit] n rabalder nt; racket m
radiator ['reidieitə] n radiator m
radical ['rædikəl] adj radikal
radio ['reidiou] n radio m
radish ['rædiʃ] n reddik m
radius ['reidiəs] n (pl radii) radius m
raft [rɑːft] n flåte m
rag [ræg] n fille c
rage [reidʒ] n raseri nt; v rase
raid [reid] n angrep nt
rail [reil] n gelender nt, rekkverk nt
railing ['reiliŋ] n gelender nt
railroad ['reilroud] nAm jernbane m
railway ['reilwei] n jernbane m; skinnegang m
rain [rein] n regn nt; v regne
rainbow ['reinbou] n regnbue m
raincoat ['reinkout] n regnfrakk m
rainproof ['reinpruːf] adj vanntett
rainy ['reini] adj regnfull
raise [reiz] v heve; øke; dyrke; *oppdra, ale opp; *pålegge; nAm lønnstillegg nt

raisin ['reizən] n rosin c
rake [reik] n rake m
rally ['ræli] n rally nt; opptog nt; v samle seg
ramp [ræmp] n rampe c
ramshackle ['ræm,ʃækəl] adj falleferdig
rancid ['rænsid] adj harsk
rang [ræŋ] v (p ring)
range [reindʒ] n rekkevidde c; ~ **finder** avstandsmåler m
rank [ræŋk] n rang m; rekke c
ransom ['rænsəm] n løsepenger pl
rape [reip] v *voldta; n voldtekt c
rapid ['ræpid] adj hurtig
rapids ['ræpidz] pl elvestryk nt
rare [rɛə] adj sjelden; lettstekt, blodig
rarely ['rɛəli] adv sjelden
rascal ['rɑːskəl] n skurk m, slyngel m
rash [ræʃ] n utslett nt; adj forhastet, ubesindig
raspberry ['rɑːzbəri] n bringebær nt
rat [ræt] n rotte c
rate [reit] n tariff m, pris m; fart m; **at any** ~ i alle fall, i hvert fall; ~ **of exchange** valutakurs m
rather ['rɑːðə] adv temmelig, ganske, riktig; heller
ration ['ræʃən] n rasjon m
raven ['reivən] n ravn m
raw [rɔː] adj rå; ~ **material** råmateriale nt
ray [rei] n stråle m
razor ['reizə] n barberhøvel m; ~ **blade** barberblad nt

reach [ri:tʃ] v nå; n rekkevidde c
react [ri'ækt] v reagere
reaction [ri'ækʃən] n reaksjon m
***read** [ri:d] v lese
reading ['ri:diŋ] n lesning m
reading lamp ['ri:diŋlæmp] n leselampe c
reading room ['ri:diŋru:m] n lesesal m
ready ['redi] adj klar, parat; ferdig
real [riəl] adj virkelig
reality [ri'æləti] n virkelighet c
realizable ['riəlaizəbəl] adj mulig
realize ['riəlaiz] v *innse, *ha klart for seg; realisere
really ['riəli] adv virkelig, faktisk; egentlig
rear [riə] n bakside c; v *oppdra; heve; ~ **light** baklykt c
reason ['ri:zən] n årsak c, grunn m; fornuft m, forstand m; v resonnere
reasonable ['ri:zənəbəl] adj fornuftig; rimelig
reassure [,ri:ə'ʃuə] v berolige
rebate ['ri:beit] n fradrag nt, rabatt m
rebellion [ri'beljən] n oppstand m, opprør nt
recall [ri'kɔ:l] v erindre, minnes; tilbakekalle; annullere
receipt [ri'si:t] n kvittering c; mottakelse m
receive [ri'si:v] v *få, *motta
receiver [ri'si:və] n telefonrør nt
recent ['ri:sənt] adj ny
recently ['ri:səntli] adv forleden, nylig
reception [ri'sepʃən] n mottakelse m; ~ **office** resepsjon m
receptionist [ri'sepʃənist] n resepsjonist m
recession [ri'seʃən] n tilbakegang m
recipe ['resipi] n oppskrift c
recital [ri'saitəl] n solistkonsert m
reckon ['rekən] v regne; tro
recognition [,rekəg'niʃən] n

anerkjennelse m; gjenkjennelse m
recognize ['rekəgnaiz] v kjenne igjen; anerkjenne
recollect [,rekə'lekt] v huske
recommend [,rekə'mend] v anbefale; tilråde
recommendation [,rekəmen'deiʃən] n anbefaling c
reconciliation [,rekənsili'eiʃən] n forsoning c
record¹ ['rekɔːd] n plate c; rekord m; protokoll m
record² [ri'kɔːd] v registrere
recorder [ri'kɔːdə] n kassettspiller m
recording [ri'kɔːdiŋ] n opptak nt
recover [ri'kʌvə] v *finne igjen; bli frisk, *komme seg
recovery [ri'kʌvəri] n helbredelse m, bedring c
recreation [,rekri'eiʃən] n atspredelse m, rekreasjon m; ~ **center** Am, ~ **centre** rekreasjonssenter nt
recruit [ri'kruːt] n rekrutt m
rectangle ['rektæŋgəl] n rektangel nt
rectangular [rek'tæŋgjulə] adj rektangulær
rector ['rektə] n sogneprest m
rectum ['rektəm] n endetarm m
recyclable [ri'saikləbəl] adj resirkulerbar
recycle [ri'saikəl] v resirkulere
red [red] adj rød; **red tape** papirmølle c, byråkrati nt
redeem [ri'di:m] v frelse
reduce [ri'djuːs] v redusere, minske
reduction [ri'dʌkʃən] n reduksjon m, avslag nt
redundant [ri'dʌndənt] adj overflødig
reed [riːd] n siv m
reef [riːf] n rev nt
reference ['refrəns] n referanse m, henvisning m; forbindelse m; **with ~ to** vedrørende

refer to [ri'fə:] henvise til
referee [,refə'ri:] n dommer m
refill ['ri:fil] n refill m
refinery [ri'fainəri] n raffineri nt
reflect [ri'flekt] v reflektere;
gjenspeile
reflection [ri'flekʃən] n refleks m;
speilbilde nt
reflector [ri'flektə] n reflektor m
refresh [ri'freʃ] v forfriske
refreshment [ri'freʃmənt] n
forfriskning m
refrigerator [ri'fridʒəreitə] n
kjøleskap nt
refugee [,refju'dʒi:] n flyktning m
refund¹ [ri'fʌnd] v refundere
refund² ['ri:fʌnd] n tilbakebetaling c
refusal [ri'fju:zəl] n avslag nt
refuse¹ [ri'fju:z] v *avslå
refuse² ['refju:s] n avfall nt
regard [ri'gɑ:d] v *anse; betrakte; n
respekt m; **as regards** angående,
med hensyn til; **best ~** med vennlig
hilsen, mvh
regarding [ri'gɑ:diŋ] prep med
hensyn til; angående
regatta [ri'gætə] n regatta m
régime [rei'ʒi:m] n regime nt
region ['ri:dʒən] n egn m; område nt
regional ['ri:dʒənəl] adj regional
register ['redʒistə] v *innskrive seg;
bokføre; **registered letter**
rekommandert brev
registration [,redʒi'streiʃən] n
registrering c; **~ number**
registreringsnummer nt; **~ plate**
nummerskilt nt
regret [ri'gret] v beklage; n beklagelse
m
regular ['regjulə] adj regelmessig;
normal, vanlig
regulate ['regjuleit] v regulere
regulation [,regju'leiʃən] n regel m,
bestemmelse m; regulering c

rehabilitation [,ri:hə,bili'teiʃən] n
rehabilitering c
rehearsal [ri'hə:səl] n prøve c; øvelse
m
rehearse [ri'hə:s] v prøve; øve
reign [rein] n regjeringstid c; v herske
reimburse [,ri:im'bə:s] v
tilbakebetale
reindeer ['reindiə] n (pl ~) reinsdyr nt
reject [ri'dʒekt] v tilbakevise, avvise;
forkaste
relate [ri'leit] v *fortelle
related [ri'leitid] adj beslektet
relation [ri'leiʃən] n forhold nt,
forbindelse m; slektning m
relative ['relətiv] n slektning m; adj
relativ
relax [ri'læks] v slappe av
relaxation [,rilæk'seiʃən] n
avslapning m
reliable [ri'laiəbəl] adj pålitelig
relic ['relik] n relikvie m
relief [ri'li:f] n lindring c, lettelse m;
hjelp c; relieff nt
relieve [ri'li:v] v lindre; avløse
religion [ri'lidʒən] n religion m
religious [ri'lidʒəs] adj religiøs
rely on [ri'lai] stole på
remain [ri'mein] v *forbli; *bli igjen
remainder [ri'meində] n rest m
remaining [ri'meiniŋ] adj resterende
remark [ri'mɑ:k] n bemerkning m; v
bemerke
remarkable [ri'mɑ:kəbəl] adj
bemerkelsesverdig
remedy ['remədi] n legemiddel nt;
botemiddel nt
remember [ri'membə] v huske
remembrance [ri'membrəns] n
erindring c, minne nt
remind [ri'maind] v minne
remit [ri'mit] v overføre
remittance [ri'mitəns] n remisse m
remnant ['remnənt] n rest m, levning

m

remote [ri'mout] *adj* fjern, avsides

removal [ri'mu:vəl] *n* fjerning *c*

remove [ri'mu:v] *v* fjerne

remuneration [ri,mju:nə'reiʃən] *n* godtgjørelse *m*

renew [ri'nju:] *v* fornye

rent [rent] *v* leie; *n* leie *c*

repair [ri'pɛə] *v* reparere; *n* reparasjon *m*

reparation [,repə'reiʃən] *n* reparasjon *m*

*repay [ri'pei] *v* tilbakebetale

repayment [ri'peimənt] *n* tilbakebetaling *c*

repeat [ri'pi:t] *v* *gjenta

repellent [ri'pelənt] *adj* frastøtende

repentance [ri'pentəns] *n* anger *m*

repertory ['repətəri] *n* repertoar *nt*

repetition [,repə'tiʃən] *n* gjentakelse *m*

replace [ri'pleis] *v* erstatte

reply [ri'plai] *v* svare; *n* svar *nt*; **in ~** som svar

report [ri'pɔ:t] *v* rapportere; melde; melde seg; *n* rapport *m*, melding *c*

reporter [ri'pɔ:tə] *n* reporter *m*

represent [,repri'zent] *v* representere; forestille

representation [,reprizen'teiʃən] *n* representasjon *m*

representative [,repri'zentətiv] *adj* representativ

reprimand ['reprima:nd] *v* *irettesette

reproach [ri'proutʃ] *n* bebreidelse *m*; *v* bebreide

reproduce [,ri:prə'dju:s] *v* reprodusere

reproduction [,ri:prə'dʌkʃən] *n* reproduksjon *m*

reptile ['reptail] *n* krypdyr *nt*

republic [ri'pʌblik] *n* republikk *m*

republican [ri'pʌblikən] *adj*

republikansk

repulsive [ri'pʌlsiv] *adj* frastøtende

reputation [,repju'teiʃən] *n* rykte *nt*; anseelse *m*

request [ri'kwest] *n* anmodning, bønn *m*; *v* anmode, be*

require [ri'kwaiə] *v* kreve; behøve

requirement [ri'kwaiəmənt] *n* krav *nt*

requisite ['rekwizit] *adj* påkrevd

rescue ['reskju:] *v* redde; *n* redning *m*

research [ri'sə:tʃ] *n* forskning *m*

resemblance [ri'zembləns] *n* likhet *c*

resemble [ri'zembəl] *v* likne

resent [ri'zent] *v* *ta ille opp

reservation [,rezə'veiʃən] *n* reservasjon *m*; forbehold *nt*

reserve [ri'zə:v] *v* reservere; bestille; *n* reserve *m*

reserved [ri'zə:vd] *adj* reservert

reservoir ['rezəvwa:] *n* reservoar *nt*

reside [ri'zaid] *v* bo

residence ['rezidəns] *n* bolig *m*; **~ permit** oppholdstillatelse *m*

resident ['rezidənt] *n* fastboende *m*; *adj* bosatt; stedlig

resign [ri'zain] *v* *fratre; *gå av

resignation [,rezig'neiʃən] *n* avskjedssøknad *m*; avskjed *m*

resin ['rezin] *n* harpiks *m*

resist [ri'zist] *v* *gjøre motstand mot

resistance [ri'zistəns] *n* motstand *m*

resolute ['rezəlu:t] *adj* bestemt, besluttsom

respect [ri'spekt] *n* respekt *m*; ærbødighet *c*, aktelse *m*; *v* respektere

respectable [ri'spektəbəl] *adj* respektabel

respectful [ri'spektfəl] *adj* ærbødig

respective [ri'spektiv] *adj* respektiv

respiration [,respə'reiʃən] *n* åndedrett *nt*

respite ['respait] *n* henstand *m*

responsibility [ri,sponsə'biləti] *n* ansvar *nt*

responsible [ri'spɔnsəbəl] *adj* ansvarlig

rest [rest] *n* hvile *m*; rest *m*; *v* hvile

restaurant ['restərō:] *n* restaurant *m*

restful ['restfəl] *adj* beroligende

rest home ['resthoum] *n* hvilehjem *nt*

restless ['restləs] *adj* urolig; rastløs

restrain [ri'strein] *v* tøyle

restriction [ri'strikʃən] *n* innskrenkning *m*

rest room ['restru:m] *nAm* toalett *nt*

result [ri'zʌlt] *n* resultat *nt*; følge *m*; *v* resultere

resume [ri'zju:m] *v* *gjenoppta

résumé ['rezjumei] *n* resymé *nt*

retail ['ri:teil] *n* ~ **trade** detaljhandel *m*

retina ['retinə] *n* netthinne *c*

retire [ri'taiə] *v* trekke seg tilbake; gå av med pensjon

retired [ri'taiəd] *adj* pensjonert

retirement [ri'taiəmənt] *n* pensjon *m*

return [ri'tə:n] *v* vende tilbake, *komme tilbake; *n* tilbakekomst *m*; ~ **flight** tilbaketur *m*; ~ **journey** hjemreise *m*, tilbakereise *c*

reunite [ˌri:ju:'nait] *v* gjenforene

reveal [ri'vi:l] *v* åpenbare, avsløre

revelation [ˌrevə'leiʃən] *n* avsløring *c*

revenge [ri'vendʒ] *n* hevn *m*

revenue ['revənju:] *n* inntekter *pl*, toll *m*

reverse [ri'və:s] *n* motsetning *m*; bakside *c*; revers *m*; motgang *m*; omslag *nt*; *adj* motsatt; *v* rygge

review [ri'vju:] *n* anmeldelse *m*; tidsskrift *nt*

revise [ri'vaiz] *v* revidere

revision [ri'viʒən] *n* revisjon *m*

revival [ri'vaivəl] *n* gjenopplivelse *m*

revolt [ri'voult] *v* *gjøre opprør; *n* oppstand *m*, opprør *nt*

revolting [ri'voultiŋ] *adj* motbydelig, frastøtende, opprørende

revolution [ˌrevə'lu:ʃən] *n* revolusjon *m*; omdreining *m*

revolutionary [ˌrevə'lu:ʃənəri] *adj* revolusjonær

revolver [ri'vɔlvə] *n* revolver *m*

revue [ri'vju:] *n* revy *m*

reward [ri'wɔ:d] *n* belønning *c*; *v* belønne

rheumatism ['ru:mətizəm] *n* reumatisme *m*

rhinoceros [rai'nɔsərəs] *n* (pl ~, ~es) neshorn *nt*

rhubarb ['ru:bɑ:b] *n* rabarbra *m*

rhyme [raim] *n* rim *nt*

rhythm ['riðəm] *n* rytme *m*

rib [rib] *n* ribbein *nt*

ribbon ['ribən] *n* bånd *nt*

rice [rais] *n* ris *m*

rich [ritʃ] *adj* rik

riches ['ritʃiz] *pl* rikdom *m*

rid [rid] *v* befri (of fra); **get ~ of** bli kvitt

riddle ['ridəl] *n* gåte *c*

ride [raid] *n* tur *m*

*ride** [raid] *v* kjøre; *ride

rider ['raidə] *n* rytter *m*

ridge [ridʒ] *n* høydedrag *nt*

ridicule ['ridikju:l] *v* *latterliggjøre

ridiculous [ri'dikjuləs] *adj* latterlig

riding ['raidiŋ] *n* ridning *m*; ~ **school** rideskole *m*

rifle ['raifəl] *v* gevær *nt*

right [rait] *n* rettighet *c*; *adj* rett, riktig; høyre; rettferdig; **all right!** bra!; *be ~ *ha rett; ~ **of way** forkjørsrett *m*

righteous ['raitʃəs] *adj* rettskaffen

right-hand ['raithænd] *adj* på høyre side, høyre

rightly ['raitli] *adv* med rette

rim [rim] *n* felg *m*; kant *m*

ring [riŋ] *n* ring *m*; krets *m*; manesje *m*

*ring** [riŋ] *v* ringe; ~ **up** ringe opp

rinse [rins] *v* skylle; *n* skylling *c*

riot ['raiət] *n* oppløp *nt*

rip [rip] v *rive i stykker
ripe [raip] adj moden
rise [raiz] n pålegg nt, høyde m; oppstigning m; opprinnelse m
***rise** [raiz] v reise seg; *stå opp; *stige
rising ['raiziŋ] n oppstand m
risk [risk] n risiko m; fare m; v risikere
risky ['riski] adj risikabel, dristig
rival ['raivəl] n rival m; konkurrent m; v rivalisere
rivalry ['raivəlri] n rivalitet m; konkurranse m
river ['rivə] n elv m; ~ **bank** elvebredd m
riverside ['rivəsaid] n elvebredd m
roach [routʃ] n (pl ~) mort m
road [roud] n gate c, vei m; ~ **fork** veiskille m; ~ **map** veikart nt; ~ **system** veinett nt; ~ **up** veiarbeid nt
roadhouse ['roudhaus] n veikro c
roadside ['roudsaid] n veikant m; ~ **restaurant** vertshus m
roadway ['roudwei] nAm kjørebane m
roam [roum] v streife omkring
roar [rɔː] v brøle, bruse; n dur m, brøl nt
roast [roust] v steke, riste; n stek c
rob [rɔb] v rane
robber ['rɔbə] n ransmann m
robbery ['rɔbəri] n plyndring c, ran nt, tyveri nt; overfall nt
robe [roub] n lang kjole; embetsdrakt c
robin ['rɔbin] n rødstrupe m
robust [rou'bʌst] adj robust
rock [rɔk] n klippe m; v gynge
rocket ['rɔkit] n rakett m
rocky ['rɔki] adj steinet
rod [rɔd] n stang c
roe [rou] n rogn c
roll [roul] v rulle; n rull m; rundstykke nt

roller-skating ['roulə,skeitiŋ] n rulleskøyteløping c
Roman Catholic ['roumən 'kæθəlik] romersk-katolsk
romance [rə'mæns] n romanse m
romantic [rə'mæntik] adj romantisk
roof [ruːf] n tak nt; **thatched** ~ halmtak m
room [ruːm] n rom nt, værelse nt; plass m; ~ **and board** kost og losji; ~ **service** værelsesbetjening c; ~ **temperature** værelsestemperatur m
roomy ['ruːmi] adj rommelig
root [ruːt] n rot c
rope [roup] n rep nt
rosary ['rouzəri] n rosenkrans m
rose [rouz] n rose c; adj rosa
rotten ['rɔtən] adj råtten
rouge [ruːʒ] n rouge m
rough [rʌf] adj ru
roulette [ruː'let] n rulett m
round [raund] adj rund; prep om, omkring; n runde m; ~ **trip** Am turretur
roundabout ['raundəbaut] n rundkjøring c
rounded ['raundid] adj avrundet
route [ruːt] n rute c
routine [ruː'tiːn] n rutine m
row¹ [rou] n rad m; v ro
row² [rau] n krangel m/nt
rowdy ['raudi] adj ståkende, voldsom
rowing boat ['rouiŋbout] n robåt m
royal ['rɔiəl] adj kongelig
rub [rʌb] v *gni
rubber ['rʌbə] n gummi m; viskelær nt; ~ **band** strikk m
rubbish ['rʌbiʃ] n avfall nt; tull nt, sludder nt; **talk** ~ vrøvle; ~ **bin** søppelbøtte c
ruby ['ruːbi] n rubin m
rucksack ['rʌksæk] n ryggsekk m
rudder ['rʌdə] n ror nt
rude [ruːd] adj uforskammet

rug [rʌg] n rye m

ruin ['ru:in] v *ødelegge; n undergang m; ruins ruin m

rule [ru:l] n regel m; styre nt, makt c, regjering c; v regjere, herske; as a ~ som regel, vanligvis

ruler ['ru:lə] n regent m, monark m; linjal m

Rumania [ru:'meiniə] Romania

Rumanian [ru:'meiniən] adj rumensk; n rumener m

rumour ['ru:mə] n rykte nt

*run [rʌn] v *løpe; *renne; ~ into støte på

runaway ['rʌnəwei] n rømling m

rung [rʌŋ] v (pp ring)

runner ['rʌnə] n løper m

runway ['rʌnwei] n startbane m

rural ['ruərəl] adj landlig

ruse [ru:z] n list c

rush [rʌʃ] v styrte; n siv nt

rush hour ['rʌʃauə] n rushtid c

Russia ['rʌʃə] Russland

Russian ['rʌʃən] adj russisk; n russer m

rust [rʌst] n rust m

rustic ['rʌstik] adj landsens, rustikal

rusty ['rʌsti] adj rusten

S

sack [sæk] n sekk m

sacred ['seikrid] adj hellig

sacrifice ['sækrifais] n offer nt; v ofre

sacrilege ['sækrilidʒ] n helligbrøde m

sad [sæd] adj bedrøvet; vemodig, bedrøvelig, trist

saddle ['sædəl] n sal m

sadness ['sædnəs] n vemod nt

safe [seif] adj sikker; n safe m, pengeskap nt

safety ['seifti] n sikkerhet c; ~ belt sikkerhetsbelte nt; bilbelte nt; ~ pin sikkerhetsnål c; ~ razor barberhøvel m

sail [seil] v seile; n seil nt

sailing boat ['seilinbout] n seilbåt m

sailor ['seilə] n sjømann m

saint [seint] n helgen m

salad ['sæləd] n salat m

salad-oil ['sælədɔil] n matolje c

salary ['sæləri] n gasje m, lønn c

sale [seil] n salg nt; for ~ til salgs; sales utsalg nt; sales tax moms m

saleable ['seiləbəl] adj salgbar

salesman ['seilzmən] n (pl -men) ekspeditør m, butikkselger m

salmon ['sæmən] n (pl ~) laks m

salon ['sælɔ̃:] n salong m

saloon [sə'lu:n] n bar m

salt [sɔ:lt] n salt nt; ~ cellar, Am ~ shaker n saltkar nt

salty ['sɔ:lti] adj salt

salute [sə'lu:t] v hilse

salve [sɑ:v] n salve c

same [seim] adj samme

sample ['sɑ:mpəl] n vareprøve c

sanatorium [,sænə'tɔ:riəm] n (pl ~s, -ria) sanatorium nt

sand [sænd] n sand m

sandal ['sændəl] n sandal m

sandpaper ['sænd,peipə] n sandpapir nt

sandy ['sændi] adj sandet

sanitary ['sænitəri] adj sanitær; ~ towel, Am ~ napkin (sanitets)bind nt

sapphire ['sæfaiə] n safir m

sardine [sɑ:'di:n] n sardin m

satchel ['sætʃəl] n ransel m

satellite ['sætəlait] *n* satellitt *m*; ~
dish parabolantenne *c*; ~ **tv**
satellittoverføring *c*, satellitt-TV *m*
satin ['sætin] *n* sateng *m*
satisfaction [,sætis'fækʃən] *n*
tilfredsstillelse *m*, tilfredshet *c*
satisfactory [,sætis'fæktəri] *adj*
tilfredsstillende
satisfy ['sætisfai] *v* tilfredsstille;
satisfied tilfreds, tilfredsstilt
Saturday ['sætədi] lørdag *m*
sauce [sɔːs] *n* saus *m*
saucepan ['sɔːspən] *n* kasserolle *m*,
gryte *c*
saucer ['sɔːsə] *n* skål *c*
Saudi Arabia [,saudiə'reibiə] Saudi-
Arabia
Saudi Arabian [,saudiə'reibiən] *adj*
saudiarabisk
sauna ['sɔːnə] *n* badstue *c*
sausage ['sɔsidʒ] *n* pølse *c*
savage ['sævidʒ] *adj* vill
save [seiv] *v* redde; spare
savings ['seiviŋz] *pl* sparepenger *pl*; ~
bank sparebank *m*
saviour ['seivjə] *n* frelser *m*
savo(u)ry ['seivəri] *adj* velsmakende;
pikant
saw[1] [sɔː] *v* (p see)
saw[2] [sɔː] *n* sag *c*
sawdust ['sɔːdʌst] *n* sagflis *c*
sawmill ['sɔːmil] *n* sagbruk *nt*
***say** [sei] *v* *si
scaffolding ['skæfəldiŋ] *n* stillas *nt*
scale [skeil] *n* målestokk *m*; skala *m*;
skjell *nt*; **scales** *pl* vekt *c*
scandal ['skændəl] *n* skandale *m*
Scandinavia [,skændi'neiviə]
Skandinavia
Scandinavian [,skændi'neiviən] *adj*
skandinavisk; *n* skandinav *m*
scapegoat ['skeipgout] *n* syndebukk
m
scar [skɑː] *n* arr *nt*

scarce [skɛəs] *adj* knapp
scarcely ['skɛəsli] *adv* knapt
scarcity ['skɛəsəti] *n* knapphet *c*
scare [skɛə] *v* skremme; *n* panikk *m*
scarf [skɑːf] *n* (pl ~s, scarves) skjerf *nt*
scarlet ['skɑːlət] *adj* skarlagenrød
scary ['skɛəri] *adj* foruroligende; nifs
scatter ['skætə] *v* spre
scene [siːn] *n* scene *m*
scenery ['siːnəri] *n* landskap *nt*
scenic ['siːnik] *adj* naturskjønn
scent [sent] *n* duft *m*
schedule ['ʃedjuːl] *n* ruteplan *m*,
timeplan *m*
scheme [skiːm] *n* skjema *nt*; plan *m*
scholar ['skɔlə] *n* akademiker;
student *m*; elev *m*
scholarship ['skɔləʃip] *n* stipend *nt*
school [skuːl] *n* skole *m*
schoolboy ['skuːlbɔi] *n* skolegutt *m*
schoolgirl ['skuːlgəːl] *n* skolepike *m*
schoolmaster ['skuːl,mɑːstə] *n* lærer
m
schoolteacher ['skuːl,tiːtʃə] *n* lærer
m
science ['saiəns] *n* (natur)vitenskap
m
scientific [,saiən'tifik] *adj*
vitenskapelig
scientist ['saiəntist] *n*
vitenskapskvinne *c*; vitenskapsmann
(pl -menn) *m*
scissors ['sizəz] *pl* saks *c*
scold [skould] *v* skjenne på; skjelle
scooter ['skuːtə] *n* scooter *m*;
sparksykkel *m*
score [skɔː] *n* poengsum *m*; *v*
markere
scorn [skɔːn] *n* hån *m*, forakt *m*; *v*
forakte
Scot [skɔt] *n* skotte *m*
Scotch [skɔtʃ] *adj* skotsk
Scotland ['skɔtlənd] Skottland
Scottish ['skɔtiʃ] *adj* skotsk

scout [skaut] *n* speider *m*

scrap [skræp] *n* bit *m*

scrape [skreip] *v* skrape

scratch [skrætʃ] *v* skrape, rispe; *n* risp *nt*, skramme *c*

scream [skri:m] *v* *skrike, hyle; *n* hyl *nt*, skrik *nt*

screen [skri:n] *n* skjermbrett *nt*; skjerm *m*, filmlerret *nt*

screw [skru:] *n* skrue *m*; *v* skru

screwdriver ['skru:ˌdraivə] *n* skrujern *m*

scrub [skrʌb] *v* skrubbe; *n* kratt *nt*

sculptor ['skʌlptə] *n* billedhogger *m*

sculpture ['skʌlptʃə] *n* skulptur *m*

sea [si:] *n* sjø *m*; ~ **urchin** sjøpinnsvin *nt*; ~ **water** sjøvann *nt*

seabird ['si:bə:d] *n* sjøfugl *m*

seacoast ['si:koust] *n* kyst *m*

seagull ['si:gʌl] *n* havmåke *c*

seal [si:l] *n* segl *nt*; sel *m*, kobbe *m*

seam [si:m] *n* søm *m*

seaman ['si:mən] *n* (pl -men) sjømann *m*

seaport ['si:pɔ:t] *n* havneby *m*

search [sə:tʃ] *v* lete etter; ransake; *n* leting *c*

searchlight ['sə:tʃlait] *n* lyskaster *m*

seascape ['si:skeip] *n* bilde med maritimt motiv

seashell ['si:ʃel] *n* skjell *nt*

seashore ['si:ʃɔ:] *n* strand *c*; kyst *m*

seasick ['si:sik] *adj* sjøsyk

seasickness ['si:ˌsiknəs] *n* sjøsyke *m*

seaside ['si:said] *n* kyst *m*; ~ **resort** badested *nt*

season ['si:zən] *n* sesong *m*, årstid *c*; **high** ~ høysesong *m*; **low** ~ lavsesong *m*; **off** ~ utenfor sesongen; ~ **ticket** sesongkort *nt*

seat [si:t] *n* sete *nt*; plass *m*, sitteplass *m*; ~ **belt** sikkerhetsbelte *nt*

second ['sekənd] *num* annen; *n* sekund *nt*; øyeblikk *nt*

secondary ['sekəndəri] *adj* sekundær, underordnet; ~ **school** høyere skole

second-hand [ˌsekənd'hænd] *adj* brukt

secret ['si:krət] *n* hemmelighet *c*; *adj* hemmelig

secretary ['sekrətri] *n* sekretær *m*

section ['sekʃən] *n* seksjon *m*, avdeling *c*

secure [si'kjuə] *adj* sikker; *v* sikre seg

security [si'kjuərəti] *n* sikkerhet *c*; kausjon *m*

sedative ['sedətiv] *n* beroligende middel

seduce [si'dju:s] *v* forføre

***see** [si:] *v* *se; *innse, *begripe, *forstå; ~ **to** sørge for

seed [si:d] *n* frø *nt*

***seek** [si:k] *v* søke

seem [si:m] *v* *late til, synes

seen [si:n] *v* (pp see)

seesaw ['si:sɔ:] *n* vippe *c*

seize [si:z] *v* *gripe

seldom ['seldəm] *adv* sjelden

select [si'lekt] *v* *utvelge, *velge ut; *adj* utsøkt, utvalgt

selection [si'lekʃən] *n* utvalg *nt*

self [self] *n* selv; *n* selv, jeg; selv...

self-centered *Am*, **self-centred** [ˌself'sentəd] *adj* selvopptatt

self-employed [ˌselfim'plɔid] *adj* selvstendig næringsdrivende

self-evident [ˌsel'fevidənt] *adj* opplagt

self-government [ˌself'gʌvəmənt] *n* selvstyre *nt*

selfish ['selfiʃ] *adj* selvisk

selfishness ['selfiʃnəs] *n* egoisme *m*

self-service [ˌself'sə:vis] *n* selvbetjening *c*; ~ **restaurant** kafeteria *m*

***sell** [sel] *v* *selge

semblance ['sembləns] *n* utseende

nt; likhet c

semi- ['semi] halv-

semicircle ['semi,sə:kəl] n halvsirkel m

semicolon [,semi'koulən] n semikolon nt

senate ['senət] n senat nt

senator ['senətə] n senator m

*send [send] v sende; ~ back sende tilbake, returnere; ~ for sende bud etter; ~ off sende av sted

sender ['sendə] n sender m; avsender m

senile ['si:nail] adj senil

sensation [sen'seiʃən] n sensasjon m; fornemmelse m, følelse m

sensational [sen'seiʃənəl] adj sensasjonell, oppsiktsvekkende

sense [sens] n sans m; fornuft m; mening m, betydning m; v merke; ~ of honour æresfølelse m

senseless ['sensləs] adj meningsløs

sensible ['sensəbəl] adj fornuftig

sensitive ['sensitiv] adj følsom

sentence ['sentəns] n setning m; dom m; v dømme

sentimental [,senti'mentəl] adj sentimental

separate¹ ['sepəreit] v skille, separere

separate² ['sepərət] adj særskilt, atskilt

separately ['sepərətli] adv separat

September [sep'tembə] september

septic ['septik] adj septisk; *become ~ *gå betennelse i

sequel ['si:kwəl] n fortsettelse m

sequence ['si:kwəns] n rekkefølge m; serie m

serene [sə'ri:n] adj rolig; klar

series ['siəri:z] n (pl ~) serie m

serious ['siəriəs] adj seriøs, alvorlig

seriousness ['siəriəsnəs] n alvor nt

sermon ['sə:mən] n preken m

serum ['siərəm] n serum nt

servant ['sə:vənt] n tjener m

serve [sə:v] v servere

service ['sə:vis] n tjeneste m; betjening c; ~ charge serveringsavgift c; ~ station bensinstasjon m

serviette [,sə:vi'et] n serviett m

session ['seʃən] n sesjon m

set [set] n klikk m; sett nt

*set [set] v *sette; ~ menu fast meny; ~ out *dra av sted

setting ['setiŋ] n omgivelser pl

settle ['setəl] v ordne, avslutte; ~ down *slå seg ned

settlement ['setəlmənt] n ordning c, overenskomst m

seven ['sevən] num sju, syv

seventeen [,sevən'ti:n] num sytten

seventeenth [,sevən'ti:nθ] num syttende

seventh ['sevənθ] num sjuende, syvende

seventy ['sevənti] num sytti

several ['sevərəl] adj atskillige, flere

severe [si'viə] adj heftig, streng

*sew [sou] v sy; ~ up sy sammen

sewer ['su:ə] n kloakk m

sewing machine ['souiŋmə,ʃi:n] n symaskin m

sex [seks] n kjønn nt; sex m

sexual ['sekʃuəl] adj seksuell

sexuality [,sekʃu'æləti] n seksualitet m

shade [ʃeid] n skygge m; nyanse m

shadow ['ʃædou] n skygge m

shady ['ʃeidi] adj skyggefull

*shake [ʃeik] v riste, ryste

shaky ['ʃeiki] adj vaklende

*shall [ʃæl] v *skal

shallow ['ʃælou] adj grunn

shame [ʃeim] n skam c; shame! fy!

shampoo [ʃæm'pu:] n sjampo m

shamrock ['ʃæmrɔk] n trekløver m

shape [ʃeip] n form c; v forme

share [ʃɛə] v dele; n del m; aksje m

shark [ʃɑːk] n hai m

sharp [ʃɑːp] adj spiss

sharpen ['ʃɑːpən] v spisse

shave [ʃeiv] v barbere seg

shaver ['ʃeivə] n barbermaskin m

shaving brush ['ʃeiviŋbrʌʃ] n barberkost m

shaving foam ['ʃeiviŋfoum] n barberskum nt

shawl [ʃɔːl] n sjal nt

she [ʃiː] pron hun

shed [ʃed] n skur nt

*shed [ʃed] v *utgyte; spre

sheep [ʃiːp] n (pl ~) sau m

sheer [ʃiə] adj pur, absolutt; skjær, gjennomsiktig, tynn

sheet [ʃiːt] n laken nt; ark nt; plate c

shelf [ʃelf] n (pl shelves) hylle c

shell [ʃel] n skjell nt; skall nt

shellfish ['ʃelfiʃ] n skalldyr nt

shelter ['ʃeltə] n ly nt, tilfluktssted nt; v *gi ly

shepherd ['ʃepəd] n gjeter m

shift [ʃift] n skift nt

*shine [ʃain] v skinne; glinse, stråle

ship [ʃip] n skip nt; v skipe

shipowner ['ʃi,pounə] n skipsreder m

shipyard ['ʃipjɑːd] n skipsverft nt

shirt [ʃəːt] n skjorte c

shiver ['ʃivə] v *skjelve, hutre; n skjelven m

shock [ʃɔk] n sjokk nt; v sjokkere; ~ absorber støtdemper m

shocking ['ʃɔkiŋ] adj sjokkerende

shoe [ʃuː] n sko m; ~ polish skokrem m; ~ shop skotøyforretning c; gym shoes turnsko pl

shoelace ['ʃuːleis] n skolisse c

shoemaker ['ʃuː,meikə] n skomaker m

shook [ʃuk] v (p shake)

*shoot [ʃuːt] v *skyte

shop [ʃɔp] n forretning c; v handle; ~

assistant ekspeditør m, butikkselger m; **shopping bag** handlebag m; **shopping centre** kjøpesenter nt

shopkeeper ['ʃɔp,kiːpə] n kjøpmann m

shopwindow [,ʃɔp'windou] n utstillingsvindu nt

shore [ʃɔː] n bredd m, kyst m

short [ʃɔːt] adj kort; liten; ~ circuit kortslutning m

shortage ['ʃɔːtidʒ] n knapphet c, mangel m

shorten ['ʃɔːtən] v forkorte

shortly ['ʃɔːtli] adv snart, i nær fremtid

shorts [ʃɔːts] pl shorts m; underbukse c

short-sighted [,ʃɔːt'saitid] adj nærsynt

shot [ʃɔt] n skudd nt; sprøyte c; scene m

*should [ʃud] v *skulle

shoulder ['ʃouldə] n skulder c

shout [ʃaut] v *skrike, rope; n rop m

shovel ['ʃʌvəl] n skuffe c

show [ʃou] n oppførelse m, forestilling c; utstilling c

*show [ʃou] v vise; utstille, vise frem; bevise

showcase ['ʃoukeis] n monter m

shower ['ʃauə] n dusj m; regnskur m, skur m

showroom ['ʃouruːm] n utstillingslokale nt

shriek [ʃriːk] v *skrike; n hvin nt

shrimp [ʃrimp] n reke c

shrine [ʃrain] n helgenskrin nt, helligdom m

*shrink [ʃriŋk] v krympe

shrinkproof ['ʃriŋkpruːf] adj krympefri

shrub [ʃrʌb] n busk m

shudder ['ʃʌdə] n gys nt

shuffle ['ʃʌfəl] v stokke

*shut [ʃʌt] *v* lukke; **shut** stengt,
lukket; **~ in** stenge inne

shutter ['ʃʌtə] *n* vinduslem *m*, skodde
m

shy [ʃai] *adj* sjenert, sky

shyness ['ʃainəs] *n* skyhet *c*

Siamese [,saiə'mi:z] *adj* siamesisk

sick [sik] *adj* syk; kvalm

sickness ['siknəs] *n* sykdom *m*;
kvalme *m*

side [said] *n* side *c*; parti *nt*; **one-
sided** *adj* ensidig

sideburns ['saidbə:nz] *pl* kinnskjegg
nt

side street ['saidstri:t] *n* sidegate *c*

sidewalk ['saidwɔ:k] *nAm* fortau *nt*

sideways ['saidweiz] *adv* til siden

siege [si:dʒ] *n* beleiring *c*

sieve [siv] *n* sil *m*; *v* sikte, sile

sight [sait] *n* syne *nt*; skue *nt*, syn;
severdighet *c*

sign [sain] *n* tegn *nt*; vink *nt*, gest *m*; *v*
undertegne

signal ['signəl] *n* signal *nt*; tegn *nt*; *v*
signalisere

signature ['signətʃə] *n* underskrift *c*,
signatur *m*

significant [sig'nifikənt] *adj*
betydningsfull

signpost ['sainpoust] *n* veiviser *m*

silence ['sailəns] *n* stillhet *c*; *v* få til å
tie

silencer ['sailənsə] *n* lydpotte *c*

silent ['sailənt] *adj* stille, taus; ***be ~**
tie

silk [silk] *n* silke *m*

silly ['sili] *adj* dum, tåpelig

silver ['silvə] *n* sølv *nt*; sølv-

silversmith ['silvəsmiθ] *n* sølvsmed
m

silverware ['silvəwɛə] *n* sølvtøy *nt*

similar ['similə] *adj* liknende

similarity [,simi'lærəti] *n* likhet *c*

simple ['simpəl] *adj* likefrem, enkel;
vanlig

simply ['simpli] *adv* simpelthen

simulate ['simjuleit] *v* etterligne

simultaneous [,siməl'teiniəs] *adj*
samtidig

sin [sin] *n* synd *c*

since [sins] *prep* siden; *adv* siden; *conj*
siden; fordi

sincere [sin'siə] *adj* oppriktig; **yours
sincerely** med vennlig hilsen, mvh

sinew ['sinju:] *n* sene *c*

*sing [siŋ] *v* *synge

singer ['siŋə] *n* sanger *m*; sangerinne
c

single ['siŋgəl] *adj* enkel; ugift; **~
room** enkeltrom *nt*

singular ['siŋgjulə] *n* entall *nt*; *adj*
enestående

sinister ['sinistə] *adj* illevarslende

sink [siŋk] *n* vask *m*

*sink [siŋk] *v* *synke

sip [sip] *n* slurk *m*

sir [sə:] min herre

siren ['saiərən] *n* sirene *c*

sister ['sistə] *n* søster *c*

sister-in-law ['sistərinlɔ:] *n* (pl
sisters-) svigerinne *c*

*sit [sit] *v* *sitte; **~ down** *sette seg

site [sait] *n* sted *nt*; beliggenhet *c*

sitting room ['sitiŋru:m] *n* stue *c*

situated ['sitʃueitid] *adj* beliggende

situation [,sitʃu'eiʃən] *n* situasjon *m*;
stilling *c*

six [siks] *num* seks

sixteen [,siks'ti:n] *num* seksten

sixteenth [,siks'ti:nθ] *num* sekstende

sixth [siksθ] *num* sjette

sixty ['siksti] *num* seksti

size [saiz] *n* størrelse *m*, dimensjon *m*;
format *nt*

skate [skeit] *v* *gå på skøyter; *n*
skøyte *c*

skating ['skeitiŋ] *n* skøyteløping *c*; **~
rink** skøytebane *m*

skeleton ['skelitən] n skjelett nt

sketch [sketʃ] n skisse c, utkast nt; v tegne, skissere

ski¹ [skiː] v *gå på ski

ski² [skiː] n (pl ~, ~s) ski c; ~ boots skistøvler pl; ~ jump skihopp nt; hoppbakke m; ~ lift skiheis m; ~ pants skibukse c; ~ poles Am skistaver pl; ~ sticks skistaver pl

skid [skid] v *gli

skier ['skiːə] n skiløper m

skiing ['skiːiŋ] n skiløping c

skil(l)ful ['skilfəl] adj kyndig, flink, dyktig

skill [skil] n dyktighet c

skilled [skild] adj kyndig, dreven; faglært

skin [skin] n hud c, skinn nt; skall nt

skip [skip] v hoppe; hoppe over

skirt [skəːt] n skjørt nt

skull [skʌl] n skalle m

sky [skai] n himmel m; luft c

skyscraper ['skai,skreipə] n skyskraper m

slack [slæk] adj treg; slapp

slacks [slæks] pl bukse c, bukser pl

slam [slæm] v *slå igjen

slander ['slɑːndə] n bakvaskelse m

slang [slæŋ] n slang m; sjargong m

slant [slɑːnt] v skråne

slanting ['slɑːntiŋ] adj skjev, skrånende, skrå

slap [slæp] v fike; n fik m

slate [sleit] n skifer m

slave [sleiv] n slave m

sledge [sledʒ] n slede m, kjelke m

sleep [sliːp] n søvn m

*sleep [sliːp] v *sove

sleeping bag ['sliːpiŋbæg] n sovepose m

sleeping car ['sliːpiŋkɑː] n sovevogn c

sleeping pill ['sliːpiŋpil] n sovepille c

sleepless ['sliːpləs] adj søvnløs

sleepy ['sliːpi] adj søvnig

sleet [sliːt] n sludd nt

sleeve [sliːv] n erme nt; omslag nt

sleigh [slei] n kjelke m, slede m

slender ['slendə] adj slank

slice [slais] n skive c

slide [slaid] n rutsjebane m; lysbilde nt

*slide [slaid] v *gli

slight [slait] adj ubetydelig; svak

slim [slim] adj slank; v slanke seg

slip [slip] v *gli, skli; *smette; n feiltrinn nt

slipper ['slipə] n tøffel m

slippery ['slipəri] adj glatt, sleip

slogan ['slougən] n slagord nt, valgspråk nt

slope [sloup] n skråning m; v helle

sloping ['sloupiŋ] adj skrånende

sloppy ['slɔpi] adj slurvet

slot [slɔt] n myntsprekk m; åpning c; ~ machine automat m

slovenly ['slʌvənli] adj sjusket

slow [slou] adj tungnem, langsom, sakte; ~ down *sette ned farten, saktne farten; bremse

sluice [sluːs] n sluse c

slum [slʌm] n slum m

slump [slʌmp] n prisfall nt

slush [slʌʃ] n snøslaps nt

sly [slai] adj slu

smack [smæk] v smekke; n dask m

small [smɔːl] adj liten; ringe

smallpox ['smɔːlpɔks] n kopper pl

smart [smɑːt] adj fiks; smart, flink, lur

smash [smæʃ] n hardt slag m; v knuse; ødelegge

smell [smel] n lukt c

*smell [smel] v lukte; *stinke

smelly ['smeli] adj illeluktende

smile [smail] v smile; n smil nt

smith [smiθ] n smed m

smoke [smouk] v røyke; n røyk m; no smoking røyking forbudt

smoker ['smoukə] *n* røyker *m*;
røykekupé *m*

smoking compartment
['smoukiŋkəm,pa:tmənt] *n*
røykekupé *m*

smooth [smu:ð] *adj* jevn, smul, glatt;
myk

smuggle ['smʌgəl] *v* smugle

snack [snæk] *n* matbit *m*

snail [sneil] *n* snegl *m*

snake [sneik] *n* slange *m*

snapshot ['snæpʃɔt] *n*
øyeblikksfotografi *nt*, snapshot *nt*

sneakers ['sni:kəz] *plAm* tennissko
pl, joggesko *pl*

sneeze [sni:z] *v* *nyse

sniper ['snaipə] *n* snikskytter *m*

snooty ['snu:ti] *adj* hoven

snore [snɔ:] *v* snorke

snorkel ['snɔ:kəl] *n* snorkel *m*

snout [snaut] *n* snute *c*

snow [snou] *n* snø *m*; *v* snø

snowstorm ['snoustɔ:m] *n* snøstorm
m

so [sou] *conj* så; *adv* slik; så, i den
grad; **and ~ on** og så videre; **~ far**
hittil; **~ that** så, slik at

soak [souk] *v* gjennombløte, bløte

soap [soup] *n* såpe *c*

sober ['soubə] *adj* edru; nøktern

so-called [,sou'kɔ:ld] *adj* såkalt

soccer ['sɔkə] *n* fotball *m*; **~ team**
fotball-lag *nt*

social ['souʃəl] *adj* samfunns-, sosial

socialism ['souʃəlizəm] *n* sosialisme
m

socialist ['souʃəlist] *adj* sosialistisk; *n*
sosialist *m*

society [sə'saiəti] *n* samfunn *nt*;
selskap *nt*, forening *c*

sock [sɔk] *n* sokk *m*

socket ['sɔkit] *n* pæreholder *m*;
stikkontakt *m*

soda ['soudə]: **~ pop** *nAm colloquial*

brus *m*; **~ water** soda *m*, selters *m*;
naturlig mineralvann *m*

sofa ['soufə] *n* sofa *m*

soft ['sɔft] *adj* myk; **~ drink** alkoholfri
drikk

soften ['sɔfən] *v* *bløtgjøre

software ['sɔftweə] *n* programvare *m*

soil [sɔil] *n* jord *m*; jordbunn *m*;
jordsmonn *nt*

soiled [sɔild] *adj* skitten

solar ['soulə] *adj* sol...; **~ system**
solsystem *nt*

sold [sould] *v* (p, pp sell); **~ out**
utsolgt

soldier ['souldʒə] *n* soldat *m*

sole¹ [soul] *adj* eneste

sole² [soul] *n* såle *m*; flyndre *c*

solely ['soulli] *adv* utelukkende

solemn ['sɔləm] *adj* høytidelig

solicitor [sə'lisitə] *n* sakfører *m*,
advokat *m*

solid ['sɔlid] *adj* solid; massiv; *n* fast
stoff

soluble ['sɔljubəl] *adj* oppløselig

solution [sə'lu:ʃən] *n* løsning *c*;
oppløsning *c*

solve [sɔlv] *v* løse

somber *Am*, **sombre** ['sɔmbə] *adj*
dyster

some [sʌm] *adj* noen; *pron* visse,
enkelte; litt; **~ day** en gang; **~ more**
litt mer; **~ time** en gang

somebody ['sʌmbədi] *pron* noen

somehow ['sʌmhau] *adv* på en eller
annen måte

someone ['sʌmwʌn] *pron* noen

something ['sʌmθiŋ] *pron* noe

sometimes ['sʌmtaimz] *adv* av og til

somewhat ['sʌmwɔt] *adv* nokså

somewhere ['sʌmweə] *adv* etsteds

son [sʌn] *n* sønn *m*

song [sɔŋ] *n* sang *m*

son-in-law ['sʌninlɔ:] *n* (pl sons-)
svigersønn *m*

soon [su:n] adv fort, snart; **as ~ as** så snart som

sooner ['su:nə] adv heller

sore [sɔ:] adj sår, øm; n ømt sted; sår nt; **~ throat** halsesyke m

sorrow ['sɔrou] n sorg c

sorry ['sɔri] adj lei for; **sorry!** unnskyld!, beklager!

sort [sɔ:t] v ordne, sortere; n sort m, slags m/nt; **all sorts of** alle slags

soul [soul] n sjel c

sound [saund] n klang m, lyd m; v *lyde; adj sunn; pålitelig

soundproof ['saundpru:f] adj lydtett

soup [su:p] n suppe c; **~ plate** suppetallerken m; **~ spoon** suppeskje c

sour [sauə] adj sur

source [sɔ:s] n kilde m

south [sauθ] n syd m, sør m; **South Pole** Sydpolen

South Africa [sauθ 'æfrikə] Sør-Afrika

South America [sauθ ə'merikə] Sør-Amerika

southeast [ˌsauθ'i:st] n sørøst m

southerly ['sʌðəli] adj sørlig

southern ['sʌðən] adj sørlig

southwest [ˌsauθ'west] n sørvest m

souvenir ['su:vəniə] n suvenir m

sovereign ['sɔvrin] n hersker m

***sow** [sou] v så

spa [spa:] n kursted nt

space [speis] n rom nt; verdensrom nt; avstand m, mellomrom nt; v sette mellomrom; **~ shuttle** romferge c

spacious ['speiʃəs] adj rommelig

spade [speid] n spade m

Spain [spein] Spania

Spaniard ['spænjəd] n spanjol m, spanier m

Spanish ['spæniʃ] adj spansk

spanking ['spæŋkiŋ] n juling c; ris nt

spanner ['spænə] n skiftenøkkel m

spare [spɛə] adj reserve-, ekstra; v *unnvære; **~ part** reservedel m; **~ room** gjesteværelse nt; **~ time** fritid c; **~ tyre** reservedekk nt; **~ wheel** reservehjul nt

spark [spa:k] n gnist m

sparking plug ['spa:kiŋplʌg] n tennplugg m

sparkling ['spa:kliŋ] adj funklende; musserende

sparrow ['spærou] n spurv m

***speak** [spi:k] v snakke

spear [spiə] n spyd nt

special ['speʃəl] adj spesiell; **~ delivery** ekspress

specialist ['speʃəlist] n spesialist m

speciality [ˌspeʃi'æləti] n spesialitet m

specialize ['speʃəlaiz] v spesialisere seg

specially ['speʃəli] adv i særdeleshet

species ['spi:ʃi:z] n (pl ~) art m

specific [spə'sifik] adj spesifikk

specimen ['spesimən] n prøve c, eksemplar nt

speck [spek] n flekk m

spectacle ['spektəkəl] n skue nt, syn nt; **spectacles** briller pl

spectator [spek'teitə] n tilskuer m

speculate ['spekjuleit] v spekulere

speech [spi:tʃ] n tale m

speechless ['spi:tʃləs] adj målløs

speed [spi:d] n hastighet c; fart m; **cruising ~** marsjfart m; **~ limit** fartsgrense c

***speed** [spi:d] v kjøre fort; kjøre for fort

speeding ['spi:diŋ] n råkjøring c

speedometer [spi:'dɔmitə] n fartsmåler m

spell [spel] n fortryllelse m

***spell** [spel] v stave

spelling ['speliŋ] n stavemåte m

***spend** [spend] v bruke, spandere;

*tilbringe

sphere [sfiə] n kule c; område nt

spice [spais] n krydder nt; **spices** krydderier pl

spiced [spaist] adj krydret

spicy ['spaisi] adj krydret

spider ['spaidə] n edderkopp m; **spider's web** spindelvev m

*spill [spil] v søle

*spin [spin] v *spinne; snurre

spinach ['spinidʒ] n spinat m

spine [spain] n ryggrad m

spinster ['spinstə] n gammel jomfru

spire [spaiə] n spir nt

spirit ['spirit] n ånd m; spøkelse nt; ~ **stove** spritapparat nt; **spirits** spirituosa pl, alkoholholdige drikker; humør nt

spiritual ['spirit∫uəl] adj åndelig

spit [spit] n spytt nt; spidd nt

*spit [spit] v spytte

spite [spait] n ondskapsfullhet c; v være ekkel mot; **in ~ of** til tross for

spiteful ['spaitfəl] adj ondskapsfull

splash [splæ∫] v skvette

splendid ['splendid] adj praktfull, glimrende

splendo(u)r ['splendə] n prakt m

splint [splint] n beinskinne c

splinter ['splintə] n splint m

*split [split] v kløyve

*spoil [spɔil] v *ødelegge; skjemme bort

spoke[1] [spouk] v (p speak)

spoke[2] [spouk] n eike c

sponge [spʌndʒ] n svamp m

spook [spu:k] n spøkelse nt

spool [spu:l] n spole m

spoon [spu:n] n skje c

spoonful ['spu:nful] n skjefull m

sport [spɔ:t] n sport m

sports car ['spɔ:tska:] n sportsbil m

sportsman ['spɔ:tsmən] n (pl -men) idrettsmann m

sportswear ['spɔ:tswɛə] n sportsklær pl

sportswoman ['spɔ:tswumən] n (pl -women) idrettskvinne c

spot [spɔt] n flekk m; sted nt

spotless ['spɔtləs] adj plettfri

spotlight ['spɔtlait] n prosjektør m

spotted ['spɔtid] adj flekket

spout [spaut] n tut m

sprain [sprein] v forstue; n forstuing c

spray [sprei] n sprut m; spray m; v sprøyte (planter), sprute; spraye

*spread [spred] v spre

spring [spriŋ] n vår m; fjær c; kilde m

springtime ['spriŋtaim] n vår m

sprouts [sprauts] pl rosenkål m

spy [spai] n spion m

square [skwɛə] adj kvadratisk; n kvadrat nt; plass m

squash [skwɔ∫] n fruktsaft c; squash m; v kryste

squeeze [skwi:z] v presse (saft); trykke

squirrel ['skwirəl] n ekorn nt

squirt [skwə:t] n sprut m

stable ['steibəl] adj stabil; n stall m

stack [stæk] n stabel m

stadium ['steidiəm] n stadion nt

staff [sta:f] n personale nt

stage [steidʒ] n scene m; stadium nt, fase m; etappe m

stain [stein] v flekke; n flekk m; **stained glass window** glassmaleri nt; ~ **remover** flekkfjerner m

stainless ['steinləs] adj plettfri; ~ **steel** rustfritt stål

staircase ['stɛəkeis] n trapp c

stairs [stɛəz] pl trapp c

stale [steil] adj ~ **bread** gammelt brød; ~ **air** dårlig luft

stall [stɔ:l] n utsalgsbord nt; orkesterplass m

stamp [stæmp] n frimerke nt; stempel nt; v frankere; trampe; ~ **machine**

frimerkeautomat m

stand [stænd] n stand m; tribune m

*stand [stænd] v *stå

standard ['stændəd] n norm m; standard-; **~ of living** levestandard m

stanza ['stænzə] n strofe m; vers nt

staple ['steipəl] n stift m

star [stɑː] n stjerne c

starboard ['stɑːbəd] n styrbord

stare [stɛə] v stirre

starling ['stɑːliŋ] n stær m

start [stɑːt] v begynne; n start m

starting point ['stɑːtiŋpɔint] n utgangspunkt nt

state [steit] n stat m; stand m; v erklære; **the States** [ðə steits] De forente stater

statement ['steitmənt] n erklæring c

station ['steiʃən] n stasjon m; posisjon m

stationary ['steiʃənəri] adj stillestående

stationer's ['steiʃənəz] n papirhandel m

stationery ['steiʃənəri] n papirvarer pl

statistics [stə'tistiks] pl statistikk m

statue ['stætʃuː] n statue m

stay [stei] v *bli; *oppholde seg, *ta inn; n opphold nt

steadfast ['stedfɑːst] adj standhaftig

steady ['stedi] adj stø

steak [steik] n biff m

*steal [stiːl] v *stjele

steam [stiːm] n damp m

steamer ['stiːmə] n dampskip nt

steel [stiːl] n stål nt

steep [stiːp] adj bratt, steil

steeple ['stiːpəl] n kirketårn nt

steer [stiːə] v styre

steering column ['stiəriŋ,kɔləm] n rattstamme m

steering wheel ['stiəriŋwiːl] n ratt nt

steersman ['stiəzmən] n (pl -men)

rorgjenger m

stem [stem] n stilk m

step [step] n skritt nt, steg nt; trinn nt; v *tre, trå

stepchild ['steptʃaild] n (pl -children) stebarn nt

stepfather ['step,fɑːðə] n stefar m

stepmother ['step,mʌðə] n stemor c

stereo [steriou] n stereo m; colloquial stereoanlegg nt

sterile ['sterail] adj steril

sterilize ['sterilaiz] v sterilisere

steward ['stjuːəd] n stuert m; flyvert m

stewardess ['stjuːədes] n flyvertinne c

stick [stik] n stokk m

*stick [stik] v klebe

sticker [stikə] n klistremerke nt

sticky ['stiki] adj klebrig

stiff [stif] adj stiv

still [stil] adv fremdeles; likevel; adj stille

stimulant ['stimjulənt] n stimulans m

stimulate ['stimjuleit] v stimulere

sting [stiŋ] n stikk m

*sting [stiŋ] v *stikke

stingy ['stindʒi] adj gjerrig; smålig

*stink [stiŋk] v *stinke

stipulate ['stipjuleit] v *fastsette

stipulation [,stipju'leiʃən] n betingelse m

stir [stəː] v røre

stitch [stitʃ] n sting nt; hold nt

stock [stɔk] n forsyning c; v lagre; **~ exchange** fondsbørs m, børs m; **~ market** fondsmarked nt; **stocks and shares** verdipapirer pl

stocking ['stɔkiŋ] n strømpe c

stole[1] [stoul] v (p steal)

stole[2] [stoul] n stola m

stomach ['stʌmək] n mage m; **~ ache** magesmerter pl

stone [stoun] n stein m; edelstein m;

stein-; **pumice** ~ pimpstein *m*

stood [stud] *v* (p, pp stand)

stop [stɔp] *v* stoppe; avslutte; *holde opp med; *n* holdeplass *m*; **stop!** stopp!

stopper ['stɔpə] *n* kork *m*

storage ['stɔːridʒ] *n* lagring *c*

store [stɔː] *n* lagerbeholdning *m*; forretning *c*; *v* lagre; ~ **house** lagerbygning *m*

stor(e)y ['stɔːri] *n* etasje *m*

stork [stɔːk] *n* stork *m*

storm [stɔːm] *n* storm *m*

stormy ['stɔːmi] *adj* stormfull

story ['stɔːri] *n* fortelling *c*

stout [staut] *adj* korpulent, tykkfallen

stove [stouv] *n* ovn *m*; komfyr *m*

straight [streit] *adj* rak; ærlig; *adv* rett; ~ **ahead** rett frem; ~ **away** med en gang; ~ **on** rett frem

strain [strein] *n* anstrengelse *m*; anspennelse *m*; *v* overanstrenge; sile

strainer ['streinə] *n* sil *m*; dørslag *nt*

strange [streindʒ] *adj* fremmed; underlig

stranger ['streindʒə] *n* fremmed *m*

strangle ['stræŋgəl] *v* kvele

strap [stræp] *n* rem *c*

straw [strɔː] *n* halm *m*

strawberry ['strɔːbəri] *n* jordbær *nt*

stream [striːm] *n* bekk *m*; strøm *m*; *v* strømme

street [striːt] *n* gate *c*

streetcar ['striːtkɑː] *nAm* trikk *m*

strength [streŋθ] *n* styrke *m*

stress [stres] *n* stress *nt*; trykk *nt*; *v* belaste; *legge vekt på

stretch [stretʃ] *v* tøye; *n* strekning *m*

strict [strikt] *adj* streng

strike [straik] *n* streik *m*

***strike** [straik] *v* *slå; *slå til; streike; *stryke

striking ['straikiŋ] *adj* påfallende, oppsiktsvekkende, slående

string [striŋ] *n* snor *c*; streng *m*

strip [strip] *n* strimmel *m*

stripe [straip] *n* stripe *c*

striped [straipt] *adj* stripet

stroke [strouk] *n* slaganfall *nt*

stroll [stroul] *v* slentre; *n* spasertur *m*

strong [strɔŋ] *adj* sterk; kraftig

stronghold ['strɔŋhould] *n* tilfluktssted *nt*; høyborg *c*

structure ['strʌktʃə] *n* struktur *m*

struggle ['strʌgəl] *n* strid *m*, kamp *m*; *v* *slåss, kjempe

stubborn ['stʌbən] *adj* sta

student ['stjuːdənt] *n* student *m*; elev *m*

studies ['stʌdiz] *pl* studium *nt*

study ['stʌdi] *v* studere; *n* studium *nt*; arbeidsværelse *nt*

stuff [stʌf] *n* materiale *nt*; saker *pl*

stuffed [stʌft] *adj* fylt

stuffing ['stʌfiŋ] *n* fyll *nt*

stuffy ['stʌfi] *adj* trykkende; snerpet

stumble ['stʌmbəl] *v* snuble

stung [stʌŋ] *v* (p, pp sting)

stupid ['stjuːpid] *adj* dum

style [stail] *n* stil *m*

subject¹ ['sʌbdʒikt] *n* subjekt *nt*; undersått *m*; gjenstand *m*; emne *nt*; ~ **to** utsatt for

subject² [səb'dʒekt] *v* underkue

sublet [ˌsub'let] *v* fremleie

submarine ['sʌbməriːn] *n* ubåt *m*

submit [səb'mit] *v* underkaste seg

subordinate [sə'bɔːdinət] *adj* underordnet; sekundær

subscriber [səb'skraibə] *n* abonnent *m*

subscription [səb'skripʃən] *n* abonnement *nt*

subsequent ['sʌbsikwənt] *adj* følgende

subsidy ['sʌbsidi] *n* tilskudd *nt*

substance ['sʌbstəns] *n* substans *m*

substantial [səb'stænʃəl] *adj*

substansiell; virkelig; anselig

substitute ['sʌbstitjuːt] v erstatte; n erstatning m; stedfortreder m

subtitle ['sʌb.taitəl] n undertekst m

subtle ['sʌtəl] adj subtil

subtract [səb'trækt] v *trekke fra

suburb ['sʌbəːb] n forstad m

suburban [sə'bəːbən] adj forstads-

subway ['sʌbwei] nAm undergrunnsbane m

succeed [sək'siːd] v lykkes; *etterfølge

success [sək'ses] n suksess m

successful [sək'sesfəl] adj vellykket

succumb [sə'kʌm] v bukke under

such [sʌtʃ] adj sånn, slik; adv slik; ~ as slik som

suck [sʌk] v suge

sudden ['sʌdən] adj plutselig

suddenly ['sʌdənli] adv plutselig

suede [sweid] n semsket skinn

suffer ['sʌfə] v *lide; *gjennomgå

suffering ['sʌfəriŋ] n lidelse m

suffice [sə'fais] v *være tilstrekkelig

sufficient [sə'fiʃənt] adj tilstrekkelig

suffrage ['sʌfridʒ] n stemmerett m

sugar ['ʃugə] n sukker nt

suggest [sə'dʒest] v *foreslå

suggestion [sə'dʒestʃən] n forslag nt

suicide ['suːisaid] n selvmord nt

suit [suːt] v passe; tilpasse; kle; n dress m

suitable ['suːtəbəl] adj egnet

suitcase ['suːtkeis] n koffert m

suite [swiːt] n suite m

sum [sʌm] n sum m

summary ['sʌməri] n sammendrag nt

summer ['sʌmə] n sommer m; ~ time sommertid c

summit ['sʌmit] n topp m

sun [sʌn] n sol c

sunbathe ['sʌnbeið] v sole seg

sunburn ['sʌnbəːn] n solbrenthet c

Sunday ['sʌndi] søndag m

sunglasses ['sʌn.glɑːsiz] pl solbriller pl

sunlight ['sʌnlait] n sollys nt

sunny ['sʌni] adj solrik

sunrise ['sʌnraiz] n soloppgang m

sunset ['sʌnset] n solnedgang m

sunshade ['sʌnʃeid] n parasoll m

sunshine ['sʌnʃain] n solskinn nt

sunstroke ['sʌnstrouk] n solstikk nt

suntan ['sʌntæn] brunfarge m

suntan oil ['sʌntænɔil] sololje c

super ['sjuːpə] adj colloquial flott, bra; kul, kult

superb [su'pəːb] adj storartet

superficial [.suːpə'fiʃəl] adj overfladisk

superfluous [su'pəːfluəs] adj overflødig

superior [su'piəriə] adj høyere, overlegen, bedre, større

supermarket ['suːpə.maːkit] n supermarked nt

superstition [.suːpə'stiʃən] n overtro c

supervise ['suːpəvaiz] v overvåke

supervision [.suːpə'viʒən] n overoppsyn nt, oppsyn nt

supervisor ['suːpəvaizə] n kontrollør m

supper ['sʌpə] n aftensmat m

supple ['sʌpəl] adj bøyelig, smidig, myk

supplement ['sʌplimənt] n tillegg nt

supply [sə'plai] n tilførsel m, levering c; forråd nt; tilbud nt; v forsyne

support [sə'pɔːt] v *bære, *hjelpe; n støtte m

supporter [sə'pɔːtə] n tilhenger m; forsørger m

suppose [sə'pouz] v *anta; **supposing that** forutsatt at

suppository [sə'pɔzitəri] n stikkpille c

suppress [sə'pres] v undertrykke

surcharge ['sə:tʃɑ:dʒ] n ekstragebyr nt

sure [ʃuə] adj sikker

surely ['ʃuəli] adv sikkert

surface ['sə:fis] n overflate c

surfboard ['sə:fbɔːd] n surfingbrett nt

surgeon ['sə:dʒən] n kirurg m; veterinary ~ veterinær m

surgery ['sə:dʒəri] n operasjon m; legekontor nt

surname ['sə:neim] n etternavn nt

surplus ['sə:pləs] n overskudd nt

surprise [sə'praiz] n overraskelse m; v overraske; forbause

surrender [sə'rendə] v *overgi seg; n overgivelse m

surround [sə'raund] v *omgi, omringe

surrounding [sə'raundiŋ] adj omkringliggende

surroundings [sə'raundiŋz] pl omegn m

survey ['sə:vei] n oversikt m

surveillance [sə:'veiəns] n overvåking c

survival [sə'vaivəl] n overleving c

survive [sə'vaiv] v overleve

suspect[1] [sə'spekt] v mistenke; ane

suspect[2] ['sʌspekt] n mistenkt m

suspend [sə'spend] v suspendere

suspenders [sə'spendəz] plAm bukseseler pl

suspension [sə'spenʃən] n fjæring c; ~ bridge hengebro c

suspicion [sə'spiʃən] n mistanke m; mistenksomhet c; anelse m

suspicious [sə'spiʃəs] adj mistenkelig; mistenksom, mistroisk

sustain [sə'stein] v orke; *opprettholde

Swahili [swə'hi:li] n swahili m

swallow ['swɔlou] v svelge, sluke; n svale c

swam [swæm] v (p swim)

swamp [swɔmp] n myr c

swan [swɔn] n svane c

swap [swɔp] v bytte

*swear [sweə] v *sverge; banne

sweat [swet] n svette m; v svette

sweater ['swetə] n ulljakke c; genser m

sweatshirt ['swetʃə:t] n (bomulls)genser

Swede [swi:d] n svenske m

Sweden ['swi:dən] Sverige

Swedish ['swi:diʃ] adj svensk

*sweep [swi:p] v feie

sweet [swi:t] adj søt; n sukkertøy nt; dessert m; sweets sukkertøy pl; godter pl

sweeten ['swi:tən] v sukre

sweetheart ['swi:thɑ:t] n elskling m

swell [swel] adj flott

*swell [swel] v svelle

swelling ['sweliŋ] n hevelse m

swift [swift] adj rask

*swim [swim] v svømme

swimmer ['swimə] n svømmer m

swimming ['swimiŋ] n svømming c; ~ pool svømmebasseng nt

swimmingtrunks ['swimiŋtrʌŋks] pl badebukse c

swimsuit ['swimsu:t], n swimming suit nAm badedrakt c

swindle ['swindəl] v svindle; n svindel m

swindler ['swindlə] n svindler m

swing [swiŋ] n huske c

*swing [swiŋ] v svinge; huske

Swiss [swis] adj sveitsisk; n sveitser m

switch [switʃ] n bryter m; v skifte; ~ off *slå av; ~ on *slå på

switchboard ['switʃbɔːd] n sentralbord nt

Switzerland ['switsələnd] Sveits

sword [sɔːd] n sverd nt

swum [swʌm] v (pp swim)

syllable ['siləbəl] n stavelse m

symbol ['simbəl] n symbol nt
sympathetic [ˌsimpə'θetik] adj
deltakende, medfølende
sympathy ['simpəθi] n sympati m;
medfølelse m
symphony ['simfəni] n symfoni m
symptom ['simtəm] n symptom nt
synagogue ['sinəgɔg] n synagoge m
synonym ['sinənim] n synonym nt

synthetic [sin'θetik] adj syntetisk
Syria ['siriə] Syria
Syrian ['siriən] adj syrisk; n syrer m
syringe [si'rindʒ] n sprøyte c
syrup ['sirəp] n sirup m
system ['sistəm] n system nt; **decimal**
~ desimalsystem nt
systematic [ˌsistə'mætik] adj
systematisk

T

table ['teibəl] n bord nt; tabell m; ~ **of**
contents innholdsfortegnelse m; ~
tennis bordtennis m
tablecloth ['teibəlklɔθ] n duk m
tablespoon ['teibəlspu:n] n spiseskje
c
tablet ['tæblit] n tablett m; plate c
taboo [tə'bu:] n tabu nt
tactics ['tæktiks] pl taktikk m
tag [tæg] n merkelapp m
tail [teil] n hale m
taillight ['teillait] n baklys nt
tailor ['teilə] n skredder m
tailor-made ['teiləmeid] adj
skreddersydd
***take** [teik] v *ta; *gripe; *følge;
skjønne, *forstå, *begripe; ~ **away**
*ta med seg; fjerne, *ta vekk; ~ **off**
lette; ~ **out** *ta bort; ~ **over** *overta; ~
place *finne sted; ~ **up** *oppta
take-off ['teikɔf] n start m
tale [teil] n fortelling m, eventyr nt
talent ['tælənt] n begavelse m, talent
nt
talented ['tæləntid] adj begavet
talk [tɔ:k] v snakke; n samtale m
talkative ['tɔ:kətiv] adj snakkesalig
tall [tɔ:l] adj høy, lang
tame [teim] adj tam; v temme

tampon ['tæmpən] n tampong m
tangerine [ˌtændʒə'ri:n] n mandarin
m
tangible ['tændʒibəl] adj følbar
tank [tæŋk] n tank m
tanker ['tæŋkə] n tankbåt m
tanned [tænd] adj brun
tap [tæp] n kran c; lett slag; v banke
tape [teip] n lydbånd nt; bånd nt;
adhesive ~ limbånd nt, tape m;
heftplaster nt; ~ **measure** målebånd
nt; ~ **recorder** båndopptaker m
tar [ta:] n tjære c
target ['ta:git] n skyteskive c, mål nt
tariff ['tærif] n tariff m
task [ta:sk] n oppgave c
taste [teist] n smak m; v smake;
smake på
tasteless ['teistləs] adj smakløs
tasty ['teisti] adj velsmakende
taught [tɔ:t] v (p, pp teach)
tavern ['tævən] n kro c
tax [tæks] n skatt m; v *skattlegge
taxation [tæk'seiʃən] n beskatning m
tax-free ['tæksfri:] adj skattefri
taxi ['tæksi] n taxi m, drosje c; ~ **driver**
drosjesjåfør m; ~ **rank**
drosjeholdeplass m; ~ **stand** nAm
drosjeholdeplass m

taximeter ['tæksi,miːtə] n taksameter nt

tea [tiː] n te m; ~ **set** teservise nt

***teach** [tiːtʃ] v lære, undervise

teacher ['tiːtʃə] n lærer m, lektor m

teachings ['tiːtʃiŋz] pl lære c

tea cloth ['tiːkləθ] n kjøkkenhåndkle nt

teacup ['tiːkʌp] n tekopp m

team [tiːm] n lag nt

teapot ['tiːpɔt] n tekanne c

***tear¹** [tɛə] v *rive

tear¹ [tiə] n tåre c

tear² [tɛə] n rift c

tease [tiːz] v erte

tea-shop ['tiːʃɔp] n tesalong m

teaspoon ['tiːspuːn] n teskje c

technical ['teknikəl] adj teknisk

technician [tek'niʃən] n tekniker m

technique [tek'niːk] n teknikk m

technological [,teknə'lɔdʒikəl] adj teknologisk

technology [tek'nɔlədʒi] n teknologi m

teenager ['tiː,neidʒə] n tenåring m

teetotaller [tiː'toutələ] n avholdsmann m

telepathy [ti'lepəθi] n telepati m

telephone ['telifoun] n telefon m; ~ **book** Am telefonkatalog m; ~ **booth** telefonkiosk m; ~ **call** telefon m, telefonsamtale m; ~ **directory** telefonkatalog m; ~ **exchange** telefonsentral m

television ['teliviʒən] n fjernsyn nt; ~ **set** fjernsynsapparat nt

***tell** [tel] v *si; *fortelle

telly ['teli] n colloquial fjernsyn nt, TV m

temper ['tempə] n sinne nt

temperature ['temprətʃə] n temperatur m

tempest ['tempist] n storm m

temple ['tempəl] n tempel nt; tinning m

temporary ['tempərəri] adj midlertidig, foreløpig

tempt [tempt] v friste

temptation [temp'teiʃən] n fristelse m

ten [ten] num ti

tenant ['tenənt] n leieboer m

tend [tend] v *ha tendens til; passe; ~ **to** *være tilbøyelig til

tendency ['tendənsi] n tendens m, tilbøyelighet c

tender ['tendə] adj øm, myk; mør

tendon ['tendən] n sene c

tennis ['tenis] n tennis m; ~ **court** tennisbane m; ~ **shoes** tennissko pl; joggesko pl

tense [tens] adj anspent

tension ['tenʃən] n spenning m

tent [tent] n telt nt

tenth [tenθ] num tiende

tepid ['tepid] adj lunken

term [təːm] n uttrykk nt; frist m, termin m; betingelse m

terminal ['təːminəl] n endestasjon m; terminal m

terrace ['terəs] n terrasse m

terrain [te'rein] n terreng nt

terrible ['teribəl] adj fryktelig, forferdelig, grusom

terrific [tə'rifik] adj storartet

terrify ['terifai] v skremme; **terrifying** skremmende

territory ['teritəri] n område nt

terror ['terə] n redsel m

terrorism ['terərizəm] n terror m, terrorisme m

terrorist ['terərist] n terrorist m

terry(cloth) ['teri(klɔθ)] n frotté m

test [test] n prøve c, test m; v teste

testify ['testifai] v vitne

text [tekst] n tekst m

textbook ['teksbuk] n lærebok c

textile ['tekstail] n tekstil m/nt

texture ['tekstʃə] n struktur m

Thai [tai] adj thailandsk; n thailender m

Thailand ['tailænd] Thailand

than [ðæn] conj enn

thank [θæŋk] v takke; ~ **you!** takk !

thankful ['θæŋkfəl] adj takknemlig

that [ðæt] pron den, det; som; conj at

thaw [θɔ:] v tine, smelte; n tøvær nt

the [ðə,ði] art -en, -a; -et; **the ... the** jo ... jo

theater Am, **theatre** ['θiətə] n teater nt

theft [θeft] n tyveri nt

their [ðeə] adj deres

them [ðem] pron dem

theme [θi:m] n tema nt, emne nt

themselves [ðəm'selvz] pron seg; selv

then [ðen] adv da; deretter, så

theology [θi'ɔlədʒi] n teologi m

theoretical [θiə'retikəl] adj teoretisk

theory ['θiəri] n teori m

therapy ['θerəpi] n terapi m

there [ðeə] adv der; dit

therefore ['ðeəfɔ:] conj derfor

thermometer [θə'mɔmitə] n termometer nt

thermostat ['θə:məstæt] n termostat m

these [ði:z] adj disse

thesis ['θi:sis] n (pl theses) tese m; avhandling c

they [ðei] pron de

thick [θik] adj tykk; tett

thicken ['θikən] v tykne

thickness ['θiknəs] n tykkelse m

thief [θi:f] n (pl thieves) tyv m

thigh [θai] n lår nt

thimble ['θimbəl] n fingerbøl nt

thin [θin] adj tynn; mager

thing [θiŋ] n ting m

***think** [θiŋk] v tenke; tenke etter; ~ **of** tenke på; *komme på; ~ **over** tenke over

thinker ['θiŋkə] n tenker m

third [θə:d] num tredje

thirst [θə:st] n tørst m

thirsty ['θə:sti] adj tørst

thirteen [,θə:'ti:n] num tretten

thirteenth [,θə:'ti:nθ] num trettende

thirtieth ['θə:tiəθ] num trettiende

thirty ['θə:ti] num tretti

this [ðis] adj denne; pron denne

thistle ['θisəl] n tistel m

thorn [θɔ:n] n torn m

thorough ['θʌrə] adj omhyggelig, grundig

thoroughfare ['θʌrəfɛə] n ferdselsåre c, hovedvei m

those [ðouz] pron de

though [ðou] conj selv om, skjønt; adv imidlertid

thought[1] [θɔ:t] v (p, pp think)

thought[2] [θɔ:t] n tanke m

thoughtful ['θɔ:tfəl] adj tankefull; omtenksom

thousand ['θauzənd] num tusen

thread [θred] n tråd m; v tre

threadbare ['θredbɛə] adj loslitt

threat [θret] n trussel m

threaten ['θretən] v true

three [θri:] num tre

three-quarter [,θri:'kwɔ:tə] adj tre fjerdedels

threshold ['θreʃould] n terskel m

threw [θru:] v (p throw)

thrifty ['θrifti] adj sparsommelig

throat [θrout] n hals m; strupe m

throne [θroun] n trone c

throttle ['θrɔtəl] n choke m

through [θru:] prep gjennom

throughout [θru:'aut] adv overalt; heltigjennom

throw [θrou] n kast nt

***throw** [θrou] v slenge, kaste

thrush [θrʌʃ] n trost m

thumb [θʌm] n tommelfinger m

thumbtack ['θʌmtæk] *nAm* tegnestift *m*

thump [θʌmp] *v* dunke

thunder ['θʌndə] *n* torden *m*; *v* tordne

thunderstorm ['θʌndəstɔːm] *n* tordenvær *nt*

Thursday ['θəːzdi] torsdag *m*

thus [ðʌs] *adv* slik

thyme [taim] *n* timian *m*

tick [tik] *n* merke *nt*; ~ **off** krysse av

ticket ['tikit] *n* billett *m*; lapp *m*; ~ **machine** billettautomat *m*

tickle ['tikəl] *v* kile

tide [taid] *n* tidevann *nt*; **high** ~ høyvann *nt*; **low** ~ lavvann *nt*

tidy ['taidi] *adj* ordentlig; ~ **up** rydde opp

tie [tai] *v* *binde, knytte; *n* slips *nt*

tiger ['taigə] *n* tiger *m*

tight [tait] *adj* stram; trang; *adv* fast

tighten ['taitən] *v* stramme; strammes

tights [taits] *pl* strømpebukse *c*

tile [tail] *n* gulvflis *c*; takstein *m*

till [til] *prep* inntil, til; *conj* inntil

timber ['timbə] *n* tømmer *nt*

time [taim] *n* tid *c*; gang *m*; takt *m*; **all the** ~ hele tiden; **in** ~ i tide; ~ **of arrival** ankomsttid *c*; ~ **of departure** avgangstid *c*

time-saving ['taim,seiviŋ] *adj* tidsbesparende

timetable ['taim,teibəl] *n* ruteplan *m*

timid ['timid] *adj* blyg

timidity [ti'midəti] *n* sjenerthet *c*

tin [tin] *n* tinn *nt*; boks *m*, hermetikkboks *m*; **tinned food** hermetikk *m*; ~ **opener** hermetikkåpner *m*

tiny ['taini] *adj* bitte liten

tip [tip] *n* spiss *m*; drikkepenger *pl*

tire¹ [taiə] *n* dekk *nt*

tire² [taiə] *v* *bli trett

tired [taiəd] *adj* utmattet, trett; ~ **of** lei av

tiring ['taiəriŋ] *adj* trettende

tissue ['tiʃuː] *n* vev *nt*; papirlommetørkle *nt*

title ['taitəl] *n* tittel *m*

to [tuː] *prep* til, på; for å

toad [toud] *n* padde *c*

toadstool ['toudstuːl] *n* fluesopp *m*; giftig sopp

toast [toust] *n* ristet brød; skål *m*; *v* riste

tobacco [tə'bækou] *n* (pl ~s) tobakk *m*

tobacconist's tobakksforretning *c*

today [tə'dei] *adv* i dag

toddler ['tɔdlə] *n* småbarn *nt*

toe [tou] *n* tå *c*

toffee ['tɔfi] *n* en slags karamell

together [tə'geðə] *adv* sammen

toilet ['tɔilət] *n* toalett *nt*, *colloquial* do *m/nt*; ~ **case** toalettveske *c*; ~ **paper** toalettpapir *nt*

toiletry ['tɔilətri] *n* toalettsaker *pl*

token ['toukən] *n* tegn *nt*; bevis *nt*; sjetong *m*

told [tould] *v* (p, pp tell)

tolerable ['tɔlərəbəl] *adj* utholdelig

toll [toul] *n* bompenger *pl*; gebyr *nt*

tomato [tə'mɑːtou] *n* (pl ~es) tomat *m*

tomb [tuːm] *n* grav *c*

tombstone ['tuːmstoun] *n* gravstein *m*

tomorrow [tə'mɔrou] *adv* i morgen

ton [tʌn] *n* tonn *nt*

tone [toun] *n* tone *m*; klang *m*

tongs [tɔŋz] *pl* tang *c*

tongue [tʌŋ] *n* tunge *c*

tonight [tə'nait] *adv* i kveld, i natt

tonsilitis [,tɔnsə'laitis] *n* betente mandler

tonsils ['tɔnsəlz] *pl* mandler *pl*

too [tuː] *adv* altfor; også

took [tuk] *v* (p take)

tool [tuːl] *n* verktøy *nt*, redskap *nt*

toot [tuːt] *vAm* tute

tooth [tu:θ] n (pl teeth) tann c

toothache ['tu:θeik] n tannverk m; tannpine c

toothbrush ['tu:θbrʌʃ] n tannbørste m

toothpaste ['tu:θpeist] n tannkrem m

toothpick ['tu:θpik] n tannpirker m

top [tɔp] n topp m; overside c; lokk nt; øverst; **on ~ of** oppå; **~ side** overside c

topic ['tɔpik] n emne nt

topical ['tɔpikəl] adj aktuell

torch [tɔ:tʃ] n fakkel m; lommelykt c

torment[1] [tɔ:'ment] v pine

torment[2] ['tɔ:ment] n pine c

torture ['tɔ:tʃə] n tortur m; v torturere

toss [tɔs] v kaste

tot [tɔt] n lite barn

total ['toutəl] adj total; fullstendig; n totalsum m

totalitarian [,toutæli'tɛəriən] adj totalitær

touch [tʌtʃ] v røre, berøre; n kontakt m, berøring c; følesans m

touching ['tʌtʃiŋ] adj rørende

tough [tʌf] adj seig

tour [tuə] n rundreise c, tur m

tourism ['tuərizəm] n turisttrafikk m

tourist ['tuərist] n turist m; **~ class** turistklasse c; **~ office** turistkontor nt

tournament ['tuənəmənt] n turnering c

tow [tou] v taue

towards [tə'wɔ:dz] prep mot; overfor

towel [tauəl] n håndkle nt

towel(l)ing ['tauəliŋ] n frotté m

tower [tauə] n tårn nt

town [taun] n by m; **~ center** Am, **~ centre** sentrum nt; **~ hall** rådhus nt

townspeople ['taunz,pi:pəl] pl byfolk pl

toxic ['tɔksik] adj giftig

toy [tɔi] n leketøy nt

toyshop ['tɔiʃɔp] n leketøysforretning c

trace [treis] n spor nt; v etterspore, oppspore

track [træk] n spor nt; bane m

tracksuit [træksu:t] n treningsdrakt c

tractor ['træktə] n traktor m

trade [treid] n handel m; yrke nt; v *drive handel

trademark ['treidma:k] n varemerke nt

trader ['treidə] n kjøpmann m

tradesman ['treidzmən],
tradeswoman [,treidz'wumən], n (pl -men, -women) butikkeier m

trade union [,treid'ju:njən] n fagforening c

tradition [trə'diʃən] n tradisjon m

traditional [trə'diʃənəl] adj tradisjonell

traffic ['træfik] n trafikk m; **~ jam** trafikk-kork m; **~ light** trafikklys nt

tragedy ['trædʒədi] n tragedie m

tragic ['trædʒik] adj tragisk

trail [treil] n sti m, spor nt

trailer ['treilə] n tilhenger m; campingvogn c

train [trein] n tog nt; v dressere, trene; **stopping ~** somletog nt; **through ~** hurtigtog nt; **~ ferry** jernbaneferje c

trainee [trei'ni:] n lærling; trainee

trainer ['treinə] n trener m

training ['treiniŋ] n trening c

trait [treit] n trekk nt

traitor ['treitə] n forræder m

tram [træm] n trikk m

tramp [træmp] n landstryker m; **go for a ~** gå på tur

tranquil ['træŋkwil] adj rolig

tranquillizer ['træŋkwilaizə] n beroligende middel

transaction [træn'zækʃən] n transaksjon m

transatlantic [,trænzət'læntik] adj transatlantisk

transfer [træns'fəː] *v* overføre

transform [træns'fɔːm] *v* forvandle, omdanne

transformer [træns'fɔːmə] *n* transformator *m*

transition [træn'siʃən] *n* overgang *m*

translate [træns'leit] *v* *oversette

translation [træns'leiʃən] *n* oversettelse *m*

translator [træns'leitə] *n* oversetter *m*

transmission [trænz'miʃən] *n* sending *c*

transmit [trænz'mit] *v* sende

transmitter [trænz'mitə] *n* sender *m*

transparent [træn'spɛərənt] *adj* gjennomsiktig

transport[1] ['trænspɔːt] *n* transport *m*

transport[2] [træn'spɔːt] *v* transportere

transportation [ˌtrænspɔː'teiʃən] *n* transport *m*

trap [træp] *n* felle *c*

trash [træʃ] *n* rask *nt*, skrap *nt*; ~ **can** *Am* søppelkasse *c*

travel ['trævəl] *v* reise; ~ **agency**, ~ **agent** reisebyrå *nt*; ~ **insurance** reiseforsikring *c*; **travelling expenses** reiseutgifter *pl*

travel(l)er ['trævələ] *n* reisende *m*; **travel(l)er's cheque** reisesjekk *m*

tray [trei] *n* brett *nt*

treason ['triːzən] *n* forræderi *nt*

treasure ['treʒə] *n* skatt *m*

treasurer ['treʒərə] *n* kasserer *m*

treasury ['treʒəri] *n* statskasse *c*

treat [triːt] *v* behandle

treatment ['triːtmənt] *n* behandling *c*

treaty ['triːti] *n* traktat *m*

tree [triː] *n* tre *nt*

tremble ['trembəl] *v* *skjelve; dirre

tremendous [tri'mendəs] *adj* kolossal

trendy ['trendi] *adj* *colloquial* moderne

trespass ['trespəs] *v* krenke annens eiendom

trespasser ['trespəsə] *n* uvedkommende *m*

trial [traiəl] *n* rettssak *c*; forsøk *nt*

triangle ['traiæŋgəl] *n* trekant *m*

triangular [trai'æŋgjulə] *adj* trekantet

tribe [traib] *n* stamme *m*

tributary ['tribjutəri] *n* bielv *c*

tribute ['tribjuːt] *n* hyllest *m*

trick [trik] *n* knep *nt*; trick *nt*

trigger ['trigə] *n* avtrekker *m*

trim [trim] *v* klippe, stusse

trip [trip] *n* reise *c*, utflukt *c*, tur *m*

triumph ['traiəmf] *n* triumf *m*; *v* triumfere

triumphant [trai'ʌmfənt] *adj* triumferende

troops [truːps] *pl* tropper *pl*

tropical ['trɔpikəl] *adj* tropisk

tropics ['trɔpiks] *pl* tropene *pl*

trouble ['trʌbəl] *n* trøbbel *nt*, uleilighet *c*, besvær *nt*; *v* bry

troublesome ['trʌbəlsəm] *adj* brysom

trousers ['trauzəz] *pl* bukse *c*; **trouser...** bukse...

trout [traut] *n* (pl ~) ørret *m*

truck [trʌk] *nAm* lastebil *m*

true [truː] *adj* sann; ekte, virkelig; trofast, tro

trumpet ['trʌmpit] *n* trompet *m*

trunk [trʌŋk] *n* koffert *m*; stamme *m*; bagasjerom *nt*

trust [trʌst] *v* stole på; *n* tillit *m*

trustworthy ['trʌst,wəːði] *adj* pålitelig

truth [truːθ] *n* sannhet *c*

truthful ['truːθfəl] *adj* sannferdig

try [trai] *v* prøve, forsøke, anstrenge seg; *n* forsøk *nt*; ~ **on** prøve

tube [tjuːb] *n* rør *nt*; tube *m*

tuberculosis [tjuːˌbəːkju'lousis] *n* tuberkulose *m*

Tuesday ['tjuːzdi] tirsdag *m*

tug [tʌg] v taue; n slepebåt m; rykk nt

tuition [tju:'iʃən] n undervisning c; skolepenger pl

tulip ['tju:lip] n tulipan m

tumbler ['tʌmblə] n beger nt

tumo(u)r ['tju:mə] n svulst m

tuna ['tju:nə] n (pl ~, ~s) tunfisk m

tune [tju:n] n melodi m; ~ in stille inn

tuneful ['tju:nfəl] adj melodisk

tunic ['tju:nik] n tunika m

Tunisia [tju:'niziə] Tunisia

Tunisian [tju:'niziən] adj tunisisk; n tunisier m

tunnel ['tʌnəl] n tunnel m

turbine ['tə:bain] n turbin m

turbojet [,tə:bou'dʒet] n turbojet m

Turk [tə:k] n tyrker m

Turkey ['tə:ki] Tyrkia

turkey ['tə:ki] n kalkun m

Turkish ['tə:kiʃ] adj tyrkisk; ~ bath romerbad nt

turn [tə:n] v dreie; vende, svinge, *vri om; n dreining m, vending c; sving m; tur m; ~ back vende tilbake; ~ down forkaste; ~ into forvandles til; ~ off stenge av; ~ on *sette på; skru på; ~ over vende om; ~ round snu; snu seg

turning ['tə:niŋ] n sving m

turning point ['tə:niŋpɔint] n vendepunkt nt

turnover ['tə:,nouvə] n omsetning m;

~ tax moms m

turnpike ['tə:npaik] nAm bomvei m

turpentine ['tə:pəntain] n terpentin m

turtle ['tə:təl] n skilpadde c

tutor ['tju:tə] n huslærer m

tuxedo [tʌk'si:dou] nAm (pl ~s, ~es) smoking m

TV [,ti'vi:] n colloquial TV m; on ~ på TV

tweed [twi:d] n tweed m

tweezers ['twi:zəz] pl pinsett m

twelfth [twelfθ] num tolvte

twelve [twelv] num tolv

twentieth ['twentiəθ] num tyvende

twenty ['twenti] num tyve

twice [twais] adv to ganger

twig [twig] n kvist m

twilight ['twailait] n skumring c

twine [twain] n hyssing m

twins [twinz] pl tvillinger pl

twist [twist] v sno; *vri; n vridning m

two [tu:] num to

two-piece [,tu:'pi:s] adj todelt

type [taip] v *skrive på data; taste; n type m

typhoid ['taifɔid] n tyfus m

typical ['tipikəl] adj typisk

tyrant ['taiərənt] n tyrann m

tyre [taiə] n dekk nt; ~ pressure lufttrykk nt

U

ugly ['ʌgli] adj stygg

ulcer ['ʌlsə] n magesår nt

ultimate ['ʌltimət] adj siste

ultraviolet [,ʌltrə'vaiələt] adj ultrafiolett

umbrella [ʌm'brelə] n paraply m

umpire ['ʌmpaiə] n dommer m

unable [ʌ'neibəl] adj ute av stand til

unacceptable [,ʌnək'septəbəl] adj uakseptabel

unaccountable [,ʌnə'kauntəbəl] adj uforklarlig; uansvarlig

unaccustomed [,ʌnə'kʌstəmd] adj uvant

unanimous [juːˈnæniməs] *adj*
enstemmig

unanswered [ˌʌˈnɑːnsəd] *adj*
ubesvart

unauthorized [ˌʌˈnɔːθəraizd] *adj*
uten fullmakt

unavoidable [ˌʌnəˈvɔidəbəl] *adj*
uunngåelig

unaware [ˌʌnəˈweə] *adj* ubevisst

unbearable [ʌnˈbeərəbəl] *adj*
uutholdelig

unbreakable [ˌʌnˈbreikəbəl] *adj*
uknuselig

unbroken [ˌʌnˈbroukən] *adj* intakt

unbutton [ˌʌnˈbʌtən] *v* knappe opp

uncertain [ʌnˈsəːtən] *adj* uviss,
usikker

uncle [ˈʌŋkəl] *n* onkel *m*

uncomfortable [ʌnˈkʌmfətəbəl] *adj*
ubekvem

uncommon [ʌnˈkɔmən] *adj*
usedvanlig, sjelden

unconditional [ˌʌnkənˈdiʃənəl] *adj*
betingelsesløs

unconscious [ʌnˈkɔnʃəs] *adj*
bevisstløs

uncork [ˌʌnˈkɔːk] *v* *trekke opp

uncover [ʌnˈkʌvə] *v* avdekke

uncultivated [ˌʌnˈkʌltiveitid] *adj*
udyrket

under [ˈʌndə] *prep* under, nedenfor

undercurrent [ˈʌndəˌkʌrənt] *n*
understrøm *m*

underestimate [ˌʌndəˈrestimeit] *v*
undervurdere

underground [ˈʌndəgraund] *adj*
underjordisk; *n* undergrunnsbane *m*

underline [ˌʌndəˈlain] *v* understreke

underneath [ˌʌndəˈniːθ] *adv*
nedenunder

underpants [ˈʌndəpænts] *plAm* truse
c

***understand** [ˌʌndəˈstænd] *v* *forstå,
fatte

understanding [ˌʌndəˈstændiŋ] *n*
forståelse *m*

understate [ˌʌndəˈsteit] *v* underdrive

understatement [ˌʌndəˈsteitmənt] *n*
underdrivelse *m*

***undertake** [ˌʌndəˈteik] *v* *gå i gang
med

undertaking [ˌʌndəˈteikiŋ] *n* foretak
nt

underwater [ˈʌndəˌwɔːtə] *adj*
undervanns-

underwear [ˈʌndəweə] *n* undertøy *pl*

undesirable [ˌʌndiˈzaiərəbəl] *adj*
uønsket

***undo** [ˌʌnˈduː] *v* åpne, løse opp

undoubtedly [ʌnˈdautidli] *adv*
utvilsomt

undress [ˌʌnˈdres] *v* kle av seg

unearned [ˌʌˈnəːnd] *adj* ufortjent

uneasy [ʌˈniːzi] *adj* urolig

uneducated [ˌʌˈnedjukeitid] *adj* uten
utdannelse

unemployed [ˌʌnimˈplɔid] *adj*
arbeidsløs; arbeidsledig

unemployment [ˌʌnimˈplɔimənt] *n*
arbeidsløshet *c*; arbeidsledighet *c*

unequal [ˌʌˈniːkwəl] *adj* ulik

uneven [ˌʌˈniːvən] *adj* ulik, ujevn

unexpected [ˌʌnikˈspektid] *adj*
uventet

unfair [ˌʌnˈfeə] *adj* urettferdig

unfaithful [ˌʌnˈfeiθfəl] *adj* utro

unfamiliar [ˌʌnfəˈmiljə] *adj* ukjent

unfasten [ˌʌnˈfɑːsən] *v* løse, løsne

unfavo(u)rable [ˌʌnˈfeivərəbəl] *adj*
ugunstig

unfit [ˌʌnˈfit] *adj* uegnet

unfold [ʌnˈfould] *v* brette ut, folde ut

unfortunate [ʌnˈfɔːtʃənət] *adj*
uheldig

unfortunately [ʌnˈfɔːtʃənətli] *adv*
uheldigvis, dessverre

unfriendly [ˌʌnˈfrendli] *adj* uvennlig

ungrateful [ʌnˈgreitfəl] *adj*

utakknemlig

unhappy [ʌn'hæpi] *adj* ulykkelig

unhealthy [ʌn'helθi] *adj* usunn

unhurt [ˌʌn'həːt] *adj* uskadd

uniform ['juːnifɔːm] *n* uniform *c*; *adj* ensartet

unimportant [ˌʌnim'pɔːtənt] *adj* uviktig

uninhabitable [ˌʌnin'hæbitəbəl] *adj* ubeboelig

uninhabited [ˌʌnin'hæbitid] *adj* ubebodd

unintentional [ˌʌnin'tenʃənəl] *adj* utilsiktet

union ['juːnjən] *n* fagforening *c*; union *m*, forbund *nt*

unique [juː'niːk] *adj* enestående

unit ['juːnit] *n* enhet *m*

unite [juː'nait] *v* forene; **united** *adj* forent

United States [juː'naitid steits] De forente stater

unity ['juːnəti] *n* enhet *m*

universal [ˌjuːni'vɔːsəl] *adj* universell, generell

universe ['juːnivɔːs] *n* univers *nt*

university [ˌjuːni'vɔːsəti] *n* universitet *nt*

unjust [ˌʌn'dʒʌst] *adj* urettferdig

unkind [ʌn'kaind] *adj* uvennlig; ukjærlig

unknown [ˌʌn'noun] *adj* ukjent

unlawful [ˌʌn'lɔːfəl] *adj* ulovlig

unless [ən'les] *conj* med mindre

unlike [ˌʌn'laik] *adj* forskjellig

unlikely [ʌn'laikli] *adj* usannsynlig

unlimited [ʌn'limitid] *adj* grenseløs, ubegrenset

unload [ˌʌn'loud] *v* lesse av

unlock [ˌʌn'lɔk] *v* lukke opp; låse opp

unlucky [ʌn'lʌki] *adj* uheldig

unnecessary [ʌn'nesəsəri] *adj* unødvendig

unoccupied [ˌʌ'nɔkjupaid] *adj* ledig

unofficial [ˌʌnə'fiʃəl] *adj* uoffisiell

unpack [ˌʌn'pæk] *v* pakke opp

unpleasant [ʌn'plezənt] *adj* utrivelig, ubehagelig; usympatisk, utiltalende

unpopular [ˌʌn'pɔpjulə] *adj* upopulær

unprotected [ˌʌnprə'tektid] *adj* ubeskyttet

unqualified [ˌʌn'kwɔlifaid] *adj* ukvalifisert

unreal [ˌʌn'riəl] *adj* uvirkelig

unreasonable [ʌn'riːzənəbəl] *adj* urimelig

unreliable [ˌʌnri'laiəbəl] *adj* upålitelig

unrest [ˌʌn'rest] *n* uro *m*; rastløshet *c*

unsafe [ˌʌn'seif] *adj* usikker, utrygg

unsatisfactory [ˌʌnsætis'fæktəri] *adj* utilfredsstillende

unscrew [ˌʌn'skruː] *v* skru løs

unselfish [ˌʌn'selfiʃ] *adj* uselvisk

unskilled [ˌʌn'skild] *adj* ufaglært

unsound [ˌʌn'saund] *adj* usunn

unstable [ˌʌn'steibəl] *adj* ustabil

unsteady [ˌʌn'stedi] *adj* ustø; ustadig

unsuccessful [ˌʌnsək'sesfəl] *adj* mislykket

unsuitable [ˌʌn'suːtəbəl] *adj* uegnet

unsurpassed [ˌʌnsə'paːst] *adj* uovertruffen

untidy [ʌn'taidi] *adj* uordentlig

untie [ˌʌn'tai] *v* knytte opp

until [ən'til] *prep* inntil, til

untrue [ˌʌn'truː] *adj* usann

untrustworthy [ˌʌn'trʌst,wəːði] *adj* upålitelig

unusual [ʌn'juːʒuəl] *adj* uvanlig, ualminnelig

unwell [ˌʌn'wel] *adj* uvel

unwilling [ˌʌn'wiliŋ] *adj* uvillig

unwise [ˌʌn'waiz] *adj* uklok

unwrap [ˌʌn'ræp] *v* pakke opp

up [ʌp] *adv* opp, oppover

upholster [ʌp'houlstə] *v* *trekke,

polstre
upkeep ['ʌpkiːp] *n* vedlikehold *nt*
uplands ['ʌpləndz] *pl* høyland *nt*
upon [ə'pɔn] *prep* på
upper ['ʌpə] *adj* øvre, over-
upright ['ʌprait] *adj* rank; rett; loddrett
*upset [ʌp'set] *v* forstyrre; *adj* opprørt
upside down [,ʌpsaid'daun] *adv* på hodet; opp ned
upstairs [,ʌp'stɛəz] *adv* ovenpå
upstream [,ʌp'striːm] *adv* mot strømmen
upwards ['ʌpwədz] *adv* oppover
urban ['əːbən] *adj* by-
urge [əːdʒ] *v* formane; *n* trang *m*
urgency ['əːdʒənsi] *n* innstendighet *c*; viktighet *c*
urgent ['əːdʒənt] *adj* presserende
urine ['juərin] *n* urin *m*
Uruguay ['juərəgwai] Uruguay

Uruguayan [,juərə'gwaiən] *adj* uruguayansk; *n* uruguayaner *m*
us [ʌs] *pron* oss
usable ['juːzəbəl] *adj* anvendelig
usage ['juːzidʒ] *n* sedvane *m*; bruk *m*
use[1] [juːz] *v* bruke; ***be used to** *være vant til; ~ **up** bruke opp
use[2] [juːs] *n* bruk *m*; nytte *c*; ***be of ~** *være til nytte
useful ['juːsfəl] *adj* nyttig, brukbar
useless ['juːsləs] *adj* unyttig
user ['juːzə] *n* bruker *m*
usher ['ʌʃə] *v* vise veien
usual ['juːʒuəl] *adj* vanlig
usually ['juːʒəli] *adv* vanligvis
utensil [juː'tensəl] *n* redskap *nt*; kjøkkenredskap *nt*
utility [juː'tiləti] *n* nytte *c*
utilize ['juːtilaiz] *v* anvende
utmost ['ʌtmoust] *adj* ytterst
utter ['ʌtə] *adj* total, fullstendig; *v* ytre

V

vacancy ['veikənsi] *n* ledig stilling
vacant ['veikənt] *adj* ledig
vacation [və'keiʃən] *n* ferie *m*
vaccinate ['væksineit] *v* vaksinere
vaccination [,væksi'neiʃən] *n* vaksinering *c*
vacuum ['vækjuəm] *n* vakuum *nt*; *vAm* støvsuge; ~ **cleaner** støvsuger *m*
vague [veig] *adj* vag
vain {vein} *adj* forfengelig; forgjeves; **in ~** forgjeves
valid ['vælid] *adj* gyldig
valley ['væli] *n* dal *m*
valuable ['væljubəl] *adj* verdifull; **valuables** *pl* verdisaker *pl*
value ['væljuː] *n* verdi *m*; *v* taksere, vurdere

valve [vælv] *n* ventil *m*
van [væn] *n* varebil *m*
vanilla [və'nilə] *n* vanilje *m*
vanish ['væniʃ] *v* *forsvinne
vapo(u)r ['veipə] *n* damp *m*
variable ['vɛəriəbəl] *adj* variabel
variation [,vɛəri'eiʃən] *n* avveksling *c*; forandring *c*
variety [və'raiəti] *n* utvalg *nt*
various ['vɛəriəs] *adj* forskjellige, diverse
varnish ['vɑːniʃ] *n* lakk *m*; *v* lakkere
vary ['vɛəri] *v* variere; forandre; *være forskjellig
vase [vɑːz] *n* vase *m*
vast [vɑːst] *adj* vidstrakt, umåtelig
vault [vɔːlt] *n* hvelving *m*; bankhvelv

nt

veal [vi:l] *n* kalvekjøtt *nt*

vegetable ['vedʒətəbəl] *n* grønnsak *c*;
~ **merchant** grønnsakshandler *m*

vegetarian [,vedʒi'tɛəriən] *n*
vegetarianer *m*

vegetation [,vedʒi'teiʃən] *n*
vegetasjon *m*

vehicle ['vi:əkəl] *n* kjøretøy *nt*

veil [veil] *n* slør *nt*

vein [vein] *n* åre *c*; **varicose** ~
åreknute *m*

velvet ['velvit] *n* fløyel *m*

velveteen [,velvi'ti:n] *n*
bomullsfløyel *m*

venerable ['venərəbəl] *adj* ærverdig

venereal disease [vi'niəriəl di'zi:z]
kjønnssykdom *m*

Venezuela [,veni'zweilə] Venezuela

Venezuelan [,veni'zweilən] *adj*
venezuelansk; *n* venezuelaner *m*

ventilate ['ventileit] *v* ventilere; lufte,
lufte ut

ventilation [,venti'leiʃən] *n*
ventilasjon *m*; utluftning *m*

ventilator ['ventileitə] *n* ventilator *m*

venture ['ventʃə] *v* våge

veranda [və'rændə] *n* veranda *m*

verb [və:b] *n* verb *nt*

verbal ['və:bəl] *adj* muntlig

verdict ['və:dikt] *n* kjennelse *m*, dom
m

verify ['verifai] *v* kontrollere

verse [və:s] *n* vers *nt*

version ['və:ʃən] *n* versjon *m*

versus ['və:səs] *prep* kontra

vertical ['və:tikəl] *adj* vertikal

very ['veri] *adv* svært, meget; *adj*
eksakt, virkelig; absolutt

vessel ['vesəl] *n* fartøy *nt*; kar *nt*

vest [vest] *n* undertrøye *c*; vest *m*

veterinary surgeon ['vetrinəri
'sə:dʒən] dyrlege *m*

via [vaiə] *prep* via

vibrate [vai'breit] *v* vibrere

vibration [vai'breiʃən] *n* vibrasjon *m*

vicar ['vikə] *n* sogneprest *m*

vicarage ['vikəridʒ] *n* prestegård *m*

vice president [,vais'prezidənt] *n*
visepresident *m*

vicinity [vi'sinəti] *n* nabolag *nt*,
nærhet *c*

vicious ['viʃəs] *adj* ondskapsfull

victim ['viktim] *n* offer *nt*

victory ['viktəri] *n* seier *m*

video camera ['vidiou'kæmərə] *n*
video-kamera *nt*

video cassette ['vidiou'kæset] *n*
videokassett *m*

video recorder ['vidiou ri'kɔ:də] *n*
video-spiller *m*

view [vju:] *n* utsikt *m*; oppfatning *m*,
syn; *v* betrakte

viewfinder ['vju:,faində] *n* søker *m*

vigilant ['vidʒilənt] *adj* årvåken

villa ['vilə] *n* villa *m*

village ['vilidʒ] *n* landsby *m*; bygd *c*

villain ['vilən] *n* skurk *m*

vine [vain] *n* vinranke *m*

vinegar ['vinigə] *n* eddik *m*

vintage ['vintidʒ] *n* vinhøst *m*; årgang
m

violation [vaiə'leiʃən] *n* krenkelse *m*

violence ['vaiələns] *n* vold *m*

violent ['vaiələnt] *adj* voldsom, heftig

violet ['vaiələt] *n* fiol *m*; *adj* fiolett,
lilla

violin [vaiə'lin] *n* fiolin *m*

virgin ['və:dʒin] *n* jomfru *c*

virtue ['və:tʃu:] *n* dyd *m*

visa ['vi:zə] *n* visum *nt*

visibility [,vizə'biləti] *n* sikt *m*

visible ['vizəbəl] *adj* synlig

vision ['viʒən] *n* syn

visit ['vizit] *v* besøke; *n* besøk *nt*, visitt
m; **visiting hours** besøkstid *c*

visitor ['vizitə] *n* besøkende *m*

vital ['vaitəl] *adj* vesentlig

vitamin ['vitəmin] *n* vitamin *nt*
vivid ['vivid] *adj* livfull
vocabulary [və'kæbjuləri] *n* ordforråd *nt*; ordliste *c*
vocal ['voukəl] *adj* vokal
vocalist ['voukəlist] *n* sanger *m*
voice [vɔis] *n* stemme *m*
void [vɔid] *adj* ugyldig
volcano [vɔl'keinou] *n* (pl ~es, ~s) vulkan *m*
volt [voult] *n* volt *m*
voltage ['voultidʒ] *n* spenning *m*
volume ['vɔljum] *n* volum *nt*; bind *nt*
voluntary ['vɔləntəri] *adj* frivillig

volunteer [,vɔlən'tiə] *n* frivillig *m*
vomit ['vɔmit] *v* kaste opp, *brekke seg
vote [vout] *v* stemme; *n* stemme *m*; avstemning *m*
voucher ['vautʃə] *n* bong *m*
vow [vau] *n* løfte *nt*, ed *m*; *v* *sverge
vowel [vauəl] *n* vokal *m*
voyage ['vɔiidʒ] *n* reise *c*
vulgar ['vʌlgə] *adj* vulgær; simpel, ordinær
vulnerable ['vʌlnərəbəl] *adj* sårbar
vulture ['vʌltʃə] *n* gribb *m*

W

wade [weid] *v* vasse
waffle ['wɔfəl] *n* vaffel *m*
wages ['weidʒiz] *pl* lønn *c*
wag(g)on ['wægən] *n* godsvogn *c*; vogn *c*
waist [weist] *n* midje *c*
waistcoat ['weiskout] *n* vest *m*
wait [weit] *v* vente; ~ **on** oppvarte
waiter ['weitə] *n* kelner *m*, servitør *m*
waiting ['weitiŋ] *n* venting *c*; ~ **list** venteliste *c*; ~ **room** venteværelse *nt*
waitress ['weitris] *n* (*kvinnelig*) *servitør m*
***wake** [weik] *v* vekke; ~ **up** våkne
walk [wɔ:k] *v* *gå; spasere; *n* spasertur *m*; gange *m*; **walking** til fots
walker ['wɔ:kə] *n* turgjenger *m*
walking stick ['wɔ:kiŋstik] *n* spaserstokk *m*
wall [wɔ:l] *n* mur *m*; vegg *m*
wallet ['wɔlit] *n* lommebok *c*
wallpaper ['wɔ:l,peipə] *n* tapet *nt*
walnut ['wɔ:lnʌt] *n* valnøtt *c*
waltz [wɔ:ls] *n* vals *m*

wander ['wɔndə] *v* flakke, vandre
want [wɔnt] *v* *ville; ønske; *n* behov *nt*; mangel *m*
war [wɔ:] *n* krig *m*
wardrobe ['wɔ:droub] *n* klesskap *nt*, garderobe *m*
warehouse ['wɛəhaus] *n* pakkhus *nt*, lagerbygning *m*
wares [wɛəz] *pl* varer *pl*
warm [wɔ:m] *adj* varm; *v* varme
warmth [wɔ:mθ] *n* varme *m*
warn [wɔ:n] *v* advare
warning ['wɔ:niŋ] *n* advarsel *m*
wary ['wɛəri] *adj* forsiktig
was [wɔz] *v* (p be)
wash [wɔʃ] *v* vaske; ~ **and wear** strykefri; ~ **up** vaske opp
washable ['wɔʃəbəl] *adj* vaskbar
washbasin ['wɔʃ,beisən] *n* håndvask *m*
washing ['wɔʃiŋ] *n* vask *m*; ~ **machine** vaskemaskin *m*; ~ **powder** vaskepulver *nt*
washroom ['wɔʃru:m] *nAm* toalett *nt*

wasp [wɔsp] n veps m

waste [weist] v sløse bort; n sløseri nt; adj øde; ~ **separation** kildesortering c

wasteful ['weistfəl] adj ødsel

wastepaper basket [weist'peipə,ba:skit] n papirkurv m

watch [wɔtʃ] v betrakte, *iakttra; bevokte; n ur nt; ~ **for** *holde utkikk etter; ~ **out** *være forsiktig

watchmaker ['wɔtʃ,meikə] n urmaker m

watchstrap ['wɔtʃstræp] n klokkerem c

water ['wɔ:tə] n vann nt; **iced** ~ isvann nt; **running** ~ innlagt vann; ~ **ski** vannski c

watercolo(u)r ['wɔ:tə,kʌlə] n vannfarge m; akvarell m

waterfall ['wɔ:təfɔ:l] n foss m

watermelon ['wɔ:tə,melən] n vannmelon m

waterproof ['wɔ:təpru:f] adj vanntett

watt [wɔt] n watt m

wave [weiv] n bølge c; v vinke

wavelength ['weivleŋθ] n bølgelengde m

wavy ['weivi] adj bølget

wax [wæks] n voks m

waxworks ['wækswə:ks] pl vokskabinett nt

way [wei] n vis nt, måte m; vei m; retning m; avstand m; **any** ~ på hvilken som helst måte; **by the** ~ forresten; **out of the** ~ avsides; **the other** ~ **round** tvert om; ~ **back** fjern fortid; ~ **in** inngang m; ~ **out** utgang m; **one-way traffic** enveiskjøring c

wayside ['weisaid] n veikant m

we [wi:] pron vi

weak [wi:k] adj svak; tynn

weakness ['wi:knəs] n svakhet c

wealth [welθ] n rikdom m

wealthy ['welθi] adj rik

weapon ['wepən] n våpen nt

***wear** [wɛə] v *ha på seg; ~ **out** *slite ut

weary ['wiəri] adj trett, sliten

weather ['weðə] n vær nt; ~ **forecast** værmelding c

***weave** [wi:v] v veve

wedding ['wediŋ] n vielse m, bryllup nt; ~ **ring** vielsesring m

wedge [wedʒ] n kile m

Wednesday ['wenzdi] onsdag m

weed [wi:d] n ugress nt

week [wi:k] n uke c

weekday ['wi:kdei] n hverdag m

weekend ['wi:kend] n helg c

weekly ['wi:kli] adj ukentlig

***weep** [wi:p] v *gråte

weigh [wei] v veie

weight [weit] n vekt c

Welch [welʃ] adj walisisk

welcome ['welkəm] adj velkommen; n velkomst m; v hilse velkommen

weld [weld] v sveise

welfare ['welfɛə] n velferd m

well¹ [wel] adv godt; adj frisk; **as** ~ også; **as** ~ **as** så vel som; **well!** ja vel!

well² [wel] n kilde m; brønn m

well-founded [,wel'faundid] adj velbegrunnet

well-known ['welnoun] adj velkjent

well-to-do [,weltə'du:] adj velhavende

went [went] v (p go)

were [wə:] v (p be)

west [west] n vest m

westerly ['westəli] adj vestlig

western ['westən] adj vestlig

wet [wet] adj våt; fuktig

whale [weil] n hval m

wharf [wɔ:f] n (pl ~s, wharves) kai c

what [wɔt] pron hva; ~ **for** hvorfor

whatever [wɔ'tevə] pron hva enn

wheat [wi:t] n hvete m

wheel [wi:l] *n* hjul *nt*

wheelbarrow ['wi:l,bærou] *n* trillebår *c*

wheelchair ['wi:ltʃɛə] *n* rullestol *m*

when [wen] *adv* når; *conj* når, da

whenever [we'nevə] *conj* når enn; alltid når

where [wɛə] *adv* hvor; *conj* hvor

wherever [wɛə'revə] *conj* hvor enn

whether ['weðə] *conj* om; **whether ... or** om ... eller

which [witʃ] *pron* hvilken; som

whichever [wi'tʃevə] *adj* hvilken som helst

while [wail] *conj* mens; *n* stund *c*

whim [wim] *n* innfall *nt*, nykke *nt*

whip [wip] *n* pisk *m*; *v* vispe

whiskers ['wiskəz] *pl* kinnskjegg *nt*

whisper ['wispə] *v* hviske; *n* hvisking *c*

whistle ['wisəl] *v* plystre; *n* fløyte *c*

white [wait] *adj* hvit

whiting ['waitiŋ] *n* (pl ~) hvitting *m*

Whitsun ['witsən] pinse *c*

wit [wit] *n* vidd *nt*

who [hu:] *pron* hvem; som

whoever [hu:'evə] *pron* hvem (som) enn

whole [houl] *adj* fullstendig, hel; uskadd; *n* hele *nt*

wholesale ['houlseil] *n* engroshandel *m*; ~ **dealer** grosserer *m*

wholesome ['houlsəm] *adj* sunn

wholly ['houlli] *adv* helt

whom [hu:m] *pron* til hvem

whore [hɔ:] *n* hore *c*

whose [hu:z] *pron* hvis

why [wai] *adv* hvorfor

wicked ['wikid] *adj* ond

wide [waid] *adj* bred, vid

widen ['waidən] *v* utvide

widow ['widou] *n* enke *c*

widower ['widouə] *n* enkemann *m*

width [widθ] *n* bredde *m*

wife [waif] *n* (pl wives) kone *c*

wig [wig] *n* parykk *m*

wild [waild] *adj* vill

will [wil] *n* vilje *m*; testamente *nt*

*will [wil] *v* *vil

willing ['wiliŋ] *adj* villig

willow ['wilou] *n* pil *c*

willpower ['wilpauə] *n* viljestyrke *m*

*win [win] *v* *vinne

wind [wind] *n* vind *m*

*wind [waind] *v* sno seg; *trekke opp, vikle

winding ['waindiŋ] *adj* buktet

windmill ['windmil] *n* vindmølle *c*

window ['windou] *n* vindu *nt*

windowsill ['windousil] *n* vinduskarm *m*

windscreen ['windskri:n] *n* frontrute *c*; ~ **wiper** vindusvisker *m*

windshield ['windʃi:ld] *nAm* frontrute *c*; ~ **wiper** *Am* vindusvisker *m*

windy ['windi] *adj* vindhard

wine [wain] *n* vin *m*; ~ **cellar** vinkjeller *m*; ~ **list** vinkart *nt*

wing [wiŋ] *n* vinge *m*

winner ['winə] *n* vinner *m*

winning ['winiŋ] *adj* vinnende; **winnings** *pl* gevinst *m*

winter ['wintə] *n* vinter *m*; ~ **sports** vintersport *m*

wipe [waip] *v* tørke, tørke bort; tørke av

wire [waiə] *n* wire *m*, vaier *m*; ståltråd *m*

wisdom ['wizdəm] *n* visdom *m*

wise [waiz] *adj* vis

wish [wiʃ] *v* lenges etter, ønske; *n* ønske *nt*, lengsel *m*

witch [witʃ] *n* heks *c*

with [wið] *prep* med; hos; av

*withdraw [wið'drɔ:] *v* *trekke

tilbake

*withhold [wið'hould] v *holde tilbake

within [wi'ðin] prep innenfor; adv innvendig; innen

without [wi'ðaut] prep uten

witness ['witnəs] n vitne nt

wits [wits] pl forstand m

witty ['witi] adj vittig; spirituell

wolf [wulf] n (pl wolves) ulv m

woman ['wumən] n (pl women) kvinne c

womb [wu:m] n livmor c

won [wʌn] v (p, pp win)

wonder ['wʌndə] n under nt; forundring c; v undre seg

wonderful ['wʌndəfəl] adj skjønn, vidunderlig; herlig

wood [wud] n trevirke nt; skog m; ~ carving treskjærerarbeid nt

wooded ['wudid] adj skogkledd

wooden ['wudən] adj tre-; ~ shoe tresko m

woodland ['wudlənd] n skogsområde nt

wool [wul] n ull c

wool(l)en ['wulən] adj ull-

word [wə:d] n ord nt

wore [wɔ:] v (p wear)

work [wə:k] n arbeid nt; v arbeide; virke, fungere; **working day** arbeidsdag m; ~ of art kunstverk nt; ~ permit arbeidstillatelse m

worker ['wə:kə] n arbeider m

workman ['wə:kmən] n (pl -men) arbeider m

works [wə:ks] pl fabrikk m

workshop ['wə:kʃɔp] n verksted nt

world [wə:ld] n verden m; ~ war verdenskrig m

world-famous [,wə:ld'feiməs] adj

verdensberømt

world-wide ['wə:ldwaid] adj verdensomspennende

worm [wə:m] n mark m

worn [wɔ:n] adj (pp wear) slitt

worn-out [,wɔ:n'aut] adj utslitt

worried ['wʌrid] adj bekymret

worry ['wʌri] v bekymre seg; n bekymring c

worse [wə:s] adj verre; adv verre

worship ['wə:ʃip] v *tilbe; n gudstjeneste m

worst [wə:st] adj verst; adv verst

worth [wə:θ] n verd nt; *be ~ *være verd; *be worth-while *være umaken verd

worthless ['wə:θləs] adj verdiløs

worthy of ['wə:ði əv] verdig

would [wud] v (p will)

wound¹ [wu:nd] n sår nt; v såre

wound² [waund] v (p, pp wind)

wrap [ræp] v pakke inn

wreck [rek] n vrak nt; v *ødelegge

wrench [rentʃ] n skrunøkkel m; rykk nt; v *vri

wrinkle ['riŋkəl] n rynke c

wrist [rist] n håndledd nt

wristwatch ['ristwɔtʃ] n armbåndsur nt

*write [rait] v *skrive; **in writing** skriftlig; ~ down *skrive ned

writer ['raitə] n forfatter m

writing pad ['raitiŋpæd] n skriveblokk c

writing paper ['raitiŋ,peipə] n skrivepapir nt

written ['ritən] adj (pp write) skriftlig

wrong [rɔŋ] adj gal, uriktig; n urett m; v *gjøre urett; *be ~ *ta feil

wrote [rout] v (p write)

X

Xmas ['krisməs] jul c
X-ray ['eksrei] n røntgenbilde nt; v

røntgenfotografere

Y

yacht [jɔt] n lystbåt m; ~ **club**
   seilforening c
yachting ['jɔtiŋ] n seilsport m
yard [jɑːd] n gårdsplass m; hage m
yarn [jɑːn] n garn nt
yawn [jɔːn] v gjespe
year [jiə] n år nt
yearly ['jiəli] adj årlig
yeast [jiːst] n gjær m
yell [jel] v hyle; n hyl nt
yellow ['jelou] adj gul
yes [jes] ja
yesterday ['jestədi] adv i går
yet [jet] adv ennå; conj likevel,

allikevel
yield [jiːld] v yte; *vike
yoghurt ['jɔgət] n yoghurt, jogurt m
yoke [jouk] n åk nt
yolk [jouk] n eggeplomme c
you [juː] pron du; deg; dere
young [jʌŋ] adj ung
your [jɔː] pron din; dine, deres
yours [jɔːz] pron din; dine, deres
yourself [jɔː'self] pron deg; selv
yourselves [jɔː'selvz] pron dere; selv
youth [juːθ] n ungdom m; ~ **hostel**
   ungdomsherberge nt; vandrerhjem nt

Z

zeal [ziːl] n iver m
zealous ['zeləs] adj ivrig
zebra ['ziːbrə] n sebra m
zenith ['zeniθ] n senit nt; høydepunkt
   nt
zero ['ziərou] n (pl ~s) null nt
zest [zest] n lyst c; iver m
zinc [ziŋk] n sink m

zip [zip] n glidelås m; ~ **code** Am
   postnummer nt
zipper ['zipə] n glidelås m
zodiac ['zoudiæk] n dyrekretsen
zone [zoun] n sone c; område
zoo [zuː] n (pl ~s) dyrehage m
zoology [zou'ɔlədʒi] n zoologi m

Gastronomisk ordliste

Mat

almond mandel

anchovy ansjos

angel food cake sukkerbrød laget av eggehviter

angels on horseback østers rullet i baconskiver og grillstekt

appetizer snacks

apple eple
~ charlotte en slags tilslørte bondepiker stekt i ovn
~ dumpling innbakt eple
~ sauce eplemos

apricot aprikos

Arbroath smoky røkt kolje

artichoke artisjokk

asparagus asparges
~ tip aspargestopp

aspic kjøtt- eller fiskekabaret

assorted blandede

bagel ringformet rundstykke

baked ovnsbakt
~ Alaska dessert av sukkerbrød, is og marengs som gis et kort opphold i stekeovnen og deretter flamberes
~ beans ovnsbakte hvite bønner i tomatsaus
~ potato ovnsbakt potet (med skall)

Bakewell tart mandelkake med syltetøy

baloney en slags servelatpølse

banana banan
~ split dessert av forskjellige sorter is, banan, nøtter og frukt- eller sjokoladesaus

barbecue 1) sterkt krydret kjøttsaus servert på rundstykke 2) grilling, grillparty
~ sauce sterkt krydret tomatsaus

barbecued grillet over trekull

basil basilikum

bass havåbor

bean bønne

beef oksekjøtt
~ olive okserulade

beefburger hamburger (av karbonadedeig)

beet, beetroot rødbete

bilberry blåbær

bill regning
~ of fare spisekart, meny

biscuit kjeks, småkake

black pudding blodpølse

blackberry bjørnebær

blackcurrant solbær

bloater lettsaltet røkesild

blood sausage blodpølse

blueberry blåbær

boiled kokt

Bologna (sausage) en slags servelatpølse

bone ben

boned benfri

Boston baked beans ovnsbakte hvite bønner med baconstrimler, tomatsaus og sirup

Boston cream pie kake fylt med vaniljekrem eller pisket krem og dekket med sjokolade

brains hjerne

braised surret, stekt under lokk

bramble pudding bjørnebærkompott med epleskiver

braunschweiger røkt leverpølse

bread brød

breaded panert

breakfast frokost

breast bryst (fjærkre)

brisket bringe

broad bean hestebønne

broth kraft, buljong

brown Betty en slags tilslørte
bondepiker

brunch kombinert frokost og lunsj

brussels sprout rosenkål

bubble and squeak en slags pytt i
panne

bun 1) bolle med rosiner (GB) 2)
rundstykke (US)

butter smør

buttered smurt

cabbage kål

Caesar salad grønn salat med hvitløk,
brødterninger, ansjos, egg og
parmesanost

cake kake, terte

cakes småkaker, bakverk

calf kalvekjøtt

Canadian bacon røkt svinefilet skåret
i skiver

canapé smørbrødsnitte

cantaloupe kantalupp

caper kapers

capercaillie, capercailzie tiur

caramel karamell

carp karpe

carrot gulrot

cashew cashew-nøtt

casserole gryte (-rett)

catfish steinbit

catsup ketchup

cauliflower blomkål

celery selleri

cereal cornflakes

hot ~ grøt

check regning

Cheddar (cheese) hard, lett syrlig,
engelsk ost

cheese ost

~ board osteanretning

~ cake ostekake

cheeseburger hamburger med
smeltet osteskive

chef's salad grønn salat med skinke,
hårdkokt egg, tomater, kylling og ost

cherry kirsebær

chestnut kastanje

chicken kylling

chicory 1) endivie (GB) 2) sikori (US)

chili con carne krydret gryterett av
kjøttdeig og brune bønner

chips 1) pommes frites (GB) 2) chips,
potetgull (US)

chit(ter)lings innmat av svin

chive gressløk

chocolate sjokolade

~ pudding 1) ulike typer myk
sjokoladekake (GB) 2)
sjokoladepudding (US)

choice utvalg

chop kotelett

~ suey gryterett av oppskåret svine-
eller kyllingkjøtt og grønnsaker;
serveres med ris

chopped hakket

chowder tykk fiske- og skalldyrsuppe
med bacon og grønnsaker

Christmas pudding mektig fruktkake
som serveres til jul; ofte flambert

chutney sterkt krydrede, sursøte,
syltede grønnsaker eller frukt

cinnamon kanel

clam sandskjell

club sandwich dobbelt smørbrød
med kald kylling, bacon, salatblader,
tomat og majones

cobbler fruktkompott dekket med
paideig

cock-a-leekie soup hønsesuppe med
purre

coconut kokosnøtt

cod torsk

Colchester oyster engelsk østers av
høy kvalitet

cold cuts/meat kjøttpålegg

coleslaw kålsalat

compote kompott

condiment krydder

consommé buljong

cooked kokt, tillaget

cookie kjeks, småkake

corn 1) hvete, havre (GB) 2) mais (US)

~ **on the cob** maiskolbe

cottage pie ovnsstekt kjøttfarse dekket med potetmos

course (mat)rett

cover charge kuvertavgift

crab krabbe

cracker smørbrødkjeks

cranberry tyttebær

~ **sauce** tyttebærsyltetøy

crawfish 1) langust (GB) 2) sjøkreps (US)

crayfish kreps

cream 1) fløte, krem 2) fromasj 3) fin suppe

~ **cheese** kremost

~ **puff** vannbakkels med krem

creamed potatoes poteter i kremsaus

creole sterk saus av tomater, paprika og løk

cress karse

crisps chips, potetgull

croquette krokett

crumpet et slags tebrød som spises varmt med smør

cucumber slangeagurk

Cumberland sauce saus av ripsgelé tilsatt vin, appelsinjuice og krydder

cupcake småkake

cured speket

currant 1) korint 2) rips

curried med karri

curry karri

custard 1) vaniljesaus 2) eggekrem

cutlet liten kjøttskive (med eller uten ben); snitsel

dab sandflyndre

Danish pastry wienerbrød

date daddel

Derby cheese skarp, gul ost

devilled meget sterkt krydret

devil's food cake myk og mektig sjokoladekake

devils on horseback plommer kokt i vin og fylt med mandler og ansjos, rullet i bacon og grillet

Devonshire cream tykk fløte

diced skåret i terninger

diet food diettmat

dinner middag

dish rett

donut smultring

double cream tykk kremfløte

doughnut smultring

Dover sole sjøtunge (av høy kvalitet)

dressing 1) salatdressing 2) fyll i fjærkre

Dublin Bay prawn sjøkreps

duck and

duckling andunge

dumpling 1) innbakt frukt 2) suppebolle, kumle

Dutch apple pie eplepai dekket med melis og smør

éclair vannbakkels

eel ål

egg(s) egg

boiled ~ kokt

fried ~ speilegg

hard-boiled ~ hardkokt

poached ~ forlorent

scrambled ~ eggerøre

soft-boiled ~ bløtkokt

eggplant aubergine

endive 1) sikori (GB) 2) endivie (US)

entrée 1) forrett 2) mellomrett

fennel fennikel

fig fiken

fillet filet

finnan haddock røkt kolje

fish fisk

~ **and chips** frityrstekt fisk og pommes frites

~ **cake** fiskekrokett

flan fruktterte

flapjack liten, tykk pannekake
flounder flyndre
fool en slags fruktfromasj
forcemeat kjøttfarse, fyll
fowl fjærkre
frankfurter frankfurterpølse
French bean grønn bønne, snittebønne
French bread pariserloff
French dressing 1) salatdressing av olje og vineddik (GB) 2) salatdressing med majones og ketchup (US)
french fries franske poteter, pommes frites
French toast arme riddere
fresh fersk
fried stekt (i olje)
fritter innbakte og friterte biter av kjøtt, skalldyr eller frukt
frogs' legs froskelår
frosting glasur
fruit frukt
fry frityrstekt mat
galantine stykker av fugle-, kalve- eller fiskekjøtt i aspik
game vilt
gammon røke- eller spekeskinke
garfish horngjel
garlic hvitløk
garnish garnityr, pynt
gherkin sylteagurk
giblets innmat av fugl, kras
ginger ingefær
goose gås
~ berry stikkelsbær
grape drue
grated revet
gravy saus av kjøttkraft
grayling harr
green bean grønn bønne, brekkbønne
green pepper grønn paprika
green salad grønn salat
greens grønnsaker

grilled grillstekt, griljert
grilse liten sommerlaks
grouse rype
gumbo kreolsk rett med kjøtt, grønnsaker, fisk eller skalldyr og okra-skudd
haddock kolje
haggis hakket innmat av får, blandet med havregryn og løk
hake lysing
half halv, halvparten
halibut hellefisk
ham skinke
~ and eggs skinke og egg
haricot bean grønn eller gul bønne
hash rett av finskåret kjøtt
hazelnut hasselnøtt
heart hjerte
herbs krydderurter
herring sild
home-made hjemmelaget
hominy grits en slags maisgrøt
honey honning
honeydew melon melon med gulgrønt kjøtt
horse-radish pepperrot
hot 1) varm(t) 2) sterkt krydret
huckleberry blåbær
hush puppy bakverk av maismel
ice-cream iskrem
iced 1) isavkjølt 2) med glasur
icing glasur
Idaho baked potato stor ovnsbakt potet
Irish stew lammeragu med poteter og løk
Italian dressing salatdressing av olje, vineddik, hvitløk og krydderurter
jam syltetøy
jellied i gelé
Jell-O gelédessert
jelly gelé
Jerusalem artichoke jordskokk
John Dory sanktpetersfisk

jugged hare hareragu
juniper berry einebær
junket kalvedans
kale grønnkål
kedgeree en slags plukkfisk med ris
og hårdkokt egg
kidney nyre
kipper røkesild
lamb lam
Lancashire hot pot gryterett av
lammekoteletter og -nyrer, poteter
og løk
larded spekket
lean mager
leek purre
leg lår
lemon sitron
~ sole sandflyndre
lentil linse
lettuce hodesalat
lima bean en slags hestebønne
lime en slags grønn sitron
liver lever
loaf brød
lobster hummer
loin 1) kotelettrad (svin) 2) nyrestykke
(kalv)
Long Island duck and av høy kvalitet
low calorie kalorifattig
lox røkelaks
lunch lunsj
macaroon makron
mackerel makrell
maize mais
maple syrup lønnesirup
marinated marinert, nedlagt
marjoram merian
marrow marg
~ bone margben
marshmallow søtsak av maissirup,
sukker, eggehvite og gelatin
mashed potatoes potetstappe
mayonnaise majones
meal måltid

meat kjøtt
~ ball kjøttbolle
~ loaf forloren hare, en slags
kjøttpudding
~ pâté kjøttpostei
medium medium stekt (om biff)
melted smeltet
Melton Mowbray pie kjøttpai
menu spisekart, meny
meringue marengs
mince 1) hakkekjøtt 2) finhakke
~ pie pai med eplebiter, rosiner, sukat
og krydder
minced hakket
~ meat hakkekjøtt
mint mynte
minute steak raskt stekt, tynn biff
mixed blandet
~ grill forskjellige sorter kjøtt og
grønnsaker grillstekt på spidd
molasses sirup
morel morkel
mousse 1) fin farse av fugl, skinke
eller fisk 2) fromasj
mulberry morbær
mullet multe (fisk)
mulligatawny soup hønsesuppe
sterkt krydret med karri
mushroom sopp
muskmelon en slags melon
mussel blåskjell
mustard sennep
mutton fårekjøtt
noodles nudler
nut nøtt
oatmeal havregrøt
oil olje
okra abelmoskus (afrikansk grønnsak)
olive oliven
onion løk
orange appelsin
ox tongue oksetunge
oxtail oksehale
oyster østers

pancake tykk pannekake
parsley persille
parsnip pastinakk
partridge rapphøne
pastry (konditor)kake
pasty postei, pai
pea ert
peach fersken
peanut peanøtt, jordnøtt
~ butter peanøttsmør
pear pære
pearl barley perlegryn
peppermint peppermynte
perch åbor
persimmon daddelplomme,
  kakiplomme
pheasant fasan
pickerel ung gjedde
pickled marinert
pickles 1) grønnsaker eller frukt
  nedlagt i saltlake eller eddik 2)
  sylteagurker (US)
pie pai, ofte dekket med et deiglokk
pigeon due
pigs' feet/trotters griselabber
pike gjedde
pineapple ananas
plaice rødspette
plain naturell, uten saus eller krydder
plate tallerken
plum plomme
~ pudding flambert fruktkake som
  serveres i julen
poached porchert
popover lett, luftig småkake
pork svinekjøtt
porridge grøt
porterhouse steak tykk biff av
  filetkammen
pot roast grytestek med grønnsaker
potato potet
~ chips 1) pommes frites (GB) 2)
  potetgull (US)
~ in its jacket kokt potet med skall

potted shrimps reker nedlagt i
  kryddersmør; serveres kaldt
poultry fjærkre
prawn stor reke
prune sviske
ptarmigan fjellrype
pumpkin gresskar
quail vaktel
quince kvede
rabbit kanin
radish reddik
rainbow trout regnbueørret
raisin rosin
rare råstekt (om biff)
raspberry bringebær
raw rå
red mullet rødmulle
red (sweet) pepper rød paprika
redcurrant rips
relish en slags tykk kald kryddersaus
  med hakkede grønnsaker og olivener
rhubarb rabarbra
rib (of beef) oksekamstek
rib-eye steak entrecôte (biff)
rice ris
rissole krokett av kjøtt- eller
  fiskepostei
river trout bekkørret
roast 1) stek 2) stekt
Rock Cornish hen broiler, stor kylling
roe rogn
roll rundstykke
rollmop herring sammenrullet
  marinert sildefilet med løk eller
  sylteagurker
round steak lårstek
Rubens sandwich sprengt oksekjøtt
  på rugbrød med gjæret surkål, ost og
  salatdressing; serveres varmt
rusk kavring
rye bread rugbrød
saddle sadel
saffron safran
sage salvie

salad salat
~ bar salat- og grønnsakbuffet
~ cream lett sukret, kremaktig
salatdressing
salmon laks
~ trout ørret, aure
salted saltet
sandwich dobbelt smørbrød
sauce saus
sauerkraut gjæret kål
sausage pølse
sautéed lettstekt i smør eller olje
scallop kammusling
scampi sjøkrepshale
scone rundstykke av havre- eller
byggmel
Scotch broth suppe av okse- eller
fårekjøtt, grønnsaker og perlegryn
Scotch egg hardkokt egg dekket med
pølsefarse og stekt
Scotch woodcock ristet brød med
eggerøre og ansjos(postei)
sea bass havåbor
sea bream dorade (fisk)
sea kale strandkål
seafood fisk og skalldyr
(in) season (i) sesong(en)
seasoning krydder
service charge serviceavgift
service (not) included service (ikke)
inkludert
set menu fast meny
shad stamsild
shallot sjalottløk
shellfish skalldyr
sherbet sorbett (is)
shoulder bog
shredded finstrimlet
~ wheat hvetecornflakes
shrimp reke
silverside (of beef) lårtunge av okse
sirloin steak mørbradstek
skewer spidd
slice skive

sliced skåret i skiver
sloppy Joe kjøttfarse med tomat;
serveres på brød
smelt krøkle (laksefisk)
smoked røkt
sole sjøtunge
soup suppe
sour sur
soused herring nedlagt slid, sursild
spare-rib grillstekt svineribbe
spice krydder
spinach spinat
spiny lobster langust
(on a) spit (på) spidd
sponge cake sukkerbrød
sprat brisling
squash squash
starter forrett
steak-and-kidney pie paiskjell fylt
med kjøtt- og nyrestuing
steamed dampkokt
stew stuing, ragu
Stilton (cheese) bløt ost av
normannatype
strawberry jordbær
string bean grønn bønne, snittebønne
stuffed fylt, spekket
stuffing fyll, farse
suck(l)ing pig pattegris
sugar sukker
sugarless sukkerfri
sundae iskrem med frukt, nøtter,
pisket krem og fruktsauser
supper sen middag
swede kålrabi
sweet 1) søt 2) dessert
~ corn mais
~ potato søtpotet
sweetbread brissel
Swiss cheese sveitserost
Swiss roll swissroll, rullekake
Swiss steak skive av oksekjøtt surret
med tomat og løk
T-bone steak T-benstek

table d'hôte fast meny
tangerine en slags mandarin
tarragon estragon
tart terte
tenderloin filet
Thousand Island dressing
salatdressing laget av majones og
chilisaus og hakket paprika
thyme timian
toad-in-the-hole biter av oksekjøtt
eller pølse dekket med
pannekakerøre og stekt i ovn
toast ristet loff
toasted ristet
~ **cheese** ristet ostesmørbrød
~ **(cheese) sandwich** ristet dobbelt
smørbrød med skinke og ost
tomato tomat
tongue tunge
treacle sirup
trifle sukkerbrød med syltetøy dekket
med knuste mandelmakroner;
serveres med pisket krem og
vaniljekrem
tripe innmat
trout ørret
truffle trøffel
tuna, tunny tunfisk
turbot piggvar
turkey kalkun
turnip turnips; nepe
turnover liten terte med syltetøy- eller
fruktfyll
turtle soup skilpaddesuppe
underdone råstekt (om biff)

vanilla vanilje
veal kalvekjøtt
~ **birds** benløse fugler (av kalvekjøtt)
~ **cutlet** kalvesnitsel
vegetable grønnsak
~ **marrow** en slags gresskar
venison dyrekjøtt, vilt
vichyssoise kald suppe av purre og
poteter
vinegar eddik
Virginia baked ham ovnsstekt røkt
skinke dekorert med stekte
ananasskiver og kirsebær
wafer (is)kjeks
waffle vaffel
walnut valnøtt
water ice sorbett (is)
watercress vannkarse
watermelon vannmelon
well-done godt stekt
Welsh rabbit/rarebit ristet brød med
tykk ostesaus
whelk trompetsnegl
whipped cream pisket krem
whitebait småfisk, ofte sild
woodcock rugde
Worcestershire sauce sterk
kryddersaus av eddik og soja
York ham spekeskinke
Yorkshire pudding en slags pudding
av pannekakerøre som stekes
sammen med roastbiff
zucchini squash
zwieback kavring

Drikker

ale sterkt, litt søtt øl som har gjæret
ved høy temperatur
bitter ~ mørkt, beskt

brown ~ mørkt; på flaske
light ~ lyst; på flaske
mild ~ mørkt, fyldig fatøl

pale ~ lyst, med sterk humlesmak; på flaske

angostura en bitter essens som brukes i forskjellige aperitiffer

applejack eplebrennevin

Athole Brose skotsk drink av whisky, blandet med honning og havremel tilsatt vann

Bacardi cocktail drink av rom, gin, granateplesaft og limejuice

barley water drikk med fruktsmak, laget av byggavkok

barley wine mørkt øl med høyt alkoholinnhold

beer øl

  bottled ~ på flaske

  draft, draught ~ fatøl

  bitters bitre aperitiffer

black velvet blanding av champagne og *stout* (serveres ofte til østers)

bloody Mary drink av vodka, tomatjuice og krydder

bourbon amerikansk whisky laget av mais; litt søtlig smak

brandy 1) brandy; brennevin av druer eller annen frukt 2) konjakk

  ~ **Alexander** blanding av brandy, kakaolikør og fløte

British wines viner laget i Storbritannia, som regel av importerte druer

cherry brandy kirsebærlikør

chocolate sjokolade

cider sider, eplevin

  ~ **cup** drink av sider, krydder og isbiter

claret rød bordeauxvin

cobbler longdrink av vin, sitron, sukker og fruktbiter

coffee kaffe

  ~ **with cream** med fløte

  black ~ uten fløte og sukker

  caffeine-free ~ kaffeinfri

  white ~ med melk

Coke Coca-Cola

cordial likør

cream fløte

cup 1) kopp 2) sommerdrink av kald vin blandet med soda, tilsatt litt sprit eller likør og pyntet med en appelsin-, sitron- eller agurkskive

daiquiri cocktail av rom, limejuice og sukker

double dobbel

Drambuie likør laget av whisky og honning

dry tørr

  ~ **martini** 1) tørr vermut (GB) 2) cocktail av gin og tørr vermut (US)

egg-nog eggetoddi

gin and it cocktail av gin og italiensk (søt) vermut

gin-fizz cocktail av gin, soda, sitronsaft og sukker

ginger ale ingefærøl

ginger beer alkoholholdig ingefærøl

grasshopper cocktail av peppermyntelikør, kakaolikør og fløte

Guiness (stout) mørkt, fyldig øl med sterk malt- og humlesmak

half pint måleenhet, ca. 3 dl

highball whisky eller brandy blandet med soda eller ingefærøl

iced isavkjølt

Irish coffee kaffe med irsk whisky, sukker og pisket krem

Irish Mist irsk likør laget av whisky og honning

Irish whiskey irsk whisky; mildere enn skotsk whisky. Lages bl. a. av bygg-gryn, rug, havre og hvete; modnes i trefat

juice juice, fruktsaft

lager pilsenerøl

lemon squash sitronsaft

lemonade sitronbrus

liqueur likør

liquor brennevin
malt whisky skotsk whisky laget av malt
Manhattan cocktail av *bourbon*, søt vermut og *angostura*
milk melk
mineral water naturlig mineralvann
mulled wine varm, krydret vin
neat bar (uten vann eller isbiter)
old-fashioned cocktail av whisky, kirsebær, sitron, *angostura* og sukker
on the rocks med isbiter
Ovaltine Ovomaltine (sjokoladedrikk med malt)
Pimm's cup(s) en sterk longdrink med fruktsaft og soda
  ~ **No. 1** med gin
  ~ **No. 2** med whisky
  ~ **No. 3** med rom
  ~ **No. 4** med brandy
pink champagne rosa champagne
pink lady cocktail av gin, eplebrennevin (Calvados), granateplesaft, sitronsaft og pisket eggehvite
pint måleenhet, ca. 6 dl
port (wine) portvin
porter mørkt, bittert øl
quart måleenhet, 1,14 liter (US 0,95 liter)
root beer alkoholfri leskedrikk
rum rom

rye (whiskey) amerikansk whisky laget av rug; tyngre og sterkere smak enn *bourbon*
scotch (whisky) skotsk whisky
screwdriver cocktail av vodka og appelsinjuice
shandy bittert øl blandet med ingefærøl eller brus
short drink dram
shot dram
sloe gin-fizz plommelikør med soda, sitronsaft og sukker
soda water sodavann
soft drink brus, leskedrikk
sour 1) sur 2) om drink tilsatt sitronsaft
spirits brennevin
stinger cocktail av konjakk og peppermyntelikør
stout sterkt, mørkt engelsk øl
straight ublandet (rent brennevin)
sweet søt
tea te
Tom Collins cocktail av gin, soda, sitronsaft og sukker
water vann
whisky sour cocktail av whisky, soda, sitronsaft og sukker
wine vin
  red ~ rød
  sparkling ~ musserende
  white ~ hvit

Minigrammatikk

Artikler

Den **bestemte** artikkel har samme form i entall og flertall: **the.**

the room – the rooms	rommet - rommene

Den **ubestemte** artikkel har to former: **a**, som brukes foran ord som begynner med en konsonant, og **an**, som brukes foran vokal eller stum **h**.

a coat	en kåpe/frakk
an umbrella	en paraply
an hour	en time

Some angir en ubestemt mengde eller et ubestemt antall. Det anvendes foran substantiv i både entall og flertall, og tilsvarer på norsk «noen», «noe», «litt».

I'd like some tea, please.	Jeg vil gjerne ha litt te.
Give me some stamps, please.	Gi meg noen frimerker, er du snill.

Any betyr «noen»/«hvilken» som «helst», og brukes ofte i nektende og spørrende setninger.

There isn't any soap.	Det er ikke noe såpe her.
Do you have any stamps?	Har du frimerker?
Is there any mail for me?	Er det kommet noe post til meg?

Substantiver

Flertall dannes som regel ved å føye **-(e)s** til entallsformen.

cup – cups	kopp - kopper
dress – dresses	kjole - kjoler

Obs! Hvis et substantiv slutter på **-y** i entall, endres stavemåten til **-ies** i flertall hvis **y** kommer etter en konsonant. Kommer den etter en vokal, anvendes den normale flertallsendelsen **-s**.

lady – ladies	dame - damer
day – days	dag - dager

Men ingen regel unten unntak...

man – men	mann - menn
woman – women	kvinne - kvinner
child – children	barn - barn
foot – feet	fot - føtter
knife – knives	kniv - kniver

Genitiv

1. Når eieren er et levende vesen og når substantivet ikke slutter på **-s**, føyer man til **'s**.

the boy's room	guttens rom
Anne's dress	Annes kjole

Hvis substantivet slutter på **-s**, føyer man kun til apostrofen (').

the boy's room	guttenes rom

2. Hvis eieren ikke er et levende vesen, brukes preposisjonen **of.**

the end of the journey	reisens slutt (slutten på reisen)

Adjektiver

Adjektivet forblir uendret både foran substantivet og når det står alene.

a large brown suitcase   en stor brun koffert

Komparativ og **superlativ** kan dannes på to måter.

1. Adjektiver med én stavelse og de fleste adjektiver med to stavelser får endelsen **-(e)r** og **-(e)st**.

small – smaller – smallest	liten - mindre - minst
pretty – prettier – prettiest	søt - søtere - søtest

Obs! **-y** etter konsonant endres til **i** foran **-er** og **-est**.

2. Adjektiver med flere enn to stavelser og enkelte adjektiver med to stavelser (f.eks. de som slutter på **-ful** eller **-less**) danner komparativ og superlativ ved hjelp av **more** og **most**.

expensive (dyr) – **more expensive – most expensive**
careful (forsiktig) – **more careful – most careful**

Følgende adjektiver er uregelmessige:

good (bra) – **better – best**	**much** (mye)	⎫
bad (dårlig) – **worse – worst**	**many** (mange)	⎬ **– more – most**
little (lite) – **less – least**		⎭

Pronomener

	personlige nominativ	pronomer akkusativ	eiendomspronomener 1)	2)
jeg	I	me	my	mine
du	you	you	your	yours
han	he	him	his	his
hun	she	her	her	hers
den/det	it	it	its	–
vi	we	us	our	ours
dere	you	you	your	yours
de	they	them	their	theirs

Verb

Tre viktige **hjelpeverb** i presens:

to be (å være)

	sammentrukket form	sammentrukket nektende form	
I am	I'm	I'm not	–
you are	you're	you're not	you aren't
he is	he's	he's not	he isn't
she is	she's	she's not	she isn't
it is	it's	it's not	it isn't
we are	we're	we're not	we aren't
you are	you're	you're not	you aren't
they are	they're	they're not	they aren't

Spørreform: **Am I? – Is he? – Are they?**
Obs! I dagligtale brukes så å si bare de sammentrukne formene.

to have (å ha)

	sammentrukket form	sammentrukket nektende form
I have	I've	I haven't
you have	you've	you haven't
he/she/it has	he's/she's/it's	he/she/it hasn't
we have	we've	we haven't
you have	you've	you haven't
they have	they've	they haven't

Spørrende: **Have you? – Has he?**

to do (å gjøre)

I do, you, he/she/it does, we do, you do, they do

Nektende: **I do not (I don't) – He does not (He doesn't)**
Spørrende: **Do you? – Does she?**

For alle hjelpeverb gjelder:

1. Nektende form dannes med **not** (ikke).
2. Spørrende form dannes ved å sette verbet foran subjektet.

Andre verb

Engelske verb beholder samme form i alle personer i **presens,** med unntak av 3. person entall der man legger til **-(e)s.**

	to speak (å snakke)	to ask (å spørre)	to go (å gå)
I	speak	ask	go
you	speak	ask	go
he/she/it	speaks	asks	goes
we/you/they	speak	ask	go

Imperfektum og **perfektum partisipp** dannes for regelmessige verb ved å føye til endelsen **-d** eller **-ed.**

Presens partisipp dannes ved å føye endelsen **-ing** til infinitivsformen.

Nektende form dannes med hjelpeverbet **do** + **not** + infinitiv:

I do not (don't) like this hotel.   Jeg liker ikke dette hotellet.

Spørrende form dannes med hjelpeverbet **do** + subjekt + infinitiv:

Do you drink wine?   Drikker du vin?

Progressiv (pågående) form

Denne formen finnes ikke på norsk, men motsvarer «holder på med å», og dannes med hjelpeverbet **to be** fulgt av presens partisipp av verbet.

infinitiv	presens partisipp	progressiv form
to read	**reading**	**I'm reading.**
to sing	**singing**	**She's singing.**

What are you doing?   Hva er det du holder på med (å gjøre)?
I'm writing a letter.   Jeg holder på (med) å skrive et brev.

Uregelmessige verb

Her er en liste over uregelmessige engelske verb. Sammensatte verb, eller verb som har prefiks, bøyes etter samme mønster som det enkle verbet; eks.: *overdrive* bøyes som *drive*, *mistake* som *take*.

Infinitiv	Imperfektum	Perfektum partisipp	
arise	arose	arisen	*stå opp*
awake	awoke	awoken/awaked	*vekke; våkne*
be	was	been	*være*
bear	bore	borne	*bære*
beat	beat	beaten	*slå*
become	became	become	*bli*
begin	began	begun	*begynne*
bend	bent	bent	*bøye*
bet	bet	bet	*vedde*
bid	bade/bid	bidden/bid	*by (befale)*
bind	bound	bound	*binde*
bite	bit	bitten	*bite*
bleed	bled	bled	*blø*
blow	blew	blown	*blåse*
break	broke	broken	*brekke*
breed	bred	bred	*ale opp*
bring	brought	brought	*bringe*
build	built	built	*bygge*
burn	burnt/burned	burnt/burned	*brenne*
burst	burst	burst	*briste*
buy	bought	bought	*kjøpe*
can*	could	–	*kunne*
cast	cast	cast	*kaste*
catch	caught	caught	*gripe*
choose	chose	chosen	*velge*
cling	clung	clung	*klamre seg til*
clothe	clothed/clad	clothed/clad	*kle på*
come	came	come	*komme*
cost	cost	cost	*koste*
creep	crept	crept	*krype*
cut	cut	cut	*skjære*
deal	dealt	dealt	*handle*
dig	dug	dug	*grave*
do (he does*)	did	done	*gjøre*
draw	drew	drawn	*trekke*
dream	dreamt/dreamed	dreamt/dreamed	*drømme*

drink	drank	drunk	*drikke*
drive	drove	driven	*kjøre*
dwell	dwelt	dwelt	*bo*
eat	ate	eaten	*spise*
fall	fell	fallen	*falle*
feed	fed	fed	*fôre*
feel	felt	felt	*føle*
fight	fought	fought	*slåss*
find	found	found	*finne*
flee	fled	fled	*flykte*
fling	flung	flung	*kaste*
fly	flew	flown	*fly*
forsake	forsook	forsaken	*svikte*
freeze	froze	frozen	*fryse*
get	got	got	*få*
give	gave	given	*gi*
go (he goes*)	went	gone	*gå*
grind	ground	ground	*male, knuse*
grow	grew	grown	*gro*
hang	hung	hung	*henge*
have (he has*)	had	had	*ha*
hear	heard	heard	*høre*
hew	hewed	hewed/hewn	*hugge*
hide	hid	hidden	*gjemme*
hit	hit	hit	*slå*
hold	held	held	*holde*
hurt	hurt	hurt	*såre*
keep	kept	kept	*beholde*
kneel	knelt	knelt	*knele*
knit	knitted/knit	knitted/knit	*strikke*
know	knew	known	*vite*
lay	laid	laid	*legge*
lead	led	led	*lede*
lean	leant/leaned	leant/leaned	*lene*
leap	leapt/leaped	leapt/leaped	*hoppe*
learn	learnt/learned	learnt/learned	*lære*
leave	left	left	*forlate*
lend	lent	lent	*låne (ut)*
let	let	let	*la; leie ut*
lie	lay	lain	*ligge*
light	lit/lighted	lit/lighted	*tenne*
lose	lost	lost	*miste*
make	made	made	*lage*
may*	might	–	*kunne (få lov)*

mean	meant	meant	*mene*
meet	met	met	*møte*
mow	mowed	mowed/mown	*slå (gress)*
must*	must	–	*måtte*
ought* (to)	ought	–	*burde*
pay	paid	paid	*betale*
put	put	put	*legge*
read	read	read	*lese*
rid	rid	rid	*befri*
ride	rode	ridden	*ride*
ring	rang	rung	*ringe*
rise	rose	risen	*reise seg*
run	ran	run	*løpe*
saw	sawed	sawn	*sage*
say	said	said	*si*
see	saw	seen	*se*
seek	sought	sought	*søke*
sell	sold	sold	*selge*
send	sent	sent	*sende*
set	set	set	*sette*
sew	sewed	sewed/sewn	*sy*
shake	shook	shaken	*riste*
shall*	should	–	*skulle*
shed	shed	shed	*felle*
shine	shone	shone	*skinne*
shoot	shot	shot	*skyte*
show	showed	shown	*vise*
shrink	shrank	shrunk	*krympe*
shut	shut	shut	*lukke*
sing	sang	sung	*synge*
sink	sank	sunk	*synke*
sit	sat	sat	*sitte*
sleep	slept	slept	*sove*
slide	slid	slid	*gli*
sling	slung	slung	*kaste*
slink	slunk	slunk	*luske*
slit	slit	slit	*flenge*
smell	smelled/smelt	smelled/smelt	*lukte*
sow	sowed	sown/sowed	*så*
speak	spoke	spoken	*snakke*
speed	sped/speeded	sped/speeded	*haste*
spell	spelt/spelled	spelt/spelled	*stave*

* presens indikativ

spend	spent	spent	*gi ut; tilbringe*
spill	spilt/spilled	spilt/spilled	*søle, spille*
spin	spun	spun	*spinne*
spit	spat	spat	*spytte*
split	split	split	*splitte*
spoil	spoilt/spoiled	spoilt/spoiled	*ødelegge; skjemme bort*
spread	spread	spread	*spre*
spring	sprang	sprung	*hoppe opp*
stand	stood	stood	*stå*
steal	stole	stolen	*stjele*
stick	stuck	stuck	*klebe*
sting	stung	stung	*stikke*
stink	stank/stunk	stunk	*stinke*
strew	strewed	strewed/strewn	*strø*
stride	strode	stridden	*skride*
strike	struck	struck/stricken	*slå*
string	strung	strung	*tre på snor*
strive	strove	striven	*streve*
swear	swore	sworn	*banne; sverge*
sweep	swept	swept	*feie*
swell	swelled	swollen/swelled	*hovne*
swim	swam	swum	*svømme*
swing	swung	swung	*svinge*
take	took	taken	*ta*
teach	taught	taught	*undervise*
tear	tore	torn	*rive*
tell	told	told	*fortelle*
think	thought	thought	*tenke*
throw	threw	thrown	*kaste*
thrust	thrust	thrust	*støte*
tread	trod	trodden	*trå*
wake	woke/waked	woken/waked	*våkne; vekke*
wear	wore	worn	*ha på seg*
weave	wove	woven	*veve*
weep	wept	wept	*gråte*
will*	would		*ville*
win	won	won	*vinne*
wind	wound	wound	*sno*
wring	wrung	wrung	*vri*
write	wrote	written	*skrive*

---

* presens indikativ

Engelske forkortelser

A.D.	*anno Domini*	e.Kr.
Am.	*America; American*	Amerika; amerikansk
a.m.	*ante meridiem (before noon)*	mellom kl. 00.00 og 12.00
Amtrak	*American railroad corporation*	sammenslutning av private amerikanske jernbaneselskaper
Ave.	*avenue*	aveny
B.C.	*before Christ*	f.Kr.
Blvd.	*boulevard*	boulevard
B.R.	*British Rail*	Britiske statsbaner
Brit.	*Britain; British*	Storbritannia; britisk
Bros.	*brothers*	brødrene (i firmanavn)
¢	*cent*	1/100 dollar
Can.	*Canada; Canadian*	Canada; kanadisk
CID	*Criminal Investigation Department*	Det britiske kriminalpoliti
CNR	*Canadian National Railway*	Kanadiske statsbaner
c/o	*(in) care of*	adressert
Co.	*company*	kompani
Corp.	*corporation*	aksjeselskap *Am*
CPR	*Canadian Pacific Railways*	et privat kanadisk jernbaneselskap
D.C.	*District of Columbia*	Columbia-distriktet (Washington, D.C.)
DDS	*Doctor of Dental Science*	tannlege
e.g.	*for instance*	f.eks.
Eng.	*England; English*	England; engelsk
EU	*European Union*	Den europeiske union
ft.	*foot/feet*	fot (30,5 cm)
GB	*Great Britain*	Storbritannia
H.H.	*His Holiness*	Hans Hellighet
H.M.	*His/her Majesty*	Hans/Hennes Majestet
H.M.S.	*Her Majesty's ship*	britisk marineskip
hp	*horsepower*	hestekraft
i.e.	*that is to say*	dvs.
in.	*inch*	tomme (2,54 cm)
Inc.	*incorporated*	A/S
£	*pound sterling*	engelsk pund
L.A.	*Los Angeles*	Los Angeles
Ltd.	*limited*	A/S
M.D.	*Doctor of Medicine*	lege
M.P.	*Member of Parliament*	medlem av Det britisk parlament
mph	*miles per hour*	eng. mil i timen

Mr.	*Mister*	herr
Mrs.	*Missis*	fru
Ms.	*Missis/Miss*	fru/frk.
nat.	*national*	nasjonal
No.	*number*	nr.
N.Y.C.	*New York City*	byen New York
p.	*page; penny/pence*	side; $^{1}/_{100}$ pund
p.a.	*per annum*	pr. år
Ph.D.	*Doctor of Philosophy*	dr. philos.
p.m.	*post meridiem (after noon)*	mellom kl. 12.00 og 24.00
PO	*Post Office*	postkontor
P.T.O.	*please turn over*	vennligst bla om
RCMP	*Royal Canadian Mounted Police*	Det kongelige kanadiske ridende politi
Rd.	*road*	vei, veg
ref.	*reference*	referanse
Rev.	*reverend*	pastor
RFD	*rural free delivery*	postboks (på landsbygda)
RR	*railroad*	jernbane
RSVP	*please reply*	vennligst svar
$	*dollar*	dollar
Soc.	*society*	selskap
St.	*saint; street*	sankt; gate
STD	*Subscriber Trunk Dialling*	automattelefon
UN	*United Nations*	FN
US	*United States*	USA
USS	*United States Ship*	amerikansk marineskip
VAT	*value added tax*	med moms
VIP	*very important person*	betydningsfull person
Xmas	*Christmas*	jul
yd.	*yard*	yard (91,44 cm)
YMCA	*Young Men's Christian Association*	KFUM
YWCA	*Young Women's Christian Association*	KFUK
ZIP	*ZIP code*	postnummer

Tall

Grunntall

0	zero
1	one
2	two
3	three
4	four
5	five
6	six
7	seven
8	eight
9	nine
10	ten
11	eleven
12	twelve
13	thirteen
14	fourteen
15	fifteen
16	sixteen
17	seventeen
18	eighteen
19	nineteen
20	twenty
21	twenty-one
22	twenty-two
23	twenty-three
24	twenty-four
25	twenty-five
30	thirty
40	forty
50	fifty
60	sixty
70	seventy
80	eighty
90	ninety
100	a/one hundred
230	two hundred and thirty
1,000	a/one thousand
10,000	ten thousand
100,000	a/one hundred thousand
1,000,000	a/one million

Ordenstal

1st	first
2nd	second
3rd	third
4th	fourth
5th	fifth
6th	sixth
7th	seventh
8th	eighth
9th	ninth
10th	tenth
11th	eleventh
12th	twelfth
13th	thirteenth
14th	fourteenth
15th	fifteenth
16th	sixteenth
17th	seventeenth
18th	eighteenth
19th	nineteenth
20th	twentieth
21st	twenty-first
22nd	twenty-second
23rd	twenty-third
24th	twenty-fourth
25th	twenty-fifth
26th	twenty-sixth
27th	twenty-seventh
28th	twenty-eighth
29th	twenty-ninth
30th	thirtieth
40th	fortieth
50th	fiftieth
60th	sixtieth
70th	seventieth
80th	eightieth
90th	ninetieth
100th	hundredth
230th	two hundred and thirtieth
1,000th	thousandth

Klokken

Både engelskmennene og amerikanerne anvender uttrykkene a.m. (ante meridiem) om tiden etter midnatt frem til kl. 12, og p.m. (post meridiem) om tiden etter kl. 12 frem til midnatt. I England går man imidlertid mer og mer over til å bruke 24-timerssystemet.

Eksempler:

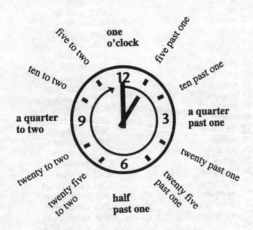

I'll come at seven a.m.	Jeg kommer kl. 7 om morgenen.
I'll come at two p.m.	Jeg kommer kl. 2 om ettermiddagen.
I'll come at eight p.m.	Jeg kommer kl. 8 om kvelden.

Dagene

Sunday	søndag	*Thursday*	torsdag
Monday	mandag	*Friday*	fredag
Tuesday	tirsdag	*Saturday*	lørdag
Wednesday	onsdag		

Conversion tables/
Omregningstabeller

Meter og fot

Tallene i midten gjelder både for meter og fot, dvs.
1 meter = 3,281 fot, og 1 fot = 0,30 meter.

Metres and feet

The figure in the middle stands for both metres and
feet, e.g. 1 metre = 3.281 ft. and 1 foot = 0.30 m.

Meter/Metres		Fot/Feet
0.30	1	3.281
0.61	2	6.563
0.91	3	9.843
1.22	4	13.124
1.52	5	16.403
1.83	6	19.686
2.13	7	22.967
2.44	8	26.248
2.74	9	29.529
3.05	10	32.810
3.66	12	39.372
4.27	14	45.934
6.10	20	65.620
7.62	25	82.023
15.24	50	164.046
22.86	75	246.069
30.48	100	328.092

Temperatur

For å regne om fra celsius- til fahrenheitgrader,
ganger en med 1,8 og legger til 32.
Omvendt - for å regne om fra fahrenheit- til
celsiusgrader - trekker en fra 32 og deler med 1,8.

Temperature

To convert Centigrade to Fahrenheit, multiply by 1.8
and add 32.
To convert Fahrenheit to Centigrade, subtract 32
from Fahrenheit and divide by 1.8.

OCEAN CRUISING
& CRUISE SHIPS

This cruise guide, updated annually, contains
more ships, more charts, more analytical
data and more advice than any other guide.

Running to more than half a million words,
it has established itself over 20 years as the
definitive reference work for both novice
and veteran passengers and for travel agents.
Its author, Douglas Ward, has spent 4,500
days at sea, aboard more than 800 cruises
and has been described by the London *Times*
as the industry's most feared critic.